Polish Contributions to International Criminal Law

Queen Mary Studies in International Law

Edited by

Malgosia Fitzmaurice

VOLUME 55

The titles published in this series are listed at *brill.com/qmil*

Polish Contributions to International Criminal Law

By

Patrycja Grzebyk, Bartłomiej Krzan and
Karolina Wierczyńska

BRILL | NIJHOFF

LEIDEN | BOSTON

Co-financed by the Polish Ministry of Justice and the Institute of Justice in Warsaw (IWS).

Ministry of Justice
Republic of Poland

35 YEARS IWS 1990-2025

Cover illustration: The Trial of Rudolf Hoess, Commander of the Auschwitz Camp, March 1947. Source: Narodowe Archiwum Cyfrowe/National Digital Archive.
Translated by IURIDICO LEGAL & FINANCIAL TRANSLATIONS SP. Z O.O.

Library of Congress Cataloging-in-Publication Data

Names: Grzebyk, Patrycja, author. | Krzan, Bartłomiej, author. | Wierczyńska, Karolina, author.
Title: Polish contributions to international criminal law / by Patrycja Grzebyk, Bartłomiej Krzan, and Karolina Wierczyńska.
Description: Leiden ; Boston : Brill Academic Publishers, Inc., 2025. | Series: Queen Mary Studies in International Law, 1877-4822 ; volume 55 | Includes bibliographical references and index.
Identifiers: LCCN 2025024545 | ISBN 9789004712683 (hardback) | ISBN 9789004712690 (pdf)
Subjects: LCSH: International criminal law. | International criminal law--Poland. | International crimes--Law and legislation--Poland. | Crimes against Humanity--Law and legislation--Poland. | Criminal justice, Administration of--Poland. | International and municipal law--Poland. | War crimes. | Criminal liability (International law) | International criminal courts. | Poland--History.
Classification: LCC KZ7000 .G79 2025 | DDC 345--DC23/ENG/20250523
LC record available at https://lccn.loc.gov/2025024545

Typeface for the Latin, Greek, and Cyrillic scripts: "Brill". See and download: brill.com/brill-typeface.

ISSN 1877-4822
ISBN 978-90-04-71268-3 (hardback)
ISBN 978-90-04-71269-0 (e-book)
DOI 10.1163/9789004712690

Published by Koninklijke Brill BV, Plantijnstraat 2, 2321 JC Leiden, The Netherlands.
Koninklijke Brill BV incorporates the imprints Brill, Brill Nijhoff, Brill Schöningh, Brill Fink, Brill mentis, Brill Wageningen Academic, Vandenhoeck & Ruprecht, Böhlau and V&R unipress.

Contents

Acronyms

AAN	Archiwum Akt Nowych (The Archives of Modern Records)
AIDP	Association Internationale de Droit Pénal
AIPN GK	Archiwum Instytutu Pamięci Narodowej – Główna Komisja (The Archives of the Institute of National Remembrance – the Main Commission)
AJIL	American Journal of International Law
AK	Armia Krajowa (The Home Army)
AP	Additional Protocols of 8.06.1977 to the Geneva Conventions for the Protection of Victims of War of 1949
APISM	The Archives of the Polish Institute and Sikorski Musem in London
CHR	Commission on Human Rights
CLF	Criminal Law Forum
Code of Crimes	Draft Code of Crimes against the Peace and Security of Mankind
Code of Offences	Draft Code of Offences against the Peace and Security of Mankind
CROWCASS	Central Registry of War Criminals and Security Suspects
DPP	Demokratyczny Przegląd Prawniczy (Journal: Democratic Review of Law)
DPT	Departament Prawno-Traktatowy polskiego Ministerstwa Spraw Zagranicznych (Legal and Treaty Department of Polish Ministry of Foreign Affairs)
Dz.U.	Dziennik Ustaw (Journal of Laws of the Republic of Poland)
Dz.Pr.P.P.	Dziennik Praw Państwa Polskiego (Journal of Laws of Polish State)
ECOSOC	United Nations Economic and Social Council
EJIL	European Journal of International Law
GA	General Assembly of the United Nations
GC	Geneva Conventions for the Protection of Victims of War of 12.08.1949
GKBZHWP	Główna Komisja Badania Zbrodni Hitlerowskich w Polsce (Chief Commission for the Investigation of Nazi Crimes in Poland)
GKBZNWP	Główna Komisja Badania Zbrodni Niemieckich w Polsce (Chief Commission for the Investigation of German Crimes in Poland)

GKBZHWP-IPN	Główna Komisja Badania Zbrodni Hitlerowskich w Polsce – Instytut Pamięci Narodowej (Chief Commission for the Investigation of Nazi Crimes in Poland – Institute of National Remembrance)
HC IV	Convention (IV) respecting the Laws and Customs of War on Land and its annex: Regulations concerning the Laws and Customs of War on Land. The Hague, 18 October 1907.
IBUCL	International Bureau for the Unification of Criminal Law (Bureau International pour l'Unification du Droit Pénal)
ICC	International Criminal Court
ICJ	International Court of Justice
ICL	International Criminal Law
ICPRD	International Commission for Penal Reconstruction and Development
ICUCL	International Conference of Unification of Criminal Law (Conférence internationale pour l'unification du droit pénal)
ICTR	International Criminal Tribunal for Rwanda
ICTY	International Criminal Trubunal for the former Yugoslavia
IDI	Institut de Droit International
IHL	International Humanitarian Law
ILA	International Law Association
ILC	International Law Commission
IPN	Instytut Pamięci Narodowej (Institute of National Remembrance)
IPN Act	Act on the Institute of National Remembrance – Commission for the Prosecution of Crimes against the Polish Nation
IUPL	International Union of Penal Law
JICJ	Journal of International Criminal Justice
KK	Kodeks karny (Polish Criminal Code)
KPK	Kodeks postępowania karnego (Polish Code of Criminal Procedure)
KRN	Krajowa Rada Narodowa (State National Council)
LON	League of Nations
MFA	Ministry of Foreign Affairs
MON	Ministerstwo Obrony Narodowej (Polish Ministry of Defence)
M.P.	Monitor Polski (Official Gazette of the Republic of Poland)
NTN	Najwyższy Trybunał Narodowy (Supreme National Tribunal)
OR	Official Records
OSN	Orzecznictwo Sądu Najwyższego (Repertory of Polish Supreme Court)

OSP	Orzecznictwo Sądów Polskich (Repertory of Polish Jurisprudence)
PCIJ	Permanent Court of International Justice
PIP	Państwo i Prawo (Journal: State and Law)
PISM	Polski Instytut Spraw Międzynarodowych (Polish Institute of International Affairs)
PKWN	Polski Komitet Wyzwolenia Narodowego (Polish Committee of National Liberation)
PPA	Przegląd Prawa i Administracji (Journal: Review of Law and Administration)
PPD	Polski Przegląd Dyplomatyczny (Journal: Polish Diplomatic Review)
PrepCom	Preparatory Committee (of the ICC)
PYIL	Polish Yearbook of International Law
RCADI	Recueil des Cours de l'Académie de Droit International
RDPC	Revue de droit pénal et de criminologie
RIDP	Revue internationale de droit pénal
RJN	Rząd Jedności Narodowej (Provisional Government of National Unity)
RPEIS	Ruch Prawniczy, Ekonomiczny i Socjologiczny (Journal of Law, Economics and Sociology)
RPW	Rocznik Prawniczy Wileński (Journal: Vilnius Yearbook of Law)
SN	Sąd Najwyższy (Supreme Court of Poland)
SM	Sprawy Międzynarodowe (Journal: International Affairs)
TK	Trybunał Konstytucyjny (Polish Constitutional Tribunal)
UNWCC	United Nations War Crimes Commission
WPP	Wojskowy Przegląd Prawniczy (Journal: Military Legal Review)
YILC	Yearbook of the International Law Commission
ZWZ	Związek Walki Zbrojnej (Union of Armed Struggle)

Introductory Remarks

1

Ever since the groundwork of international criminal law began to take shape, Polish scholars, Polish diplomats and Polish institutions have contributed to its development, in some cases playing key roles. Suffice to mention the instrumentality of Emil Stanisław Rappaport in the creation and development of the International Association of Penal Law (AIDP/IAPL), Rafał Lemkin's endeavours towards the prohibition of the crime of genocide, or Stefan Glaser and Jerzy Litawski's activities within the United Nations War Crimes Commission (UNWCC) with the goal of codification of international crimes and principles of liability for them, or Jerzy Sawicki and Tadeusz Cyprian's efforts to bring individual Nazi criminals to justice before a court. Last but not least, one could not possibly omit the judicial *acquis* of Polish courts with respect to judging international crimes, in particular decisions of the Supreme National Tribunal (*Najwyższy Trybunał Narodowy*). It was before Polish courts, after all, that for the first time (!) in human history the responsibility for initiating and prosecuting a war of aggression, for genocide, or for crimes against humanity was pondered and more types of war crimes were defined.

Despite the indubitable achievements of Polish diplomacy, scholarship and jurisprudence, Polish contributions to the development of international criminal law are sometimes ignored.[1] It is not rare for the subject literature to mention the role of Poland, albeit without giving the names of the Polish delegates, whereas the representatives of other states are not similarly clothed in anonymity. Here and there, the labours of many Polish scholars and diplomats are credited to one individual, such as in the case of the Convention on the Prevention and Punishment of the Crime of Genocide of 1948 (hereinafter Genocide Convention) and the role of Rafał Lemkin.

It is the intention of this monograph to cast a new light on the development of international criminal law, accentuating the achievements of Polish diplomacy, scholarship and judiciary, naming the persons involved. The authors demonstrate that, since the restoration of independence in 1918, Poland and her citizens have undertaken numerous initiatives contributing

1 Cf. Reginbogin, Safferling (2006); Kreß, Barriga (2016), *passim*. Among the positive examples of appreciation of the importance of the efforts of Polish diplomats and scholars one could note Fleming (2022a); Tallgren, Mégret (2020); and Sands (2018).

to the development of the new subdiscipline within international law: international criminal law. Polish diplomats and scholars alike have time and again served as the original creators of solutions ultimately adopted in, for example, international conventions or resolutions of international organizations. Through their engagement in the international forum, Poles (whether in private capacity or as official members of Polish delegations to diplomatic conferences tasked with devising the contents of treaties)[2] have made a significant imprint on the current shape of international law, its substantive scope – contents of definitions of crimes and principles of international criminal responsibility, as well as procedural solutions.

The research goals of this monograph are firstly to pinpoint the contributions of Polish scholars and diplomats in the shaping of international law, as well as the achievements of Polish jurisprudence in shaping the framework of responsibility for international crimes; secondly, to identify the leading individuals of Polish nationality, as well as Polish initiatives, having contributed to the development of international criminal law; thirdly, to highlight the reasons behind Polish involvement (or lack thereof) in the various initiatives in the field of international criminal law.

In the creation of this work, it was necessary to adopt certain preliminary assumptions intended to facilitate overcoming the difficulties entailed by a suitable and fair presentation of the subject matter.

The delineation of an appropriate time-frame for the monograph was troublesome. The starting date – 1918 – appeared to be self-evident, as the year when Poland's independence was restored after the Great War. The achievements of individuals and institutions since that time can, therefore, be reputed as unquestionably Polish, i.e. linked to Poland as a full-fledged subject of international law. Nevertheless, there had been prior publications by authors writing in Polish and self-identifying as Poles. By way of example, one could mention Jan Gottlieb Bloch.[3] In 1899, as a subject of Russian Tsar Nicholas II, he published the last volume of his monumental treatise titled *Przyszła wojna pod względem technicznym, ekonomicznym i politycznym. Wnioski ogólne z dzieła*[4], importantly written in Polish before being translated into several languages (into English as the W.T. Stead (transl.), *War of the Future in its Technical, Economic and Political Relations*, London: Grant Richards). Bloch pointed out the necessity of creating a court of

2 At the same time, we are aware that sometimes the roles – private and official – cannot easily be separated; this problem is described, among others, by Schachter (1977): 217ff.

3 More on Jan G. Bloch see Kołodziejczyk (1983).

4 Bloch (1899): 66; a digitized version of the original is available at www.polona.pl.

arbitration for states to avert interstate conflicts and the arms race. Furthermore, he highlighted the necessity of establishing a separate chamber for the punishment of the press if its activities were to have procured the outbreak of a war through agitation. Such a court would be empowered to impose fines as punishment; the relevant regulations, according to Bloch, ought to be placed in domestic criminal codes. Noting the danger associated with critical attitudes of the press towards the decisions of international courts, which could constitute a form of agitation for war (in present terminology, incitement to the crime of aggression),[5] he won his place among the forerunners of the field of international criminal law. Significantly, he influenced the shape taken by international law at the time – it was Bloch who inspired Tsar Nicholas II to convene the first Hague conference in 1899.[6] It was during that conference that the first agreements were adopted with a view to limiting the options for starting a war and methods of waging it.[7]

Other Polish scholars having published works of importance prior to the cut-off date set by the title of this monograph include Antoni Białecki (*Zadanie prawa międzynarodowego i obowiązki stron wojujących* [*The task of international law and the obligations of the belligerent parties*], 1875), Roman Buczyński (*O jurysdykcji karnej w stosunkach międzynarodowych* [*On criminal jurisdiction in international relations*], 1872) and Franciszek Kasparek (*O wydawaniu przestępców* [*On the surrender of criminals*], 1882). Particular distinction, however, belongs to Gustaw Roszkowski, a professor of the University of Lviv, whose publications include *O azylach i ekstradycji: ze szczególnym uwzględnieniem stosunków Austro-Węgierskiej Monarchii* (1882a) [*On asyla and extradition: with special emphasis on the relations of the Austro-Hungarian Monarchy*]; *O najnowszych traktatach Austro-Węgierskiej Monarchji z Belgją i Holandją z 1880 i 1881 roku w przedmiocie wydawania przestępców* (1882b) [*On the most recent treaties of the Austro-Hungarian Monarchy with Belgium and Holland* of 1880 and 1881 on extradition of

5 Bloch (1899): 306.

6 Bloch (2010): 419; see also http://www.bloch.org.pl/images/pliki/Szkic.pdf.

7 The Conference adopted: (i) the Convention on the Pacific Settlement of International Disputes; (ii) Convention Respecting the Laws and Customs of War on Land; (iii) Convention for the Adaptation to Maritime Warfare of the Principles of the Geneva Convention of 22.08.1864; Declaration concerning the Prohibition of the Discharge of Projectiles and Explosives from Balloons or by Other New Analogous Methods; Declaration concerning the Prohibition of the Use of Projectiles with the Sole Object to Spread Asphyxiating Poisonous Gases; Declaration concerning the Prohibition of the Use of Bullets which can Easily Expand or Change their Form inside the Human Body such as Bullets with a Hard Covering which does not Completely Cover the Core, or containing Indentations.

criminals]; *O oxfordzkim projekcie prawa wojny lądowej w porównaniu z prawem francuzkiem, hollenderskiem i rosyjskiem oraz z deklaracyą brukselską* (1881a) [*On the Oxford draft of the law of war on land as compared to French, Dutch and Russian law and to the Brussels Declaration*], *O poglądach Moltkego na prawo wojny* (1881b) [*On Moltke's views on the law of war*], *O Konwencyi Genewskiej* (1887) [*On the Geneva Convention*] and *O zmianach projektowanych w konwencyi genewskiej r. 1864* (1900) [*On proposed amendments to the Geneva Convention of 1864*]. It is worth noting that Roszkowski was not only a fertile author but also an internationally renowned scholar of international law, as confirmed by his membership in the Institut de Droit International (IDI) – as a corresponding member in 1882 and an active member in 1891.[8]

The end of this book's timeline can raise certain doubts, although the symbolic significance of the centenary of the independence of the Polish state (2018) cannot be ignored. Nonetheless, we signal key events having occurred before this book went into print in 2025.

There were (and still are) difficulties deciding who can be identified as a Pole. Until 1918, Poland had remained for more than 100 years under partitions. As a result, many of the individuals mentioned in this monograph were born as the subjects of the Russian Tsar or the Emperors of Germany or Austria-Hungary (and thus in a different legal system). Even if some of them decided to live in Poland after World War I and became Polish citizens, at a later time (because of warfare, persecution or considerations of economic or academic nature) they decided to emigrate and never lived in Poland again. Sometimes, they still regarded themselves as Poles (e.g. Wacław Komarnicki, Rafał Lemkin and Stefan Glaser), at other times, however, they did not disclose their Polish ties (Hersch Lauterpacht[9]) or even

8 Redzik (2020a): 1.

9 References to Poland in the memories compiled by Lauterpacht's teachers deal with his place of origin – Kelsen (1961), activity in Jewish associations, as well as the climate of hostility towards Jewish students at the JCU – McNair (1961): 4. As noted by Elihu Lauterpacht in his biography of his father, Hersch Lauterpacht's links to Poland were limited. Any realistic link, in the sense of having a personal attachment to the state bearing the name, is confined solely to the period between the formation of the Polish state and Lauterpacht's departure for studies in Vienna. After leaving Lwów in 1919, Lauterpacht never came back to live there again. Formally, in July 1922, he applied for a Polish passport, which he would use until naturalization in the United Kingdom in 1931. Before taking the oath of fealty to the Crown on 12.06.1931, he procured a certificate of renunciation of Polish citizenship from the Consulate General. On the other hand, he paid two visits to the reborn Polish state and occasionally wrote on legal topics for Polish journals (importantly, in the Polish language!). He ardently encouraged his parents to move to the United

tried to extricate themselves from their Polishness (Helen Silving[10]), or their relationship with Poland could be regarded as 'complicated' (Theodor Meron[11]) – in those cases it is difficult to claim that we are dealing with the legacy of Polish scholarship, for which reason such persons are named in the introductory notes but their achievements are not analysed more extensively in the remainder of this work. Obtaining degrees and titles from Polish universities or working for them was somewhat of an indicator, provided that e.g. the John Casimir University in Lviv (Lwów) or Jagiellonian University in Cracow had been Polish halls of learning even before independence, as the lectures had been in Polish and the overwhelming majority of lecturers had been of Polish origin. In turn, at the Imperial University of Warsaw, Poles also studied and lectured, but the Russian was the exclusive language of instruction.

In principle, we decided that if a person was born in the territory of Poland (within its borders either prior to World War II or after its conclusion) or accepted Polish nationality during the relevant period, then they fall within the thematic scope of this book, as long as their activities coincide with the titular timeline. Where the nationality is not certain, we acknowledge as much and proceed with caution.

The title of this monograph refers to the international criminal law. It will be expedient, however, to emphasize already from the onset the difficulty of

---

Kingdom, albeit to no avail, due to siblings remaining in the old country. In Elihu Lauterpacht's account, Hersch Lauterpacht never suggested that he did not hail from Poland. See E. Lauterpacht (2010): 17–18, 38. See also Sands (2018): 123. See also Nahlik (1987b): 241, where the author emphasizes that when Lauterpacht and Winiarski sat together on the ICJ, they conversed in Polish.

10 It is worth recalling an excerpt from the preface to Helen Silving's memoirs by her husband, Paul K. Ryu, where he stresses the identity problems faced by the scholar of international criminal law: "She notices with sadness that she was treated as a 'Jew' in Poland and Nazi Austria, as a 'refugee from Europe' as well as a female intruder into the legal profession during and after World War II in the United States, as 'esta Americana' or 'gringa' in Puerto Rico, and as 'an American' (miguk saram) in Korea, as an 'American' also in Europe after WWII" – Silving (1988): 15. It would be problematic to count Silving among Polish lawyers, with her having neither studied nor written in Poland. She was, however, the first female law professor in the United States and for many years the only woman in international criminal law; more: Garcia-Salmones Rovira (2013): 167, Paz (2014): 1123–1146; Silving furthermore appears in numerous citations, e.g. Cryer (2005): 344; Glennon (2001): 191.

11 Meron (2021): 4 – "My departure from Poland after the war was followed by a deliberate disconnect, rejection, denial. I did not want to hear of Poland or talk of my wartime experience".

speaking, with regard to the interwar period, of the existence of an independent subdiscipline within public international law that international criminal law is today. That was a time of debate on the necessity of unification of criminal law and establishment of a universal criminal code but not the laying of the groundwork of a new discipline with the resulting development of studies in it. At that stage, there had not yet been a consistent distinction between the *droit pénal international* (criminal international law – a derivative of domestic criminal law and product of interstate co-operation primarily on extraditions and the exercise of jurisdiction) and the *droit international pénal* (international criminal law – linked to the development of public international law and thus setting forth the definitions of international crimes and the principles of responsibility for them). The purpose of the debates held throughout the Interwar period was to develop and adopt common solutions in domestic law and not to create norms of international law to take precedence before domestic norms. Nonetheless, it was precisely during the interwar period that the first initiatives sprung up that several decades later would bear fruit in the adoption of international treaties and creation of institutions nowadays regarded as being of key importance to international criminal law.

2

To paint a full picture of Polish achievements in the field of international law, this monograph was divided in two principal parts.

The first part discusses the activities of Polish authorities, diplomatic service, courts and scholars from 1918, paying attention to the historico-political background. It identifies Polish initiatives (individuals acting in private capacity or as official representatives of the Polish state) in the area of international criminal law. It includes the analysis of Polish involvement in the initiation of the works on and shaping of the contents of international conventions and resolutions passed by organizations. The chapter in question also outlines the scope in which Poland was bound by the various international treaties or, where not party to the specific convention, the reasons for non-accession, as well as Poland's stance on the obligations contained therein. For each of the discussed periods, attention is paid to domestic legislation adopted during the time, making it possible to discern the way in which Polish domestic law influenced the shape of international regulation and *vice versa*. The role of the judiciary in the shaping of principles of responsibility for international crimes is also identified. The importance of the analysis of Polish legislation, jurisprudence and official positions taken by authorities consists in its utility to the assessment of the role in shaping of international customary law. Specific individuals are also named – international lawyers and diplomats who, in our opinion, had the greatest impact (also in the light of the reception of their publications and their participation in the works on specific documents) on the debate on international criminal law unfolding during the period. Endeavours were made to identify those academic centres in which studies into international criminal law took place.

The first (historical) part of this monograph distinguishes four periods. The first one coincides with the interwar period – 1918–1939, i.e. the time when the works were initiated on cataloguing and defining international crimes and establishing the principles of responsibility for them. It is also a time during which the efforts of states were focused primarily on the unification of criminal law. The question of accountability for the crimes committed during World War I and the subsequent fights for the Polish Republic's borders also surfaced.

The second period – 1939–1944/1945 – begins with the outbreak of World War II and witnesses the initiatives of Polish government-in-exile for documenting and judging the crimes committed by the Nazis and their allies. That part of the book also describes the efforts of the underground state to bring those guilty of the crimes to judgment, as well as the innovative legislative solutions adopted either by the government-in-exile or by the communist authorities.

The third period spans the years 1945–1989. In the corresponding passages, we outline the efforts to exact the accountability of those guilty of crimes committed during World War II and to agree on the contents of so-called Nuremberg law. The special achievements of Polish courts in the development of the principles of accountability are recounted. There is a particular focus on Poland's role in the adoption of the specific conventions regulating international criminal law. Considerable attention is paid to the activities of the judiciary, i.e. special courts, Supreme National Tribunal, common courts and the Supreme Court, to which holding the Nazis accountable for crimes committed during World War II was a priority. The end date – 1989 – is conventional, marking the end of the Cold War and of the Polish People's Republic.

The passages dealing with the fourth of the periods, viz. 1989–2025 (post-Cold War period), highlight the acceleration of the already pending works on the definitions of international crimes and principles of responsibility for them but also developments in criminal jurisdiction over international crimes of domestic and international nature, especially with regard to the establishment of the International Criminal Court (ICC). They also discuss procedures involving responsibility for communist crimes, as well as for Nazi crimes and ones unconnected with the historical events of the World War II era, such as the problem of the execution of penalties imposed by the International Criminal Tribunal for the former Yugoslavia (ICTY), or the matter of the responsibility of Polish soldiers for the events in Nangar Khel (Afghanistan) in 2007 resulting in civilian fatalities and injuries.

Whereas the purpose of the first part of this work is to outline the scope of Polish contributions to the development of international criminal law in general, from a historical perspective, the second part deals with specific problems. Its goals are to highlight Polish achievements with regard to the problem of criminalization of the most important international crimes – 'core' crimes – i.e. those covered by the jurisdiction of the ICC (i.e. crime of aggression, war crimes, crimes against humanity, and the crime of genocide). Notice is made, however, of Poland's stance on the crime of terrorism, the incorporation of which into the catalogue of international crimes is a subject of ongoing debate, as well as on so-called transnational crimes focusing the attention of international lawyers and adepts of criminal law in the Interwar period. Moreover, the second part analyses principles of key importance to the prosecution of international crimes. Thus, it discusses the topic of the lack of a statute of limitations on the crimes, as well as criminal jurisdiction and its exercise, and the principles of criminal responsibility. Those are essential to the delineation of the terms and methods of accountability for international crimes.

3

Both the thematic scope and the timeline make it necessary to transcend the classic dogmatic method. In a natural way, to be able to encapsulate the essence of the impact and influence, one has to apply the historical method, albeit not in isolation from other research methods and techniques. We accept with humility the admonition of the 16th-century French humanist François Baudouin: without history, jurisprudence is blind – *sine historia caeca est iurisprudentia*! Thus, we acknowledge the feedback loop between law and history, and, in consequence, recognize historical interpretation as an element that is necessary to the comprehension of law.

For the purpose of studying the legacy left by Polish scholars, diplomats and institutions, we generally analysed, *inter alia*, the *travaux préparatoires* of the various international conventions or United Nations General Assembly (GA) resolutions, works of such bodies as the International Law Commission (ILC), IDI, International Law Association (ILA), International Union of Penal Law (IUPL), IAPL, International Commission for Penal Reconstruction and Development (ICPRD) and UNWCC, as well as the decisions of the various international or domestic Polish courts, and the official positions presented by Polish representatives within e.g. the ICC Assembly of States Parties. We also analysed the subject literature, as well as historical literature providing the context for the relevant events.

While working on the book, we had precious conversations with persons such as Władysław Czapliński, Maria Frankowska, Piotr Hofmański, Józef Koredczuk, Jerzy Kranz, Leszek Kubicki, Marek Madej, Jerzy Menkes, Renata Szafarz, Anna Wyrozumska and Beata Ziorkiewicz. We also completed research queries in such foreign institutions as the Wiener Library for the Study of the Holocaust and Genocide in London; Archive of the Polish Institute and Sikorski Museum (APISM) in London, Peace Palace Library in the Hague, UN Library in Geneva, as well as other libraries in Berlin, Cambridge, Geneva and Paris, not to mention the libraries of Polish academic institutions.

During our studies, we discovered the importance and the achievements of Polish academics and diplomats, so often overlooked or unrecorded by the literature. It must be noted, however, that the stymied access to Poland's official negotiating positions following 1945 did not make the goals set before this monograph any easier to achieve. This is also the effect of the frequent disappearance, from the various Polish institutions, of the good practice of detailed note-taking in negotiations. The present project proves the existence of numerous other areas deserving of study. Although we spared no efforts to give prominence to the achievements of the individual Polish scholars, we are aware that certain publications or persons may have eluded our attention. Therefore, we will be grateful for any feedback concerning the necessary supplementations.

All hyperlinks, unless specified otherwise, were accessible as at 27.02.2025. The decisions of the various courts and tribunals were analysed on the basis of the texts of judgments available on the forum's website or in its official digests.

We wish to thank our Reviewers and the series editor – Professor Malgosia Fitzmaurice. We also desire to give words of gratitude to Piotr Rylski, Agnieszka Mikos-Sitek and other staff members of the Polish Institute of

Justice, who for several years supported our work on the monograph. At Brill, special thanks are due to Ms. Ingeborg van der Laan. Last but not least, we extend the expressions of our gratitude to our families having gamely braved the discomforts of our work on this book.

Patrycja Grzebyk authored Chapters Two, Three, Six and Seven and Introduction; Bartłomiej Krzan wrote Chapters Five, Eight, Eleven, Twelve and Final Conclusions; Karolina Wierczyńska is the author of Chapters One, Four, Nine and Ten.

PART 1

History of Polish Involvement in the Development of International Criminal Law

CHAPTER 1

Interwar (1918–1939)

1 Restoration of Independence

Poland reclaimed her independence on 11.11.1918, but already on 7.10.1918, the Regency Council exercising the supreme authority in the Kingdom of Poland (pending the appointment of a regent) issued a proclamation titled *To the Polish Nation*[1], in which, with the words: 'Let there fall silent all that which can divide us from each other and let there one great voice resound: A United Independent Poland,' it proclaimed Polish independence. By the same proclamation, it dissolved the Council of State and resolved to form a cabinet and convoke parliament as soon as possible. On 12.10.1918, the Regency ordered a new wording of the military oath and took over the control of the armed forces.[2]

One month later, in Compiègne, the Entente signed the truce with Germany ending World War I. To Poland, that was an especially symbolic moment. After 123 years of partitions, the country was returning to the map of the world. The Regency Council, 'in the face of the looming danger external and internal, for the harmonization of all military ordinances and to keep order in the country,' by its decree placed the military authority and supreme command of Polish armed forces (and thereafter the mission of forming a cabinet) to Józef Piłsudski.[3] One day prior, Piłsudski had returned to Warsaw. In the words of Stanisław Kutrzeba: 'the day 11 November 1918 is the day of the establishment of an independent Polish State.'[4]

1 Proclamation of the Regency Council of 7.10.1918, Kumaniecki (1920), 119–120.

2 *Ibidem*: 120.

3 Decree of the Regency Council to the Polish nation on the transfer of military power to Józef Piłsudski on November 11, 1918 [*Dekret Rady Regencyjnej do narodu polskiego o przekazaniu władzy wojskowej Józefowi Piłsudskiemu 11 listopada 1918*], Dz.Pr.P.P.1918.17.38, see also Ajnenkiel (1997): 52.

4 Kutrzeba (1935): 99. It is worth pointing out, however, that only to years before WWII did the Sejm (lower chamber of Polish parliament) of the Polish Republic adopt an Act of 23.04.1937 on the Independence Day (Dz.U.33.255), noting as follows: 'the day 11 November as the anniversary of the resumption by the Polish National of an independent statehood and as a day for all time connected to the great name of Józef Piłsudski, the victorious Leader of the Nation in the struggle for the freedom of the Homeland – is a solemn Independence Day.'

 | DOI:10.1163/9789004712690_003

The new state's situation was a highly complicated one. The country was devastated by warfare, the borders of the state were indeterminate, and for the several years to come they presented the cause of military conflicts and plebiscites. It will not be an exaggeration to state that as far as the state borders of Poland were concerned, World War I ended only in the 20s. of the 20th century, i.e. after they were finally determined. The nascent statehood witnessed numerous tragic events implicating accountability. On 22–24 November, following the withdrawal of Ukrainians from Lviv, a pogrom of the Jewish population took place amid accusations of having supported the Ukrainian armed forces during the fights for the city.[5] Poland was also involved in an armed conflict with Czechoslovakia over the Cieszyn Silesia region in 1919–1920.

Part of the population inhabiting the territory of the Polish Republic did not speak Polish.[6] The year 1921 brought the First General Census of the Polish Republic,[7] which, although it did not include territories allocated to Poland only at a later time,[8] saw 70% of the population declare Polish ethnicity, 15% Ukrainian, 8% Jewish, 4% Belarusian and 3% German. Russians, Lithuanians, Czechs and some of the persons identifying as 'locals' did not exceed 1%.

It is not known how many of those spoke Polish. That was asked in a second general census, of 1931. At that time, Polish was claimed as the mother tongue by almost 70% of the population, Ukrainian by 10%, Jewish and Hebrew by more than 8%, Ruthenian by almost 4%, Belarusian by 3%, German by a little more than 2%, and Russian by just short of 0.5%.[9]

The partitioning powers left behind different legislative systems, and the shape of the judiciary also differed among the partitioning zones. The June of 1919 saw the appointment of a Codification Commission[10] tasked with:

5 Gauden (2019): 47–49; Hagen (2018): 123ff.

6 It should be recalled that the partitioning powers restricted the use of Polish in schools and the administration.

7 See The 1919 Act on the organization of administrative statistics (*Ustawa o organizacji statystyki administracyjnej*), Dz.U.1919.85.464, as amended.

8 For example, contested territories – Gawryszewski (2005): 111.

9 Central Statistical Office, Department of Statistical Studies, *100 years of Poland in numbers. 1918–2018*; [*Główny Urząd Statystyczny, Departament Opracowań Statystycznych,* 100 lat Polski w liczbach. 1918–2018] online at: https://stat.gov.pl/obszary-tematyczne/inne-opracowania/inne-opracowania-zbiorcze/100-lat-polski-w-liczbach-1918-2018,30,1.html?pdf=1.

10 The 1919 Act on the codification commission [Ustawa z dnia 3 czerwca 1919 r. o komisji kodyfikacyjnej], Dz.Pr.P.P.1919.44.315.

'preparation of drafts of a uniform legislation for all the lands (...) in the area of civil and criminal law,' as well as, 'other legislative drafts such as the Codification Commission shall elaborate either in effect of a resolution of the Sejm or in consultation with the Ministry of Justice.' The unification and codification of the law, in the face of the existence of the different legal systems of the partitioning powers, brought extraordinarily momentous legislative effects in the form of a series of codes enacted into force; a new, unified judicial system was built from the ground up in the following couple of years.

Members of the Commission's criminal division, established in order to codify substantive and procedural criminal law, included Edward Krzymuski (vice chair) i Emil Stanisław Rappaport (secretary), Juliusz Makarewicz and Wacław Makowski.[11] Among the members of the civil division was, for example, Michał Rostworowski. Those eminent jurists were responsible for the subsequent development of international law, including international criminal law.[12]

2 Treaty of Versailles

In January 1919 in Paris began the peace conference leading up to the signature of the peace treaties by the belligerent states and allied and associated powers.

The Polish delegation to the conference in Versailles incorporated mainly the members of the Polish National Committee, an organization founded by Roman Dmowski in 1917 in Lausanne and operating in Paris. The delegates plenipotentiary were Dmowski himself, Ignacy Jan Paderewski and Władysław Grabski. Kazimierz Dłuski was appointed a deputy delegate. Besides them, a number of advisors and experts were appointed; among others, Stanisław Kutrzeba was responsible for legal affairs, Franciszek Bujak for economic ones, and the issue of responsibility for the outbreak of the war was entrusted to Konstanty Skirmunt and later Leon Łubieński and Kazimierz

11 Markiewicz (2010): 116.

12 As far as the Commission's achievements in the field of criminal law are concerned, it will be expedient to mention the adoption of the Code of Criminal Procedure in 1929 (drafters included Makowski, Mogilnicki and Śliwiński) and of the Criminal Code in 1932 (Makarewicz and Makowski), the latter of which marked the apex achievement of its era and is until now the point of reference in numerous scholarly discussions (Dz.U.1932.60.571; see Koredczuk (2011): 45ff, Markiewicz (2010): 118).

Rybiński.[13] The congress works bureau also included Bohdan Winiarski, who dealt with legal and historical matters.[14] As an aside, it might be noted that the Commission on Reparation of Damage included Zygmunt Chamiec and Kazimierz Olszowski, with Jan Żółtowski joining the Commission on International Labour Legislation.[15]

A Commission on the Responsibility of the Authors of the War and the Enforcement of Penalties (hereinafter the 'Commission on Responsibilities') was also created during the peace conference.[16] Its task was to investigate the responsibility for the war. It included 15 members – two each from the great powers, i.e. United States of America, United Kingdom, France, Italy and Japan, and one each from selected states holding a particular stake. Those were Poland, Belgium, Romania, Greece and Serbia.[17] The Polish member was Skirmunt, and after him, from February onward, Łubieński; Rybiński became the secretary.

---

13 A detailed list can be found in Skoczek (2019): 34–42; Documents were placed in the collection titled Treaty of Peace with Germany, Hearings before the Committee on Foreign Relations United States Senate, 66th Congress, 1st session, on the Treaty of Peace with Germany, signed at Versailles on June 29, 1919 and submitted to the Senate on July 10, 1919, by the President of the United States (hereinafter: the 'Treaty of Peace with Germany'), Washington: Government Printing Office 1919, 314; Report Presented to the Preliminary Peace Conference by the Commission on the Responsibility of the Authors of the War and on Enforcement of Penalties (hereinafter: the 'Commission's report'): 316ff. It will be expedient to note that the works of the Commission are discussed also by Cyprian, Sawicki (1948b: 6ff). The Commission's report also in: Commission on the Responsibility of the Authors of the War and on Enforcement of Penalties, AJIL, vol. 14 (1–2): 95–154.

14 Bohdan Winiarski was active in the national movement, collaborating closely with Dmowski. In the Congress of Oppressed Nationalities in 1919 in Rome, preceding the peace talks in Versailles, he actively campaigned for the inclusion of Polish interests – cf. Sandorski (2004): 54–55.

15 Members of the various commissions in: Treaty of Peace with Germany, Annex 7: 309ff.

16 Cybulski (1987): 251 – that author provides an extensive discussion of the works of the Commission for the Examination of Violations of Customary and International Law by Foreign Authorities and Armed Forces in Polish Territories (*Komisja Badania Pogwałceń Prawa Zwyczajowego i Międzynarodowego przez Władze i Wojska Obce na Ziemiach Polski*). The Commission was tasked with the gathering of documentation of violations of international and domestic law during the armed conflict. It contributed to the complication of a Polish list of Germans whom we expected to be handed over pursuant to the provisions of the Versailles Treaty (Cybulski (1987): 253).

17 Treaty of Peace with Germany, Annex 7: 313ff.

The Commission on Responsibilities worked to develop the principles to govern the responsibility for war crimes committed during the war. The main tasks in its purview were to identify the persons responsible for the outbreak of the war; the facts constituting violations of the laws and customs of war by the Germans and forces allied to them on land and sea and in the air; the responsibility of specific individuals for those acts, mainly members of high commands and other high-profile persons; the matter of the establishment of a tribunal and procedures for the judgment of such persons; other related matters such as would arise during the Commission's works.[18]

On 29.03.1919, the Commission on Responsibilities presented its unanimously adopted report. The latter was of great significance to the development of the concept of individual responsibility and international criminal law, for it laid the groundwork for the first trial in history in which a head of state was to be judged and provided for the lesser criminals to be judged by military courts. Most of all, however, it broke the monopoly of a state on the exercise of criminal jurisdiction with respect to its citizens and accepted the assumption that individuals may be held accountable for their acts before international courts. Cherif Bassiouni called the report 'the greatest development for its time'.[19]

With regard to state responsibility for leading to the war, after analysis of the documents, the Commission pointed to Germany, Austria, Turkey and Bulgaria as the perpetrators. It was emphasized that the aforementioned states had rejected the proposals for peaceful resolution of the conflict, advanced by the Entente, and refused peace negotiations.[20]

In respect of the violations, the Commission took into consideration the reports of the British and French delegations, as well as memoranda from Greece, Belgium and Serbia and documents submitted by the Polish delegation, referring to violations of international law. At first, on 26.02.1919, the Polish delegation (the letter is undersigned by delegate Łubieński) offered information on crimes committed by German and Austrian armed forces, noting their premeditation and methodical execution – meaning the destructive forcible subjugation of terrorized populations and induction of economic supremacy; mass executions of civilian population; forced labour and deportations of civilian population; hostage taking; introduction of counterfeit currency; divestment of the population of its national identity by

18 *Ibidem*: 313.

19 Bassiouni (2011): 656.

20 Commission's report: 316–321.

prohibiting new Polish schools from being opened, closing existing ones and banning Polish books; supporting the Bolsheviks, Russians and Ukrainians with the simultaneous demilitarization of Polish militias.[21] The same allegations were also raised in the report of 5.03.1919 (*Note Sommaire*). The report was submitted by the Polish delegation,[22] with Łubieński's signature, and contained an elaboration on the aforementioned violations committed by German authorities in Polish territory. The violations concerned the introduction of a new currency, viz. the Polish mark, which significantly impoverished the population, putting it at the mercy of profiteers; deforestation had begun, with the cut wood being transported to Prussia; the same applied to other drains on the resources of the economy, including minerals, as well as food products, resulting in physical devastation of the inhabitants. All this was to ruin the country and lead to the extermination (in the original French: *exterminer*) of the population.[23] The report also mentions the denationalization of Poles in Lithuania as particularly harmful to the population. It involved the prohibition against opening new schools in Lithuania and the necessity of closing the existing ones. Moreover, the report mentioned the cruel attacks by the Bolsheviks (supported by the Germans and Austrians) on the civilian population.[24] Attached with the document was a report on prisoners of war by a government committee led by Czesław Knichowiecki.[25]

That document and the other ones allowed the Commission on Responsibilities to draw up a list of war crimes.[26] Before the commission outlined examples of crimes, it devoted a paragraph to noting that unprecedented

21 Note de la délégation polonaise in: Conférence de la Paix 1919–1920, Recueil des actes de la conférence, Partie IV, Commissions de la conférence, Commission des responsabilités des auteurs de la guerre et sanctions, Paris: Imprimerie nationale 1922: 347.

22 Note Sommaire sur les exactions commises, contrairement au droit des gens en Pologne par les armées ennemies de 1914 à 1918 (hereather: Note Sommaire) in: Conférence de la Paix 1919–1920, Recueil des actes de la conférence, Partie IV, Commissions de la conférence, Commission des responsabilités des auteurs de la guerre et sanctions, Paris: Imprimerie nationale 1922: 474–478, on works of Poles see also Cybulski (1987).

23 Note Sommaire: 477.

24 *Ibidem.*

25 Rapport de la Commission gouvernmentale des prisoners de guerre, Varsovie, À la délégation polonaise a la conférence de la paix, 4.02.1919, in: Conférence de la Paix 1919–1920, Recueil des actes de la conférence, Partie IV, Commissions de la conférence, Commission des responsabilités des auteurs de la guerre et sanctions, Paris: Imprimerie nationale 1922: 480.

26 The Commission's report: 326–327. The list of crimes was incorporated directly into the body of the report, but it also exists as a separate document in the form of annex.

cruelty could be observed during the war – neither prisoners of war, nor women and children were spared. They fell victim of murder, torture and mass executions. Hospital ships were attacked, vessels of the merchant marine were destroyed, wells were poisoned. The commission noted the 'number and gravity' of the crimes. The list was not complete or exhaustive, but it covered all the most important violations (32 items) featured in the reports and memoranda submitted by the states, including murders, massacres, well poisoning, theft, confiscations of property, systematic terrorism, killings of prisoners of war, torture of civilians, rapes, deportations of the civilian population, and internments. The charges submitted by the Poles in their documentation (apart from the allegation of supporting the Bolsheviks, Russians and Ukrainians), overlap in many places with the list. The list of 32 crimes (more on them in subchapter 7.1) was an important point of reference for proceedings before the Nuremberg tribunal; hence, Bogdan Cybulski remarks that Poland, whose representatives had worked on the commission's report: 'contributed to the actual placement of the principal Nazi criminals before the Nuremberg Tribunal.'[27] The conclusions of the relevant part of the Commission's report contained the summation that the war had been waged with the use of unlawful and barbaric methods, in violation of existing laws and customs of war and, 'elementary laws of humanity.'[28]

The next part of the report dealt with individual responsibility for the violations. The Commission made it clear that holding high positions in the state cannot justify any exemption from responsibility or protect those holders after the responsibility is confirmed by a suitable tribunal. Interestingly, the Commission observed that such a person (holder of a high office, e.g. head of state) could be exempted from being held responsible, but their position would be different in the light of international law.[29] In a later part, the Commission referred to the necessity of creating a high tribunal composed of judges from different states and subsequently noted that invoking immunity, so that the most egregious violations of laws and customs of war could not be judged, would: 'shock the conscience of civilized mankind.' The Commission also underscored that it was intolerable for a high-ranking official to avoid responsibility due to holding one position and not another. Mitigation of the responsibility would, however, be for the court to decide. The conclusions affirmed the individual responsibility of

27 Cybulski (1987): 256.
28 Commission's report: 327.
29 *Ibidem*: 328.

persons having violated the laws and customs of war, irrespective of the positions they had held.

On the matter of the establishment, organization and procedure of the competent tribunal, the Commission deemed it proper to consider the competence of such a tribunal with regard to two types of violations – those having caused the outbreak of the war, as well as violations of the laws and customs of war and laws of humanity. Concerning the violations having led to the war, the Committee decided against specifying that the persons having contributed to the outbreak (the former Kaiser) ought to be held responsible before such a tribunal. The emphasis was made that a war of aggression was not necessarily incompatible with positive law. Unquestionably, however, a contravention of international law had taken place, due to the violation of its overarching principle, i.e. that of the independence of states. The conclusions stated that, in the future, criminal responsibility and criminal sanctions should be established for serious violations of the basic principles of international law.[30]

As for the violations of the laws and customs of war and laws of humanity, it was recalled that the belligerent parties had the right to judge the violators, although with the emphasis that in certain situations a high tribunal should be appointed for that purpose. Such a tribunal should be established for the perpetrators of the most serious mass crimes; perpetrators whose orders had been applicable not to one theatre but to multiple territories of the Allied states; persons who had had the opportunity (on account of their position) to prevent violations; others who for various reasons should be judged by a high tribunal.[31]

The body, according to the Commission's proposal, should incorporate the representatives of several powers, apply the law of nations and decide its own procedure. It was proposed that the national courts ought not to proceed if a given case were to fall within the purview of the high tribunal (in a sense, therefore, the tribunal was accorded priority to the exercise of penal jurisdiction); it was also suggested that an individual's conviction by a domestic court must not pose a bar to their prosecution by the high tribunal or the court of an Allied state. The conclusions of the relevant part of the report also referred to issues other than mentioned above, namely that the individuals charged with such type of crimes should not be granted amnesty and should be prosecuted before the tribunal.[32] The main body of

30 *Ibidem*.
31 *Ibidem*: 331ff.
32 *Ibidem*: 332ff.

the Commission's report only raised the problem of the immunity without discussing amnesty. Moreover, the Commission made references to the obligations of the states deemed hostile with regard to the provision of information on the activities of persons who had been in command of any places of detention, such as prisoner-of-war camps, civilian camps or labour camps. The purpose of such information was to be used in order to secure the convictions of such persons and determine the degree of their respective responsibility. The Allied states, on the other hand, were to adopt such legislative solutions as to facilitate the jurisdiction of the international tribunal and its operations (it is noteworthy that only in the conclusions of the report does the matter of an international tribunal rather than high tribunal feature for the first time). Last but not least, the Commission also specified that the Allied states should expect neutral states to extradite those who committed crimes for the purpose of their prosecution.[33]

Concerning the related issues, the Commission – in Annex IV to the report – formulated proposals of provisions concerning the obligations of the hostile states and the jurisdiction of the tribunal, for inclusion in the peace treaties.[34] The report was signed by the representatives of 10 states, among them Łubieński for Poland.

The report, in the preparation of which Poland had been highly involved thanks to participation in the Commission's works and submission of a list of war crimes committed, had largely, albeit not completely, translated into the contents of the provisions of the Treaty of Versailles, signed on 28.06.1919.[35] Not only did the latter spell the end of World War I, it also imposed on the acceding states an obligation to resolve their disputes peacefully, refrain from restoring to war and have recourse to courts of arbitration in the event of disputes arising among the states (Article 10–12).[36]

Part III Section VIII of the Treaty referred to Poland, with Article 87 addressing the borders. Among other things: 'Germany (…) recognizes the complete independence of Poland.' The nature of the Treaty provisions dealing with Poland's borders was thus not clear or final. The borders other than set by the Treaty would be demarcated at a later time. The remainder of the articles on Poland referred to the right of transit through Polish territory

33 *Ibidem*: 333.

34 Annex IV, Provisions for Insertion in Treaties with Enemy Governments in: Treaty of Peace with Germany, Hearings before the Committee on Foreign Relations United States Senate … : 377–378.

35 Dz.U.1920.35.200.

36 Dz.U.1920.35.

from East Prussia to Germany and back, telegraphic freedom (Article 89), Polish nationality (Article 91), as well as mutual recognitions and settlements between Poland and Germany (Article 92). A very interesting picture is painted by the provisions of Article 93, which provided the basis for being bound by the Minority Treaty:

> Poland accepts and agrees to embody in a Treaty with the Principal Allied and Associated Powers such provisions as may be deemed necessary by the said Powers to protect the interests of inhabitants of Poland who differ from the majority of the population in race, language or religion.
>
> Poland further accepts and agrees to embody in a Treaty with the said Powers such provisions as they may deem necessary ….

Poland also had to accept the provisions of the Little Treaty of Versailles,[37] the so-called Polish Minority Treaty, which referenced the provisions and institutions of the Treaty of Versailles. Article 1 bound Poland not to take any such legislative action as might be contrary to the provisions of Articles 2–8. Those provisions were to deal with the rights and freedoms accorded by the Polish state to its citizens irrespective of their ethnicity, language, race or religion, such as equality before law, equal civil and political rights, the same treatment and legal and factual guarantees, including the right to incorporate and operate institutions and schools. Poland's signature of the Treaty was the fruit of the efforts – among others – of the President of the United States of America, Woodrow Wilson,[38] who had harboured certain

37 Dz.U.1920.110.728.

38 In the subject literature, however, we will find numerous unfavourable references to that fact, based on the criticism of the circumstance that Germany (the Weimar Republic) was not covered by the obligations of that agreement and furthermore that it undermined and restricted the sovereign rights of the Polish state; cf. Drozdowski in: Skoczek (2019): 8. That argument may have been rooted in the fact that the Treaty imposed obligations on the states with regard to minorities and, in practice, on the basis of the Treaty, other states were empowered to notify the League Council and the latter to issue instructions to Poland with regard to the protection of minority rights. Disputes concerning the implementation of the Treaty could be referred to the jurisdiction of the PCIJ. Other than cases involving the provisions of the Treaty (see Rights of Minorities in Upper Silesia (Minority Schools) Judgment of 26/04/1928 (Series A, No. 15)), the PCIJ also handed down advisory opinions on the interpretation of the provisions of the Treaty (see German Settlers in Poland Advisory Opinion of 10/09/1923 (Series B, No. 6); Acquisition of Polish Nationality, Advisory Opinion of 15/09/1923 (Series B, No. 7). A little fewer than 30% of all complaints filed during the life of that

justified concerns, pressing for its adoption. For he was familiar with the problem of pogroms in Poland,[39] as well as the surge in anti-Semitism throughout Europe.[40]

The crucial provisions of the Treaty of Versailles[41] from the perspective of the matters here being discussed, contained in Articles 227–230, addressed the responsibility for violations of the laws and customs of war. They provided for the accountability of the criminals, including the German Kaiser Wilhelm II Hohenzollern, accused by the associated and allied powers 'for a supreme offence against international morality and the sanctity of treaties' (Article 227 of the Treaty). The Treaty provided for the creation of a tribunal composed of five judges appointed by the USA, United Kingdom, France, Italy and Japan, and thus an international court. Article 228 stipulated that the German perpetrators of crimes would be tried before the military tribunals of the various powers for acts 'in violation of the laws and customs of war.' The German government was to extradite them if such were the will of the powers. Article 229 discussed the composition of the military tribunals, specifying that for those perpetrators who acts involved several of the powers, military tribunals composed of the representatives of the same powers should be established. Article 230, in turn, bound the

instrument concerned the representatives of the German minority in Poland, whereas the Jews almost never availed themselves of the Treaty solutions. It will be expedient to observe that a large role in respect of the protection of minority rights was played by the Upper Silesian Mixed Commission, established in 1922 pursuant to the Polish-German treaty dealing with the division of Upper Silesia. Its president, Felix Calonder, viewed its mechanism as the most refined instrument for the protection of minority rights, including the temporary suspension of anti-Jewish legislation in the German part of Upper Silesia; cf. Erpelding (2017).

39 Lundgreen-Nielsen (1982): 105–126.

40 An account from the Congress of Versailles in 1919 concerning Dmowski is interesting. Supposedly, when inquired by Wilson regarding the Jewish question, he replied that 10% of Poland's population were Jews and that was about 8% too many (Leuprecht (2001): 115).

41 Before the adoption of the Treaty, the USA and Japan submitted reservations as to the Commission's report. The reservations submitted focused on the assumption that the Kaiser bore moral responsibility for not having prevented the violations committed by his subordinates but himself had not committed any crimes. Those reservations were not heeded in the Treaty. Annex II, Memorandum of reservations presented by the Representatives of the United States to the Report of the Commission on Responsibilities, April 4, 1919, in: Treaty of Peace with Germany, Hearings before the Committee on Foreign Relations United States Senate … : 371; Annex III, Reservations by the Japanese Delegation, in: Treaty of Peace with Germany, Hearings before the Committee on Foreign Relations United States Senate … : 376.

German government to co-operate and render assistance with the pending proceedings, provide evidence, and so on.

The German delegation protested against the provisions of the Treaty[42] but signed it on 28.06.1919. The Allies, on the other hand, commenced their efforts to bring those accused of crimes to trial. They did not succeed either in having the Kaiser judged or in bringing the lesser perpetrators before the Allied military courts. The Kingdom of the Netherlands, not party to the Treaty, refused to extradite the former monarch, who had found refuge in its territory and been granted asylum.[43]

As for the lesser perpetrators, Germany forcibly criticized the possibility of the extradition of the offenders; on 13.12.1919, a statute was passed conferring the exclusive jurisdiction for the judgment of the German perpetrators on the court in Leipzig.[44] The Allies consented, submitting a list of persons who, in their opinion, should be judged. Those were almost 900 people (including 50 nominated by Poland),[45] out of whom 45 were eventually selected and the cases forwarded by the Allies together with the evidence to the court in Leipzig. During the trials, the Belgians and the French withdrew, unwilling to continue to participate in what they termed, 'the farce.'[46] Suffice to say that 12 people were ultimately judged, out of whom 6 acquitted. Those convicted of war crimes were given absurdly low sentences (the most severe was 4 years' imprisonment for the sinking of a hospital ship).

Because not one of the 900 persons mentioned on the list was extradited to Poland, it would be difficult to speculate on what the trials could have looked like there, had the offenders against the law of nations been tried at the time.

---

42 Cyprian, Sawicki (1948b): 18.

43 *Ibidem*: 19–21.

44 *Ibidem*: 22.

45 There are different accounts as to the contents of the list – this is described e.g. by Bassiouni (2011): 656; also concerning the number of persons wanted by the various states. Cyprian and Sawicki (1948b: 23) report that the Polish list comprised 51 names, while according to Kubicki (1963) those were 425 names subsequently reduced to 51. A publication in the *Kurjer Poranny* of 13.01.1920 gives the number at 50. We were unable to locate the list during our inquiries. Cybulski mentions the following names, among others, as having been on the list: Hans von Beseler, Etzdorf von Rummel and Wolfgang von Kriss. See also Cybulski (1986): 334, where he recounts almost the entire 'Polish' list, and Cybulski (1987): 255. None of the offenders from the Polish list were judged.

46 Cyprian, Sawicki (1948b): 31–33; more on the trials on the charges submitted by the United Kingdom: *German War Trials. Report of Proceedings before the Supreme Court in Leipzig. With appendices*, His Majesty Stationery Office: London 1921.

Nonetheless, it is to the Poles' credit that they took an active part in the peace conference and the works on the project of the first international criminal tribunal. Those achievements should be viewed as fundamental, to the point that they provided the ideological basis for the creators of the permanent criminal court, to whom the assurance that serious crimes would never again go unpunished was a principal point of concern.

3 Poles' Activities in International Organizations

Poles took an active part in the works of international organizations and associations, now and then even initiating their establishment. It is worth recalling at in 1923 the Polish Branch of ILA was formed. Chairing its first board was Zygmunt Cybichowski, with Ignacy Szebeko – diplomat and member of the Sejm – as vice chair. Other board members included Julian Makowski, Michał Rostworowski and Szymon Rundstein. Since the onset of the 20th century, the ILA has occupied itself with the problem of the establishment of an international criminal court. The matter had been raised already during the 1922 conference in Buenos Aires, where a draft was prepared that would subsequently be refined and adopted in the Vienna conference in 1926.[47] As the Polish section came to life one year after the first initiative relating to the establishment of the tribunal, it is difficult to determine the degree of Polish participation. Nevertheless, Poles did participate in the talks on the matter, as attested by the fact that the ILA's 35th Conference took place in Warsaw on 9–15.08.1928, drawing approximately 200 participants from 25 states. It passed two resolutions: *Draft Convention on Extradition* and *Rules for the Government of Territory Occupied by Hostile Forces*. The list includes as many as 45 names from Poland, including Zygmunt Cybichowski, Cezary Berezowski, Ludwik Ehrlich and Stefan Glaser.[48]

The matter of the creation of an international criminal court was also the subject of the works of dedicated criminal-law associations such as the AIDP. Its co-founder in 1924[49] was Emil Stanisław Rappaport. Rafał Lemkin

47 Grzebyk (2013a): 83.

48 Równy (2003): 39–42.

49 AIDP "replaced" the International Union of Penal Law. Already before World War I, several Polish criminal lawyers attempted to create a Polish group within that body, established in 1889 in Vienna by Franz von Liszt, Gerard van Hamel and Adolphe Prins. The Polish motion, however, despite having garnered the support of the French,

became the secretary of the Polish group. The Association's purpose was to harmonize the principles underlying the domestic legislations of the various states, so as to achieve the adoption by all of them of a common set of general principles of penal repression.[50] Lemkin was also a member of the International Bureau for the Unification of Criminal Law,[51] whereas Rappaport, in 1928–1939, served as its Vice President.

The AIDP's Polish group was somewhat active. During the first congress in Brussels, in 1926, Rappaport became the leader of the Polish delegation comprising, among others, Wacław Makowski, Juliusz Makarewicz and Aleksander Mogilnicki. Rappaport presented a report, titled *Ètat législatif actuel dans la République polonaise*, on the works on the codification of Polish law.[52] The congress also discussed the subject of the application of protective measures, prison labour, and creation of an international criminal court, at the time hypothesized as a chamber of the Permanent Court of International Justice (PCIJ) operating at the League of Nations. The plans were for that court to be given the powers to punish states and individuals for violations of international criminal law on the basis of previously adopted international conventions. The congress was of the opinion that the goal in the form of the establishment of an international institution of criminal justice should be achieved in a gradual manner by way of detailed agreements among the states. In the end, a resolution was adopted in favour of the unification of criminal law and recognition of universal principles of penal repression, noting the high desirability of the

was rejected – mainly by German vote, for political reasons. The official explanation was that a nation without a state could not have its own national group within the organization, even though a Croatian group was accepted in identical circumstances. A breakthrough was made thanks to contacts with Garçon, who invited Rappaport to become a member of *La Société Générale des Prisons*. Rappaport was then able to extend the invitation to other Polish lawyers and jurists. Garçon's work was thereafter continued by Henri Carton de Wiart (Belgium), Louis Hugueney (France) and Quintiliano Saldaña (Spain). Together with Rappaport, they on 14.03.1924 created the International Association of Penal Law/Association Internationale de Droit Pénal (IAPL/AIDP), Rappaport was not only the AIDP's co-founder but also its Vice President of many years (1924–1961) and thereafter an honourary member – see extensively Grzebyk (2020a): 104; see also Kunicka (2013): 1063ff.

50 Rappaport (1929b): 20.

51 Lemkin (2018): 63.

52 AIDP, Premier congrès international de droit pénal, Bruxelles (26–29.07.1926), Paris 1927.

adoption of common, uniform rules,[53] and agreeing that the states should convene in a conference devoted to the harmonization of the principles of penal repression (which gave the beginning to unification congresses, as discussed below).[54]

The congress in Bucarest in 1929 was attended by Rappaport, Glaser and Helena Wiewiórska. Among other topics, it discussed the criminal responsibility of bodies corporate, the use of foreign criminal law by a domestic judge, and the collegiality of judicial panels.[55]

The third congress took place in Palermo, in 1933, and, among others, dealt with what crimes should be subject to universal jurisdiction. Other topics included the crime of defamation and the matter of the executive criminal code (regulating the enforcement of penalties). Rappaport, Lemkin, Leon Rabinowicz, Glaser and Mogilnicki presented reports from Poland.

The fourth congress was convened in Paris (initially planned to be Athens), 1937. Its agenda focused on how states were to protect peace through criminal law. Discussions also covered the mutual notice of offenders' past histories with the justice system, punishment by analogy of a crime not stipulated in the criminal code, and procedural guarantees for the defendant in pretrial proceedings.[56] Glaser, Mogilnicki and Wolter delivered papers on the subject of *Légalité des délits*.[57] Speakers included Glaser, Rappaport, Wiewiórska and Lemkin. The last one's paper was titled *La protection de la paix par le droit pènal interne*.[58] He stressed that the role of criminal law in the prevention of war was secondary, whereas the protection of peace instead called for the existence of a harmonious international co-operation. Pointing towards the goal of world peace, he accentuated the necessity of the states' acting to oppose the outbreak of another armed conflict.[59] Lemkin's emphasis on the role of international co-operation

53 AIDP, Résolutions des Congrès AIDP (1926–2004), ReAIDP/e-RIAPL, 2006, D-01, 13, https://www.ehu.eus/documents/1736829/2010409/O+23+Resolutions+des+Congres+de+lassociation+internationale+de+droit+penal.pdf.

54 Rappaport (1929b): 20.

55 Second International Congress of Penal Law (Bucharest, 6–12.10.1929) (2015), 86 (1) RIDP, 31.

56 Fourth International Congress of Penal Law (Paris, 26–31.07.1937) (2015), 86(1) RIDP, 41.

57 Glaser also *Garanties de la defense*; see Stefan Glaser (1937b): 874; Mogilnicki's paper in: Mogilnicki (1935): 341–343.

58 Lemkin (1938a): 95–126.

59 *Ibidem*: 123–124.

highlights the development course his interests had taken in the preceding decade, having previously centred firmly on criminal law (in that, he was not alone – Glaser underwent a similar transformation). Lemkin became an advocate for international criminal law.

The most time in Paris was consumed by the matter of the applicability of analogy in the context of the principle of *nullum crimen, nulla poena sine lege.* That principle had been repealed by the criminal code of Soviet Russia in 1922, allowing the full extent of the application of analogy by the judge. Germany, in turn, enabled the imposition of a penalty even for an act not foreseen by the statute, as long as it was, 'deserving of punishment.'[60] Symptomatically, representatives of those countries did not attend.[61] The congress, however, did pass a resolution to confirm that the principle of legality of crimes and penalties, the necessary guarantee of individual rights, had as its consequence the exclusion of the method of analogy from the interpretation of criminal statutes, and that it extended equally to protective measures as to penalties.[62]

Among the international congresses that were instrumental in the development of the discipline of international criminal law, one also needs to mention the unification congresses of criminal law. The idea of such meetings had been borrowed from AIDP congresses and was intended as a reflection of the European states' aspirations to harmonize the provisions regulating criminal justice. The first conference on the unification of criminal law took place in 1927 in Warsaw.

At the time, Rappaport wrote about the goals that should be guiding the international community – goals of which he himself was a great promoter: 'The international criminal tribunal, or the criminal chamber of the current Permanent Court of International Justice (…) this is a great way to expand the criminal liability of individuals and communities organized in a strictly international manner.'[63] Apart from the institutionalization, the discussion also focused on the harmonization of criminal law. The goal, however, was not to create 'United States of Europe' and give them a common criminal code (that vision was not alien to Rappaport, though rather as a solution for the future), but to aspire to the universalization of the criminal law of nations within existing structures and under the auspices of the League of

60 Kulesza (2021): 267.

61 Rappaport (1937): 172–177.

62 Glaser (1937b): 879.

63 Rappaport (1929b): 38.

Nations, as well as for the states to harmonize their respective legislations in such fragments as would be amenable to such unification.[64]

The congress in Warsaw managed to agree on a list of international delicts – *delicta juris gentium*. Those included:

a) piracy,
b) forgery of coin, public securities or banknotes,
c) slave trade,
d) trafficking in women or children,
e) intentional use of any means capable of causing a universal danger,
f) drug production and trafficking,
g) production and distribution of pornographic printed materials
h) other criminal offences stipulated by the international conventions entered into by the State.[65]

According to the assumptions of the resolution passed in the congress, crimes of that kind were to be punishable according to the law of a given state, irrespective of the perpetrator's nationality or the place of commission of the crime. Thus, penalization on the basis of universal jurisdiction was expected.

The congress also approved the concept of attempt and aiding and abetting; legitimate defence and dire necessity were also discussed. Moreover, Rappaport tabled a motion to include the propaganda of a war of aggression as such a *delictum juris gentium*. The main goal was to initiate a discussion among prominent jurists on the necessity of penalization of that type of crime and its addition to the criminal codes of the states.[66]

Participants of the congress in Warsaw included Quintiliano Saldaña, Henri Ferri, Jean-Andre Roux, Simon Sasserath, Vespasian Pella, Toma Givanovitch, and, on the Polish side, Emil S. Rappaport, Wacław Makowski and Aleksander Mogilnicki.

The second unification congress in Rome, in 1928, saw the establishment of the International Bureau for the Unification of Criminal Law, so as to provide for the continuity of the unification works. The Belgian representative, Henri Carton de Wiart, became the President, and the Polish member, Rappaport, a Vice President. The remaining Vice Presidents were Mario d'Amelio, Megalos Calloyani, Simon Sasserath, and Vespasian Pella the secretary gen-

64 *Ibidem*: 39.

65 *Ibidem*: 118ff.

66 Motion for the Warsaw Conference concerning the crime of propaganda of a war of aggression; *Ibidem*: 98ff.

eral.[67] Apart from Rappaport, the Polish representatives attending in Rome included Mogilnicki, Makowski and Glaser. The congress saw the adoption of resolutions concerning protective measures and international recidivism.[68]

Subsequent congresses took place in Brussels (1930), Paris (1931), Madrid (1933), Copenhagen (1935) and Cairo (1938).[69] In Brussels, the attempt was made to codify the crime of terrorism and add it to the 'Warsaw' list of *delicta juris gentium*. Eventually, it was added in a parenthesis – in category e, i.e. 'intentional use of any instrument capable of producing a public danger.' The lack of a definition of terrorism did, however, pose a problem. Therefore, the discussion continued in the congress in Paris, with the decision to appoint a group tasked with presenting its conclusions to the congress in Madrid.[70] As Lemkin wrote, however, the consensus could not be reached on a definition of terrorism as it 'embraces a large variety of different criminal acts.'[71]

In Paris, remaining within the topic range of terrorism, Lemkin presented a paper titled: *Emploi intentionnel des tous moyens capables de faire courir un danger commun*.[72]

In Madrid, he did not attend,[73] but he had been able to have his paper printed in time, by the Pedone publishing house, to be sent to the congress. It bore the title *Les actes constituant un danger général (interétatique) considérés comme délits des droit des gens*. It is probably one of Lemkin's best-known texts outside of his canonical *Axis Rule in Occupied Europe: Laws of Occupation, Analysis of Government, Proposals for Redress* of 1944. While the word 'genocide' is not used in the text, references are made to the crimes of barbarity and vandalism, linked to the protection of the collective in both an existential and a spiritual sense – doubtless providing a direct inspiration for the eventual definition of genocide.[74] In his Madrid paper, Lemkin

67 *Ibidem*: 150.

68 *Ibidem*: 141ff.

69 Informations from the League of Nations search engine: http://www.lonsea.de/pub/org/775.

70 Callahan (2018): 127.

71 Rafał Lemkin, *Acts Constituting a General (Transnational) Danger Considered as Offences Against the Law of Nations* online at: http://www.preventgenocide.org/lemkin/madrid1933-english.htm.

72 Szawłowski (2014): 299.

73 Lemkin (2018): 65, Sands (2018): 204.

74 The idea of punishing barbarity had surfaced before Lemkin mentioned it in his paper – concerning the conflict between Vespasian Pella and Lemkin in this matter see Mamolea (2020): 82.

suggested that, in the legal circumstances of the time, the codification of a new criminal offence in the law of the nations under the name of terrorism would be futile and superfluous. In his opinion, there was a necessity to return to the 'Warsaw formula' and create provisions addressing acts so harmful and dangerous to the international community that their nature as crimes against the law of nations would be regarded as expedient and necessary and would avoid provoking reservations. Lemkin enumerated, in order: acts of barbarity, acts of vandalism, preparation of catastrophes in international communication, intentional interruption of international communication, and dissemination of a human, animal or plant epidemic disease.

Barbarity was to denote acts of extermination directed against specific groups (Lemkin mentioned ethnic, social and religious groups), for political, religious or other reasons; vandalism to any forms of organized destruction of art and cultural legacy.[75]

In pointing out the necessity of covering such crimes with universal jurisdiction,[76] Lemkin appealed to the conscience of the international community. He noted that only the most serious crimes were met with universal repression. He encouraged the states to adopt an international convention providing for penal repression against the aforementioned crimes.[77] To Lemkin, the report marked his contribution to the discussion of the necessity of expansion of the list of crimes against the law of nations. Accordingly, he would draw attention to the contents of the original list and acknowledge Rappaport's earlier attempts to expand it to include the crime of propaganda of a war of aggression. Lemkin had not yet realized at the time that his document would constitute the conceptual beginning of a normative process to be finalized 15 years later in the form of a Genocide Convention.

In the congress in Copenhagen in 1935, Lemkin once again returned to the topic of terrorism, delivering a paper titled *Teroryzm*. He published an abstract in the *Gazeta Sądowa Warszawska*.[78] Referring to a diversity of terrorist acts, he pointed out that they consisted primarily in the intimidation

75 Lemkin, *Les actes constituant …*

76 Lemkin goes as far as recommending a specific shape of provisions dealing with such crimes.

77 Thus, things were different from what was claimed by Szawłowski (2014: 300): 'Therefore, in 1933, Lemkin had not yet postulated entering into some international convention on "punishing the crime of barbarity."'

78 Lemkin (1935): 561–564.

of the population, whereas international terrorism had as its goal harming the interests of the state of presenting a threat to the entire international order. There, he referred to internal and international terrorism according to concepts formulated by Rappaport and Givanovitch. At the end, similarly to his Madrid report, he proposed a specific wording of provisions dealing with both types of terrorism. In the 7th congress in Cairo, which took place in 1938, Lemkin redirected his interests to the crime of forgery of passports[79] and was the rapporteur on the subject.

It will also be expedient to note the 2nd International Congress of Comparative Law in 1937 in The Hague. Although the latter congress combined all legal disciplines, the problems of criminal law and procedure proved to be the most captivating to the observers. Lemkin served as the secretary of the criminal law section. Other Poles in attendance included Glaser and Rappaport. Moreover, a dozen or so papers were sent in from Poland, among them those by Antoni Deryng and Władysław Wolter.[80] The greatest emotion was roused by the topic of adherence or non-adherence to the principle of *nulla poena sine lege* in domestic legislation. The German delegates present in the congress stood in defence of the German reform repealing the application of the aforementioned rule, justifying that with the 'healthy national sense.' The academic society attending the congress voiced a categorical objection to the repeal and spoke in favour of retention of the principle (only the Germans abstained and no one voted against). A firm resistance to the use of analogy in criminal law came from the Polish participants – Wolter, Glaser and Lemkin.[81]

It is also fitting to recall the initiatives of the League of Nations involving the participation of experts from Poland. Among the most important ones was the attempted creation of an international criminal tribunal for the purpose of fighting terrorism. Together with the draft convention on the repression of terrorism, designs on the creation of a permanent criminal court took shape. November 1937 saw an international conference in Geneva on the repression of terrorism. Although the proposal of adopting such a convention failed to garner broad support, it was probably one of the most significant prewar activities in international humanitarian law with Poles

79 *Falsification of Passports as an International Crime: Towards an International Convention for the Protection of Passports*. Report to the Sixth International Conference for the Unification of Penal Law, held in Cairo in January 1938.

80 Glaser (1937b); Lemkin (1937): 178–181.

81 Glaser (1937b): 885–886; Lemkin (1937): 181.

participating. Documents of the League of Nations mention an employee of Polish Ministry of Justice, Lucjan Bekerman, who took part in the works of the League's terrorism committee in 1936.[82]

Last but not least, one could not possibly omit the fact of Poland's participation in the founding 'conference' of Interpol in 1923 in Vienna. Police chiefs from 20 nations, invited by the Austrian chief of police, Johann Schober (who subsequently led the organization until 1932), decided to develop international co-operation in fighting terrorism, money laundering, crimes against the legacy of mankind, but also war crimes (the term was employed in the broad sense, extending to crimes against humanity and genocide).[83]

4 Treaty Obligations

Poland, as a fully fledged participant of international relations, acceded in 1918–1939 to a considerable number of international conventions. Besides the aforementioned Treaty of Versailles, one has to mention in particular the conventions in international humanitarian law, which were of importance to later commitments. The list includes, among others: the Convention on Hospital Ships of 1904;[84] the Convention for the Amelioration of the Condition of the Wounded and Sick in Armies in the Field of 1906[85] replaced by the Geneva Convention for the Amelioration of the Condition of the Wounded and Sick in Armies in the Field of 1929;[86] the Convention for the Pacific Settlement of International Disputes of 1907;[87] the Convention respecting the Laws and Customs of War on Land of 1907;[88] the

82 See Report: https://www.legal-tools.org/doc/502186/pdf, also Historical Survey of the Question of International Criminal Jurisdiction – Memorandum submitted by the Secretary-General, A/CN.4/7/Rev.1, 16–18.

83 Fooner (2009): 7.

84 Online at: https://ihl-databases.icrc.org/en/ihl-treaties/hague-conv-1904; Dz.U.1936.60.439.

85 Online at: https://ihl-databases.icrc.org/assets/treaties/180-IHL-GC-1906-EN.pdf; Dz.U.1927.28.225.

86 Online at: https://ihl-databases.icrc.org/assets/treaties/300-IHL-GC-1929-1-EN.pdf; Dz.U.1932.103.864.

87 Online at: https://cil.nus.edu.sg/wp-content/uploads/2019/02/1907-The-Hague-Convention-for-the-Pacific-Settlement-of-International-Disputes-1-1-1.pdf; Dz.U.1930.9.64.

88 Online at: https://ihl-databases.icrc.org/assets/treaties/195-IHL-19-EN.pdf; Dz.U.1927.21.161.

Convention relative to the Opening of Hostilities of 1907;[89] the Convention relative to the Rights and Duties of Neutral Powers and Persons in case of War on Land of 1907;[90] the Convention relative to the Legal Position of Enemy Merchant Ships at the Start of Hostilities of 1907;[91] the Convention relating to the Conversion of Merchant Ships into War-Ships of 1907;[92] the Convention concerning Bombardment by Naval Forces in Time of War of 1907;[93] the Convention for the Adaptation to Maritime Warfare of the Principles of the Geneva Convention of 1907;[94] the Convention relative to Certain Restrictions with regard to the Exercise of the Right of Capture in Naval War of 1907;[95] and the Protocol for the Prohibition of the Use in War of Asphyxiating, Poisonous, or Other Gases, and of Bacteriological Methods of Warfare of 1925;[96] the Convention for the Amelioration of the Condition of the Wounded and Sick in Armies in the Field of 1929;[97] the Convention relative to the Treatment of Prisoners of War of 1929.[98]

Apart from the ratification of the treaties on the law of war, Poland joined initiatives taken with a view to preventing future global armed conflicts, ratifying both the General Treaty for Renunciation of War as an Instrument of National Policy of 1928,[99] and the Convention for the Definition of Aggression of 1933.[100] She also acceded to the Litvinov Protocol – a multilateral pact relating to the coming into force of the aforementioned General Treaty (a document in the nature of a non-aggression pact). It was

89 Online at: https://ihl-databases.icrc.org/assets/treaties/190-IHL-18-EN.pdf; Dz.U.1927.21.159.

90 Online at: https://ihl-databases.icrc.org/assets/treaties/200-IHL-20-EN.pdf; Dz.U.1927.21.163.

91 Online at: https://ihl-databases.icrc.org/assets/treaties/205-IHL-21-EN.pdf; Dz.U.1936.6.64.

92 Online at: https://ihl-databases.icrc.org/assets/treaties/210-IHL-22-EN.pdf; Dz.U.1936.6.65.

93 Online at: https://ihl-databases.icrc.org/assets/treaties/220-IHL-24-EN.pdf; Dz.U.1936.6.66.

94 Online at: https://ihl-databases.icrc.org/assets/treaties/225-IHL-25-EN.pdf; Dz.U.1936.6.67.

95 Online at: https://ihl-databases.icrc.org/assets/treaties/230-IHL-26-EN.pdf; Dz.U.1936.6.68.

96 Online at: https://ihl-databases.icrc.org/assets/treaties/280-IHL-36-EN.pdf; Dz.U.1929.28.278.

97 118 LNTS 303; Dz.U.1932.103.864.

98 118 LNTS 343; Dz.U.1932.103.866.

99 94 UNTS 57; So-called Kellogg-Briand Pact, notably signed by the then-foreign minister, August Zaleski, Dz.U.1929.63.489.

100 148 LNTS 211; Dz.U.1933.93.712.

signed on 9.02.1929 by Poland, the USSR, Romania, Estonia and Latvia.[101] Additionally, due to the insufficiency of the guarantees offered by the Litvinov Protocol, Poland entered on 25.07.1932 into a non-aggression pact with the USSR,[102] providing that, should one of the parties be attacked by a third state, the parties would neither directly nor indirectly involve themselves by assisting the attacker. The pact was initially made for three years and subsequently prolonged for until 1945. The USSR self-evidently violated the terms of the pact by entering with the Germans into a secret protocol to the Molotov-Ribbentrop Pact (an international treaty between the Third Reich and the USSR, of 23.08.1939), and thereafter committing an act of aggression against Poland on 17.09.1939.

Poland also signed on 26.01.1934, a non-aggression declaration with Germany,[103] intended to normalize the relations between the two states for at least 10 years – those were to be based on the principles of the Kellogg-Briand Pact of 1928. Germany, however, repudiated the declaration on 28.04.1939.

It is furthermore noteworthy that when Adolf Hitler became the German Chancellor, Germany left the League of Nations on 21.10.1933. As an expression of objection to that decision, the Polish foreign minister, Józef Beck, withdrew Poland from the dispute-resolution mechanism of the Little Treaty of Versailles (Article 12).

5 Polish Legislation

As noted beforehand, Poland's situation upon the resumption of independence was complex. Among others, dynamic works began within the Codification Commission to provide the new state with legislative cohesion (uniform legislation to replace the several different legal systems left behind by the partitioning powers). That was a one-of-a-kind chance to create the law from scratch, incorporating the progressive solutions actively promoted at the time in international congresses. Thanks to that, the Criminal Code of 1932,[104] owing to the involvement of Makarewicz, Makowski and Rappaport, until this day shines as an example of a modern code.[105] For example, it

101 Dz.U.1929.29.283.
102 136 LNTS 41; Dz.U.1932.115.951.
103 Online at: https://avalon.law.yale.edu/wwii/blbk01.asp; Dz.U.1934.16.124.
104 Dz.U.1932.60.571.
105 Uczkiewicz (2022): 37.

accounted the possibility of judging offenders on the basis of universal jurisdiction. Article 9 of the Code provided for the judgement of a foreign national who were not to be extradited for the commission of any of the following offences:

> (a) robbery at sea; (b) counterfeiting of money, public securities or banknotes; (c) slave trade; (d) trafficking in women or children; (e) use of a means capable of presenting a general danger with the intention of bringing about such danger; (f) drug trafficking; (g) trafficking in pornographic publications; (h) another criminal offence provided for by international treaties entered into by the Polish State.

That was an enlightened solution, especially in view of the fact that even today some states do not recognize the exercise of their jurisdiction on the basis of universal repression. Moreover, Article 113(2) of the Code espoused an innovative approach to the incitement of war, uniquely stipulating as follows: 'whoever publicly calls for a war of aggression shall be liable to imprisonment of up to 5 years.' Before World War II, out of all other European states, only Romania criminalized the propaganda of a war of aggression.[106] Suffice to say that that the 1932 Code remained in force until 1969, and some of its solutions have found their continuation in the Criminal Code of 1997.

6 The Judiciary

After 1918, Polish courts formally did not occupy themselves with issues relating to international crimes.[107] While the Allied governments endeavoured to bring the perpetrators from World War I to judgement, the matter was not brought to conclusion.

Even through during World War I and after its formal end (e.g. during the Silesian Uprisings and the Polish-Soviet War) war crimes were committed in territories ultimately falling within the borders of the Polish Republic – both by the nationals of the neighbouring states and Polish citizens[108]

---

106 It was dubbed the *Lex Rappaport*; see more Grzebyk (2020a): 102, 105.

107 This subchapter was authored by Patrycja Grzebyk.

108 See the protestation note of the government of the Russian Soviet Federative Socialist Republic of 3.06.1919 to the government of the Polish Republic and the governments of the Allied Powers against the murders and violence perpetrated by Polish armed

– one cannot speak of systematically holding the guilty responsible before Polish courts.

The literature mentions isolated examples of cases in which such crimes can be surmised to have taken place, but the courts classified them as ordinary rather than international crimes. The most notorious case is the trial of Edward Antoniowski, Marian Lasocki, Zygmunt and Albin Lewicki, Kazimierz Kasior and Tomasz Cyndler in the murder on 2.01.1919 of the members of the Russian Red Cross mission having arrived to provide care for Russian prisoners of war.[109] The domestic courts were lenient to the Polish perpetrators: The Regional War Court in Warsaw, on 6.03.1920, acquitted Antoniowski and sentenced the rest to short prison terms – not exceeding 2 years – for, respectively, the incitement or commission of murder and appropriation of cash. The execution of the penalty was suspended. The above trial (as well as the others cited in the literature) did not, however, formally involve international crimes.

There were no extradition requests with regard to perpetrators from neighbouring states. That was the result of the Polish state's amnesty policy (decrees of the Chief of State of 8.02.1919, Act of 10.03.1921[110] and act of 24.05.1921[111] on Amnesty), as well as the respective treaties between the Poland and Germany of 1.10.1919[112] and Soviet Russia of 18.08.1921.[113] It can thus be assumed that the lack of procedures involving criminal responsibility for war crimes was a conscious decision by Polish authorities in line with the global standards of the time. For Poland, the priority was to settle the country's borders and not to judge the crimes perpetrated while fighting for them.

---

forces in the occupied territories of Lithuania and Belarus, in: Bierzanek (1967), vol. II: 183–187.

109 Those killed included Bronislav Vesolovsky, Lyudovik Klocman, Maria Alter and Magdalena Aivazova. They were executed by firing squad near Mień. Leon Alter escaped death because his would-be killers failed to notice he was only wounded. See Protestation note of 8.01.1919 from the People's Commissar for Foreign Affairs, Georgy Chicherin, to Polish foreign minister L. Wasilewski in connection with the murder of the members of the Russian Red Cross Mission in: Bierzanek (1967), vol. II: 162–163; see also Szymborski (2019); Targański (2019) and https://historiamniejznanaizapomniana.wordpress.com/2016/01/03/mord-na-czlonkach-delegacji-rosyjskiego-czerwonego-krzyza-w-1919-r/.

110 Dz.U.1921.29.163.

111 Dz.U.1921.42.261.

112 Dz.U.1922.11.85.

113 Dz.U.1921.49.300.

7 Academic Life

In order to describe Polish academic life of the interwar period, one must first at least briefly discuss the circumstances of the time, noting certain processes, events and political concerns (from the restoration of independence, through the May Coup in 1926 which resulted in an overthrow of the democratically-elected government caused hundreds of fatalities to the Sanation authoritarian rule) closely intertwined with the fates of the scholars described in this work. The awakening of a new statehood to life following 123 years of partitions inspired enthusiasm for independence and new challenges in the areas of lawmaking, with the settling of the borders, political reforms leaning towards autocracy, anti-Semitic pogroms and harassment of the intelligentsia opposing the authorities.

Academic life under the Second Polish Republic concentrated mainly around the existing universities. During the first years of regained independence, considerable changes can be seen in the staffing of professorial chairs, which must be connected with significant staff shortages in newly created institutions of higher learning.[114]

In the 20s of the 20th century, five public universities and one non-public university were functioning (or beginning to function). The public ones were: Jagiellonian University in Cracow, Stephen Báthory University in Vilnius, John Casimir University in Lviv, Józef Piłsudski University in Warsaw and Polish University in Poznań. The non-public one was the University of Lublin. It is also fitting to mention the *Wolna Wszechnica Polska* (literally 'Polish Free University') – a private higher school playing a great role in the continued education of the workforce – and the *Wyższa Szkoła Handlowa* (Higher School of Commerce), to which the international lawyers described in this work had ties.

Lviv was place of singularly academic atmosphere, attracting eminent intellectuals. Located in the Austrian partition prior to Poland's independence, it had been the mainstay of academic education. Apart from the University of Lviv, four other higher schools were in operation in the city. Lviv was Poland's largest academic centre, both in terms of the number of schools and the number of students.[115] The University of Lviv gained the name of Universitas-Joannes-Casimiriano Leopoliensis (John Casimir

114 As noted by Bajerski (2017: 87ff), the worst staffing situation was at the Stephen Báthory University in Vilnius, where in 1923 almost a third of the chairs was held by deputy professors (not exceeding 3% in the universities in Galicia).

115 *Ibidem*: 62.

University) pursuant to the order of the Chief of State of 8.11.1919.[116] In the first years of independence, it had only four active faculties – theology, law, medicine and philosophy, the legal one with the largest headcount.[117] John Casimir University's Faculty of Law was the *alma mater* of numerous prominent lawyers and jurists, who later made international careers.[118] Prior to independence, one of the pioneers of modern international law, Zygmunt Cybichowski, served as its professor extraordinarius in 1912–1917; in 1919, he accepted a professorship at the University of Warsaw .

As at 1939, the staff of John Casimir University's Department of Law of Nations and General Theory of State included Professor Extraordinarius Ludwik Ehrlich as the chair; Doc. Dr Stanisław Hubert and Dr Władysław Rębisz as salaried or fixed-rate assistants, as well as Józef Giebułtowicz, Doc. Dr Zenon Wachlowski, Doc. Dr Kazimierz Grzybowski, Dr Lesław Adam, Jan Edward Juźwiak, Kazimierz Witold Hoffman (later under the family name Kocot) as volunteer assistants. Graduates included Stanisław Edward Nahlik, who until 1936 served as an assistant to Professor Ludwik Ehrlich, similarly to Antoni Deryng, who worked there at the Faculty of Law first as a senior assistant and later, as a docent, and in 1936 he became the vice dean and in 1937 the dean of the Faculty of Law and Socio-Economic Sciences of University of Lublin.[119]

The John Casimir University's Faculty of Law was also home to a three-year School of Diplomacy, the main organizer and head of was (until the outbreak of World War II) was Ehrlich.[120] Among the lecturers were Karol Bertoni, Wachlowski, Hubert and Grzybowski. Graduates included Jan Kozielewski, subsequently known as Jan Karski, Sohn, Giebułtowicz and Nahlik.[121]

116 M.P. 1919.255.

117 Redzik (2004). In the winter semester of 1924/25, there were 1846 students (while humanities had 1861 and mathematics and natural science had 1180). Kronika UJK we Lwowie za rok szkolny 1924/25, Lviv 1925, 158 [Chronicle of the JCU in year 1924/25]

118 Other than the lawyers and jurists discussed in this book, one should also mention Ludwik Sohn. Conferred his doctorate in legal sciences in 1935, he left Poland several weeks before the German invasion; all of his subsequent career would be abroad. Sohn was a scholar of international law with a vast range of academic interests. After the war, his work concentrated on international institutions, the law of the sea, use of armed force, human rights, and state responsibility – see Buerghenthal (2006): 623–628; Sands (2012): 11–28. Another native of Lviv was Karol Aleksandrowicz (Charles Henry Alexandrowicz), an eminent legal historian – see Armitage, Pitts (2022): 23.

119 Staszewski (2006): 93 and *idem* (2008): 33.

120 Redzik (2006): 121–149 i (2020b); Pugacewicz (2010): 133–143, 140.

121 List of students in 1932 (including 7 women!) see: Redzik (2020b): 279.

Although Ehrlich himself had studied under Stanisław Starzyński (eminent constitutionalist dubbed a 'leading character not only among the Lwovian constitutionalists but also of the entire Polish constitutionalism of the Second Republic),[122] he made his own career as an expert in international law and creator of his own school of the law of nations.

Rafał Lemkin, in turn, began his studies at the Jagiellonian University, where, among others, he attended the lectures given by Edmund Krzymuski. In the aftermath of a disciplinary action in 1921, he transferred to the John Casimir University, attending the lectures of Ludwik Ehrlich and Piotr Stebelski (the latter in criminal procedure). For several years, he participated in a seminar led by Juliusz Makarewicz, a leading scholar of criminal law and the principal author of the 1932 Criminal Code (informally known as 'Makarewicz Code'). It appears that the latter was also the greatest influence on the course taken by Lemkin's scholarly interests, as it was in his that Lemkin's first academic works came to life. In his memoirs concerning conversations with the professors about Soghomon Tehlirian's trial for the killing of Talaat Pasha, Lemkin recounts that they invoked the argument of state sovereignty. One can hardly resist wondering whether that remark concerned Makarewicz[123] or the classic lecture in the law of nations delivered by Ehrlich, where the latter certainly discussed state sovereignty and may have broached the subject of the Armenian genocide.[124]

Lviv was also the city in which Hersch Lauterpacht began his studies,[125] which he later interrupted in circumstances on which he commented as follows:

> I had not been able to take the final examinations because the University has been closed to Jews in Eastern Galicia.[126]

His son Elihu, on the other hand, notes that Hersch passed some of the examinations with the grade of 'good' (*dobry*), so the quoted words do not ring completely true. As Hersch wrote them in 1920, having already for a year stayed in Vienna, perhaps what he had in mind were the events

122 Redzik (2007): 130.

123 As suggested in Redzik (2018): 246, entry: Lemkin.

124 Lemkin (2018): 62; see also Kowalski (2020): 369.

125 He frequently omitted this part from his biographical note, as he never finished his Lviv studies; see e.g. the bio in the Hague courses: Lauterpacht: (1930).

126 Lauterpacht (2000), citing Hersch's *Letter from Hersch Lauterpacht to Zionist Executive*, 10.06.1920, 15.

following the pogrom of the Jews in Lviv in November 1918. In order to protect the city's Jewish population locked in a clinch between the Poles and the Ukrainians, Lauterpacht joined the Jewish militia. The militia patrolled the Jewish quarters, watching over the inhabitants. Although Lauterpacht's family did not suffer in the November pogrom, in which several hundred people died,[127] he himself was a witness of the events. Doubtless, the experience of anti-Semitism affected his life choices. Lauterpacht departed Lviv in the summer of 1919 and made his way to Vienna, where he continued his education under the care, among others, of Hans Kelsen. From that time onward, his ties to Poland, other than having family here, would be marginal. The atmosphere in Vienna, on the other hand, was saturated with anti-Semitism in such a degree that Lauterpacht and his wife moved to England. In 1928, when in conference in Warsaw, he was asked where his good command of Polish came from. Allegedly, he retorted: 'Thanks to your *numerus clausus*.'[128] The regulations concerning the *numerus clausus* (understood to mean an absolute limit of scholarships available to Jewish students) were never enacted into statutory law in Poland, but Lauterpacht may have been referring to the broadly understood discrimination of students of Jewish origin, which presented a serious problem of the era.[129] It is another thing that the possible reasons for his move to London probably venture beyond the aforesaid matter. Lauterpacht was active in the Zionist movement,[130] and thus his activities must have brought reservations from Polish authorities. This prompts the reflection that his departure from Poland had a more complicated context and the decision was urged by a larger number of reasons of strictly political and academic or scholarly nature, of which anti-Semitism and the experience of the pogrom may also have been an important part. From Nahlik's account it occurs that in the same year 1923 Lauterpacht had applied for a chair at University of Lviv, which was ultimately given to Ludwik Ehrlich. Nahlik also reminisced about his relationship with Jerzy Sawicki – an older colleague from the law faculty of University of Lviv (later professor of criminal law at the University of

127 Gauden (2019).

128 Lauterpacht (2000): 21.

129 More: Osęka (2018); Dąbrowska (1936), Majewski (2016): 141–154; Ogonowski: (2012): 144; Michalski, Podemski: (2022), see also Zofia Trębacz, *Antysemityzm uniwersytecki w dwudziestoleciu międzywojennym*, https://www.jhi.pl/artykuly/antysemityzm-uniwersytecki-w-dwudziestoleciu-miedzywojennym,3634.

130 Loeffler (2019): 31.

Warsaw and participant of the Nuremberg trials), with whom he attended some of the lectures of the School of Diplomacy.[131]

Stefan Glaser's academic path was the inverse of Lauterpacht's. He first read law in Vienna (1914–1916) and only later in Lviv (1916–1918), where he was awarded his doctorate in legal sciences. According to his own account, Glaser attended Juliusz Makarewicz's seminar[132] (Redzik, on the other hand, reports[133] that Glaser was a participant in the seminar led by Piotr Stebelski).[134] A short while after receiving his degree, he was also able to obtain habilitation from the Jagiellonian University.

Although **Cracow** was not as great a hub of higher learning as Lviv, its university is the oldest one in Poland[135] and one of a few oldest in the world. During the partitions, it remained a vibrant academic centre. During the time, the Jagiellonian University's Chair of the Law of Nations was headed by Michał Rostworowski, having succeeded to that position after Franciszek Kasparek's death in 1903 and occupied it until appointment as a judge of the PCIJ. In 1908, he became professor ordinarius; he was also a member of the IDI and of the Permanent Court of Arbitration. In a similarity to many other luminaries of the era, his academic interests were vast, from criminal jurisdiction on mercantile ships in foreign ports (the topic of his habilitation in 1896), through war studies (*Wojna a społeczeństwo polskie*, 1915), to peace treaties (*Wojna a traktat pokojowy*, 1916). As his perspective was informed by the war raging at the time, in his publications he attempted to predict how it should end from the perspective of international law.

The studies, however, did not concern the international criminal responsibility of an individual. The source of the beginnings of that topic lies with the academic circles of criminal law. Stefan Glaser, who would later be among those developing international criminal law as an academic discipline, was linked to those rather than the circles of international law. He received his habilitation in 1921 at the Chair of Criminal Law and Procedure led by Edmund Krzymuski. The latter eminent jurist held the chair from 1884 to his sudden death in Ostend in Belgium in 1928. He was a savant of

131 Nahlik (1987b).

132 Evidence from Glaser's personnel file in the author's possession.

133 Redzik (2018): 115.

134 Wierczyńska, Wierczyński (2020): 306–334.

135 The Jagiellonian University was founded in 1364 by King Casimir the Great. It initially comprised three faculties: liberal arts, medicine and law. The name of Jagiellonian was given to it in 1817 in order to emphasize the links to the Jagiellonian dynasty.

criminal law and also the author of the first commentary on the system of criminal law published in Polish in 1885 (*Wykład prawa karnego ze szczególnem uwzględnieniem ustaw austriackich*). With his outlooks linked to the classical school of criminology, he had a great influence on Glaser and the latter's views on punishment and prevention. It was Krzymuski who commended Glaser to the rector of the University of Lublin, where he went to work as a deputy professor of criminal law and procedure even before his habilitation, after which he took the position of professor extraordinarius. In 1924, in turn, he transferred to the University of Vilnius, where he would take the Chair of Criminal Law and Procedure.[136]

Graduates of the Jagiellonian University include Manfred Lachs, who in 1937 took from there his degree of doctor of laws. Marek Korowicz, too, completed his legal studies with the Jagiellonian University even obtaining a doctorate in 1929. Already before World War II did he publish works on the subjecthood of an individual in international law.[137]

Accompanying the Jagiellonian University already under the partitions was the Polish School of Political Sciences (*Polska Szkoła Nauk Politycznych*) which gathered together lecturers from the University and others from the outside. Its authorities included Michał Rostworowski as a member and director. The school's character changed after World War I – it operated as a university school within[138] the structure of the Faculty of Law. Rostworowski's closest collaborators, working as lectures of the school already prior to the outbreak of World War II, were Roman Rybarski and Bohdan Winiarski; in the academic year 1934/1935, the latter taught postwar international problems as a subject and also served as the school's secretary. Others lecturers included Zygmunt Sarna, Stanisław Kutrzeba, Stanisław Estreicher and Władysław Wolter. After Edmund Krzymuski's death, Wolter took over the Chair of Criminal Law at the Jagiellonian University; at the school, he gave lectures in the international law against war and international criminal law. As early as 1939, Wolter published his lecture titled, 'International Criminal Law,' discussing the terminology and issues

136 Interestingly, Glaser, who wrote his doctoral dissertation under Makarewicz and his habilitation dissertation under Krzymuski, had the opportunity to meet the two great scholars who were in a conflict with each other. Their decades-long dispute is described by: Pol (2000): 474ff.

137 Korowicz (1938): 41. More extensively on Korowicz see: Przyborowska-Klimczak (2022a): 242ff and the literature referenced therein.

138 Jagiellonian University School of Political Sciences (1920–1949), https://inp.uj.edu.pl/historia-instytutu2.

such as the sense of existence of an international criminal court.[139] Wolter also studied totalitarian systems. His publications included a paper titled *Prawo karne pod znakiem swastyki*[140] ('Criminal law under the sign of the swastika'), in which he explained the arcana of the criminal policy of national socialism in Germany.

Zygmunt Sarna was the school's next director after Rostworowski from 1936 onward, having previously served as vice director since 1931. Like many other professors of Jagiellonian University, he was targeted by the Sonderaktion Krakau (a German operation against the Cracow academic circles, as part of which members of university staff and those of the Mining Academy were deported to the Sachsenhausen Camp), although he was later freed thanks to his family's connections. Other professors were not so lucky (a total of 155 academics from Jagiellonian University were arrested at the time).[141] Władysław Wolter remained imprisoned at Sachsenhausen until 1940, and Stanisław Estreicher died there in 1939. Professor Rostworowski, as a judge of the PCIJ rather than professor of a university, was not subjected to the Sonderaktion Krakau but died during the occupation.

The University in **Lublin** was created after the formation of an Organization Committee for a Catholic University in Saint Petersburg in 1918, with plans of opening of such a university. Shortly thereafter, the project won the acceptance of the episcopate, and the university was inaugurated.[142] The new institution had to employ staff from other universities. The initial lecturers hailed from different origins, though most were from the John Casimir University of Lviv and the University of Warsaw and many had worked for several universities and higher schools in parallel. The initial years of Lublin's Chair of the Law of Nations are characterized by high staff fluctuation.

The first lecturer in the law of nations at the University of Lublin was Zygmunt Cybichowski. He had been invited to lead the Chair of the Law of Nations in 1919 and worked there until the end of the academic year 1922/23.[143] At the same time, he was also in the University of Warsaw's employee.

The first academic teacher of criminal law was Stefan Glaser, employed from 1920/21 onward as deputy professor of criminal law, and from 1922/29

139 Wolter (1939): 1–3, 77–80.

140 *Ibidem*: 231–246.

141 Gawęda (1986): 35ff.

142 Bajerski (2017): 67–68; the name 'Catholic University of Lublin' has been in use since 1928.

143 Przyborowska-Klimczak, Staszewski (2008): 325; more extensively on the Lublinian professors: Staszewski (2022): 261ff.

as professor extraordinarius; in 1923/24, following the departure of Cybichowski, he took the position of professor extraordinarius of the law of nations.[144] After him, the Chair of the Law of Nations was occupied by Bronisław Bouffałł, lecturing in parallel at the Wolna Wszechnica Polska in Warsaw.[145] He broached the topics of war e.g. in the article titled *Wyjęcie wojny z pod prawa w pakcie Kellogga*.[146] In the academic year 1928/29, Cezary Berezowski took the position of deputy professor of the law of nations. His contract would be terminated in 1932.[147]

In 1932/33, the position of deputy professor of the law of nations was taken by Henryk Dembiński, who remained there until World War II broke out. In 1935,[148] he published *Wojna jako narzędzie prawa i przewrotu* – a book in which he discussed not only restrictions on the right to wage war but also the idea of repression against hostilities, and actions for peace. He examined the paradigm of the just war and the matter of recognition of the lawlessness perpetrated by armed aggression as legal facts, entering the topic range explored during the time by the academics of Vilnius.

The Stephen Báthory University in **Vilnius** was a continuation of the institution of higher learning originated by King Stephen Báthory in 1579 by allocating funds to the transformation of the Jesuit College in Vilnius into a Jesuit Academy and University of Vilnius (*Academia et Universitas Vilnensis Societatis Jesu*). Under the Russian partition, the university operated as the Imperial University of Vilnius, and after the fall of the November Uprising it was closed as part of the repressions, to be reopened in an independent Poland. On 28.08.1919, Józef Piłsudski issued a decree establishing a university in Vilnius,[149] and on 11.10.1919 a solemn inauguration took, place during which the institution was named in honour of Stephen Báthory.

In the Faculty of Law and Social Sciences of the University of Vilnius, the law of nations was the province of three academics – Professor Wacław Komarnicki and two docents: Michał Król and Wiktor Sukiennicki.[150]

---

144 Przyborowska-Klimczak, Staszewski (2008): 328.

145 *Ibidem*: 329.

146 Bouffałł (1930): 502–519.

147 The circumstances are explained by Przyborowska-Klimczak and Staszewski: (2008) 332.

148 Zob. Henryk Dembiński (1900–1949) in: Szlachta, Bieroń (ed.) (2004): 132ff.

149 Gawrońska-Garstka (2016): 22–39.

150 Michał Król died under the occupation, Komarnicki lived until 1954 and Sukiennicki would die in 1983 in the United States. Sukiennicki's career was not firmly bound to international law. He considered himself as a Sovietologist; as he writes in his

However, a chair occupied strictly with the law of nations was never formed.[151] Komarnicki held the Chair of State Law and Science, which is reflected by his bibliography, in which publications in the law of nation share the pride of place with those on constitutional topics.

Out of the three academics, the studies of only the former two could in any significant way be linked to the problems of international criminal law from today's perspective. At the time, their interests fell within the purview of classic international law. The deliberations of the Vilnian scholars on the topics of aggression, the aggressor state, or international responsibility, brought no shame to the them in comparison to the foreign journals of the period.[152] For example, shortly after the adoption of Convention for the Definition of Aggression in 1933, Komarnicki published his article titled *La définition de l'agresseur*,[153] as the aftermath of the conference on collective security in London, where, as a member of the Polish delegation, he delivered a paper in contribution to the ongoing debate on the definitions of the aggressor state and aggression itself.

Perhaps it was under the influence of those thoughts that Król published his *Zagadnienie agresji w prawie międzynarodowym* ('The topic of aggression in international law') one week before the German invasion of Poland. Therein, he discussed the meaning of the term aggression under the different international conventions mentioning it; he pointed out the problems relating to the interpretation of those definitions, their fragmentary nature, and problems with the qualification of preparation for aggression, as well as noting the problems arising from the desire to have everything defined. He moreover disputed Komarnicki's views, positioning the latter as an adherent of the concept of the territorial aggression in its most liberal version – Król criticised this position.[154]

memoirs: 'To the law of nations, with the theory of which I have mainly occupied myself with thus far, I had become averse in a certain degree – I had increasingly realized that *who* speaks is more important than the *what* in it (...)' – Sukiennicki (1967): 36.

151 Chairs of international law existed at the University of Warsaw and the University of Poznań, Lviv, as noted before, had a chair of the law of nations and general theory of state and the Jagiellonian University a chair of political law and the law of nations; see also Żukowski (2016): 425ff, Balcerzak (2022): 177.

152 Balcerzak (2022).

153 Deryng (1935): 73–84.

154 Król (1939): 247–260.

Despite certain 'international elements', the fault of the Vilnian researchers' prewar activities was their local character. Komarnicki and Król published in a journal of which Komarnicki was the editor-in-chief and which was published by the Faculty of Law and the Daniłowicz Law Society in Vilnius – the *Rocznik Prawniczy Wileński*. All of Król's works concerned with the subject of international responsibility or aggression were published there. In a voluminous article constituting a reprint of his doctoral dissertation titled *Odpowiedzialność państw w prawie międzynarodowem*[155] ("States' responsibility in international law'), the academic explored topics such as the *locus standi* of an individual, predicting that individual subjecthood under international law would eventually crystallize. However, the young scholar's theses delivered as part of extraordinarily extensive studies had no prospects of broad dissemination because of having been published in a niche journal and in the Polish language; hence, they had no chance to exist in an international forum, were resonating only in domestic academia.[156]

Since 1924, the Chair of Criminal Law and Procedure at the Stephen Báthory had been held by Stefan Glaser, the importance of which consists in that his interests during that time had still not concentrated on international law, albeit his writings of the time manifest elements we today associate with international criminal law. Nowadays, Glaser – along Vespasian Pella, Emil Stanisław Rappaport, Henri Donnedieu de Vabres and Rafał Lemkin – is reputed one of the precursors of the new discipline.[157] Glaser was a most prolific author, having published several dozen books and articles, often quoted until the present day in either criminal or international law.[158] During his university work in Vilnius, however, he had still been a specialist in criminal law with a very broad perspective encompassing international relations and international co-operation among states in criminal cases.

155 Król (1929): 177–416 (doctoral dissertation).

156 See a review of Król's published doctoral dissertation, H. Dembiński (1930): 497–503; Król's other important works include *Represalia i wyższa konieczność w prawie międzynarodowym* [The represalia and dire necessity in international law] – Król (1930): 15–99 (habilitation); or *Próby kodyfikacji zasad międzynarodowej odpowiedzialności państw* [Attempts to codify the principles of the international responsibility of states] – Król (1936): 174–284; *Zagadnienie agresji w prawie międzynarodowym* [The topic of aggression in international law] – Król (1939): 167–312.

157 Tallgren, Megret (eds.) (2020).

158 See Glaser (1929a), (1929b), (1929c), (1929d) and *Nullum crimen sine lege* – Glaser (1942); *Prawo karne na kongresach międzynarodowych* (Paryż, Haga) [Penal law at international congresses (Paris, the Hague)]– Glaser (1937).

This can be seen clearly in his chosen subjects of study and his inclination towards international issues, still perceived through the lens of domestic law at the time.[159] For example, the inauguration lecture he gave in Vilnius in 1924 concerned extradition. Later, he continued the studies into extradition with a series of articles in the *Palestra*, titled *Nowe kierunki w międzynarodowem prawie karnem a ekstradycja* ('New directions in international criminal law and extradition'). There, he wrote about an idea of international justice transcending the territorial confines of the states and linked to it the necessity of uniformization (harmonization) of the legal provisions and 'internationalization of the administration of criminal justice.' He was clearly for the unification of criminal law[160] and appreciated the gradual changes in the states' conduct. Glaser believed that the states ought to punish the perpetrator regardless wherever the act may have been committed.[161] To him, one of the signs of the aspirations to internationalization were the international community's efforts to establish an international criminal court. In that regard, he referred to the texts of 19th-century conventions.[162] He was sceptical of the use of the institution of extradition in the context of political crime, stressing that the perpetrator's activities did not stem from malice.[163] In the context of extradition, he explored the principles of speciality, criticizing its application from the teleological or the equitable position, venturing the suggestion that it would be more reasonable to be guided by the states' mutual confidence in each other's justice systems.[164] Simultaneously, he believed that the application of the principle of reciprocity in the context of the harmonization of legal orders with regard to extradition, i.e. making its implementation contingent on the existing practice, ought not to be taking place.[165]

Glaser was stripped of his university position as a consequence of political events. Following the May Coup and the resignation of prime minister Wincenty Witos's cabinet in 1926, the Sanation camp took over the government of the country. The opposition called for resistance to increasingly authoritarian rule. In response, the authorities commenced a series of arrests of politicians affiliated with the oppositions. Those were kept at the

159 Wierczyńska, Wierczyński (2020): 306ff.
160 Glaser (1929a): 136–137.
161 *Ibidem*: 145.
162 *Ibidem*: 142–143.
163 Glaser (1929c): 270.
164 Glaser (1929d): 364–365.
165 Glaser (1929e): 552.

fortress in Brześć.[166] A place of seclusion was also established for them in Bereza Kartuska, where they were mistreated, beaten and tortured; part were judged, part kept without conviction or sentence.[167] The academic circles were opposed to such repressions.[168] The government, in response, decided to retire the academics who had signed the so-called Brześć Protest. A reform of the education system was carried out, as the existing law had guaranteed to professors the security of tenure outside of exceptional situations that did not, however, include political criticism. Article 3 of the new Act on Academic Schools[169] authorized the minister of education to establish and abolish chairs and departments, which resulted in the Minister of Religious Denominations and Public Enlightenment's liquidation of more than 50 university chairs, retiring 30 professors.[170] As one of the authors of the Brześć Protest, Glaser fell victim of those activities. In consequence, his chair was liquidated and he himself, at the age of 39, became a retired pensioner. He moved to Warsaw, where he took up legal practice, representing the political opposition in court cases.[171]

The sole university in all of Western Poland was the one in **Poznań,** established in the spring of 1919 and since 1955 known as the Adam Mickiewicz University in Poznań.[172] Its Chair of International Law was created as one of the first 18 chairs of the Law Faculty of the University of Poznań.

Initially, the Chair remained vacant, to be occupied on the break of 1922–1923 by Bohdan Winiarski with the title of professor extraordinarius, having taught public international law there since 1921. From 1923 onward, Winiarski served as the first professor and head of the Chair of International Law, and in March 1929 he was promoted to professor ordinarius. Immediately before World War II, he served as the dean of the Faculty of Law.

166 Being an inconvenience to the regime, members of the opposition were held criminally responsible. However, the charges adduced against them were of political nature. By way of example, it can be noted that Witos was convicted but did not submit to the penalty and instead migrated out of the country. In connection with the outbreak of WWII, the President of Poland issued a decree extending amnesty to the former Brześć prisoners, including Witos. Paradoxically, therefore, what freed him of criminal responsibility for his activities in opposition to the Sanation's dictatorial rule was Hitler's aggression against Poland. See Decree of the President of the Republic of 31.10.1939 on Amnesty for the Former Brześć Prisoners, Dz.U.1939.100.1000.

167 Szreffel (2010): 207–219.

168 Glaser (1974): 15ff.

169 Dz.U.1933.29.247.

170 Glaser (1974): 22.

171 *Ibidem*: 26.

172 See: https://bip.amu.edu.pl/podstawy-prawne-dzialania-uam.

Already before the war, in 1936, he published a monograph titled *"Obrona konieczna" w prawie narodów* ('"Legitimate defence" in the law of nations'), discussing, among other topics, that of preventive war.

Winiarski expressed dissatisfaction with the mass codification of international law leading towards a universal unification and filling of gaps in international law. Above all, he feared the possible departure from state autonomy in favour of individuals or organizations. He appeared as a defender of state sovereignty, not realizing the opportunity presenting itself at the time in connection with universal codification and departure from the absolute judicial jurisdiction of the state. He saw only danger in it, heralding the end of state sovereignty and even of international law.[173]

In 1915, **Warsaw** saw the opening ceremeony of the University of Warsaw – one of the first national institutions operating in the Polish language despite the ongoing war. It is at the University of Warsaw that Zygmunt Cybichowski worked in 1916–1936 and served three terms as the dean of its law faculty. From 1917 onward, he became involved in international law.[174] Participants in his extraordinarily popular seminars in constitutional and international law included Cezary Berezowski (who, in 1937, would be appointed the faculty's professor extraordinarius). As early as 1914, Cybichowski published the *Międzynarodowe prawo wojenne z uwzględnieniem przesilenia bałkańskiego* ('The international law of war including the Balkan Breakthrough'), and one year later a coursebook titled *Prawo narodów. System prawa międzynarodowego* ('The law of nations. The system of international law'), subsequently reprinted several times. In 1926, he delivered a Hague lecture titled *La compétence des tribunaux a raison d'infractions commises hors du territoire*. His most important works include the *Międzynarodowe prawo karne. Kompetencja sądów do ścigania przestępstw zagranicznych* ('International Criminal Law. The competence of the courts to prosecute foreign crimes'), which he himself describes as a monograph based on Hague lectures.[175] It is not, however, a series of lectures in international criminal law as we see it today; Cybichowski defined it differently: 'it is that part of international private law which concerns itself with criminal law.' In the course of the lecture, he discussed the powers of the domestic courts to prosecute foreign crimes under the principle of territoriality. The work was also a rather systematic lecture on international law. The discussion of the state's territorial jurisdiction marked the

173 Winiarski (1930): 158.

174 Izdebski (2008): 99.

175 Cybichowski (1927a): 7.

point of departure for the discussion of the state's jurisdiction with regard to its territory, seas and vessels. He also described the modes of liability relating to the various stages of *iter criminis*, as well as accessory liability, mentioning piracy as a crime of the law of nations. The summation revealed his expectations of the future development of international law, headed towards – in his opinion – the uniformization or harmonization of domestic provisions (i.e. the way in which the European criminal law of the present day is developing). Before the war, Cybichowski published extensively on matters relating to armed conflicts, including occupation,[176] as well as jurisdiction in foreign crimes.[177] Casting a blot on his legacy are, however, his anti-Semitic views and collaboration with the Germans during World War II.[178]

Cybichowski's assistants and attendees of his seminars include Edward Muszalski, who, in 1926, published his doctoral disseration titled *Rozpoczęcie i wypowiedzenie wojny w prawie państwowem i prawie narodów*[179] ('The start and declaration of war in state law and the law of the nations'), with Cybichowski's preface. In 1938, Remigiusz Bierzanek began his work at the University of Warsaw as assistant to Berezowski, receiving his doctoral degree almost immediately before the outbreak of World War II.[180]

In the **Szkoła Główna Handlowa** (Warsaw School of Economics), operating under this name since 1933, international law was taught by Julian Makowski – an extraordinarily versatile scholar and an active diplomat of many years (for more than a decade, he led the Treaty Department at the Polish MFA). In 1915, he published an academic coursebook titled *Zasady prawa międzynarodowego* ('Principles of International Law'), and in 1918 another one titled *Prawo Międzynarodowe* ('International Law'), continuing and developing on the *Zasady*. In 1931, he delivered a Hague lecture titled *L'organisation actuelle de l'arbitrage international*; during the Interwar period, he lectured at the Free Polish University [Wolna Wszechnica Polska].

The latter was a private institution of higher learning formed in 1919 by transformation of the Society for Academic Courses (formerly the 'Flying University') into an academic school. After World War II, its branch campus was transformed into the University of Łódź. In 1921–1927, its Chair of

176 Cybichowski (1927b) i (1927c).
177 Cybichowski (1927a).
178 Salomonowicz, Serczyk (2003): 46–47.
179 Muszalski (1926).
180 Bierzanek (2006): 87.

the Law of Nations was led by Szymon Rundstein,[181] of whom Krzysztof Pol wrote: 'one could without fear hazard the assertion that in the history of Polish legal thought of the 19th and 20th centuries, there was hardly a more versatile academic to be found than Szymon Rundstein.'[182] The scholar had outstanding achievements of both national and international standing, in the fields of legal theory, civil law, philosophy of law, and international law. Of those, international law had been the subject of his academic work since World War I, and his publications include *"Szkody wojenne". Teorya nadzwyczajnych indemnizacyj w prawie publicznem*[183] ('War damages. Theory of extraordinary indemnizations in public law'). Therein, among other topics, Rundstein discusses the matter of an individual's claim against the state arising from the state's responsibility for a breach of its own statutorily regulated obligations. Rundstein pondered whether a concept of objective (i.e. relating to the object) liability of the state was not perhaps taking shape in international law.[184] In his *Szkody wojenne a współczesne prawo narodów*[185] ('War damages and modern law of the nations'), he continued that exploration, revisiting the question of state liability and the principles for determining that liability and types of damages. He also considered by subjecthood of individuals, asking himself whether an individual could venture claims against a state in damages and whether individuals could be regarded as subjects of international law. For he noted that certain rights were forming for individuals, though not easy to bring to fruition. Rundstein also noted the sole exception relating to the existence of an international prize court (involving the seizure of ships on the basis of letters of marquee), giving individuals the opportunity to complain directly to the tribunal.[186] It is noteworthy that Rundstein's observations had preceded the outbreak of World War I. At the time, no one had supposed that the Allies states would attempt to place the German Kaiser before an international court and the discussion of individual subjecthood would acquire another dimension.

Apart from his rich academic achievement, Rundstein served in a number of important and prestigious positions in international institutions, such

181 Rundstein was a cousin to Ludwik Ehrlich.

182 Pol (2000): 950. Rundstein was also frequently cited by international publications; see e.g. Korowicz (1959): 172, 208, 330; furthermore, his ideas of the development of international law continue to resonate abroad: Reisman (1992): 49–50; Fripp (2016): 1.35.

183 Rundstein (1916).

184 *Ibidem*: 10ff.

185 Rundstein (1917).

186 *Ibidem*: 105–110.

as the Committee of Experts for the Progressive Codification of International Law (*Comité d'Experts pour la Codification progressive du droit international*) of the League of Nations, tasked with inquiring as to what matters should be the subject of international codification.[187] The Committee formulated a dozen or so problems calling for action in the form of international codification, such as extradition, the penal competence of the states with regard to crimes committed outside their territory, the repression of piracy, and diplomatic immunity. As a rapporteur, Rundstein dealt with the topic range of: 'such conflicts of state affiliation (nationality) as the resolution of which would not procure difficulties of political nature.' He was also a co-rapporteur on the subject of the possibility of agreeing on provisions concerning the procedure for international conferences, necessary for the conclusion and drafting of treaties.[188] Moreover, in 1928, he gave a Hague lecture devoted to topics of arbitration in private law, titled *Arbitrage international en matière privée*, and in 1933 one on the PCIJ – *La Cour permanente de Justice internationale comme instance de recours*. He also served as a judge of the Permanent Court of Arbitration. Together with his family, he died at the extermination camp in Treblinka.

Though the **Wolna Wszechnica Polska** was the employer of a considerable number of eminent scholars, the institution deserves a mention also on other accounts. According to Artur Bajerski's observation, it was, 'a centre of progressive social thought and scholarly research.'[189] An outstanding number of women studied there – 75% of in the academic year 1919/1920. It will be expedient to recall that women gained the active and passive suffrage in 1918 and were proclaimed equal in rights to men by art. 96 of the March Constitution of 1921.[190] In the interwar period, restrictions on women's access to education and specific professions, including the legal professions, existed almost everywhere in the world. By contrast, the professional careers

187 Rundstein (1928): 1–43, 9–10; Finch (1925): 534–542.

188 Rundstein (1928): 13.

189 Bajerski (2017): 67.

190 Dz.U. 1921.44.267, suffrage was granted by Piłsudski's Decree on the Election System, and March Constitution in turn, affirmed that all citizens were equal in the eyes of the law, but only several years thereafter did the Supreme Court, in a decision of 16.02.1924, identify that article as repealing the legal provisions imposing restrictions on the public rights of women. In some regions, legislation openly discriminatory to women continued to exist, such as provisions on inheritance in the eastern voivodeships, where Russian law was applied (see Pietrzak (2000): 83), or the so-called Celibacy Act (Act concerning the termination of a teacher's service relationship as a result of marriage, enacted by the Silesian Sejm on 29 March 1926, in force until 9 April 1938 – see Łysko (2015): 390).

of certain Polish women, despite clearly evident legal or practical obstacles, paint an outright impressive picture.[191] It would be difficult, on the other hand, to judge how many careers may have been stifled as a result of the existing limitations.

Neither did the Wszechnica ever see anti-Semitic excesses or 'Ghetto benches.' Its lecturers included Emil Stanisław Rappaport and, as his assistant, Rafał Lemkin, the subsequent author of the definition of genocide, as well as Leon Radzinowicz (Rabinowicz), a prominent criminologist.[192]

Rappaport was among the co-founders of Polish Society for Criminal Legislation and of the AIDP. For decades, he remained a judge on active duty, starting from 1917, when he was appointed a justice of the Court of Appeals in Warsaw and later as a justice of the Criminal Chamber of the Supreme Court. In the interwar period he also participated in the works of the criminal section of the Codification Commission. His draft of a criminal code prepared together with Aleksander Mogilnicki became the point of departure for the Makarewicz Code of 1932, which reflects some of Rappaport's positions, such as the penalization of the propaganda of an aggressive war (Article 113). The latter was dubbed the *lex Rappaport*.[193] The Polish regulations were innovative on a global scale, and they also demonstrate how extraordinarily progressive, ahead of their era, were the views held by their author, nowadays regarded as one of the precursors of the discipline of international criminal law.

---

191 The first legal profession to open its ranks to women was the advocates' bar. The first woman to enter the roll of advocates, in 1925, was Helena Wiewiórska, having completed her legal studies and advocacy traineeship in Saint Petersburg. She commanded recognition abroad, participated in international congresses (as discussed above) and was a contributor to the 1931 *Encyklopedja podręczna prawa karnego* ['Handy Encyclopaedia of Criminal Law'] edited by Wacław Makowski. The first woman judge in Poland was Wanda Wóytowicz-Grabińska, appointed on 6 March 1929 to a juvenile court. She was engaged in numerous international organisations as e.g. the International Bureau for the Suppression of Traffic in Women and Children or International Committee of the Howard League, see Fleming (2022a): 80. The first one to be assigned to the cases of adults was Maria Hasińska in 1937 – see Stypułkowska (1994): 141. Concerning the obstacles to the exercise of the legal professions by women see Łysko (2015): 393ff; see also Pietrzak (2000): 80.

192 Radzinowicz, having published a book titled *Mesures de sûreté. Ètude de politique criminelle* abroad (Radzinowicz (1929)), returned to continue his academic career in Poland. In 1929, he passed his *rigorosa* (doctoral examinations) at the Jagiellonian University, and his book was accepted as a doctoral dissertation on the basis of a positive opinion from Władysław Wolter; more extensive see Widacki (2019): 365; and Hood (2001): 648; see also subchapter 11.4.

193 Kornat (2010): 68.

Rafał Lemkin took his doctorate in law from the John Casimir University in 1926 and went to work as a public prosecutor at the District Court in Brzeżany. Subsequently, he moved to Warsaw, becoming a deputy prosecutor there. Thereafter, probably from 1934 onward, he came to lead a prosperous law firm. Lemkin had had Rappaport's acquaintance from his Lviv times, as suggested by Ryszard Szawłowski[194] The life stories of both were at the time closely intertwined; probably, they had a great influence on each other's views, or at least Rappaport on Lemkin's, as the former had been 23 years the latter's senior, so a master-student relationship may have existed between them. Lemkin collaborated with Rappaport in the Codification Commission, where Rappaport served as the secretary of the criminal section and Lemkin the reporting clerk (in a word, they were connected with the bonds of a comprehensive collaboration in several fields, and thanks to that Lemkin took an active part in the country's academic life and international congresses). By the September of 1939, Rafał Lemkin had published a considerable body of works, including commentaries on statutes, as well as articles written in foreign languages.[195]

At the time, some Poles sought education abroad – it is worth mentioning Kopek Mikliszański, who, in a monograph developing on a dissertain from 1933, *Le droit pénal international d'après la législation polonaise*,[196] promoted the vision of a universal criminal law binding on all states at all times.

8 Conclusions

The first years of Polish statehood after 1918 were characterized by an extraordinary level of scholarly and diplomatic activity in the creation of law and participation in international congresses and organizations. While discussing the various international law issues of that era we observe that the problems discussed by the internationalists paint a more modest picture than the initiatives undertaken by those specializing in criminal law, who showed more panache. They travelled to international congresses, delivered reports, participated in an animated international exchange of thought on matters pertaining to the nascent discipline. Thanks to the

194 Szawłowski (2014): 291.

195 Among others, a commentary on amnesty and criminal-fiscal law Lemkin (1936); Lemkin (1938b), as well as a work on international payments – Lemkin (1939).

196 Mikliszański (1935); see also, Kuczma (1937): 259, and Preuss (1936): 178.

industriousness of Rappaport, who involved himself in the initiative of creating the AIDP and its Polish branch, as well as organizing its conference, Poles participated in the crucial initiatives linked to international criminal law.

Simultaneously, the activities of jurists specializing in either international or criminal law somewhat strongly reflect the emergence of a new statehood with the associated dangers. The scholars' ponderings often take up the problems of the illegality of aggression, the definition of the aggressor state, the right to wage war, and the propaganda of a war of aggression. Diligent observes of the reality surrounding them as they were, the Polish academics embarked on topics that were fundamental to their era, dealing with guarantees of individual rights, the individual's hypothetical subjecthood under international law and the associated rights. At the same time, scholars and diplomats voiced determined criticism of the authoritarian changes unfolding in the criminal legislation of the USSR and Germany, manifested by the application of analogy and departure from the principle of *nullum crimen sine lege*. Protection of civil rights, protection of the rights of the various groups, the principle of humanity – those were not alien problems to the academics of the time.

CHAPTER 2

World War II (1939–45)

1 The Road to Nuremberg

Germany launched a war of aggression against Poland on 1.09.1939, and a little more than a fortnight later, on 17 September, so did the Soviet Union. At the beginning of October 1939, together with the capitulation of the last troops of Polish Armed forces at Kock, regular fights ended. The entire territory of the Polish Republic found itself under occupation. That, however, did not spell the end of the crimes committed by both aggressors in the territory of Poland; on the contrary, it meant escalation. Thus, the proactivity of Polish efforts to promote the idea of judging the German and Soviet crimes can hardly be surprising. In the case of the USSR's crime, however,[1] the discussion became difficult after 1940, because the Soviet Union became a key member of the anti-Nazi coalition. The members of Polish government-in-exile were aware that raising the issue of the USSR's responsibility could lead to the interruption of the works on holding the Nazi criminals accountable, and thus they oftentimes made the conscious decision to refrain from actively demanding justice for Soviet crimes.[2] They also knew that after the German invasion of the USSR, improving their relationship with the latter was a priority to the Brits, one for the sake of which they were willing to sacrifice good relations with the Polish government.[3]

Members of Poland's highest authorities – President Ignacy Mościcki, Prime Minister Felicjan Sławoj-Składkowski and Commander-in-Chief Edward Rydz-Śmigły – were interned by the authorities of Romania. Nonetheless, on the basis of Article 13(2)(b) of the Constitutional Act of 23.04.1935,[4] Mościcki appointed Władysław Raczkiewicz to be his successor, who then appointed a new prime minister for the government-in-exile (in France) in the person of General Władysław Sikorski.[5]

1 Szawłowski (1995), vol. 1: 351ff and vol. 2: 191ff.

2 See e.g. protocol of Polish inter-ministerial conference of 9.10.1943, PRM-K/74 doc. 5, 13, 17 (APISM).

3 Kochavi (1998): 10.

4 Dz.U.1935.30.227.

5 See more Michowicz (1999): 136ff.

 | DOI:10.1163/9789004712690_004

From June 1940 onward, the seat of the government-in-exile was in London, and it is from that there the main actions to bring judgment for the crimes were taken. It is noteworthy that the new cabinet included lawyers and jurists specializing in international law – suffice to mention Wacław Komarnicki (who became the minister of justice in Sikorski's cabinet in 1942 and continued to serve in that capacity until 1944) and Stefan Glaser (who became the chair of the criminal-law section in the commission for legislative works at the Ministry of Justice).

Already on 28.11.1939 Sikorski emphasized in a speech the problem of German crimes.[6] Edward Raczyński – the Republic's ambassador to the United Kingdom – submitted on 2.12.1939 to the British Foreign Ministry, a protest against the arrest of the professors of Jagiellonian University and their subsequent deportation to the Sachsenhausen concentration camp.[7] In turn, on 15.12.1939, the Polish Council of Ministers adopted a resolution concerning German crimes in Poland, proclaiming: 'Following victorious war, the Polish State will apply retorsions against Germans, especially against the Germans' leading circles, for the innocent Polish victims.'[8] Upon orders from the Committee for Home Affairs (*Komitet dla spraw Kraju* established on 8.11.1939), headquartered in Angers in France, Michał Potulicki developed a draft instruction concerning the documentation of the occupying state's activities in Poland.[9] Thus, from April 1940 onward, Polish authorities were gathering investigative materials in a systematic manner.[10]

In parallel, Polish authorities strived to persuade other states to issue appropriate common declarations condemning the German criminal activities. The efforts bore fruit, among others, in the Anglo-Franco-Polish declaration of 17.04.1940, expressing a deep shock in connection with the reports of German crimes in Poland. The declaration was intended as a protest to the conscience of the world.[11] It emphasized that Nazi Germany aspired not only to the destruction of people and things but also of the cultural and

6 Pasek (2002): 14; Jonca (1987): 46 (where the date 29.11.1939 is provided).

7 Pilichowski (1980c): 65; Gelewski (1976): 342–343.

8 M.P.1939.285.1.

9 Zob. Jonca (1987): 47; szerzej Kobierska-Motas (1995): 175ff.

10 Rojowska (2013): 15ff; Ryszka (1982): 99.

11 See "Palestine Post" of 18.04.1940; Goryński (1944): 16–17 who cites the mentioned statement but with the date of 20.04.1940; see also Herzog (1975): 47; Kubicki (1987): 28; Szerer (1948b): 113ff. Certain authors' attempts to reproach Poland with having delayed for months before requesting France or the United Kingdom to condemn the crimes, as if the preceding steps taken by Polish authorities without French or British support were meaningless, must be regarded as an absurdity – Segesser (2005): 362.

religious existence of the defenceless Polish population currently finding itself in its power. In November 1940, the Polish and Czechoslovak governments issued a common declaration condemning the German occupier and pointing out several violations of the Hague Convention with Respect to the Laws and Customs of War on Land (HC IV) of 1907 in the occupied territories, and in December 1940, in another joint official statement, they referred to the unlawful German policy of denationalization. Statements of that kind were unprecedented and clearly demonstrative of that neither the Polish nor the Czechoslovak governments would desist from pursuing justice for the crimes perpetrated by the Nazis.[12] More statements would be issued in the following months, such as the one of 24.09.1941 demanding equitable compensation for the evil, or the one of 4.12.1941 (jointly with the USSR), anticipating the punishment of Nazi criminals in order to safeguard a lasting and just peace.[13]

Time after time, through diverse channels, including the media, did the representatives of Polish government emphasize the scale of the German crimes and the associated violations of the applicable norms of international law.[14] Polish authorities paid scrupulous attention to how the matter of the crimes was portrayed in British press and published appropriate statements, such as the one of 20.12.1940 in *The Times*, accentuating the incompatibility of the actions undertaken with a view to the destruction of the Polish nation with the provisions of the Hague Conventions of 1907.[15]

Beyond any doubt, it was the Polish government's priority to bring those suspected of international crimes to justice, as expressed in the programmatic declaration of Sikorski's cabinet of 24.02.1942, with the following words:

> The government will demand a complete and successful – preventing aggression for the future – disarmament of the aggressors and severe punishment of those guilty of the present war, [that is] Germany and is allies. For the wrongs done, for the crimes committed and destruction wrought, they must suffer the [well-]deserved

12 Plesch (2011): 104; Plesch, Sattler (2014): 21; Kochavi (1998): 3, 10.

13 Cyprian, Sawicki (1956a): 703; Cyprian, Sawicki (1962b), part I: 9–10; Goryński (1944): 18.

14 See statement of Władysław Raczkiewicz in BBC cited by Finder, Prusin (2018): 15 – "not a single German, whether he gave or executed a criminal order, will escape the punishing hand of Justice".

15 Doc. A 11E/124 (APISM).

> punishment, simultaneously providing those wronged with complete material and moral redress. That is the command of elementary historical justice that must prevail in international relations.[16]

To achieve the goal of bringing the Nazis to justice, however, one first had to convince a greater number of states to take joint action.

On 5–21.11.1941, a conference of nine occupied states was held in London, with Raczyński presiding. The conference emphasized the necessity of gathering the evidence of the crimes and developing common principles for holding the criminals responsible.[17] One particularly significant initiative taken by Polish authorities[18] was the holding in St James Palace in London (hence the name of the adopted instruments – St James Agreement/St James Declaration) on 12–13.01.1942 of a conference of representatives of governments-in-exile, i.e. Belgium, Czechoslovakia, France, Greece, the Netherlands, Yugoslavia, Luxembourg, Norway, and, of course, Poland. The conference was opened by Anthony Eden, who spoke very sparingly, noting that the initiative did not come from the United Kingdom.[19] Presiding over the conference, Sikorski stressed that there could be no crime without punishment and that the punishment had to be meted out for the acts of violence perpetrated by the enemy. For it was not fitting that any suffering be left without redress.[20]

According to the first document, adopted on 12.01.1942 by the participants of St James Conference, the signatories (including, besides the aforementioned nine occupied states, the United Kingdom and Australia, Canada, New Zealand, Union of South Africa and representatives of General Charles de Gaulle) undertook a commitment to joint fight against the aggression and declared that the true basis for a lasting peace was found

16 Dz.U.1943,8.40.

17 Ryszka (1982): 101ff.

18 Goryński (1944): 19 – emphasizing that the initiative of convening the conference came from the Free French National Committee following the execution of hostages in France in October 1941, though noting that the text of the declaration was drafted jointly by Poland and Czechoslovakia.

19 Lingen (2014): 55 – the author stresses that the United Kingdom and the USA (and likewise the USSR, China, Australia, Canada, New Zealand, Union of South Africa, and India) had the status of observes, assuring for them a more neutral position with regard to the initiative; Kochavi (1998): 18–20.

20 A document issued by the Inter-Allied Information Committee, London, *Punishment for War Crimes. The Inter-Allied Declaration Signed at St. James's Palace, London on 13th January 1942 and relative documents,* His Majesty's Stationery Office, https://nla.gov.au/nla.obj-648522001/view?partId=nla.obj-648522929#page/n6/mode/1up.

in the co-operation of free nations in a world free of aggression, where everybody could benefit from economic and social safety, and for that purpose to be achieved, collaboration was necessary in both war and peace.[21]

The second document, of 13.01.1942, the original text of which had been drafted by the legal advisors of Polish Ministry of Justice – Michał Potulicki and Władysław Kulski – and the representative of the Czechoslovak foreign minister, Adolf Prohazka,[22] dealt with the problem of punishment for those guilty of war crimes.[23] It asserted that the then-present conflict was the outcome of German politics of aggression and that Germany had imposed a regime of terror on the occupied states, including mass imprisonments, expulsions, executions of hostages, and massacres. It was recalled also that, in line with HC IV, to which Germany was party, the occupier was prohibited from using violence against the civilian population, repealing binding law or modifying national institutions, whereas those were the acts committed in the occupied territories by the Third Reich and its allied states. What is especially significant, however, is the emphasis laid in the preamble to the declaration on that international solidarity required not the public revenge but the meting out of justice in keeping with the requirements of the civilized world. The declaration stated that violence against the civilian population constituted neither an act of war nor a political crime, the way those were understood by civilized nations. One of the goals of the war waged by the allies was to be the punishment of those guilty of crimes, whether having issued orders or carrying them out and participating in the crimes. The signatories underscored that they entrusted to the spirit of international solidarity the apprehension, extradition and trial and judgment of the guilty, as well the execution of their sentences. Therewith, it was clearly indicated by the signing parties that neither an order nor the position of the person issuing it should exclude responsibility. As emphasized by Tadeusz Gelewski, the declaration distinguished three categories of persons responsible for war crimes: (1) those who prepared and gave the order; (2) the direct perpetrators; (3) persons who participated in the crimes as the perpetrator's lower-raking executors and accessories.[24]

21 The Inter-Allied Conference, 13.01.1942, "Bulletin of International News" 19, no. 2 (24.01.1942 r.): 50.

22 Uczkiewicz (2020): 243.

23 Text available at https://nla.gov.au/nla.obj-648522001/view?partId=nla.obj-648522082#page/n0/mode/1up. Declaration gained suport of Chinese delegate King Wunsz.

24 Gelewski (1976): 345.

The declaration of 13.01.1942 was signed by representatives of nine states (with Poland represented by Prime Minister Sikorski and by Raczyński as acting foreign minister). Representatives of the United States and of the United Kingdom received it with mixed feelings. They preferred not to address the crimes committed in e.g. Czechoslovakia, which they regarded as an internal matter of Germany, given that the partial annexation of Czechoslovakia had been sanctioned in Munich in 1938 and given the fear of reprisals against their soldiers held in captivity.[25] The Brits realized, however, that they were not in a position to be able to weaken the Polish and Czechoslovak efforts to bring the suspects to justice.[26] The declaration clearly stated that the criminals were to be met with legal, not political responsibility. In Sikorski's view, the declaration changed the direction taken by the development of international law, recognizing the criminality of acts committed during war. Raczyński, in turn, pointing directly towards Hans Frank, emphasized that the evil done to the civilian population would be treated as 'offences against the common law.' With that, the possibility of classifying war crimes as political crimes was excluded, contrary to the desires of the Belgian prime minister, Hubert Pierlot.[27]

Poland was the first to demand the punishment of those guilty of crimes, and the conference organized by the Polish government along with the St James Declaration of 13.01.1942 produced a strong impulse for further action (e.g. inspiring the open condemnation of the Japanese crimes as well).[28] Since the spring of 1942, both the United Kingdom and the USA had been practically flooded with the systematic reports on Nazi crimes submitted by the Polish side.[29]

The London conference involved a certain incident reflecting the state of tension in Polish-Jewish relations. Namely, Jewish circles reproached Polish authorities with failure to forward to the participants of the London conference the report transmitted to Sikorski by the Joint Foreign Committee, the Board of Deputies of British Jews, and the Anglo-Jewish Association, signed by Selig Brodetsky and Leonard Stein, detailing the fate of the Jews under German occupation.[30] The Polish side, however, explained that the letter (dated 12.01.1942) containing the report arrived too late to be able to be

25 Lingen (2014): 55.
26 Segesser (2005): 370–371; Kochavi (1998): 26, 28, 32.
27 Pol (1987): 50.
28 *Ibidem*.
29 Finder, Prusin (2018): 15.
30 Matthäus *et al.* (2013): 279–280.

distributed among the participants. It is remarkable, however, that Sikorski formulated a response only 4 months later.[31] The tone of the report, as well as the reaction to its not being forwarded for distribution, demonstrate that the problem of 'rivalry' among the victims (whose injuries are greater, who is the main victim of Nazi crimes, etc.)[32] and of a certain distrust from Jewish circles[33] had already existed at the time. That is understandable given the tense Polish-Jewish relations preceding the outbreak of the war. It did little to help the building of a common front on the matter of justice for Nazi crimes,[34] though it must be emphasized that Polish authorities made efforts to publicize the crimes committed against the Jews (e.g. the famous Jan Karski report for US President Franklin Delano Roosevelt[35] and especially Karski's book *Story of a Secret State* of 1944 or Witold Pilecki's reports of 1943 on the situation at Auschwitz-Birkenau[36]), and the various government agencies occupied themselves with documenting the crimes committed against the Jews, as will be discussed below[37]. It was on Polish initiative that, on 17.12.1942, the Allied Nations issued a joint declaration on German crimes perpetrated on the Jews in the occupied territories, anticipating the inevitability of retribution and the necessity to expedite the practical preparations to that affect ('They re-affirm their solemn resolution to ensure that those responsible for these crimes shall not escape retribution, and to press on with the necessary practical measures to this end.')[38].

The importance placed by the Polish Republic on the matter of judgment for the crimes is attested by the fact that the topic was the subject of inter-ministerial conferences discussing, among other things, the role that could be played by the new bodies whose establishment was anticipated by the British authorities. Karol Jonca reports that particularly innovative ideas were submitted in those conferences by Tadeusz Cyprian and Stefan Glaser.[39] According to the representatives of Polish ministries, it was necessary to focus on the crimes and not on the names of the perpetrators

31 *Ibidem*: 281–282.

32 *Ibidem*: 306.

33 See also Stola in: Michowicz (1999): 666ff.

34 See also Miszewski (2016): 64.

35 Published by Republic of Poland, Ministry of Foreign Affairs (1942).

36 See Pilecki (2017).

37 See also Długołęcki (2022).

38 Parliamentary Debates, House of Lords [Jews (German Barbarities)], vol. 385, 17.12.1942, https://hansard.parliament.uk/Commons/1942-12-17/debates/a2c7d178-71a7-4896-8839-3771d89f52c9/Jews (GermanBarbarities); see also Goryński (1944) 22.

39 Jonca (1987): 50.

(later, the two would no longer be separated) and that ought to be handled by the United Nations War Crimes Commission, whereas a separate body (a technical committee) should be created for the purpose of the preparation of the theoretical framework of the procedure for the trials (what procedural model to adopt, what type of court, etc.).[40]

Polish authorities decided that it was necessary to commission a body to gather information about the crimes; that was to be co-ordinated by Glaser.[41] It was realized that the materials on the crimes were scattered across different ministries. The main documents were found in the Ministry of the Interior and in the Ministry of Congress Affairs, but the Ministry of Industry, Commerce and Navigation and the Ministry of the Treasury also held some of the requisite documents. To prepare for the anticipated trials, one had to gather the evidence of individual culpability and identify the direct perpetrators, as well as those who gave the orders and issued the relevant regulations. To secure their ability to judge the perpetrators of the crimes, the Polish representatives undertook the negotiation of a general extradition treaty with the relevant states and lobbied for the principle that the domestic courts of the state in whose territory the crimes had been committed were to have the jurisdiction to judge those suspected of the crimes.[42] The matter was determined by a declaration of the four powers, i.e. United States, United Kingdom, USSR and China, of 30.10./1.11.1943, according to which the four nations would continue their joint activities, 'pledged for the prosecution of the war against their respective enemies,' which included preparation for holding responsible those guilty of the outbreak of the war. A separate statement by Roosevelt, Churchill and Stalin communicated that the Allies had been given abundant evidence of crimes, massacres and mass executions perpetrated by the Nazi forces in the conquered states, and the Nazis' brutality was without precedent. The document anticipated that the German officers and men, as well as members of Nazi parties responsible for the crimes or having knowingly taken part in them would be handed over to the states where they had committed their crimes and there judged pursuant to the laws of the liberated states (Poland was mentioned in the context). Interesting, a direct reference was made to

---

40 See protocol of 17.09.1943, PRM-K/74, doc. 4, p. 8 (17 (APISM). The following persons took part in the meeting: Adamkiewicz, Cyprian, Glaser, Krajewski, Kulski, Potulicki, Piotrowski, Sokołowski, Sukiennicki.

41 Meeting of 9.10.1943, PRM-K/74, doc. 5 (APISM).

42 See e.g. Rutczyński (1944): 11ff.

the responsibility of the Germans who had participated in the mass shootings of Polish officers, as well as those responsible for butchering the civilian population; this bears testimony to the tenacity with which the Poles pressed the issue in their talks with the representatives of the great powers. The promise was made that those guilty would be chased to the end of the world so as for them to be brought to the prosecutors to be held responsible. Simultaneously, it was noted that the above did not apply to those German criminals whose offenses had no particular geographical localization and who would therefore be punished according to the joint decision of the Allied governments.[43]

In the spring of the same year, the signatories of the declaration of 13.01.1942 established an Inter-Allied Conference (later transformed into the War Crimes Commission)[44] tasked with documenting the war crimes committed in occupied Europe, preparing joint statements by the governments-in-exile concerning the German crimes, as well as concrete legal solutions enabling the perpetrators to be brought to justice. The Belgian representative, Georges Kaeckenbeeck, led the Commission, with Michał Potulicki serving as its secretary.[45] The Commission functioned until August 1943, i.e. the beginning of the works leading up to the establishment of the UN War Crimes Commission.

Polish representatives also participated in the debates within the other bodies of crucial importance to the shaping of the framework for the responsibility for the crimes, such as the London International Assembly or the International Commission for Penal Reconstruction and Development.[46]

The London International Assembly was a body established in September 1941 upon the initiative of Robert Cecil. It was intended for the replacement of the Assembly of the League of Nations as a forum for the exchange of thoughts and discussions, provided that the participants took part in the works as private individuals, on account of their expertise and renown, rather than as representatives of their governments. Those involved in its works included August Zaleski, at the time the Chief of the Civil Chancellery of the President of the Republic. The purpose of such a formula was to

43 See documentation on: https://history.state.gov/historicaldocuments/frus1943v01/d684.

44 Inter-Allied Information Centre, Punishment for war crimes. Collective notes presented to the governments of Great Britain the USSR and the USA and relative correspondence, London 1942.

45 Uczkiewicz (2020): 240.

46 Lingen (2014): 45ff; Plesch (2011): 103; Uczkiewicz (2020): 249.

assuage the concerns of the British foreign minister, Anthony Eden, who was afraid that talks in the assembly could be detrimental to his own independent negotiations. The London Assembly was an important body in how its purpose was to develop the principles to inspire international politics after the end of the war. In total, the Assembly met more than 300 times, and in December 1943 it adopted final reports on its works (*Reports on the punishment of war crimes*). It included Marcel de Baer's subcommittee tasked with considering the matter of the codification of international criminal law and procedure. Its purpose was to apply incessant pressure on the British diplomatic service and especially the War Crimes Committee led since July 1942 by John Simon.

The International Commission for Penal Reconstruction and Development, which also formed in 1941 out of so-called Cambridge Conference (and included, besides Stefan Glaser, Hersch Lauperpacht, Bohdan Winiarski and others),[47] appointed a committee tasked with examining the possibility of holding war criminals accountable before domestic courts,[48] which the Polish government especially desired. There, in April 1942, a questionnaire was developed on the rules and procedures applicable to the ongoing war; Poland, Belgium, Czechoslovakia, France, Greece, the Netherlands, Luxembourg, Norway and Yugoslavia responded.[49] The responding states identified their legislative provisions enabling them to confront the challenge of judging the crimes of World War II (WWII), as opposed to international law.

Poland was keen on adopting the principle that the relevant crimes were to be judged in chronological order, meaning that Poland would have the priority.[50] In a committee meeting at the Polish Institute in London, in July 1942, subcommittees were created to examine legal issues, and although the Poles were not presiding at the works, the remarks made by Glaser and Lauterpacht carried much consequence.[51] Glaser, among other things, drew attention to the new forms of commission of crimes, noting the mass scale of certain activities (concentration camps, mass executions, forced resettlements), as well as economic violence, imposition of destructive labour, and

47 Uczkiewicz (2020): 245.

48 Garrod (2016): 349; Lingen (2014): 56–57.

49 Goold Adams (1948): 96ff.

50 See PRM-K/74, doc. 5 (APISM). It might be questioned whether Poland or Austria and Czechoslovakia were the first victims of WWII. The answer would have impact on the priority in judging criminals.

51 Lingen (2014): 59.

extermination of the population. He pointed out the role played by Nazi law, which legitimized the majority of the German authorities' actions.[52] Lauterpacht, on the other hand, prepared a memorandum titled *Punishment of War Crimes*, intended as a summation the works, in which he argued for the establishment of an international court, by which to overcome the difficulties identified in the domestic laws. Some of the other members did not concur with his opinion, including the chair – Arnold McNair – bearing in mind the futility of the attempts made during the Interwar period.

On the initiative of the Polish government and in a collaboration with the governments of 16 Allied states (Australia, Belgium, China, Czechoslovakia, France, Greece, the Netherlands, Yugoslavia, Canada, Luxembourg, Norway, New Zealand, the USA, the Union of South Africa, and Poland, the latter represented by Raczyński and Glaser),[53] on 20.10.1943, the UN War Crimes Commission was created and tasked not only with documenting the crimes committed during WWII but also identifying the perpetrators and providing the governments with the evidence.

The Commission's works began in January 1944. The Briton, Cecil Hurst, became its Chairman (in 1945, following his resignation in response to the rejection by the British and the American governments of the Commission's draft statue of a UN Criminal Tribunal, he would be replaced by Robert A. Wright), which was consistent with the Poles' desires, as they believed the British leadership would provide the Commission's works with greater stability.

Three committees were created within the UNWCC: The Committee I on Facts and Evidence (chaired by Marcel de Baer), tasked with determining the facts and gathering the evidence in specific cases, with Jerzy Litawski, Chief of the Polish War Crimes Office in 1943–1945, participating in the works; Committee II on Means and Methods of Enforcement (chaired by Herbert C. Pell) dealt with the discussion of the rules for extradition, principles governing the punishment of the guilty, procedures for the collection of evidence in occupied territories, draft statute of an international court (adopted by the Commission on 26.09.1944 but ultimately rejected by the UK and the USA); and Committee III on Legal Affairs, to determine the principles of responsibility and other legal issues relating to the crimes.

Glaser, as the head of the criminal-law section in the commission on legislative works at the Ministry of Justice, appeared to be the natural

---

52 Glaser's report for the Cambridge Commission for Penal Reconstruction and Development, "National Laws and Jurisdictions", 22.10.1942 r., TNA, LCO 2/2973.

53 UNWCC (1948): 112.

candidate for Poland's representative in the Commission.[54] In testimony to the recognition of his competence (as well as the importance of Poland), he was appointed to chair Committee III.[55] Attesting to the significance of that role is the fact that the Commission's recommendations were more persuasive than those offered by the individual states.[56] Glaser, however, served in it only briefly, until August 1944, when upon his resignation, it went to Bohuslav Ečer from Czechoslovakia. Following Glaser's departure, Cyprian became Poland's representative in the Commission.[57] Litawski and Lachs, as representatives of the national office, also took an active part in the works (e.g. during the UNWCC conference on 31.04.-2.06.1945 with the national war crimes offices). Litawski was a key figure in Committee I, appreciated to the extent that when recognition was withdrawn from the Polish government-in-exile, he went on to be employed by the Commission's secretariat (in May 1945 as legal counsel and thereafter secretary of Committee I, and from July 1947 onward as senior legal counsel, replacing Egon Schwelb).[58]

The UNWCC met for the first time on 18.01.1944. Since the beginning, there were doubts as to whether the Commission should occupy itself solely with war crimes *stricto sensu* or also with other atrocities committed on racial, political or religious grounds.[59] Despite controversy, the Commission also worked on crimes against humanity, doubtless influenced by the position of Glaser, who emphasized that it had to address: 'acts incompatible with a given country's criminal statute that are simultaneously a violation of international law but also other, more serious crimes, of racial, political or religious nature – especially the crimes on German Jews in Germany.'[60] Glaser also campaigned for the list of war crimes to include mass arrests,

54 See letter of W. Komarnicki (Ministry of Justice) to Romer (MFA) of 9.08.1943, PRM-K/74, doc. 1, p. 10 (APISM).

55 UNWCC, Minutes of the seventh meeting, 1.02.1944, available at https://www.legal-tools.org/doc/a3c690/pdf/.

56 Karska (2009): 45.

57 See PRM-K/74, doc. 3, 18.09.1944 (APISM).

58 UNWCC (1948): V; Litawski authored chapters II, III i IX *History of the United Nations War Crimes Commission and the Development of the Laws of War* (1948).

59 See letter of Cecil Hurst, 1.06.1944 to governments, PRM-K/74, doc. 7, p. 29 (APISM).

60 PRM-K/74, doc. 7, p. 22, 5.06.1944 (APISM). Such a position run counter of the approach taken by the USA or the UK, and the expansion of the thematic range to crimes against humanity committed before the war resulted in cuts to the Commission's budget and the recall of the American representative, Herbert Pell – see Plesch (2011): 110–111.

hostage taking and issuing legal acts targeted against human dignity.[61] He submitted a draft of the principles of individual responsibility of the war criminals, according to which both those issuing the order to commit a crime and those carrying such an order out were to be held responsible.[62] Of particular value was the indication of the responsibility of the occupation authorities' officials for the issue and implementation of unlawful legal acts, orders, etc., as well as the responsibility of judges for issuing judgments in contravention of international law and engaging in so-called judicial crimes. The Polish draft also specified that the administrative superior would be responsible for the crimes committed in their district.

One unquestionably Polish contribution to the understanding of war crimes was the raising of the issue of crimes against culture (in this context, one has to mention Karol Estreicher and Stanisław Lorentz, who strove to protect cultural property and publicize the problem of their destruction and appropriation),[63] which, in Poland's opinion, ought to include not only attacks on the artists and academics but also the destruction or appropriation of art and other property, including sacred art. The above approach was emphasized by submitting the appropriate charge files, such as charge file 7 of February 1944, concerning the destruction of the monument of Boleslaus the Brave in Gniezno, which was part of the general German policy of destruction of any signs of Polish culture; charge file 12 of March 1944 concerning the deportation of Cracow scholars to Nazi camps, described in the context of fighting Polish culture; charge file 21 concerning the destruction of churches, synagogues, etc.; charge file 33 concerning Jewish property (see also file 1508); charge file 36 concerning private property; or charge file 40 concerning the destruction and theft of libraries and archives; and many more.[64]

Poland appreciated the Commission's importance and financed its activities without objections.[65] The Commission's works were diligently followed and discussed in the aforementioned inter-ministerial conferences, especially whenever the subject of the draft convention on an inter-Allied tribunal to judge war crimes or draft convention on the extradition of criminals

61 UNWCC, Proposal by the Polish representatives for adding items to the list of war criminals (Minutes of the 17th meeting, 9.05.1944): 3.

62 AIPN GK 159.125, k. 220–221, Glaser's paper of 7.04.1944; AAN 2/133/0/6/44, Protocol of the meeting ot the Section of Criminal Law Criminal Procedure and Penology, 15.05.1942.

63 Waltoś (2015).

64 See more Fleming (2022a): 294; Fleming (2022b).

65 According to UNWCC resolution of 22.03.1944, Poland paid 400£ a year.

surfaced.[66] From the picture painted by the documents of the inter-ministerial conferences, accents were placed by Polish authorities on guaranteeing that a command from a superior should be no bar to responsibility; the ability to hold responsible the persons administrating the relevant territory if the direct perpetrators are not known; holding both the issuer and the executor of an order responsible but also holding a judge responsible for the consequences of the judgments issued. Realizing that in the German case, the legislative underpinnings of the Nazi crimes were of great significance, the members of the conference considered the utility of the construct of culpable incitement for the evaluation of the character of German legislation.[67] Precisely on account of hypothetical reliance on domestic legislation to avoid responsibility, Glaser proposed in February 1944 that the International Commission for Penal Reconstruction and Development gather information concerning the law in force in Germany. The other issues being discussed included the problem of immunities, acting in a state of necessity, retroactivity, as well as conflict between domestic and international jurisdiction.[68] The problems discussed found reflection in the legislative drafts submitted by Glaser and Komarnicki (drafters of the Decree of 1943, more on which below), as well as Mieczysław Siewierski and Jerzy Śliwowski.

Realizing that, with time, the problem of crimes committed in Soviet territories (including Polish eastern territories occupied by the Soviets) and of the jurisdiction over them would come to surface, the Polish government preferred that the UNWCC discuss the crimes in a chronological order, thus delaying the issue of Soviet crimes.[69]

When the Commission began to gather information about specific crimes, verify the evidence, identify the perpetrators, etc., in which included Litawski (among others) took part, it became evident how important the ongoing gathering of information on the perpetrators had been. Poland made an enormous effort in submitting a list of crimes along with the supporting evidence. In the Ministry of the Interior (which supervised the clandestine administration in the occupied territories), a War Crimes Commission was established, incorporating two sections – general and Jewish. A specialized agency was also created in Scotland, systematically recording testimony from individuals who had been pressed into the German army,

66 See e.g. PRM-K/74, doc. 5, p. 12ff; PRM-K/74, doc. 13 (APISM).

67 See PRM-K/74, doc. 2, 20.09.1943 (APISM).

68 AAN, 2/133/0/6/44, k. 469.

69 See PRM-K/74 doc. 5, p. 12ff. (APISM).

then taken prisoner and, following liberation of France and Italy, come to Scotland to serve in Polish Armed Forces. Accepted in total were a thousand affidavits selected out of statements given by 30 thousand potential witnesses. The office, led by Litawski and headquartered at 16 Thorney Court, Palace Gate, employed 6 lawyers (3 barristers, 1 investigative judge, 1 prosecutor and 1 junior lawyer), as well as support staff.

Meticulous collection of evidence was necessary because, in line with the recommendation of 16.05.1944, merely providing the names and formulating suppositions of culpability did not suffice – in the UNWCC's opinion – for the case to proceed. It was further necessary to identify all persons occupying the relevant positions in the administration and the army.[70]

Poland systematically referred the cases of the various crimes, provided that by 13.06.1944 it had been possible to submit documentation on 21 cases involving murders, massacres, systematic terrorism, torture, robbery, endangering the lives of hostages, deportations, concentration camps, use of collective punishment, destruction of property, and ill-treatment of prisoners of war; it was noted that the worst abuses were occurring in the death camps for the Jews. The Poles, moreover, prepared a separate publication on the crimes against the Jews, which they forwarded to the UNWCC, titled *The Persecution of Jews in German-Occupied Poland*, as well as chapters in *The German Attempt to Destroy the Polish Nation* and *The German New Order in Poland* (Polish Government Information Office). Some of the charge files focused solely on crimes against the Jewish population (e.g. files no. 29, 33 and 34). Poland also submitted a list of concentration camps; among others, file 20 pertained to the camps in Bełżec, Sobibór, Majdanek, Kosów Podlaski, Chełmno (Kulmhof) and Oświęcim (Auschwitz).[71]

Polish War Crimes Office emphasized that[72] it had materials on the legal position of the Jews in occupied Poland and the legislation discriminating against them, including violations of their dignity; treatment of Jewish women and children; restrictions of access to professions, occupations and trades; confiscations of Jewish property; persecution of the Jewish religion; forced labour; expulsions; establishment of ghettoes and concentration camps; killings, murders, massacres and biological extermination. Litawski stressed that his office was co-operating with Jewish organizations and it was Poland's position that her courts had the jurisdiction to judge not only crimes committed within the territory of the Republic of Poland but also

70 PRM-K/74, doc. 7, p. 33 (APISM)

71 Doc. 160/44, 21.07.1944 (Wiener Library).

72 See doc. 37/44, 29.04.1944, (Wiener Library).

abroad, with regard to crimes targeting Polish nationals and the Polish state. Multiple times did Polish representatives underscore the legal obligation incumbent on their state to judge the crimes against the Jews. They also emphasized their particular desire to judge the crimes against prisoners of war (here, one can notice the indubitable influence of Komarnicki,[73] though it is worth emphasizing that other lawyers and jurists among the Polish exiles, too, had traumatizing experiences behind them, such as Winiarski, who had been arrested by the Germans in 1939 and held as a hostage[74]).

Polish authorities realized that if the negotiations concerning the appointment of an inter-Allied tribunal were to be handed over to diplomatic representatives rather than an international commission, there was a small chance of Polish presence in the adjudicating panels (as the reality proved later).[75] Some of the members of the inter-ministerial conferences, e.g. Włodzimierz Adamkiewicz, voiced their dissatisfaction with the tendency towards judging the Germans not on the basis of domestic law but 'unfamiliar' or 'unknown' international law, the 'unbeaten tracks, in this field, of international law,' – in which the Anglophones saw the possibility of circumventing the ban on retroaction. Cyprian, in turn, pointed out that the judges in international bodies would certainly be dependent on their governments, appointed on short commissions and obliged soon to return to their countries. There was a difference of opinions in the Polish government concerning the American-inspired Indian proposal, submitted in a UNWCC subcommittee, for military tribunals to be established by allied supreme commands. While Litawski supported that solution, the ministerial representatives took a critical view. There was the resurfacing problem of a draft convention on the extradition of war criminals, which provided for the use of an administrative procedure in relations among the Allies (i.e. excluding the neutral states). It was agreed, however, that the convention should not apply to prisoners of war. Polish representatives in the inter-ministerial conference also wondered, already in November 1944, how to approach the qualification of the then-ongoing war as a type of war crime and decide when it began. They saw the problematic nature of recognizing the criminality of such actions of the Reich as the occupation of the Sudetsko (Sudetenland in German). Hence, attempts were made to separate the causation

73 See PRM-K/74, doc. 11, 30.06.1944, (APISM).

74 Sandorski (2004): 77.

75 See protocols of inter-ministerial conferences of 21 and 28.11.1944, PRM-K/74, doc. 13 (APISM).

of the war from the preparation. In principle, Poland assumed that the war had begun on 1.09.1939 but, for diplomatic reasons, did not want to frustrate the Czechs' efforts to have also the actions taken against them recognized as a war crime *lato sensu*.

Poland attempted to demonstrate the existence of a special character of the crimes targeted against Polish nationals. Thus, for example, in the UNWCC conference on 6.05.1945, Cyprian stressed that Poles had suffered more than any other nation, whether in terms of the number of victims or the scope of the crimes. As examples he gave the murder of the professors from Cracow; the shooting of 140 Poles in Anin on 26–27.12.1939 as part of German reprisals for a drunken civilian's attack; the extermination of the intelligentsia, officers and clergy; mass deportations, including for the purpose of slave labour – which affected 2.5 to 3.5 million people; the organization of concentration camps in Treblinka, Bełżec and Majdanek; and the experiments at the camp in Ravensbrück[76].

In a conference of the national offices (31.05–2.06.1945),[77] with Litawski, Cyprian and Lachs attending on behalf of the Polish office, Cyprian presented the issue of recognition of the criminality (in the light of the information supplied by the Underground State) of actions taken with a view to completely annihilating the Polish population. The latter was supposed to happen, among other ways, through starvation and slave labour (characteristically, Lachs provided the same examples during the postwar negotiations of the Genocide Convention). Placing the emphasis on the scale of the crimes against the Poles was to facilitate the building of a strong negotiation position for Poland with regard to the determination of the principles for the bringing of the suspects to justice. The problem of rivalry over who was to judge the perpetrators did not escape notice, and although Cyprian underscored that – as in any other extradition case – the ultimate decision as to where a given suspect was to be tried would depend on diplomatic negotiations, Lachs noted that the lack of codified rules of extradition would spark conflicts and thus the matter ought to be resolved by the Commission. Lachs also stressed that some crimes, such as those committed against the Jews, bore similarities, so it was worth judging them jointly in order to avoid the duplication of efforts. In the aforementioned conference,

76 UNWCC, Record of the Conference held on May 6th, 1945, between members of the UNWCC and members of the United States Senate and House of Representatives, doc. C115, 24.05.1945: 6.

77 UNWCC – National Offices Conference, London, 31 May-June 1945, Minutes and Documents, 15825–00001, eg. at 11.

it became clear that the American aspiration was to establish an international tribunal, whereas the Brits were content with leaving the matter of responsibility for the crimes to the executive power. All of the states participating in the conference appreciated the necessity of gathering evidence of the crimes. At the end of the conference, the proposal was tabled to adopt a commitment (*voeu*) under which one or more offices would be created (Central Recording Office – Lachs's own proposal) and tasked with the apprehension and handing over of the defendants; all but major criminals were to be dispatched to the states requesting them, according to a list approved by the UNWCC, and any disputes would be arbitrated by the Commission; the Commission would also be vested with the right to bring indictments before any tribunal of the United Nations, whereas the remaining defendants were to be prosecuted by the national offices; it was also emphasized that the Soviets had to co-operate or they would be in violation of the terms of the Moscow Declaration of 30.10.1943; the same terms of responsibility would be applicable to European and to Japanese perpetrators; for the recording and indexing of the crimes, the American system would be followed. Cyprian (like other state representatives) emphasized, however, that it was beyond his powers to become bound by the *voeu* on Poland's behalf without instructions from his government.

Poland, as a result of Glaser's persuasion, decided to participate in the works and finance the UN War Crimes Commission's subcommittee tasked with the investigation of Japanese crimes in the Far East.[78] The Polish representative in that subcommittee was Alfred Emeryk Poniński, a member of the Polish Embassy in Chongqing, who served until July 1945, i.e. the Polish government-in-exile's loss of international recognition. Here, it should be added that there were no prospects of a separate panel for crimes committed in Soviet territories, as the USSR saw no such need.[79]

2 Polish Legislation

Polish authorities highlighted the legislative preparations for the judgment of those suspected of international crimes, as in addition to the Criminal Code of 1932, the President – on 30.03.1943 – issued a Decree on Criminal Responsibility for War Crimes[80] (the works had already been pending since

78 See PRM-K/74, doc. 8, 12.06.1944; PRM-K/74, doc. 9, 14.06.1944 (APISM).

79 PRM-K/74, doc. 4(11) – APISM.

80 Dz.U.1943.3.6. See more Goryński (1944): 24.

1942),[81] which provided for the criminal responsibility of: 'persons belonging to the German Reich or states allied to or collaborating with the same,' as well as: 'other persons acting in the interest of the Reich or the said states, for offences committed after 31 August 1939, notwithstanding the place of commission of the act' (Article 1). The Decree invoked international law (Articles 2, 5, 6 and 7) and referred to acts injuring the Polish state, Polish legal persons and Polish nationals (Article 2), including resettlements (Article 3), causing a general danger to human life or health in Poland (Article 4), compelling a Polish national to join foreign armed forces or provide labour for the enemy (Article 5), injuring a Polish citizen with judicial decisions (Article 6), as well as robbery, theft, destruction of or significant damage to public property or private property representing a value to the nation as a whole (Article 7). Importantly, the Decree emphasized that both those ordering the commission of the acts described in it and those executing such orders were to be held responsible (Article 10). Therewith, already in 1943 did Polish legislation contain a provision for the criminal responsibility of those executing orders. In many ways, the Decree had a pioneering role, being the first instrument of domestic legislation to set forth a legal framework for the responsibility of war criminals.[82] As stated by Komarnicki in the Decree's explanatory memorandum authored by himself, the purpose of the instrument was to assist with demonstrating that the German terror was aimed at the biological and cultural eradication of entire communities.[83]

Subsequent key decrees were already issued by communist authorities, who distanced themselves from the legislation of the government-in-exile; hence, in the trials conducted after the war, the Code of 1932 was cited but the Decree of 1943 was not.

Polish Committee of National Liberation (PKWN) – provisional executive organ operating from July to December 1944 in the territory occupied by the Red Army; on 31.08.1944, it adopted a Decree on the Sentencing Guidelines for Fascist-Nazi Criminals Guilty of Homicide and Ill-Treatment of the Civilian Population and Prisoners of War, and for Traitors to the Polish Nation, so-called August Decree (*Dekret Polskiego Komitetu Wyzwolenia Narodowego z dnia 31 sierpnia 1944 r. o wymiarze kary dla faszystowsko-hitlerowskich zbrodniarzy winnych zabójstw i znęcania się nad ludnością cywilną i jeńcami oraz dla zdrajców Narodu Polskiego*) – *sierpniówka*.[84] The authorship of the

81 See more Goryński (1944): 87ff.
82 Uczkiewicz (2020): 246; Kubicki (1987): 29.
83 AAN, 2/133/0/6/44, k. 28–30.
84 Dz.U.1944.4.16.

text of the Decree is attributed to Leon Chajn, although his substantive role was minimal. That is because the Decree was a copy of the Soviet solutions, so one can hardly look to it for original Polish legal thought.[85] However, the vagueness of the terminology left openings for a greater role of Polish courts' decision-making in the application of the Decree.[86]

The August Decree provided for punishment for – as long as such actions assisted the occupying authorities – 'participation in the commission of homicide of persons from among the civilian population or prisoners of war or ill-treatment or harassment of the same,' and, 'actions injurious to persons staying within the territory of the Polish State, especially through the apprehension or deportation of persons wanted or persecuted by the occupying power for any reasons (excluding prosecution for common crimes)' (Article 1).

The Decree targeted only one aggressor and occupier – the Nazi Germany (which was secured through the use of the adjective 'fascist-Nazi,' rather than e.g. 'national-socialist,' so as to avoid the implication of the existence of any links between German and Soviet socialists).

The Decree was exceptionally repressive – firstly, because of the retroactivity. For it applied all the way back to 1.09.1939. Secondly, the same punishment was threatening for participation in homicide (including incitement or an accessory role) as for e.g. harassment or denunciation. That motivated some of the courts to acquit the defendants due to the excessive severity of even the lower sentencing limit.[87] Thirdly, the Decree's Article 3 emphasized that acting in the service of the hostile occupying power, on its order or due to its coercion was no bar to liability.

3 The Judiciary

Polish courts continued to operate in occupied Poland, but for the obvious reasons they did not judge the war crimes committed by the Nazis. Directorate of Diversion of the Supreme Command of the Home Army (*Kierownictwo Dywersji* – 'Kedyw') carried out actions consisting in the physical liquidation of German criminals (e.g., the one targeting Franz Kutschera on 1.02.1944), but such assassinations – despite the misleading information in some historical publications and on certain websites – can hardly be

85 Lityński (1999): 63; Machnikowska (2008): 260.
86 Pasek (2002): 35–36.
87 Lityński (1999): 67.

regarded as the execution of court judgments. They were the outcome of a political decision taken by the Supreme Command of the Home Army in consultation with the government-in-exile.[88] Hence, they constituted an example of armed operations (elimination of specific personal targets) rather than judicial activities.

The Underground State somewhat quickly developed military judicial structures. On 16.04.1940, the Committee for the Country adopted a resolution establishing secret courts (at supreme, regional and area commands of the Union of Armed Struggle – Związek Walki Zbrojnej, ZWZ),[89] tasked with: 'judging and sentencing in cases of the crimes of treason, espionage, denunciation, as well as inhuman persecution and abuse of the Polish population.'[90] Considering the high degree of generality of the language used in the definition of the crime, viz.: 'persecution and abuse of the Polish population,' that could extend to war crimes and crimes against humanity.

The adjudicating panel included the respective supreme, regional or area commander, a representative of the 'social factor' (society), and a person with legal education. Courts of that type could either acquit or impose a death sentence. Given the realities of life under the occupation, the enforcement of any other type of punishment (such as imprisonment) was not feasible. Where the circumstances of the case called for the imposition of a prison term, the final decision was deferred until after the war. While the military secret courts considered the crimes committed by current or former members of the ZWZ (even after their leaving the organization), crimes committed by other persons not belonging to the ZWZ – be they Polish nationals or the occupiers or other foreigners – were to be judged by the secret courts of the Government Delegation for Poland. Pending their formation or in the absence of a delegation in a given area, the aforementioned crimes were to be examined by the secret court of the appropriate territorial command of the ZWZ.[91] In practice, the entire civil wing of the judiciary formed with two years' delay compared to the military

88 That was part of the Home Army's operation codenamed "Główki" ("Heads"), of which the objective was the elimination of high-ranking members of German occupation authorities. See Stachiewicz (1987): 65; Morzycki-Markowski (2017): 19; Strzembosz (1983): 401ff.

89 ZWZ was established based on the order of Commander-in-chief – general Władysław Sikorski, of 13.11.1939. ZWZ was transformed into the AK on 14.02.1942.

90 Texts of 1940 code reprinted in Gondek (1988): 148. On ZWZ courts see more: Machnikowska (2008): 256ff; Burczyk (2010): 292; Pasek (2002): 16; Szyprowski (2012): passim; Kurkowska (2012): passim; Gondek (1988): 37; Lisiewicz (1988): 15ff.

91 See more Wołkonowski (2007): 123.

wing. Thus, for a long time the military courts held a broad scope of *ratione personae* jurisdiction.[92]

Near the end of the 1941, the secret courts (whose Polish name carried negative associations with German Vehmic courts) were renamed to special military courts at the level of the Supreme Commander and Area Commanders of the Home Army, with by-laws adopted on 26.11.1941.[93] They had the same jurisdiction as the late secret courts, viz. prosecution of crimes: 'against the safety of the Armed Forces in the country,' defined by applicable criminal provisions, committed or attempted by members of the military after 4.12.1939. They were also competent to impose prison terms. Following another wave of organizational changes, the special military courts dealt with any crime targeting the safety of Polish armed forces within the country or committed by military personnel.[94] In December 1942, separate special civilian courts were established[95] to judge Polish and foreign nationals for such grave crimes against the interests of the state, nation and citizens as called for immediate punishment.[96] Those courts, adjudicating in panels of three – only one member had to have legal education – upon finding the accused guilty of the crimes charged, could only impose the death penalty.[97] In practice, they usually heard cases of denunciation, espionage and provocation.[98] It must be noted that on 3.05.1944 the Council of Ministers at Home issued an interim regulation on special criminal courts operating at the level of government delegations.[99] On that basis, those courts had jurisdiction in criminal cases concerning: 'acting for the benefit of the occupier or to the detriment of the Polish state or Nation.'[100] In practice, similarly to the preceding special/secret courts, they dealt with cases of collaboration with the enemy and blackmail (*szmalcownik* cases). Dariusz Burczyk counts the special courts' caseload at approximately 5 thousand cases, with 3 to 3.5 thousand death sentences, of which 2.5 thousand were carried out.[101] Those data are only estimates, as the case records have

92 Gondek (1988): 59.

93 Text of the Statute of ZWZ-AK special military courts available in Gondek (1988): 152ff.; see also Pasek (2002): 17.

94 Pasek (2002): 17–18.

95 Kurkowska (2012): 167; Gondek (1984): 650.

96 Gondek (1988): 98.

97 Korboński (1991): 108.

98 Gondek (1988): 100 and 106ff.

99 Dz.U.1944.1.6.

100 Text in: Gondek (1988): 168ff.

101 Burczyk (2014): 293.

not been preserved, and historians have to rely on announcements and reports published by the underground press.

With the end of 1944, the activities of the underground courts ceased.[102] Along with the communist takeover, the organization of the court system and the method of prosecution of criminals – especially those responsible for international crimes and collaboration – changed completely.[103]

To the communists, the matter of bringing the criminals to judgment was a priority. In the PKWN Manifesto of 22.07.1944, the communists emphatically proclaimed: 'It will be the task of the independent Polish courts to ensure the swift administration of justice. No German war criminal, no traitor to the nation can escape punishment!.'[104] The communist authorities intended to use the punishment of the crimes as leverage to legalize and legitimize their takeover of power.[105]

On 12.09.1944, the PKWN issued a Decree on Special Criminal Courts for Cases of Fascist-Nazi Criminals (*Dekret o specjalnych sądach karnych dla spraw zbrodniarzy faszystowsko-hitlerowskich*)[106] According to the Decree, in the territory of every court of appeals there was to be created a special criminal court for the judgment of the crimes covered by Articles 1–4 of the August Decree (i.e., other that the aforementioned crimes, viz. participation in homicide, persecution, etc., the jurisdiction also extended to blackmail against the same persons or those close to them with the threat of apprehension and delivery to the occupying authorities) – Articles 1–2.

On the basis of the Decree, on the same day, the first special criminal courts were created in Lublin and Warsaw (the latter temporarily seated in Siedlce).[107] Apart from the above, the special courts were also formed in Gdańsk, Cracow (with an off-campus division in Rzeszów), Toruń, Wrocław, Poznań, Katowice and Łódź (with off-campus divisions in Warsaw and Białystok).

The panel of such a special court was to include a judge (appointed by the Praesidium of the State National Council – *Krajowa Rada Narodowa* (KRN) – at the recommendation of the Head of the Department of Justice from among persons holding legal qualifications)[108] and two lay judges (the

102 Machnikowska (2008): 258.

103 *Ibidem*: 10ff.

104 Dz.U.1944.1.annex.

105 Birt (2019): 81. Kuisz (2020).

106 Dz.U.1944.4.21.

107 Machnikowska (2008): 260.

108 The KRN was established by the Act of 11.09.1944 on the Organization and Scope of Operation of the National Councils (Dz.U.1944.5.22; consolidated text: Dz.U.1946.3.26);

list of lay judges was to be determined by the Praesidium of the KRN from among candidates recommended by voivodeship national councils). The Decree of 12.09.1944 determined the requirements to be met by the lay judges; those could be persons who: 'have taken or are still taking an active part in either armed struggle against the German occupier or civil action of defence and resistance, including propaganda actions, or in the action of restoration of Polish statehood in the political, economic or cultural scope, provided they shall be at least 21 years of age.' Persons accused of collaborating with the German occupier, as well as persons suspected of having acted within the structures of the Polish Underground State during the occupation or co-operated with the pro-independence underground forces after the war were unable to serve as lay judges. Importantly, judges having worked in courts controlled by the occupation administration were not excluded, as the new authorities decided that the former had not acted against the Polish reason of state or their professional ethics.[109] The presiding judge of the special court reported directly to the PKWN's head of justice department. The judges and prosecutors of the special criminal courts were put an equal footing with the judges and prosecutors of courts of appeals.

In addition to the crimes covered by the Decree of 31.08.1944, the jurisdiction of the special courts also covered cases involving the abandonment of Polish nationality (ethnicity) and citizenship, in line with the Decree of 4.11.1944 on Protective Measures with regard to Traitors to the Nation (*Dekret o środkach zabezpieczających w stosunku do zdrajców Narodu*).[110]

The procedure before the special courts – in accordance with the Decree on Special Criminal Courts for Cases of Fascist-Nazi Criminals[111] – was to follow the prewar Code of Criminal Procedure,[112] albeit with certain excep-

Article 1 of the Act provided: 'Pending the appointment of a permanent political representation of the nation according to the principles of the Constitution of 17.03.1921, national councils shall act as interim legislative and self-government bodies in territories of the Republic of Poland liberated from the occupation.' Hierarchically, the KRN was at the apex, then the voivodeship (province-level), *powiat* (county, district), municipal and communal national councils. See the Act of 11.09.1944 on the Powers of the President of the State National Council (Dz.U.1944.5.23). More Machnikowska (2008): 11ff.

109 Machnikowska (2008): 62.

110 Dz.U.1944.11.54.

111 Dz.U.1944.4.21.

112 Code of 19.30.1928 (*Rozporządzenie Prezydenta Rzeczypospolitej – Kodeks postępowania karnego*), Dz.U.1928.33.313.

tions. The indictment did not require a statement of reasons and had to be filed no later than 14 days of the apprehension of the suspect (Article 12); in the event of the suspect's absconding, the indictment and the trial could proceed *in absentia*, and the resulting judgement did not have the status of a default judgment.[113] An 'objection' (motion to dismiss) was not available against the indictment (Article 14(3)). The judgments of the special courts were final and unappealable – legally binding (Article 18). Only a convict sentenced to death could petition the President of the KRN for clemency (Article 19). The proceedings were single-instance, and only the conferral of certain powers on the Supreme National Tribunal (which will be discussed below) introduced an illusion of two instances.[114]

The aforementioned exemptions from the provisions of the Code of Criminal Procedure, especially the lack of guaranteed participation of defence counsel at trial or option to appeal the conviction, prove that the special courts did not meet the standards currently understood to belong to the canon of a fair trial. For that reason, and because of the very high rate of capital convictions (only Soviet courts were characterized by greater severity),[115] it is nowadays somewhat easy to discredit them and regard them as show trials, even though a good number of the defendants certainly merited a conviction.

The first and one of the most celebrated cases coming up before the special courts[116] was the case of the staff of KL Majdanek (Konzentrationslager der Waffen SS Lublin). It was tried from 27.11. to 2.12.1944 before the Special Criminal Court in Lublin.[117] The lawyers were conscious of its importance; the prosecutors said: 'we are at a turn of the development of international law, which is being created by the new democracies,'[118] and: 'the peoples cannot go back to the norm ere a forest of gallows sprouts up.'[119] In essence, the defendants were to brought to account for the deaths of 1.5 million people.

113 See also Article 10 of the Act of 27.04.1949 (*Ustawa o zmianie przepisów postępowania karnego*), Dz.U.1949.32.238.

114 Birt (2019): 73.

115 Biegański (2004): 175ff.

116 For greater publicity, the trial was filmed; see Kuisz (2020): 299. Henryk Świątkowski, the Minister of Justice at the time, sat in the first row.

117 *Majdanek. Rozprawa przed Specjalnym Sądem Karnym w Lublinie* (1945); see also Finder, Prusin (2018): 29ff.

118 *Majdanek. Rozprawa przed Specjalnym Sądem Karnym w Lublinie* (1945): 11.

119 *Ibidem*: 82.

Composing the panel were Bohdan Zembrzuski (presiding) and lay judges Genowefa Nadulska and Tadeusz Dymowski. The Special Court Prosecution Service were represented by Henryk Cieśluk and Jerzy Sawicki. Sitting in the defendants' dock were Hermann Vögel (camp guard, SS-Oberscharführer), Anton Thernes (deputy commandant of Section IV, SS-Obersturmführer), Wilhelm Gerstenmeier (administrative worker, SS-Hauptscharführer), Heinz Stalp (kapo), Theodor Schöllen (SS-Rottenführer) and Edmund Pohlmann (kapo). The defence counsel (Wojciech Jarosławski, Kazimierz Krzymowski, Tadeusz Krystoń and Aleksander Kunicki) asked to be excused, which was not granted by the court. The trial transcripts reveal, however, that the defence counsel complied with their duty, insisting, for example, that in each and every case individual culpability had to be established, whereas the witnesses called by the prosecution gave evidence only of specific cases of ill-treatment and not of responsibility for the operation of the camp as a whole. The counsel also noted that some of the defendants had been subjected to intense indoctrination, while others had been camp prisoners themselves. Eventually, in Pohlmann's case, the court was obliged to order a discontinuance on 30.11.1944 due to his suicide. All the other defendants were convicted and sentenced to death by hanging, which was carried out by a public execution on 3.12.1944, at 11.00 AM, at the site of KL Majdanek.

That was the first of the Majdanek trials and the first of all trials of this type. In deciding the guilt and punishment, the court relied solely on the provisions of the August Decree, but the prosecutors' speeches reflected numerous angles of international law interpreted in a similar way in later trials. During the trial, the prosecutors invoked treaty law (the Hague Conventions of 1907 and the Geneva Convention of 1929 on prisoners of war – ratified both by Poland and Germany), as well as customary law, including the: 'usages established between civilized nations, from the laws of humanity and the requirements of the public conscience.' Prosecutor Sawicki pointed out that as the German service people had violated international law, then in the light of the aforementioned conventions imposing on combatants the obligation to follow the customs of war, the defendants ought to be dealt with not as prisoners of war but as common criminals[120] (the

120 *Ibidem*: 14, where the prosecutor emphasized that the defendants were tormentors dressed in military uniforms, doing tasks having nothing to do with the conduct of war, and their actions stood in contrast with international law and international

significance of which was that prisoners of war should be judged before a military court, not a special court).

Invoking the Regulations concerning the laws and customs of war on Land, of 1907, annexed to the HC IV, it was argued that the punishment of the civilian population without conducting a trial and without establishing guilt, as well as treacherous killings of persons belonging to the enemy nation or armed forces, dispossession of Polish citizens of their property, and imposition of collective responsibility for the actions of individuals were all unlawful. The prosecutor argued that in accordance with the Reichsgericht's judgment of 16.07.1921 in the HMHS Llandovery Castle case, the German crimes at the time (in the form of the destruction of a hospital ship) were classified as common crimes, with the associated finding that following orders did not waive responsibility. Somewhat characteristically, the prosecutors were convinced that it was in the interest of justice to demonstrate that the crimes committed were in the nature of common crime (in that context, the prosecutor cited the St James Declaration). The court concurred with that position and ruled that the defendants were not prisoners of war and even should one have regarded them as such, the Hague Convention did not preclude their trial for common crimes. Of great import was the argument concerning the defendants' responsibility for the operation of the camp in Majdanek as a whole (corresponding to the modern notion of so-called second model of joint criminal enterprise).[121] Prosecutor Cieśluk proclaimed: 'I accuse and render them guilty by complicity of all crimes committed at Majdanek. They are guilty, for as members of the SS or merely as kapo they were the mainstay of the Nazi system.'[122] Prosecutor Sawicki used the term *współprzysięga* (roughly: oath-bound conspiracy) and insisted: 'who in that death mill was the millstone, who the turbine and who the propelling current? In that mill of death, every little screw had its purpose.'[123]

---

morality, so the provisions of the conventions on combatants should not be applied to them; he also stressed the necessity of observing the principle of clean hands, whereby the defendants were not in a position to invoke the conventions they themselves had violated (*Ibidem*: 15).

121 See Bassiouni (2013): 377; Sliedregt (2007): 186.

122 *Majdanek. Rozprawa przed Specjalnym Sądem Karnym w Lublinie* (1945): 75.

123 *Ibidem*: 27, see also 25 – 'co-participates in a crime not only he who murders but also he who stands at the door and lets not the victim out or the help in. Responsible for the crime is he also who previously makes an agreement to use the robbed property. He too is a partaker of the crime'; cf. 26 and 81.

4 Academic Life

The war and the resulting occupation made it impossible for universities to function in the territory of the Polish Republic in the old form. In German-occupied Poland, the universities were closed; in the part occupied by the Soviets, Polish lecturers were systematically removed. Both of the occupying powers engaged in the extermination and repression of the intelligentsia.[124] For example, Emil S. Rappaport, who remained in Warsaw, was arrested because it had been decided that as a judge he was passing judgements unfavourable to the Germans. He spent a year in a cell and was released thanks to the intercession of Edmund Mezger, whom he had known from the AIDP.[125] Mezger was good acquaintances with Hans Frank (together, they had published a book titled *Nationalsozialistisches Handbuch und der strafrechtliche Schutz von Staat, Partei und Volk*), who in years 1939–1945 served as the Generalgouverneur of the occupied Polish territory. Ludwik Ehrlich, in turn, was with his wife in Bergen (Norway) at the time WWII broke out. He managed to return to Lviv before the city's capitulation and assisted with the drafting of the terms. From October to December 1939, he lectured on the law of nations and political law and served as the vice dean of the Faculty of Law and head of the School of Diplomacy at the John Casimir University. In January 1940, he was dismissed from the university by the new Soviet authorities. He transferred to the Generalgouvernement (to Falejówka, where had a landed estate) and there co-operated with the Underground State. Warned of his impending arrest, in 1942, he escaped to the Zamojszczyzna, where he served in an important role in the Home Army, as attested by the fact that following his eventual arrest, a daring operation was carried out to break him out of Biłgoraj Prison. The two cases – Rappaport's and Ehrlich's (both met acting in different roles at the trial of Arthur Greiser before the Supreme National Tribunal) – distinctly demonstrate that the continuation of normal academic or professional (as legislators, judges or civil servants) activities in occupied Poland was not possible until 1945.

Scholars attempted to continue their research and converse about developments in science abroad, especially in the United Kingdom. Glaser's efforts towards the integration of the academic circles were of considerable consequence here. Within the British Association for the Advancement of Science, he was commissioned to lead the Committee on Post-War

124 More Walczak (1995): passim.

125 Siewierski (1965): 543.

University Education,[126] which discussed (similarly to the UN conferences of ministers of education taking place since 1943) how science was to develop after the war.

Glaser also initiated, in 1942, the establishment of the Association of University Professors and Lecturers of Allied Countries in Great Britain,[127] which facilitated the building of a common position in a given case in a broader circle and was intended to assist with the reconstruction of the academic world after the war and with the formation of closer ties with British academia. Glaser also presided over the Association of Polish Professors and Docents, which he had established already in France in 1940 for the purpose of propagation of Polish academic thought.

Internationalists played a key role in the creation of a Polish Faculty of Law at the University of Oxford,[128] the organization committee of which was selected during the so-called professors' meeting on 21.03.1944.[129] It was Glaser himself who headed the new faculty in 1944. He was replaced by Tadeusz Brzeski and subsequently Wiktor Sukiennicki. The lecturers included Wacław Komarnicki[130] – therewith, it can be surmised that Oxford became the refuge of the Vilnius school of international law.

Despite the highly difficult wartime conditions, valuable academic works came to life and without any doubt influenced the formation of international criminal law. First of all, one has to mention Rafał Lemkin's *Axis Rule in Occupied Europe: Laws of Occupation, Analysis of Government, Proposals for Redress*, published in 1944 in the USA. A strong response was also attracted by texts authored abroad by Manfred Lachs, i.e. *War crimes and political offences* (1944) and *The Unwritten Laws of Warfare* (1945). Those two publications on the topics of war crimes are among those often cited in foreign literature.[131]

It is also necessary to mention the Polish-language (and thus of more limited influence on the development of global scholarship) publication by Zenon Goryński (pseudonym adopted by three people working on the monograph on behalf of the Polish Lawyers Association),[132] titled *Zbrodnie*

126 It will be expedient to note that Glaser was also the dean of the Faculty of Law and Economics of the Polish University Abroad in Paris.

127 Glaser (1974): 93–95; see also *Association ...* (1942).

128 See Presidential decree of 14.04.1944, Dz.U.1944.5.11.

129 Mierzwa (2018): 83ff.

130 Góras (2019): 265–286, 283.

131 Appleman (1954/1971): 377; Herzog (1975): 140.

132 Uczkiewicz (2022): 246.

wojenne. Szkic prawny ('War crimes. A legal outline'). Published in 1944 in Jerusalem, the book reflected (and still does) an impressive level of scholarship.

5 Conclusions

From the beginning of WWII, the Polish authorities strove to make the matter of bringing crime suspects to justice a priority for the Allied states. To that end, they undertook comprehensive activities involving participation in all sorts of forums in which the matter of responsibility was discussed, including the most important one, the UNWCC; it was also of importance to recall the prewar provisions capable of facilitating the judgment of those accused of international crimes and the creation of new legal frameworks, both substantive and procedural. The trials conducted before the Polish underground courts in the initial years of WWII concerning primarily the cases of collaboration with the enemy, blackmail and denunciation, hence not the typical war crimes. That, however, changed with the creation of special courts by the communists. Here, it must be noted that the matter of bringing those guilty of international crimes to justice was a priority both to the government-in-exile and the government established by the communists in Lublin. Despite the lack of a consensus among the politicians in exile as to whether the international criminals should be judged solely on the basis of domestic law or also international law (which certain Polish representatives believed to be underdeveloped and unclear), when it became possible to place the suspects before a court, the Polish prosecutors abundantly relied on references to international law, as evidenced by the first Majdanek trial. In defiance of the unfavourable wartime conditions, the flagship works of Lemkin or Lachs became widely echoed in global scholarship.

CHAPTER 3

The Cold War (1945–1989)

1 The Nuremberg Trial

The ultimate negotiations concerning the principles to govern the judgment of the major criminals of the European Axis played out among the representatives of France, USA, United Kingdom and USSR.[1] The other states (including those having experienced long years of brutal occupation) were excluded from the process.[2] It cannot be ruled out, however, that the solutions adopted in the end had been influenced by prior discussions, especially considering that the Americans valued the opinion of the Polish jurists – for example, recommending Litawski to high positions within the UNWCC.[3]

The other occupied states could only accede to the eventual London Agreement by the Government of the United Kingdom of Great Britain and North Ireland, the Government of the United States of America, the Government of the French Republic and the Government of the Union of Soviet Socialist Republics for the Prosecution and Punishment of Major War Criminals of the Axis Powers.[4]

The aforementioned treaty established an International Military Tribunal (IMT) tasked with judging the major war criminals. The terms of the Tribunal's functioning were defined by the Charter of the IMT, annexed to the Agreement. Article 6 emphasized an important aspect from the Polish perspective: 'Nothing in this Agreement shall prejudice the jurisdiction or the powers of any national or occupation court established or to be established in any Allied territory or in Germany for the trial of war criminals.'

In accordance with the Charter, only the representatives of the four powers were to sit as judges (Article II) or serve as lead prosecutors (Article XIV) allowed, among other things, to speak in court. That meant the representatives of many states (including Poland) in the territories of which Germans had committed crimes – states having first called for the criminals to

1 Sellars (2014): 84ff.
2 Potyrała (2010): 71–72.
3 See also Lingen (2020): 512; Fleming (2022a): 9.
4 Dz.U.1947.63.367.

be brought to justice – were unable to appear independently before the Tribunal. From the perspective of decades, the lack of inclusiveness in such a solution is all the more appalling.

The issue of aggression against Poland fell within the purview of the American and British prosecutors, who were responsible for the drafting of the indictment for crimes against peace (war of aggression and war in violation of treaties, respectively). War crimes and crimes against humanity within the territory of the Polish Republic were assigned to the Soviet prosecutor, who naturally focused on crimes against the population of the USSR and was not necessarily interested in highlighting such German crimes (among them the destruction of Warsaw) as would draw the attention to the Soviet passivity (for when the part of Warsaw situated on the left bank of the Vistula bled to death, and the German criminals were systematically destroying the city along with its inhabitants, on the other side of the river stood a Soviet army that provided no assistance to the Warsaw Uprising).[5]

The question of justice for the crimes committed in Polish territory and against Polish nationals was complicated by the existence of two governments at the time – the government-in-exile and the Provisional Government of National Unity (*Rząd Jedności Narodowej* – RJN), the latter established by the communists. With the recognition of the RJN on 6.07.1945 by the United Kingdom, the Polish representative in UNWCC, Tadeusz Cyprian, lost his mandate, as he had been the representative of the exiles.[6] Only in October 1945 was a representative of the new government officially delegated to the UNWCC[7] – initially once more Cyprian, after him Mieczysław Szerer, with Cyprian as his deputy (in February 1947 Szerer was replaced by Marian Muszkat, who served until the closing of the office of the Polish delegation on 30.04.1948).[8] Neither of them, however, were in a position to add any new evidence that could be used by the prosecution in the Nuremberg Trials.[9] Thus, at the time when the UNWCC was occupied with drafting a preliminary bill of indictment (prepared in the main between July and September 1945, published on 6.101945 and filed on 14 October) and decided whom to charge, there was

5 On the gaps in charges presented in Nuremberg, see Cyprian, Sawicki (1967a): 164ff; Małcużyński (1989): 69ff; Grzebyk (2019a).

6 Cyprian (1977): 114.

7 Kubicki (1987): 29.

8 Rojowska (2013): 22.

9 Szerer (1977): 125.

no Polish representative in its ranks.[10] Hence, although Manfred Lachs compiled a report titled *German Crimes against Poland. Official Report of the Polish Government to be submitted to the International Military Tribunal* (London–Nurnberg, December 1945), his findings could affect the presentation of the cases in court only in an insignificant degree (though it is noteworthy that the report e.g. raised the issue of intentional systematic genocide).[11] The aforementioned report was admitted by the Tribunal into evidence. However, it did not extend e.g. to the matter of the Warsaw Uprising and could not account for all the witness testimonies and official documents gathered to date.[12] Nonetheless, the aforementioned document was invoked by the Soviet prosecutors in the context of the accusation of waging a war of aggression against Poland or the treatment of Polish prisoners of war, Germanization of Polish law, mass executions, appropriation of property, destruction of cultural property, deportations, and crimes against humanity (the example of Treblinka and Auschwitz).[13] Interesting, the British, American or French prosecutors never invoked the Polish document in court, and out of all six national reports, the IMT only cited the Czech one.[14]

Attempts to salvage that disadvantageous state of affairs were made by the Polish delegation in Nuremberg, composed of four representatives: Stefan Kurowski (head of the delegation), Jerzy Sawicki, Stanisław Piotrowski and Tadeusz Cyprian (apart from them, Rafał Lemkin was present with the American delegation and Hersch Lauterpacht with the British). Initially, the Polish delegates had to content with a hostile attitude towards their very presence at Nuremberg.[15] When they arrived on 19.11.1945, they were permitted to stay only for 10 days.[16] Later, mostly thanks to Soviet support,[17] their permit was formally extended by one month for the purpose of handing over the documents brought with them (including the reports submitted by the Jewish Historical Committee).[18] However, one could not possibly count on all of the documents being duly analysed by the prosecutors, if it all they

10 Cyprian, Sawicki (1962), part I: 21; Cyprian, Sawicki (1956a): 709; Cyprian (1977): 111; Kubicki (1963): 49.

11 See also Finder, Prusin (2018): 57.

12 Cyprian, Sawicki (1956b): 23–24.

13 Finder, Prusin (2018): 67ff.

14 *Ibidem*: 98.

15 Cyprian, Sawicki (1967a): 111; Małcużyński (1989): 79.

16 Cyprian, Sawicki (1962), part I: 21–22.

17 Finder, Prusin (2018): 54.

18 *Ibidem*: 184.

could be exhibited into evidence.[19] It is worth recalling that in the Heidelberg Documentation Centre alone the Americans gathered together 170 tonnes of documents concerning the functioning of the Third Reich, which they were unable to study despite the work of a delegation comprising several hundred members.[20]

The representatives of the four powers feared that granting official status to the Polish delegation would encourage other states to send theirs.[21] Accordingly, Polish efforts for the members of the delegation to be allowed to appear before the court as assistant counsel for the prosecution were futile, as the powers decided that only their own nationals could serve as official assistants. Neither did an attempt to appear in the capacity of *amicus curiae* bear any fruit, because the tribunal rejected the petition.[22] Polish delegates could only support the prosecutors from the four powers without an independent right to present evidence in the courtroom[23] and participate in the preliminary interrogations, such as Sawicki in the case of Josef Bühler, Heinz Guderian, Ernest Rode and especially Erich von dem Bach-Zelewski.[24] The Poles, however, soon proved their usefulness.[25] Especially, the analysis of Hans Frank's journals done by Piotrowski proved to be of utility. Those were among the crucial evidence in the case. Not without their own significance were the delegates' good private contacts with those involved in the trial, as well as proficient command of several languages.[26] It will be expedient to recall the words of Elwyn Jones, stating emphatically that the Polish delegation's contributions to the international experiment in Nuremberg was one of the most valuable.[27]

Ultimately, in Room 600 of the Nuremberg Palace of Justice, only a total of two Poles spoke: Seweryna Szmaglewska (recorded in the transcripts as 'Severina Shmaglevskaya') – a former prisoner of Auschwitz-Birkenau[28] – and Samuel Rajzman, deported from the Warsaw Ghetto to Treblinka Camp.[29] Both of the testimonies were universally perceived as stirring.

19 Małcużyński (1989): 72–73.
20 Cyprian (1977): 117; Aleksandrow (1974): 5.
21 Cyprian, Sawicki (1967a): 113.
22 Article 15(e) IMT Charter; Cyprian, Sawicki (1956b): 24–25.
23 Cyprian (1977): 120–121.
24 Sawicki (1968): 17ff.
25 Jones (1948): 112.
26 Cyprian (1977): 110.
27 Jones (1948): 112–113.
28 See also Szmaglewska (1976); Szmaglewska (1945).
29 Transcript available at: https://avalon.law.yale.edu/imt/02-27-46.asp.

Szmaglewska spoke of the fate of children at the camp in Auschwitz and Rajzman of the organization of the camp in Treblinka, citing examples of inhuman cruelty.

The Nuremberg trial (to the surprise of the Americans, who had expected swift proceedings taking no more than several weeks) took almost a year to complete (from the beginning on 20.11.1945 to the judgment and sentence of 1.10.1946). Poland attempted to influence the judgment by publicizing the trials taking place before the Supreme National Tribunal (NTN), which had been established on 22.01.1946[30] and which conducted the trials of high-profile Nazi officials, demonstrating the true scale of the crimes in Poland. Its first judgments were delivered even before the Nuremberg judgment – on 9.07.1946, Arthur Greiser received his death sentence, and on 5.09.1946 the same penalty was imposed on Amon Leopold Göth. It is in those judgments of the NTN that the foundations were expounded of responsibility for a war of aggression and for crimes against the Jewish population, described explicitly as genocide in language taken straight from Lemkin's publications. The opportunity was also seized to publicize the manner of organization of the Generalgouvernement and of the death camps. The trials were reported in several languages, and the information about the Tribunal's findings certainly must have reached those involved in the great Nuremberg trial and the subsequent Nuremberg trials conducted before American war tribunals (Telford Taylor, the lead prosecutor in the subsequent Nuremberg trials, was an observer at the trials of Höss and Fischer).[31]

The Nuremberg judgment itself devoted considerable space to the analysis of the aggression on Poland, the manner of organization of the Generalgouvernement, the treatment of the Polish forced labourers in Germany, the incorporation of Gdańsk and certain other territories into the Reich, as well as plans of liquidation of Polish intelligentsia, nobility and Jews (Action AB). The description of the fate awaiting Poland and Poles was extraordinarily brutal. The Tribunal recalled that in the Germans' opinions, the Poles were to become their slaves working on starvation food rations and subjected to executions and deportations under any pretext.[32] To

30 Dz.U.1946.5.45.

31 Prusin (2013): 121; Lubecka (2021): 92; Fleming (2022a): 240.

32 For example, citing Hans Frank's statement of 6.02.1940 – when asked for a comment on the posters hanged out on orders from Konstantin von Neurath considering the execution of Czech students, Frank retorted that if he were to order posters to be hanged out for the shooting of every seven Poles, there would not be enough forests in Poland to make the paper.

emphasize the criminality of the war waged by the Germans, the Polish-German declaration of non-violence of 26.01.1934 was invoked. It also important what did not find its way into the judgment but had been the subject matter of the Tribunal's deliberations – namely, the Katyń Massacre, the responsibility for which the USSR attempted to place on Germany.[33] The examination of the Katyń Massacre took two days (1–2.07.1946). The Soviet prosecutor, however, did not manage to persuade the court of the Germans' guilt and thus, even the dissenting opinion of Soviet judge Iona Nikitchenko said not a word about Katyń. It is also worth noting that Göring's defence counsel considered calling Władysław Anders (Polish general captured and tortured by Soviets, released in 1941 after the conclusion of Sikorski-Maisky Agreement based on which 40.000 strong army under General Anders' leadership) as a witness, among others, but such a co-operation never materialized. Anders's assistant, however, claimed that the general was ready to hand over the relevant documents to the Tribunal if formally summoned.[34] The abortive attempt to implicate Anders in the Nuremberg trial could be interpreted as evidence of the equivocality of the approach taken by the Polish émigré government to the aspirations to judge the Katyń Massacre. The Polish representatives were conscious of the realities of the policy followed by the great powers, who did not intend to hold fellow Allies responsible for their crimes, or at least not in the 40s of the 20th century. Henryk Świątkowski, the RJN justice minister, and Wacław Barcikowski, President of the Supreme Court, were in the audience when the Nuremberg judgment was read out.[35]

2 Co-operation after Nuremberg

The Nuremberg trial was to be one of several trials initially expected to proceed before the International Military Tribunal. However, the realities of the Cold War – mutual distrust and the Americans' reluctance to finance subsequent trials in the existing form – scrapped any prospects of continued co-

33 Hirsch (2019): 177. The initial intention was to accuse the Germans of the murder of 925 Polish officers, as that was the number of bodies exhumed by Nikolay Burdenko's commission; later, the Soviets compelled the revision of the indictment to attribute to the Germans the killings of 11 thousand Poles – *ibidem*, 182 and 184; see also Schabas (2015): 249ff; Basak (1993) and (2009); Heydecker, Leeb (2006): 341ff; Kulesza (2006).

34 Schabas (2015): 271.

35 Cyprian, Sawicki (1962a), part I: 20.

operation among the great powers.[36] Of crucial importance were, therefore, the trials held before domestic courts; the ability of those to proceed, however, necessitated co-operation with respect to extraditing the criminals and securing the evidence.

In February 1945, the State National Council (KRN) passed a resolution establishing the Commission for the Investigation of German Crimes in Poland attached to the Praesidium of the KRN, based on the foundations created by members of the commission investigating the crimes at Auschwitz-Birkenau. A proper legal basis for the Commission's functioning, however, only came with the KRN Decree of 10.11.1945, establishing not only a Chief Commission but also Regional Commissions.[37]

When the first Praesidium of the Chief Commission formed in May 1945, it was led by Deputy Prime Minister Stanisław Janusz, with Minister of Foreign Affairs Wincenty Rzymowski and Minister of Justice Henryk Świątowski as his deputies. In turn, pursuant to the November Decree, the Chief Commission was to be chaired at each time by the Minister of Justice. The involvement of such high-profile dignitaries in the Praesidium bore testimony to the serious and priority treatment accorded to the Commission's works. The Commission's first Director-in-Chief became Alfred Fiderkiewicz, replaced near the end of 1945 by Janusz Gumkowski, who would serve until 1965.

The Chief Commission's tasks were as follows (Article 3):

> examine and gather evidence concerning the German crimes committed in 1939–1945 in Poland or outside of her borders with regard to Polish citizens or people of Polish ethnicity and with regard to foreigners staying in Poland at the time; chairing and reconciling the works of the Regional Commissions and all institutions of related scope of operations, as well as collaboration with the Institute of National Remembrance attached to the Praesidium of the Council of Ministers; publishing the materials and results of the investigations into the German crimes and publicizing the same in-country and abroad, as well as sharing materials with similar foreign institutions.

---

36 *Final Report to the Secretary of the Army on the Nuernberg War Crimes Trials Under Control Council Law No. 10 by Telford Taylor, Brigadier General, U.S.A. Chief of Counsel for War Crimes*, Washington, D.C., 15.08.1949: 272.

37 Dz.U.1945.51.293. See Pilichowski (1980c): 28ff. It will be expedient to note that earlier on, in August 1944, a Polish-Soviet extraordinary commission was created to investigate the German crimes committed at Majdanek – Pilichowski (1980c): 23.

The Commissions and their delegated bodies had the: 'right to conduct investigations and examine witnesses' (Article 4). To that end, they were to apply the: 'relevant provisions of the Code of Criminal Procedure,' and while exercising such activities, they held the powers belonging to judicial authorities; as emphasized by Article 4 of the Decree: 'The activities undertaken by the members of the Chief Commission and of the Regional Commission holding judicial or prosecutorial qualifications shall have the force of judicial procedures and the transcripts shall have the force of judicial transcripts.'

As soon as July 1945 the decision was made for the Commission to be an organ of the Ministry of Justice and for the materials to be gathered by judges and prosecutors. The necessity of co-operation and properly securing the sites of the former prisoner-of-war camps was self-evident. Accordingly, the first conference of delegates in Warsaw discussed the need for the appointment of an International Commission for the Investigation of German Crimes to provide suitable protection for the camp site in Majdanek or that in Auschwitz Birkenau.

It will be expedient to recall that it was the Chief Commission who prepared the materials concerning the activities of the former Generalgouverneur Hans Frank and forwarded them to the International Military Tribunal for the Nuremberg trial.[38] For the latter, the Commission also compiled the data on the loss of life among the teachers (of schools of all tiers) and the wartime fates of the professors of institutions of higher learning.[39] Moreover, it prepared the evidence for the trials of Friedrich Flick, Oswald Pohl, IG Farben leadership, and Alfred Krupp (before the American tribunals as part of the subsequent Nuremberg trials).[40] It also published bulletins in foreign languages, the first of which (*German Crimes in Poland*, Warszawa 1946–1947) was distributed during the Nuremberg trial.[41] In the bulletin, Jan Sehn[42] published the outcome of his investigation of the crimes committed

38 Jasiński (2018): 132.

39 Pilichowski (1975): 9.

40 Jasiński (2018): 134.

41 Pilichowski (1980c): 25. Bulletin was also published in French: La Commission Générale d'Enquête sur les Crime Allemands en Pologne, "Les crimes allemands en Pologne", Varsovie 1948, vol. I–II.

42 Gańczak (2020). Sehn conducted documentation works in Germany; among his other occupations, he campaigned – unfortunately, without success – for the extradition of Hans Ehlich, an employee of the Reichssicherheitshauptamt (RSHA, Reich Security Main Office), and Hermann Krumey, regarded as a close collaborator of Adolf Eichmann.

at the camp in Auschwitz-Birkenau.[43] It is also there where we can find the two paramount sources documenting the Holocaust of the Jews in Poland, viz. Jürgen Stroop's report on the liquidation of the Warsaw Ghetto (*Es gibt keinen jüdischen Wohnbezirk in Warschau mehr!*)[44] and excerpts from Friedrich (Fritz) Katzmann's report on the extermination of the Jews in Galicia (as part of Action Einsatz Reinhardt),[45] as well as the outstanding criminological analysis by Stanisław Batawia[46] based on his numerous conversations with Rudolf Höss,[47] the Camp Commandant of Auschwitz-Birkenau.

During the first years after the war, the activities of the Chief Commission concentrated on matters of the extradition of the criminals and legal assistance for courts and prosecutors in cases against the extradited suspects.[48] For example, in 1949, the Commission investigated Ernst Boepple,[49] Wilhelm Burger[50] and Gerhard Maurer;[51] their extradition was requested, among others, by the investigative judge of the Regional Court in Cracow, Jan Sehn. All of the criminals were extradited to Poland and there convicted of their crimes. The Commission also investigated the extermination of Soviet prisoners of war in German camps in Poland.

In 1945, on the initiative of the Chief Commission, the Provisional Government of National Unity dispatched a Polish Military Mission (with more

43 Persuasive of the value represented by those inquiries are their numerous citations in foreign literature, see Pelt (2016): 216ff; Nagorski (2017): 63ff.

44 Biuletyn GKBZHwP (1960), no. 11: 113–199.

45 Biuletyn GKBZHwP (1951), no. 6: 171–187.

46 Biuletyn GKBZHwP (1951), no. 7.

47 Primomo (2020): 188–189.

48 Pilichowski (1975): 14.

49 Among his other functions, Ernst Boepple was deputy to Josef Bühler, convicted by the NTN. He was one of those responsible for the implementation of the Holocaust. Boepple was extradited to Poland in October 1947 by the authorities of the American occupation zone. He received a death sentence on 14 December 1949, and the execution was carried out one year later.

50 Wilhelm Burger – an SS-Sturmbannführer and camp-administration official. Member of the NSDAP and of the SS, from 1936 in the administration of Dachau and Oranienburg camps, later in charge of the administration of Auschwitz-Birkenau. After the war, he was convicted, among others, by the Voivodeship Court in Cracow.

51 Gerhard Maurer – employee of the SS administration as Head of the *Amstgruppe D II*. He dealt with matters relating to the forced labour of the camp inmates. After Arthur Liebehenschel's appointment as Camp Commandant of Auschwitz-Birkenau, Maurer became the deputy of Richard Glücks, to whom the authorities of German concentration camps reported. In 1947, he was handed over to the Polish authorities, sentenced to death by the Voivodeship Court in Cracow in 1951, and executed two years later.

than 100 members in 1946), led by Colonel Jakub Prawin, to the Allied Control Council.[52]

In theory, the Polish Military Mission was to perform a co-ordinating and supervisory role with regard to the other missions, including the War Crime Investigation Mission attached to the British Army at the Rhine, established by command of the Minister of National Defence no. 29, of 23.01.1946, in the British occupation zone.[53] That mission was led by Lieutenant Colonel Henryk Zapolski-Downar. Its consultant was Lieutenant Colonel Marian Muszkat. As per the command, the mission was supervised by the Chief Commission. It was to be responsible for extraditions from the occupation zones in Germany. As noted by Czesław Pilichowski, the mission's operations were to cover all criminals of whose guilt sufficient evidence had been gathered. Among its other successes, the Military Mission's department in charge of collection of documents managed to secure the documentation of the destruction of Warsaw Ghetto, Jürgen Stroop's report and notes from Adolf Hitler's conversations with Wilhelm Keitel; in a word, passing through the Mission's hands were documents of enormous probative value.[54] The decision was made that the extradition requests would be submitted only by the leadership according to a set procedure – the goal was to avoid duplication.

Also in 1946 (the invitation from the Americans arrived on 15.01.1946), a Mission 'for the investigation of war crimes in the European continent' was established (by command of the Minister of National Defence no. 57 of 15.11.1946), operating in the American occupation zone, albeit reporting to the Commander-in-Chief rather than the Ministry of Justice and the Chief Commission.[55] Corresponding missions could not be established in the French and Soviet zones,[56] although in May 1947, a subunit of the mission operating in the American zone was created in the French zone.[57] The aforementioned missions in the American and British zones (with field units subordinated to them) were referred to under the joint name of Polish Military Mission for the Investigation of War Crimes in Europe, whose works formally ended at the beginning of 1951.

---

52 Radomski (2013): 423. Kobierska-Motas (1991): 90ff; Lubecka (2011): 27.

53 Gondek (1981): 27.

54 Pilichowski (1975): 13.

55 IPN GK 162/286, k. 189–190.

56 Materski in: Materski, Michowicz (2010): 205.

57 Rojowska (2013): 25.

Although the Chief Commission co-operated with its Soviet counterparts (the Extraordinary State Commission for the Establishment and Investigation of the Atrocities of the German Fascist Invaders and Their Accomplices and the Damage They Caused to Citizens, Collective Farms, Public Organizations, State Enterprises and Institutions of the USSR, as well as the USSR prosecution service and archives)[58] without major hurdles, there could be no question of extensive international co-operation with the Western states.

In years 1948–1949, the Polish authorities systematically abolished the Regional Commissions. The longest-operating one was the Regional Commission in Cracow (until 1953). In December 1949, the Chief Commission was renamed to the Chief Commission for the Investigation of Nazi Crimes in Poland (GKBZHwP) in connection with the division of Germany into West and East Germany and reluctance to stigmatize the new partner in the Soviet Bloc – the GDR. In 1984, the Chief Commission was transformed into the Chief Commission for the Investigation of Nazi Crimes in Poland – Institute of National Remembrance.[59]

According to the Moscow Declaration of 30.10–1.11.1943, the criminals were to be handed over to the states in which they had committed their crimes. The great powers' Berlin Declaration, of 5.06.1945, emphasizing that all of the named Nazi criminals would be apprehended and handed over to the Allied states, was kept in a like tone.[60] The tone of the Potsdam Declaration of 21.07.1945 was also similar. In accordance with all the aforementioned declarations, the criminals were to be handed over to the states in which they had committed their crimes and would be judged by the courts there. The London Agreement of 8.08.1945 and the Law no. 10 of the Allied Control Council (Article IV) of 20.12.1945 also followed the same spirit.[61] The last-mentioned instrument introduced a uniform extradition system throughout Germany.[62] Its Article 4 specified that persons having committed crimes listed in Article 2 (i.e. crimes against peace, war crimes and

58 Baskow (1987): 131.

59 Dz.U.1984.21.98.

60 *Declaration regarding the defeat of Germany and the assumption of supreme authority with respect to Germany by the Governments of the United States of America, the Union of Soviet Socialist Republics, the United Kingdom and the Provisional Government of the French Republic*, 5.06.1945, https://avalon.law.yale.edu/wwii/ger01.asp, także Szpak (1979): 12.

61 Text available at https://avalon.law.yale.edu/imt/imt10.asp.

62 Control Council Law No. 10, Punishment of Persons Guilty of War Crimes, Crimes Against Peace and Against Humanity, https://www.legal-tools.org/doc/ffda62/pdf/.

crimes against humanity) might be arrested and delivered to the zone or state where the crimes had been committed.

In theory, the extradition procedure as a whole was clear and not supposed to take up much time. The appropriate documents concerning the defendant's guilt were submitted to the UNWCC, which – if the crime was sufficiently established as probable and the acts charged unquestionably fell within the category of war crimes – put the relevant individual on the list of criminals (it will be expedient to note that Poland was highly active in nominating criminals for inclusion on the list and did not hesitate to name the highest representatives of Germany, including Hitler himself, as proposed by Cyprian,[63] which demonstrated that, in Poland's view, the immunity enjoyed by an incumbent head of state offered no protection from responsibility for international crimes). Thereafter, the request went to the Central Registry of War Criminals and Security Suspects (CROWCASS) in Paris, and, if the location of the accused could be determined, the request for extradition was forwarded to the competent occupation authority.[64]

Unfortunately, the collaboration between Poland on the one side and the UNWCC and the occupying powers after the war on the other side was rendered difficult and collapsed entirely in 1947,[65] despite issues being raised within the UNWCC by Polish and Yugoslavian representatives.[66]

The takeover of the responsibility for co-operation on the extraditions by the new communist authorities of Poland was not without its own problems. For example, on 26.11.1945, Kent wrote to Litawski as the former representative in the UNWCC that for weeks the Commission had not been in receipt of any information coming from the Polish office, no answers to inquiries as to whether Poland was interested in judging the arrested individuals. Kent emphasized that the last letter on record was one of 7.09.1945, undersigned, 'K. Epler.'[67] From January onward, on the other hand, a number of notices were sent concerning the trials proceeding against the criminals in France and Yugoslavia. On 3.12.1945, Litawski replied that the office had been in liquidation since the end of September 1945 and that all cases had been handed over to Szerer, the new representative of the Polish

63 Kochavi (1998): 108.

64 Cyprian, Sawicki (1956a): 751.

65 Cyprian (1971): 337; Pilichowski (1980b): 28, points towards 1949 as the end of the cooperation, which is when extraditions were suspended altogether; until November 1947, requests could still be filed. He states that in 1946–1947, a total of 1683 criminals were extradited out of West Germany, and after 1947, only 93.

66 UNWCC (1948): 149.

67 Doc. XX/PHBK (Wiener Library).

government in the UNWCC. He also suggested contacting Lachs, who was the head of the delegation at the time, and whom Litawski had informed of Kent's request. On 22.12.1945, Kent wrote back that he had been able to get in touch with Szerer. That does not mean the co-operation was smooth. For it was clear that the matter of war crimes was being used for political purposes; hence, in his letter to Lachs dated 20.12.1945, H.H. Wade (Chief Research Officer) of the UNWCC emphasized that the Commission's resources could be used but sensitive information ought not to be publicized before the trial.[68]

In the coming months, the mutual trust among the former Allies dwindled. Formally, Poland continued to function in the established structures and requested the extradition of more individuals (e.g. on 4.11.1946, Szerer requested the extradition of Richard Wedemeyer, Marta Puretz, Stefanie Brandstätter, and, on 28.11.1946, von dem Bach-Zelewski – in that matter, he wrote to Colonel George Ledingham), but despite the Americans' response that Wedemeyer and von dem Bach-Zelewski indeed should be put on trial, the extradition did not materialize. Sometimes, the reasons given by the Americans were absurd; for example, in their letter to the Polish authorities concerning the refusal to extradite Joseph Muehlmann, Wilhelm Fischer, Mikołaj (Nikol) Terlecki and Roman Worobkiewicz, the American forces in Austria asserted that the appropriation of works of art was not a war crime.[69] Moreover, in the same latter, the Americans stressed that the Polish demands were based on testimony from, 'resettled Jews,' who, in the opinion of the USA, lacked reliability and impartiality.

Starting from 1946, Polish authorities sent complaints to the UNWCC and to the authorities of the individual occupation zones, insisting that failure to extradite criminals constituted the violation of a basic international obligation.[70] It was noted that individuals from Dachau, Ludwigsburg and Zuffenhausen were being released on a mass scale and that the UNWCC should take a position as to their possible arrest.[71] Such arguments, however, could not persuade the American commanders. The head of the American office responsible for war affairs in Germany did not trust the entries on the list of war criminals made by the UNWCC and, as he expounded in a letter of

68 Letter available in Wiener Library.

69 Letter AG.000.5/ACA/L of 17.07.1947 (Wiener Library).

70 Doc. A6L., ref. 3187/47, 16.12.1947 (Wiener Library); doc. No. 3091/47, 18.11.1947 (Wiener Library). See Robert Criaigie comments on the improvements in British occupation zone, doc. A.60, 24.11.1947 (Wiener Library).

71 Letter of Szerer to Wright of 8.07.1946. See also Kobierska-Motas (1991): 99.

29.05.1947, he demanded evidence of guilt.[72] The regulations introduced in the American zone on 17.11.1947 stipulated that extradition requests were to be granted only on an exceptional basis, and a proper request had to be very detailed, specifying e.g. the defendant's eye colour and weight. Everything was to be decided by the legal department of the US military administration,[73] and thus the position of the UNWCC entirely lost prominence. The Brits also refused to extradite Erich von Manstein and Albert Kesselring.[74] Von Manstein was judged in England and Germany, but the evidence supplied by Poland was not relied on, and he was ultimately acquitted of the 'Polish' charges.[75]

The Polish authorities wrote reports on the progress made in bringing the criminals to judgment.[76] For example, in a letter from Muszkat (the Polish representative at the UNWCC at the time) to Wright, Muszkat stated that there is a need to confront the dilemma of revenge and prevention of impunity, but also re-education, prevention and general prevention (so as to instil the fear in other potential criminals of being held responsible). The failure to judge the crimes could become the source of new wars and new crimes – thus, efforts to judge the crimes were an element of the struggle for peace. He emphasized that the Poles had been made to suffer some of the greatest sacrifices by the Nazis, with nearly a fourth of the nation dying and a half of the property being stolen or destroyed (the data are, of course, exaggerated, but such were the data cited by Muszkat in his letter). Realizing the problem of the impossibility of a precise assessment of the losses or of identifying the perpetrators by name, Muszkat preferred to focus on the responsibility of camp staff and groups (Gestapo), noting the Polish efforts to bring the criminals to judgement before the NTN (one of the trials dealt with the responsibility of Auschwitz camp staff) and openness to foreign observers. He mentioned legislative amendments (Muszkat referred to Journal of Laws (*Dziennik Ustaw*) of 15.12.1946, publishing, among others, the consolidated text of the Decree of 31.08.1944). In his letter of 6.12.1947 to Robert Craigie (no. 3176/47), Muszkat emphasized that until 1.10.1947, it had not been possible to verify all of the persons intended to be released.

72 Cyprian, Sawicki (1956a): 752 and (1956b): 138.

73 Cyprian, Sawicki (1956a): 753.

74 Cyprian, Sawicki (1956a): 755. See Text of Polish Governments Note regarding the German War Criminals Rundstedt, Manstein and Strauss, Droit au Service de la Paix 1949, no 1.

75 Cyprian, Sawicki (1956b): 148ff; Cyprian (1971) 361ff.

76 See e.g. report of 11.03.1947.

Replying on 29.01.1948 to Muszkat's letter of 6.12.1947, Wright offered assurances that he recognized the existence of a problem with the extradition of criminals from the British zone and that he had contacted the authorities of the United Kingdom on the matter. Simultaneously, he noted the absence of requests from Poland for the extradition of individuals from A List (individuals from B List had committed their crimes in Germany, which was where they should be judged). He also emphasized that, for example, the Polish authorities had not been interested in judging Fritz Branch, and in three other cases, the Poles themselves had ceased to pursue the matter, which showed that the author of the letter was not aware of all the circumstances. Wright pointed out that of all 13 surnames on the Polish list, as many as 8 were written with errors or with the wrong given names, impeding an effective co-operation; in the case those allegedly responsible for crimes against humanity – viz. Hermann Eyer, Gerhard Hoppe and Fritz Weiss – the Commission did not have evidence of their guilt, for which reason the extradition was not warranted. Moreover, the Commission did not have sufficient staff to search for the criminals wanted by Poland.[77] There were also cases in which the Polish authorities returned individuals extradited by mistake.

There existed an irreconcilable difference of opinion between the Polish authorities and the UNWCC. Whereas Poland's position was that all staff of camps such as Auschwitz-Birkenau or Stutthof ought to be judged,[78] the UNWCC's Committee I precluded the possibility of prosecuting the entire staff of a camp. According to the latter, only in the case of smaller units, such as the Institute of Anatomy in a given camp, it was possible for the entirety of a small staff to be entered on the list of criminals. It was emphasized that the quality of the documentation forwarded to the UNWCC was increasingly poor, as complained by Litawski (who worked there as legal counsel).[79] It was also clear that the communist authorities had more interest in the prosecution of the alleged collaborationists than Nazi criminals (especially after 17.11.1946, which is when the special courts were shut down).

77 Doc. 3176–47 (Wiener Library).

78 UNWCC, Minutes of the Meeting of Committee I, doc. 84, 4.12.1946; and doc. 78, 16.10.1946; Finder, Prusin (2018): 24 cited data according to which Poland, by 1947, had requested the extradition of e.g. 437 persons from the Auschwitz camp administration and 249 staff from KL Majdanek. Out of a total of 7405 names submitted by Poland to the UNWCC, the number of successful extraditions was only 1.8 thousand.

79 Letter of Litawski to Muszkat of 20.06.1947.

Technical difficulties with the transport of the defendants were not without consequence, either. The initial assumption was that a 'mass extradition' would take place.[80] Thus, the necessity of ensuring organization and transport vehicles, as well as appointing special teams to pick up the defendants was reckoned with. However, somewhat soon, the German prisoners began to be released on a mass scale in the American zone,[81] and the end of November 1946 marked the end of the Poles' efforts to organize their own transport.[82] American trains from Dachau to the Polish-Czech border were relied on at the time. The American and British authorities, who had been very accommodating in the period up to 1947, however, refused to provide technical assistance with the extraditions of war criminals as soon as 1948,[83] even though the Polish authorities had since 1947 only requested the extradition of major criminals and refrained from requesting those whom other states would put on trial.[84]

Pilichowski, Szpak and Birt[85] provide the same information that within the span of two years (1944–1946), Poland submitted 8413 extradition requests, out of which 7405 were recorded in the UNWCC's register. During the period from April 1946 to December 1950, a total of 1803 war-crime suspects were extradited to Poland. Of those, 1325 were from the American zone, 392 from the British, 51 from the Soviet and 35 from the French. Different data are provided by Kobierska-Motas, whose studies include a register of extradited individuals (including information such as date of birth, where the extradition was from and on the basis of what crimes, who judged the individual and what sentence was given),[86] resulting in more punctilious data. According to her, 1817 individuals were extradited.

Despite the aforementioned problems with the extraditions, one must emphasize the enormous effort made by the Polish justice system to judge the German criminals, considering the tens of thousands of cases and thousands of judgments, according to the statistics below (see subchapters 2.3 and 3.5). The last trials held in connection with German crimes were those of Paul Otto Geibel (extradited to Poland in 1947, tried since 1954 before the

80 Kobierska-Motas (1991): 96–97.

81 *Ibidem*: 99.

82 *Ibidem*: 101.

83 *Ibidem*: 101–111.

84 *Ibidem*: 101–102.

85 Pilichowski (1971b); Szpak (1979): 25; Birt (2019): 75.

86 Kobierska-Motas (1992): 28–252. For example, the register opens with Josef Abbot, sentenced by the Court of Appeals in Gdańsk to 7 years' imprisonment, and closes with Józef Żółty, sentenced by the Regional Court in Cracow to death.

Regional Court in Warsaw, convicted and sentenced on 31.05.1954; upheld by the Court of Appeals on 22.09.1954) and Erich Koch, the latter from 20.10.1958 to the judgment of the voivodeship court on 9.03.1959.[87]

Notably, although Poland promulgated an amnesty on 27.04.1956,[88] the latter did not extend to those guilty of crimes under Article 1a (killings of civilians and prisoners of war) of the August Decree, so it did not cover the entirety of the sentences imposed on Geibel and Koch.[89]

In numerous trials pending before foreign courts, Poles appeared as witnesses and victims of crimes, judges (e.g. in the trial of Otto Thielke) but also perpetrators (e.g. the trial of Kazimierz Cegielski, a kapo at the Bergen-Belsen camp in Germany, convicted on 18.06.1947 in Lüneberg of war crimes committed at the camp and sentenced to death).

Although the official co-operation died down after 1947, Polish authorities did not deny assistance when Nazi criminals were being put on trial e.g. in France, Belgium or West Germany.[90] Particularly noteworthy in this context is the example of Sehn, who assisted with the organization of the visits of Western German prosecutors in Poland and had previously made sure the site of the Auschwitz-Birkenau camp had been suitably secured, as there was a chance that the evidence could be destroyed or stolen.[91] Sehn's co-operation with the Germans immediately after the war can only be seen as a unique development, as the relations between Poland and West Germany (the Federal Republic of Germany) were always somewhat cautious. Only in the mid-60s of the 20th century can one speak of somewhat intensified co-operation. Polish authorities provided legal assistance in the form of e.g. loans of documents concerning the crimes committed, the circumstances of their commission, witness interrogations of Polish citizens, as well as service of process.[92] On-site visits by juries from the courts of the Federal Republic

87 More Majewski (2008).

88 Dz.U.1956.4.11.

89 Murzynowski, Rezler (1972): 77; Finder, Prusin (2018): 226. Geibel initially was to be released on the basis of the aforementioned amnesty, but the Supreme Court on 19 December 1959 quashed the amnesty decision of the court in Opole (where Geibel was serving his term). Eventually, Geibel committed suicide on 12.10.1966.

90 Szulc (1980): 846; Pilichowski (1980c): 31, 33, 45ff. Poland offered assistance in 1959, but the Federal Republic of Germany began to use it only in 1964. Poland forwarded the documentation to Ludwigsburg (Zentrale Stelle der Landesjustizverwaltungen zur Aufklärung Nationalsozialistischer Verbrechen), Polish witnesses went to trials, on-site visits were conducted, etc. See more Bielawski (1980): 854ff

91 More Gańczak (2020).

92 Szulc (1980): 846ff.

of Germany were also organized.[93] Employees of the Chief Commission for the Investigation of Nazi Crimes in Poland went for consultations to the Federal Republic of Germany, Austria and West Berlin to examine various evidence gathered and shared by prosecutors and courts.

Despite this co-operation – well-received, in principle – extraditions of criminals wanted by Poland continued to be denied in the decades to come (e.g. of Franz Stangl, the commandant of the camps in Treblinka and Sobibór; Hermine Braunsteiner-Ryan, a supervisor at the camp in Majdanek; or Heinz Reinefarth, responsible for the Wola Massacre – killing of around 40–60.000 civilians), as a result of the lack of confidence in the communist justice system. Unfortunately, Polish court proceedings were regarded on par with the celebrated Soviet show trials, such as the one of the Japanese war criminals judged in Khabarovsk.[94]

3 Treaty Obligations

On 25.09.1945, Poland acceded to the Agreement for the Prosecution and Punishment of the Major War Criminals of the European Axis.[95] Ratification followed in June 1947 and promulgation in the Polish Journal of Laws in October 1947.[96] As, however, emphasized by Jerzy Sawicki, by sending a Polish delegation to Nuremberg, indirectly participating in the trial and providing materials, we had recognized the force the Agreement *per facta concludentia* already since September 1945 rather than 25.06.1947, i.e. the date of ratification (entry into force with regard to Poland).[97]

When the Nuremberg judgment came down, Poland supported the adoption of the Nuremberg principles by the UNGA, which took place by Resolution no. 95 (I) of 11.12.1946. Together with the USSR, Poland was unsupportive of joining the problem of the Nuremberg principles to the discussion on the Code of Offences./Crimes Against the Peace and Security of Mankind[98] or the concept of an International Criminal Court due to concerns of creating a platform to attack the USSR and its allies.[99]

93 Bielawski (1980): 854ff.

94 Bílková (2014): 719; Pławski (1950).

95 Dz.U.1947.63.367.

96 Dz.U.1947.63.367 and 368.

97 Sawicki (1948): 55; Pasek (2002): 100.

98 A/C.6SR 160, 14.10.1949: 6; see also Cyprian, Sawicki (1956a): 726; (1956b): 72–73; (1967): 221–222.

99 Cyprian, Sawicki (1956a): 724, 731.

Later, Polish delegates persistently demanded the universal recognition of the Nuremberg principles.[100] Poland also supported the adoption of the UNGA resolutions concerning the extradition and punishment of war criminals, i.e. 3(I) of 13.02.1946 and 170 (II) of 31.10.1947, and it was on Poland's initiative that in the Declaration on Territorial Asylum, adopted by the UNGA on 14.12.1967, emphasis was placed on not granting asylum to war criminals.[101]

The Polish representatives did not succeed at persuading the other states to adopt an international extradition convention, the draft of which had been prepared during WWII, but the problem of the extradition of criminals continued to surface in the debates in UNGA thanks to Polish efforts among others.

It must be noted that, apart from the conventions mentioned above, the majority of the works contributing to the development of international criminal law in the 1947–1989 period took place in the International Law Commission (ILC). Unfortunately, during the time of debates on e.g. the merits of the creation of a permanent international criminal court, the Nuremberg principles, the definition of aggression or the *Draft Code of Offences against the Peace and Security of Mankind*, the Commission lacked a representative from Poland. When Manfred Lachs and Stanisław Pawlak sat in the Commission (1962–1966 and 1987–1991 respectively), those were not periods of working on problems from the area of international criminal law, outside of the matter of the statute of limitations, discussed since 1965 in other bodies of the UN. Indeed, the works were pending on the definition of aggression, but those ground down to a halt at the beginning of the 60s of the 20th century, and as far as the International Criminal Court is considered, the talks only really began after 1989.

Thus, when problems relating to the development of international criminal law were discussed in the ILC, Poland only had the opportunity to comment on specific drafts as part of general consultations among the states or make statements on them in the Sixth Committee, which notably Lachs was on several occasions elected to preside over (1949, 1951 and 1955).[102] The Polish representatives, for example, emphasized the necessity of prevention, which translated into the punishability not only of the commission but also preparation of the conditions for the commission of such type of crimes. They insisted on punishment for incitement to war even without any other

100 Cyprian, Sawicki (1956b): 66.
101 Resich (1980): 804.
102 Abraszewski (1975): 133.

accompanying violation; they also emphasized the necessity of criminalization of any forms of hatred on national, racial or religious grounds; they argued for the need to punish the preparation of any sort of plans of an aggressive war, plans of use of weapons of mass destruction or incitement of chauvinist tendencies aimed at the disruption of peaceful and friendly relations among the nations.[103] Commenting on those proposals, the American member of the ILC, Manley O. Hudson, emphasized that in Poland's opinion, it was crucial to punish not only the incitement or commission but also the propagation of nationalist, racial or religious hatred and prohibit weapons of mass destruction, which was consistent with the proposals of another member of the ILC – Shushi Hsu from China.[104] The example of Poland also surfaced in the arguments offered by the Soviet representative, Vladimir Koretsky, who, noting the criminalization of international crimes by the Polish Criminal Code, emphasized the doubts as to the necessity of the creation of an international criminal code.[105] At the same time, until the end of the Cold War, Poland consistently opposed the creation of an international criminal court, asserting that such a solution violated Polish sovereignty.[106] It is, however, noteworthy that some Polish academics residing abroad, e.g. Glaser, supported the works on an international criminal court,[107] whereas others, such as Lemkin, regarded any such solution as premature.[108]

A treaty shaping the framework of international criminal law influenced in a great degree by Poland and individual Poles is the Genocide Convention. In this context, one has above all to mention the role of Rafał Lemkin,[109] who, as an émigré Polish scholar working for the American government, spearheaded the debate around the necessity of codification of a new crime – genocide – with the publication of his own voluminous work titled *Axis Rule in Occupied Europe: Laws of Occupation, Analysis of Government, Proposals for Redress*, of 1944, as well as other publications,[110] noted also in the Polish literature of the time.[111] When he failed to persuade the American delegation to introduce a definition of the crime of genocide to

103 YILC (1950), vol. II, 250ff.
104 YILC (1950), vol. I, 162, §82.
105 YILC (1949), vol. I, 218, §48.
106 Cyprian, Sawicki (1956b): 110ff; Muszkat (1954): 338.
107 Glaser (1952).
108 Abtahi, Webb (2008): 246.
109 Lewis (2014): 195ff.
110 E.g. Lemkin (1947).
111 Cyprian, Sawicki (1956a): 765; see also (1956b): 164ff.

the London Agreement of 1945, he focused on the promotion of his idea in the newly formed UN. Paradoxically, however, the resolution on genocide was tabled by Cuba, Panama and India and not by Poland or the USA.

A subcommittee was appointed to draft the resolution, comprising the representatives of Saudi Arabia, Chile, France, India, Cuba, Panama, Poland, the USA, United Kingdom and USSR. The subcommittee deliberated on 2–5.12.1946. Within it, Poland proposed to regard the propagation and dissemination of hate against ethnic, racial or religious groups as a form of preparation for the commission of the crime. Members of the subcommittee regarded the proposal as interesting in itself but decided that the matter should be examined within the framework of the works and studies undertaken after the enactment of the relevant resolution.

The UNGA adopted Resolution no. 96(I), The Crime of Genocide, on 11.12.1946. In it, it recognized genocide as a crime under international law, encouraged the states to adopt suitable domestic legislation for the prevention and punishment of the crime, recommended the organization of international co-operation for the purpose of facilitation the swift prevention and punishment of the crime of genocide until its elimination but also requested the Economic and Social Council (ECOSOC) to undertake the appropriate works for the purpose of the preparation of a suitable draft convention to be tabled in the next session of the UNGA.

The first stage of the works was the compilation by the Secretariat, with the participation of three experts (acting on their own behalf rather than that of the individual states) – Rafał Lemkin, Vespasian Pella and Henri Donnedieu de Vabres – of a compendium of ideas for use by the UNGA. At that stage, practically all options were on the negotiation table. The proper works took place in an *ad hoc* committee composed of the representatives of states, i.e. China, France, Lebanon, Poland, the USA, USSR and Venezuela. It was the draft prepared by that committee which was debated in the Sixth Committee of the General Assembly.

The Polish representatives spoke numerous times, especially Aleksander Bramson (who recalled that genocide could be committed not only in a time of war but also in a time of peace and emphasized that history preceding WWI knew examples of cultural genocide, citing the practice of *ausrotten* used by Otto von Bismarck, i.e. the ban on the use of Polish in schools as a language of instruction of otherwise);[112] Juliusz Katz-Suchy, Manfred Lachs (sometimes mistakenly recorded as 'Laks' in the documents), Oskar

112 UN Doc. A/AC.10/SR.28, 13.06.1947 and 24.06.1947.

Lange, Stefan Litauer and, above all, Aleksander Rudziński. All of them emphasized the severity of Poland's experience of genocide during WWII. The Polish delegates were desirous for the convention to include the issue of destruction of culture (thus understanding genocide more broadly than biological extermination alone)[113] and preparation for genocide (in this context, the example of the infamous manufacture of soap out of human remains was raised especially by Lachs).[114] They were sceptical, on the other hand, of the creation of an international criminal court and lack of a mention of fascist regimes, while mentioning the problem of the impunity of many of the criminals.[115] That scepticism, however, was the result of the necessity of arguing in line with the position held by the USSR.

The Polish delegation's contribution to the discussion was so significant and regarded as so valuable that when the *ad hoc* Committee decided to establish a subcommittee for the drafting of the articles of the convention, its members, beside the USA (John Maktos) and USSR (Platon D. Morozov) included Poland (Rudziński). Thus, one cannot overestimate the significance of how the representative of Poland achieved an equal footing with those of the two great powers of the time, and the *travaux préparatoires* reflect that Rudziński's opinions enjoyed considerable recognition. However, in publications dealing with genocide, his contribution goes unnoticed. This is provided that while Rudziński played a leading role in the *ad hoc* Committee's subcommittee, within the Sixth Committee the distinction belongs to Lachs.

The Convention was adopted on 9.12.1948,[116] and Poland ratified it as soon as 18.07.1950.[117] Poland submitted two reservations to the Convention, concerning the non-recognition of the mandatory jurisdiction of the International Court of Justice (Article IX)[118] and the need to apply the Convention to non-independent territories, including mandates (Article XII).[119]

113 Cyprian, Sawicki (1956b): 171–174.

114 *Ibidem*: 184.

115 *Ibidem*: 176–177.

116 It is characteristic that Poland (similarly to the other states of the Eastern Bloc, as well as Saudi Arabia and Union of South Africa) abstained from the vote on 10 December 1948 on the adoption of the Universal Declaration of Human Rights, because, as argued by Modzelewski, Poland's achievements had significantly outpaced the proposals of the declaration. So he made the supercilious remark: 'For us, that document will not suffice.' – *Zbiór Dokumentów* (1948), no.12: 867–883; Parzymies (2012): 81.

117 Dz.U.1952.2.9.

118 Polish government withdrawn its reservation concerning Article IX on 16.10.1997.

119 78 UNTS 277.

When the issue of the reservations to the Convention came up before the ICJ, Poland submitted on 13.01.1951 a written statement to the effect that the matter of the submission of the reservations had been resolved favourably to them and that the ICJ should not issue an advisory opinion on it at all.[120] Naturally, Poland ended up being among the states voting against the adoption of the UNGA's Resolution no. 598/VI of 12.01.1952 concerning reservations to international treaties.

In the case of the Geneva conventions of 1949 on the protection of war victims, Poland did not send an official delegation to the conference. Stanisław Kalina (the second secretary of the Polish legation in Bern) thus only held observer status. Kalina himself and Julian Przyboś were authorized to sign the text of the Convention on behalf of the Polish People's Republic, which they did on 8.12.1949 (the text itself had been adopted on 12.08.1949).[121] A Polish representative, Przyboś, submitted reservations to GC, among which the most prominent one in the context of the thematic scope of this monograph was the one dealing with Article 85 GC III, whereby prisoners of war convicted of war crimes and crimes against humanity in line with the principles established during the Nuremberg trials would forfeit their right to the protection of the Convention, so that the penalty imposed on them could be executed in accordance with the regulations of the interested state. Similar reservations were submitted by the other states remaining in the orbit of the USSR. Poland ratified the GCs in September 1954.[122] The meagre contribution to the development of the ultimate shape of the GCs must come as a surprise in the light of Poland's experiences from the time of WWII. It must be noted, however, that among those who had a realistic impact on the preparation of the GC drafts was Hersch Lauterpacht.[123]

A significant contribution from the Polish delegation can be traced, on the other hand, in the negotiations leading up to the Hague Convention for the Protection of Cultural Property in the Event of Armed Conflict (adopted on 14.05.1954),[124] with the particularly active involvement of Stanisław Lorentz, whose achievements in the field of protecting cultural property during

120 *Pleadings, oral arguments, documents. Reservations to the Convention on the Prevention and Punishment of the Genocide*: 283–285.

121 *Final Record of the Diplomatic Conference of Geneva 1949*, Vol. I, Federal Political Department, Berne.

122 Dz.U.1956.38.171.

123 Lewis (2014): 257ff.

124 Dz.U.1957.46.212.

WWII and documenting the destruction wrought by the Germans are inestimable.[125] It is also worth noting that the protective sign of the blue shield used to mark cultural property was designed by a Pole – Jan Zachwatowicz (Conservator General of Monuments in Poland at the time), a participant in the Hague Conference.

Other significant involvement of Poland in the creation of the framework of international criminal law should be noted in the context of the Convention on the Non-Applicability of Statutory Limitations to War Crimes and Crimes Against Humanity of 1968. Numerous times did Poland make statements concerning the inaction of the bodies of the German justice system and the problem of statute of limitations running on the crimes. The Chief Commission for the Investigation of Nazi Crimes systematically appealed for the non-application of statutes of limitations.[126] On 22.04.1964, Poland adopted an Act on Halting the Course of Prescription in Respect of the Perpetrators of the Gravest Nazi Crimes Committed in the Period of the World War II (*Ustawa w sprawie wstrzymania biegu przedawnienia w stosunku do sprawców najcięższych zbrodni hitlerowskich popełnionych w okresie drugiej wojny światowej*).[127] The topic of the statute of limitations was raised by Polish academics in the context of the steps taken by the German authorities to provide the criminals with impunity under the pretext of the passage of time.[128]

Of especial importance in the international forum was the fact of holding the academic conference on the statute of limitations in Warsaw in June 1964.[129] At the conclusion of the Conference, the so-called Warsaw Declaration was adopted, calling for, among other things, the exclusion of the applicability of statutes of limitations to the prosecution and punishment of international crimes on the basis of norms of domestic law. Additionally, Poland submitted a memorandum on statutes of limitations in March 1965[130] and, in August 1965, materials prepared by the Chief Commission for the Investigation of Nazi Crimes in Poland.[131] Poland also

125 Lorentz (1970).

126 Pilichowski (1980a): 13–17.

127 Dz.U.1964.15.86.

128 Rotfeld, Ryszka (1965): 13; see also Daszkiewicz (1970): 4–5 i (1972).

129 Grosescu (2019): 242–243.

130 Resich (1981): 87.

131 Pilichowski (1980c): 70; Resich (1980): 793 (the author emphasizes that Poland's actions were motivated not by revenge but by a historical and moral duty owed to humanity, considering that Poland, beside the USSR, suffered the greatest losses during World War II).

exerted pressure for the matter to be dealt with by the Human Rights Commission, which, on 9.04.1965, adopted the relevant Resolution no. 3 (XXI), and, in 1966, in the 22th and 23rd sessions of the Commission, the agenda included discussion of the study on statutes of limitations commissioned by the UN Secretary General and a draft convention on the non-applicability of statutes of limitations.[132] Subsequently, the topic was raised in the UNGA, which – under the influence of the conclusions of the working group of Committees III and VI – adopted on 18.12.1967 the Resolution no. 2338, whereby the works on the relevant convention were assigned a high priority. The Convention was adopted by resolution no. 2391 of 26.11.1968, mainly by the votes of the socialist states.[133] It is noteworthy that in the Convention – in line with Poland's position – the crime of genocide is dealt with as a type of crime against humanity and not as a separate type of crime.[134]

In 1969, by UNGA Resolution no. 2583 (invoking, among others, the St James Declaration), the states were encouraged to ratify the Convention, and an appeal was made to the states having decided against ratifying the Convention to refrain from acting contrary to its goals. The UNGA recalled that in accordance with the Convention, the states should investigate war crimes and crimes against humanity and make the appropriate arrests and extraditions and secure the convictions of those guilty of the crimes.

Poland signed the Convention on 16.02.1968 and was the first state to ratify it, on 29.01.1969,[135] later also undertaking other activities to propagate the idea of non-applicability of statutes of limitations. Suffice to recall the submission of documents by the Chief Commission for the Investigation of Nazi Crimes in Poland to the AIDP conference in 1969 in Rome or the promotion of the resolution on the non-applicability of statutes of limitations to Nazi crimes in the International Conference of the Red Cross in Stambul in 1969.[136]

As regards other initiatives, it will be expedient to mention Poland's especially active participation in the works on the Declaration on the Elimination of All Forms of Racial Discrimination, of 20.11.1963,[137] which Poland

132 See also UN Doc. E/CN.4/1966, 15.02.1966.

133 Convention was adopted with 58 votes. 7 states were against (Australia, Honduras, Portugal, Salvador, South Africa, UK, USA), 36 states abstained. See also Resich (1980): 794.

134 E.g. Cyprian, Sawicki (1956b): 191.

135 Dz.U.1970.26.208.

136 Pilichowski (1980c): 57–58.

137 Cf. Pawlak (2019): 276; Resich (1981): 64ff.

ratified on 7.03.1966.[138] The Polish delegates (Sławomir Dąbrowa, Zofia Dembińska and Zbigniew Resich) submitted numerous amendments (usually without success) aimed at the opening of the Convention to non-member states or the punishment of the incitement of racial discrimination, and the outlawing of racist and neo-fascist organizations.[139] Given the opportunity, they emphasized the extent to which Poland had suffered as a result of the Nazi racial policy.[140]

There is also a clearly noticeable Polish influence on the shape taken by the additional protocols to the GCs of 1949, adopted in 1977. The distinction belongs to the Polish representatives who took part in the final drafting, including Tadeusz Malik and Stanisław Edward Nahlik, who chaired the works of Committee II (Malik the first session and Nahlik the second, third and fourth); Nahlik, as a representative of the group of states of Eastern Europe, also participated in the Drafting Committee and was its rapporteur. With regard to highly consequential expert input, the distinction goes also to Remigiusz Bierzanek (often recorded as 'Bierzaneck'), Marian Flemming and Andrzej Górbiel.

Poland, similarly to the entire communist bloc, pressed for solutions strengthening the protection of the civilian population, as well as definitions of war crimes and responsibility for them. Interestingly, however, Poland ratified the protocols only on 23.10.1991 and recognized the jurisdiction of the International Fact-Finding Committee only in 1992.[141]

It ought to be noted that during the negotiations of the International Convention against the Taking of Hostages, of 17 December 1979, Poland – together with the communist block – objected to its adoption. Therefore, it can hardly be surprising that we ratified the Convention only in 2000.[142] By contrast, with regard to the Convention against Torture and Other Cruel, Inhuman or Degrading Treatment or Punishment, of 10.12.1984, which Poland signed in January 1986, the ratification was relatively swift and accomplished in 1989.[143] With regard to the Convention against Torture, Poland decided to submit reservations to the effect of not recognizing the jurisdiction neither of the Committee (Article 28), recognizing its

138 Dz.U.1969.25.187.

139 E.g. UN Doc. A/C.3/SR.1366, 6.12.1965.; A/C.3/SR.1220, 3.10.1963; A/C.3/SR.1167, 30.10.1962, https://hr-travaux.law.virginia.edu/racial-discrimination.

140 UN. Doc. A/C.3/SR.1215, 30.09.1963.

141 Dz.U.1992.41.175.

142 Dz.U.2000.106.1123.

143 Dz.U.1989.63.378.

jurisdiction for individual claims only on 12.05.1993, nor of the ICJ (Article 30(1)). Poland submitted those reservations when signing the Convention, but they were not confirmed at the time of ratification. In consequence, the Polish MFA claims that those reservations are not valid.

4 Polish Legislation

Of crucial importance after 1945 was the aforementioned August Decree, with several subsequent amendments. The amendment of 16.02.1945[144] enabled the Supreme National Tribunal (NTN) to judge those of the war criminals extradited to Poland by other states whose cases fell within the NTN's jurisdiction (although there was the possibility of delegating them to special criminal courts); and persons prosecuted on the basis of the Decree of 28.06.1946 on Criminal Responsibility for the Abandonment of Nationality during the War of 1939–1945 (*Dekret o odpowiedzialności karnej za odstępstwo od narodowości w czasie wojny 1939–1945*). The power to impose punishment other than death penalty was also added, which was of great significance because – as noted above – in its original version, the Decree provided for the death penalty equally for direct participation in killings, maltreatment and persecution (Article 1(a)) as for acting to the detriment of wanted or persecuted persons by their apprehension, deportation or persecution (Article 1(b)). Following the amendment, the Decree covered actions to the detriment of persons wanted by the occupation authorities for any reasons (other than prosecution for common crimes) through their identification, apprehension or deportation – the penalty was death; as well other actions to the detriment of the Polish State or persons from among the civilian population or prisoners of war – the penalty was 3 to 15 years' imprisonment, life imprisonment or death. For extorting benefits from those wanted or persecuted, with the threat of apprehending them or handing them over to the occupation authorities and for other actions detrimental to such persons by taking advantage of the situation created by the occupation, the amendment set the sentencing limits at 3 to 15 years' imprisonment. The amendment also made it possible to judge crimes not targeting persons who were staying within the territory of Poland at the time of the act.

By decree of 10.12.1946,[145] the NTN's jurisdiction *ratione materiae* was extended to the killings of not only civilians or prisoners of war but also of

144 Dz.U.1946.41.237.

145 Dz.U.1946.69.376.

'military persons'. As a follow-up to the IMT's judgment, the Decree introduced the type of crime defined as: 'participating in a criminal organization created or recognized by the authorities of the German state or of a state allied thereto or by a political association acting in the interest of the German state or of a state allied thereto.' Simultaneously, the Decree defined such groups or organizations as ones having as their objective the commission of crimes against peace, war crimes or crimes against humanity or, having a different objective, pursuing it through the commission of the aforementioned crimes. The December Amendment specified that the following were among such organizations: National Socialist German Workers' Party (NSDAP) – key positions; Protection Squads (*Schutzstaffel*, SS); Secret State Police (Gestapo); Security Service (*Sicherheitsdienst*, SD). It also introduced the principle that an action or omission under the influence of a threat, command or order posed no exemption from criminal responsibility but could result in more lenient sentencing (i.e. the Nuremberg solution). Interestingly, the December Amendment replaced the phrase, 'in the interest of the German occupation authorities,' with: 'in the interest the authorities of the German state or of a state allied thereto,' so as to cover also the activities having taken place before or after the occupation. Adam Lityński, however, rightly emphasized, that such language theoretically made it possible to judge the communist authorities – at least until the beginning of Operation Barbarossa, concerning the making of the Molotov-Ribbentrop Pact.[146] The Decree also provided for the extraordinary mitigation of punishment due to the perpetrator's personal circumstances or the circumstances of the act, if the action or omission had been influenced by a threat, command or order. That was a significant change, considering that the August Decree initially stipulated a mandatory death sentence for homicide. The identification or handing over to the authorities of the German state or of a state allied thereto of a person wanted for common crimes was also depenalized where the perpetrator had been acting in an overarching public or private interest. It was no longer required for an act committed abroad to be regarded as a criminal offence by the law of the place of its commission.

The Decree of 22.10.1947[147] included detailed regulation of the matter of confiscation of property, and the Decree of 3.04.1948[148] the matter of retrial and increased availability of special mitigating circumstances.

146 Lityński (1999): 66.

147 Dz.U.1947.65.390.

148 Dz.U.1948.18.124.

Among other legal instruments, not necessarily dealing exclusively with the crimes of the period of WWII, one needs to mention the Decree of 13.06.1946 on Criminal Offences Particularly Dangerous in the Period of Reconstruction of the State (*Dekret o przestępstwach szczególnie niebezpiecznych w okresie odbudowy Państwa*), called the, 'Small Criminal Code.'[149] The significance of the Decree consists in that some of the crimes listed in it potentially fell within the scope of crimes against peace (Article 1 – assault on a unit of Polish or allied armed forces) or crimes against humanity or genocide (Article 30 – incitement or praise of ethnic, religious or racial conflicts; Article 31 – public disparagement, ridicule or humiliation of a group or of individuals due to their national, ethnic, religious or racial affiliation; Article 32 – an act against the aforementioned groups or persons if resulting in death, severe impairment of the body, disruption of the normal course of political life, or a threat to public safety; as well as the following, related articles 33–35). The adoption of the Act of 22.04.1964 on Halting the Course of Prescription in Respect of the Perpetrators of the Gravest Nazi Crimes Committed in the Period of World War II (*Ustawa w sprawie wstrzymania biegu przedawnienia w stosunku do sprawców najcięższych zbrodni hitlerowskich popełnionych w okresie drugiej wojny światowej*) was of great importance in practice.[150]

The decision was made for the new Criminal Code of 19.04.1969 not to contain a part devoted to international crime, as the intention was to regulate those by a separate statute, which, however, did not ultimately happen.[151]

5 The Judiciary

5.1 *Special Courts*

As noted above, on 12.09.1944, the PKWN established special criminal courts for the cases of fascist-Nazi criminals. There are significant controversies with regard to the quantitative and qualitative assessment of the special court's judicial decisions. Aleksander Pyszkowski reports that the special courts received a total of 22 thousand cases, of which 12 thousand on the basis of the August Decree and 10 thousand under the Decree of 4.11.1944.[152]

149 Dz.U.1946.30.192.
150 Dz.U.1964.15.86.
151 Kubicki (1987): 45.
152 Pyszkowski (1946): 37.

Of all indictments submitted under the August Decree, more than 7 thousand cases were heard, with approximately 750 death sentences handed down, and 400 prison terms exceeding 10 years, as well as 2.5 thousand terms of up to 10 years[153]. Zdzisław Biegański, on the other hand, claims that a total of 8838 arrived in the special courts, out of which 4593 were decided and 3954 individuals were convicted.[154] The same data are stated by Leszek Kubicki (for the period from 22.07.1944 to 22.07.1946); he also specifies that the special courts convicted 2471 people, out of whom 631 received the death penalty, 306 prison terms in excess of 10 years, and 1534 prison terms of up to 10 years.[155] Dariusz Burczyk, however, emphasized that in the latter half of 1946 many a judgment was still passed that the statistics cited by Biegański and Kubicki do not include[156]. Kazimierz Bogucki specified that the special courts judged a total of 6,169 individuals in 1944–1946.[157] Anna Machnikowska, in turn, gives the August Decree's figure at 3954 convictions, including 721 death sentences.[158]

Unfortunately, with regard to the special courts – and generally Polish court system after 1944 – it is difficult to trust the data cited in the various documents because the same courts and on the basis of the same legal provisions judged both war criminals and so-called traitors to the Nation. Accusing the opposition (or members of the Home Army in general, whom the communist propaganda dubbed the 'bespittled dwarves of reaction')[159] of collaboration with the Nazis was standard fare. The provisions of

153 *Ibidem*: 39.

154 Biegański (2003): 121, 123.

155 Kubicki (1963): 40–41.

156 Burczyk (2014): 295.

157 Bogucki (1973): 238.

158 Machnikowska (2008): 269. This chapter omits the partial statistics forwarded to the UNWCC, such as those submitted on 28.11.1946 by Cyprian (Trials of War Criminals in Poland, UNWCC, A.27), who identified 44,762 arriving cases, out which 9,449 had gone to the special courts. Cyprian states that the special courts had judged 4593 cases, imposing the death penalty in 631, a prison term exceeding 10 years in 306 cases, a prison term shorter than 10 years in 1534 cases, with the remainder ending in acquittals. He notes, however, that the above statistics include both typical war crimes and cases of treason and collaboration, as the official data did not distinguish the two types of cases.

159 The term 'bespittled dwarf of reacton' was used on a propaganda poster by Włodzimierz Zakrzewski, titled *Olbrzym i zapluty karzeł reakcji* ('A giant and a bespittled dwarf of reaction'), printed in February 1945. The poster depicted a soldier of the Polish People's Army and a dwarfish human figure spitting at him, with a tag captioned 'AK' (Polish acronym for the Home Army) hanging down the latter's neck.

the August Decree [as well as those of the subsequently adopted Decree on Responsibility for the September Defeat and Fascization of State Life (*Dekret o odpowiedzialności za klęskę wrześniową i faszyzację życia państwowego*)][160] were weaponized to prosecute the political opposition: 'as an instrument of not only repression but also of moral annihilation against the activists of the Home Army underground.'[161] According to Machnikowska,[162] the above happened: 'in line with the thesis that the defendants (…) killed and persecuted the members of left-wing organizations, on whom rested the brunt of the armed resistance to the occupation authorities.'[163]

As opposed to the NTN, which will be discussed below, the judicial activities of the special courts are controversial in that testimony was not infrequently forced by intimidation or beating; the prosecutors but also the judges resorted to emotional phrasing and insults; the defendants' objections as to the manner in which the proceedings were conducted were ignored; unreliable witnesses were relied upon; the defence counsel did not endeavour to save the defendants from the death penalty; the language of the judgments was laconic and often did not refer to the defendant's individual guilt but only the broader context of the Third Reich's crimes.[164]

According to the available statistics, in 1944–1969 (thus not only before the special courts but also the common courts), a total of 17,845 people were convicted of crimes from the time of the occupation, out of whom only 5432 were German and the remaining 12,413 were Poles, Ukrainians, Belarusians, Jews and others.[165] Does this mean that collaboration with the enemy occurred on such a great scale? Not necessarily. Firstly, one has to consider that the Polish courts were not in a position to judge a great number of German criminals because the extraditions were not forthcoming (even so, the achievements of the Polish justice system in that regard are much more impressive than those of e.g. the Belgian or Dutch systems);[166] secondly, many were accused of collaboration with the Germans and sentenced to death solely because they opposed the new communist power – the judgments were rendered on the basis of the same August Degree to

160 Dz.U.1946.5.46.
161 Steinsbergowa (2016): 100–101.
162 Machnikowska (1999): 393; Machnikowska (2008): 310ff.
163 Birt (2019): 72.
164 Lubecka (2011): 38.
165 Pilichowski (1980c): 73.
166 Ruckerl (1980): 82.

make the emphatic statement that individuals linked to the government-in-exile collaborated with the Nazis.[167]

Apart from the above-discussed trial of Majdanek staff (see subchapter 2.3), another celebrated trial, now before the special court in Gdańsk, was that of Stutthof staff, held between 25.04. and 1.06.1946.[168] The panel included Józef Tarczewski (legal practitioner; presiding) and Józef Iżycki (editor of *Wieczór* newspaper) and Tadeusz Tylewski (composer, orchestra director, former inmate of Stutthof – the fact may have impacted his impartiality) as lay judges; Stanisław Stachurski appeared for the prosecution. There were 15 defendants (Johann Pauls, Jenny-Wanda Barkmann, Elizabeth Becker, Wanda Klaff, Ewa Paradies, Gerda Steinhoff, Aleksy Duzdala, Tadeusz Kopczyński, Kazimierz Kowalski, Wacław Kozłowski, Józef Reiter, Franciszek Szopiński and Marian Ziółkowski, who died in prison before the trial began, Erna Beilhardt, and kapos Jan Preiss and Jan Breit). They were charged with maltreatment of the camp inmates, causing the deaths of many. Eleven of the defendants received death sentences. Beilhardt and Kowalski were given prison terms and two individuals – Duzdala and Preiss – were acquitted.

In subsequent Gdańsk trials taking place on 5–10 and 19–29.11.1947, another 40 individuals were judged, most of whom would be sentenced to death, though the rare acquittals also happened. The executions were carried out by public hanging. The former camp prisoners or members of their families, who had volunteered to participate, acted as the executioners, dressed in camp uniforms.

Even though the special courts' judgments came down by the hundreds, they were of no greater consequence to the shaping of the doctrines of international criminal law. In the UNWCC's cycle of publications titled *Law Reports of Trials of War Criminals*, although several NTN judgments were discussed, there was no mention of proceedings before the 'ordinary' special courts or common courts. That is probably the result of Polish omissions and failure to forward the relevant summaries in the English language. Hence, the Polish efforts to judge the crimes have not been suitably highlighted. It is worth noting, however, that the same series describes the

167 To further humiliate the soldiers of the Home Army, they were often imprisoned together with Nazi criminals; for example, Kazimierz Moczarski was locked in the same cell with Jūrgen Stroop who was responsible for liquidation of Warsaw ghetto.

168 More Burczyk (2014) and (2022).

trials before the domestic courts of other states, in which Poles provided key testimonies; for example, the Belsen case.[169]

The special courts were abolished by the Decree of 17.10.1946.[170] Cases initiated before the Decree came into force were to proceed according to the old law, and in those cases the NTN prosecutor retained the ability to lodge an appeal-in-cassation with the Supreme Court. The short deadlines, single-instance proceedings and severity of the judgments, though acceptable in wartime were not met with understanding in a time of peace. Nor were there sufficient reasons to warrant the retention of a judicial structure parallel to the common judiciary.

The *ratione materiae* jurisdiction of the special courts were taken over by Regional Courts in compositions defined by the Decree of 13.06.1946 (Small Criminal Code),[171] viz. one professional judge presiding and two lay judges from a list agreed by the praesidium of the voivodeship national council competent *ratione loci* for the regional court's seat.

5.2 *The Supreme National Tribunal*

With its Decree of 22.01.1946, the PKWN established the Supreme National Tribunal and its prosecution service[172] (with a position equal to that of the Supreme Court; sometimes, for reasons of its nature, the NTN was classified as a special court).[173]

The First President of the Supreme Court (which had several presidents) served as the President of the NTN. As opposed to the other special courts, the NTN procedure required the attendance of defence counsel at trial. The defendant had no right of appeal but could petition the President of the State National Council (KRN) for clemency. Thus, the NTN proceedings were a single-instance procedure.

Its jurisdiction covered: 'cases of the criminal offences of persons who, in accordance with the Moscow Declaration of the three Allied powers: United States of America, Union of Soviet Socialist Republics and [the United Kingdom of] Great Britain [and Northern Ireland] on the Nazis' responsibility for the atrocities committed by them w[ould] be remanded to the organs of the prosecution service of the Polish Republic for crimes

169 Case of Josef Kramer et al. before British military court in Luneburg, 17.09–17.11.1945, UNWCC (1947), 2 *Law Reports of Trials of War Criminals* 1.

170 Dz.U.1946.59.324.

171 Dz.U.1946.30.92.

172 Dz.U.1946.5.45.

173 Jakubowski (2002): 35–37.

committed in the territory of the Polish State during the occupation,' and: 'cases of crimes specified by the Decree of 22 January 1946 on Responsibility for the September Defeat and Fascization of State Life' (Article 13). Throughout its entire history, the NTN did not hear a single case under the January Decree (there was no such indictment).[174]

By the Decree of 17.10.1946, the jurisdiction was expanded so as to include not only the criminal offences specified by the Decree of 22.01.1946 but also cases of: 'criminal offences committed by such persons as, for the crimes committed by them, may in accordance with the Moscow Declaration (…) be handed over to the authorities of the Republic' – thus, not only crimes committed within the territory of Poland but also crimes committed either before or after the occupation. The same decree removed from the NTN's jurisdiction cases dealing with the exclusion of hostile elements from Polish society.

Until the October amendment, the NTN had priority of jurisdiction before other special courts. It was also the NTN that decided on retrials in its own cases. Pursuant to Article 15 of the aforementioned Decree, the NTN prosecutor could challenge a special court's judgment within 3 months if there were grounds for an appeal-in-cassation or retrial.[175] In theory, therefore, the NTN had judicial supervision over the special courts and their prosecutors. On a successful appeal-in-cassation, the NTN would quash the disputed judgment, and the retrial would proceed before the NTN itself. In practice, the supervision was illusory, given that only the President of the NTN served on a permanent basis and different adjudicating panels, as well as different prosecutors, were appointed on a case-by-case basis. The NTN never exercised its powers with regard to the special courts, and by an amendment of the Decree, dated 17.10.1946, it was stripped of those powers in favour of the Supreme Court.[176]

The NTN's panels included 3 professional and 4 lay judges (3 judges for *in camera* proceedings) – Article 3 of the Decree on the Supreme National Tribunal. While the professional judges were appointed by the Praesidium of the KRN out of a list submitted by the Minister of Justice, the lay judges were appointed by the same body from among the members of parliament (Article 4). The involvement of lay judges was intended to add a social

174 Although the NTN did not judge anyone for responsibility for the September defeat, it remanded the indictments to the common courts – see Machnikowska (2008): 273.

175 Decree of 22.01.1946 on Supreme National Tribunal (*Dekret o Najwyższym Trybunale Narodowym*) Dz.U.1946.5.45.

176 Decree of 17.10.1946, Dz.U.1946.59.325.

factor, theoretically with the highest qualifications.[177] And yet, combining membership in the Tribunal with membership in parliament, so that the lay judges were simultaneously active politicians, unquestionably raises doubts with regard to independence (formally guaranteed by the Decree) and the separation of powers. Nevertheless, in practice, care was taken that the individual judges, prosecutors, expert witnesses and defence counsel held high qualifications.[178]

The aforementioned October Decree introduced important procedural guarantees: participation of defence counsel throughout the entire judicial proceedings; the defence counsel accorded the rights of a party; the defendant, as well as the defendant's parent, guardian, spouse, child or sibling with the right to choose the counsel. In the absence of counsel by choice, one was appointed by the court. A retrial was available in favour of the defendant on account of facts or evidence previously unknown to the court and excluding or mitigating the criminality or punishability of the act. The trial could begin no earlier than 60 days after the proper announcement.

A total of 7 trials took place before the NTN, in which a total of 49 individuals were judged.[179] Characteristically, the first judgments in the cases of Arthur Greiser (in connection with the crimes for which he was responsible as the Reichsstatthalter of the Reichsgau Wartheland)[180] and Amon Leopold Göth (camp commandant in Płaszów) were entered, respectively, on 9.07.1946 and 5.09.1946, thus before the Nuremberg judgment. The Polish authorities perfectly realized that the judgments could influence the jurisprudence of the Nuremberg tribunal; that is the reason for the meticulous analyses of the issues of responsibility for aggressive war in the above trials, citing the expert studies of the internationally reputed Ludwik Ehrlich, or the detailed discussion of the criminal character of the occupation rule and the scope of the persecutions that befell the population of the occupied territories, especially the Jews, including the organization of the labour camps.

Subsequent trials focused on proving the crimes perpetrated by the occupation forces in Warsaw and its vicinity, including the scope of the

177 Cyprian, Sawicki (1949): 3.

178 *Ibidem*: 3, 9; Prusin (2010): 4–5.

179 The NTN judgments were published in: Cyprian, Sawicki (1962c): 1ff; in the later part of this work, citations refer to the versions published therein. For a discussion of the trials of Arthur Greiser, Rudolf Höss, Auschwitz staff, and Josef Bühler, see also Gumkowski and Kułakowski (1961).

180 More Drumbl, Epstein (2010); Łuczak (1997), Kulesza, Schenk (2023); *Proces Greisera ...* (1946).

persecutions targeting the Polish and Jewish population, as well as the scale of destruction visited on Warsaw, including the murder of 790 thousand inhabitants out of 1.25 million (the trial of Ludwig Fischer, Ludwig Leist, Josef Meisinger and Maks Daume, ending with the judgment of 3.03.1947); the organization of the concentration camps, including Auschwitz, and the medical experiments performed there (the trials of Rudolf Höss,[181] judgment of 2.04.1947, and of Auschwitz staff, viz. 40 individuals, including Arthur Liebehenschel – Höss's successor in office – ending with the judgment of 22.12.1947); actions taken with a view to the annexation of Gdańsk to the Reich, and occupation rule in Pomerania (the trial of Albert Forster,[182] judgment of 29.04.1948); the criminal responsibility of the administration of the occupied territories of the Generalgouvernement (the trial of Josef Bühler, judgment of 5.08.1948).

There were plans of a trial focusing on the liquidation of the Warsaw Ghetto and destruction of Warsaw during the 1944 Uprising and in its aftermath – potential defendants included Erich von dem Bach-Zelewski, Erich von Manstein, Heinz Guderian, Heinz Reinefarth and Erich Koch.[183] Precisely because of the preparations for that trial, Telford Taylor decided against holding a trial concerning the destruction of Warsaw before the American military courts in the subsequent Nuremberg trials.[184] However, no trial occurred either before the NTN or any other Polish court in the crimes perpetrated during the Warsaw Uprising because of the non-extradition of the defendants (von dem Bach-Zelewski merely testified in the trial of Fischer and others[185]); the decision was made against proceeding *in absentia*, even though the option was on the table.

Some of the NTN judgments were discussed in the aforementioned *Law Reports of Trials of War Criminals* series, namely those in the cases of Amon Göth (case 37, vol. 7), Rudolf Höss (case 38, vol. 7), Arthur Greiser (case 74, vol. 13) and Josef Bühler (case 85, vol. 14) – those cases are cited in foreign literature[186] and in the judgments of courts both Polish[187] and international

181 Lubecka (2019).
182 Podgóreczny (1975b): 20ff; (1975a).
183 Cyprian, Sawicki (1960): 367ff.
184 Heller (2011): 64.
185 Erich von dem Bach-Zelewski testified in case of Fischer et al., see Sawicki (1968): 244ff.
186 Drumbl (2013); Prusin (2010).
187 See e.g. Judgment of Criminal Law Division of the Supreme Court, 923/49 z 25.06.1949 r.; OSN(K): 1949/1/1, Lex no. 161330.

ones.[188] However, the cases of Fischer and others or of the Auschwitz camp staff also attracted some interest. Simultaneous interpretation was provided into English, French, German and Russian during the proceedings.[189]

The authorities of Poland at the time, as well as the lawyers taking part in the proceedings were aware of the momentous significance of the trials. Examples include judge Alfred Eimer's letter of 9.10.1947 to the MFA, mentioning the necessity of ensuring space for foreign press in the trials of Höss and Auschwitz staff.[190] Those cases had the potential to influence the shaping of the foundations of international criminal law. After all, the decisions of domestic courts could later be relied on by the International Military Tribunal, of which several were expected to follow.[191] In order to be able to gain influence on international jurisprudence, one had to attract the interest of foreign media and, more importantly, the persons who could influence the selection of cases and the shaping of the rules of responsibility. The Polish trials were intended to highlight the scale of crimes, as well as the involvement of both individuals and corporations (e.g. IG Farbenindustrie, Union-Werke and Friedrich Krupp AG, Siemens).[192] The selection of the cases to proceed before the NTN by design was to be, and was indeed, symbolic; so was the choice of the locations where the trials and the executions were taking place.[193] Jurists of international repute were assigned to con-

188 See e.g. ICTY, *Prosecutor v. Momčilo Krajišnik*, IT-00-39-T, 27.09.2006, footnote 1645; *Prosecutor v. Mladen Naletilić and Vinko Martinović*, IT-98-34-A, Separate and Partly Dissenting Opinion of Judge Schomburg, 3.05.2006, §12; *Prosecutor v. Milomir Stakić*, IT-97-24-A, 22.03.2006, §29; *Prosecutor v. Radislav Krstić*, IT-98-33-T, 2.08.2001, footnote 1132 *Prosecutor v. Drago Josipović et al.*, IT-95-16-T, 14.01.2000, §600 and footnote 904; *Prosecutor v. Tihomir Blaškić*, IT-95-14-T, 3.03.2000, §223; *Prosecutor v. Radislav Krstić*, IT-98-33-T, 2.08.2001, footnotes 1132, 1282; *Prosecutor v. Radislav Krstić*, IT-98-33-T, 2.08.2001, footnote 1282.

189 See Tryuk (2021): 88ff, who notes that the interpreters participating in the trials had often been serving in that role for the first time in their lives, without the benefit of training and experience, in extraordinarily difficult circumstances, given the great political, propaganda and international importance of the trials (87).

190 AIPN, IPN/GK 196/8; see Tryuk (2014): 83.

191 Klafkowski (1968a): 15.

192 See NTN, Auschwitz case: 181ff; NTN, Höss case: 107ff; Cyprian, Sawicki (1949): 10–13, 31.

193 Trials took place in Poznań (Greiser), Cracow (Göth, Bühler, Auschwitz), Warsaw (Fischer, Höss), Gdańsk (Forster). Höss was executed within the Auschwitz concentration camp he commanded, while Greiser was publicly executed in the spot in Poznań, where usually Nazi criminals executed their own verdicts.

duct the trials, such as the appointment of Emil Stanisław Rappaport as judge in Greiser's trial.[194]

In part, the attempt to attract the interest of foreign observers was a success.[195] Attending Höss's trial, in addition to foreign correspondents, was a US delegation of eight members, including General Telford Taylor, the lead prosecutor in the later Nuremberg trials (he also observed Fischer's trial), as well as observers from Norway and France. Those in attendance at the trial of Auschwitz staff, in turn, included Lieutenant Yves Lemerle, who was the president of the French military tribunal in Rastatt.[196]

In its judgments, the Tribunal did not hesitate to use terms such as crime against peace, genocide, crimes against humanity or war crimes. In the classification of the individual acts, however, it referred primarily to specific provisions of the Criminal Code of 1932 and to the August Decree of 1944. Nevertheless, it analysed the aforementioned crimes under international law and formulated the principles of responsibility for them.

The NTN was the first court in history, before the IMT's judgment of 1.10.1946, to judge an individual (Greiser) for a crime against peace. On the basis of Ehrlich's expert opinions,[197] it was demonstrated that the war waged by the Third Reich was an act of aggression incompatible with the international law then in force, i.e. Article 104 of the Treaty of Versailles and the Paris Agreement between the Polish Republic and the Free City of Gdańsk of 9 November 1920.[198] Greiser was found guilty of crimes against peace due to having, as the President of the Free City of Danzig (Gdańsk) Senate, and as the Deputy Gauleiter of Gdańsk, in concert with Forster and other members of the NSDAP, prepared, led and waged a war of aggression against Poland in keeping with the party line. He violated the Free City's Charter and Poland's internationally recognized rights, especially considering that the Senate Resolution of 23 August 1939 appointing Albert Forster to the newly created position of mayor, was signed by Greiser. In NTN's

194 See also Prusin (2013): 121 who emphasizes in total 37 judges, prosecutors, counsels for defence had PhD degree.

195 Kuisz (2020): 323ff.

196 Tryuk (2021): 89, 91.

197 Ludwik Ehrlich, "Agresja III Rzeszy Niemieckiej na Polskę – pogwałcenie norm prawa międzynarodowego" and "Zagadnienie wojny we współczesnym prawie międzynarodowym", in: *Ekspertyzy i orzeczenia przed Najwyższym Trybunałem Narodowym. Część I. Agresja III Rzeszy Niemieckiej na Polskę i okupacja hitlerowska w Polsce w świetle prawa międzynarodowego*, MS, GKBZHwP 1979: 11ff. See also Grzebyk (2020b); *Proces Greisera (Sprawozdanie prawnicze)* (1946): 63–91.

198 NTN, Greiser case: 4–5.

opinion, it was Forster who bore the main responsibility for the separation of Gdańsk (Danzig) from Poland and its transformation into a German base, from which aggression was waged against Poland, but Greiser, as a person in close relations with Forster, also bore the responsibility.

Following the IMT's judgment (i.e. in cases of Forster, Bühler, Ludwig Fischer and others), the NTN's judgments no longer delved into the legality of the war conducted against Poland or definition of war of aggression as such, deciding that the IMT's judgment had settled the matter. It was thus assumed as an obvious fact that any planning, preparation, commencement and prosecution of an aggressive war constituted a crime against peace.[199] In Forster's case, three stages of involvement in a crime against peace were distinguished, covering also the period before 1.09.1939. In the first stage, in years 1930–1933, i.e. between Forster's arrival in Gdańsk and the Nazi takeover, Forster prepared the local structures of the NSDAP for the takeover, initiated the preparations for the violation of international treaties and agreements, attempted to eliminate the opposition, changed the laws and regulations, and organized SS units. During the second stage, from 1933 to 1.09.1939, Forster's activities had the goal of incorporation of Gdańsk into the Reich, as evidenced by the enactment of the Decree of 23.08.1939. With that, a violation of international obligations took place. Forster was responsible for the training of the Nazi units stationed in Gdańsk and the visits of naval ships such as the Schleswig-Holstein, which on 1.09.1939 began the bombardment of the Westerplatte and Gdynia. In the third stage, from the incorporation of Gdańsk into the Reich to the liberation of the city in April 1945, Forster's involvement in the commission of crimes against peace consisted in his appointment as the head of the civilian administration. His holding that position in the awareness that all of the decrees incorporating Gdańsk into the Reich were incompatible with international treaties, was an aggravating circumstance. NTN deemed Forster to have been one of the co-authors of Nazi policies, as attested, among others, by his having been authorized by Hitler to conduct direct talks in July 1938 with politicians in England.[200] Greiser's responsibility was of a different nature, as he in principle served in an executive role, and yet, he was found guilty of a crime against peace. In Fischer's case, the responsibility for a crime against peace was inferred from the fact alone of his membership in a specified group of party leaders. With that, the NTN found that from a certain position in the hierarchy upward, a person had to be knowingly and

199 NTN, Fischer et al. case: 57.

200 NTN, Forster case: 295.

deliberately, with a purpose, participating in the planning, organization and commission of a crime against peace within the criminal organization that was the NSDAP.[201] In the case of Bühler, in turn, the responsibility for crimes against peace derived from his having wielded occupation authority, which – given that it had constituted the result of a war of aggression – was, in the NTN's opinion, unlawful by design. For to the Tribunal, a crime against peace was – owing to the occupation – a continuous crime, lasting until the end of the occupation of Poland.[202] According to the NTN, which also resurfaced in the subsequent decisions of the common courts and of the Supreme Court, the Nazi occupation authorities only had obligations and no rights in the light of the law.[203]

From today's perspective, the NTN's judgments concerning the individual responsibility for a crime against peace merit certain criticism. Namely, the Tribunal (similarly to the other special and common courts) did not draw a clear distinction between individual responsibility and state responsibility.[204] Thus, for example, in Forster's case, the Tribunal's judgment referred to such historically distant events as the invitation of the Teutonic Order to Polish territory in AD 1226.[205] (Similar remarks were made by the prosecutors of the Special Court in Lublin during the trial of KL Majdanek staff.) Likewise, the Tribunal's conclusions as to the rights or powers of the occupation authorities were not reflected by the regulation adopted following WWII, in which the matters of the legality of the use of force as such were distinguished from the principles of conduct in war.[206] However, that was a rather frequent 'affliction' of the domestic courts of the former occupied states.[207]

---

201 NTN, Fischer et al. case: 58–59. See also Grzebyk (2013a): 185ff.

202 NTN, Bühler case: 360–362.

203 See more Kubicki (1963): 85; (Lord) Wright (1948): 87ff. Fortunately, in the end, the Supreme Court in its judgment of 11.10.1949 (Wa. K 1103/49, *Rocznik Prawa Międzynarodowego* (1949), 237–240), withdrew from that interpretation and acknowledged that the Hague Convention was also applicable to the German occupier ('the Hague Regulations are applicable to any occupation, even an unlawful one, such as the German occupation in Poland was').

204 NTN, Forster case: 264, 268.

205 NTN, Forster case: 269; NTN, Auschwitz case: 171.

206 See Preamble of 1977 AP I.

207 See e.g. Netherlands Special Court in Amsterdam, Case of Willy Zuehlke, 3.08.1948 and in the same case Netherlands Special Court of Cassation, 6.12.1948, UNWCC (1949), 14 *Law Reports of Trials of War Criminals* 139; 15 *Law Reports of Trials of War Criminals* 150.

The NTN was the first court to have used the term 'genocide' and progressively referred to the Nazi crimes with it, invoking the definition proposed in Lemkin's publications.[208] The defendants, as noted above, were convicted on the basis of specific provisions of domestic law, which, of course, did not yet define the crime of genocide, but the fact itself of the use of the term is noteworthy. The NTN's judgments analysing the crime of genocide preceded the UNGA's adoption of its Resolution no. 96 (I) on genocide of 1946, and the Convention on the Prevention and Punishment of the Crime of Genocide, of 1948, (and thus they may have influenced the shape taken by their provisions), as well as the judgments of the International Military Tribunal of 1.10.1946, and of the International Military Tribunal for the Far East, of 12.12.1948, as well as of the American military tribunals in the subsequent Nuremberg trials. Those tribunals made references to a genocidal policy but did not use the term in their judgments.

Already in the first trial concerning Greiser's responsibility did the tribunal point towards the: 'new crime against the interests of humanity and requirements of national and international conscience, in the form of genocide (according to the latest Anglophone terminology),'[209] referring to individuals (Forster in Pomerania, Bracht in Silesia, Greiser in the Warthegau and Frank in the Generalgouvernement) as perpetrators of genocide.[210] Göth's trial could be termed the first ever to have been wholly devoted to genocide,[211] in which the court explicitly referred to the policy of extermination of the Jews and Poles as genocide, taking the biological and the cultural dimensions into account.[212] In turn, in Höss's trial, it was underscored that the greatest genocide in history had taken place at Birkenau.[213] Thus, not the Nuremberg but the Polish tribunal found the Nazi policy with regard to the Jews to have been genocide.

On the formal side, the NTN regarded genocide as a special type of crime against humanity,[214] characterized by the selection of the victims for their membership in a specific nation, ethnicity or race.[215] The Tribunal emphasized that the defendants had been members of larger teams operating with

208 NTN, Greiser case: 13; NTN, Bühler case: 8; NTN, Forster case: 274.
209 NTN, Greiser case: 13.
210 *Ibidem*: 19–20.
211 Klafkowski (1968a): 17.
212 NTN, Göth case: 26–27; NTN, Bühler case: 341, 344. See also Cyprian, Sawicki (1949): 28.
213 NTN, Höss case: 111; NTN, Auschwitz case: 179.
214 See e.g. NTN, Bühler case: 326, 329.
215 NTN, Höss case: 113–114. In its judgment, the NTN also noted the existence of *dolus specialis* characteristic of genocide in the German activities, manifest in that: 'merely

a view to the commission of genocide.[216] In the contrary case, the killing of a given group on such a mass scale would not have been possible. The NTN analysed the policies against Polish nationals of Jewish ethnicity or origin (murder, concentration in ghettoes, maltreatment) and against the Polish population as such. It stressed on numerous occasions that both Jews and Poles were being subjected to genocide,[217] though the respective methods may have differed.

As typical acts of genocide, the NTN mentioned individual and mass murders of civilians and prisoners of war; maltreatment; persecution and infliction of bodily injuries; injuries resulting in health disorder in such persons; protracted deprivation of civilians of liberty applied against civilians – death camps, concentration camps and forced resettlements, as well as: 'deportation of Polish children and youth, against the will of their parents and guardians, and their placement, for the purposes of complete Germanization, in German foster families and public educational facilities in the Reich heartlands, severing all connection with [their] families and [their] Polishness, giving them German names and family names';[218] 'impeding Polish reproduction, restricting food for sick children and pregnant women, etc.';[219] and medical experiments intended to procure artificial infertility and thus assist with the annihilation of entire nations.[220] Moreover, it regarded the following as acts of genocide: 'systematic destruction of Polish culture, theft of Polish cultural property, and Germanization of the country and of the Polish population, and the unlawful seizure of public property,' as well as: 'systemic, unlawful divestment of the Polish population of its private property.'[221]

The NTN judgments involving genocide typically considered the repression of Polish culture as evidence of the genocidal nature of the German policy.[222] The NTN emphasized that, for example, in Greiser's case we had to do with a criminal conspiracy: 'against the basic interests of universal human culture and civilization; meaning martial and biological aggression,'

belonging to a specific nation or race was the reason for placing them in a camp as a protective measure.'

216 NTN, Fischer et al. case: 58; NTN, Höss case: 134.

217 NTN, Göth case: 24–25.

218 NTN, Greiser case: 7; cf. NTN, Forster case: 265, 295, 305.

219 NTN, Greiser case: 19.

220 NTN, Höss case: 132–133.

221 NTN, Greiser case: 6.

222 NTN, Göth case: 27; NTN, Forster case: 308; NTN, Greiser case: 9, 14; NTN, Bühler case: 378; NTN, Fischer et al. case: 69–70.

as well as: 'cultural annihilation (genocide) of neighbouring nations, especially the Polish Nation, execrated so much by the Germans.'[223] In the case of Fischer and others, the NTN paid especial attention to the fact of the destruction of culture, academic and scientific institutions, education, etc.[224] It underscored the practices of 'racial Germanization' and Germanization achieved by the: '[d]eportation of adult Poles and Jews, Germanization of racially amenable Polish children, by method of biological destruction of the Polish and Jewish populations, as well as utter liquidation of Polish culture and Polish political thought, that is by way of physical and spiritual genocide.'[225] In the Tribunal's opinion, in the territory of Greater Poland (Wielkopolska), Greiser pursued a: 'general Nazi-Hitlerite genocidal attack on the right to existence, right to the separate national [existence] and culture of small and middle-sized nations.'[226] In Göth's case, the NTN found: 'such eradication of Polishness had all characteristics of genocide, in the biological sense together with the cultural annihilation of said nations.'[227] It emphasized the starvation rations.[228]

In Höss's trial, the NTN explicitly stated that it was in Auschwitz-Birkenau that the greatest genocide in human history had taken place,[229] for the *Lager Auschwitz* was intended to become the world's greatest slaughterhouse. In the NTN's opinion, the programmatic nature of the eradication of humanity (genocide) in the death camps, provided every ground for the following conclusion: 'the camps, in the Hitlerite system, were one of those means which were to lead to the implementation of the criminal goals underpinning Hitlerism and constituting an attack on the most constitutional bases of human co-existence, the rights to existence and life.'[230]

By contrast, in the trial of Auschwitz camp staff, the NTN did not throw the term 'genocide' around. It referred to the concentration camps as, 'factories of death,' but classified the acts perpetrated in them as crimes against humanity and war crimes.[231] The restraint may have been prompted by a desire to fall in line with the Nuremberg judgment, in which the term

223 NTN, Greiser case: 10–11.

224 NTN, Fischer et al. case: 49.

225 NTN, Greiser case: 13–14.

226 *Ibidem*: 14.

227 NTN, Göth case: 27.

228 NTN, Göth case: 30; NTN, Auschwitz case: passim (especially concerning Liebehenschel); NTN, Bühler case: 354.

229 NTN, Höss case: 111, 113.

230 *Ibidem*: 133.

231 NTN, Auschwitz case: 252–253.

'genocide' had not been used. In its subsequently issued judgments, the NTN noted that the relegation of a given nation to the category of slaves (the distinction between 'German masters' and 'Polish servants'), the exploitation of that nation's labour, preventing it from engaging in religious cult and depriving it of its temples, constituted genocide.[232] The same was the case when destroying the organization of Polish life and evidence of Polish culture was accompanied by economic impairment relative to the German population.[233] However, in the judgment in Forster's case (following in time after the UNGA resolution of 1946), the NTN, referring to genocide as, 'the most abominable crime,'[234] emphasized that the goal of that crime was the destruction of the, 'biological substance.'[235] Similarly, in Bühler's case, the Tribunal found that the entire area of the Generalgouvernement ('GG') had been: 'one great concentration camp in which, by different methods, gradually, like in the ghettoes, people were being eliminated because the entire population of the GG had been destined for biological destruction.'[236]

With regard to crimes against humanity, NTN merely quoted from the IMT Charter, emphasizing that crimes against humanity covered any persecution on political, racial or religious grounds pursued in connection with a crime against peace or with war crimes, even where such a crime against humanity had preceded the war.[237] As the NTN would underscore, a crime prohibited by the criminal codes of all civilized nations.[238]

The analysis of the judgments reveals the existence of a difficulty drawing a clear distinction between the fragments supposed to refer to crimes against humanity from those dealing with war crimes. For the Tribunal interpreted the elements of such criminal offences as unlawful deportations to labour camps in the context of the prohibition of slavery,[239] or such as torture, including psychological torture, e.g. in the form of forcing individuals to sing joyful songs.[240] Detailed descriptions of torture were quoted in nearly every judgment of the NTN, and torture, after all, may be classified – depending on the circumstances – as war crimes or as crimes against humanity, or as genocide.

232 NTN, Greiser case: 18.
233 NTN, Fischer et al. case: 60–61.
234 NTN, Forster case: 287.
235 *Ibidem*: 295.
236 NTN, Bühler case: 344.
237 NTN, Fischer et al. case: 57.
238 NTN, Auschwitz case: 253.
239 NTN, Fischer case et al.: 57.
240 NTN, Auschwitz case: 188.

In the case of war crimes, the Tribunal specified typical acts identifiable as such, including murder, bodily injury, restriction of liberty, theft of public or private property, or destruction of cities and settlements without a military necessity.[241] The following were also classified as crimes: the desecration of corpses, the conduct of medical experiments without the patients' consent, even if done in the interest of humanity as a whole,[242] and destruction of cultural property.[243] It also discussed the criminality of the practice of hostage taking, on the basis of Ehrlich's expert opinions filed in connection with Fischer's trial.[244]

With regard to the principles of responsibility for international crimes (see also Chapter 12), it will be expedient to note the way in which the NTN dealt with the issue of participation in a criminal union or execution of orders. Already before the IMT's judgment, the NTN considered the fact of membership in certain groups classified as criminal to be a separate crime, as long as the given individuals had discharged specific functions.[245] Interestingly, the NTN did not feel bound by the list of organizations deemed criminal by the IMT.[246] It also regarded as criminal the authorities of the Generalgouvernement (from the Kreis- Stadthauptmann tier up).[247] The NTN also regarded the authorities of a concentration camp as a criminal group (at least in respect of camps created within the territory of Poland).[248] It pointed out that the camps were an instrument of systematic commission of crimes against humanity, with the goal of unlawful imprisonment and deprivation of health, property and life of specified persons and groups, on account of their race, ethnicity, religion or political beliefs.[249] The difference compared to the trial of Majdanek staff was that the NTN explicitly defined the criminal group as including the German authorities, camp administration and staff, outside of the prisoners compelled to

241 NTN, Fischer case et al.: 57; NTN, Höss case: 124.

242 NTN, Auschwitz case: 186; NTN, Höss case: 128.

243 NTN, Forster case: 273–274, 295, 298; NTN, Bühler case: 326–327; NTN, Fischer case et al.: 60–61; NTN, Greiser case: 14, 18.

244 Cyprian, Sawicki (1962a): 134.

245 NTN, Fischer case et al.: 50–52 (Fischer), 53 (Meisinger), 74 (Leist), 83 (Meisinger), 83 (Daume). See also NTN, Greiser case: 4; NTN, Göth case: 24–25; NTN, Höss case: 93, 99; NTN, Auschwitz case: 145; NTN, Forster case: 263; NTN, Bühler case: 325.

246 NTN, Auschwitz case: 251–252. IMT did not recognize as criminal the following organizations: the Reich Cabinet, the SA, the General Staff and High Command of Wehrmacht. Polish courts respected those findings in their jurisprudence.

247 NTN, Fischer case et al.: 57.

248 NTN, Auschwitz case: 255; Klafkowski (1968a): 26–27.

249 NTN, Auschwitz case: 252–253.

discharge certain administrative functions.[250] It was on the occasion of the Auschwitz trial that the NTN emphasized that, just as the SS as a whole, so should the Auschwitz staff be regarded as a criminal organization, entailing criminal responsibility on the basis of membership alone. The responsibility was, therefore, borne by individuals who 'only' performed the selection, took the prisoners' food away, injected the Zyklon-B or transported corpses to the crematories.[251] The Tribunal emphasized that the 20th century was a century of collective human agency in every field of life, and the commission of crimes in a group was an aggravating circumstance, as crimes of that type were even more dangerous than crimes committed by individuals.[252] The NTN also held that the criminal responsibility was incurred by all individuals having assisted the commission of the crimes[253] or encouraged or incited them.[254]

When considering the responsibility for membership in a criminal group or conspiracy against the achievements of general human culture and civilization,[255] the NTN believed that the defendant's individual acts did not have to be proven, but what was important was to identify the acts of the criminal conspiracy and the degree of the defendant's participation.[256] It clearly noted, however, that the goal was not to depart from the necessity of attributing individual culpability when determining the individual's guilt or to impose responsibility on behalf of others. The goal was only to affirm that modern crimes required the participation of more or less numerous groups of perpetrators and communities of diverse kinds and diverse degrees of direct co-operation.[257] If one acceded to a group in which co-operation, assistance and obedience – and initiative, on command levels – were the obligations of membership, one accepted responsibility for everything the group did, from which personal responsibility derived.[258] However, it remained to be determined whether the individual acceded to the organization of their own volition or by compulsion and what position

250 *Ibidem*: 254.

251 *Ibidem*: passim (see excerpts concerning Koch, Götz, Medefind, Möckel, Mandl, Kraus, Kremer, Büntrock).

252 NTN, Fischer et al. case: 58–59.

253 NTN, Bühler case: 374–375.

254 NTN, Fischer et al. case: 53; NTN, Greiser case: 16; NTN, Auschwitz case: 242.

255 NTN, Greiser case: 10.

256 NTN, Höss case: 134; Cyprian, Sawicki (1949): 11.

257 NTN, Greiser case: 16; Cyprian, Sawicki (1949): 19.

258 NTN, Greiser case: 16–17; NTN, Fischer et al. case: 58.

they held.[259] Without a doubt, a command role determined responsibility for the activities of the group (as in the case of Arthur Liebehenschel[260]), whether or not one participated in the specific acts.[261] In every case, the NTN verified that the members had been aware of the activities of the organization of which they had been members and that they had ways of influencing those activities.[262] The NTN's adherence to the principle of individual culpability is demonstrated by the acquittal of Hans Münch. He was acquitted because it had been demonstrated that he had been ordered to work at the camp against his will and attempted to help the camp inmates.[263]

Already prior to the first trial before the NTN, it was feared that the defendants would attempt to evade responsibility by claiming to have acted in the execution of orders.[264] The NTN, however, explicitly stated that an unlawful order led to the responsibility of both the issuer and the executor,[265] thus ruling that the doctrine of blind obedience to orders (*Kadavergehorsam*) could not apply.[266] The matter of orders was associated with the one of membership in a criminal union. For the NTN emphasized that if one had acceded to a group in which absolute subordination had been required, then one thereby had accepted the responsibility for executing the orders issued within that group.[267] Thus, the key moment was that of joining the group, not of taking the order. In the NTN's opinion, in the case of individuals holding high positions, who were fully aware of the unlawfulness of the order, acting in the execution of orders could not even serve as a mitigating circumstance.[268] On the contrary, the fact that the defendants complied with their orders eagerly, even demonstrating initiative of their own, constituted an aggravating circumstance.[269]

Some defendants – Greiser and Höss – claimed that they could not be held responsible for the crimes committed by everyone who had formally

259 NTN, Bühler case: 380.
260 NTN, Auschwitz case: 195.
261 NTN, Greiser case: 14–15; NTN, Bühler case: 359.
262 NTN, Höss case: 95; NTN, Forster case: 278.
263 NTN, Auschwitz case: 258.
264 Bartoszkiewicz (1946): 301.
265 NTN, Greiser case: 17; NTN, Bühler case: 369, 379; see also Sawicki (1968): 270.
266 NTN, Greiser case: 16.
267 NTN, Fischer et al. case: 58–59.
268 NTN, Auschwitz case: 259; NTN, Bühler case: 369, 371.
269 NTN, Höss case: 134; NTN, Fischer et al. case: 67.

been subordinate to them.[270] However, the Tribunal attributed to them intention in the form of *dolus eventualis*, whereby even if a person did not intend to commit the crime but foresaw and accepted the possibility of its commission, then they may be attributed the responsibility for the crime.[271] The Tribunal developed upon the doctrine of command responsibility, concluding that where the individuals concerned had the opportunity to prevent the crimes or were aware of the possibility that the crimes would occur but did not react to that possibility,[272] or they approved of the crimes upon becoming aware of them,[273] they were fully responsible. Venturing even further, the NTN found Greiser responsible for the crimes inspired by him intellectually,[274] as well as for the transmission of the orders alone, as in Daume's case.[275] The Tribunal also rightly stressed the key role of the 'simple clerks' such as Bühler, who composed the criminal system and ensured the effective operation of the criminal machinery.[276]

As one can see, therefore, the NTN's decisions were highly influential when it came to the interpretation of the elements of the criminal offences classified as international crimes, as well as responsibility for them, especially with regard to the concept of a criminal organization/criminal union and command responsibility, including civilian superiors, such as Bühler, the 'office criminal'.[277] Thus, the emphasis of Cyprian and Sawicki, writing of the NTN's work as the, 'apex achievement of Polish judiciary,' can hardly be surprising.[278] That was noted, among others, also by Gabriel Finder and Alexander Prusin, who warned against the perception of postwar Polish court decisions as the typical Stalinist show trials,[279] although they were correct in pointing out certain inadequacies of the procedure (insufficient time for the defence to prepare for the trial and inability to call all the witnesses; in the case of the Auschwitz trial, also the excessive workload on the defence counsel).[280]

270 NTN, Höss case: 132.
271 NTN, Fischer et al. case: 69, 71.
272 NTN, Auschwitz case: 196; NTN, Bühler case: 351.
273 NTN, Fischer et al. case: 68.
274 NTN, Greiser case: 16.
275 NTN, Fischer et al. case: 86.
276 NTN, Bühler case: 343, 371.
277 NTN, Bühler case: 343; see also Lubecka (2021): passim; Weichert (1948): 120ff.
278 Cyprian, Sawicki (1962c): XI.
279 Finder, Prusin (2018): 6.
280 *Ibidem*: 127; Prusin (2013): 136.

The NTN ceased to operate after handing down its last judgment in 1948, albeit the legal basis for its functioning had not formally been repealed.[281]

5.3 *The Common Courts*

On the basis of the Decree Abolishing the Special Criminal Courts, the cases referred to them were taken over by regional courts.[282] In July 1949, there was a reshuffle in the *ratione materiae* jurisdiction of common courts on the basis of amendments to the Code of Criminal Procedure, Regulation on the Common Court System and other legislation.[283] The court of appeals became the first-instance court for cases of acts mentioned by the August Decree and chapter II of the small criminal code. With the reform of 1950,[284] courts of appeals (*sądy apelacyjne*) were abolished, as were regional courts (*sądy okręgowe*) and municipal courts (*sądy grodzkie*). In their place, voivodeship courts (*sądy wojewódzkie*), which took over the proceedings under the August Decree and *powiat* courts (*sądy powiatowe*) were established. In 1975, the latter were replaced by district courts (*sądy rejonowe*), following changes to the administrative subdivision of the country.[285]

Several problems must be mentioned with regard to the conviction statistics under the August Decree. The statistics are imprecise, data are missing for certain periods, and the distinction is not drawn between collaboration and war crimes or the courts entering the judgments.[286] And thus Marcin Birt, relying on data from the Statistics Section of the Ministry of Justice, concluded that by January 1948, a total of 9463 individuals had been convicted, of whom the majority – 7427 people – received prison terms up to 10 years, and 981 were given prison terms exceeding 10 years; and 1055 were sentenced to death. The data covered both special and common courts.[287] Andrew Kornbluth gives the number of persons accused before various courts (whether special or common) of war crimes or collaboration under the August Decree in the 12 years starting from 1946 at 32 thousand,

---

281 Jakubowski (2002): 50.

282 This subchapter was authored by Karolina Wierczyńska.

283 Dz.U.1949.33.243.

284 The 1950 Act amending the Law on the System of Common Courts, Dz.U.38.347 (*Ustawa z dnia 20 lipca 1950 r. o zmianie prawa o ustroju sądów powszechnych*).

285 The 1975 Act on The Two Tiers of Administrative Subdivision of the State and amending the Act on the National Councils, Dz.U.1975.16.91 (*Ustawa z dnia 28 maja 1975 r. o dwustopniowym podziale administracyjnym Państwa oraz o zmianie ustawy o radach narodowych*).

286 Kubicki (1963): 178–180.

287 Birt (2019): 72.

resulting in 20 thousand convictions, including 1835 capital sentences.[288] According to Anna Machnikowska, when it comes to the statistics from common courts, the vast majority of death sentences came down in cases of crimes classified under the August Decree,[289] but – as she notes – the statistics are not precise. Other sources claim 5463 August Decree convictions by the end of 1947, out of which 305 death sentences, yet others 3690 convictions, out of which 143 capital.[290]

As far as the defendants' nationalities are concerned, according to Leszek Kubicki's estimates, a total of approximately 18 thousand individuals were convicted under the August Decree in 1946–1960, of whom 25% (approximately 4.5 thousand) were German nationals.[291] According to Czesław Pilichowski, a total of 5340 German nationals were sentenced in 1944–1970.[292]

The data provided by Elżbieta Kobierska-Motas appear to be the most accurate, challenging some of the calculations done by Kubicki or Pilichowski. For she acknowledges that some of the records have been destroyed or gone missing or are incomplete.[293] Given the lack of complete archival data, the ultimate numbers and nationalities of those judged under the August Decree are difficult to determine. On the basis of the annual reports compiled by the Ministry of Justice, Kobierska-Motas estimates a total of approximately 20 thousand convictions under the August Decree in 1944–1988. Apart from the 3954 convictions handed down by the special courts and the 49 convictions in the 7 cases tried by the Supreme National Tribunal, the regional courts issued 12,247 judgments, and the remainder (i.e. more than 3.5 thousand) came from courts of appeals, voivodeship courts and *powiat* courts.[294]

One has to emphasize very clearly that the postwar justice system was used in the persecutions of persons regarded as enemies of the communist system. The communist authorities visited repressions upon the members of the structures of the Underground State. In the common courts, their cases neighboured those of the Nazis, which in a way was to elevate the

288 Kornbluth (2021): 7.

289 Machnikowska (2008): 312.

290 *Ibidem.*

291 Kubicki (1963): 182, similarily Brewing (2022): 279. This means that a great number of cases involved Polish nationals – some involving collaboration or other offences common at the type, and some the activities of the Underground State.

292 After Jasiński (2018): 113.

293 Kobierska-Motas (1991): 19.

294 Kobierska-Motas (1992): 18.

profile of the case and create a 'presumption of similar gravity of crimes.'[295] For example, it was on the basis of the August Decree that a death sentence was imposed on General August Emil Fieldorf (*nom de guerre* 'Nil'),[296] the organizer and commander of the Home Army's Directorate of Diversion and Deputy Commander-in-Chief. The execution was carried out in 1953. The Supreme Court's panel was composed of Emil Merz, Gustaw Auscaler and Igor Andrejew.[297] The Decree on Responsibility for the September Defeat and Fascization of State Life also served as the basis for the conviction and 6-year prison sentence of Mieczysław Siewierski, the first prosecutor of the Supreme Court and prosecutor of the NTN (he prosecuted Arthur Greiser and Albert Forster, among others) for the fascization of political life.[298] Apparently, the authorities intended to discredit his conspirational activities within the Government Delegation for Poland. The trial itself came as a shock, for Siewierski had seemed to be trusted by the authorities.[299] He was imprisoned in the same block with Forster, whom he had prosecuted before the NTN.[300] Similar examples of judicial crimes,[301] unfortunately, abound.[302]

Approximately 20 thousand trials of Nazis suspected of crimes were carried out before Polish common courts. The defendants were allowed to contact their families, receive letters and parcels, and had constant medical care.[303] The conditions in the prisons were poor; equally poor for all inmates. They certainly were not treated worse than members of the Polish opposition. Kazimierz Moczarski, who spent almost a year in the same cell

295 Machnikowska (2008): 312; Paczkowski (2019): 167ff.

296 Those convicted and executed on the basis of the same provisions include not only General Fieldorf 'Nil' but also Bolesław Kontrym 'Żmudzin' and Bronisław Chajęcki, Municipal President Starzyński's deputy during the days of the defence of Warsaw in September 1939; life terms were handed out to Kazimierz Moczarski, Jerzy Czekanowski, Stanisław Cybulski and other members of the resistance and soldiers of the Home Army – Steinbergowa (2016): 101.

297 Those judges, when hearing a revision appeal against the General's capital conviction, upheld the judgment passed by the voivodeship court following a staged trial – Gardocki (1997): 218.

298 Prusin (2013): 139.

299 Siewierski was later rehabilitated by the Supreme Court – see Lubecka (2021): 212–213.

300 Finder, Prusin (2018): 130.

301 A judicial crime occurs when an act of justice is transformed into an act of repression performed in violation of the basic principles of fair trial and becomes an abuse of judicial power, and the judgement constitutes the implementation of a previously made political decision. See more: Zdrójkowski (2022): 179ff.

302 Machcewicz mentions 300 individuals in: Jasiński (2018): 10.

303 Lubecka (2011): 41.

with Jürgen Stroop, responsible for the liquidation of Warsaw Ghetto, recalled that the latter officially received a double food ration and was entitled to a bed, the latter of which he proposed to give up for Moczarski.[304] Stroop's charges included membership in the SS – an organization deemed criminal by the Nuremberg judgment. Moreover, he was accused of having, with his orders, procured the murders of at least 56,065 people and the deaths of tens of thousands more in the burning underground sewers and other hideouts. He was also accused of the destruction of the ghetto building complex and destruction of a synagogue located outside of the ghetto. Stroop provided the evidence of his own crimes, compiling the documentation of the liquidation of the ghetto – the aforementioned Stroop report (used as evidence in the Nuremberg trial).[305]

Stroop was not the only high-ranking Nazi judged by Polish common courts for war crimes (sentenced to death and executed in 1952[306]). His collaborator and executor of the liquidation of the ghetto, Franz Konrad, was judged in the same trial and executed together with Stroop.

Another high-profile defendant was Erich Koch – the Oberpräsident for East Prussia and Reichskommissar for Ukraine. Charged with crimes under Articles 1, 2 and 4 of the August Decree, he was convicted and sentenced to death on 9.03.1959 (the execution was not carried out; the criminal died in 1986 in prison in Barczewo). Paul Otto Geibel, in turn, who had been the commandant of the SS and police for the Warsaw district from March 1944 and participated in quelling the Warsaw Uprising, was judged by the Voivodeship Court for the Capital City of Warsaw in 1954 and sentenced to life in prison[307] for crimes committed while putting down the Warsaw Uprising (in the same cell with him was Bogdan Deczkowski, a soldier of the Home Army Directorate of Diversion). Geibel later committed suicide while serving his term. It is also worth mentioning Erich Engels, who was imprisoned in the same cell with Władysław Bartoszewski, a member of the Polish resistance movement.[308] Engels was sentenced to death on 13.03.1950 and

---

304 Moczarski (2018): 11 and 13; Gustav Schielke, who shared a cell with them, had a straw mattress instead of a bed.

305 See also Finder, Prusin (2018): 152ff.

306 Earlier, in March 1947, the American military tribunal in Dachau had sentenced him to death for having issued the orders for the murder of Allied parachutists. Subsequently, however, he was extradited to Poland to stand trial for the liquidation of the Warsaw Ghetto and the murder of almost 60 thousand people. His trial began on 1951 before the Voivodeship Court for the Capital City of Warsaw.

307 Finder, Prusin (2018): 2013.

308 *Ibidem*: 133.

executed in 1951 at Mokotów Prison in Warsaw for war crimes committed in the Generalgouvernement. On 29.01.1949, Josef Grzimek, the commandant of several Nazi labour camps in the occupied territory of Poland and 'ghetto liquidator', as he had been called, was sentenced to death by the Regional Court in Warsaw for war crimes.[309] Kurt Ludwig Burgsdorff, the last governor of the GG's Cracow district, accused, among other things, of having participated in the works of the NSDAP, was sentenced by the Regional Court in Cracow to 3 years' imprisonment. His lack of demonstrated ill will towards the Poles was considered by the court as a mitigating circumstance.[310] After completing his term, he returned to Germany.

The situation of the Nazi criminals convicted by Polish courts or awaiting trial changed as a result of amnesties. With Article 4 of the Amnesty Act of 22.11.1952, penalties already imposed were reduced (the death penalty commuted to 15 years' imprisonment, and life in prison to 12 years' imprisonment). However, the Act excluded its own application to crimes under Article 1 (killings of civilians, members of the military or prisoners of war) and 4 (membership in criminal groups) of the August Decree (Article 9(1)(3)).[311] Article 8(1) of the Amnesty Act of 27.04.1956[312] stipulated that proceedings should not be initiated and if already initiated, the discontinued, with regard to the crimes specified in the August Decree, except for the crimes set out by Article 1(1) of the Decree. As a result, it was no longer possible to judge criminals for membership in criminal groups. Those affected favourably included Erich Koch.[313] The Amnesty Decree of 19.07.1977[314] similarly excluded its own application to the crimes set out by Article 1(1) of the August Decree, concerning the killings of the civilian population, military persons and prisoners of war.

The Polish courts did not manage to judge all of the major criminals, e.g. obtain the extradition of and bring to justice those responsible for the theft

309 *Ibidem*: 136.

310 Detailed study on a proces: *Więzienne zapiski Kurta von Burgsdorff – krakowskiego Gubernatora czasu schyłku listopad 1943 – styczeń 1945* [The Prison Notes of Kurt von Burgsdorff – the Kraków Governor in the latter years of November 1943 – January 1945] online at: https://niemieckikrakowblog.wordpress.com/2020/01/17/wiezienne-zapiski-carla-von-burgsdorff-krakowskiego-gubernatora-czasu-schylku-12-1944-01-1945/.

311 Dz.U.1952.146.309.

312 Dz.U.1956.11.57.

313 Majewski (2008): 50; Kubicki (1963): 184.

314 Dz.U.1977.24.102.

of works of art, such as Kajetan Mühlmann.[315] The Americans rejected the extradition request in his case, claiming that the theft of works of art was not a war crime. Efforts towards the extradition of Eberhardt Lütze, accused of the theft and confiscation of Veit Stoss's altarpiece from Saint Mary's Basilica in Cracow, were also met with refusal. Extradition was also denied in the case of Walter Huppenhothen – the head of the Gestapo in Lublin (the American authorities denied the requests despite the evidence of guilt provided by the Polish authorities – at present, Huppenhothen's collaboration with US military intelligence is a known fact).[316]

Justice was also denied to the victims of the crime committed in the Wola part of Warsaw.[317] Erich von dem Bach-Zelewski, the criminal whose role in the Nuremberg trial was that of a witness and not a suspect, was never held criminally responsible for his bloody suppression of the Warsaw Uprising and crimes committed during World War II on the civilian population – Jews, Poles and Russians, despite his name being listed at UNWCC list no 50, at number 8.[318] Similarly, Heinz Reinefahrt, whose troops took part in the murder of tens of thousands of Wola inhabitants, was never punished for his crimes, his extradition to Poland having been repeatedly denied.[319] Today, outside of isolated cases,[320] there is no possibility of judging the suspects, as they are no longer among the living – Article 17(1) of Polish Code of Criminal Procedure provides for a mandatory discontinuance on the defendant's (suspect's) death. Many of the potential witnesses have also died.

As noted by the subject literature, Soviet crimes have not been brought to trial,[321] whether during that period or at any time ever. Furthermore, the political entanglement of the courts and instrumentalization of the justice system cast a shadow on the achievements of the postwar justice system,

---

315 Michałowska (2017): 39, extensively on German policy of looting works of art Kudelski (2005).

316 Kobierska-Motas (1991): 139–140.

317 Broader on Wola massacre and perspectives on prosecution: Grzebyk (2019b): 107; Kuczyńska (2019a): 123; Krzan (2019): 157; Wierczyńska (2019): 175.

318 Kobierska-Motas (1991): 140.

319 *Ibidem*: 141, broader on problems with extradition and prosecution of Reinefahrt see: Martii (2016).

320 Such as that of Irmgard Furchner, the shorthand typist of Stutthof sentenced in Germany to 2 years imprisonment for participation in the murder of more than 10 thousand camp inmates, see: Paul Kirby, Robert Greenall, *Irmgard Furchner: Nazi typist guilty of complicity in 10,500 murder*, 20.12.2022, https://www.bbc.com/news/world-europe-64036465.

321 Kowalski (2019): 235.

especially in the context of the Cold War and the accompanying critique of the 'European achievements of socialism.'

5.4 *The Supreme Court*

When it comes to the judgments of the courts in cases of violations of the August Decree and certain other provisions, attention is drawn to the judgments of the Supreme Court, as they informed the decision-making of the lower courts and influenced the development of Polish legal scholarship.[322]

The Supreme Court's judgment must be considered in the context of the Nuremberg judgment, as the latter constituted the point of reference for the judgment of individuals for the crimes committed. With its judgments, the Supreme Court rather dynamically enriched the discussion on participation in the crimes, sparked by the Nuremberg judgment. Referring to the list of criminal organizations provided in the latter, the Supreme Court specified – invoking Article 10 of the IMT Charter – that the criminal nature of those organizations would be regarded as proved and not to be doubted.[323]

It expanded the list of the organizations it regarded as criminal, in which the membership alone was thus subject to punishment.[324] It also discussed organizations that could not be regarded as criminal. Among other points, the Supreme Court noted that in judging the individual's membership in criminal organizations, one had to examine whether it was voluntary, whether the individual had been aware of the organization's objectives, was ideologically bound to the organization and had consent to the co-operation within it. In the Supreme Court's opinion, in such cases, free will was crucial to the determination of responsibility.[325] This is with the caveat that the Supreme Court also acknowledged that: 'the responsibility for participation in a criminal group [wa]s, however, a responsibility separate from the responsibility for one's own committed criminal acts.'[326] It stipulated moreover, that: 'the burden of proof that the induction had been forcible is, in the relevant case, incumbent on the defendant.'[327] The Supreme Court would additionally remark as follows: 'membership in the "Waffen S.S." military formations of the Protective Squadrons constitutes the criminal offence

322 This subchapter was authored by Karolina Wierczyńska.

323 SN, Judgement, 10.02.1948, LuK 197/47.

324 Kubicki (1963): 146–155.

325 SN, Judgement, 25.06.1948, K 582/47, OSN(K) 1948/4/115.

326 *Ibidem*.

327 SN, Decision, 15.03.1948, K 1112/47, OSN(K) 1948/2/31.

set out in Article 4(3)(b) of the Decree of 31 August 1944 (…) with the exclusion of those individuals who were inducted by force and did not commit war crimes.'[328]

Apart from the organizations deemed criminal by the Nuremberg judgment, the Supreme Court regarded as such the leadership of the administration of the Generalgouvernement, the camp structure, the Ukrainian SS formation,[329] as well as the Ukrainian Insurgent Army, which it deemed to have been created by an association acting in the German interest for the purpose of: 'eradicating the Polish element and the anti-fascist elements within the territory of Ukraine, as well as fighting the Soviet Union in reliance on the Nazi Third Reich, whereby it constitute[d] a criminal organization within the meaning of Article 4 of the August Decree.'[330] As for the SA assault troops, though the Supreme Court initially excluded their criminal nature,[331] it noted that while SA membership did not in itself constitute a crime within the meaning of the August Decree, the affiliation of a Polish national with the SA created the: 'presumption of having claimed German nationality' (Article 1(1) of the Decree of 28.06.1946).[332] The caveat was also made that although the Nuremberg tribunal had excluded the SA from its list of criminal organizations the membership in which constituted a criminal offence, cases had been noted of SA members committing crimes. The Supreme Court acknowledged: 'it cannot, however, be claimed that members of the SA universally participated in the commission of criminal acts or even knew of those, i.e. that their acts can be attributed a universal character and thus the implementation of an organizationally predefined purpose or plan.'[333] However, it did not exclude the recognition of the specific activity of one of the SA troops as a criminal group.'[334]

The court did not regard as criminal such organizations as the order-keeping police (Ordnungspolizei), the fire police (Feuerschutzpolizei), building police (Baupolizei), field and forest police (Feld-und Forstpolizei), as it had not been their objective to commit crimes.[335] Accordingly, service in an ordinary police force could not be understood as: 'tantamount with

328 *Ibidem.*

329 Kubicki (1963): 147–150.

330 SN, Judgement, 22.09.1950, K 1147/50.

331 SN, Decision, 6.10.1947, K 666/47; see also Pasek (2002): 100ff.

332 SN, Decision, 6.10.1947, K 666/47.

333 *Ibidem.*

334 Kubicki (1963): 149–150.

335 SN, Judgement, 27.02.1948, K 164/47.

participation in the criminal organization known under the name of Secret State Police (Gestapo).' Polish Auxiliary Battalions in German Service and Volunteer Polish Corps assisting the German army were not regarded as criminal organizations, either, albeit it was found that the voluntary accession of a Polish national to such an organization could be regarded as the crime defined in Article 101(1) of the Criminal Code.[336] The Supreme Court also made findings relating to positions of leadership – namely that the position of Ortsgruppenkassenleiter was not a leadership position, while Reichsleiters, Gauleiters, Kreisleiters and Ortsgruppenleiters, members of the Reichsleitung and office heads in the clerical staffs of Reichsleitung, Gauleitung and Kreisleitung tiers of the NSDAP should be regarded as positions of leadership (in the light of Article 4(3)(a) of the August Decree).[337] The Supreme Court also decided that having served as an interpreter or translator at the Gestapo could imply involvement in that criminal organization within the meaning of Article 4 of the August Decree.[338]

The Supreme Court also addressed the activities of the confidential informers, finding that they could be regarded as criminal where the perpetrator had acted with the intention of acting in the interest of the authorities of the German state.[339] In another case, the court held that reporting to a German village foreman on Soviet soldiers arriving in a village could be classified as a crime within the meaning of Article 1(2) of the August Decree.[340] Acceptance of the role of a confidential Gestapo informant was regarded in the same manner.[341] The court even found that acting in the interest of the occupation authorities by reporting to the German military police on German deserters, who were subsequently shot, was a criminal offence because contributing to: 'the punishment of German deserters prevented the spread of desertion and therewith the earlier disintegration of the German Army.'[342] As for a person who beat and reported on German labourers, the Supreme Court noted that acting to the detriment of the civilian population for the purpose of acting in the occupier's interest did not necessarily have to be limited to death or bodily injury alone but could

336 SN, Decision (7 judges), 25.05.1948, K 205/48.

337 SN, Decision, 23.02.1948, K 949/47, OSN(K) 1948/1/1; also extensively Pasek (2002): 101–102.

338 SN, Judgement, 6.06.1950, K 576/50, OSN(K) 1950/2/8.

339 SN, Decision, 24.06.1949, K.800/49.

340 SN, Judgement, 22.08.1951, II K 531/51.

341 SN, Judgement, 10.08.1951, II K 530/51, OSN(K) 1952/2/16.

342 SN, Judgement, 6.06.1950, K 374/50, OSN(K) 1950/2/12.

apply to any case in which the perpetrator had had the intention – even *dolus eventualis* – of harming the victim.[343]

The Supreme Court, and especially its Military Chamber, did not escape the instrumentalization of the justice system (let it be recalled that the Supreme Court did not grant the revision appeal from the capital conviction of General Fieldorf 'Nil'). Unfortunately, that casts a shadow on the achievements of the postwar justice system. It cannot, however, be ignored that the Supreme Court developed on the stipulations of the Nuremberg judgment, expounding a clear interpretation of the principles of responsibility for the crimes committed during WWII.

6 Academic Life

The Polish Faculty of Law at Oxford University in the **United Kingdom** was closed on 5.10.1946 (some sources specify 31.03.1947). On 9.12.1949, on the other hand, Polish University Abroad/Polish University in Exile (*Polski Uniwersytet na Obczyźnie*, PUNO) was established. Stefan Glaser, Wacław Komarnicki and Wiktor Sukiennicki were among those lecturing at its Faculty of Law and Social Science, of which Jerzy Gawenda became the dean.[344] From 1945 onward, Glaser (in connection with his diplomatic mission in Brussels) formed increasingly close ties to **Belgium** and its universities in Liège, Leuven and Ghent. Considering the powerful assistance he later provided in the professional development of academics from the Polish People's Republic (e.g. Leszek Kubicki and Marian Cieślak), the Belgian foothold must be regarded as an important point on the map of Polish scholarship of international criminal law in the postwar period, with authors such as Sawicki and Cyprian quoting abundantly from Glaser's works.[345] After the war, Glaser published a number of highly cited works such as: *Les infractions internationales, les délits politiques et l'extradition* (1949); *Introduction à l'étude du droit international pénal* (1954); *Infraction internationale: ses éléments constitutifs et ses aspects juridiques: exposé sur la base du droit pénal comparé* (1957); the two-volume *Droit international pénal conventionnel* (1970/1978); *Culpabilité en droit international pénal* (1960); and *The Charter of the Nuremberg Tribunal and New Principles of International Law Perspectives on the Nuremberg Trial* (1947/2008).

343 SN, Judgement, 30.11.1948, LuK 495/48.

344 Mierzwa (2018): 91.

345 Cyprian, Sawicki (1956b): 61ff.

Come the end of WWII, Polish scholars staying abroad feared returning home. An interesting case was that of Wacław Komarnicki, who tried to find employment in Warsaw. For on 18.12.1945, he was unanimously recommended by the appropriate selection board for the position of professor and head of the University of Warsaw's Chair of Theory and Law of State, in which regard the dean, Stefan Zaleski, contacted him. In 1946, Komarnicki confirmed his willingness to take the position and, on 14.06.1947, he wrote to the dean that he would be returning to the country and able to start teaching with the beginning of the academic year 1947/48, but before his arrival he would insist on receiving an official nomination from the ministry of education. Komarnicki was eager to settle the matter quickly, as with the closing down of the Polish faculty at Oxford, his prospects of employment had greatly diminished. He insisted that, since his nomination was late in coming, perhaps there was the possibility of contracting him to teach some lectures. In July 1947, he also asked for his travel expenses to be paid (invoking his professorial statute, high costs and lack of income).

The new dean of the Faculty of Law, Jan Wasilkowski (Zaleski, from September 1946, went on to serve as vice rector) in his letters of 11 (no. 387/47) and 19.09.1947, recalled the Ministry of Education circular of 4.06.1947 whereby the chairs of the professors who had failed to repatriate by 1 February 1947 were to be deemed vacant. The same applied also to the professors of the universities in Lviv and Vilnius, as the staff had been transferred to Wrocław and Toruń, respectively. In October, Wasilkowski notified Komarnicki that there was no possibility of obtaining an official nomination without arriving in Poland. Komarnicki decided against taking the risk of repatriation. He tried to leave for the USA,[346] but there were no perspectives of his finding employment in one of the universities there, even though he did command some recognition, as illustrated by the fact that he was invited to lecture at the Hague Academy in 1949 (he published a lecture titled *La définition de l'agresseur dans le droit international moderne*) and by his activities in the International Association of University Professors and Lecturers. He co-operated with Glaser in the establishment of the Polish Society of Arts and Sciences Abroad. He also worked at the British Museum. He died in 1954 in London.

The scholarly émigrés (in this case, in the USA) also included Lemkin, who published several articles on genocide after the war: *Genocide – a modern crime* (1945); *Genocide* (1946); *Le génocide* (1946); and *Genocide as a*

346 See letter of W. Komarnicki to the Executive Committee of the Central European University Professors and Lecturers Association. 7.09.1951.

Crime Under International Law (1947). Too preoccupied with his efforts for the adoption of the Genocide Convention and subsequent ratification by the individual states, he was unable to gain a permanent footing in the academic circles of America.

Also abroad during the postwar period, Krystyna Marek – graduate of the Jagiellonian University and author of publications in the fields of the *jus cogens* (1968) and criminal responsibility of a state (1978) – conducted her research in Geneva in **Switzerland** (at the University of Geneva and in the Graduate Institute of International and Development Studies).

The end of the war allowed academic centres to be rebuilt and academic activities to be resumed in Poland. Due to the destruction of Warsaw, the initial seat of government immediately after the war was **Łódź**. It cannot be surprising, therefore, that the University of Łódź, established by decree of 24.05.1945, was where the lawyers and jurists involved in the works of the Supreme Court, Ministry of Justice, etc., once again found academic employment. Such was the case with Rappaport (who remained in Łódź until the end of his life) and Jerzy Sawicki (who taught there since 1948). In the postwar period, Rappaport focused on executive criminal law (enforcement) and his translation of Beccaria, albeit one cannot possibly ignore his monograph titled *Naród-Zbrodniarz: przestępstwa hitleryzmu a naród niemiecki: szkic analityczny przestępczości i odpowiedzialności osobowo-zespołowej* (1945) ('A Nation-Criminal: the crimes of Hitlerism and the German nation: an analytical sketch of personal and team criminality and Responsibility'). Academics linked to the University of Łódź also included Jan Waszczyński, the author of an article titled *Zbrodnie przeciw ludzkości* (*narodziny i rozwój pojęcia*) (1986) ('Crimes against humanity (birth and development of the term').

In **Warsaw** – at the **University of Warsaw** – the main personality in the field of international criminal law, cited with relative frequency by foreign literature,[347] was Jerzy Sawicki. He served in a number of functions at the Ministry of Justice (as head of special supervision from 1945 and from 1946 as Director of the International Co-operation Bureau), Supreme Court and Supreme National Tribunal (as one of the prosecutors). Sawicki was the Polish delegate to the International Congresses of Democratic Lawyers (Paris 1946, Brussels 1947, Prague 1948) and representative at the Commission Internationale Pénale et Pénitentiaire. In 1947, at the Jagiellonian University, he defended his doctoral dissertation on the sociological-legal foundations of the responsibility of fascist criminals; it is also there that he gained the

347 Herzog (1975): 75.

position of docent on the basis of a work titled *Zbrodnie przeciwko ludzkości – rozwój i definicja* ('Crimes against humanity – development and definition'). From 1950 onward, he was employed by the University of Warsaw. In 1954, he took the Chair of Criminal Law, which he led until 1967. He published a number of monographs in the Polish and foreign languages: *Ludobójstwo: od pojęcia do konwencji 1933–1948* (1949) ('Genocide: from the term to the convention, 1933–1948); *Przestępstwo podżegania do wojny* (1951) ('The crime of incitement of war'); *De Nuremberg à la nouvelle Wehrmacht* (1958b); *Als sei Nürnberg nie gewesen. Die Abkehr von den völkerrechtlichen Prinzipien der Nürnberger Urteile* (1958a); and, together with Tadeusz Cyprian, *Agresja na Polskę w świetle dokumentów* (1946, co-authored also by Henryk Świątkowski) ('The aggression against Poland in the light of the documents'); *Prawo norymberskie* (1948) ('Nuremberg law'); *Głos ma prokurator …* (1962; co-authored also by Mieczysław Siewierski) ('The prosecutor may speak … '); *Nieznana Norymberga; dwanaście procesów norymberskich* (1965) ('The unknown Nuremberg: twelve Nuremberg trials'); *Ludzie i sprawy Norymbergi* (1967a) ('The people and cases of Nuremberg'); and *Nazi rule in Poland, 1939–1945* (co-authored also by Edward Rothert).

In the 50s of the 20th century, academics with ties to the University of Warsaw included Stanisław Pławski, the author of *Proces japońskich zbrodniarzy w Chabarowsku* (1950) ('The trial of the Japanese criminals in Khabarovsk'), who in the 60s migrated to France and publish, among other works, the *Étude des principes fondamentaux du droit international pénal* (1972). Manfred Lachs (also linked to the Institute of Law Studies of the Polish Academy of Sciences), having published his principal works in the field of international criminal law already during his wartime exile, also continued his research at the University of Warsaw. Although his postwar academic works rarely revisited the matter of responsibility for international crimes (despite his active involvement in the negotiation of the leading international documents in the field).

Another scholar with ties to the University of Warsaw was Marian Muszkat, who finished his legal studies there but took his doctoral degree in 1936 from the University of Nancy. He returned to Warsaw for his habilitation process on the basis of a dissertation titled *Międzynarodowe prawo karne, rozwój nowej dziedziny* (1950) ('International criminal law: the development of a new discipline'), which was never published.[348] It must be noted that the University of Warsaw Library collections do include his work from 1949,

348 Karski (2007a): 77.

titled *Zarys wykładu międzynarodowego prawa karnego* ('A lecture outline in international criminal law'), but it is not clear whether that served as the formal basis for his habilitation. His published works deal primarily with Nuremberg law and were published in Polish, as well as English and French. When, in 1957, he moved to Israel, as Marion Mushkat he advised the Yad Vashem on preparations for the trial of Adolf Eichmann. It is notable that Muszkat published in a number of languages (English, Chinese, Czech, French, German, Russian and Hungarian) and his bibliography includes several hundred entries, though of variable quality.

Those employed by the University of Warsaw further included Franciszek Ryszka, who wrote a number of works historical in nature but containing a great deal of legislative analysis: *Noc i mgła: Niemcy w okresie hitlerowskim* (1962/1966/1997) ('Night and mist: Germany during the Nazi period'); *Państwo stanu wyjątkowego: rzecz o systemie państwa i prawa Trzeciej Rzeszy* (1964/1974/1985) ('A state of emergency powers: the matter of the constitutional and legal system of the Third Reich'); *U źródeł sukcesu i klęski: szkice z dziejów hitleryzmu* (1972/1975) ('At the fount of success and defeat: sketches in the history of Hitlerism'); *"Sprawa polska" i sprawy Polaków: szkice z lat 1944–1946* (1966) ('The "Polish cause" and the cases of Poles: sketches from 1944–1946'); he also wrote a preface for Kazimierz Moczarski's *Conversations with an Executioner* (edition of 1983) and a number of other works on the various criminals and criminal organizations.

Another one was Remigiusz Bierzanek, also with links to the University of Łódź in the postwar period, the author of works such as *Ekstradycja w traktatach zawieranych przez państwa hetyckie* (1958) ('Extradition in treaties concluded by the Hittite states'); *Sur les origines du droit de la guere et de la paix* (1960); *Prawa człowieka w konfliktach zbrojnych* (1972) ('Human rights in armed conflicts'); *Represalia wojenne jako środek zapewniający przestrzeganie prawa międzynarodowego* (1978; in English as *Reprisals as a Mean of Enforcing the Laws of Warfare: The Old and the New Law*, 1979); *Wojna a prawo międzynarodowe* (1982) ('War and international law').

Other scholars lecturing at the University of Warsaw included Cezary Berezowski, the author of *Ochrona prawno-międzynarodowa zabytków i dzieł sztuki w czasie wojny* (1948) ('The protection of monuments and artworks in wartime under international law'); Ludwik Gelberg, the author of *Piractwa na morzach chińskich: próba analizy prawnej* (1956) ('Piracy in the Chinese seas: an attempt at legal analysis') and *Die Nürnberger Prinzipien und das moderne Völkerrecht* (1978); and Lech Gardocki, the author of *Zagadnienia internacjonalizacji odpowiedzialności karnej za przestępstwa popełnione za granicą* (1979) ('Problems in the internationalization of criminal responsibility for offences committed abroad') and *Zarys prawa karnego międzynarodowego* (1985) ('An outline of international criminal law'), who also published in German, e.g. *Über den Begriff des internationalen Strafrechts* (1986). In years 1962–1968, academics linked to the University of Warsaw also included Juliusz Katz-Suchy (also the Director of the Polish Institute of International Affairs), who often spoke on behalf of the MFA in discussions on drafts relating to international criminal law. It was he who, as the Polish representative, abstained from voting on the adoption of the Universal Declaration of Human Rights in 1948.[349] Another employee of the University of Warsaw was Roman Piotrowski, whose knowledge of international criminal law was relied on primarily in the works of the government-in-exile during WWII.

Warsaw was also home to the scholars of the **Institute of Law Studies of the Polish Academy of Sciences (PAN)**, such as Leszek Kubicki, the author of a monograph titled *Zbrodnie wojenne w świetle prawa polskiego* (1963) ('War crimes in the light of Polish law'), also cited in foreign works,[350] and co-author of the *System Prawa Karnego* (1985) ('Criminal law system'), in which he discussed the history of international criminal law; as well as Czesław Pilichowski of the PAN's Institute of History, but above all those of the **Chief Commission for the Investigation of Nazi Crimes in Poland.** Pilichowski was the author of numerous publications such as *Trybunał Norymberski i zasady norymberskie a sprawa ścigania i karania hitlerowskich zbrodniarzy wojennych w latach 1945–1971* (1971) ('The Nuremberg tribunal and Nuremberg principles and the matter of prosecution and punishment of Nazi war criminals in 1945–1971'); *Badanie i ściganie zbrodni hitlerowskich 1944–1974* (1975) ('Investigation and prosecution of Nazi crimes, 1945–1971); *No time-limit for these crimes* (1980a); and the editor of such important works as *Ekspertyzy i orzeczenia przed Najwyższym Trybunałem Narodowym* (1979–1981) ('Expert studies and rulings before the Supreme National Tribunal'); *Zbrodnie i sprawcy: ludobójstwo hitlerowskie przed sądem ludzkości historii* (1980) ('Crimes and perpetrators: Nazi genocide before the court of humanity and history'); *Ściganie i karanie sprawców zbrodni wojennych i zbrodni przeciwko ludzkości: (wybór dokumentów)* (1978) ('The prosecution and punishment of the perpetrators of war crimes and crimes against humanity: (selection of documents)'). Another scholar associated with the Chief Commission was Janusz Gumkowski, the co-author – together with Tadeusz Kułakowski – of *Zbrodniarze hitlerowscy*

349 Karski (2008): 320.

350 E.g. Herzog (1975): 140.

przed Najwyższym Trybunałem Narodowym (1961) ('The Nazi criminals before the Supreme National Tribunal').

It is also worth mentioning the **Polish Institute of Foreign Affairs**, headquartered in Warsaw, at one point (1950–1951) led by Muszkat, whose 'contributions' included struggle for the purity of the Marxist science of international law.[351] The Institute's staff included the aforementioned Ryszka (in 1961–1965) and Alfons Klafkowski, whose main works are *Okupacja niemiecka w Polsce w świetle prawa narodów* (1946) ('The German occupation in Poland in the light of the law of nations'); *Zasady norymberskie a rozwój prawa międzynarodowego* (1966) ('The Nuremberg principles and the development of international law'); *Obozy koncentracyjne hitlerowskie jako zagadnienie prawa międzynarodowego* (1968a) ('The Nazi concentration camps as a problem of international law') and *Ściganie zbrodniarzy wojennych w Niemieckiej Republice Federalnej w świetle prawa międzynarodowego* (1968b) ('The prosecution of war criminals in the Federal Republic of Germany in the light of international law'); as well as Renata Sonnenfeld, the author of an article titled *Pojęcie "międzynarodowego prawa karnego publicznego"* (1984) ('The notion of "public international criminal law"').

The aforementioned Klafkowski's primary ties, however, were with the **Adam Mickiewicz University in Poznań**, with which Bohdan Winiarski[352] also had some ties in the postwar period, limited as they were on account of his duties as a judge of the International Court of Justice. Poznań was also home to the **Institute for Western Affairs (Instytut Zachodni)**, of which Tadeusz Cyprian (also linked to the Adam Mickiewicz University and, as noted below, the Maria Curie-Skłodowska University in Lublin) served as deputy director in 1956–1957. The Institute's staff often discussed the legal aspects of the German occupation in their articles published in the *Przegląd Zachodni* ('Western Affairs Review').

The most notable among the internationalists of the **Jagiellonian University in Cracow** was Ludwik Ehrlich, who, however, outside of his expert opinions for the NTN, did not deal more extensively with the responsibility for international crimes. Among other academics, it is worth mentioning: Stanisław Nahlik, the author of, among other works, *L'extension du statut de combattant à la lumière du protocole I de Genève de 1977* (1979) and *La protection internationale des biens culturels en cas de conflit armé* (1967); Teofil Leśko (having played a reprehensible role in handing out capital convictions to members of the Polish Underground), who authored works such as *Konflikty*

351 Karski (2007a): 78; Kulski (1952): 543ff.

352 Sandorski (2004): 105–106.

zbrojne w świetle prawa międzynarodowego (1976) ('Armed conflicts in the light of international law') and *Międzynarodowe prawo konfliktów zbrojnych* (1979, and a number of subsequent editions) ('The international law of armed conflicts') and translated Lev Smirnov and Evgeny Zaitsev's *Przed tokijskim trybunałem* (1983) ('Before the Tokyo Tribunal'); as well as Andrzej Górbiel, the author of *Konieczność wojskowa w prawie międzynarodowym* (1970) ('Military necessity in international law').[353] Another academics with ties to the Jagiellonian University were Władysław Wolter or Andrzej Spotowski and the forensic researcher, Jan Sehn, who published *Obóz koncentracyjny Oświęcim-Brzezinka (Auschwitz-Birkenau): na podstawie dokumentów i źródeł* (1956 and later editions) ('The Oświęcim-Brzezinka (Auschwitz-Birkenua) concentration camp: on the basis of the documents and sources'.

The academics in **Wrocław**, at the **University of Wrocław**, included the aforementioned Franciszek Ryszka, as well as Kazimierz Kocot, Ludwik Ehrlich' assistant in 1938–1940 and author of works such as *Zagadnienie źródeł prawa międzynarodowego na tle współczesnej walki o pokój* (1953) ('The problem of the sources of international law against the background of the modern fight for peace'); as well as Jan Kolasa, who published an article titled *Proces Norymberski – aspekt proceduralny* (1988) ('The Nuremberg trial – the procedural aspect'). Under the tuition of Karol Wolfke, doctoral dissertations were defended by Adam Basak and Leon Szpak, both publishing in the field. Neither could one possibly ignore the activities of Karol Jonca and the importance of the *Studia nad Faszyzmem i Zbrodniami Hitlerowskimi* ('Studies into Fascism and Nazi Crimes') – a journal he founded and published from 1974 (in 2011, renamed to *Studia nad Autorytaryzmem i Totalitaryzmem* – 'Studies into Authoritarianism and Totalitarianism'). Last but not least, the aforementioned Sonnenfeld, linked since the mid-80s of the 20th century to the **University of Łódź**, completed her studies and defended her doctorate at the University of Warsaw. It is worth noting here that she herself fell victim of postwar anti-Semitism resulting in delays with her habilitation process and professorship, despite her meeting all of the requirements.[354] Luckily to Poland, Sonnenfeld opted against emigration and obtained her deserved degrees and titles, but a number of other valuable individuals (such as Jerzy Sztucki) preferred to emigrate, to the detriment of the Polish academia.

In **Toruń**, at the **Nicolaus Copernicus University**, notable scholars included Janusz Symonides, who had ties to that university for a long time

353 Barcik (2018): 72.

354 Menkes (2012): 244.

until 1989. Among other works, he published a chapter titled *Współpraca międzynarodowa w zwalczaniu przestępczości na morzu otwartym* (1985) ('International co-operation in fighting crime in the open sea').

In **Lublin**, at the **Maria Curie-Skłodowska University**, the main personalities linked to the development of international criminal law were Tadeusz Cyprian (1950–1953) and Aleksander Bramson (in the 50s of the 20th century also tied to the Polish Institute of International Affairs), the latter of whom had assisted Lachs in the preparation of the Polish indictment[355] and after the war published works on Nuremberg law, he also restored Polish Group of ILA;[356] and Jan Balicki, the author of a monograph titled *Pojęcie agresji w prawie międzynarodowym* (1952) ('The notion of aggression in international law'); *Apartheid: studium prawno-polityczne rasizmu w Afryce Południowej* (1967) ('The apartheid: a politico-legal study in racism in South Africa'); *Dyskryminacja rasowa w świetle prawa międzynarodowego* (1972) ('Racial discrimination in the light of international law'); *Dyskryminacja rasowa – przeszłość i teraźniejszość* (1986) ('Racial discrimination – the past and the present').

In **Katowice**, the **University of Silesia** employed Roman Jasica (also linked for some time to the University of Warsaw and the Polish Institute of International Affairs), who published works in international humanitarian law.

Last but not least, it is worth noting the activities of the Polish representatives in the **International Association of Penal Law** – **AIDP** (of which the Polish section was affiliated with the Committee of Legal Sciences of the Polish Academy of Sciences), which especially Rappaport was so eager to continue after the war (e.g. he led the Polish delegation to the congress in Athens in 1957).[357] The Polish delegates were also the main initiators of the adoption of a 1947 resolution on the protection of peace in law; they also emphasized the necessity of punishing war propaganda (similar initiatives were undertaken as part of the International Association of Democratic Lawyers) and of taking action to preclude the statute limitations from affecting international crimes, as discussed in other parts of this book (see subchapter 3.3 and chapter X).[358] However, it should be noted that after the

355 Cyprian, Sawicki (1962), part I: 22. It concerns the raport: *German Crimes against Poland. Official Report of the Polish Government to be submitted to the International Military Tribunal* (London–Nurnberg, December 1945).

356 Równy (2003): 39ff; Przyborowska-Klimczak (2022a): 253ff.

357 Rappaport (1958): 12.

358 Not infrequently, the Polish delegates attempted to leverage the AIDP conferences for political purposes, as in the case of Muszkat and Sawicki's paper on the lack of basis for German claims to Polish Recovered Territories in the light of international criminal

war, the AIDP focused not only in international criminal law but primarily on studies in comparative criminal law. In the latter respect, one could mention the involvement of e.g. Jan Skupiński and Stanisław Waltoś in the preparation of the *Diversion and Mediation* report of 1982.[359]

As regards the International Bureau for the Unification of Criminal Law, which had been the arena of a dynamic co-operation before the war, Polish scholars such as Sawicki and Cyprian insistently termed it a 'reactionary' body whose activities were targeted against the USSR in the afterwar period.[360] Of course, those were opinions consistent with the Communist Party's line.

7 Conclusions

After the war (and even during it, as one cannot ignore the Lublin trial of KL Majdanek staff), the Polish justice system made an impressive effort to bring international crimes to judgement, though, unfortunately, only those committed by the Nazis. The Soviet crimes, such as the Katyń Massacre, remained a taboo subject and attempts to investigate them led to repressions. As that was realized by Jan Sehn and his team, they conducted their investigations into the Katyń crime in secret from the Soviet authorities.[361]

The justice system's efforts were impressive not only on account of the number of the cases proceeded but also the quality of the legal argumentation especially before the NTN. The quality of the latter's opinions does not fall below the level represented by those handed down in the Nuremberg and subsequent Nuremberg trials. The NTN's discussion of the nature of the various specific crimes and principles of responsibility for them (especially with regard to membership in a criminal organization, command responsibility, including the responsibility of civilian superiors, as well as the non-recognition of unlawful orders or legal acts as a justification or excuse) may be interesting both from the perspective of domestic and international law. Thus, there can be no surprise that monographs have been written in the West on the works of Polish courts, such as Finder and Prusin, *Justice Behind the Iron Curtain: Nazis on Trial in Communist Poland* (2018), and their other

law. Their presentation was received by Roux and Calloyani as having a weak legal basis and purely political nature; see the report in 3 PiP 1947, 103.

359 Correspondence in the authors' possession.

360 Cyprian, Sawicki (1956b): 168.

361 Gańczak (2020): 177ff.

publications cited in this book, as well as Andrew Kornbluth, *The August Trials. The Holocaust and Postwar Justice in Poland* (2021). On the other hand, one can wonder why the Polish courts could pass such judgments on international crimes as are even today capable of making an impression with their legal reasoning but at the same time judge the members of the Polish Underground in show trials conducted on the basis of the same legislation. The answers must be sought in the composition of the panels and the timings of the judgments. The judgments dealing with international crimes were for the most part handed down before 1948, by judges educated before WWII. Thus, it becomes fitting to regard the achievements of the NTN as, in essence, the swan song of prewar judiciary and scholarship and not a success of People's Poland.

Polish diplomatic activities of the 1945–1989 should be filtered through the sieve of co-operation with the USSR. Whether they wanted it or not, Polish diplomats were cogs in the Soviet voting machine.[362] For example, they remained sceptical of the idea of creation of an international criminal court or restricted the applicability of the Genocide Convention to protect Soviet criminals and, at the time, the *de facto* decision makers of Polish foreign policy. The double standards, i.e. on the one hand taking a principled approach to the judgment of Nazi crimes and on the other hand protecting the Soviet criminals came to the Polish diplomats and scholars all the easier considering how they had already been compelled to such conduct by the circumstances of WWII, when, in the interest of preserving the unity of the anti-Nazi coalition, the Soviet crimes were to be left unspoken.

Nonetheless, certain initiatives or positions taken were the fruit of Polish academic and diplomatic thought, such as part of the regulation in the Genocide Convention of 1948 or the concept itself of the Convention on the Non-Applicability of Statutory Limitations of 1968, as well as a number of provisions from the protocols additional to the HC.

The experience of World War II made research into international criminal law and international humanitarian law flourish in multiple Polish academic centres. Though the initial years after the war were dominated by Sawicki and Cyprian (whose government functions facilitated their access to the documents), many other Polish academics within the country engaged in valuable studies in international criminal law. Abroad, on the other hand, still identifying themselves as Poles, Glaser, Lemkin and others continued their academic work.

---

362 Materski in: Materski, Michowicz (2010): 265.

CHAPTER 4

After the Cold War (1989–2025)

1 Constitutional and Legal Changes

After the fall of the communist regime in 1989, Poland underwent a political transformation resulting in democratic government. An enormous change was taking place in international relations and foreign policy, including accession to international organizations of fundamental importance to international obligations, the development of human-rights protection and global safety and security. The new foreign minister was Krzysztof Skubiszewski (serving until the autumn of 1993), who summarized the Polish reason of state as follows: 'Poland's reason of state demands that in the coming years the regained sovereignty be reinforced, the safety and security of the state be built, the economic and civilizational development of the nation and society be supported and that our position be strengthened in the international arena, especially in Europe.'[1]

In keeping with those goals, in 1991, Poland acceded to the Council of Europe, joining the ranks of states protecting human rights and democratic standards. A Europe Agreement establishing an association between Poland and the European Communities was signed (an accession treaty took force in 2004, which is when Poland became a member of the European Union). The process of recovery of political independence and reconstruction of democracy was symbolically accomplished with the withdrawal of Soviet forces in 1993. In 1999, Poland acceded to the North Atlantic Treaty Organization – NATO. Poland also became very actively involved on behalf of the structural institutionalization of the Conference for Security and Co-operation in Europe, which, in 1995, was transformed into the Organization for Security and Co-operation in Europe.[2]

In 1997, Poland adopted a new Constitution,[3] Article 9 of which provides that the Republic of Poland respects the international law binding on it. That obligation extends also to customary international law. In consequence, acts of domestic law should conform to the obligations of

1 Bieńczyk-Missala, Kuźniar (2020): 10.
2 Zięba (2020): 275.
3 Constitution of the Republic of Poland of 2.04.1997, Dz.U.78 483, as amended.

DOI:10.1163/9789004712690_006

international law. In 1997, a new Criminal Code was adopted,[4] with provisions governing the exercise of universal jurisdiction with regard to a foreign national in respect of whom the decision has been made against extradition, in the case of a criminal offence committed abroad that the Republic of Poland is obliged to prosecute under international treaties (Article 113).[5]

Chapter XVI of the 1997 Code, titled *Crimes against peace, crimes against humanity and war crimes*, regulates *inter alia* punishment for the crime of aggression (Article 117), crime of genocide (Article 118), crime against humanity[6] (Article 118a), and war crimes (Articles 119–126c) (as discussed extensively in the later chapters of this book).

The initial decades following the fall of the communist system were an extraordinarily dynamic period, both with regard to the state's internal policy and its external relations. Poles became actively involved in numerous fields. The areas of that involvement included initiatives relating to international criminal law and especially the creation of the ICTY and ICC, as well as inclusion of a definition of the crime of aggression in the ICC Statute (and exercise of jurisdiction with regard to that crime). Poland participated in the ILC's works on Draft Code of Crimes against the Peace and Security of Mankind and the principle of *aut dedere aut judicare*.

Poland also monitored the implementation of previous undertakings, permanently supporting the adoption by the UNGA of resolutions concerning the Genocide Convention. The purpose of the resolutions was to affirm that genocide was a crime under international law, to condemn it, and to encourage the states not having acceded to the Convention to so accede.[7] The sense of the practice of adopting, year after year or every two years, a resolution kept in the same or similar wording is that while the international situational keeps changing as a result of the evolution of the international environment, establishment of new states or transformation of existing ones or of their political systems, such a resolution makes it possible to reaffirm the position taken by the state promoting it – the state's invariable position on matters of fundamental importance to international law.

---

4 Dz.U.1997.88.553, as amended.

5 Following accession to the Rome Statute of the ICC, Article 113 was amended to include the provision that Polish criminal law shall apply to a foreign having committed: 'a criminal offence specified in the Rome Statute of the International Criminal Court, done at Rome on 17.07.1998 (Dz.U.2003.708 and of 2018.1753).'

6 Introduced to the Criminal Code with the 2010 Amendment (Dz.U.98.626).

7 See e.g. UN Doc. A/C.3/47/L.39, 19.11.1992, similarily: A/C.3/45/L.69, 21.11.1990.

2 Mazowiecki, the Conflict in the Former Yugoslavia, and the Creation of the ICTY

In 1995, as a gesture of protest, Tadeusz Mazowiecki, the Special Rapporteur of the UN Commission on Human Rights (CHR) at the time,[8] resigned from the position he had accepted 3 years prior.[9] In the opinion of Roman Wieruszewski, Mazowiecki's resignation as rapporteur, 'was the first stone that launched an avalanche, as a result of which a few months later a peace agreement in Dayton was concluded.'[10]

To the rapporteur, the scale of the crimes committed in the Srebrenica area was the last chord in his mission of several years during which he not only documented the crimes committed but also attempted to alert the international community to them, insisting also on the creation of a tribunal to judge the war crimes. His resignation was prompted by the failure of the safe zone in Srebrenica – the zone of which the establishment he, as the special rapporteur, had recommended in his reports, in the belief that it would protect the Muslim Bosnians from the Serbs. In actuality, the functioning of the zone facilitated the murder of the Bosniak minority by the Serbs, as the defenceless population had been concentrated there. In July 1995, the greatest mass crime of the last decades in Europe took place there, later recognized both by the ICTY[11] and the ICJ[12] as genocide. Nearly 8 thousand men were killed in that crime. As at the time of his resignation, Mazowiecki did not have the full picture of the scale of the crimes, but it was Srebrenica – along with his frustration with the inaction of the international community – that was the driving motive in his decision.

The term 'ethnic cleansing' owes its entry into broad circulation to Mazowiecki, in whose eyes it had been not so much the consequence or by-product of the conduct of the war but its very purpose. He noted:

8 E/CN.4/RES/1992/S-1/1, par. 12ff.

9 UN Doc. E/CN.4/1996/9, 22.08.1995. Interviewed by Dawid Warszawski, Mazowiecki commented: 'For me, Srebrenica was the last straw. Once again promises had been broken and values betrayed. It is hard to be the voice of hope when one is forced into a posture of complete helplessness,' see *Will to disaster*, 24(5) Index on censorship 1995, 67.

10 Wieruszewski (2019): 246.

11 See e.g. ICTY, *Prosecutor v. Krstic*, IT-98-33-A, 19.04.2004.

12 ICJ, Application of the Convention on the Prevention and Punishment of the Crime of Genocide (Bosnia and Herzegovina v. Serbia and Montenegro), Judgement, ICJ Reports 2007, 43.

> "Ethnic cleansing" may be equated with a systemic purge of the civilian population with a view to forcing it to abandon the territories in which it lives. This practice has been described many times. It has beed accompanied by mass killings, rape, the destructions of houses, mosques and churches, the terrorist shelling of cities, and, what is more, the forcing of people to declare that they are forsaking their homes voluntarily.[13]

In his report of 17.11.1992, he wrote: 'term «ethnic cleansing» refers to the elimination by the ethnic group exercising control over the given territory of members of other ethnic groups'.[14] That was not the only thing he noted – extensive parts of the reports dealt with information on rapes of women. To Mazowiecki, the rapes were a method of ethnic cleansing and a war crime.[15] The team of experts appointed to examine the situation of women, in a report from their mission on 12–13.01.1993, attached report on their mission as Annex II to Mazowiecki's report, emphasized:[16]

> Those responsible for human rights abuses should be held accountable. In the present situation there is no recourse to justice for victims of human rights violations inside the country. An international tribunal should be established to bring to justice the perpetrators of all war crimes and crimes against humanity, including rape. Those who committed rape, those who ordered it, or those in positions of authority who failed to prevent it should be brought to justice.

Mazowiecki's reports were used in the trials before the ICTY[17] not only as a point of reference with regard to the documentation of the crimes committed but also in the capacity of specific source documents. The reports also influenced the development of the scholarship and are frequently cited in the subject literature.[18]

---

13 S/PV.3134, 13.11.1992, 39.

14 UN Doc. A/47/666, §9.

15 UN Doc. E/CN.4/1993/50, §§82–89.

16 *Ibidem*: §72.

17 See ICTY, Separate Opinion Of Judge Li On The Defence Motion for Interlocutory Appeal on Jurisdiction, 2.10.1995.; ICTY, Prosecutor v. Šešelj, Decision on Prosecution's Motion for Admission of Evidence from the Bar Table, IT-03-67-T, 19.12.2010.

18 The subject literature highlighting Mazowiecki's influence is very extensive; here, only by way of example, Schabas (2014): 39–60; Ramcharan (2011): 48 summarized that

Mazowiecki insisted on the establishment of a Commission of Experts to analyse information on violations of humanitarian law.[19] The latter was created in 1992 by UN Secretary General Boutros Boutros-Ghali and led by Frits Kalshoven, later replaced by Cherif Bassiouni.[20] In his activities, the Commission made use of Mazowiecki's reports. Today, they constitute some of the most important documents in the matter of establishing the proof of ethnic cleansing.[21]

The reports were also cited by the Republic of Poland's then-foreign minister, Krzysztof Skubiszewski, who emphasized in the UNGA session[22] that the Polish government saw the necessity of closing the detention camps for civilians and prisoners of war in the territory of former Yugoslavia and releasing the detainees. He also recalled the necessity of bringing to justice those responsible for violations of humanitarian law.

The Security Council heeded the Special Rapporteur's remarks and those of the Commission of Experts, and, in May 1993, by the Resolution no. 827, decided to establish the ICTY. Mazowiecki can thus be credited with momentous impact not only with regard to the documentation of the crimes but also the establishment of the first international institution since the time of WWII to judge the perpetrators of international crimes, as well as long-term impact on the development of international criminal law.

Poland has signed an agreement with the UN with regard to the implementation of the ICTY's judgments.[23] On its basis, those convicted by the Tribunal can serve their terms in Polish prisons. Those situations are described below (see subchapter 4.6). However, despite the somewhat fruitful collaboration with the ICTY, Poland has never had a judge in the tribunal (though Jan Skupiński was once a candidate, SC Res. 1104(1997)). Nor has any Pole ever judged in the International Criminal Tribunal for Rwanda (ICTR), which also came to life by way of the Security Council's Resolution no. 955 of 1994. Poland, however, has supported initiatives relating to the operations of both of the *ad hoc* tribunals. For example, while a member of the SC, in the Resolution 1048 (1996), Poland supported the appointment of

Mazowiecki had had 'historic contribution in alerting the international community of what had taken place.'

19 SC Res. 771(1992); SC Res. 780(1992); E/CN.4/1992/S-1/10, §19.

20 Extensively: Bassiouni (2017).

21 See UN Doc. S/1994/674, Commission's report is the annex to the letter.

22 UN Doc. A/47/PV.7: 72–77.

23 Agreement between the Government of the Republic of Poland and the United Nations on the enforcement of sentences of the International Criminal Tribunal for the former Yugoslavia, 18.10.2008 (Dz.U.2009.137.1123).

Louise Arbour as the Chief Prosecutor of the ICTY and of the ICTR to replace Richard Goldstone, whose term was ending. In the SC meeting, the Polish representatives, Paweł Radomski and later Joanna Wronecka, provided assurances of support and readiness for collaboration with the International Residual Mechanism for Criminal Tribunals, which replaced both of the *ad hoc*[24] tribunals.

3 Polish Engagement and the International Criminal Court

In the 80s of the past century, the works were resumed on a Draft Code of Offences (which quickly transformed into a Draft Code of Crimes) against Peace and Security of Mankind.[25] During the works in the UNGA's Sixth Committee, the Polish representative took the position that the drafting of the statute of the international criminal court should be separate from the drafting of the Code of crimes.[26] For both had been joined together since the very beginning (with a view to the possible use of the code in designing the provisions of the statute of the permanent ICC), resulting in a drafting impasse on both fronts. It also discouraged the states unwilling to support one of the documents.[27]

In 1989, Sixth Committee discussed in a meeting what crimes should be included in the draft code and what their definitions should be. The representative of the Polish MFA, Janusz Mickiewicz,[28] communicated the Polish delegation's position in favour of taking as the point of reference the concepts of the gravity of the crimes according to the GCs of 1949 and their API of 1977. The Polish delegates noted that the general definition of war crimes should be supplemented with a list of acts constituting war crimes. They also supported the separation of crimes against humanity from war crimes – with the assumption that the future definition of the former should cover not only mass crimes but also those taking the form of systematic prosecution if committed by an individual.[29] They also insisted on separate provisions dealing with the crime of genocide, based on the respective

24 UN Doc. S/PV.8278, 6.06.2018, S/PV.8416, 11.12.2018.

25 GA Res/36/106 (1981).

26 E.g. Janusz Mickiewicz, Director of MFA Legal Department; UN Doc. A/C.6/44/SR.29, 1.11.1989, §§104–105.

27 Sixth Committee, A/C.6/47/SR.28, 4.11.1992, statement of Janusz Stańczyk §70.

28 A/C.6/44/SR.29, §99ff.

29 *Ibidem*: §103.

Genocide Convention. They believed that the crimes of apartheid, slavery and all other forms of servitude, such as forced labour, and other inhuman acts, should be included in the draft. They suggested the addition of destruction of property, noting that doing so would be consistent with the spirit of the Nuremberg principles and that the description of the crime should refer to the cultural and spiritual heritage of mankind. The desire was also to include environmental damage and the use of weapons of mass destruction, believing that the inclusion of such crimes would strenghten the effectiveness of their prevention.[30]

In 1991, our then-candidate to the International Law Commission, Renata Szafarz, spoke during the deliberations of Sixth Committee.[31] She observed that the majority of provisions dealing with specific crimes were a reflection of generally applicable norms of customary international law having in some cases the character of *jus cogens*. She noted that sentencing limits should be provided for each of the crimes individually, rather than a single catalogue of penalties applicable to all crimes. However, she remarked that the entire discussion appeared to be illogical without a mechanism to implement the provisions through specific regulation. There, she highlighted the necessity of the creation of an international criminal court with jurisdiction over the crimes mentioned in the draft code.

She also stressed the need to reject the argument relating to the costs of establishing such a tribunal, noting that the benefits of creating such an institution would have outweighed the anticipated costs. Moreover, she suggested that the jurisdiction of such a court should be exclusive with regard to crimes against peace and concurrent with the jurisdiction of the state in the case of crimes against the security of mankind.

One year later, in the deliberations of Sixth Committee, the representative of Polish MFA, Janusz Stańczyk, reiterated that Poland supported the idea of the creation of an international justice system for criminal cases.[32] He referred to the activities of the working group, identifying certain solutions Poland was ready to support. During that time, the Polish representative expressed the belief that an international criminal court did not have to be a fully fledged permanent court. At that point, however, the concurrent jurisdiction of the court and of the states was already assumed, without identifying any specific ways of dealing with that concurrence. It

30 *Ibidem*: §§104–105.

31 A/C.6/46/SR.29, 5.11.1991, 19–20; in the end, Szafarz fell two votes short of joining the ILC.

32 A/C.6/47/SR.28: 15ff.

was also believed that the hypothetical court should not have close relations with the ICJ and above all judges should not be able to sit in both courts. It was emphasized that the court's statute should be adopted by the states in the form of international agreement and should provide for jurisdiction in the most serious crimes, including drug trafficking. Expansion of the catalogue of crimes following the entry into force of the Code of crimes also was contemplated.[33]

In 1993, during the works on the Code of Crimes, the Polish representative was of the opinion that the system of punishment should specify the lower and upper sentencing limits for each type of crime. The system should include life imprisonment and prison terms from 10 to 35 years. He specified that a single body to decide on the criminal responsibility of the perpetrators of crimes against peace and security of mankind would be extraordinarily difficult to establish. He stressed that the hypothetical court should, in the assessment of the crime of aggression, rely on the position taken by the Security Council. In the absence of that, however, the court should have the right to consider on its own the classification of specific actions as an act or threat of aggression.[34]

Many of the proposals supported by the Polish delegates found reflection in the Code of Crimes, such as the elements of the definitions of crimes or their separate definitions. The idea of specifying the sentencing limits individually for each specific type of crime was completely scrapped.

The text of the Code of Crimes was adopted by the International Law Commission in 1996 and submitted to the UNGA. The latter was to decide the form in which the new code should come to life – whether as an international convention or through incorporation into the Statute of the ICC. In the end, the decision was not made.

During the time, the works on the creation of the ICC were also pending.[35] The idea of its creation had been revisited in 1989.[36] The initial works on the Statute proceeded in the ILC, which compiled both a draft statute and recommendations on matters of the international administration of justice. The Commission adopted the draft statute in 1994 and proposed to

33 *Ibidem.*

34 A/CN.4/448/Add.1: 93ff.

35 Schabas (2011): 16ff, Wierczyńska (2016a): 30ff.

36 With the contribution of the then-prime minister of Trinidad and Tobago, Arthur Robinson. In the 44th session of the UNGA, he tabled the motion to create an international criminal court with jurisdiction over drug trafficking. On 4.12.1989, the UNGA adopted Resolution 44/39 on the international criminal responsibility of individuals and entities engaged in illicit trafficking in narcotic drugs across national frontiers.

convene an international conference of plenipotentiaries to proceed with the draft statute and sign the convention establishing the international criminal court. By Resolution 49/53 of 17.02.1995, the UNGA decided to appoint an *ad hoc* Committee open to all states and members of specialized agencies. The Committee was to deal with the substantive matters relating to the ILC's draft and consider the preparation of a conference to adopt the statute. The states were invited to submit comments on the draft, and 'Establishment of an International Criminal Court' was put on the agenda of the anticipated 50th session of the Assembly in order to consider the *ad hoc* Committee's remarks and the comments submitted by the states.

The leadership of the *ad hoc* Committee for the establishment of the ICC included: Adriaan Bos of the Netherlands as Chairman; Cherif Bassiouni of Egypt, Silvia A. Fernandez de Gurmendi of Argentina and Marek Madej of Poland[37] as Deputy Chairs, and Kuniko Saeki of Japan as Rapporteur. The Committee's report[38] dealt with numerous points of substantive law and procedure but also of the nature of the court itself and its function. Some were dealt with laconically, such as the role of the prosecutor, and some – such as the problem of complementarity – were expounded in detail. First of all, as we known from the *ad hoc* Committee's report (which, however, does not provide the specific positions taken by the participating delegates), the states were not in agreement as to the nature the anticipated court's jurisdiction should take. Some of the states were of the opinion that the principle of complementarity ought to be followed, structured so as to concede priority to domestic jurisdiction.[39] Others, on the other hand, were desirous to emphasize the presumption of their jurisdiction to judge the perpetrators in the strongest terms possible. Yet others were in favour of the priority of the international jurisdiction. Although there were voices criticizing the foundation of the court's jurisdiction on the principle of complementarity, the deliberations at the time already reflected a strong tendency among states to rely on that principle, narrowing down precisely the situations in which the court would be exercising the jurisdiction in preference to a state. The proposal was for the court to act when the perpetrators of serious crimes cannot be properly judged before domestic courts or when there has been an unwarranted conviction or acquittal.

37 Marek Madej was at the time legal counsel to Poland's permanent mission in New York.

38 Report of the Ad Hoc Committee on the Establishment of an International Criminal Court, No. 22 (A/50/22), hereafter: Report of the Ad Hoc Committee.

39 Report of the Ad Hoc Committee: 6.

The *ad hoc* Committee's report also recorded that the states that discussed, apart from the complementarity itself, the matter of the catalogue of crimes the anticipated court's jurisdiction should cover. Interestingly, some states suggested the expansion of the scope of the groups protected by the Convention on the Prevention and Punishment of the Crime of Genocide. It was noted, however, that a definition having the status of customary law should not be modified on that path. Some states were of the opinion that the court's jurisdiction should also extend to the crime of aggression, but the lack of the latter's definition posed a problem. It was clear that no definition could be agreed in a short time-frame, especially given the problematic role of the Security Council in deciding whether aggression had taken place. Already by that point had proposals been tabled to adjourn the works on the definition of the crime of aggression and, consequently, its inclusion in the statute. More space was devoted to the Security Council, including whether it should refer cases to the court, thus avoiding the establishment of further *ad hoc* tribunals under Chapter VII of the UN Charter.[40] Many states voiced reluctance to concede any role to the SC in the context of the court's functioning. In their opinion, the SC's hypothetical powers: 'would reduce the credibility and moral authority of the court,' or even forfeit the court's independence.

Much space in the document was also claimed by procedural issues, such as the departure from the traditional extradition model, collaboration between the court and the domestic authorities, recognition of court judgments and decisions, and financial matters. In the conclusions of its report, the *ad hoc* Committee stated that the works should continue. Attached with the report was a list of issues to be addressed in such continued works on the adoption of a statute for the court. Those included the problem of non-retroaction, non-applicability of statutes of limitations, and corporate responsibility.[41]

The report recounted the activities of all of the participating states as a whole. It would be difficult to trace precisely what influence Poland may have had on its actions and proposed solutions. From a conversation with the Polish delegate, Marek Madej, it occurs that Poland was in the group of states whose proposals garnered the most support. Due to her own wartime experience, Poland was in favour of the establishment of a permanent criminal court to judge the most serious crimes of international law (including the crime of aggression). Nor did the recourse to the principle

40 *Ibidem*: 12–26.

41 *Ibidem*: 27–60.

of complementarity with regard to the court's jurisdiction incur any reservations from the Polish delegates. Poland also supported the retention of the court's relationship with the Security Council. Poland's sentiment was in favour of the SC's bringing to the court's attention such situations as might possibly fall within the scope of the court's interest.[42]

In December 1995, the UNGA adopted the Resolution 50/46 titled: 'Establishment of an International Criminal Court,' whereby the decision was made to establish a Preparatory Committee (PrepCom) open to all states and specialized agencies. PrepCom was tasked with the examination of the remarks submitted in the *ad hoc* Committee's report and the written comments from the states and consolidation of the different ideas surfacing in the debates. Its purpose was to prepare a universally accepted text of the draft convention establishing an international criminal court. In particular, that meant the PrepCom was to submit a consolidated draft. As a consequence of the PrepCom's works, the agenda of the 51th session of the ILC included discussion of the PrepCom's report and the adoption of a convention text.[43]

The leadership of the PrepCom did not change compared to the *ad hoc* Committee, and thus the Pole, Marek Madej, kept the position of deputy chairman, but the rapporteur changed, with Jun Yoshida, also of Japan, replacing Kuniko Saeki.[44]

The PrepCom's report of 13.09.1996 discussed the matters of the court's objectives, the perpetrator's individual responsibility, and the crimes to fall within the court's jurisdiction. In the context of genocide, the definition in the Convention was deemed sufficient, although there was a discussion of the necessity of narrowing down certain terms used in it, such as mental harm.[45] In the context of crimes against humanity, specific examples were given for consideration from the perspective of the definition. The discussion on the definition of the crime of aggression was resumed, but once again no definition had been agreed. There had even been proposals to abandon the attempts to define it and leave it up to the Security Council to define specific situations as aggression. Some of the delegations, however, perceived any such solution as dangerous, noting the necessity of avoidance

42 Interview with Marek Madej, 11.05.2020, in the author's possession.

43 Res GA 50/46, §5.

44 Report of the Preparatory Committee on the Establishment of an International Criminal Court, (A/51/22), 13.09.1996, hereafter: PrepCom's report.

45 PrepCom's report: 18.

of a situation in which a veto in the SC could prevent a person from being charged before the court with the crime of aggression.[46]

New problems, which in the *ad hoc* Committee's report had been no more than signalled, also entered the discussion; for example, the irrelevance of the position held and immunity; corporate responsibility; and a number of procedural matters.[47] Poland, among others, opted for the lack of head-of-state or head-of-government immunity in proceedings before the anticipated court.[48]

The first part of the Committee's report emphasized the need for the continuation of the works, involvement of as many states as was possible, and introduction of a co-operation procedure for working groups. The Committee decided that the conference for the adoption of the statute could take place in 1998. The second part of the report is a collation of the proposals arriving from the ILC, the Committee and the individual states. The report makes no specific mention of any Polish proposals, but not because there had not been any. On the contrary, the Polish government attached significant importance to the anticipated conference. Already before the organization of the conference did the works proceed within a special inter-ministry team of experts appointed by the MFA. A negotiation instruction was prepared. The delegates were to strive to secure the strongest possible and the most independent position for the court. Among other aspects, that meant providing the prosecutor with the broadest possible scope of independence and the power to initiate proceedings *ex proprio motu*; the adoption of automatic jurisdiction whereby the states having ratified the statute were to be bound by it without need of any separate declarations. The goal was also for the court to have complementary jurisdiction in the event of futility or impossibility of state proceedings. Last but not least, the Polish delegation was to support providing the court with jurisdiction also for crimes committed during non-international conflicts.[49]

Poland's delegation for the Rome Conference, commenced in June 1998, comprised Minister of Justice Hanna Suchocka as delegation head; Undersecretary of State Janusz Stańczyk as deputy delegation head; employees of Polish Embassy to Italy: Maciej Górski, Tomasz Orłowski and Lech Kubiak;

46 *Ibidem*: 19.

47 *Ibidem*: 45ff.

48 Interview with Marek Madej, 11.05.2020, in the author's possession.

49 Response by the Minister of Justice to Interpellation no. 909 concerning the initiative for the establishment of an International Criminal Court, 8.10.1998, http://orka2.sejm.gov.pl/IZ3.nsf/main/2316DD44.

Director of the MFA Legal Department, Jerzy Kranz; Director of the Office of the Minister of Justice, Wojciech Kijowski; Agnieszka Dąbrowiecka of the Ministry of Justice; Maria Frankowska of Southern Illinois University; Michał Płachta of the University of Gdańsk, Anna Wyrozumska of the University of Łódź; and Katheryn Legomsky as the secretary of the delegation. The members of the Polish delegation did not hold high-profile positions in the conference, but their presence was visible; they participated in plenary discussions and in the teams working on the content. Poland nominated a candidate to the Drafting Committee, in the person of Maria Frankowska. The Committee's task was to co-ordinate and refine the drafting without reopening the discussion on the merits and without altering the contents, in line with the instructions from the Committee of the Whole,[50] i.e. give the final shape to the provisions agreed. In a certain sense, therefore, it was the last stage of a complicated process of international legislation. As regards the positions taken on specific topics, Poland submitted together with other states – including Israel, Canada, Finland, France and Germany – a working document on the prosecutor's role in the commencement of pretrial proceedings; and individually Polish representatives took part in the discussion on the necessity of narrowing down the provisions on evidence gathering, as well as the matter of extradition and surrender.[51]

Poland belonged to the so-called like-minded states (also including Canada, Germany and the United Kingdom, among others) – an informal group of more than 60 states opting for the adoption of specific solutions in the coming statute.[52] Those dealt with the jurisdiction on the core crimes, including the crime of aggression, as well as the ban on the submission of any reservations with regard to the provisions of the statute by the states. In the assessment of William Schabas: 'while operating relatively informally, the like-minded quickly dominated the structure of the Conference,'[53] especially from the moment when Philippe Kirsch of Canada, also in the group, became Chairman of the Committee of the Whole.

In the plenary discussion, the Polish positions had been consistent with the solutions that were subsequently adopted. However, the Polish

50 Draft Final Act of the United Nations Diplomatic Conference of Plenipotentiaries on the Establishment of an International Criminal Court, UN Doc. A/CONF.183/13 (vol. III), 82.

51 Working Group on Procedural Matters, see: A/CONF.183/C.1/WGPM/L.18, initiatives concerning evidence A/CONF.183/C.1AVGPM/LJ1; question of surrender and extradition A/CONF.183/C.1/L.93; UN Doc. A/CONF.183/13 (vol. III): 294, 335.

52 Schabas (2011): 18–22.

53 *Ibidem*: 19.

representatives had recommended a uniform jurisdiction of the anticipated court for all of the crimes over which it would have jurisdiction.[54] They also noted that establishing the court would reinforce the rule of law by enforcing individual responsibility and would create a mechanism for combating genocide, war crimes and crimes against humanity. In that respect, they agreed with the adoption of the definition of genocide from the Genocide Convention.[55] They believed the court's *ratione materiae* jurisdiction should extend to the crime of aggression.[56] The court was to be complementary to the domestic jurisdictions[57] and have all the necessary powers to determine whether a state has properly complied with its obligations. They emphasized that a relationship should be established between the court and the Security Council for the purposes of determining whether the crime of aggression had taken place; while the SC's role should not be diminished, its activities ought not to have a detrimental impact on the court's exercise of its powers. Furthermore, the prosecutor should have the power to bring the proceedings *ex officio*, and the states party should be obliged to co-operate closely with the court. The Polish delegates also emphasized that the statute should deal with the responsibilities of individuals, not legal persons; replacement of the term 'criminal organisations' with 'legal persons' would have necessitated the use of the vague term 'group' in the statute. In the opinion of Maria Frankowska, the inclusion of the responsibility of bodies corporate in the statute would have introduced a lack of consistency – if organizations could be held responsible, then why not the states?[58] In procedural matters, Anna Wyrozumska was of the opinion that both the accused individuals and the states should be able to raise objections to the court's jurisdiction and admissibility of the proceedings. In her view, the prosecutor should also hold that power.[59] Dąbrowiecka noted that the matter of the elements of the definitions of the crimes should not delay the adoption of the text of the statute itself,[60] whereas the expansion of the *ratione materiae* jurisdiction, especially with regard to the use of prohibited weapons as a category of war crimes,

54 UN Doc. A/CONF.183/13 (vol. II), Suchocka: 93, Wyrozumska: 314, 333.

55 Delegate Frankowska concurred with the German position expounded by Judge Kaul: 'consensus with respect to the crime of genocide had already been reached, and the 1948 Genocide Convention contained a generally acceptable definition that could be used in the Statute' in: UN Doc. A/CONF.183/13/ (vol. II): 147.

56 *Ibidem*, Suchocka: 93, Frankowska: 147, Dąbrowiecka: 286.

57 *Ibidem*, Suchocka: 93.

58 *Ibidem*: 136.

59 *Ibidem*: 217.

60 *Ibidem*: 286.

should be left for the review conference to resolve. Frankowska also voiced the opinion that the court's jurisdiction should apply to persons who had been at least 18 years old when the crime was committed.[61]

The statute was opened for signatures in July 1998 and entered into force 4 years later – on 1.07.2002, upon achieving 60 ratifications. The Polish Minister of Justice, Hanna Suchocka, signed the statute on 9.04.1999 on behalf of the Republic of Poland. In line with the government statement of 31.07.2002,[62] consent was given to the ratification of the Rome Statute of the ICC by the Act of 5.07.2001.[63] The President of the Republic of Poland ratified it on 9.10.2001, and on 12.11.2001, the ratification document was submitted to the UN Secretary General as the depositary of the treaty.

The Explanatory memorandum of the motion to Sejm for consent to ratify the Statute noted: 'The Court's success, however, is contingent on the manifestation of the strong political will of a sufficiently large group of states, manifested not only in the signature and ratification of the ICC but also the correct shaping of domestic legislation so as for the latter to enable the full co-operation of state bodies with the Court and provision of assistance to the court in the widest possible scope.'[64]

The memorandum mentioned Poland's obligations arising from the statute with regard, among other issues, to co-operation with the Court, concession of privileges and immunities to the Court's staff in Polish territory, and bearing the costs of the implementation of requests for assistance. Some of the obligations required legislative amendments, such as the expansion of the catalogue of crimes stipulated in Polish criminal law; some even required a constitutional amendment, i.e. those dealing with extradition.[65]

The aforementioned document also noted that the court did not present a threat to the state's sovereignty, emphasizing that even in the case of the Court's automatic jurisdiction (in the meaning of its exercise of jurisdiction with regard to the most serious crimes): 'the principle of complementarity gives effective protection from the infringement of state sovereignty in the area of the administration of justice on condition that it be used within the limits specified by the Statute.'[66] The necessity of a swift ratification

61 UN Doc. A/CONF.183/13/ (vol. II): 136.

62 Dz.U.2003.78.709.

63 Dz.U.2001.98.1065.

64 Explanatory memorandum, see online at: http://orka.sejm.gov.pl/Rejestrd.nsf/wgdruku/2431/$file/2431.pdf, 1.

65 Ziorkiewicz (2005): 295ff.

66 Explanatory memorandum: 13.

was also stressed. It was accentuated that Poland had been among the 'like-minded states' and, given fast ratification of the Statute, would be able to have on influence on the functioning of the Court and the shape of the first Assembly of States Parties to the ICC. At the time, emphasis was also placed on the necessity of becoming bound by the Statute in order to expedite Poland's accession to the European Union, in connection with the European Parliament's resolution of 6.05.1999 on the ratification of the Statute of the International Criminal Court.[67] The document called upon the Council and the European Commission to make the signature and/or ratification of the ICC Statute an essential element of negotiations with third parties.[68]

The Statute was ratified by the Sejm and under Polish law, it is a ratified international treaty within the meaning of Article 91(2) of the Constitution, with precedence before acts of parliament. The provisions of the Statute have partially been incorporated as into the Code of Criminal Procedure and the Criminal Code. Amendments to the Criminal Code included the modification of Articles 113 and 117, as well as addition and modification of some provisions of Chapter XVI *Crimes against peace, crimes against humanity and war crimes*, chapter XXIII *Crimes against freedom*; Chapter XXV *Crimes against sexual freedom and morality*; Chapter XXVI *Crimes against family and guardianship*; Chapter XXX *Crimes against the administration of justice*.[69] In the Code of Criminal Procedure, a new Chapter 66a was added, with Articles 611g–611s on co-operation with the International Criminal Court.[70] Whether that was done properly is up to debate. The very definition of crime against humanity in the Criminal Code already differs from the one in the Statute. On the one hand, the provisions of the Statute are somewhat casuistic and diverge from the nature of the provisions of a criminal code. On the other hand, the latter ought to reflect the contents of the treaty with the best precision achievable. In the contrary case, the ICC could regard domestic conduct based on defectively implemented provisions as not genuine proceedings.[71]

67 Official Journal of the European Communities, C 279, 1.10.1999: 425–426.

68 The need to ratify the Statute was also signalled by the Council of Europe – see: International Criminal Court – Recommendation 1408 (1999) of the Parliamentary Assembly and UN – GA Res/53/105 (1998).

69 The details are in the 2010 Act amending the Criminal Code, the Act on the Police, the Act Implementing the Criminal Code and the Code of Criminal Procedure, Dz.U. 2010.98.626.

70 Dz.U.2004.240.2405, extensively Grzegorczyk (2009).

71 See Article 17 of the Rome Statute and the principle of complementarity therein, also Wierczyńska (2012): 263, (2016b): 255.

In 2008, the Sejm passed an act to ratify the Agreement on the Privileges and Immunities of the ICC.[72] On 3.12.2024 Poland has entered into an agreement with the ICC concerning the implementation of the Court's judgments. Additionally, Poland supports the Court financially and had no arrears, which is of key importance to the Court's ability to perform the tasks for which it has been established. As occurs from an interview with the Court's former President, Piotr Hofmański, Poland even overpays when needed.[73]

The explanatory memorandum of the motion for the ratification of the Rome Statute noted that the institution of surrender, stipulated by the Statute, was a qualitatively new form of co-operation with the states, different from extradition (handing over) and applicable only in relationships between the ICC and the states.[74] As stated in the explanatory memorandum, the surrender is mandatory. The Statute does not enable any grounds of refusal the state could rely on, whereas there is an extensive list of possible bars to extradition. It was consistently pointed out that there was no incompatibility between the institution of surrender and Article 55(1) of the Polish Constitution of 1997, which banned the extradition of a Polish citizen.

In connection with the introduction of the institutions of the European Arrest Warrant (EAW) and surrender to the ICC, it became necessary, however, to test their constitutionality. In 2005, the Polish Constitutional Tribunal handed down a judgment[75] that, although referring in principle to the constitutionality of Article 607t(1) of Code of Criminal Procedure of 1997, allowing a Polish citizen to be handed over to a European Member State under a European Arrest Warrant, was indirectly of fundamental importance to the assessment of the constitutionality of the surrender stipulated in the ICC Statute. The Constitutional Tribunal found the Code provision to be unconstitutional; although the Court was sympathetic to lifting the bar on the extradition of own nationals to EU member states, it noted that could not be accomplished through a mere dynamic interpretation of Article 55(1) of the Constitution. In consequence, a constitutional amendment was proceeded. The 2006 Amendment[76] allowed, among other things, the

72 Dz.U.2008.220.1430.

73 The authors of this book interviewed Piotr Hofmański on 12.12.2022.

74 See the explanatory memorandum and Article 102 of the Statute.

75 TK, judgement, 27.04.2005, P 1/05 (Dz.U.2005.77.680).

76 Dz.U.2006.200.1471.

extradition of a Polish citizen 'upon a request made by (…) an international judicial body if such a possibility stems from an international treaty ratified by Poland,' satisfying the obligations of the Statute (also of the EAW Framework Decision).

Article 123 of the Statute of the ICC provides for review conferences in order to discuss amendments. In particular, that refers to the list of crimes. The underlying reason is primarily that the text adopted in the Rome Conference did not define the crime of aggression. The states had not been ready to adopt such a definition in 1998.

In 2002, a Special Working Group on the Crime of Aggression began energetic activities in a series of meetings between the sessions of the Assembly of States Party to the ICC, including work on a definition of aggression and terms of extradition with regard to it. The meetings were regular enough to gain the name of Princeton Process.[77] Participants on Poland's behalf included Andrzej Makarewicz[78] for the MFA, Piotr Dolata of the Permanent Mission to the UN, and Władysław Czapliński,[79] also for the MFA. The definition worked out in the meetings was presented to the Review Conference in Kampala in Uganda. Adoption by the Review Conference of the terms of the exercise of the Court's jurisdiction developed by the group appeared to be problematic, however, as the group itself had not been in full agreement as to what that should look like in the absence of a decision by the SC on the qualification of a situation as an act of aggression;[80] as a result, the group developed alternative solutions.

Ultimately, in the Review Conference on 31.05-11.06.2010, Poland's representatives were: Krzysztof Kwiatkowski of the Ministry of Justice; Maciej Szpunar – Undersecretary of State in the MFA; Remigiusz Henczel – Director of the MFA Legal Department; Anna Grupińska – Polish Ambassador to the Republic of Uganda; Marek Madej of the MFA Legal Department; and Beata Ziorkiewicz of the Ministry of Justice. Władysław Czapliński attended as an advisor; organizational assistance was provided by Ryszard Sosiński of the Polish Embassy to the Republic of Kenya.

Poland (together with Portugal) lobbied strongly for the provisions of the amendments concerning the crime of aggression not to be overly casuistic

77 More extensively on the works: Grzebyk (2013): 118ff.

78 ICC-ASP/3/SWGCA/INF.1.

79 ICC-ASP/8/INF.2.

80 Grzebyk (2013): 121.

but rather for more abstract language to be used. However, that was not met with broad support.[81]

The Review Conference adopted amendments dealing with the definitions of war crimes, expanding the jurisdiction of the Court onto non-international conflicts (Resolution no. 5), and a definition of the crime of aggression (Resolution no. 6). Moreover, it agreed on the terms of the exercise of the Court's jurisdiction over the crime of aggression, as well as a solution allowing the states not to be bound by the provisions concerning the crime of aggression. In consequence, the amendment was ratified by several dozen states – fewer than 1/3 of the parties to the Statute. On 14.07.2014, the President of the Republic of Poland ratified the amendments from the Resolutions no. 5 and 6, which came into force in respect of Poland on 25.09.2015.[82]

4 Treaty Obligations and Polish Participation in Initiatives on International Criminal Law

Apart from ratifying the ICC Statute and amendments to it, Poland acceded to a number of other treaties fundamental to the development of international humanitarian law and international criminal law. Among those, it is worth mentioning the Protocols additional of 1977 to the Geneva Convention of 1949 (Protocol I relating to the Protection of Victims of International Armed Conflicts; and Protocol II relating to the Protection of Victims of Non-International Armed Conflicts);[83] and Protocol III relating to the Adoption of an Additional Distinctive Emblem);[84] the Convention on the Prohibition of the Development, Production, Stockpiling and Use of Chemical Weapons and on their Destruction of 1993;[85] Additional Protocol of 1995 to the Convention on Prohibitions or Restrictions on the Use of Certain Conventional Weapons which may be deemed to be Excessively Injurious or to have Indiscriminate Effects, ('Protocol on Blinding Laser Weapons');[86] the International Convention for the Suppression of the Financing of Terrorism of 1999.[87]

81 From the conversation held with Beata Ziorkiewicz on 12.11.2020.
82 Dz.U.2018.1754.
83 1125 UN 609; Dz.U.1992.41.175, annex.
84 2404 UNTS 261; Dz.U.2010.70.447.
85 1975 UNTS 45; Dz.U.1999.63.703, annex.
86 1380 UNTS 370; Dz.U.2007.215.1583.
87 2178 UNTS 197; Dz.U.2004.263.2620.

Poland has also acceded to several conventions of the Council of Europe, e.g. the European Convention on Extradition of 1957, with protocols;[88] the European Convention on the Suppression of Terrorism of 1977;[89] the Convention against Torture and Other Cruel, Inhuman or Degrading Treatment or Punishment of 1987.[90]

Since the ratification of the amendment on the crime of aggression, there have been no other equally spectacular matters supported by Poland in reference to the development of international criminal law. Polish representatives made remarks concerning the obligation to 'either extradite or prosecute' (*aut dedere aut judicare*) with regard to areas still not covered by that obligation, e.g. some of the crimes against humanity, war crimes other than serious violations, and war crimes in non-international conflicts.[91]

As far as independent initiatives are concerned, it will certainly be expedient to note that Poland submitted the idea of a convention targeting organized crime. The draft was presented to the UNGA in 1996 by President Aleksander Kwaśniewski. The UN Convention against Transnational Organized Crime, adopted by the UNGA on 15.11.2000, was ratified by Poland in 2001 (more extensively on this convention and the protocols to it see subchapter 5.3).[92]

Poland has also participated in works on the initiative of other states, such as the MLA initiative, concerned with a Multilateral Treaty for Mutual Legal Assistance and Extradition for Domestic Prosecution of the Most Serious International Crimes.[93] The text was adopted in May 2023 in Slovenia[94] and Poland signed it in February 2024.

Poland hardly ever benefited of extensive experience when it comes to participation in the international administration of justice in criminal

88 ETS 24; Dz.U.1994.70.307.

89 1137 UNTS 93; Dz.U.1996.117.557.

90 ETS 126; Dz.U.1995.46.238.

91 Compilation of Government Reactions to the International Law Commission's Project on Crimes Against Humanity, prepared by the Whitney R. Harris, World Law Institute, 3.01.2019, https://cpb-us-w2.wpmucdn.com/sites.wustl.edu/dist/b/2004/files/2019/04/6thCommitteeGovernmentalResponses2013-2018_-1.3.19.pdf.

92 Dz.U.2005.18.158.

93 Poland is one of states supporting this initiative: https://www.centruminternationaalrecht.nl/documents/1304248/1549530/List+of+supporting+States.pdf/7875bb48–723a-ece9-5d96-bd9afdfcfd12?version=1.5&t=1606990329794&download=true.

94 Convention on International Cooperation in the Investigation and Prosecution of the Crime of Genocide, Crimes against Humanity and War Crimes, https://www.centruminternationaalrecht.nl/mla-initiative, see also https://www.gov.si/en/registries/projects/mla-initiative/diplomatic-conference-for-formal-negotiations/

cases. Polish representative never sat as judges either in the ICTY or the ICTR. From the beginning of the existence of the ICC, however, Poland has nominated candidates. The first one was Eleonora Zielińska (2002), followed by Władysław Czapliński (2011), followed by Piotr Hofmański, who was elected for the 2015–2024 term. In March 2021, he became the President of the ICC.[95] Since his appointment, Judge Hofmański served in the Appeals Chamber, of which he had become the head. Among others, he had judged the cases of Laurent Gbagbo and Charles Blé Goudé, as well as Jean-Pierre Bemba Gombo.

With regard to Polish participation in the international administration of justice in criminal cases, one should first of all note the European Union Rule of Law Mission in Kosovo, with the participation of Polish judges. Those were Agnieszka Klonowiecka-Milart, Anna Bednarek, Anna Adamska-Gallant, Mariola Paśnik, Arkadiusz Semeniuk, Piotr Bojarczuk, Cezary Łubowski, Dariusz Sielicki, Witold Jakimko and Arkadiusz Sędek.

Klonowiecka-Milart had also from 2006 been an *ad hoc* judge, and since 2010 a permanent judge, of the Extraordinary Chambers in the Courts of Cambodia to judge the crimes committed by the Khmer Rouge regime, and Bednarek, in 2019, was sworn in as a Trial Chamber judge of the Special Tribunal for Lebanon.

As for participation in other international bodies, in 1997, Professor Zdzisław Galicki (University of Warsaw) was elected to the International Law Commission, where he served until 2011. In 2004, the ILC decided to take on the topic/principle of *aut dedere aut judicare*, and Galicki was appointed special rapporteur in 2005.[96] In his preliminary report, he observed that the main issues for the rapporteur concerned whether *aut dedere aut judicare* ought to be inferred only from such treaties as provide for it or perhaps should be viewed also as a binding norm of customary law. He also noted that the states had the obligation to either prosecute or extradite the perpetrator but there was also a third option, connected with the hypothetical jurisdiction of the ICC to adjudicate on the crimes.[97] In his capacity as special rapporteur, Galicki submitted four reports: in 2006, 2007, 2008 and 2011 (more in subchapter 11.2).

In 2015, as part of the works of the International Law Commission, the Polish MFA Advisory Legal Committee submitted an opinion dealing

95 New ICC Presidency elected for 2021–2024, 11.03.2021: https://www.icc-cpi.int/Pages/item.aspx?name=pr1576.

96 GA Res/60/22.

97 YILC 2004 – Vol.II(2): 124.

with the immunities of state officials in the context of foreign criminal jurisdiction.[98]

It will also be expedient to mention Council of Europe initiatives relating to works on the states' international co-operation in criminal cases. For example, Hofmański was involved in some of the Council of Europe's projects as a member of the Committee of Experts of the Council of Europe known as the Reflection Group on the Developments in International Co-operation in Criminal Matters from 2001 to 2002; subsequently also in the Committee of Experts on Transnational Justice, created for the purpose of continuing the works of the Group of Reflection, serving in 2004–2006.

5 The Chief Commission and the Institute of National Remembrance

The end of the Cold War and the fall of communist rule in Central Europe did not make it easier to judge the Nazis, not only because doing so was not the priority for the authorities of European states but also because many of those guilty were no longer among the living.

For several years, relations with Germany have been developing somewhat dynamically with regard to the investigation of crimes. The prosecutors from the Institute of National Remembrance actively co-operate with the Central Office of the State Justice Administrations for the Investigation of National Socialist Crimes in Ludwigsburg – a specialized unit within the German prosecution services, tasked with investigating the crimes committed by German citizens during WWII.[99] As for relations with Russia, despite several, 'thaws,'[100] they remain sense, and there can be no question of the prosecution of crimes for the time being.

---

98 Opinion by Legal Advisory Committee to the Minister of Foreign Affairs of the Republic of Poland on immunities of State officials from foreign criminal jurisdiction, 27.04.2015, https://legal.un.org/ilc/sessions/67/pdfs/english/iso_poland.pdf.

99 Nowotnik (2018).

100 Involving e.g. Mikhail Gorbachev's admission that the USSR was behind the Katyń Massacre, though a counterbalance had already been sought in the USSR for it, in the form of so-called Anti-Katyń which referred to allegations of crimes committed by Polish nationals on Russian prisoners of war in January 1919 when the Polish-Soviet war took place, the name of Anti-Katyń, was a part of a Russian propaganda effort to relative the Katyn Massacre. The goal was to juxtapose the Katyń Massacre with the alleged intended crimes perpetrated by Poles on Russian prisoners of war. Incidents of sadism against Russian prisoners in POW camps were met with condemnation and could hardly be regarded as the norm. The literature cites isolated

With an amendment of 1991 the law on Chief Commission for the Investigation of Nazi Crimes in Poland – Institute of National Remembrance was changed,[101] the Chief Commission's tasks were specified to include the investigation of Nazi crimes, Stalinist crimes and other crimes constituting war crimes or crimes against humanity. Article 2b(1) of the law on Chief Commission after amendment included provisions on the crimes to be investigated, viz. non-applicability of statutes of limitations with regard to war crimes and crimes against humanity. Article 2b(2) defined crimes against humanity: 'crimes of genocide (…) and other serious persecutions due to the victims' affiliation with a specific ethnic, social, racial or religious groups, if implemented by state authorities or inspired or tolerated by them.' The innovative nature of the amendment is noteworthy. It introduced the possibility of investigative activities but also archive works and research into Stalinist crimes, which were defined as committed against individuals or groups of the population up to 31.12.1956 by the communist authorities or tolerated and inspired by them (Article 2a).

In 1998, the Sejm enacted the Act on the Institute of National Remembrance – Commission for the Prosecution of Crimes against the Polish Nation (the 'IPN Act'),[102] whereby the 1984 Act on the Chief Commission was repealed. The new act renamed 'Hitlerite' crimes to Nazi crimes and 'Stalinist' crimes to communist crimes. The later were defined as: 'acts committed by officials of the communist state during the period from 17 September 1939 to 31 December 1989, consisting in repression or other forms of violation of human rights with regard to individuals or groups of population or in connection with repression, constituting crimes according to the Polish criminal law applicable at the time of their commission' (Article 2(1)). The definition of a crime against humanity was copied over from Article 2b of the above-cited act (and renumbered to 3). The definition differs completely from the one in Article 118a of the Criminal Code of 1997, to which it was added by an amendment in 2010.[103] The purpose

examples such as the trial of Second Lieutenant Malinowski for the killing of Soviet prisoner of war Arnold Lahzis (Wyszczelski (2013): 65). Zbigniew Karpus mentions the trials of Wagner and Malinowski for abuse of the prisoners of the camp in Strzałkowo – see interview of 18.05.2011, *Katyń jak obozy dla jeńców z Rosji w 1920?*, https://www.rp.pl/publicystyka/art14519621-historia-katyn-jak-obozy-dla-jencow-z-rosji-w-1920, also Korkuć (2020): 7.

101 Amendment of 1991 (Dz.U.1991.45.195), referred to the act of 1984 (more in subchapter 3.2).

102 Dz.U.1998.155.1016.

103 Dz.U.2010.626.

of the provisions of the Criminal Code regarding crimes against humanity was to reflect the provisions of the Rome Statute. In domestic law, similarly to international law, those are regarded as a separate category of crime from genocide, with altogether differently defined elements.[104] The complex *chapeau* of the crimes against humanity defined in[105] Articles 118a(1), 118a(2) and 118a(3) stipulates identically: 'who, participating in a mass attack or at least one of repeat attacks targeted against a group of the population, undertaken for the purpose of implementing or supporting the policy of a state or organization' – thus, it does not refer to the crime of genocide. At the time of the adoption of the IPN Act, a similar definition of crimes against humanity was provided in the Convention on the Non-Applicability of Statutory Limitations of 1968.

In cases of the crimes specified in the IPN Act, the investigations are led by a specially appointed prosecutor of the Regional Commission (which is regulated by Article 45 of the Act). In cases specified in Article 1(1)(a), i.e. concerning the scope of the act's regulation with regard to the crimes mentioned in the act,[106] the special prosecutor has all of the powers of a prosecutor, also in cases within the jurisdiction of military courts. The purpose of the investigation is also to explain the circumstances of the case, in particular to identify the victims; hence, the investigation may proceed despite the alleged perpetrator's death.

Although the prospects of identifying the perpetrators dwindle increasingly with time, as at the end of February 2004, as provided by Andrzej Rzepliński,[107] the IPN prosecutors were conducting as many as 1295 investigations. Those included 335 cases Nazi crimes (25.9% of all), 878 of

104 See Article 118 (enumerating the elements of genocide) and 118a (enumerating the elements of a crime against humanity) (Dz.U.2022.1138).

105 See. art. 118a §1, 2 i 3 Criminal Code.

106 The regulatory scope includes registering, gathering, storing, preparing, securing, sharing and publishing documents created or gathered from 22.07.1944 to 31.07.1990 by the security organs of the state, as well as the security organs of the German Third Reich and Union of Soviet Socialist Republics, concerning:
a) the following crimes, committed against Poles or Polish citizens of other ethnic (national) affiliation, during the period from 8.11.1917 to 31.07.1990:
   - Nazi crimes;
   - communist crimes;
   - crimes of Ukrainian nationalists and members of Ukrainian formations collaborating with the German Third Reich;
   - other criminal offences constituting crimes against peace, crimes against humanity or war crimes.

107 Rzepliński (2004).

communist crimes (67.85% of all) and 82 other cases involving war crimes and crimes against humanity (6.3%). The mechanism guaranteed by the IPN Act allows investigations to be led in cases as yet unexplained.[108]

By comparison,[109] in 2010, the prosecutors of the Regional Commissions had a total of 1141 cases pending, including 697 of communist crimes, i.e. 61%; 391 into Nazi crimes, i.e. 34% of all cases; and 43 cases of war crimes and crimes against humanity, including genocide, i.e. 3.7%; the remaining 10 cases involved acts specified by Articles 54 and 55 of the IPN Act (provisions criminalizing certain conduct relating to such documents as should be or already are in the IPN's archives, and counterfactual public denial of crimes against the Polish nation).

According to statistics published at the end of 2018, the Regional Commissions – as at 1.01.2018 – had 562 cases pending, out of which 407 (more than 72%) concerning communist crimes, 130 (more than 23%) concerning Nazi crimes, and 25 (4.4%) concerning other types of criminal offences constituting crimes against peace, crimes against humanity or war crimes, including 14 cases under Articles 54–55 of IPN Act. In 2018, the Commission registered 1140 new cases, including 768 (more than 67%) dealing with communist crimes, 280 (24.5%) dealing with Nazi crimes, and 92 (8%) dealing with other crimes, out of which 65 cases concerned Articles 54–55 of the IPN Act.[110]

Without delving into statistical details concerning the finalization of cases handled by the IPN, the majority of cases end in a discontinuance (due to failure to identify the perpetrator or other reasons), few perpetrators (several p.a., statistically speaking) are charged, and in the majority of cases the decision is a refusal to investigate, joinder to other pending investigations or remand to another authority according to jurisdiction.

As can be observed, many of the cases currently dealt with by the IPN concern not Nazi crimes or crimes against humanity and war crimes, but communist crimes. However, the circumstances of crimes committed during WWII continue to be actively explained. Currently, the Regional Commissions of the IPN continue to lead investigations into crimes against

108 Kuczyńska (2019b): 149–150.

109 Information on the activities of the IPN between 1.01.2011 and 31.12.2011, https://ipn.gov.pl/pl/o-ipn/informacje-o-dzialalnos/24311,w-okresie-1-stycznia-2011-r-31-grudnia-2011-r.html, 144.

110 Information on the activities of the IPN between 1.01.2018 and 31.12.2018, https://ipn.gov.pl/pl/o-ipn/informacje-o-dzialalnos/70546,w-okresie-1-stycznia-2018-r-31-grudnia-2018-r.html.

humanity or war crimes, albeit those do not end in indictments but rather serve the in-depth explanation of the acts committed. For example, the investigations pending at the Regional Commission in Gdańsk[111] currently concern the mass killings of Polish citizens in the autumn of 1939 in Piaśnica near Wejherowo (Case S 56.2011.Zn); Nazi crimes constituting crimes against peace committed by the officials of the German Third Reich during WWII at the site of the Stutthof German concentration Camp in Sztutowo together with its subcamps (resulting in the death of more than 60 thousand people, with no fewer than 110 thousand inmates subjected to torture and inhuman treatment, Case S 10.2018.Zn); Nazi crimes constituting crimes against humanity committed by the officials of the German Third Reich on 8 and 29.09.1939 in Gdańsk, consisting in the death sentences passed by the Eberhardt Group's Field Court Martial on the 38 defenders of the Polish Post building in Gdańsk.[112]

The investigations pending before the Regional Commission in Cracow[113] currently concern Nazi crimes against humanity committed in Oświęcim and other localities, consisting in the deprivation of Polish citizens of their freedom by placing them at the KL Auschwitz-Birkenau concentration camp, where they were killed and tortured. The goal of the investigation is, among others, to determine the organization and functioning of the KL Auschwitz-Birkenau death camp in the light of the functioning of the other concentration and death camps, the number of victims, the details of the camp prisoners and the circumstances of their deaths. The Cracow commission also has a pending investigation into the Nazi crime against humanity consisting in the mass executions of Polish citizens in Przegorzały in 1939–1944 by the officials of the German state (Case S 61.2012.Zn).[114]

---

111 See Gdańsk website of the Commission: https://ipn.gov.pl/pl/sledztwa/sledztwa/oddzialowa-komisja-w-gdansku-s/31537,Sledztwa-w-toku.html.

112 The Eberhardt Group was a formation comprising the different German police and military troops stationed within the Free City of Danzig (Gdańsk). Those were subordinated to the German 3rd Army command, and their commander was Friedrich Eberhardt; more extensively Ordon (1974): 211–222.

113 See Cracow website of the Commission: https://ipn.gov.pl/pl/sledztwa/sledztwa/oddzialowa-komisja-w-krakowie/31558,Sledztwa-w-toku.html.

114 Other prior investigations are discussed by Rzepliński (2004). It is also worth noting that the information on the IPN's activities published by the institution itself directly concern those of its investigations attracting public interest, e.g. case S 38/04/Zk – the investigation of the Katyń Massacre, constituting a war crime and crime against humanity (mass murder of no fewer than 21,768 Polish citizens from 5 March to an unidentified day and month of 1940 in the territory of the USSR by the officials of that state), or S 19/05/Zn – the investigation into the killing of the municipal president of

The Regional Commission in Warsaw, in turn, is in charge of an investigation into the Katyń Massacre (Case S 38/04/Zk) with regard, among other things, to the determination of the list of victims and all circumstances of the crime, and archivization of the documents. The investigation concerns the murder of about 22 thousand Polish citizens. In this regard, the IPN provided assistance to the plenipotentiary of the Minister of Foreign Affairs in the case before the ECtHR (as discussed below).[115]

6 The Judiciary

Cases concerning the crimes investigated by the IPN fall within the jurisdiction of the common courts (with a possible appeal-in-cassation to the Supreme Court under Article 523 of the Code of Criminal Procedure of 1997). However, the structure of the provisions governing the IPN is somewhat unfortunate and has been the subject of critical analysis in the subject literature.[116] The problem largely concerns the definition of the crimes specified by the IPN Act, which defines the international crimes in a completely different manner from the Criminal Code's. The crime definitions from the IPN Act diverge very significantly from the statutory definitions in the Criminal Code and those in international legislation. Suffice to say that the definition of a crime against humanity in the IPN Act comprises the crime of genocide, whereas for decades now, the crimes have had independent definitions in international law and unquestionably are not synonymous (e.g. the definitions in the Rome Statute).

As a result, it cannot be said that Polish common courts (when acting on the basis of the IPN Act) apply international legislation consistently with their original 'international' wording; rather, they attempt, with varying degrees of success, to reconcile the language of the domestic statutes to the norms of international law.[117]

Another problem linked to the IPN Act concerns the application of its definition of a crime against humanity to the judgment of the perpetrators

Warsaw, Stefan Starzyński. Both of the cases are described in the information on the activities of the Institute of National Remembrance – Commission for the Prosecution of Crimes against the Polish Nation, for the period from 1.01.2011 to 31.12.2011: 152.

115 The IPN has created a special website for initiatives dealing with the investigation of the crime: katyn.ipn.gov.pl.

116 Grzebyk (2017).

117 See. Grzebyk (2017): 287–300; Wierczyńska (2017a): 275–286, (2022).

of communist crimes. As a result, the courts rule that, for example, a crime against humanity has occurred with regard to internments several days long[118] or the political persecution of individuals in the 40s of the 20th century.[119] Such a practice ought to be met with a critical eye. In the 40s of the 20th century, Poland was only party to the London Agreement of 1945, an Annex to which – the IMT Charter – defined crimes against humanity. Since 1969, in turn, Poland had been party to the Convention on the Non-Applicability of Statutory Limitations, which contained definition of crimes against humanity, but a different one from the IMT Charter's. Moreover, the IMT Charter does not constitute a universal document on the basis of which perpetrators of crimes could be charged. Its application was limited to the major criminals of the European Axis. By contrast, the Convention on the Non-Applicability of Statutory Limitations does not at all concern itself with the judgment of individuals – it only deals with regulations preventing the statute of limitations from running on the crimes. However, Polish courts judge communist crimes as crimes against humanity in violation of the principle of legality; furthermore, they do so, citing the ICC's judgments inconsistently with the purpose and subject-matter of the Rome Statute, which entered into force in 2002 and which mandates the applicability of the ICC's operations only to the most serious crimes committed after the date of the Statute's coming into force. Such activities (i.e. judging communist crimes as crimes against humanity in reference to the events of the Martial Law (12.12.1981- to 22.07.1983) or the political events of the 40s of the 20th century) violate the principle of legality and are out of agreement with scholarly findings.[120] The above-described situation will continue to exist for as long as there exist two legal instruments each defining international crimes differently. While the regulation contained in the Criminal Code already does not sufficiently reflect the international legislation, the IPN Act

118 E.g. the Regional Court in Białystok, judgment, 18.10.2016, VIII Ka 414/16, Regional Court in Gorzów Wielkopolski, judgment, 15.10.2015, II K 62/11, IPN –S87/06/Zk – the last judgment can be found e.g. at https://www.legal-tools.org/doc/a98935/pdf.

119 E.g., District Court in Legionowo, judgement, 16.11.2011, II K 679/17.

120 E.g. Piątek (2004): 258. That author expressly remarks: 'one cannot, through the interpretation of Article 3 of the IPN Act, modify and expand the definitions arising from international law'; that, however, is what is done when the courts interpret the provisions of the Rome Statute, in a way contrary, as it were, to established international practice, just to force them to match the *a priori* thesis that the criminal offence of internment for several days or prosecution of a single individual can be classified and judged as a crime against humanity.

introduces complete terminological confusion, and the recommendation should be for it to be amended.

The cases proceeding under the IPN Act are not the only situations in which the common courts contend with the application of international criminal law. Another example are the provisions concerning the taking over of individuals convicted and sentenced by an international court. Polish courts have issued decisions agreeing to transfers of ICTY convicts and adapting their sentences to Polish laws and regulations.[121] The first of the ICTY's convicts to be transferred to Poland for the service of their prison term was Radislav Krstić, convicted of the crime of genocide for his participation in the massacre of civilians in Srebrenica.[122] Polish courts issued orders accepting his transfer to Poland for the service of his prison term.[123] Later, Krstić, serving his time in the Polish prison in Piotrków Trybunalski, was joined by other persons convicted by the ICTY, viz. Sreten Lukić,[124] Mićo Stanišić and Stojan Župljanin,[125] which were serving their terms in Poland since 8.08.2019. Pursuant to the provisions of Division XIII of Polish Code of Criminal Procedure, Poland was to adapt the imposed prison terms to the upper sentencing limit provided for by Polish statute. Thus, even though Krstić had been sentenced to 35 years' imprisonment, the Polish court found that his conduct exhausted the elements of criminal offences regulated by Polish Criminal Code and accepted his transfer for the 25 years available in Poland (this sentence was already served in Poland). The sentence imposed by the ICTY on Lukić had been 20 years, whereas the Polish upper sentencing limit for the relevant types of crimes was 15 years, and such became the period for which his transfer was agreed. On 7.10.2021, the President of the International Residual Mechanism for Criminal Tribunals decided to release Lukić from the remainder of his sentence.[126] As for

121 That is the consequence of mentioned above Poland's agreement with the UN, Dz. U.2009.137.1123; the adaptation of the prison terms imposed by international courts is done on the basis of Polish provisions – Chapter XIII of the Code of Criminal Procedure.

122 ICTY, Prosecutor v. Krstić, Judgement, 19.04.2004, IT-98-33-A.

123 See Regional Court in Warsaw, VIII KOP 222/12, order of 6.12. 2012, confirming the legal admissibility of the transfer of Radislav Krstić's sentence to be served in Poland, and VIII KOP 49/14, order of 26.05.2014.

124 ICTY, Prosecutor v. Šainović, Pavković, Lazarević, Lukić, Judgement, 23.01.2014, IT-05-87-A.

125 ICTY, Prosecutor v. Stanišić, Župljanin, Judgement, 30.06.2016, IT-08-91-A.

126 MICT, Prokurator v. Sreten Lukić (Decision on the Application for Early Release of Sreten Lukić), 7.10.2021, MICT-14-67-ES.4

Stanišić and Żupljanin, whom the ICTY had sentenced to 22 years each, the Regional Court in Warsaw decided that 15 years could be served in Poland.

Polish courts have also made an attempt to judge crimes committed by Polish soldiers abroad. This refers to the events of August 2007, when Polish soldiers of the International Security Assistance Force opened machine-gun and mortar fire on the Afghan village of Nangar Khel. Six persons died and three were injured. As a result, Polish military courts held the first trials since WWII in war crimes consisting in the killing of civilians and opening fire at an undefended object, violating Articles 25 and 23(b) of the Hague Regulations of 1907; Article 3(1)(a) of the GC IV of 1949 relative to the Protection of Civilian Persons in Time of War, and Article 4(2)(a) and Articles 13(1) and 13(2) of AP II to the GC of 1949. The military prosecutors charged seven soldiers: the group commander who issued the order, the commander of the patrol sent to the site, and five subordinate soldiers – a warrant officer, senior corporal and three privates. In June 2011, the Military Regional Court in Warsaw acquitted all 7 soldiers due to the lack of sufficient evidence to demonstrate that the opening of fire on the village was intentional.

On 14.03.2012, the Supreme Court[127] on appeal acquitted one of the commissioned officers (the former base commander) and two of the privates (the SC found the Military Regional Court in Warsaw to have acted correctly in excluding the *dolus directus* and the *dolus eventualis* in respect of those individuals with regard to the crimes charged and in holding that they had been acting in the execution of an order from their commander without realizing the order to be unlawful). The case of the remaining two soldiers was remanded to the Military Regional Court for retrial at the first instance. That court, on 19.03.2015, ruled that persuasive evidence of the commission of a war crime by the defendants was lacking. The court emphasized that did not mean they had not committed a criminal offence. The court held them responsible for having executed the order inconsistently with its meaning and with the rules governing the use of weapons by the Polish Military Contingent in Afghanistan. One of the defendants was also convicted of careless handling of a weapon (the LM-60 mortar), resulting in the death and severe injury of other persons. Three of the defendants were sentenced to suspended prison terms ranging from 6 months to 2 years, and the fourth received a conditional discontinuance. On 17.02.2016, the Military Chamber of the Supreme Court[128] upheld the first-instance

127 SN, Judgement, 14.03.2012, WA 39/11.

128 SN, Judgement, 17.02.2016, WA 16/15.

judgment of 19.03.2015, simultaneously announcing that the defendants were not guilty of a war crime.

It will also be expedient to refer to some cases that, although they potentially involve international crimes, were not judged by Polish courts. One of the cases still demanding explanation is the responsibility of Polish authorities for the CIA prison in Kiejkuty, where, in 2003–2005, individuals suspect of terrorism were held on behalf of the American authorities and tortured as part of 'enhanced interrogation techniques' such as waterboarding. Polish authorities consistently claimed that they had not been aware of any torture and the premises of the base in Kiejkuty had effectively been under American control.[129] Applicants Al Nashiri[130] and Abu Zubaydah, kept at the prison, filed an application with the European Court of Human Rights against Poland, alleging violations of Articles 3, 5 and 8 ECHR. The ECtHR found that Poland was responsible for the violations. In the judgment *Abu Zubaydah v. Poland*,[131] the ECtHR assessed that Poland is responsible for violations applicant's rights under art. 3, 5 and 8 of the Convention. In the Court's opinion, Poland had not managed to conduct an effective investigation in accordance with the requirements set out in Articles 3 and 13 of the Convention, either. Furthermore, the ECtHR found a violation of the applicant's rights under Article 8 and held Poland responsible for enabling the CIA's transfer of the applicant out of the territory despite the existence of a serious risk of manifestly unfair trial in the light of Article 6(1) of the Convention.[132] By contrast, the investigation, which should have included President Aleksander Kwaśniewski, Prime Minister Leszek Miller and Intelligence Agency Chief Zbigniew Siemiątkowski,[133] had already been discontinued by the prosecution service in 2020, citing the lack of evidence, according to press reports.[134] The domestic proceedings did not explain the

129 It is worth noting that this angle is an element of proceedings pending before the ICC; see: ICC, Judgment on the appeal against the decision on the authorisation of an investigation into the situation in the Islamic Republic of Afghanistan, 5.03.2020, ICC-02/17-138.

130 ECtHR, Al Nashiri v. Poland, App. No. 28761/11, Judgement, 24.07.2014.

131 ECtHR, Husayn (Abu Zubaydah) v. Poland, App No. 7511/13, Judgement, 24.07.2014.

132 *Ibidem* §566.

133 See also Wierczyńska (2011): 276.

134 Żytnicki (2022). The Committee of Ministers of the Council of Europe, which monitors the states' compliance with the judgments, has received information about the partial suspension of the proceedings. In statements dating from January 2022, the Polish authorities noted that the prosecutorial order partially discontinuing the investigation had been upheld by the Regional Court in Warsaw on 7 September 2021 and was thus legally binding (final and unappealable), https://hudoc.exec.coe.int/eng?i=004-20624.

matter of the responsibility of the Polish officials who ought to have exercised effective control.

An equally controversial matter demanding explanation is the in-depth investigation of the crime committed in 1940 by the NKVD. The crime of the execution by shooting of about 22 thousands of Polish citizens deemed 'enemies of the Soviet power' and buried in mass graves has not yet been explained. An exhaustive investigation has not been completed, all evidence has not been presented, and no specific individuals have been convicted (although in 1990 the Soviet authorities officially confirmed their responsibility for the shootings of Polish prisoners of war and an official investigation was initiated, and in 2010 the Russian Duma adopted a resolution concerning the Katyń tragedy, in which it confirmed that the: 'mass extermination of Polish nationals in the territory of the USSR during World War II,' had taken place on Stalin's orders[135]). Outside of the thaw periods, the Russian Federation has for many years made the co-operation difficult if only with regard to at least identifying all of the victims' burial locations or granting access to the documents. The relatives of the victims attempted to prove before the ECtHR that Russia had violated Articles 2, 3 and 38 ECtHR. On 16.04.2012, the ECtHR Chamber ruled that there had been a violation of Article of the Convention and that Russia had breached the obligation of Article 38 ECHR (the obligation to facilitate the examination of the case). The Court also found itself to lack the competence to examine the merits of the alleged violation of Article 2 of the Convention.[136] The Grand Chamber affirmed the lack of the *ratione temporis* jurisdiction in the context of the alleged violation of Article 2 and that the alleged violation of Article 3 had not taken place, only finding Russia to have violated its obligations under Article 38 of the Convention.[137]

7 Academic Life

At present, within many faculties and without, works are taking place on international criminal law, concerned with its beginnings, institutionalization

135 Russian State Duma's resolution concerning the Katyń massacre, at: https://dzieje.pl/aktualnosci/rosja-uchwala-dumy-panstwowej-ws-katynia.

136 ECtHR, Janowiec and others v. Russia, App. No. 55508/07 and 29520/09, Judgement, 16.04.2012.

137 ECtHR, Janowiec and others v. Russia, App. No. 55508/07 and 29520/09, Judgement 21.10.2013.

and challenges awaiting it.[138] After 1989, the first publications at least indirectly relating to the criminal responsibility of an individual in international law or the international administration of justice in criminal cases appeared in the early 90s of the 20th century. Those were primarily journal articles, chapters in monographs, rarely complete monographs, unfortunately written mostly in Polish. Authors of the first monographs in the field include: Władysław Czapliński (*Skutki prawne nielegalnego użycia siły w stosunkach międzynarodowych*, 1993 – 'Legal effects of unlawful use of force in international relations') and Joanna Nowakowska-Małusecka (*Odpowiedzialność karna jednostek za zbrodnie popełnione w byłej Jugosławii i w Rwandzie*, 2000 – 'Criminal responsibility of individuals for crimes committed in the former Yugoslavia and Rwanda).

With the beginning of the 21st century, research and publications in international criminal law flourished. International criminal law also became an element of the classic lecture in public international law or criminal procedure, as well as disciplines other than legal. Numerous researchers took on international criminal law even outside of lectures or seminars with the students.

Nearly all Polish universities (including private ones) provide lectures on international criminal law and confer doctorates and habilitations in this area. In addition to traditionally existing universities, private law schools have flourished after 1989. However, no faculty other than the Faculty of Law and Administration of the University of Łódź has had a dedicated chair of international criminal law. In **Łódź**, the Chair of International Criminal Law of the Faculty of Law and Administration of the University of Łódź was first headed by Krzysztof Indecki (1952–2021) and thereafter transformed into a Department of the International Administration of Justice. Moreover, the following scholars have researched international criminal law: Anna Wyrozumska, who participated in the works leading to the adoption of the ICC Statute, Tomasz Ostropolski, Justyna Jurewicz, Tomasz Lachowski and Witold Kulesza. In **Lublin** (**Catholic University of Lublin**), international criminal law was the area of expertise of Kinga Stasiak, while in **Poznań**, at **Adam Mickiewicz University**, international criminal law is the field

138 A questionnaire was designed for the purpose of obtaining detailed information from the individual universities and sent out via official channels as well as the Polish section of the AIDP, and private channels. The Google questionnaire was answered by 17 persons, and 4 additional questionnaires were sent by e-mail. The section description reflects the data obtained. Some of the faculties did not return the questionnaires.

researched by Paweł Wiliński and Anna Potyrała. In Toruń, at **Nicolaus Copernicus University**, works in international criminal law are published by Agnieszka Szpak. In Warsaw, several academic institutions are home to researchers in international criminal law. At the **University of Warsaw**, works in this field are published by Patrycja Grzebyk, Karol Karski and Michał Królikowski, while at **Cardinal Stefan Wyszyński University**, Elżbieta Karska (she published her works also as Elżbieta Socha at the University of Wrocław), as well as Krzysztof Masło. The researchers at the **Institute of Law Studies of the Polish Academy of Sciences** included Leszek Kubicki and nowadays Hanna Kuczyńska, Celina Nowak, Karolina Wierczyńska; one of the academics with ties to the Institute was Jerzy Kranz, who participated in the works on the ICC. At the **War Studies University** works on international criminal law published Piotr Milik. The **University of Wrocław** is home to the publications of Karolina Kremens and Bartłomiej Krzan. Among authors dealing with international criminal law, it will be expedient to mention Joanna Małusecka-Nowakowska and Ilona Topa of the **University of Silesia in Katowice.** At the **University of Gdańsk** the scholar who researched international criminal law and took part in the adoption of the ICC Statute was Michał Płachta.

Coursebooks on international criminal law include: Michał Królikowski, Paweł Wiliński, Jacek Izydorczyk *Podstawy prawa karnego międzynarodowego* (2008) ('Essentials of international criminal law'); Lech Gardocki, Teresa Gardocka, Łukasz Majewski, *Prawo karne międzynarodowe. Zarys systemu* (2017) ('International criminal law. A system outline'); Piotr Hofmański and Hanna Kuczyńska (*Międzynarodowe prawo karne* – 'International criminal law').

As far as participation in **international associations** participating in the development of international criminal law is concerned, one should first of all mention the ILA, in which Poles are actively involved. The Committees having at least marginally dealt with the international administration of justice in criminal cases are: Committee on the Procedures of International Courts and Tribunals (members include Joanna Gomuła and Aleksandra Mężykowska); Commitee on Complementarity in International Criminal Law (members included Elżbieta Karska and Karolina Wierczyńska, the latter a co-author of the Sydney group report (2018) and Lisbon final report (2022)); Committee on the Use of Force: Military Assistance on Request (members include Michał Kowalski and Patrycja Grzebyk; the Committee's previous composition in 2005–2011 included Władysław Czapliński and Elżbieta Mikos-Skuza).

As for the AIDP, active members of the section formerly included Marian Cieślak, Jan Skupiński, Barbara Kunicka-Michalska, Stanisław Waltoś and Lech Gardocki; in the recent two decades, however, for various reasons, the Polish group had not shown activity – to the extent that the country membership fee was no longer paid – until reactivation of Polish branch in March 2021. It is worth mentioning, however, that its Polish members are successfully active abroad. Stanisław Tosza became Secretary General of the AIDP for the 2019–2024 term.

Members of the IDI include Kazimierz Lankosz, Jerzy Makarczyk as a member emeritus, and Malgosia Fitzmaurice elected from the United Kingdom, according to her academic affiliation. Previously, Krzysztof Skubiszewski remained an active member of the IDI until his death. On numerous occasions, the institute has dealt with issued relating to the development of international criminal law. For example, its Cracow session in 2005 bore fruit in the adoption of a resolution, for which Christian Tomuschat acted as the rapporteur, titled *Universal criminal jurisdiction with regard to the crime of genocide, crimes against humanity and war crimes*.[139]

8 Conclusions

Since 1989, Poles have actively supported initiatives in favour of the establishment of an international justice system for criminal cases. Here, one must mention in particular the reports and missions of Tadeusz Mazowiecki, who, as a UN Special Rapporteur, advocated for the establishment of an international tribunal for the former Yugoslavia. Poles also participated in the works leading to the creation of a permanent International Criminal Court, supporting the 'like-minded states,' i.e. mainstream proposals.

Although Poland did not have judges in the ICTY or the ICTR, Polish judges sat in international and hybrid courts, and Polish scholars are active in international associations, such as the ILA and the AIDP, whose activities involve international criminal law and international co-operation in criminal cases. Monographs and coursebooks on international criminal law are coming to life, and a majority of universities offer lectures in international criminal law. The discipline is now present in many institutions of higher education.

139 IDI Resolution of 26.08.2005, https://www.idi-iil.org/app/uploads/2017/06/2005_kra_03_en.pdf.

PART 2

International Crimes and Principles of Their Prosecution and Punishment

CHAPTER 5

International Crimes and Their Prosecution

1 Determining the Scope of Criminalization

Essential to the reflection on international criminal law is the specification of the punishable act the commission of which triggers the application of the norms of that law. There exists a considerable divergence in this regard, both terminological and conceptual. Defining an international crime or an international criminal offence is task fraught with difficulties. One could call upon diverse and often divergent criminological findings and look to the protected interest (or 'good' – *Rechtsgut*) infringed against, or the nature of the criminality, or, last but not least, the social point of reference.

In the first order, we are going to consider the bases and scope of international criminalization. The latter is of fundamental significance to the distinction between international crimes and transnational ones. Separate attention is given to international terrorism, which eludes unequivocal classifications, but – as demonstrated by not only Polish specialists in international criminal law – has large potential for being regarded as an international crime *stricto sensu*, irrespective, of course, of the futile attempts at its penalization and establishment of an international criminal court for it near the end of the 30s of the 20th century, or the activities of the contemporary Special Tribunal for Lebanon.[1]

The following chapters will analyse the individual core international crimes: crimes against peace (aggression), genocide, crimes against humanity, and war crimes. This systematization coincides with the scope of *ratione materiae* jurisdiction of the International Criminal Court and, in a significant degree, of the international tribunals created before it.

The literature notes that the process of internationalization and harmonization of criminal law is the consequence of the transfer of criminal-law powers to a supranational level, and the ultimate shape of the criminalization depends on (results from) the consensus among the states. Therefore, the internationalization of criminal repression is a reflection of the internationalization of crime and a necessary consequence of the latter.[2]

---

1 See STL, AC, Case no. STL-11–01/I, 16.02.2011, §83f.; cf. Krzan (2009), (2020).

2 Gardocki (1979): 15.

Already from the beginning, the relationship between international crimes and international peace had been considered. In the fourth international congress of criminal law, which took place in July 1937 in Paris, a report on the subject was delivered by Kopek Mikliszanski.[3] The problem discussed in that report vividly resembles the correlation on which the Security Council relied to create *ad hoc* tribunals, treating the commission of international crimes as a violation of international peace or safety.

International crimes themselves must be regarded as an infringement of the international community's basic interests. To look no further, this understanding of the correlation is confirmed in the preamble to the Rome Statute of the ICC, the third paragraph of which specifies that the crimes falling within the Court's jurisdiction: 'threaten the peace, security and well-being of the world'. A similar position had previously been taken by the judges of the ICTY who ruled that the crimes the Tribunal had been established to judge: 'affect the whole of mankind and shock the conscience of all nations of the world'.[4]

We are referring here to the core issue of the infringed legal interest. It seems natural from the perspective of international law to refer to peremptory norms. We could thus regard the prohibitions relating to the crimes as peremptory international law. The perfect affirmation of such an approach is the judgment of the in Zoran Kupreškić's case, finding that the majority of international humanitarian law, especially those prohibiting war crimes, crimes against humanity and genocide, are also non-derogable (*ius cogens*) norms of international law.[5] In this regard, the achievements of Polish scholars are indisputable, albeit not necessarily directly translatable into international criminal categories. By way of example, one could mention the widely quoted publications of Krystyna Marek,[6] Jerzy Sztucki[7] or Karol Wolfke,[8] and, contemporarily, Władysław Czapliński[9] and Cezary Mik.[10] Rarely, however, do they take up the problem of the correlation involving

3 Mikliszanski (1938): 56.

4 ICTY, *The Prosecutor v. Dusko Tadic* (Decision on the Defence Motion on Jurisdiction), IT-94-1-T, 10.08.1995, §42.

5 ICTY, *The Prosecutor v. Kupreskic* et al. (Judgment), 14.01.2000, IT-95-16-T, §520.

6 Marek (1968).

7 Sztucki (1974).

8 Wolfke (1972): 206, cf. a more cautious position by the same author Wolfke (1974): 158.

9 Czapliński (2006), (2016).

10 Mik (2010), (2013).

the peremptory prohibition against the infringement of specified legal interests precisely as international crimes.

It would be difficult to disagree with Tomasz Kaczmarek, whose belief it is that Polish scholarship, aside from the fundamental opus of Juliusz Makarewicz,[11] has not approached the problem of the protected legal interest in a systemic and complex manner for decades.[12] The aforementioned corypheus, taking note of historical, ethnographic and comparative source studies, outlined the evolution of the substantive understanding of a criminal offence as an attack on nature-given goods essential to development of the individual and to the survival of the social group.[13] They formulated the thesis that the institutions of criminal law are historically variable sociological phaenomena. The continued validity of Makarewicz's findings is not disputed; the quality and innovativeness of his research secure for him a lasting place on the firmament of world's criminal-law studies. His preceding work on the essence of a criminal offence was also of paramount significance.[14] Therein, he demonstrated that a criminal offence is a social phaenomenon, and thus criminality occurs not only in a state but also in any other community capable of reacting to it. He regarded a criminal offence as an act: 'by a member of a given group, such that the rest of the members thereof considers so harmful thereto that it comes forward against the perpetrator with a public, external and common reaction by abridging one of his goods.'[15] This coincides with the approach presented by the Supreme Court after having considered in the Military Chamber the case of a person convicted under Article 276(1) of the Criminal Code of 1967 in conjunction with Article 48(2) and Article 48(4) of the Decree on Martial Law:

> A criminal offence is an act (…) striking at the substantial social goods recognized by society and remaining under the protection of not only criminal law but also other normative systems, including morality, duty arising from a sense of tradition and national identity. The act must manifest an objective asociality, in the sense that it always transgresses against the values accepted by the given collective.[16]

11 Makarewicz (1906): 26f.
12 Kaczmarek (2014): 140.
13 Makarewicz (1906): 26–31, 136f.
14 Makarewicz (1896).
15 Makarewicz (1896) quoted after Pasek (2002): 164.
16 SN, Judgment of 26.09.2003, WK 18/03, LEX152034.

In Polish literature, the early studies did not approach this topic completely in the abstract, outside of the context of the ICC Statute.[17] During the Interwar period, however, Zygmunt Cybichowski categorically emphasized: '[an international crime] is an unlawful violation of international law, in which the state is culpable,' where the subject could only be an independent state: 'whereas the act of an individual cannot be an international crime.'[18] The perspective at the time focused primarily on the category of the *delicta juris gentium* – 'punishable acts of particular importance from the standpoint of their international (universal) harmfulness.'[19] In committing such acts, an individual (natural person) could realistically affect the shape of international relations.

In this range of topics, high prominence from both the academic and the organizational perspective belongs to Emil Stanisław Rappaport. It is thanks to his determination[20] that the first International Conference for the Unification of Criminal Law was held in Warsaw. In it, Poles read a number of papers.[21] It is also on Rappaport's initiative that the Conference agreed on a list of crimes subject to universal repression. Let us recall that the following were mentioned as the *delicta juris gentium*:

> (a) piracy; (b) forgery of coin, public securities or banknotes; (c) slave trade; (d) trafficking in women and children; (e) intentional use of any means capable of causing a universal danger; (f) production and distribution of narcotic drugs; (g) production and distribution of pornographic printed materials; (h) other criminal offences stipulated by the international conventions entered into by the State.[22]

Additionally, a consensus on the codification of the principles of nationality and personality of criminal repression was attempted.[23]

Rappaport called attention to the various fields of the: 'codification work of the 20th century in the area of criminal legislation.' In the first order, he pointed to the discipline of international criminal law *stricto*

17 Cyprian, Sawicki (1948c).
18 Cybichowski (1928): 277.
19 Rappaport (1931): 248
20 Grzebyk (2020a).
21 More in chapter 1.
22 Rappaport (1929b): 134f.
23 *Ibidem*: 132, 135.

sensu: 'still practically untilled, still in some degree a music of the future.' He noted, however, that the codification work of the: 'expansion of the criminal responsibility of individuals and collectives, organized in a strictly international manner,' was not aimed at the unification of the laws of the individual states but rather concerned itself with a: 'codification creativity – jointly of all civilized states in the world.'[24] In writing about the responsibility of a collective for criminal offences, Rappaport had in mind the responsibility of states and the corresponding international penal sanctions. A similar approach was taken by Hersch Lauterpacht in Oppenheim's coursebook.[25]

Almost in parallel, for in the August of 1928, Rappaport presided over a subcommittee of the 35th Conference of the International Law Association in Warsaw, which was to develop a list of criminal offences entailing the criminal's extradition under the extradition convention being in the works at the time. He acknowledged the difficulties with such an enumeration, given the substantive and formal differences from one code to the next.[26]

In Lemkin's outlook, the notion of a crime of the law of nations (*delictum juris gentium*) is a manifestation of the solidarity of the entire civilized humanity in the fight on crime. That solidarity is based on the principle of universal repression, which consists in the ability to prosecute and judge the offender at the venue of apprehension (*forum loci deprehensionis*), notwithstanding the place of commission of the crime and the criminal's nationality.[27]

The principle of universal repression, according to Lemkin, should be applied not to all criminal offences but only those having been recognized as offences infringing on the substantive or ideal interests of the entire civilized international community (the *delicta juris gentium*). The perpetrator of such offences is deemed an enemy of the entire international community and thus ought to be prosecuted and judged wherever they can be found. The principle of universal repression is thus based on a certain juridical sense common to the international community as a whole. That juridical sense is manifested through a special sensitivity to human suffering, to crimes and lawlessness in diverse parts of the world.[28]

---

24 *Ibidem*: 38; Rappaport (1929a): 32–33.
25 Lauterpacht (1955): 355.
26 Rappaport (1929b): 40, (1929a): 35.
27 Lemkin (1933): 598; cf. Glaser: (1929a–e).
28 Lemkin (1933): 598.

The first ICUCL mentioned among the international criminal offences (*delicta juris gentium*) the knowing use of means capable of causing a universal danger. The codification of that topic was to become the work of the third ICUCL in Brussels in 1930. The Polish representatives included Emil Stanisław Rappaport and Supreme Court Justice Waldemar Sokalski, accompanied by Aleksander Lednicki, Rafał Lemkin and Edward Neymark.[29] The organizational committee followed the defined term with the word 'terrorism' in parentheses, as a result of which the climate and the tempo of the debate changed entirely. The codification of a crime so defined was not achieved either by the Brussels Conference or the subsequent one, in Paris (1931).

Lemkin noted terrorism's lack of fitness for a: 'synthetic codifying approach.'[30] In lieu of that, he suggested a return to the concept from the Warsaw conference and the suitable: 'creation of a series of sets of facts containing conduct so harmful and dangerous to the international community that their character as *delictum juris gentium* be universally acknowledged and not incur any special reservations.'[31] He also noted the necessity of the introduction of a notion of interstate danger as a criterion for the creation of a *delictum juris gentium*. He defined it as threatening, at least in a potential way, the interests of a number of states or their inhabitants. Referencing the Warsaw formula, he proposed – with regard to the use of means capable of causing an interstate danger – the inclusion of the following acts: barbarity, vandalism, causing a catastrophe and interruption in international communication (telegraph, post or radio), and spread of pestilence.

In general, it can be observed that the Interwar period entailed a focus of attention primarily on international crimes understood as transnational crimes. A turn came with World War II. That was when the strictly understood international crimes came to the fore.

Stefan Glaser referred to their definition variously. In his *Introduction a l'étude du droit international pénal* (1954), he wrote: 'An international criminal offence is a fact contrary to international law; moreover, so harmful to the interests protected by that law that a rule is established in relations among the states attributing to it a criminal character, which is to say, compelling or justifying its penal repression.'[32] Three years later, in turn, in a monograph on the subject, he mentioned five elements defining an

29 Actes de la III Conference Internationale pour l'Unification du Droit Pénal.

30 Lemkin (1933): 599.

31 *Ibidem*: 600.

32 Glaser (1954): 11, cf. Glaser (1970): 49.

international criminal offence:[33] the substantive element, the legal element, unlawfulness, the moral element (culpability) and the penal element.

Stanisław Pławski, by contrast, defined an international criminal offence through three elements: 'An international criminal offence is an illicit act of culpable individuals, punished and sanctioned by criminal law, harmful to interpersonal relations in the international community.'[34]

In Marian Muszkat's opinion, in turn, an international criminal offence will not be any act contrary to the law of nations but only such a violation of that law as constitutes an attack on the foundations of peaceful international relations, as is, therefore, dangerous to the collective safety of the international community as a whole and as the commission of which is threatened with punishment either by virtue of treaty or customary norms or only according to the legal principles accepted by civilized societies.[35] Thus, Muszkat regarded Vespasian Pella's concept treating the international criminal offence as any action or omission prohibited by the law of nations as too broad and ignoring the essence of the problem. Instead, Muszkat accentuated the substantive side, i.e. the determination of a danger of to the foundations of the peaceful existence of the international community and determination that the protection of the peaceful order in international relations is effected by the imposition of a criminal sanction. Thus, the *delicta juris gentium* are not international criminal offences, as they: 'are not harmful to the peaceful relations among the nations.'[36]

In Renata Sonnenfeld's view:

> an international crime is an act, constituting the violation of an imperative norm of international law protecting the highest values of humanity. From its character and intensification, it follows at the same time that it cannot be committed by an individual, by a private person. It is indeed committed by an individual, but the latter acts as an organ of the state, often the supreme one (…). An act classified as an international crime, therefore, is marked by overlap of state conduct – an act *de iure imperii* – and the conduct of the individual who is the author and executor of such an act. The responsibility arising from the

33 Glaser (1957): 10ff.

34 Plawski (1972): 74: 'L'infraction international est un acte illicite des individus coupables, réprimé et sanctionné par le droit international, étant nuisible aux rapports interhumains dans la communauté internationale'.

35 Muszkat (1949): 309.

36 *Ibidem*: 309–310.

> conduct is also shaped on two planes: the responsibility of the state as a person and subject of international law and responsibility of the individual as a subject of the norms of international law.[37]

Sonnenfeld notes that for a given act to be classified as an international criminal offence, it will not suffice that it be condemned by an international instrument. The relevant treaty ought to contain a formula binding each State party to prosecute and punish the perpetrators of such acts.[38] Sonnenfeld also stated emphatically: 'only on the basis of the norms of international law does a criminal offence gain the classification of an international crime, provided that it is irrelevant whether the prosecution of it in a specific state may occur by virtue of an international norm or only following the incorporation thereof into domestic law.'

The most complete perspective on criminalization is expounded by Stefan Glaser in his *Droit international pénal conventionnel*, the first volume of which he published in 1970. Therein, he regarded an international criminal offence as a: 'fact (action or omission) contrary to international law and harmful to the community's interests or goods protected by the law that the conviction is solidified in the relations among the states that it must be punished.'[39] Such a conviction is manifested through a rule believed to conform to reason, to equity. Next, Glaser argues that since the universal consent of all states is not required for the binding force of custom, neither is it necessary for the conviction of the criminal character of violations of international law to be unanimous, but a more or less general conviction of conformity to the idea of justice will suffice. Accordingly, it follows that the notion of an international criminal offence does not have a fixed, unchanging value.

From the systematic perspective, Glaser divided facts into those having impact on values common to all states and those regarded on that account as international criminal offences according to various criteria. As his point of departure, he took the subject of the criminal offence, opposing the criminal offences committed by a natural person, especially such that cannot be committed by a state, to criminal offences that cannot be committed in any other way than on behalf of a state. Other criteria, in his view, are the perpetrator's motives, in particular the existence or non-existence of an ideological element. The latter is, of course, present in the crime of genocide,

---

37 Sonnenfeld (1984): 68.

38 *Ibidem*: 69–70.

39 Glaser (1970): 49.

crime against humanity, and terrorism. In turn, e.g. piracy or drug trafficking will be devoid of such an element. Another criterion will be the time when the crime is committed (peace or war).

The most space Glaser devoted to the distinctions among the international crimes according to the nature of the protected interest. In that regard, he distinguished two categories: intangible and tangible values. The first group could be considered from the perspective of impact on the international order (international peace) and human nature, encompassing war and international terrorism, as well as the harm done directly to a human being (war crimes, crimes against humanity and genocide, human trafficking, slavery, forced labour, drug trafficking and pornography). With regard to tangible values, Glaser distinguished attacks on cultural property, property useful or even indispensable to all people (telegraph, undersea cables), goods consisting in the freedom of safety of movement in the open sea and in air, as well goods the authenticity and maintenance of which are important both to the community of states and to all people individually (currency).[40]

Glaser's perspective provided an excellent overview of the phenomenon but, in comparison to the preceding findings of Quintiliano Saldaña, it did not introduce such far-reaching categorial distinctions within international crimes.

The concepts did not translate automatically into an understanding of domestic criminalization and in reference to the domestic plane. The literature witnesses the presentation of more or less expansive theories. In Polish literature, a full (complex) concept of the process of criminalization is provided by Lech Gardocki in his *Zagadnienia teorii kryminalizacji*[41] ('Problems in the theory of criminalization'). His studies were also published in continued studies, also in German,[42] whereby they had a better chance of provoking responses. It should be borne in mind that a more deliberate and profound reflection on the postulates advanced by the normative science of criminalization may constitute a method of fighting the phaenomenon of penal populism.[43] The understanding of criminalization is twofold: as the establishment or modification of existing types of offences in order to expand the limits of punishability, or as the retention of existing generic

40 *Ibidem*: 53f.

41 Gardocki (1990b).

42 See also Gardocki (1989b): 59f.; (2005): 1335f., (1990a): 17f.

43 Dębski (2013): 32.

types.[44] In later studies, other scholars[45] suggested a five-stage concept of the theory of criminalization. The first stage would be the finding in the social realities of a conduct perceived by society as dangerous to the legally protected interests, i.e. infringing on them or endangering them in a degree crossing the accepted limits. The second stage would require the consideration of the issue of necessity of a penal response. The third stage would be the assessment of the utility of the establishment of a sanctioning norm. The fourth would be the assessment of the proportionality of the penal response. The fifth would be the possibility of formulating the ban in a manner conforming to the principles of criminal law, with the principle of *nullum crimen sine lege* at the front.

Gardocki distinguished between rational and emotional criminalization (the latter based solely on the intuitively felt punishworthiness of a specific type of conduct).[46] Rational criminalization was based in particular on the following goals: (a) protection of the legal interest; (b) cementing of moral attitudes; (c) unloading of social tensions; (d) symbolic criminalization; (e) simplified criminalization; (f) doctrinal criminalization; (g) disciplining criminalization. Gardocki notes, however, that the emotional grounds of criminalization mix with the rational ones, and that the character alone does not mean the criminalization does not deserve approval.[47] As rightly emphasized by Kaczmarek: 'The social danger in an act constitutes an objective characteristic because of which a human act presents a threat to specific social interests protected by criminal law.'[48]

Of paramount importance to the criminalization under discussion here was a questionnaire survey conducted in the latter half of the 80s of the 20th century within the AIDP, with Professors Otto Triffterer and Lech Gardocki as rapporteurs. The former dealt with the subject of the efforts for the recognition and codification of international crimes, the other with the problems of implementation. In the Polish rapporteur's opinion, the most important problem of the criminalization of international crimes is whether the domestic lawmaker should always create new criminal provisions or perhaps the application of existing provisions will suffice – this is in part a problem of legislative technique, and in part a problem linked to a given

44 Gardocki (1990b): 7–9.
45 Kulesza (2014): 87f.; cf. Kulesza (2017).
46 Gardocki (1990b): 53f.
47 *Ibidem*: 78f.
48 Kaczmarek (2009): 62.

lawmaker's attitude to international crimes.[49] Himself, he opted for literal special criminalization as emphasizing the criminal character of the conduct and having an element of deterrence. Explicit criminalization increases compliance with international law and restricts the dangers relating to the interpretation of an overly narrow domestic provision.[50] Professors Marian Cieślak and Jan Waszczyński, reporting on the situation in Poland, appeared to be in agreement with the above proposition.[51] As for the sanction, Gardocki recognized the general conclusion arising from international conventions that they leave such matters to domestic law.[52]

For Polish accents, it will be expedient to recall that the national report for Canada was compiled by Louis Kos-Rabcewicz-Zubkowski,[53] and the French one by Stanisław Pławski, as an emeritus professor extraordinary of the University of Lille and dedicated to Glaser as the master of the field of international criminal law.[54] Venturing outside the Canadian experience, on the other hand, Kos-Rabcewicz-Zubkowski outlined from a more universal perspective the extensive taxonomy of the treaty sources for international crimes.[55]

The above-cited Gardocki, publishing mainly in Polish and German, played an important role in the analysis of this topic, but primarily in classic domestic criminal law (which, of course, does not undermine the significance of his findings on the plane that is of the most interest to us). Nonetheless, a much larger response was attracted by Theodor Meron's article titled *International Criminalization of Internal Atrocities*, published at the AJIL.[56] Long before his reconciliation with Poland, which he manifested clearly in his 2021 book titled *Standing up for Justice: The Challenges of Trying Atrocity Crimes*,[57] he had written:

> once internal atrocities are recognized as international crimes and thus as matters of major international concern, the right of third states to prosecute violators must be accepted. Typically, these would be offenses of such significance that the international community would

---

49 Gardocki (1989a): 101.
50 *Ibidem*: 102.
51 Cieslak, Waszczynski (1989): 436.
52 Gardocki (1989a): 104.
53 Kos-Rabcewicz-Zubkowski (1989): 195.
54 Plawski (1989): 556.
55 Kos-Rabcewicz-Zubkowski (1989): 196–199.
56 Meron (1995): 554f.
57 Meron (2021): 4–5.

> have an important interest in prosecuting the violators, especially when the criminal justice systems of the state where the offenses were committed and or the state of nationality have failed to act.[58]

In more recent literature, the problems of criminalization and its scope have been addressed, among others, by Elżbieta Dynia,[59] Tomasz Iwanek,[60] Justyna Jurewicz,[61] but also – incidentally, for the most part – other authors. It is telling that none of the major coursebooks on international criminal law explores this topic in more depth – both in Lech Gardocki's (including the second, expanded edition co-authored with Teresa Gardocka and Łukasz Majewski),[62] as well as in Piotr Hofmański and Hanna Kuczyńska's,[63] the topic of criminalization is covered narrowly at most. A more extensive discussion is contained in the work of Michał Królikowski, Paweł Wiliński and Jacek Izydorczyk.[64]

2 *Nullum crimen sine jure*

One of the fundamental principles of substantive criminal law[65] is the principle of legality. It constitutes a core element of the system of protection of human rights but also an element of justice itself and a leading rule in criminal policy.[66] We owe the *nullum crimen, nulla poena sine lege* combination of maxims to Johann Paul Anselm Feuerbach.[67] It expresses a number of postulates characteristic for written law. It imports the value of legal certainty, prohibition against analogy, and non-retroaction. In principle, it contains four aspects (more detailed rules) – two commands and two prohibitions: the command to establish punishability by (written) law – the *lex scripta*; the command to describe the criminal offence in a precise manner –

58 Meron (1995): 576.
59 Dynia (1999).
60 Iwanek (2015).
61 Jurewicz (2008).
62 Neither Gardocki (1985), nor Gardocki, Gardocka, Majewski (2017), nor Hofmanski, Kuczynska (2020).
63 Hofmański, Kuczyńska (2020).
64 Królikowski et al. (2008).
65 One may distinguish between a procedural understanding of legality and opportunistic prosecution – see Tylman (1965); Rogacka-Rzewnicka (2007).
66 See, e.g., Królikowski (2011): 62–63.
67 Feuerbach (1801): 113 (§24); Feuerbach (2007): 1005f.

lex certa; the ban on retroaction in penal law (*nullum crimen sine lege praevia, lex retro non agit*); and the ban on the use of analogy detrimental to the accused. One may also identify the fifth element, namely the command that the punishment for the criminal offence be specified and provided for in a previously enacted statute.[68] The above formulation, however, does not account for the specificity of the sources of international law, which results in the necessity of modifying it so as to incorporate also unwritten (uncodified) juridical points of reference.[69] Postulates to use a different form of the principle of legality in the international context – *nullum crimen, nulla poena sine jure* – should not, therefore, come as a surprise.[70]

The Polish voice in this regard was powerfully heard in the international works on the subject. A series of studies were prepared for the AIDP's fourth congress. Preliminary individual papers were written by Mogilnicki,[71] Glaser[72] and Wolter.[73] In the conference itself, as Rappaport observed, the Polish voices were not unanimous. Similarly to Wolter, also Śliwowski believed that the use of analogy to only a certain extent could be expedient.[74] The other delegates, including prosecutor Sieroszewski and advocate Wiewiórska, objected to the use of analogy, as was reflected in the corresponding final resolution of the congress, of which the first item emphasized the principle of legality of court proceedings as an, 'indispensable guarantee of individual right,' which had to translate into the exclusion of the application of analogy an interpretative method in criminal law.[75]

In the 2nd International Congress of Comparative Law, taking place in August in 1937 in the Hague, the Polish delegates – Walter, Glaser and Lemkin – spoke against the principle of analogy.[76] Also in the later period reflection was undertaken on the exclusivity of the statute in the sphere of criminal law occupied by the statutory specificity of the offence and punishment.

The principle of legality reflects the universally accepted international standard.[77] As Marian Cieślak wrote in 1995: 'the goal is for all that on

68 E.g. Gardocki (2008): 14.
69 Krzan (2018): 345.
70 Glaser (1970): 24, Glaser (1957): 50f.; cf. the earlier, more rigid approach.
71 Mogilnicki (1937): 1.
72 Glaser (1937a).
73 Wolter (1937).
74 Rappaport (1937): 174.
75 (2015) 86/1–2 RIDP 267.
76 Lemkin (1937): 181.
77 See Kunicka-Michalska (1993): 55; Grześkowiak (1991): 506.

which the inconvenience in the form of penal sanction depends and what it realistically means be as specified as strictly and precisely as possible.'[78] This corresponds perfectly to the position expressed 60 years prior by the PCIJ in its advisory opinion in the matter of the compatibility of certain legislative decrees of Gdańsk (Danzig) with the Free City's constitution. The Hague Court held succinctly: 'The law alone determines and decrees an offence. The law alone decrees the penalty. A penalty cannot be inflicted in a given case if it is not decreed by the law in respect of that case.'[79]

International military tribunals were strongly criticized for failure to adhere to this principle. In particular, the legitimacy of both of them to judge crimes against peace (and, to a lesser extent, also against humanity) was challenged. In respect of aggression, the Nuremberg Tribunal (IMT) found:

> the maxim *nullum crimen sine lege* is not a limitation of sovereignty, but is in general a principle of justice. To assert that it is unjust to punish those who in defiance of treaties and assurances have attacked neighboring states without warning is obviously untrue, for in such circumstances the attacker must know that he is doing wrong, and so far from it being unjust to punish him, it would be unjust if his wrong were allowed to go unpunished.[80]

It can be concluded, therefore, that the Nuremberg judgment conceded priority to the doctrine of real justice before the ideal of legality. Already in 1947, Hans Kelsen believed that the punishment of those responsible for the international crime of WWII could evidently be regarded as more important than the rather relative rule restricting *ex post facto* regulation, which admitted of multiple exceptions.[81] Antonio Cassese encapsulate the matter in similar terms: 'In other words, substantive justice punishes acts that harm society deeply and are regarded as abhorrent by all members of society, even if these acts were not prohibited as criminal when they were performed.'[82] It is also beyond any doubt that the Tribunal rejected the

78 Cieślak (1995): 120.

79 PCIJ, *Consistency of Certain Danzig Legislative Decrees with the Constitution of the Free City*, Advisory Opinion, 4.12.1935, Series A/B, Judgments, Orders and Advisory Opinions,1935, vol. 3, No. 65, 51.

80 *International Military Tribunal* (Nuremberg), Judgment and Sentences, 41 AJIL (1947) 217.

81 Kelsen (1947): 165.

82 Cassese (2009): 439.

doctrine of state sovereignty in favour of an individual's international criminal responsibility.[83]

Nor should one, however, be too precipitous in this regard. In the context of complaints about retroaction, it will be expedient to recall the position expounded by Henri Donnedieu de Vabres, who in the 20s of the 20th century had written on aggressive war,[84] and from the Polish perspective one cannot ignore Article 113 of the 1932 Criminal Code, penalizing public calls for a war of aggression.

References to the principle of *nullum crimen, nulla poena sine lege* can also be found in the Universal Declaration of Human Rights – Article 11(2). They can also be found in Article 15(1) of the International Covenant on Civil and Political Rights, although one can neither ignore the second paragraph of the same article: 'Nothing in this article shall prejudice the trial and punishment of any person for any act or omission which, at the time when it was committed, was criminal according to the general principles of law recognized by the community of nations.'[85] The above is a self-evident borrowing from the Nuremberg principles, including the possibility of the exercise of jurisdiction with regard to the perpetrators of international crimes.

During the preparatory works on the Covenants, the Polish representative, Dembińska, argued forcefully that criticism of the Nuremberg Tribunal could not be reconciled to the mandate of Committee III, which was the protection of human rights. Acknowledging the argument of the creation of the IMT as a court of the victors, she emphasized that it administered justice on behalf of all people, and the victory over Nazism had been paid a great price for. The expounded position emphasized the necessity of maintaining the consistency of response with regard to future cases of war crimes.[86] Once again, therefore, one can indirectly invoke the obligation of criminal prosecution.[87]

A slightly modified Nuremberg clause also found reflection on the regional level.[88] The requirement of legality with regard to the penalty is

83 See Indecki (2005): 144.
84 Donnedieu de Vabres (1928): 426.
85 Dz.U.1994.23.80.
86 UN Doc. E/C.3/SR.1008, 133.
87 See: Tylman (1965); Rogacka-Rzewnicka (2007).
88 The European Convention on Human Rights (Article 7(1)) and the American Convention on Human Rights (Article 9).

explicitly emphasized in the judgments of the European Court of Human Rights.[89]

3 International and Transnational Crimes

In the theory of international law, transnational crimes are held separate from international crimes. The line between the two categories is not always an easy one to draw. Often, the *ratione materiae* scope of jurisdiction of the international courts is invoked as the more important criterion. That is, of course, not the most fortunate classification, primarily on account of the arbitrary nature of the distinction but also the possibility of fluctuations. Should one take the Rome Statute as the core point of reference, there too one could notice a fluidity manifested, for example, in proposals to expand the scope of the ICC's jurisdiction.

Aside from the various constellations of the scopes of the *ratione materiae* jurisdictions of international criminal courts, the distinction between international crimes and transnational ones assumes that, rather than before international courts, the transnational crimes are to be judged by domestic courts, subject to the principle of *aut dedere aut judicare*, arising from multiple international conventions stipulating the prosecution of such crimes.[90]

The lack of consistency in the distinction between international and transnational crimes is even more strongly visible in the case of internationalized tribunals of mixed international-domestic jurisdiction (and composition, although the latter aspect could be ignored with no consequences to the context here analysed). With regard to the former issue, the hybrid nature is manifested in the combination of acts criminalized in international law and those criminalized in domestic law. A clear example is provided here especially by the Special Tribunal for Lebanon, the jurisdiction of which is limited to the crime of terrorism.[91]

Notwithstanding the nature of the crimes and the hypothetical international or internationalized character of the forum before which they are prosecuted, one must not forget that any criminal offence, including international crimes, may and even ought to be prosecuted before domestic

89 See e.g. *Baskaya and Okcuoglu v. Turkey*, App. Nos. 23536/94 & 24408/94, 31 Eur. H.R. Rep. 10, §36).

90 See, e.g. Głogowska-Balcerzak (2019): 87.

91 See Art. 1 of the STL Statute, UN Doc. S/RES/1757 (2007), annex.

courts. The triggering of external (international) jurisdictions is precisely the consequence of the shortcomings of the domestic justice system. In this context, it is worth mentioning the Polish efforts for domestic courts to be able to judge international crimes, discussed in preceding chapters.

While in international crimes the criminalization arises directly from the norms of international law, in treaty crimes, the specific basis for criminalization is stipulated in internal law. The distinction comes down to the criterion of directness. International crimes are criminalized directly under the norm of international law; by contrast, the international treaties dealing with transnational crimes stipulate only the obligation to criminalize specific types of conduct in domestic law. In this context, one can draw the distinction between international crimes (in the strict sense, narrowed to a set number of categories of acts)[92] and crimes of an international character.

An extensive classification of crimes of international nature according to the criterion of the legal nature of the corresponding regulation is provided by Zdzisław Wyrwas. He distinguishes, firstly, universally repressed crimes, which may be prosecuted by any state, notwithstanding the place of commission, the law applicable there, or the perpetrator's nationality. Those are identified with the *delicta juris gentium*. By way of example, one could mention attempts on the safety of air traffic; illegal production, smuggle and trade in narcotic drugs; counterfeiting of currency; human trafficking; or piracy at sea. The second group included crimes with elements specified in multilateral treaties imposing on the states the obligation to prosecute such crimes solely within their national jurisdiction arising from territorial or personal supremacy or that of the flag state, such as racial discrimination, pollution of the sea by ships, or damage to undersea cable. The third group of crimes of international character, by contrast, includes criminal offences defined by domestic criminal law, which typifies conduct dangerous to the international community but without directly calling them crimes, although it binds the states to suppress them, not necessarily through the use of penal legislation – for example, the prevention of illegal import, export of transfer of ownership of cultural property or infringement of industrial property through falsification of origin marking. The fourth group, according to Wyrwas, includes those of which the subject is a person, place or thing covered by immunity under international law, or crimes committed by persons enjoying international immunities and privileges, including acts against the members of foreign armed forces and their

92 Wyrwas (1989):112 mentions 5 major international crimes: crimes against peace, war crimes, crimes against humanity, genocide and apartheid.

family members, as well as crimes committed by those persons. The fifth group is crimes containing a foreign element entailing the need for international legal assistance. In the last, sixth group Wyrwas allocated those crimes that according domestic law are directed against the interests of a foreign state (e.g. espionage, smuggle). Their criminalization is justified by the protection of political and economic interests against the harmful actions of other states – in that manner, domestic norms influence international (interstate) relations.[93]

Irrespective of natural similarities manifested, for example, in the political nature of both of the categories, in comparison to international crimes, crimes of international nature have lower specific gravity, i.e. they violate the international legal order, in principle, in a low degree, are committed by private individuals and do not give rise to international responsibility.

In the literature, the hierarchy of supranational crimes has been ordered as follows: the poisoning of waters; sale of harmful substances; theft of cultural property; pollution of air; kidnapping; currency crimes; crimes relating to fishing at sea, and tax crimes, as well as breach of the terms of trade exchange.[94] The above list does not exhaust all of the acts, and deals with the international character of the corresponding acts somewhat arbitrarily. One must bear in mind that not all international treaties concerning attempts on legally protected interests contain provisions on criminalization; instead, they can 'merely' impose the obligation to co-operate with regard to specific events, legal assistance and extradition.

Concerning treaty crimes, Lech Gardocki emphasized that the reason for transcending the sphere of interests of the individual states might be the conviction that such crimes infringe on the common good or interest of the states, though at the same time he observed: 'such a good or interest cannot always be identified.'[95] He suggested that the manner and circumstances of the commission of the relevant crimes gave them their international character.[96] Hence the belief in the necessity of their prosecution and punishment as a: 'shared task of the international community.'[97] Gardocki's original list of conventional crimes (piracy at sea, slave trade, human trafficking, trade in pornography, currency counterfeiting, damage to sea cables, pollution of

93 Wyrwas (1989): 112–116.
94 Hołyst (1978): 32.
95 Gardocki (1985): 118.
96 *Ibidem*.
97 *Ibidem*: 117.

the sea with oils, drug trafficking, air terrorism, racial discrimination and international terrorism) was expanded by him in a new edition in 2017.

A different breakdown was suggested by Celina Nowak, who proposed an extensive taxonomy/catalogue of transnational and European crimes. She divided that category into acts against human rights or the security and safety of the citizens (terrorism, organized crime, digital crime, sexual abuse of minors, slavery, human trafficking, domestic violence and propagation of racism and xenophobia), economic crimes (money laundering, corruption, attempts on the financial interests of the European Union, counterfeiting of currency, other crimes against currency) and other types of crimes (crimes against the natural environment, and crimes linked to narcotic drugs). The cited author also highlighted areas of criminalization not yet pursued by Poland.[98] In this context, it is worth mentioning Poland's long delay in ratifying the Convention on Preventing and Combating Violence Against Women and Domestic Violence.[99] The latter was ratified in 2015, and the reservations were published in the government notice of 30.04.2015.[100] Subsequently, by order of 27.01.2021, the President of the Republic of Poland modified the scope of application through the modification of two reservations, extension of a reservation and withdrawal of a reservation.[101] Things were similar with the Council of Europe Convention on Cybercrime of 2001.[102] It was ratified in 2015, together with the Additional Protocol to the Convention on Cybercrime, concerning the criminalisation of acts of a racist and xenophobic nature committed through computer systems of 2003.[103]

The distinction between core international crimes and transnational crimes incurs criticism for its artificiality, rigidity and the associated simplifications.[104] The lines between political crimes and organized transnational crime are becoming blurred.

The brunt of conventions adopted in recent decades deals not so much with international crimes in the sense of core crimes as crimes against internationally protected interests. If, with regard to the first category, the criminalization follows directly from international law itself, treaty-based crimes entail the obligation of criminalization of specific types of conduct in

98 Nowak (2014): 315.
99 3010 UNTS 107.
100 Dz.U.2015.962.
101 Dz.U.2021.844.
102 Dz.U.2015.728.
103 Dz.U.2015.730.
104 Wilt (2016).

international law. Thus, a distinction is suggested between international and transnational criminal law.

The last-mentioned term is regarded as a neologism.[105] In Polish literature, Celina Nowak suggests translating 'transnational criminal law' not as *transgraniczne prawo karne* (literally: transboundary or cross-border criminal law) but rather *transnarodowe prawo karne* (literally 'transnational criminal law') by analogy to *międzynarodowe prawo karne* for, 'international criminal law.'[106] She regards transnational criminal law as a: 'complex branch of law characterized by a specific matter and manner of regulation, encompassing treaty norms imposing on the states party the obligation to criminalize specific types of conduct in domestic law, as well as regulating the principles of responsibility for those acts and co-operation in their prosecution.'[107]

It is, however, difficult to agree with her following claim: 'matters relating to the most recent achievements of foreign literature and expansion of the conceptual framework of international problems in criminal law are almost completely outside of the interests of Polish scholarship.'[108] That refers to the indirect restriction through international law of criminal acts actually or potentially having transboundary consequences, via domestic criminal law.[109] The criminalization takes place only in domestic (internal) law. Thus, we are excluding direct criminal responsibility on the plane of international law. Despite the claims of low responsiveness of Polish scholarship (Nowak), many crimes have become the subject-matter of not only articles but even monographs dealing with air terrorism,[110] money laundering,[111] and human trafficking.[112]

Transnational criminal law is looking towards the harmonization of criminal provisions and facilitation of co-operation among the states with regard to the suppression of crime. In May 1996, during the 5th Session of the Commission on Crime Prevention and Criminal Justice, Poland sponsored the initiative of drafting a convention against organized crime. The draft of a framework convention was presented in a session the UNGA in 1996 by

105 Płachta (2009): 11.
106 Nowak (2012): 5.
107 *Ibidem*: 13.
108 *Ibidem*.
109 Boister (2003): 953.
110 Galicki (1981); see also Marcinko (2008).
111 Bieniek (2010).
112 Głogowska-Balcerzak (2019); Jurewicz (2011).

President Aleksander Kwaśniewski.[113] The draft became the subject matter of the works of *ad hoc* Committee established on the basis of the UNGA Resolution 53/11 of December 1998. Following two years' negotiations, the final text of the draft was adopted on 28.07.2000 together with two additional protocols dealing with human trafficking, with emphasis on women and children, as well as migrant smuggling. On behalf of Poland, the convention was signed at Palermo in 2000 by the then-justice minister, Lech Kaczyński. The treaty was ratified in 2001.[114]

The UN Convention against Transnational Organized Crime is an example of complex regulation aimed at preventing, prosecuting and punishing organized crime. It binds the states party to penalize the following crimes: participation in an organized criminal group (Article 5), money laundering (Article 6), active and passive corruption of public officials (Article 8), and crimes against the administration of justice (Article 23).

Article 2(a) of the aforementioned Convention defines an 'organized criminal group' as:

> a structured group of three or more persons, existing for a period of time and acting in concert with the aim of committing one or more serious crimes or offences established in accordance with this Convention, in order to obtain, directly or indirectly, a financial or other material benefit.

Pursuant to article 3(2) of the Convention, on the other hand:

> an offence is transnational in nature if: (a) it is committed in more than one State; (b) It is committed in one State but a substantial part of its preparation, planning, direction or control takes place in another State; (c) It is committed in one State but involves an organized criminal group that engages in criminal activities in more than one State; or (d) It is committed in one State but has substantial effects in another State.

The Convention is supplemented by three Protocols: (1) Protocol to Prevent, Suppress and Punish Trafficking in Persons, Especially Women and Children; (2) Protocol against the Smuggling of Migrants by Land, Sea and Air; and (3) Protocol against the Illicit Manufacturing of and Trafficking in

113 UN Doc. A/C.3/51/7, annex.

114 Dz.U.2005.18.158.

Firearms, Their Parts and Components and Ammunition. The last one was adopted by the UNGA on 31.05.2001. Poland ratified the first and second Protocols on 26.09.2003.[115] The third Protocol was signed on 12.12.2002 and ratified on 4.04.2005.[116]

The Palermo protocol contains the first complex definition of the crime of human trafficking. According to that definition, human trafficking means:

> the recruitment, transportation, transfer, harbouring or receipt of persons, by means of the threat or use of force or other forms of coercion, of abduction, of fraud, of deception, of the abuse of power or of a position of vulnerability or of the giving or receiving of payments or benefits to achieve the consent of a person having control over another person, for the purpose of exploitation[117].

Exploitation was narrowed down ('exploitation of the prostitution of others or other forms of sexual exploitation, forced labour or services, slavery or practices similar to slavery, servitude or the removal of organs').[118] It must be emphasized that the Convention separates human trafficking from prostitution and other forms of sexual exploitation. At present, it is held to include human trafficking for the purpose of forcing slave labour. The definition of the unlawfulness of human trafficking under the Palermo Protocol thus encompasses also conduct consisting in the illegal renting of foreign workers and sale of children to adoptive families.

As noted in the literature,[119] Polish interpretation of the term: 'organized group with the purpose of committing a criminal offence,' is narrower, whereas the Convention assumes: 'a clear move downward, towards co-operation.'[120] Thus, the distinctions between a group and co-operation are becoming blurred.

In Polish criminal law, one must note Article 258 of the Criminal Code of 1997.[121] In this context, it is worth mentioning that the first use of the term

115 Dz.U.2005.18.160, Dz.U.2005.18.162.

116 Dz.U.2005.252.2120.

117 2237 UNTS 319; Art. 3(a).

118 *Ibidem.*

119 Kurowski (2006): 30.

120 Płachta, Zalewski (2003): 20.

121 '§1. Anyone who participates in an organised group or association whose purpose is to carry out criminal offences is liable to imprisonment for three months to five years.

§2. If the group or association specified in §1 uses weapons or have terrorist aims, then the offender is liable to imprisonment for six months to eight years.

'organized crime' (without a precise definition) was in Article 5 of the Act on Protecting the Economic Circulation of 1994.[122] One must consider both aspects – the functional (an organized criminal offence) and the structural (a criminal organization).

On the basis of the taxonomy established by the Criminal Code, one can identify the following list of treaty crimes entailing the obligation to criminalize: attempts on the Republic of Poland, general security/safety, the environment, liberty, sexual freedom and morality, activities of public administrative institutions and the justice system; the public order, protection of information, credibility of documents, property, commerce, as well as the circulation of currency and securities. Let us also bear in mind, however, that part of the treaty crimes is criminalized by legislation found outside of the Criminal Code (slave trade, criminal offences relating to narcotic drugs or the pollution of the sea, as well as infringements on rights of authorship and related rights committed with the use of an IT system).

In general, with regard to the implementation of transnational crimes, it should be noted that the Polish Criminal Code criminalizes traditional treaty crimes. The Code also typifies such criminal offences as are difficult to classify either as international crimes or treaty crimes. For example, the use of torture. On the one hand, it is evident that torture may constitute a structural element of crimes against humanity if committed as part of a deliberate and widespread or systematic attack against the civilian population. Article 7(2)(e) of the Rome Statute defines torture as the: 'intentional infliction of severe pain or suffering, whether physical or mental, upon a person in the custody or under the control of the accused; except that torture shall not include pain or suffering arising only from, inherent in or incidental to, lawful sanctions.' On the other hand, the obligation to criminalize the use of torture is imposed on Poland, for example, by the Convention against Torture and Other Cruel, Inhuman or Degrading Treatment or Punishment, adopted by the UNGA on 10.12.1984 (Article 4), which Poland ratified in 1989.[123] Article 1 of that treaty defines torture as follows:

---

§3. Anyone who sets up or leads a group or association specified in §1 that uses weapons, is liable to imprisonment for between one and 10 years.

§4. Anyone who sets up or leads a group or association with the intention of carrying out a terrorist attack is liable to imprisonment for at least three years'.

122 Dz.U.1994.126.615.

123 Dz.U.1989.63.378.

> any act by which severe pain or suffering, whether physical or mental, is intentionally inflicted on a person for such purposes as obtaining from him or a third person information or a confession, punishing him for an act he or a third person has committed or is suspected of having committed, or intimidating or coercing him or a third person, or for any reason based on discrimination of any kind, when such pain or suffering is inflicted by or at the instigation of or with the consent or acquiescence of a public official or other person acting in an official capacity.

That excludes pain and suffering arising solely from lawful sanctions, inherent or incidental to them. A number of other international treaties ratified by Poland also refer to the prevention of the use of torture, e.g. the European Convention for the Prevention of Torture and Inhuman or Degrading Treatment or Punishment, done at Strasbourg on 26 November 1987.[124] A clear prohibition of torture is mandated by Article 3 of the European Convention for the Protection of Human Rights and Basic Freedoms[125] and Article 7 ICCPR.[126]

The Polish legislator should take note that not all types of acts classifiable as torture according to definitions in multilateral international treaties have a direct counterpart in the detailed part of the Criminal Code in the shape envisaged by the relevant convention.

4 An Excursus: Terrorism

The challenge of defining terrorism has attracted the attention of numerous eminent international lawyers and[127] diplomats. The AIDP took note of the problem and organized a conference on it in Brussels already in 1930.[128]

The League of Nations Convention on the Prevention of Terrorism of 1937 was the first instrument of international law in the fight on international terrorism. Its Article 1(2) defined terrorism as: 'criminal acts directed against a State and intended or calculated to create a state of terror in the

124 Dz.U.1995.46.238.

125 Dz.U.1993.61.284.

126 Dz.U.1977.38.167.

127 Skubiszewski (1989): 42.

128 Szafrański (2007): 15.

minds of particular persons, or a group of persons or the general public.'[129] Article 2(1) regarded as a terrorist act any: 'wilful act causing death or grievous bodily harm or loss of liberty,' to the highest officials or undertaken with a view to threatening their lives. Article 2(2) placed on the same footing the: 'wilful destruction of, or damage to, public property,' as well as: 'the manufacture, obtaining, possession, or supplying of arms, ammunition, explosives or harmful substances,' for such activities.

Poland was an active participant in the *travaux préparatoires* preceding the Convention. Although not ultimately ratifying the Convention, Poland signed it, disputing first of all the establishment of the tribunal envisaged by another convention designed in parallel.[130] The Polish Republic was in favour of the suppression of terrorism with the use of domestic courts and mutual assistance in the fight of terrorism together with the necessary implementing measures.[131] It was noted that reciprocity would not be forthcoming from Germany or the USSR.

Terrorism is rather difficult to define. Controversies did not only surface during the Interwar period, they compounded the difficulty of the task in the decades that followed. One could, of course, rely on sectoral definitions in treaties made in the course of several decades. In the sixth session of the ILC in 1954, the proposal was made to recognize a terrorist act as a crime of international law.[132]

The Convention on Offences and Certain Other Acts Committed on Board Aircraft of 1963,[133] is the first international and multilateral legal instrument dealing exclusively with the security and safety of aircraft. It will be expedient to note that already in 1956, in the 4th International Congress of Penal Law in Athens, the Polish delegation proposed important provisions for inclusion in the future convention in that regard. The Polish delegates (among them Remigiusz Bierzanek[134]) advocated for the mandatory punishment of acts recognized as the most serious crimes, endangering the safety of air traffic. They additionally postulated that the future convention should bind the states to extradite criminals to states competent to punish

129 Lech (2014): 148.
130 Convention pour la création d'une cour pénale internationale, LN Doc. C.547(I) 1937.
131 Kornat (2008): 91.
132 UN Doc. A/2693.
133 704 UNTS 219.
134 Cf. Bierzanek (1956).

them, regardless of the motives of the crime.[135] In the end, the Convention was ratified by Poland only as late as 1971.[136]

The European Convention on the Suppression of Terrorism of 1977 recognized as terrorist acts the crimes mentioned in the Hague (1970)[137] and Montreal (1971)[138] Conventions concerning piracy in the air, as well as grave crimes involving an attempt on the life, bodily integrity or freedom of persons enjoying international protection, including diplomats, as well as crimes involving kidnapping, hostage taking or serious unlawful imprisonment, as well as crimes connected with the use of firearms and explosives, on condition that the use thereof endanger the lives of persons. Poland ratified the Convention in 1995,[139] and entry into life (with regard to Poland) followed on 1.05.1996. No reservations were submitted from the Polish side.

The end stage of the works on the ICC in the Rome Conference in 1998 saw the adoption of Resolution E,[140] which concerned terrorist acts and trafficking in illicit narcotic drugs. Those were not included in the scope of the ICC's jurisdiction, however, because of the inability to agree on universally accepted definitions of such crimes; accordingly, they were recommended for inclusion by a review conference.

During the review conference in Kampala, a proposal surfaced to include the topic in the conference agenda. Not being a supporter of that solution, Poland did not uphold the initiative, which was ultimately rejected. The reasons can be found, again, in the lack of a generally accepted definition of terrorism and fears of possible politicization of the Court. It is not without its own significance that the ICC does have the ability to judge acts of terrorism fulfilling the elements of the other crimes falling within the Court's jurisdiction.

On the level of **Polish law**, a 2004 amendment introduced in Article 115(2) of the Criminal Code the statutory definition of a 'criminal offence of terrorist nature.'[141] It does not list types of criminal offences but only refers to criminal offences already penalized, identifying the criterion of an upper

135 Galicki (1981): 58.

136 Dz.U.1971.15.147.

137 Convention for the Suppression of unlawful seizure of aircraft, 860 UNTS 125.

138 Convention for the suppression of unlawful acts against the safety of civil aviation, 874 UNTS 177.

139 Dz.U.1996.117.557.

140 See *United Nations Diplomatic Conference of Plenipontaries on the Establishment of an International Criminal Court*, OR, Vol. 1:71.

141 Dz.U.93.889.

sentencing limit of at least 5 years, were the criminal offence is committed or a threat of its commission is offered for the purpose of: (1) serious intimidation of a multitude of persons; (2) compelling an organ of the political authorities of the Republic of Poland or other state or organ of an international organization to undertake or refrain from specific activities; or (3) causing a serious disturbance in the constitutional order or the economy of the Republic of Poland or other state or international organization. As observed by Oktawia Górniok, the provision cited here does not require the fruition of such purposes but specifies the degree of intimidation constituting an element of the perpetrator's criminal offence, which must be serious. Facilitating the assessment of that degree may be the personal ('multitude of persons' according to the cited provision) or spatial reach (effect) of the intimidation, as well as a high degree of the fruition of the events causing the fears, or the size alone of the event causing the fear.[142]

A crime of terrorist nature is mentioned as an element of the criminal offences defined in Articles 165a, 240(1), 255a(1) and 255a(2), 258(2) and 258(4), 259a, and 259b of the Criminal Code. It would be difficult to regard the above list as exhausting all of the attacks Poland is bound to criminalize by multilateral international agreements on the suppression of the various forms of terrorism. There can be no doubt that a crime of terrorist nature eludes the classic rules of typification (definition) of criminal offences.

In Polish **legal literature**, Rappaport mentioned terrorism in the category of *delicta juris gentium*.[143] Among the first authors to study the concept of terrorism was Rafał Lemkin,[144] defining it in 1935 as a criminal activity evoking universal anxiety, targeted against the health, life or freedom of persons on account of their belonging to a different social group.[145] As part of the works on the convention in the International Bureau for the Unification of Criminal Law conference in Copenhagen, Lemkin delivered a paper on terrorism. He asserted, with regard to domestic terrorism: 'the terrorist's criminal activity is targeted directly against the public order.' He excluded the understanding of terrorism as an attack on the state as such or on its political order, as that would have the effect of making terrorism a *par excellence* political crime. He emphasized, forcefully: 'The political changes that in a certain objective course of events may follow a terrorist act ought not yet to

142 Górniok (2004).
143 Rappaport (1931): 248.
144 Lemkin (1935): 561.
145 Lech (2014): 43.

bestow that act with the character of an intentional action with a political purpose.'[146]

Both with regard to domestic and international terrorism, Lemkin acknowledged the possibility of a graduation of the terrorist's goals. In the case of international terrorism, the direct goal of the terrorist's conduct is to evoke anxiety and disturb international relations, while the ultimate (programmatic) goal can be a specific solution to an either domestic or international issue. In Lemkin's opinion, the protected legal interest ('good') in the crime of international terrorism will be the: 'international tranquility, proper forms of international co-existence, all that which fulfils the substance of the so-called international public order.'[147] Thereby, he ventured beyond the narrow understanding of terrorist activities solely as targeted against the public security of a given state.

For the crime of international terrorism, he distinguished three elements: '(1) the perpetrator's nationality of a state; (2) the state affiliation of the territory in which the crime was committed; and (3) the victim's nationality of a state.' For the terrorism to be international, Lemkin required that at least one of the three refer to a different state than the rest.[148] In his report, he also mentioned a specific manifestation of international terrorism, in the form of the use of generally dangerous means against the property of any state (own or foreign) in foreign territory or against the property of a foreign state in a state's own territory, as well as causing a catastrophe or spreading pestilence in the territory of a foreign state.

Lemkin advocated for the inclusion of both domestic and international terrorism in criminal codes as *delicta communia* (crimes that can be committed by anyone). With that, he proposed some specific language. For international terrorism, recommended the following two articles:

> Whoever, for the purpose of evoking a universal anxiety or for the purpose of disturbing international relations, undertakes within the territory of their own state criminal conduct against the life, health or freedom of heads of states or persons exercising the powers thereof, members of cabinets, diplomatic representatives, members of legislatures or judicial bodies, belonging to another state, or whoever undertakes the same acts in the territory of another state against any of the

146 Lemkin (1935): 561.

147 *Ibidem*: 562.

148 *Ibidem*: 563.

> persons aforesaid belonging to any state whatsoever, shall be liable to the penalty …

And:

> Whoever, for the purpose of evoking a universal anxiety or for the purpose of disturbing international relations: (1) uses universally dangerous means against the official seats of diplomatic representatives; (2) being within the territory of their own state, uses universally dangerous means against the property of a foreign state or, being in the territory of a foreign state, against the property of any other state; (3) procures a communication disaster or flood or spreads pestilence in the territory of a foreign state, shall be able to the penalty …[149]

Among other works of Polish authors, it is worth noting Jerzy Waciórski's *Le terrorisme politique*, published in Paris in 1939 with a preface by Donnedieu de Vabres. That constitutes yet another proof of the presence of Poles in the global academic discourse, facilitated if publishing in French or English.

Much space was devoted to reflection on terrorism by Stefan Glaser. He accentuated the characteristic element of that crime consisting in intimidation by force.[150] Within international terrorism, of which either a state or an individual could be the subject, Glaser distinguished terrorism threatening peace and terrorism threatening the safety of humanity.[151]

Academic works by Polish authors also discussed the individual aspects of the crime, without, however, foregoing to the opportunity to offer a more general perspective. In his *Terroryzm lotniczy w świetle prawa międzynarodowego* ('Air terrorism in the light of international law'), Zdzisław Galicki distinguishes as international terrorism criminal offences meeting the following conditions:

> (a) being common crimes according to the legislation of the individuals states; (b) characterized by a twofold object of the attack, including both the interest of a state or international organization and the life, health or freedom of individuals; (c) involving an international factor as a core element manifested through the mutual international configuration – from the international point of view – of the subject and of

149 Lemkin (1935): 563–564.

150 Glaser (1954): 17, (1970): 71–72.

151 *Ibidem.*

> the objective elements; (d) prosecuted and punished on the basis of international treaties engaging the principle of universal repression.[152]

In this context, it is worth noting the rich bibliography of Marek Żylicz.[153]

A somewhat capacious definition of international terrorism was offered by Bogdan Wierzbicki, who included in it crimes against the security/safety of civil aviation, crimes against life, health and freedom and rooms and means of transport of persons enjoying special protection in international law, as well as hostage taking.[154]

Tadeusz Hanausek, in turn, defined terrorism as the: 'planned, organized and usually ideologically motivated activities of persons and groups with the purpose of compelling specific benefits, conduct or attitudes from state authorities, society of individual persons, taking criminal forms calculated on evoking wide and maximally intimidated publicity.'[155] The above definition has much in the common with the view expounded by Stanisław Pikulski, who pinpointed the most relevant elements of terrorist acts from the perspective of the sciences focusing on criminal law: the subject (agent), the motivation (usually complex), the method (consisting in violence directed towards the evocation of fear, panic or social disturbance for the purpose of influencing the development of a situation desired by the terrorists), the object of the attack, its motivation with a specific ideology, and the criminalization of the act.[156]

Much attention was given to terrorism in the studies of Krzysztof Indecki,[157] also noting the links to organized crime,[158] as well as Krzysztof Wiak.[159]

In Poland, the greatest intensity of crimes viewed as terrorist acts occurred in 1944–1947 and in the 80s of the last century.[160] Andrzej Górbiel postulated the intensification of, 'systematic academic research work,' with a view to: 'effecting a diligently drafted international instrument resolving in a precise and at once exhaustive manner the full picture of juridical problems of terrorism in all of its forms.' Leaving aside the question of the

152 Galicki (1981): 31.
153 Żylicz (2014): 36f. See also Osiecki (2022).
154 Wierzbicki (1985): 190f.
155 Hanausek (1980): 30.
156 Pikulski (1993): 32f; cf. Pikulski (1991): 25.
157 See, e.g., Indecki (1998), (2018): 237f.
158 Indecki, Pływaczewski (2006): 48.
159 Wiak (2009), (2012).
160 Sławik (1993): 12.

viability of such an undertaking, it is worth noting the proposal of the establishment of a domestic: 'study team, perhaps of inter-university nature, acting in a close association with the Ministry of Foreign Affairs, Ministry of the Interior and Ministry of Justice.'[161]

5 Conclusions

By way of a summary, it will be fitting to emphasize Poles' leading role in defining the scope and theoretical basis of the criminalization, especially during the initial period, in which the attention of diplomacy and scholarship had been focused around the category of the *delicta juris gentium*. Of fundamental importance were the initiatives undertaken by Rappaport. In the periods that followed, although the topic range continued to be studied, it translated into practice to a decidedly lesser extent.

There can be no doubt that the above-cited publications written in the Polish language have a limited reach, for which reason it is difficult to compare Poles' postwar endeavours with the contributions of the professors from the Interwar period (Lemkin and others). Closing this part of the discussion, it will be worth bearing in mind that the prosecution and punishment of terrorism can take place also without the separation and emancipation into an autonomous category of a crime that does, after all, contain the defining elements of other – less controversial, so to say – international crimes.

161 Górbiel (1993): 25.

CHAPTER 6

The Crime of Aggression

1 Responsibility for Aggression after World War I

The matter of responsibility for aggressive war surfaced in the deliberations of the Commission on Responsibilities established by the Paris Conference in the aftermath of World War I. Within the Polish delegation to the Paris Conference (1919–1920), a team was created to deal with the issue of responsibility for causing the war; besides Konstanty Skirmunt and Leon Łubieński, it included also Kazimierz Rybiński (more extensively see Chapter 1). Poland, however, was not overly influential in the discussions concerning aggression (Polish representatives were present in a subcommittee dealing with war crimes). It must be noted, however, that it was the Polish delegation (Kazimierz Olszewski, Zygmunt Chamiec, Stefan Markowski) who a compiled a draft addressing reparations for war damage (*Annexe III: Principes généraux concernant la réparation des dommages de guerre* i *Annexe V: Mode d'évaluation des dommages de guerre*).

In its report of 29.03.1919, the Commission on Responsibilities came to the conclusion that the responsibility for causing the war rested completely on the side of the powers having declared the war, i.e. Germany and Austria, and secondly Turkey and Bulgaria – in connection with the objective of pursuing their policy of aggression, which imbued the war with the character of a: 'dark conspiracy against peace in Europe.'[1] The actions described, in the Commission's opinion, were for a certainty to be condemned by history; nevertheless, in the state of legal affairs existing at the time, it was not possible to claim that the conduct of a war of aggression was contrary to positive law and capable of providing the basis for an indictment before a tribunal convened to deal with war crimes.[2] The Commission, however, noted that despite the impossibility of formulating criminal charges against the responsible authorities and individuals for having procured the war, the peace conference, on account of such a significant violation of the law of nations and international good faith, should firmly condemn such type of

1 Commission on the Responsibility of the Authors of the War and on Enforcement of Penalties, *Report Presented to the Preliminary Peace Conference, March 29, 1919*, (1920) 14(1/2) AJIL: 95, 98.

2 *Ibidem*: 118–120.

conduct. The Commission also emphasized that penal sanctions should be foreseen in the future for such serious violations of the basic principles of international law. In the end, Article 227 of the Treaty of Versailles (ratified by Poland) contained the following statement: 'The Allied and Associated Powers publicly arraign Wilhelm II Hohenzollern, formerly German Emperor, for a supreme offence against international morality and the sanctity of treaties.' In the light of the Commission's conclusions and the specific language used in the Treaty, it would be difficult to interpret Article 227 as hard evidence of the establishment of individual criminal liability for the crime of aggression.[3] However, the problem of the definitive recognition of the unlawfulness of aggression and creation of a basis for individual responsibility for it began to resurface regularly during the Interwar period.

2 Initiatives of the Interwar Period

To the Polish state, having only just regained its independence and still fighting for several years to come for the shape of its borders, the criminalization of aggression was a crucial matter. It cannot be surprising that in the Interwar period Polish scholars and diplomats became involved in a number of initiatives to prohibit and to define aggression as such.

In the forum of the Assembly of the League of Nations, Poland advocated from 1923 onward for aggressive war to be recognized as unlawful. The subject came back in 1927, when Poland noted the necessity of the adoption of a non-aggression pact (to balance the lack of a counterpart of the Locarno Treaties for the states of Eastern Europe). Given the lack of support for that idea,[4] it was on Polish initiative (submitted by Franciszek Sokal)[5] that on 24 September 1927 the Assembly adopted a resoluton stating: "all wars of aggression are, and shall always be, prohibited"[6] and thereby, in accordance with a prior resolution of the Assembly of the League of Nations adopted on 25 September 1925, constituted a crime.[7] Although the significance of the resolution was more moral than legal,[8] and the resolution itself did not

3 Dinstein (2005): 117; Simons (1919): 957, 960; Willis (1976): 199; Grzebyk (2013a): 81.

4 Wehberg (1931): 42.

5 Rifaat (1979): 59–60; Brownlie (1968): 71–72.

6 League of Nations, *Declaration Concerning Wars of Aggression*, League of Nations Official Journal (Special Supplement nr 53), 24.09.1927, 22. Available at: https://www.derechos.org/peace/dia/doc/dia11.html.

7 A.1925.C.I, 25ff.

8 Herzog (1975): 33.

define aggression, giving rise to complaints from some members of British Parliament among others, the value of the statement of criminality of aggressive war in international law was in itself appreciated.[9]

Also in 1927, in a conference of the International Bureau for the Unification of Criminal Law, organized in Warsaw on the initiative of Rappaport, the topic of criminalization of war propaganda was explored. The subject continued to be discussed in the next conference, held in 1930 in Brussels. Thanks to Rappaport, the matter of the criminality of war propaganda not only became the topic of discussion in the fora of AIDP and IBUCL, the appropriate provisions were introduced to the criminal codes of Poland, Brazil and Romania.

Poland was eager to sign treaties capable of at least limiting the possibility of the use of force in international relations or provide suitable guarantees of safety in the event the use of force were actually to happen (*vide* the mutual guarantees exchanged by France and Poland as a result of the Locarno Conference in 1925 and between Poland and Romania in 1926 and 1931).[10] Polish authorities signed the Kellogg-Briand Pact of 1928[11] without hesitation, realizing, however, the limitations of its significance arising from the vaguness of its provisions.[12] Particularly important, however, were the London Conventions for the Definition of Agression.[13] Poland was one of the driving forces behind both their adoption and the expansion of their personal scope. The initiative came from Maxim Litvinov – the Soviet People's Commissar for Foreign Affairs, who already in April 1933 approached Poland with the proposal of entering into a Convention for the Definition of Aggression with the states in Eastern Europe with which the USSR had non-aggression treaties in place, namely Finland, Latvia, Estonia and Poland.[14] Poland responded positively and pressed for the implementation of the Soviet idea to occur as soon as possible but under one condition – Romania also was to become party to the treaty. In consequence, on 3.07.1933 a Convention for the Definition of Aggression was entered into among Romania, Estonia, Latvia, Poland, Turkey, the USSR, Persia and Afghanistan. On 22.07.1933, Finland acceded to the Convention.

9 HC Deb 16.11.1927, vol. 210 cc: 1001–1003.
10 See list of treaties in: Ferencz (1975).
11 Treaty was ratified by Poland on 13.02.1929, Dz.U.1929.63.489.
12 Wysocki (1974): 64; see more Korczyk (1993).
13 Dz.U.1933.93.712.
14 W. Komarnicki (1949): 50.

On 4.07.1933, in turn, also in London, another Convention on the Definition of Aggression was signed among Czechoslovakia, Romania, Turkey, the USSR and Yugoslavia.[15] The Convention was opened for signature by other states. Poland, however, decided against acceding, for two reasons. Firstly, the nature of the Convention was intended to be not regional but universal, and Poland believed that entering into such a treaty fell within the purview of the Disarmament Conference. Secondly, one of the parties was Czechoslovakia, with regard to which Poland did not want to limit the options available for the use of force to implement desirable territorial changes. On 5.07.1933, a Convention on the Definition of Aggression was concluded between the USSR and Lithuania.[16]

The aforementioned treaties were of key importance to the shaping of the customary norm prohibiting the use of force for the purpose of aggression. In this context, however, it is necessary to note that Poland's annexation of the Vilnius Region in 1920, and the attack on Czechoslovakia for the purpose of annexing the Trans-Olza in 1938, were regarded by some as acts of aggression, and those two examples of the use of force were given in the postwar debate to undermine the existence of a customary ban on aggressive war.[17]

The definition of aggression from the Convention on the Definition of Aggression (so-called London Definition) was met with almost unanimous approval from legal circles.[18] However, its self-evident weakness lies in the the fact that the London Conventions are binding only on their states parties. Thus, the definition is only of regional significance.[19] Nonetheless, references to it have been made whenever the matter of the criminalization of aggression has been discussed, from the IMT Charter to the ICC Statute.

According to the London Conventions, that state is to be regarded as the aggressor which is the first to commit one of the following (subject to treaties applicable in the relationships among the parties):

(1) Declaration of war upon another State;
(2) Invasion by its armed forces, with or without a declaration of war, of the territory of another State;

15 148 LNTS 79.
16 148 LNTS 211.
17 Hankey (1950): 13. On legality of annexation of Vilnius see W. Komarnicki (1949): 54; Amado (1952): 149.
18 Diamandesco (1935): 173.
19 London definition was included in Article 1 of the first protocol to Balkan Pact of 9.02.1934 adopted between Greece, Romania, Turkey, and Yugoslavia. 153 LNTS 156.

(3) Attack by its land, naval or air forces, with or without a declaration of war, on the territory, vessels or aircraft of another State;
(4) Naval blockade of the coasts or ports of another State;
(5) Provision of support to armed bands formed in its territory which have invaded the territory of another State, or refusal, notwithstanding the request of the invaded State, to take, in its own territory, all the measures in its power to deprive those bands of all assistance or protection.

Importantly, the conventions categorically proclaimed: 'No political, military, economic or other considerations may serve as an excuse or justification for the aggression' (Article 3). The Annex mentioned examples of such pretexts, classified as: 'the internal condition of a State' or 'the international conduct of a State'.

The above definition formed the basis of the Soviet disarmament proposal submitted in the Disarmament Conference in Geneva, were the subject of the definition of aggression was undertaken within the Political Commission. At that time, Poland consistently supported the Soviet-proposed definition of aggression.[20] The Polish representative, Edward Raczyński, emphasized that the Soviet proposal was linked to the language of Article 10 of the Covenant of the League of Nations and the accepted principles of the London Conventions. Raczyński, however, stressed that the definition of aggression or of the aggressor state was only one of the elements of the security system that had to be built and that consequences could be derived from. The Polish diplomats also noted the necessity of criminalization of public propaganda of a war of aggression, which was the fruit of the aforementioned efforts by Rappaport.[21]

3 Responsibility for Aggression after World War II

When the problem of the penalization of aggression came up during WWII, Poland invariably supported initiatives undertaken with a view to the

20 Rifaat (1979): 90.

21 LoN – Conference for the Reduction and Limitation of Armamens, Series D, Vol. 5, Minutes of the Political Commission, 8th mtg, 10.03.1933 (Definition of Aggression: Draft Declaration Proposed by the Delegation of the Union of Soviet Socialist Republics: General Discussion); see also 69th mtg, 29.05.1933 (Report of the Committee on Security Questions: Definition of the Aggressor).

punishment of those guilty of aggression.[22] The Declaration of 12.06.1941, adopted at St James's Palace in London, proclaimed the fight against German and Italian oppression, as well as mutual assistance. However, it was also noted that a lasting peace could only be founded on the co-operation of free peoples in a world free of the menace of aggression.

Poland supported the so-called Minority Report by the Czech, Bohuslav Ečer, of March 1944 (*Scope of the Retributive Action of the United Nations according to their official declarations*),[23] which stated that initiating and prosecuting WWII was a crime for which the responsible individuals should be held criminally responsible and be suitably judged.[24] And, despite the lack of success getting the UNWCC as a whole to adopt a resolution formally recognizing the crime of aggression as a separate crime or one of the types of war crimes (though that is the way it was treated in the Commission's works), Ečer's report with strong support coming also from Poland[25] had

22 Segesser (2005): 372.

23 Kochavi (1998): 99; Minear (1971): 50.

24 UNWCC (1948): 180. In response to the report, on 6.06.1944, the Committee adopted the draft of a resolution titled *Scope of the Retributive Action of the United Nations*, in which it was suggested that aggressive war ought to be recognized as war crimes and therewith fall within the scope of the Commission's investigations. In consequence, in the Committee's opinion, crimes committed for the purpose of the preparation or initiation of war should be regarded as war crimes, irrespective of the territory in which they had been committed, which could also include crimes committed in order to prevent the establishment of peace (text of the resolution in: Ferencz (1980), vol. 1: 425ff). Nevertheless, in June 1944, the Plenary Commission regarded the aforementioned proposals as too far-reaching and decided that the problem of penalization of the war itself should be once again considered by the Legal Committee (UNWCC (1948: 181). The Committee established a Subcommittee, resulting in two reports. In the majority report, it was concluded that acts committed by an individual solely for the purpose of preparation or initiation of aggressive war were not, *de lege lata*, war crimes. However, due to the gravity of the acts of such kind, especially attacks on the principles of the law of nations and international good faith, committed by the leaders of the Axis states and their satellites for the purpose of preparing and initiating the war, they should be met with formal condemnation in the peace treaties, and in the future, criminal sanctions should be envisaged for such serious violations of the fundamental principles of international law (UNWCC (1948): 182). The majority report was adopted by the representatives of the United Kingdom, the Netherlands and the USA. The minority report, prepared by Ečer, contained the conclusion that aggressive war was a crime for which the individual was responsible. However, Ečer stressed that he was not referring to the criminality of every aggressive war but a specific war – WWII, started by the Germans.

25 Cyprian, Sawicki (1956): 9–10. The authors emphasize that only thanks to Poland and Czechoslovakia's hard line, on 27.09.1944, it was not possible in the UNWCC to adopt a

the result that in the final negotiations of the texts of the London Agreement and the IMT Charter, the inclusion of responsibility for aggression was no longer as controversial. Although Polish representatives were excluded from the direct negotiation of the IMT Charter, the influence of the thoughts exchanged within the UNWCC and other institutions of the WWII period (with Polish contribution) on the shape of Nuremberg law should not be downplayed.

After the end of WWII, as noted in subchapter 3.5, the Polish courts often held German criminals responsible for a crime against peace, even before the Nuremberg judgment. Crucially instrumental in that were the expert opinions written by Ludwik Ehrlich,[26] who had to answer the question whether a prohibition of aggression could be derived from the Kellogg-Briand Pact of 1928 and from the Polish-German Declaration of 1934. Ehrlich confirmed that until the early 20th century, the legality of war had been recognized in the law of nation.[27] However, a conditional and limited obligation to avoid war began to be introduced in the Interwar period, as confirmed by the provisions of the Covenant of the LoN, especially Article 10,[28] of the Resolution of the LoN Assembly of 24.09.1927 prohibiting aggressive war. Of crucial importance was the Kellogg-Briand Pact of 1928, having

resolution to the effect that acts committed with a view to the preparation and initiation of aggressive war were not to be regarded as crimes.

26 The expert opinions were published by: Ministry of Justice, Chief Commission for the Investigation of Nazi Crimes in Poland, Internal notice no. 59, *Ekspertyzy i orzeczenia przed Najwyższym Trybunałem Narodowym, vol. 1.* ('Expert opinions and Judgments before the Supreme National Tribunal'), selection by Czesław Pilichowski, Warszawa 1979. The nature and extent of the contributions made by Professor Antoni Peretiatkowicz (judge of the Supreme Administrative Court until 1947; Rector of the University of Poznań in 1936–1939) is not clear. From the transcripts of the proceedings in Arthur Greiser's trial, it occurs that the opinions delivered by Ehrlich before the Supreme National Tribunal were co-authored, see GKBZNwP, *Proces Artura Greisera przed Najwyższym Trybunałem Narodowym* ('The trial of Arthur Greiser before the Supreme National Tribunal'), Warszawa 1946: 130. *Ibidem*: 'Presiding Judge: Calling Professor Ehrlich and Professor Peretiatkowicz. Which one of you, Professors, will be speaking? Is the opinion on the question a joint one? May I have your gracious answer. Expert Professor Ludwik Ehrlich (Professor of the Jagiellonian University): A joint one.'

27 Pilichowski (1979): 45.

28 *Ibidem*: 50. Article 10 LoN Covenant: "The Members of the League undertake to respect and preserve as against external aggression the territorial integrity and existing political independence of all Members of the League. In case of any such aggression or in case of any threat or danger of such aggression the Council shall advise upon the means by which this obligation shall be fulfilled."

the effect of prohibiting – according to Ehrlich – '[a]ny war, thus also a defensive war in the proper sense, i.e. a war began in one's own defence but conducted not as self-defence but as a war in the proper sense, in any case, war conducted outside of the limits of defence, e.g. in the territory of the other state.'[29] Ehrlich emphasized: 'a treaty has to be interpreted in a manner allowing its fulfilment (…), rejecting the interpretation from which it would follow that the treaty or its individual provisions were to be of no consequence.'[30] Therefore, according to Ehrlich: 'by virtue of the Kellogg Pact, the commencement of war by any of its parties was inadmissible as contrary to a definitive obligation of that part, so that by commencing an action contrary to the Pact, the party could never claim to be waging a war permitted by the law of nations, such as it had been permitted e.g. in the 19th century.'[31] In Ehrlich's opinion, the good-faith obligation to refrain from prosecuting a war of aggression, because doing so would be contrary to the obligations arising from the Kellogg-Briand Pact, cannot be undermined by calling upon necessity.[32] In his opinion: 'not only armed operations but any commencement of hostilities, provided that hostilities are understood to mean the unlawful, i.e. contrary to the law of nations, infliction of harm: political, economic /military, among others/ on the other side, for the purpose of forcing it to accept terms rejected by it.'[33] With that, Ehrlich supplied the foundations for the conclusion that also the actions taken against Austria or Czechoslovakia could be called aggression.[34]

Ehrlich observed: 'The common law of nations does not have direct criminal sanctions for that type of action of individuals.'[35] At the same time, he emphasized, however, that whether it was admissible under international law for Polish courts to punish that action on the basis of Polish law, i.e. domestic law, was a different issue.[36] That question Ehrlich answered in the affirmative, albeit with certain doubts with regard to responsibility for aggressive war. He emphasized that, as opposed to the violations of HC IV of 1907, the judgment of which was, 'old international practice,' the

29 Pilichowski (1979): 46.

30 *Ibidem*: 47, 71.

31 *Ibidem*: 48.

32 *Ibidem*: 50.

33 *Ibidem*.

34 Cf. Raczkowski (1938): 117–118 on Anschluss of Austria.; Kumaniecki (1939): 131ff on the annexation of Czechoslovakia and Moravia.

35 Pilichowski (1979): 37.

36 *Ibidem*: 39.

judgment of individuals for the planning, preparation, initiation or waging of aggressive war was a certain *novum*.[37]

It cannot be excluded that the opinions submitted by Ehrlich for the NTN's purposes inspired the prosecutors and the adjudicating panels in the Nuremberg Trials, considering that the proceedings were translated into other languages, including English, and widely reported by the press. Jackson was invited to observe Greiser's trial but declined due to his obligations at Nuremberg.

Not all Polish jurists were of the opinion that aggression should be regarded as a separate crime. Litawski, in his postwar publication on human rights, asserted that whatever did not fall within the category of war crimes (and it is worth bearing in mind that the question of aggression was discussed at the UNWCC precisely under this category), should be regarded as a crime against humanity.[38]

4 Defining Aggression

Whereas the decision was not made to define aggressive war for the purposes of the Nuremberg and the Tokyo trials, the need for the adoption of a precise definition was understood in a situation in which the responsibility for aggression were to be enforced not only against the nationals of defeated Germany and Japan and their allies but potentially also against nationals of all other states of the world. Without defining aggression by a state, it would not be possible to develop the principle of individual responsibility for the crime of aggression.

When the question of defining aggression came during the San Francisco negotiations in 1945, Poland was not in a position to speak on the matter, lacking official representatives in the Conference. Nor was there a Polish delegate in the International Law Commission when the discussion on aggression began or during the debate on the first draft of the Code of Crimes against Peace and Security of Mankind, during which the question of the crime of aggression was discussed. Polish representatives, however, were in a position to comment to the ILC's works in the Sixth Committee, and they availed themselves of that option, advocating firmly for the need

37 *Ibidem*: 96.

38 *Report: Human Rights in the Nuremberg Trial*, 18.07.1947 (AIPiMGS).

to develop a definition of aggression, which – in their opinion – should be based on the Soviet proposal.[39]

When the UNGA decided to establish a committee to define aggression,[40] Poland initially was among the members. Such was the case with the committee created by Resolution 688/VII of 20.12.1952 (the 15-member committee met from 24.08. to 21.09.1953) and the committee established by Resolution 895/IX of 4.12.1954 (the 19-member committee met from 8.10. to 9.11.1956). Unfortunately, Poland was not represented in the subsequently Special Committees for Defining Aggression established at a later time.

The Polish delegation did not always take an official position during consultations on the proposals with the states,[41] and thus the Polish influence on the ultimate definition of aggression is not very visible. Nonetheless, certain returning points can be identified in the Polish representatives' arguments.

In the discussion in the UN (especially the UNGA and its committees), Poland ceaselessly advocated for the continuation of the works on the definition of aggression and for the discussion of the various proposals.[42] In the opinion of the Polish representatives, the adoption of a definition was necessary in order to prevent future aggressions[43] and for the decisions of the UN bodies to be less arbitrary;[44] the definition should be enumerative,[45] because a generally worded one would be completely useless.[46] The Polish delegates consistently supported the USSR's proposal of a definition[47] in which the key importance belonged to the principle of the first use of force.[48] According to the Polish representatives – in line with the rest of the Eastern Bloc – the definition also ought to cover indirect, economic and ideological aggression.[49] The necessity of penalizing the crime of aggression

39 Sawicki (1968): 554.

40 Based on GA resolution 897/IX, 4.12.1954, works on the code were postponed till the Special Committee would present its report.

41 Poland did not send its comments in response to the SG's report, UN Doc. A/2162 and add.1, 27.08.1952.

42 Broms (1968): 71.

43 UN Doc. A/8525, 8; A/9890; Wilson (2009): 78; Stone (1958): 55.

44 Nyiri (1989): 119.

45 UN Doc. A/C.6/L.273 do A/C.6/L.269/Rev.1 and Rev.l/Corr.; UN Doc. A/2638: 4–5 (Józef Winiewicz); Wilson (2009): 76–77; Nyiri (1989): 166–167; Rifaat (1979): 233; Broms (1968): 61.

46 UN Doc. A/2638 (Józef Winiewicz).

47 Žourek (1974): 773.

48 UN Doc. A/3574, 17; Rifaat (1979): 421.

49 UN Doc. A/3574, 14; Rifaat (1979): 241.

was pointed out; that should include cases of propaganda of aggressive war, which ought to be perceived as a form of preparation for aggression (i.e. one of the stages of the *iter criminis*). The Polish delegates stressed that, for example, war propaganda was a form of psychological armament and had been punishable as preparation for aggression in the light of Article 6a of the IMT Charter; accordingly, it should also be included in the Code of Crimes against Peace and Security of Mankind.[50] It could be noted here that the persistent determination of the Polish representatives was among the things that led to the inclusion of a prohibition against war propaganda in Article 20 of the ICCPR.[51]

The Polish representatives noted that the penalization of preparations for crimes was also important, including the creation of conditions for the commission of such crimes.[52] Thus, it was crucial to prevent and punish the propaganda of war or other crimes and any forms of spreading national, racial or religious hatred, preparation of plans for an aggressive war or use of weapons of mass destruction (nuclear weapons especially),[53] as well as to penalize the evocation of chauvinist tendencies with a view to disturbing peaceful relations among the nations.[54] They pointed out the need to distinguish the aggressor from the victim and to appreciate the culpability of those who support the aggressor under the guise of neutrality.[55] Multiple times did the Polish representatives made calls for fascism to be regarded in the given negotiations as a type of war ('fascism means war')[56] and as its cause, noting the connection between human rights and the guarantee of peace (that particular angle will be discussed again with the works on the recognition of the right to peace as a human right).[57] The Polish delegates invoked the prohibition of aggressive war in the discussions surrounding the adoption of the resolutions condemning the war in Korea (although those were, of course, extremely politicized statements).[58] They noted that the UN Charter was a certain system; hence, it was crucial to refer to the provisions of Articles 1(2), 2(1), 2(2), 2(4) and 2(7) UN Charter when

---

50 UN Doc. A/AC.10/46.
51 UN Doc. A/C.3/SR.291; Kearney (2007): 92, 96, 108–109, 113, 120.
52 See also Barcikowski (1946): 304.
53 UN Doc. A.PV.227 (1949) (Stefan Wierbłowski).
54 YILC (1950), vol. II: 250.
55 UN Doc. A.PV.82 (1947) (Zygmunt Modzelewski).
56 UN Doc. A.PV.40 (1946) (Wincenty Rzymowski).
57 See Janusz Symonides (1980a) and Adam Łopatka (1980).
58 E.g. UN Doc. A.PV.382 (1952) and UN Doc. A/2229, 18.10.1952 (Stanisław Skrzeszewski).

evaluating whether specific actions were aggressive.[59] At the same time, they emphasized that fighting for independence from foreign dominance could never be regarded as aggression.[60] The legality of preventive war was also excluded.[61] The Polish delegation also stressed that it could not be in doubt since the time of the Nuremberg trial that aggression was a crime and entailed individual responsibility.[62]

In the end, the definition of aggression adopted on 14.12.1974 by consensus in the UNGA Resolution no. 3314 was satisfactory to Poland, as demonstrated by the fact that the Polish delegate to the Stockholm Conference pointed out the need to refer to this definition in the text of the APs of 1977.[63] However, Resolution no. 3314 did not develop upon the principles of criminal responsibility for the crime of aggression compared to the IMT Charter, as it only stipulates in its Article 5 that war of aggression is a crime against international peace.

5 Defining the Crime of Aggression

The problem of defining aggression and the crime of aggression appears multiple times in the ILC's works, especially those on the Draft Code of Offences/Crimes against the Peace and Security of Mankind or the discussions on the principle of *aut dedere aut judicare*. It is characteristic that although the predominating view in the ILC had been that the aforementioned principle and the concept of universal jurisdiction should not apply to crimes against peace/the crime of aggression,[64] Poland has consistently mentioned crime against peace on parity with other *core crimes*, without making any distinction among them.[65]

---

59 Solera (2008): 127–128.

60 YILC 1951, vol. II: 55 (Lachs).

61 *GAOR, Sixth Session, Sixth Committee, Ibidem*, 283rd mtg and 292nd mtg (Przemysław Ogrodziński).

62 UN Doc. SR.236, 177–178 (Lachs).

63 *OR 1974– 1977*, vol. XIV: 129 (Remigiusz Bierzanek). As a marginal note, at a later time, a draft Declaration on the Preparation of Societies for Life in Peace was sponsored by Poland and ultimately adopted as UNGA Resolution 33/73 of 15.12.1978 (with only the USA and Israel voting against). The draft was part of Poland's wider efforts to eliminate aggression from international relations; see Pawlak (2019): 274.

64 Article 9 of 1996 Code of Crimes against Peace and Security of Mankind and UN Doc. A/CN.4/571, §51.

65 UN Doc. A/CN.4/579 and Add.1–4, 2008, UN Doc. A/CN.4/599; UN Doc. A/CN.4/612.

The question of defining a framework of responsibility for the crime of aggression returned with negotiations on a statute for the ICC. Poland, under the clear influence of Germany, and specifically Hans-Peter Kaul,[66] supported placing the crime of aggression within the jurisdiction of the ICC with the preservation of the role of the Security Council in determining whether an act of aggression has taken place and with only the most serious and manifest violations of the prohibition against the use of force to qualify as aggression.[67] While not having any original proposals pertaining to the judgment of the crime of aggression, Poland was of the opinion that the crime should be subjected to the ICC's jurisdiction.

The efforts made in the Rome Conference to define the crime of aggression and the terms of exercise of jurisdiction over it were not successful. The task was entrusted to a Special Working Group, the meetings of which were attended, among others, by Andrzej Makarewicz,[68] Remigiusz Henczel and Beata Ziorkiewicz;[69] details of their activity in this regard, however, are difficult to ascertain (it was not recorded in the documentation). What is especially concerning is that there was not a single representative of Poland attending the works of the ILA committee on the use of force, which dealt aggression in 2010–2018.

The eventual amendments defining the crime of aggression (Article 8*bis*) and the terms of exercise of jurisdiction over it (Articles 15*bis* and 15*ter*) were adopted by consensus during the Review Conference in Kampala in 2010. During the discussions, the Polish delegation was in favour of restrictively narrowing the jurisdiction of the ICC for the crime of aggression only to those cases in which the victim state and the aggressor state had ratified the relevant amendments to the ICC statute.[70]

In Kampala, it was decided that the ultimate decision as to whether the ICC was to exercise jurisdiction with regard to the crime of aggression would be made in 2017 in the Assembly of States Parties of the ICC, which indeed happened by consensus. In consequence, the Court may exercise its jurisdiction over the crime of aggression from 2018.

66 Anna Wyrozumska's statement during the interview of 10.05.2019 (authors' archives).

67 Solera (2008): 356, 361, 369; United Nations Diplomatic Conference of Plenipotentiaries on the Establishment of an International Criminal Court, Rome 15.06–17.07.1998, OR, vol. 2, 181 (Maria Frankowska); 286 (Agnieszka Dąbrowiecka), 333 (Anna Wyrozumska).

68 ICC-ASP/4/SWGCA/INF.1 and ICC-ASP/5/SWGCA/INF.1

69 ICC-ASP/6/SWGCA/INF.1.

70 Kreß (2018): 9.

Poland ratified the amendments in 2014,[71] thus before their entry into force (the threshold had been set at 30 ratifications and was achieved in June 2016). At present (22.08.2025), the relevant amendments to the ICC Statute concerning the crime of aggression have been ratified by 49 states, and thus the ICC's opportunities to judge the crime of aggression are very limited.

6 Polish Legislation

As early as 1932, on the initiative of Rappaport, the crime of war propaganda was defined in the Criminal Code. Article 113 provided: '(1) Whoever publicly calls for a war of aggression shall be liable to imprisonment of up to 5 years. (2) The prosecution shall only proceed when the act set out in section 1 is penalized by the statutes of states against which the propaganda is directed.'

As noted in his commentary by Makarewicz, propaganda was not the same as incitement: 'it is not direct to a specific person but, on the contrary, to a greater number of not individually identified persons.'[72] The act, therefore, had to be committed in public, in a place generally accessible to the public; it could involve the use of the press or other printed materials intended for public distribution. Makarewicz, however, noted that the term 'aggressive war' was rather flexible, considering that the party initiating a war, rather than regarding itself as the aggressor, attributes provocation or an insult to the other side.[73] He described Article 113 of the Criminal Code as a pacifist provision.

Makowski, in turn, in his commentary, observed that Article 113 of the Criminal Code was: 'the sign of a new concept founded upon the principle of international solidarity and the fact of the recognition of war as an international crime by the civilized states.'[74] Makowski stressed that the aforementioned provision was the natural consequence of the criminality of aggressive war, and the propaganda of aggressive war was an attack on the premises of the international order (similarly to how calling for a crime to be committed was an attack on the public order). In his opinion, therefore, 'the object of the crime here [wa]s the order of the international co-

71 Dz.U.2014.500.

72 Makarewicz (1932): 195.

73 *Ibidem*: 195–196.

74 Makowski (1937): 380.

existence.' He associated the notion of aggressive war itself with the: 'initiative of an armed violation of the international order,' although with the caveat that the qualification should be *ad casum*.

Article 93 of the same Criminal Code penalized the so-called crime of state, consisting in attempts to deprive the Polish state of its independent existence or part of its territory. In essence, therefore, it was an attempt at the penalization of aggressive war against Poland. Some commentators, however, such as Makarewicz, interpreted the meaning of the provision in the context of, for example, internal forces calling for international involvement with a view to holding plebiscites with the result of loss of territory by Poland.[75] Likewise, Makowski saw Article 93 in the context of the crime of state, of a coup directed against the state's internal system.[76]

The aforementioned *lex Rappaport* was the first regulation of that type in the world, and the subsequent adoptions of similar provisions in Romania (Article 229 of the Criminal Code of 1936) and Brazil (Article 508 of the Criminal Code of 1940), as explicitly stated by the authorities of the aforementioned states, had been inspired by Rappaport and the Polish legislative experience.[77]

The next legislative instrument to deal indirectly with the scope of aggression was the Decree of the President of the Republic of Poland of 30.03.1943,[78] Article 2 of which dealt with responsibility for act contrary to the norms of international law against the interests of the Republic of Poland, a Polish legal person or Polish national. The crime of aggression could fall under that definition, especially considering the language of Article 4, aggravating the penalty for acts causing a general danger to life or health in Poland.

The August Decree of the PKWN – in its original version of 31.08.1944 – bears no trace of the criminalization of the crime of aggression as such. However, the amendment of 16.02.1945 contains the following language: 'Whoever, in the interest of the German occupational authorities, has acted or is still acting, in a manner other than set out in section 1, to the detriment of the Polish State (...),' which can already be interpreted as an indirect reference to, among others, a crime against peace directed against Poland.

The Decree on the Supreme National Tribunal, on the other hand, mentioned: 'cases of the criminal offences of persons who, in accordance

75 Makarewicz (1932): 180.

76 Makowski (1937): 319.

77 Rappaport (1929a): 48–49.

78 Dz.U.1943.3.6

with the Moscow Declaration of the three Allied powers: United States of America, Union of Soviet Socialist Republics and [the United Kingdom of] Great Britain [and Northern Ireland] on the Nazis' responsibility for the atrocities committed by them will be remanded to the organs of the prosecution service of the Polish Republic for crimes committed in the territory of the Polish State during the occupation.' As discussed more extensively in subchapter 3.5, the NTN – drawing extensively upon the IMT Charter and thereafter the Nuremberg judgment – analysed the matter of responsibility for crimes against peace.

In turn, in the Decree of 13.06.1946 on Criminal Offences Particularly Dangerous in the Period of Reconstruction of the State,[79] Article 1 ('Whoever commits a violent attempt on a unit of Polish or allied armed forces (...)') and Article 2 ('Whoever publicly calls for the commission of the crime set out in Article 1 (...)') referred indirectly to the matter of responsibility for crimes against peace/the crime of aggression. The Act of 29.10.1950 on the Defence of Peace introduced criminal sanctions for war propaganda.[80]

The Criminal Code of 1969 did not contain provisions dealing with crimes against peace/the crime of aggression. Only the Criminal Code of 1997, following the legacy of Nuremberg, expressly regulated the matter of responsibility for crimes against peace/the crime of aggression. Its Article 117 provides:

> (1) Whoever initiates or wages a war of aggression shall be liable to no less than 12 years' imprisonment, 25 years' imprisonment or life-time imprisonment. (2) Whoever makes preparations for the commission of the offence set out in section 1 shall be liable to no less than 3 years' imprisonment. (3) Whoever publicly calls for the initiation of a war of aggression or publicly praises the initiation or waging of such war shall be liable to from 3 months' to 5 years' imprisonment.[81]

The language of Article 117 is based on the terminology of the IMT Charter; hence, following Poland's ratification of the ICC Statute in 2002 several

79 Dz.U.1946.30.92.

80 Article 1: 'Whoever, by speech or writing, through the press, radio, film or in any other manner engages in war propaganda, commits a crime against peace and shall be liable to up to 15 years' imprisonment.' Article 2 clarified: 'Whoever incites or calls for war commites a crime against peace' (Dz.U.58.521). See also Muszkat (1956): 334; Grzybowski, Pundeff (1952): 537.

81 §2 was abolished, Dz.U.88.553ff.

attempts were made to update the language in order to accommodate it to the norms of international law binding on Poland and penalize not only aggressive war but also any act of aggression. Unfortunately, no such amendment has been enacted to date, bar one of 7.07.2022, which entered into force on 1.10.2023[82] and by which the option of 25 years' imprisonment is to be eliminated. As from the entry of the amendment into force, the flexible sentencing limit will be 12 to 30 years with the alternative of life imprisonment.

7 Polish Scholarship

Polish scholarship has a long history of studies into the legality of the use of of force, starting with the Polish school of international law, which was established by Stanisław of Skarbimierz (Stanislaus de Scarbimiria) and Paweł Włodkowic (Paulus Vladimiri), and propagated by Ludwik Ehrlich.[83] Voluminous treatises on the legality of war and the security (safety) system were also published during the period discussed in this book, i.e. 1918–2019 – suffice to mention the works of Zygmunt Cybichowski (1914), Władysław Kulski (1927 and 1950), Tytus Komarnicki (1923), Bohdan Winiarski (1936), Krzysztof Skubiszewski (1959), and Władysław Czapliński (1993). Thus, it cannot come as a surprise that Polish scholars had contributions to make to the international debate and negotiation of the relevant norms with regard to matter and definition of aggression and punishment for the crime of it.

Especially notable in the scholarly debate of the Interwar period are Rappaport's works on the penalization of war propaganda (1927), printed both in Polish and in French, as well as Wacław Komarnicki's *La définition de l'agresseur* (1935 and 1936), being the aftermath of the conference on collective safety in London, on the basis of which Rappaport, as a member of the Polish delegation, delivered a paper on the subject.[84] A significant publication, though – unfortunately – published only in Polish, was Michał Król's monograph titled *Zagadnienie agresji w prawie międzynarodowym* (1939) ('The problem of aggression in international law'), which appeared one week prior to the German aggression against Poland, followed a fortnight later by Soviet aggression. In that publication, Król referred to international conventions dealing with the notions of aggression or of the aggressor state

82 Dz.U.2022.2600.

83 Ehrlich (1955).

84 Balcerzak (2022): 182.

or only referencing those terms. He highlighted the interpretative problems surfacing in the legal state of affairs at the time and the general difficulties defining the phaenomenon of aggression, especially given the attempts at the criminalization also of preparations for it. Król disputed the views of Komarnicki, whom he regarded as an adherent of the territorial concept of aggression in its most liberal flavour.[85]

From among the publications dealing with responsibility for the crime of aggression during the 1939–1989 period, it will be expedient to note a series of works concerning the prohibition of aggressive wars by Jan Litawski (1943), Stefan Glaser (1953) and (1961), Wacław Komarnicki (1949), Marian Muszkat (1956),[86] Tadeusz Cyprian and Jerzy Sawicki (1960), as well as Jan Balicki (1952), Wojciech Morawiecki (1956), Aleksander Bramson (1952) and Remigiusz Bierzanek (1970). Interestingly, Polish-language positions were cited by foreign authors,[87] probably due to featuring in the UN Secretariat's official source list on aggression.[88] Authors of notable publications after 1989, on the other hand, include Władysław Czapliński (2008), Patrycja Grzebyk (2010 and 2011) (including in English – 2013; 2017b, 2022b), as well as Eleonora Zielińska (2010), Tomasz Iwanek (2013), Jakub Olejniczak (2010), and Katarzyna Banasik (2012).

8 Conclusions

During the Interwar period and the time of WWII, Polish diplomats and scholars had a meaningful influence on the criminalization of aggression. Suffice to mention the initiatives of Sokal and Rappaport in the League of Nations or the AIDP. Polish diplomats took an active participation in the drafting of the regional definition of aggression within the London Conventions of 1933, and the Polish Criminal Code of 1932 introduced the criminalization of war propaganda. The criminalization – in the views of Polish commentators – was the confirmation of the illegality of aggressive war as such. After WWII, it was a Polish court in Athur Greiser's case to

85 Król (1939): 259–260.

86 That is, however, a highly ideologized position and focused on the contributions of Soviet rather than Polish scholarship; however, at p. 329, the author emphasizes that the crime against peace criminalized by the IMT Charter: 'encompasses both direct and indirect, as well as ideological aggression, and thus also activities preparatory to a war of aggression.'

87 Nyiri (1989); Žourek (1974); Aroneanu (1958).

88 ST/LIB/32, 24.10.1973.

hand down the first judgment holding an individual responsible for crimes against peace. One could have thought that, after 1945, Polish diplomacy would play an especially active role in the efforts to define aggression within the UNGA. That, however, did not materialize. Due to the political situation, the Polish representatives limited themselves to supporting the Soviet proposals, which became transparent to the point that, for a certain time, they ceased to be included in the works of the relevant committees, being unable to contribute anything meaningful to the discussion. After 1989, in the case of the negotiation of the Rome Statute, the Polish representatives limited themselves to supporting the German proposals without drawing upon their prior experience, which could have proven to be extraordinarily valuable in the context of delineation of the circle of those bearing responsibility for the crime.

Despite the ratification of the relevant amendments to the ICC Statute, a corresponding amendment of the Criminal Code so as to bring the definition from the Polish Code to conformity with the one adopted in the Rome Statute were not introduced. From time to time, there are proposals of amendments significantly diverging from the ICC definition in attempting, for example, to criminalize activities in the economic sphere. Nevertheless, it will be fitting to mention that when Russian invasion against Ukraine took place in February 2022, the Polish prosecution opened an investigation into the aggressive war commenced by the authorities of the Russian Federation against Ukraine, precisely on the basis of the aforementioned Article 117(1) of the Criminal Code. The Polish Office of the Prosecutor, emphasized that the Russian activities: 'threaten European and international security.' They are directed against the interests of the international community, including the Republic of Poland.'[89]

89 See: https://www.gov.pl/web/sprawiedliwosc/dzialania-ministerstwa-sprawiedliwosci-i-polskiej-prokuratury-wobec-wojny-na-ukrainie.

CHAPTER 7

War Crimes

1 Responsibility for War Crimes of the World War I

The Polish delegation in the peace conference in Paris called at the end of WWI participated in the works of the Commission on Responsibilities (in the so-called Committee of Fifteen).[1] The Commission compiled the first known list of war crimes, noting the utility of documents submitted, among others by Poland ('abundant evidence of outrages of every description committed on land, at sea, and in the air, against the laws and customs of war and the laws of humanity').[2] When it came to developing a definition of war crimes and principles of responsibility for them, the contributions made by the Poles were doubtless significant, should one consider that Konstanty Skirmunt and his successor, Leon Łubieński,[3] worked in a subcommittee dealing with responsibility for violations of the laws and customs of war.

In the final version of its report, the Commission mentioned the practice of currency counterfeiting and deliberate, methodical destruction of industry, which had been mentioned by the Poles. However, the *Mémoire de la Délegation polonaise,* filed on 5.03.1919[4] and forwarded by the Polish delegation, also mentioned a number of other violations perpetrated by the German and Bolshevik authorities, subsequently included in the Commission's list. A detailed description was provided of the crimes of the troops commanded by Major Hermann Preusker in Kalisz (causing a panic by the bombardment of an undefended Kalisz, followed by setting it on fire, as well as destruction and pillage, opening machine-gun fire at persons walking in a park – those actions led to the dwindling of the city's population from 75 thousand to 35

1 See Rhea (2014): 163.

2 *Report presented to the Preliminary Peace Conference, March 29, 1919,* (1920): 14(1/2) AJIL 95, 113.

3 In conference's documents, they are referred as C. Skurmunt and L. Lubienski.

4 *Note sommaire sur les exactions commises, contrairement au droit des gens en Pologne par les armées ennemies de 1914 à 1918: Annexe I. Rapport addressé par le Président de la ville de Varsovie au sujet de dommage causes à la ville de Varsovie par l'occupation allemande,* 19.12.1918, no. 6850/B; *Annexe II. Rapport de la commission gouvernementale des prisonniers de guerre, Varsovie à la délégation polonaise à la Conference de la paix,* 4.02.1919, no. 1038, published in: *Recueil des Actes de la Conférence. Partie IV. Commissions de la Conférence (Procès-verbaux, Rapports et Documents). B. Questions Générale* (2) *Commission des Responsabilités des Auteurs de la Guerre et Sanctions,* Paris Imprimerie Nationale 1922: 474ff.

thousand); the practice of denying payments to the families of mobilized conscripts, which compounded the mortality rates; shifting war expenditure onto the local governments; prohibiting transactions in roubles and introducing a new currency; systematic destruction of forests; increase taxation and complete and systematic draining of all factory production; forced labour in inhuman conditions; excessive requisitions leading the population to starvation; unlawful arrests and imprisonments. The above-described activities had the purpose of exterminating the Polish population (*elle tendait sciemment à exterminer la population*). Data from Warsaw were cited in the context. The particularly systematic denationalization (de-ethnicization) of the population in Lithuania, as well as massacres committed by Austrian and German forces (especially during retreat) and the German, Austrian, White Russian and Ukrainian forces' prevention of the local population from organizing itself properly, which compounded the losses incurred when the Bolsheviks were committing their atrocities. On the basis of the testimony offered by Czesław Knichowiecki, a description was provided of the barbaric treatment of the inmates of the Russenlager bei Polizeipräsidium internment camp in Hannover-Linded, which included confiscation of all property, forced labour, tortures (beating with a handgun, pulling hair, insults), lack of hygiene or suitable health-care. In describing the situation of occupied Warsaw, note was taken of the starvation caused by excessive requisitions, by the imposition of additional burdens and by deportations of the population.

When the British delegation submitted a proposal of violations of the laws and customs of war, Łubieński – in a note from the Polish delegation, signed by himself – took a favourable view, albeit stipulating the caveat that it should be expanded to include such actions as had taken place during the war and especially during the Austrian and German occupation, such as: systematic and premeditated ruination with a view to facilitating the subjugation of a terrorized and pauperized population and to ensure the economic supremacy of Germany after the war; mass executions of the civilian population; forced labour, deportations and inhumane treatment of civilians; hostage taking; issuing counterfeit currency and prohibition of transactions in local currency; denationalization (de-ethnicization) of the population, prohibiting the opening of Polish schools and closing the existing ones, as well as prohibiting the circulation of books in the Polish language; providing military assistance in the form of weapons and ammunition to the Bolsheviks, Russians and Ukrainians while disarming the Polish militias.[5]

5 Note de la délégation polonaise déposée le 26 février 1919.

In the end, the Commission's list of violations of the laws and customs of war included (the ones described in the Polish memorandum are in bold font): (1) **murders and massacres; systematic terrorism;** (2) putting hostages to death; (3) **torture of civilians;** (4) **deliberate starvation of civilians;** (5) rape; (6) abduction of girls and women for the purpose of enforced prostitution; (7) **deportation of civilians;** (8) **internment of civilians under inhumane conditions;** (9) **forced labor of civilians in connection with the military operations of the enemy;** (10) **usurpation of sovereignty during military occupation;** (11) compulsory enlistment of soldiers among the inhabitants of occupied territory; (12) **attempts to denationalize the inhabitants of occupied territory;** (13) **pillage;** (14) **confiscation of property;** (15) **exaction of illegitimate or of exorbitant contributions and requisitions;** (16) **debasement of the currency, and issue of spurious currency;** (17) imposition of collective penalties; (18) **wanton devastation and destruction of property;** (19) **deliberate bombardment of undefended places;** (20) **wanton destruction of religious, charitable, educational, and historic buildings and monuments;** (21) destruction of merchant ships and passenger vessels without warning and without provision for the safety of passengers or crew; (22) destruction of fishing boats and of relief ships; (23) **deliberate bombardment of hospitals;** (24) attack on and destruction of hospital ships; (25) breach of other rules relating to the Red Cross; (26) use of deleterious and asphyxiating gasses; (27) use of explosive or expanding bullets, and other inhumane appliances; (28) directions to give no quarter; (29) **ill-treatment of wounded and prisoners of war;** (30) **employment of prisoners of war on unauthorized works;** (31) misuse of flags of truce; (32) poisoning of wells.[6]

Having regard to the progress on the works done by the Commission on Responsibilities, Łubieński persuaded the Polish Bureau for Congress Affairs to notify, on 10.03.1919, the other ministries of having commenced the: 'examination of the violations of the law of the nations by the German and Austro-Hungarian authorities and armies in Polish territories,' listing among those:

> 1/ systematically terrorizing the population; 2/ deliberate devastations, destructions of property and pillage; 3/ illegal contributions and levies; 4/ unlawful executions; 5/ deportation of civilians and forced labour; 6/ killing of hostages; 7/ aerial bombardment without warning; 8/

6 Commission on the Responsibility of the Authors of the War (1920): 114–115.

> deliberate and unneeded bombing of hospitals; 9/ illegal pressing and ill-treatment of prisoners of war; 10/ instructions to take no prisoners; 11/ general use of illegal methods of warfare.[7]

The Bureau assumed that the relevant documentation, for the purpose of exacting the criminal responsibility of the most offending individuals and giving the picture of the general methods of operation of the German and Austro-Hungarian authorities and armies, could be gathered within 8 days. Such an assumption was, of course, wrong, and no wonder that the Section for the Investigation of Violations of the Law of the Nations by the German and Austrian Authorities and Armies in Polish Territories, specially established at the Bureau for Congress Affairs, was unable to meet the task.[8]

The aforementioned Bureau for Congress Affairs had to assemble with great urgency the list of the criminals who – in Poland's view – should be judged pursuant to Article 228 of the Treaty of Versailles (the states had a month after the ratification of the Treaty to compile and submit such lists).[9] The information gathered from the courts revealed that, in their opinion, the need was to prosecute a list of crimes against civilians, e.g. terrorizing – understood very broadly, from crucifixions to demanding a bow before an officer; executions, rapes, extortions of bribes, abuse of censorship, and incitement of racial hate; crimes against combatants, e.g. murder of prisoners of war; announcement that no quarter will be given and consequent refusal to take prisoners; refusal to deliver post; use of poisonous gas; as well as a number of crimes against property, e.g. imposition of new taxes, pillage, destruction, profanation; destruction of state, communal and private forests.

As rightly noted by Cybulski, the list of 'crimes' mentioned by Polish courts was significantly wider than that adopted in the Treaty of Versailles.[10] In the end, Poland's list submitted to the Allies in December 1919 featured 51 or 57 names, depending on the source, including persons such as General Hans Hartwig von Beseler, Ulrich von Etzdorf Rummel (governors of Warsaw), General Ernst Reinhold Gerhard von Glasenapp (President of

---

7 Cybulski (1987): 252.

8 In July 1919, the Bureau for Congress Affairs also proposed the establishment of a permanent Commission for the Investigation of Violations of Ordinary and International Law by the Foreign Authorities and Armies in Polish Territories (involving primarily the ministries of justice, internal affairs and armed forces in the gathering of the relevant documentation).

9 Dz.U.1920.35.200.

10 Cybulski (1987): 254.

the Police in Warsaw), Wolfgang Ludwig Moritz von Kries (head of the civilian administration in German-occupied Kalisz and subsequently in Warsaw; head of the German Imperial Civil Administration in the General Governorate of Warsaw).[11]

Unfortunately, the Allies' final list for the Reich included only 45 persons, including those accused of the devastation of Kalisz, as the 39th–41st. During the trials in 1921 before the *Reichsgericht* in Leipzig, however, those guilty of the crimes in Kalisz were not judged, which shows that – according to the German court – either the evidence submitted by the Poles or the gravity of the crimes had been insufficient.[12]

2 Responsibility for the War Crimes of the Interwar

For several years after Poland regained independence in 1918, Poles were involved in armed conflicts (Silesian and Greater-Polish Uprisings, Polish-Soviet War, Polish-Lithuanian conflict with the occupation of Vilnius, and Polish-Czech conflict over Cieszyn Silesia).

In the case of the armed operations against the German state in 1919–1921, war crimes appear to be a marginal question.[13] The text of Polish-German amnesty agreements does not reveal typical war crimes as their

11 The number 51 is given, among others, by Cybulski (1987): 255; Rafałowski (1980): 834; the number 57 by, among others, Gelewski (1976): 96; Goryński (1944): 49; the *Kurjer Poranny* of 13.01.1920 claimed that the original length had been 425 names, reduced later to 50. Andrejew, Kubicki, Waszczyński (1985): 143, citing the *Kurjer*, give the number at 51. See also: Cybulski (1986): 334, who, also citing the *Kurjer Poranny*, states that the original Polish list had included even as many as 375 names.

12 Mullins (1921): 35ff. As the analysis of the Leipzig Trials demonstrates, one had to show a great deal of determination even to get the German criminals indicted, and even so, the penalties were disproportionately mild, as attested by the so-called British cases. Interestingly, one of the persons listed by the Brits as guilty of war crimes, Heinrich Trinke, allegedly could not be judged because he was in Poland and the time and his arrest warrant was not enforced; see: *Current Notes: German War Trials* (1922) 16 (4) AJIL 628: 629–630.

13 Acts of terror against the civilian population were the direct causes of e.g. the 1st Silesian Uprising (1919), and a number of crimes against civilians by the German side occurred especially after the 3rd Silesian Uprising (1921), but due to the timing (before or after the armed conflict) and the nature of the conflict (non-international), those were not war crimes in the light of the law at the time. Concerning the repression and torture of the 'prisoners', see: Kaczmarek (2019): 190, 195, 506, 512 and 513, where German accusations are discussed. Cf. also Kania (2021).

objects.[14] Each side only wanted to procure the freedom of persons detained due to affiliation with the relevant armed forces or military activity undertaken for political or ethnic reasons on behalf of either side of the conflict.[15] During the Polish-Lithuanian conflict (in 1920, General Lucjan Żeligowski occupied Vilnius), neither were there any violations of the law of war serious enough to provoke the discussion of exacting responsibility for war crimes. Things were different with the Polish-Czech conflict. While the Czechs were accused of crimes on Polish prisoners of war (e.g. the murder of prisoners of war in Stonawa),[16] the authors of this book could not find information on any attempts to bring the perpetrators to judgment.

During Russian (Bolshevik) operations against Poland, numerous crimes were committed on Polish prisoners of war and civilian population.[17] Particularly noted are the crimes of Semyon Budyonny's mounted force (e.g. burning a hospital with 600 wounded soldiers and medical staff in Berdyczów (Berdychiv), committing the murder of surrendering Polish soldiers in the village of Bystrzyk or in the neighbourhood of Fastów) or the cavalry corps of Gai Dmitrievich Gai (murdering the wounded in the hospital in Płock, murdering prisoners of war – estimates mention approx. one thousand, mostly officers). Not infrequently, in retaliation, Polish forces shot the prisoners, and cruel treatment in prisoner camps was not rare.[18] Although, main reasons of the death of several-dozen-thousand Soviet prisoners of war in Polish PoW camps were the difficult sanitary conditions.[19]

In the peace treaty among Poland and Russia (together with Ukraine), signed at Riga on 18.03.1921,[20] both sides guaranteed complete amnesty for political crimes (defined as: 'acts directed against the political system or security of the state, as well as all acts committed for the benefit of the other party') – Article X. The amnesty extended to acts prosecuted on an administrative or other non-judicial path, as well as breaches of provisions applicable to prisoners of war, as well as interned persons and nationals of the other party. That was explained as not opening new investigations, discontinuing the ones already opened, and not enforcing the penalties already

---

14 See statement of Polish government of 31.01.1922, Dz.U.1922.11.85.

15 Cybulski (2014): 163ff.

16 *Zaolzie. Polski Biuletyn Informacyjny* (2006), no. 1 (25). Characteristically, however, the matter of any war crimes is not discussed by the works describing the course of the conflict; see e.g. Przybylski (1932).

17 Chwalba (2020): 310.

18 See e.g. Szymowski (2021).

19 Sienkiewicz (2010/2011): 195ff.

20 Dz.U.1921.49.300.

imposed. With that, the Treaty of Riga precluded the prosecution of war criminals and confirmed that amnesty could cover such crimes.

3 Responsibility for the Crimes of World War II

An impressive Polish contribution was made to the definition of war crimes and to the development of the principles of responsibility for them during WWII and in its aftermath. The UNWCC emphasized that the Polish-Czechoslovak statement published in *The Times* on 12.11.1940, pointing towards crimes such as forced resettlement, deportation for forced labour in Germany, mass executions, deportations to concentration camps, unlawful appropriation of public and private property, extermination of the intellectual elite and destruction of cultural life, confiscation of cultural property, and persecution of religion, as well as another statement published in *The Times*, on 20.12.1940, describing the unlawfulness of the denationalization policy, initiated the process of condemnation of those crimes.[21] The UNWCC added that reforging political statements into concrete frameworks was crucial to the matter of exacting the perpetrators' responsibility for the crimes; that is what happened on Poland's initiative, through the adoption of the St James Declaration of 13.01.1942.[22]

In the Interwar period, discussions of a general definition and list of war crimes took place in the various bodies of which Poles were active members. The International Commission for Penal Reconstruction and Development, on the basis of a confidential report prepared by Lauterpacht, identified war crimes with such violations of the rules of the law of war as were of criminal nature due to their reprehensibility, brutality, ruthless disregard of the sanctity of human life and personality, as well as the inviolability of property, which could not be justified by military necessity. The Commission's Subcommittee for War Crimes, in the works of which Glaser took part, developed the distinction among: firstly, crimes relating to the conduct of armed operations (e.g. the use of a specific type of weapon, such as poisonous gas, or attacks on hospital ships); secondly, crimes not connected with armed operations, whether without any authorization, such as killings and rapes, or those having the approval of the competent authorities, such as mass killings, murder of hostages, and deportations; thirdly, serious crimes against property, both with the authorities' permission, such

21 UNWCC (1948): 87.

22 *Ibidem*: 89.

as destruction and seizure of works of art, or without that permission – pillage.[23] For the last-mentioned type of crimes, against property, only Poland was legally prepared to judge the perpetrators of such type of crimes perpetrated abroad, whether or not they could be classified as crimes directed against the security of the state.[24]

Those involved in the works of another subcommittee – dealing with the issue of acting on orders – included Hersch Lauterpacht. There, it was decided that every case should be considered individually but citing orders alone ought not to lead to an automatic exemption from responsibility. Works on principles to govern the judgment of war criminals were also taking place in the London International Assembly, in which Zygmunt Nagórski participated from Poland,[25] and subsequently in the UNWCC.

In the UNWCC, Polish voices were heard in the discussion concerning the responsibility for war crimes, such as those of Bohdan Winiarski, whose spoke about the possibility of the establishment of an international criminal tribunal,[26] or Jerzy Litawski, who emphasized that military necessity had already been considered within the regulations of the law of war and thus ought not to be regarded as a separate ground of exemption from responsibility.[27] It is of special significance that the chapter concerning the development of the law of war in the publication summarizing the UNWCC's works was written by Litawski. It should be borne in mind, however, that within the UNWCC, the notion of war crime was referred both to violations of the laws and customs of war, i.e. war crimes *stricto sensu*, and to the planning, initiation and waging of a war of aggression and acts performed also prior to the war but contrary to the elementary legal principles binding on civilized nations, i.e. crimes against humanity.

Crucially, the Poles' documentation of the crimes committed in the territory of Poland and reporting them appropriately to the Commission made it possible not only to determine the scale of the crimes but also to distinguish their various types. Ultimately, the UNWCC did not opt for a general definition of war crimes; already in December 1943, however, it compiled a working list of examples of war crimes (on the basis of the results of the works of the Commission of Fifteen, operating as part of the framework of the peace conference in 1919).

---

23 *Ibidem*: 96–97.

24 *Ibidem*: 97.

25 *Ibidem*: 99.

26 *Ibidem*: 102.

27 *Ibidem*: 28.

It is also worth noting that when it comes to German criminals accused by the governments and inducted on lists by the UNWCC, Poland had submitted as many as 7805. Only France reported more (12,546).[28] It was the Polish documentation that made it possible to comprehend the scale of the crimes committed in the concentration camps.[29] In the spring of 1944, the Polish delegation (Glaser) noted that the catalogue of war crimes had to encompass the different methods of terrorization and extermination of the inhabitants of the occupied territories, including mass arrests, hostage taking, which was argued to be contrary to Article 46 of the Hague Regulations of 1907 and the Martens clause; as well as any acts of systemic violence in the form of the use of procedures, laws and regulations discriminating against the population of the occupied territories and striking against human dignity.[30] The direct outcome of those activities was the organization of separate trials focused on the crime of hostage taking.[31]

Polish authorities held the first war-crimes trials already during WWII, and the postwar legacy of tens of thousands of judgments is extraordinarily abundant and valuable (see Subchapter 3.5).

4 The Geneva Conventions and Their Additional Protocols

The Convention relative to the Treatment of Prisoners of War, of 27.07.1929,[32] did not contain any provisions regulating individual responsibility for war crimes. In the Convention for the Amelioration of the Condition of the Wounded and Sick in Armies in the Field, adopted on the same day,[33] the states decided to incorporate provisions obliging the parties to issue appropriate penal provisions (which had to be notified within 5 years of the ratification of the Convention) and to punish those guilty of the violation of any of the provisions of the Convention (Articles 29–30). During the negotiations on the text of the Convention, it was noted that some legal

---

28 *Ibidem*: 509–510.

29 *Ibidem*: 490.

30 *Ibidem*: 171. See also UNWCC, Proposal by the Polish representatives for adding items to the list of war criminals (Minute of the 17th meeting, 9.05.1944), 3; and Polish Charge against German war criminals no. 3 (mass arrests) and 33 i 34 (law discriminating Jewish population).

31 See US v. Wilhelm List et al., 19.02.1948, summary available in UNWCC (1949), 8 *Law Reports of Trials of War Criminals* 34.

32 Dz.U.1932.103.866.

33 Dz.U.1932.103.864.

systems, including Poland's (!), had already introduced the relevant provisions to prohibit the use of signs capable of potentially being mistaken for the Red Cross emblem.[34]

A Polish delegation took part in the adoption of the Convention, and signatures were placed by Colonel Józef Gabriel Pracki and Lieutenant Colonel Wincenty Jerzy Babecki on behalf of Poland. Considering the delegates' professional profile (physicians), a significant contribution to the shape of the provisions governing criminal responsibility could scarcely be expected. It can only be regretted that Poland had not appreciated the need to promote the relevant solutions while negotiating the Geneva Conventions of 1929.

Despite the unquestionably extensive body of legislation and court decisions dealing with war crimes committed during WWII, it is difficult to pinpoint any realistic contribution by the Polish delegation to the development of the catalogue of war crimes during the negotiation of the conventions on the protection of war victims, which were ultimately adopted on 12.08.1949 in Geneva[35] and incorporate a catalogue of grave breaches. The above was the result of the fact that Poland did not formally have a delegate to the conference[36] but only an observer in the person of Stanisław Kalina, and even the signature under the conventions (placed on 8.12.1949) is accompanied by an annotation to the effect of signing late due to the lack of suitable credentials. Kalina limited himself to invoking the loss of millions of Polish lives during WWII (the famed 6 million victims) in order to amplify the impact of the Polish support for the USSR's proposals.[37]

Poland ratified the Geneva Conventions of 1949 on 26.11.1954, sustaining the reservations made by Julian Przyboś while signing, which were similar to those made by the USSR and other states of the Eastern Bloc.[38]

Of key importance to war crimes was the reservation to Article 12 GC III and Article 45 GC IV, whereby according to Poland a state could not be exempted from responsibility for compliance with the Convention from the time of handing over the protected persons to the receiving state even with respect to the time during which such persons are in the power of a party consenting to receive them. Even more important was the reservation to

34 See Presidential ordinance of 1.09.1927, Dz.U.1927.79.689; des Gouttes (1930): 1999.

35 Dz.U.1956.38.171.

36 Dijk (2022): 44.

37 *Final Record of the Diplomatic Conference of Geneva of 1949*, vol. II, Federal Political Department, Berne, 718.

38 *Final Record of the Diplomatic Conference of Geneva of 1949*, vol. I, Federal Political Department, Berne, 350–351. See 75 UNTS 444.

Article 85: Poland did not deem it legal for a prisoner of war convicted of war crimes and crimes against humanity in accordance with the principles of the Nuremberg trials to benefit from the protections offered by the Convention; such a prisoner should be subjected to the regulations governing the enforcement of penalties in the state concerned. In 2004, Poland withdrew the above reservations.[39]

Following the adoption of the GCs, it turned out rather quickly that the adopted norms were not sufficient to protect the civilian population from the effects of armed conflicts; accordingly, the International Committee of the Red Cross undertook more initiatives to strengthen the protection. During the discussion in 1957 in New Delhi on the ICRC-proposed draft rules on the protection of civilians during war, the Polish delegate, Juliusz Katz-Suchy, raised the issue of the enormous civilian losses in WWII, the need to ban nuclear weapons and delayed-action mines.[40] The key proposal from the perspective of responsibility for war crimes was for the states becoming party to the proposed rules to enact sanctions in their domestic provisions against the violators.[41] The draft, however, was not adopted, and the matter of the appropriate sanctions had its next opportunity to be discussed only during the negotiation of the Protocols Additional to the GC.

In the Diplomatic Conference on the Reaffirmation and Development of International Humanitarian Law Applicable in Armed Conflicts in Geneva in 1974–1977, a sizeable Polish delegation took part.[42] For the Ministry of Justice, Jan Witek; for the Ministry of Foreign Affairs, Juliusz Biały (recorded as 'Bialy' in the official documentation of the conference), Andrzej Kąkolecki and Stanisław Łopuszański; for the Ministry of National Defence, Marian Flemming, Kazana (the given name could not be confirmed) and Jan Ziewiński. Also part of the delegation were members of the staff of the Polish People's Republic's permanent mission at the United Nations in

39 2283 UNTS 215.

40 *XIXth International Conference of the Red Cross New Delhi, October–November 1957, Final Record concerning the Draft Rules for the Limitation of the Dangers incurred by the Civilian Population in Time of War,* International Committee of the Red Cross Geneva, April 1958, 49–51.

41 *Ibidem*: 52, 132, 136 (Article 20: "All States or Parties concerned shall introduce legal provisions bringing into force on their respective territories the present Rules and establishing penal sanctions against persons having committeed, or ordered to be committed, any infringement of the present Rules").

42 *Official Records of the Diplomatic Conference on the Reaffirmation and Development of International Humanitarian Law Applicable in Armed Conflicts, Geneva (1974–1977)* (hereafter: *OR 1974–1977*), vol. II, 252.

Geneva, i.e. Stanisław Topa and Mieczysław Paszkowski. The Polish Red Cross was represented by Tadeusz Malik (whom the documentation mistakenly records as 'Mallik') and Danuta Zys. The delegation also included Marek Lewicki in the capacity of an advisor. The key role was played, however, by the experts, who were authors of numerous works on international humanitarian law also in foreign languages – Stanisław Nahlik (Jagiellonian University),[43] Remigiusz Bierzanek (University of Warsaw),[44] and Andrzej Górbiel (recorded as 'Gorbiel'; from the University of Łódź).[45] Particular distinction must go to Nahlik, who chaired Committee II (replacing Tadeusz Malik, who had presided over the first session), having previously served as a member of the Drafting Committee and rapporteur.

The Polish delegation submitted a number of amendments concerning, among others, perfidy (i.e. a situation when a person invokes the protection of a specific category of persons under international humanitarian law for the purpose of deceiving or attacking the enemy),[46] the status of members of the resistance;[47] environmental protection, especially with regard to works on new weapons and possible consequences of their use;[48] prohibition of chemical and laser weapons, and necessity to include the perspective of the victims;[49] signage on medical vehicles;[50] neutralized zones;[51] prohibition against the execution of pregnant women, and general prohibition against the death penalty;[52] scope of the term 'religious personnel',[53] extent of the territorial application of international humanitarian law,[54] prohibition of requisitions in occupied territories.[55] Poland's past experience was invoked,[56] with special emphasis being placed on the need to protect cultural property[57] (it is also worth noting that the Polish delegation had been

43 Nahlik (1958), (1967): 61ff, (1974): 100ff.

44 Bierzanek (1960). (1968), (1975).

45 Górbiel (1970).

46 CDDH/III/I05, CDDH/IIII/93, *OR 1974– 1977*, vol. XIV, 256–257, 312.

47 CDDH/III/94, *OR 1974–1977*, vol. XIV, 321, 457.

48 CDDH/III/92, *OR 1974–1977*, vol. XIV, 250.

49 *OR 1974–1977*, vol. XVI: 13 (Flemming).

50 *OR 1974–1977*, vol. XI: 510 (Malik).

51 CDDH/III/97, *OR 1974–1977*, vol. XIV: 208–209 (Bierzanek); *OR 1974–1977*, vol. XV: 287.

52 CDDH/III/102, CDDH/III/322, *OR 1974–1977*, vol. III: 298 and vol. VIII: 364 (Łopuszański).

53 *OR 1974–1977*, vol. XI: 25 (Nahlik).

54 *OR 1974–1977*, vol. XI: 59 (Nahlik).

55 *OR 1974–1977*, vol. XI: 133 (Zys).

56 *OR 1974–1977*, vol. V: 111 (Kąkolecki).

57 CDDH/437, *OR 1974–1977*, vol. VI: 234 and vol. VII: 182 (Nahlik).

active in the negotiations preceding the HC of 1954). It was not without its own significance that Poland had made attempts to hold responsible those guilty of the destruction of cultural property during WWII.[58] The Polish representatives pointed out doubts relating to the presumption of civilian status in every situation[59] (those remarks, however, arose from the lack of distinction between the situation of a person being attacked in ongoing hostilities and a person already in the hands of the enemy). Interestingly, Flemming strongly emphasized that the ICRC's proposal for the regulation of the principle of proportionality conceded unlimited rights to the combatants, while civilian suffering and military interest were not comparable, especially given the role of terror and psychological impact on the civilian population.[60] Bierzanek raised similar arguments against the 'vague' character of the phrase 'military interest' and insisted that perhaps 'military character' or 'military nature' could be the better term.[61] The Polish side ardently campaigned for the inclusion of an absolute ban on reprisals.[62] Bierzanek emphasized that reprisals should not be used against civilian objects, as those could not be attacked without civilian harm.[63] Flemming, in turn, pointed out that reprisals only led to greater cruelties.[64] There ought to be a similarly absolute prohibition against attacking undefended places, the protection of which must not depend on the assent of the state.[65]

The matters that were discussed were of considerable importance to the definition of the various war crimes.[66] As for the list of war crimes itself, the Polish delegation stressed that the list should be merely exemplary rather

58 E.g. Karol Estreicher inspired establishment of the Commission for the Protection and Restitution of Cultural Material (the Vaucher Commission) which identified forty individuals guilty of crimes against cultural property. Poland unsuccessfully requested the extradition of Kajetan Mühlmann, Joseph Mulmann and Professor Dagobert Frey. Wilhelm Ernst Palézieux was extradited to Poland from the French occupation zone and sentenced to five years' imprisonment for pillaging cultural property. See: Nahlik (1987a): 194. Nahlik published a number of works on the protection of cultural property, also in foreign languages; see e.g. Nahlik (1988), (1986).

59 *OR 1974–1977*, vol. XIV: 20, 39 (Flemming).

60 *OR 1974–1977*, vol. XIV: 61 (Flemming).

61 *OR 1974–1977*, vol. XIV: 129.

62 CDDH/III/103 and CDDH/I/GT/113 (Polish-Syrian proposal); *OR 1974–1977*, vol. IX: 63, 77, 452; vol. X: 219; vol. XI, vol. XVI: 13. Cf. Nahlik (1978): 36ff.

63 *OR 1974–1977*, vol. XIV: 129.

64 *OR 1974–1977*, vol. XVI: 13.

65 *OR 1974–1977*, vol. XIV: 208 (Bierzanek).

66 In addition to the matters mentioned above, Poland underlined the importance of the dissemination of international humanitarian law, strengthening of the system of protective powers and substitutions, and the rights of Red Cross associations in non-

than enumerative, and thus deportations and other unlawful resettlements should certainly be mentioned among war crimes,[67] which were indeed mentioned in Article 85(4)(a) AP I, as well as attacks on cultural goods,[68] mentioned in Article 85(4)(d) API. The Polish delegation also noted the necessity of criminalization of forcible blood collection,[69] which eventually came to be regulated by Articles 11(2) and 11(3) API.

Poland was intent on the protocols emphasizing that the penalization must extend to participating in grave breaches, attempting them, as well as direct incitement or conspiracy to commit grave breaches, where those are in fact committed. That was supposed to underscore the importance of Nuremberg law.[70] Poland also highlighted the necessity of adopting provisions for a person not to be judged twice for the same act.[71] Eventually, API did not regulate the forms of participation and stages of war crimes, so the proposal was not reflected in the final version of the protocol. Likewise, the states did not opt for the protocol do regulate the matter of acting on orders, which – as emphasized by Kąkolecki – was too often raised as a defence in order to avoid responsibility.[72]

Together with Bulgaria, Belarus and Czechoslovakia, Poland also advocated for narrowing down the terms of co-operation in respect of extradition.[73] In Poland's opinion, priority to judge crimes should belong to the state in whose territory the crimes took place.[74] As emphasized by Kąkolecki, that was not about identifying the state having suffered the most to the crime but about the state in whose territory the crimes occurred having the easiest access to the evidence.[75] Poland preferred to retain the principle of *aut dedere aut judicare*, but with a provision for the priority of the state of the place of commission of the crime, in accordance with the UNGA resolution on the Principles of international cooperation in the detection, arrest, extradition and punishment of persons guilty of war crimes and crimes

international military conflicts; see e.g. *OR 1974–1977*, vol. VIII: 82, 92, 125, 281, 304 (Kąkolecki, Łopuszański); vol. XII: 271 (Malik).

67 *OR 1974–1977*, vol. IX: 56 (Biały).

68 *OR 1974–1977*, vol. XIV: 129.

69 *OR 1974–1977*, vol. X: 296 (Zys).

70 CDDH/I/304, *OR 1974–1977*, vol. X: 117 and vol. VI: 309 (Kąkolecki).

71 CDDH/III/320, *OR 1974–1977*, vol. XV: 28 (Kazana).

72 *OR 1974–1977*, vol. IX: 134.

73 See CDDH/I/310, *OR 1974–1977*, vol. X: 188.

74 *OR 1974–1977*, vol. VI: 336–337.

75 *OR 1974–1977*, vol. IX: 149.

against humanity, adopted on 3.12.1973.[76] Poland desired to preclude the ability of those guilty of war crimes to take advantage of the milder legal regime. Of course, the wish to regulate the aforementioned issues arose from Poland's negative postwar experience, when the lack of co-operation frustrated the ability to judge many of the crimes committed during WWII. Those proposals, however, were not met with a favourable reception by most of the states. Another proposal (later withdrawn) was to emphasize that for prisoners of war convicted of war crimes or crimes against humanity, the regime of the state in which they are serving the penalty should apply, in line with the Nuremberg principles.[77]

Although some of the proposals submitted by the Polish delegation were not reflected in the APs, Poland advocated very actively for the adoption of provisions on responsibility for war crimes. Nahlik expounded the need for sanctions to be introduced in international law. He emphasized that leaving those matters to domestic law was out of correspondence with the gravity of the violations, even to the point of a declaration of impunity. He maintained that the point of reference should be the Nuremberg judgment, which, in his opinion, had created international criminal law. He also stressed that grave breaches should be termed war crimes [Article 85(5) API affirmed that 'grave breaches' of the GC and API constituted war crimes], in order to highlight the relationship between the protocol and Nuremberg law, facilitating homogeneity and contributing to crime prevention.[78]

The importance of the adopted regulations on war crimes was similarly emphasized by Biały and Łopuszański, according to whom the purpose of the conference was the development of international humanitarian law, thus the need to regulate the matter of war crimes.[79] Although the Polish delegation lamented the lack of provisions on superior orders and co-operation, it was generally satisfied with the solutions that were adopted.[80]

A certain inconsistency also needs to be pointed out. Although the Polish delegates raised the point of the importance of exacting the responsibility for war crimes, they simultaneously argued that the fact-finding commission foreseen by the API should be optional, and in the event of their suggestion being rejected, they threatened that Poland would raise the seemingly

76 *OR 1974–1977*, vol. IX: 172 (Kąkolecki).

77 CDDH/II/312, *OR 1974–1977*, vol. X: 189.

78 *OR 1974–1977*, vol. VI: 293.

79 *OR 1974–1977*, vol. VII: 209; vol. VIII: 349; vol. IX: 56, 317.

80 *OR 1974–1977*, vol. IX: 415 (Kąkolecki).

closed question of reprisals.[81] They also insisted on not including any special norms relating to reservations.[82]

5 The Statute of the International Criminal Court

During the discussions in the International Law Commission and the preparatory conference preceding the conference establishing the ICC (in which Marek Madej participated on behalf of Polish MFA), the Polish voice was not heard so much when it came to the definitions of war crimes. Similar situation took place during the discussions on amendments to Article 8 of the Rome Statute, which were adopted in 2010 (extension onto non-international conflicts of the penalization of the use of poison or poisoned weapons, asphyxiating or poisonous or other gasses, as well as any analogous liquids, materials or appliances; 'bullets which expand or flatten easily in the human body, such as bullets with hard envelope which does not entirely cover the core or is pierced with incisions' – currently Articles 8(2)(e)(xiii, xiv, xv));[83] in 2017 (penalization of the use, in any armed conflict, of: 'weapons which use microbial or other biological agents, or toxins,' regardless of their origin or method of production – currently Article 8(2)(a)(xxvii) and Article 8(2)(e)(xvi);[84] and the penalization of the use of 'weapons the primary effect of which is to injure by fragments undetectable by x-rays in the human body' – currently Article 8(2)(b)(xxviii) Article 8(2)(e)(xvii);[85] penalization of the use of laser weapons designed so that their only fighting function or one of the fighting functions is to cause permanent blinding of the naked eye or eye with sigh correction – currently Article 8(2)(b)(xxix) and Article 8(2)(e)(xviii)[86]); and in 2019 (penalization of the intentional starvation of civilians in non-international conflicts as a method of conducting armed operations by depriving civilians of the necessities needed by them for survival, including deliberate obstruction of aid deliveries – currently Article 8(2)(e)(xix)[87]).

81 *OR 1974–1977*, vol. IX: 417 (Kąkolecki).

82 *OR 1974–1977*, vol. IX: 504.

83 2868 UNTS 195.

84 ICC-ASP/16/Res.4, C.N.116.2018, Treaties XVIII–10, 8.03.2018.

85 ICC-ASP/16/Res.4, C.N.125.2018, Treaties XVIII–10, 8.03.2018.

86 ICC-ASP/16/Res.4, C.N.126.2018, Treaties XVIII–10, 8.03.2018.

87 ICC-ASP/18/Res.5, C.N.394.2020, Treaties XVIII–10, 15.09.2020.

Poland ratified the 2010 amendments on 25.09.2014[88] but did not ratify the amendments of 2017 and 2019, the latter not because of a lack of intention to ratify them but due to not placing appropriate importance on the matter. Poland did not join any of the groups proposing the aforementioned amendments, believing that the proliferation of legal regimes was doing no service the cohesion of the ICC Statute; however, Poland did not oppose the amendments.[89] During the discussions in the review conference and subsequent conferences of states party, the Polish delegation limited itself to supporting the ICC in general without any attempts to amend the Statute.

6 Polish Legislation

For the Criminal Code of 1932, the decision was made against having a separate part on war crimes (understood narrowly as violations of the laws and customs of war). The legal instruments enacted during the WWII were the first to take on the subject of the definition of war crimes and the principles of the responsibility for them.

The first such instrument was the Decree of the President of the Republic of Poland of 30.03.1943 on the Criminal Responsibility for war Crimes. Its Article 2 stipulated: 'Whoever, contrary to the norms of international law, commits an act harmful to the Polish State, a Polish legal person or Polish national, shall be liable to imprisonment.'[90] If the act: 'caused death, especial torment, mutilation, lasting physical or mental disease, permanent incapacity for occupational work, subjection to a lewd act or forced transfer of a Polish national,' the perpetrator was liable to life imprisonment or the death penalty – Article 3; similarly if the act: 'caused a general danger to life or health in Poland' – Article 4. Moreover, the Decree penalized: 'coercing a Polish citizen to join foreign armed forces or, contrary to the norms of international law, work for the enemy' – Article 5; 'issuing decisions on behalf of the occupation authorities on the basis of laws and regulations enacted contrary to the norms of international law,' with the result of harming a Polish citizen – Article 6; pillage, theft, destruction of or infliction of significant damage on public or private property where such property represented a value to the nation as a whole – Article 7. Article 10 of the Decree provided

88 Dz.U.2018.1753.

89 Information conflirmed with MFA.

90 See first commentary to this act – Foryński (1944): 87ff.

for the responsibility of both the issuer and the executor of orders ('who orders the commission of an act set out in this Decree and who carries out such order').

Thus, the Decree made the responsibility conditional on a finding that the act was unlawful under international law, and the intentional vagueness of the definitions of war crimes was the product of the conviction that a typology of war crimes could not be successfully created in the Decree; accordingly, it was a better choice to rely on a general reference.[91] The latter approach would find systematic use throughout the entire history of Polish legislation on war crimes.

Although the Decree of 1943 did not serve as a basis for the judgment of war criminals due to the communist authorities' rejection of any legislation created by the government-in-exile, the importance of the Decree consisted in the ability to demonstrate during the works of the UNWCC, among others, that the various states already had the relevant legislative provisions for the prosecution of war crimes and to a wider extent than foreseen by the works of the Commission on Responsibilities established in the aftermath of WWI. It is not an insignificant fact that the Decree mentioned the type of war crime consisting in issuing decisions contrary to international law.

Moving on to legal instruments issued by the communist authorities, the Decree of 30.05.1944 on the Punishment of German Nazi Malefactors Guilty of Killing and Tormenting the Civilian Population and Prisoners of War, of Spies and Traitors to the Polish Nation among Polish Citizens, and of their Supporters (*Dekret o wymiarze kary dla niemiecko-faszystowskich złoczyńców winnych zabójstw i znęcania się nad ludnością cywilną i jeńcami wojennymi, dla szpiegów i zdrajców Narodu Polskiego spośród obywateli polskich i dla ich popleczników*), issued by the War Council of Polish Armed Forces (established by the Union of Polish Patriots), is in essence the translation of a Soviet legal instrument.[92] Thus, it can hardly be recognized as a Polish contribution to the development of the concept of war crimes. Nevertheless, its Article 1 provides: 'malefactors of different nationalities guilty of killing and tormenting the civilian population and prisoners of war, and spies and traitors among Polish citizens, shall be liable to death by handing,' and Article 2 establishes a sentencing limit of 15 to 20 years of hard labour for supporters (accessories) from among the location population. The Decree was not applied in practice.

---

91 Pasek (2002): 15.

92 Lityński (1999): 63.

Of much more important significance were the decrees of the Polish Committee of National Liberation – the so-called August Decree (*sierpniówka*), more extensively discussed in Subchapter 2.2. Initially, its Article 1 specified two rather capaciously defined acts that could be classified as war crimes and had to be committed: 'in the interest of the German occupational authority' (which excluded the judgment of any crimes committed by the USSR):[93] participating in the killings of civilians or prisoners of war, or in the torture or persecution of such persons; 'actions injurious to persons staying within the territory of the Polish State, especially through the apprehension or deportation of persons wanted or persecuted by the occupying power for any reasons' (excluding prosecution for common crimes). Additionally, Article 2 penalized the extortion of benefits from such persons (i.e. those wanted or persecuted by the occupation authorities) or from persons close to them with the threat of apprehension and delivery to the occupation authorities. In addition to direct perpetration, provisions were made for the criminalization of attempts, accessory liability and incitement; being in the service of the enemy occupation power, superior orders or compulsion did not provide for an exemption from liability.

The August Decree received numerous amendments, and the numbering of the articles changed. Here, it will be worth recalling that as a result of the subsequent amendments, the forms of acting to the injury of persons wanted or persecuted came also to include: 'denunciation' – acting in the interest of the German occupation authority in a manner other than specified in section 1 of the Decree, to the injury of the Polish State or civilians or prisoners of war. Apart from extorting benefits from the wanted or persecuted persons or those close to them, other ways of wronging them through the abuse of the circumstances created by the war were also penalized. It was emphasized that the acts could be committed not only in the interest of the German state but also any state allied to Germany, and military persons were mentioned alongside civilians and prisoners of war as potential victims of homicide or other wrongs; the latter, of course, enabled prosecution solely for the conduct of armed operations and the killing of persons who qualified as combatants. Denunciation or apprehension of persons wanted or persecuted by the authorities had to have taken place on political, ethnic, religious or racial grounds. Not only the Polish State, civilians or prisoners of war but also military personnel and Polish legal entities (e.g. the army) could be the victims of those crimes. The extortion of benefits by

93 Pasek (2002): 58.

taking advantage of the circumstances created by the war came with the attached condition of a: 'threat of triggering persecutions from the authorities of the German state or a state allied thereto.' A completely new type of crime was added under the influence of the IMT's judgment: 'participating in a criminal organization created or recognized by the authorities of the German state or of a state allied thereto or by a political association acting in the interest of the German state or of a state allied thereto.'

The August Decree and its several subsequent amendments were of crucial importance in the judgment of war crimes after WWII; on its basis, court decisions developed a detailed taxonomy of types of war crimes (see Subchapters 2.3 and 3.5), which must be recognized as a meaningful contribution to the development of international criminal law.

The critics are correct in pointing out that the postwar legislative provisions and judgments handed down on their basis were extraordinarily stringent. For example, accessories and inciters were held responsible on the same terms as perpetrators and, in accordance with the August Decree, sentenced to death. The responsibility for the crimes was, furthermore, interpreted very broadly,[94] as the goal was to criminalize any participation in the: 'machinery of death, even not consisting in deliberate physical violence intended to result in the loss of life.'[95] Thus, 'participation in killings,' according to Polish courts, included e.g. passing judgments as part of a German occupation, '*ad hoc* police court,' as well as the carrying out of such judgments and the escorting of the condemned the members of the occupation forces to the place of execution.[96]

The 'Small Criminal Code' of 1946 did not mention war crimes (as the situation in the aftermath of WWII was not characterized as an international armed conflict). Nor did the Criminal Code of 19.04.1969[97] contain a separate chapter on international crimes, such as war crimes. As reminisced by Kubicki, the anticipation was that a separate statute would regulate such type of crimes, which never materialized.[98]

Only the Polish Criminal Code of 1997[99] received a Chapter XVI, titled *Crimes against peace, crimes against humanity and war crimes*, which

94 See e.g. SN, judgment, 25.05.1949, K 478/49, PiP (1949), no. 9–10, 197.

95 SN, judgment, 25.05.1949, K/478/49.

96 SN, judgment, 13.02.1948, K 33/48, Zb.Orz. (Collection of Judgments) 44/48; SN, judgment, 29.08.1948, WAK 338/48, DPP (1948) no. 9, 47–48.

97 Dz.U.1969.13.94.

98 Kubicki (1987): 45.

99 Dz.U.1997.88.553.

contained a number of provisions falling within the scope of the term, 'war crime.' The Code covers not only grave breaches of the GCs and APs but also other violations of international humanitarian law and breaches of international regulations.[100] Thus, Polish courts have the jurisdiction to judge violations of Article 3 GCs in a non-international conflict, for example.

The Criminal Code contains provisions criminalizing e.g. any use of a means of mass destruction prohibited by international law (Article 120), as well as the production, stockpiling, acquisition, alienation, storage, transport or transfer of such means of mass destruction or means of combat, or conducting research with a view to the production or use of such means (Article 121). The penalization is not limited to armed conflicts. Thus, the provision extends both to conduct classifiable as a war crime and conduct constituting a different type of crime.

The Criminal Code also criminalizes attacks on undefended places, sanitary, demilitarized or neutralized zones or the use of any other method of combat prohibited by international law or use of a means of combat prohibited by international law during armed operations (Article 122). The following are also prohibited if done in violation of international law: homicide, causing severe damage to health, torture, cruel or inhuman treatment, experimentation even with consent, use of persons to protect a specific site or object from armed operations or from their own forces with their presence; holding as hostages persons who surrendered giving up weapons or not having means of defence, wounded, sick, wreck survivors, medical or religious staff, prisoners of war, civilians of occupied or controlled territory or territory in which armed operations are taking place or other persons enjoying international protection during armed operations (Article 123). Furthermore, the following are criminalized: coercing such persons – in violation of international law – to serve in enemy armed forces or participate in armed operations against their own country; corporal punishment; use of violence, unlawful threats or deceit in order to induce such persons to sexual intercourse or submit to or perform another sexual activity; attacks on personal dignity, in particular by degrading and humiliating treatment; deprivation of freedom; deprivation of the right to an independent and impartial court of law or curtailing such persons' right to mount a defence in criminal proceedings; declaring the rights or claims of the nationals of the opposing side to be expired, suspended or

100 More Grzebyk (2023): 6.

inadmissible to pursue before a court of law; delaying – in violation of international law – the repatriation of prisoners of war or civilians; transfer, resettlement or deportation of civilians; induction or recruitment of persons below the age of 18 to the armed forces or factual use of such persons in armed operations (Article 124). The following were criminalized (as a *występek*, so lesser offences, rather than the more serious *zbrodnia*, i.e. crime category), if contrary to international law: destruction, damage, seizure or appropriation of property or cultural property in occupied or controlled territory or territory in which armed operations are taking place (Article 125); use of the Red Cross or Red Crescent emblem, protective emblem for cultural property or other protective signs recognized by international law or use of a flag or military sign belonging to the enemy or a neutral state or an international commission (Article 125).

As can be seen, the Polish lawmaker opted for a very general definition of the offences, referring in each case to armed operations (and thus not a type of armed conflict, which means that the relevant types of criminal offences include those committed in an international as well as non-international armed conflict or even outside of an armed conflict) and to international law, which permits the Polish courts to make direct references to international humanitarian law, human rights and international criminal law.

The Criminal Code of 1997 had been adopted before the ICC Statute. Thus, the ratification of the latter gave rise to the need for adaptations to bring the Criminal Code in line with the Statute (also to able to take full advantage of the principle of complementarity expounded in the Statute). The relevant amendments, however, have never been enacted.

Only once under the Criminal Code of 1997 – in the case of the so-called Nanghar Khel Incident – was the decision made to bring proceedings in the matter of war crimes under Article 122(1) (attacking an undefended place), Article 123(1)(4) (killing of civilians) and Article 123(2) (serious damage to the health of civilians) – a potential violation of Articles 23b and 25 of the Hague Regulations of 1907, Article 3(1)(a) of the HCIV of 1907, Article 3(1)(a) of the GCIV, Article 4(2)(a) and Articles 13(1) and 13(2) of the APII. In the end, none of the defendants was convicted under the aforementioned provisions (all were either acquitted or convicted of carrying their orders out in a manner inconsistent with those orders and with the regulations governing the use of weaponry by the Polish Military Contingent in Afghanistan).[101]

101 SN, judgment, 14.03.2012, WA 39/11; SN, judgment, 17.02.2016, WA 16/15.

7 Polish Scholarship

The Polish scholarship of the Interwar period (whether Polish- or foreign-language works) did not occupy itself much with the topic of war crimes,[102] although the law of war was, of course, discussed in publications dealing more generally with international law.[103] The topic of responsibility (including individual responsibility) for war crimes appeared in Ludwik Ehrlich's standard coursebook *Prawo narodów* ('The Law of Nations') of 1927. From a general perspective, he observed: 'An individual guilty of a violation of the norms of the law of nations is responsible on the basis of domestic law. (...) It is possible to refer violations of the law of nations to ordinary courts for punishment. In such cases, the state, by acting against the individual, fulfils its obligation arising from the law of nations (...).'[104] The above-cited excerpt refers to jurisdictional matters, and it is on the problem of the exercise of jurisdiction, extradition and harmonization of domestic criminal law that jurists such as Rappaport and other Polish participants of AIDP meetings of the Interwar period focused their interest. This also explains why, for the Criminal Code of 1932, the decision was made against having a separate part on war crimes (understood narrowly as violations of the laws and customs of war), albeit some of its provisions did refer to the crime of aggression. Of course, such an approach gives rise to certain questions, especially given how obvious it was, after the experience of WWI and the subsequent conflicts over the shape of the borders, that the Hague Conventions of 1899 and of 1907 were not sufficient with regard to the scope of criminal responsibility for violations of the law of war.[105]

Works from the WWII period focusing on the legal framework of the criminalization of war crimes include Zenon Goryński's *Zbrodnie wojenne. Szkic prawny* ('War crimes. A legal outline'), published in 1944 in Jerusalem, analysing the domestic legislations of the various states and the international scholarship.[106] Goryński noted that the matter of war crimes was regulated primarily by international criminal law, rather than domestic law, and he defined war crimes as: 'violation of the norms of international law

102 Characteristically, monographs on the law of war were written before WWI rather than after it; see: Cybichowski (1914); Roszkowski (1881a), (1881b) and (1887), and his article on sanctions (1894).

103 E.g. Klafkowski (1979): 400ff.

104 Ehrlich (1927): 381–382.

105 The war prevented the organization of a third Hague conference, which had been anticipated to discuss sanctions for violations of the Hague Conventions.

106 Goryński (1944): 28.

relating to the conduct of war and behaviour of the enemy in occupied countries.'[107]

Under the influence of the trial of KL Majdanek staff, Józef Giebułtowicz wrote a monograph titled: *Odpowiedzialność przestępców wojennych w świetle prawa narodów* (1945) ('The responsibility of war criminals in the light of the law of nations'), where he emphasized that war crimes constituted a violation of international and domestic norms[108] and analysed both the matter of the responsibility of the state[109] and that of an individual, in particular the head of state.[110] In the context of the responsibility of Germany, he noted that Germany had accepted the principle of responsibility for war crimes by ratifying the 1919 peace treaty.[111]

Among those publications written by Poles during the WWII period which certainly influenced the international debate on war crimes, one should first of all mention Manfred Lachs's monograph *War Crimes. An Attempt to Define the Issues*, published by Stevens & Sons Limited in 1945. One year prior, in the *Juridical Review*, Lachs had published a thematically connected article titled *War Crimes and Political Offences* (published nearly at the same time as Hersch Lauterpacht's *The Law of Nations and the punishment of war crimes* in "British Yearbook of International Law").

In the aforementioned monograph on war crimes, Lachs argued that civilized states had reached the consensus that even in a time of war – which he termed the symbol of disorder – order had to be imposed, leading to the adoption of a number of instruments of international law listed by him in detail. Referring to the Martens Clause, Lachs invoked the unwritten laws of war (undoubtedly a reference to his work published in New Orleans in 1945 under the title *The Unwritten Laws of Warfare*), especially where the appropriate codification had not taken place – such as the rules of aerial warfare. Lachs pointed out that the existing criminal codes criminalized the relevant acts irrespective of their commission in a time of war or not; furthermore, a number of states, including Poland (where Lachs cites the Decree of 24.10.1934), had adopted special regulations relating to the security of the state. Lachs also mentioned the US-adopted *Articles of War*, starting from the famed Order no. 100 (so-called Lieber Code), as confirming the binding rules of the law of war. The German *Kriegsbrauch in Landkrieg*, by

107 *Ibidem*: 41.
108 Giebułtowicz (1945): 82.
109 *Ibidem*: 41.
110 *Ibidem*: 47.
111 *Ibidem*: 57.

contrast, he cited as an example of a challenge thrown in the face of law, and a parody.

Lachs noted that war crimes were committed during war and in connection with it, with its course and with the rights and obligations of the belligerents. He made an attempt to define war crimes, providing examples from both World Wars. He identified the following characteristics of war crimes: (1) they are acts of violence (and thus penalized by norms of domestic law applicable in wartime), including refusal to perform one's duties, such as denial of delivery of food supplies; (2) are committed in the special circumstances created by war, with their perpetrators not exposed to a danger and thus finding themselves in an advantageous situations – thus Lachs asserted that the killing of Inspector Friedrich Krüger was not a war crime because the attackers risked their lives and did not enjoy the favour of the occupation authorities; (3) are committed by a special group of persons, viz. military commanders, occupation authorities, commandants of PoW camps and many others serving in special political, legal or economic functions; in Lachs's opinion, members of paramilitary organizations *stricto sensu* but also *largo sensu*, such as marauders, can be guilty of war crimes. He submits, however, that, in the end, anyone could commit a war crime, but the aforementioned categories of persons could invoke the laws of war to have their actions judged in the correct context; (4) war crimes occur in a time of war; (5) they are committed within the battlefield and without, both in the perpetrator's state and in occupied territories, so *mutatis mutandis*, they can be committed in other territories; (6) they are committed against soldiers and members of armed forces (though with protection depending on status) against civilians, property and other targets, and are not covered by exemptions arising from the law of war. Lachs identified the following goals of war crimes: extermination, destruction of monuments, works of art and culture, of the whole organization of the state; infliction of unnecessary suffering on the belligerents.

From today's perspective, of course, Lachs's writing sometimes appears to be imprecise or chaotic. However, it is worth observing that Lachs took note not only of the responsibility of the perpetrators but also of their accessories (whether before or after the commission of the crime), and thus everyone involved in the commission of war crimes. He emphasized the applicability of war crimes as a category whether a given war was lawful or unlawful, for declared or not; he added that a conquest achieved through unlawful war could not transform into sovereignty, and he highlighted the role of the connection between war crimes and armed conflict. His definition of a war crime – 'any act of violence, qualified as crime committed during and in connection with a war under specially favourable conditions created by the war and facilitating its commission; the act being directed against the other belligerent State, or its interests; against its citizens or their interest, as well as against Stateless individuals or their interests' – came to be regarded as classic and continues to provide a point of reference.[112]

Among the authors publishing in the postwar period, one should mention Litawski, who authored a few chapters of the monograph – *History of the United Nations War Crimes Commission* of 1948 and a report titled *Human Rights in the Nuremberg Trial*, of 18.07.1947, in the Archive of the Polish Institute and Sikorski Museum. It is difficult to ascertain the breadth of the report's circulation. Therein, Litawski observed that any war crime (or crime against humanity) was directed against the integrity of a human being as an individual or a group of people or property. Without a doubt drawing upon his experience from the UNWCC, he distinguished the individual groups of war crimes: '(a) murder and ill-treatment of civilian population of, or in, and on the high seas; (b) deportation for slave labour and for other purposes of the civilian population of, and in, occupied territories; (c) murder and ill-treatment of prisoners of war and of other members of the armed forces of the countries with whom Germany was at war and of persons on the high seas; (d) killing of hostages; (e) plunder of public and private property; (f) the exaction of collective penalties, pecuniary or otherwise; (g) wanton destruction of cities, towns and villages and devastation not justified by military necessity; (h) conscription of civilian labour; (i) forcing civilians of occupied territories to swear allegiance to a hostile power; (j) Germanization of occupied territories'.[113] It is also worth recalling his article of 1948 dealing with the classifiability of breach of capitulation terms as a war crime.[114]

One should also mention Kazimierz Rutczyński's monograph titled *Zbrodnie wojenne. Studjum w skali międzynarodowej* (1946) ('War crimes. A study in the international scale'), published in Glasgow. For definitional issues, Rutczyński relies primarily on the works by Lauterpacht.[115] How-

112 La Haye (2008): 104; Segesser (2005): 366.

113 UNWCC: Human Rights Report: Preparatory Papers, Human Rights in the Nuremberg Trial (excepting crimes against Germans), UNWCC Doc. III/102, 18.07.1947.

114 See also articles authored by Litawski and published in "Polish Fortnightly Review", e.g. *German Legislation for Foreign Workers* (1943) or *The Property Rights under German Occupation* (1944).

115 Rutczyński (1947): 20.

ever, he takes up the issue of justifications, excuses and mitigating circumstances, among which he mentions superior orders, the lack of definition of certain terms, and the use of repression.

Numerous articles on the responsibility for war crimes were published after the end of WWII; their authors include: Wacław Barcikowski,[116] Marian Muszkat,[117] Antoni Landau and Czesław Wasilkowski,[118] and Aleksander Rogalski.[119] Authors of monographs on the German crimes of the WWII period include Franciszek Ryszka,[120] Alfons Klafkowski,[121] and Karol Pospieszalski.[122]

However, the main personages writing on the responsibility for war crimes in the context of the Nuremberg principles were Cyprian and Sawicki, having published a total of several dozen works devoted to exacting the responsibility for the war crimes of the WWII period.[123] The publications of Leszek Kubicki[124] were also of crucial importance, but from the perspective of global reach, works by Stefan Glaser were key. Glaser divided international crimes between the crimes of peacetime and the crimes of wartime. Among the latter category, he distinguished delicts of the common law (*droit commun*) – theft, pillage, arson, homicide, and delicts of military nature, being violations of the laws and customs of war by military personnel, whether following superior orders or not, e.g. the use of prohibited weapons, bombardment of open cities, use of asphyxiating gasses, ill-treatment of wounded and sick combatants, abuse of the Red Cross emblem, and ill-treatment of prisoners of war.[125] Glaser undertook a review of the conventions in international humanitarian law for provisions defining war crimes, noting at the same time that international criminal law was

116 Barcikowski (1946).

117 Muszkat (1947), (1948).

118 Landau, Wasilkowski (1946).

119 Rogalski (1947).

120 Ryszka (1982), (1985).

121 Klafkowski (1968a).

122 Pospieszalski (1946); Pospieszalski (1948) – there, the author observes that the relative scarcity of studies on the Nuremberg judgment was the result of its lack of broad accessibility; and Pospieszalski (1952).

123 A list of all publications by the duo of Cyprian and Sawicki would probably consume more than a dozen pages of text; thus, I will only mention here Cyprian, Sawicki (1960): 97–98, where they describe various war crimes including the process of Germanization or the removal of children from their parents.

124 E.g. Kubicki (1961).

125 Glaser (1954): 21.

constantly in development and thus the catalogue of war crimes was expanding.[126] Glaser's works have been cited frequently throughout the world.[127]

For topics relating to war crimes, key importance also belongs to publications in international humanitarian law addressing usually the matter of responsibility for war crimes; in that context, one should mention the scholars having the benefit of the experience of participation in the 1974–1977 conference, viz. Stanisław Nahlik,[128] Remigiusz Bierzanek (who, it is worth noting, became in 1986 a member of the Executive Board of the International institute of Humanitarian Law in Sanremo),[129] as well as Julian Makowski[130] and Teofil Leśko.[131] The topic of responsibility for war crimes was also mentioned e.g. by Kazimierz Kocot.[132] In the period after 1989, subchapters devoted to war crimes were included in general works in international law[133] and on international courts,[134] especially in the context of the latter's judgments,[135] as well as in works in international humanitarian law[136] and comments on the Criminal Code, among which Flemming's studies andare especially deserving of a mention.[137] As they were for the most part written in Polish, their influence on global scholarship has been limited.

8 Conclusions

The experiences of both World Wars have influenced the development of Polish scholarship, legislation and judgments on war crimes, as well as inspiring the Polish diplomacy's efforts towards the criminalization of the various types of war crimes. The diplomatic always had to run along several

126 *Ibidem*: 31.

127 Herzog (1975): 134.

128 Mostly Nahlik (1984), (1991): 165ff.

129 Mostly Bierzanek (1982).

130 Makowski (1953).

131 E.g. Leśko (1976).

132 Kocot (1956): 351.

133 Królikowski, Wiliński, Izydorczyk (2008): 127; Gardocki, Gardocka, Majewski (2017): 180ff.; Hofmański, Kuczyńska (2020): 126ff.

134 Stasiak (2012): 142; Milik (2012): passim; Płachta (2004): 391, Jakubowski, Wierczyńska (2017), (2020).

135 Nowakowska-Małusecka (2000): passim; Szpak (2011): passim.

136 E.g. Nowakowska-Małusecka (2012).

137 Flemming, Wojciechowska (1999): 66ff; cf. Grzebyk (2023): 3ff.

lines. Firstly, one had to raise awareness of what crimes actually happened and point out the threat posed by the relevant acts. The solid arguments prepared by the Polish authorities in both the WWI and the WWII periods enabled influence on the shape taken by the catalogue of international crimes eventually adopted by the Allied powers. Secondly, it was necessary to involve new legal instruments in the negotiations and to develop principles of the responsibility. Thirdly, one had to identify the bases being created in parallel for the judgment of those guilty of war crimes in domestic law and the attempts to judge those accused of the crimes, all of which to reinforce the credibility of arguments invoking the existing norms of customary law.

Although, for political reasons, the Polish representatives did not leave their mark on the Geneva Conventions of 1949, their involvement in the preparation of the Protocols Additional of 1977 is already considerable, especially in the context of the principles of responsibility for war crimes. A large Polish delegation was dispatched for the negotiations in Stockholm and included truly eminent scholars of international humanitarian law and responsibility for war crime (such as Bierzanek and Nahlik), which translated into concrete proposals and participation in the debate. After 1989, it is difficult to identify any real efforts by the Polish diplomacy concerning the principles of responsibility for war crimes and the catalogue of those crimes, which necessarily leads to a certain disappointment, considering the experiences of the preceding periods. However, one should note the presence of a separate chapter on offences against peace, humanity and war offences, among others, in the Criminal Code of 1997.

CHAPTER 8

Crimes against Humanity

1 The New Category of Crime and Its Development after World War II

There can be no doubt that crimes against humanity did not share the fate of genocide and war crimes, which were codified near the end of the 40s of the past century. The lack of suitable codification casts a shadow not completely dispersed by the adoption, in 1998, of the Rome Statute,[1] if only because of the limited support garnered by the idea of a permanent international criminal court. Exacting the responsibility of individuals for crimes against humanity is, of course, much less controversial at present than in the aftermath of WWII, but it continues to evoke several specific doubts surfacing, for example, in the efforts on behalf of the codification of international criminal law.[2]

The introduction of a category of crimes against humanity means breaking with the cardinal principle of international criminal law that the relations between a state and its nationals are the state's internal matter to be shaped as the state sees fit, with unfettered discretion, and any interference with the internal matters of a state is inadmissible.[3] On the same account, one must appreciate the twofold danger associated with crimes against humanity: for the individuals, due to the lack of a strict formulation of the charges, but also for the states, due to providing a pretext to interfere with the internal affairs of weaker states.[4] No current relevance is lost by the position of Polish authors who regarded the birth of the concept of crimes against humanity:

> as a compromise between the burning need to punish those guilty of racial, religious, ethnic or political persecutions who were not war criminals in the strict sense of the expression, on the one hand, and the other hand, the inhibition arising from the highly sensitive

1 Dz.U.2003.78.708.
2 Stasiak (2014); Krzan (2020a).
3 Waszczyński (1986): 63.
4 Donnedieu de Vabres (1947): 833.

> necessity of undermining state sovereignty with respect to the state's ability to regulate freely the status of its inhabitants.[5]

The universal international law has not developed a single precise definition of crimes against humanity.[6] Nonetheless, the term itself is not a complete novelty. In his Hague lecture, Jean Graven went as far as claiming that crimes against humanity were as old as humanity itself.[7] References to the rights of humanity appeared in the Petersburg Declaration Renouncing the Use, in Time of War, of Explosive Projectiles Under 400 Grammes Weight, of 29.11./11.12.1868.[8] The preamble of the HCIV of 1907 incorporated references to a desire to serve the interests of humanity and the increasing demands of civilization, as well as the Martens Clause,[9] repeated after the Hague Convention I on the laws of war, of 1899. A more forceful reference was included in the declaration of 28.05.1915 in which the governments of France, Russia and the United Kingdom referred to the massacres of the Armenian population in Turkey as, 'crimes against humanity and civilization,' for which: 'they w[ould] hold personally responsible (…) all members of the Ottoman government and those of their agents who are implicated in such massacres.'[10]

In this context comes to mind Hitler's secret speech of 22.08.1939, in which he announced a ruthless plan of the extermination of all Poles, comparing it to the Turkish massacre of the Armenians:

> Our strength is swiftness and brutality. Genghis Khan procured the slaughter of millions of women and children – with premeditation and with a happy heart. History sees in him only the founder of a state. It is indifferent to me what the weak civilization of Western Europe will say of me. I have given an order – and anyone who says even a word of criticism will be executed by the firing squad – that our war goal

5 Cyprian, Sawicki (1948b): 287.

6 Płachta (2004): 381.

7 Graven (1950): 433.

8 Text in: Kocot, Wolfke (1976): 337.

9 "Until a more complete code of the laws of war has been issued, the High Contracting Parties deem it expedient to declare that, in cases not included in the Regulations adopted by them, the inhabitants and the belligerents remain under the protection and the rule of the principles of the law of nations, as they result from the usages established among civilized peoples, from the laws of humanity, and the dictates of the public conscience".

10 Schwelb (1946): 181.

> consists not in the achievement of certain boundaries but in the physical destruction of the enemy. In this connection, I am keeping my skull formations in readiness – for now, only in the East – with orders to mercilessly and without compassion send men, women and children of Polish origin and language to their deaths. Only in this manner can we gain the living space (*Lebensraum*) that we need. After all, who speaks of the annihilation of the Armenians today?[11]

The report of the Commission on the Responsibilities voiced the somewhat categorical conclusion of the necessity of holding individually responsible: '[a]ll persons belonging to enemy countries, however high their position may have been, without distinction of rank, including Chiefs of States, who have been guilty of offences against the laws and customs of war or the laws of humanity.'[12] The separate treatment of the respective categories attracts some attention. However, the position taken by the American delegates – Robert Lansing and James Brown Scott – was decidedly opposed to such a view of the matter. They argued that the laws and principles of humanity differed depending on who was applying them and also differed depending on the time, place and circumstances and even perhaps the conscience of those making the decision, for which reason there was no single unchanging standard of humanity.[13]

The building of legal foundations for the punishment of the crimes against humanity committed during WWII was entrusted to the UNWCC. The Polish representatives (Glaser, Litawski and Lachs) played a pivotal role in its works, as discussed in more detail in the previous parts of this book (especially Chapter 2).

The matter of crimes against humanity in the UNWCC's works was an extraordinarily contentious one. Particularly worth accentuating is Glaser's advocacy for the treatment of the crimes against the Jews and other minorities persecuted in Germany as included in the Commission's mandate. Glaser emphasized that the Commission's works should cover: 'acts incompatible with a given country's criminal statute that are simultaneously a violation of international law but also other, more serious crimes, of racial, political or religious nature – especially the crimes on German Jews in

11 Cited after: Mazurkiewicz (2021): 191–192.

12 14 AJIL (1920): 117.

13 Memorandum of reservations presented by the Representatives of the United States to the Report of the Commission on Responsibilities, 4.04,1919, 14 AJIL (1920): 144.

Germany.'[14] He also campaigned for the expansion of the list of war crimes to include mass arrests, hostage taking and enactment of laws and regulations targeted against human dignity.[15]

Within the UNWCC, the aspirations to include crimes against humanity were met with opposition from its chairman, Cecil Hurst. He recalled the scope delineated in the invitation and create and participate in the works of the Commission, which covered only war crimes.[16] Hurst's critical stand was supported by his deputy, Herbert C. Pell, the American, Lawrence Preuss, and the representatives of Greece (Constantin Stavropoulos) and China (Liang Yunli). Aside from the distrust experienced by Pell from the US Department of State,[17] one should note the highly restrained position taken on crimes against humanity by the Brits and Americans.

While analysing the works of the UNWCC, one could not possibly ignore Jerzy Litawski's advocacy on behalf of the penalization of crimes against humanity. He was the author of a report on human rights in the Nuremberg trial (excluding crimes committed against the Germans).[18] Proceeding from the general assumption that almost any crime violated the law, including human rights in a broader, not technical meaning, the report emphasized that the foregoing applied to almost all violations of the laws and customs of war, as well as all acts falling within the notion of crime against humanity as defined by the IMT Charter. Moreover, the assertion was added that also planning, preparating, initiating and prosecuting a war of aggression, recognized by the Nuremberg tribunal as the highest international crime, constituted – in a general, non-technical meaning – a crime against humanity with the resulting violations of human rights. Litawski noted in the report that, in a technical sense, all war crimes and crimes against humanity were crimes constituting an attack on the physical integrity of individuals, groups of people, and property. For a general picture of violations of human rights, he proposed to consider twelve categories of criminal offences, most of which constituted war crimes but the last pair was classifiable as crimes against humanity: '(k) Murder, extermination, enslavement, deportation and

14 PRM-K/74, doc. 7, 5.06.1944: 22 (APISM).

15 UNWCC, Proposal by the Polish representatives for adding items to the list of war criminals (Minutes of the 17th meeting, 9.05.1944): 3.

16 Kochavi (1998): 145.

17 Plesch (2011): 110, Cox (2014): 77.

18 UNWCC: Human Rights Report: Preparatory Papers, Human Rights in the Nuremberg Trial (excepting crimes against Germans), UNWCC Doc. III/102, 18.07.1947.

other inhuman acts committed against populations before and during the war; (l) Persecution on political, racial and religious grounds'.[19] Litawski regarded the enumeration as being of primary importance in the light of the lacunae existing in the law. He also emphasized the necessity of taking the legacy of the IMT into account and addressing the problem of retroactive legislation and the principles of legality (*nullum crimen, nulla poena sine lege*).

In another document prepared by Litawski for he UNWCC, he outlined the historical overview of the problem of crimes against humanity and continued on his path of reasoning. Referring to war crimes and crimes against humanity, he highlighted their: 'particular interest to (…) and bearing on (…) the question of the protection of human rights. By their very nature these rules either constitute evidence of an already existing system or contain the nucleus of a system of provisions which, if properly developed, would lead to the better protection of fundamental human rights and minimum human standards in time of war and in peace, including the protection of populations against the abuse of sovereignty by their own authorities (…) irrespective of whether or not the abuse of sovereignty and inhuman acts are committed in violation of the domestic law of the country where they were perpetrated.'[20] He emphasized the importance of such a generally worded definition of crime against humanity, irrespective of the time and place and of the sovereignty of a given state, to the propagation of respect for human rights and fundamental freedoms without regard to race, sex, language or religion.[21]

In the end, Article VI of the London Agreement of 8.08.1945 provided for the IMT's jurisdiction, apart from crimes against peace and war crimes, also for:

> Crimes against humanity: namely, murder, extermination, enslavement, deportation, and other inhumane acts committed against any civilian population, before or during the war or persecutions on political, racial or religious grounds in execution of or in connection with any crime within the jurisdiction of the Tribunal, whether or not in violation of the domestic law of the country where perpetrated.

19 UNWCC Doc. III/102, 3.

20 UNWCC Doc. III/107 (Historical Survey of the Problem of Violations of Human Rights (War Crimes and Crimes against Humanity): 2.

21 *Ibidem*: 3.

It is difficult to determine how exactly the term 'crimes against humanity' found its way to the text of the IMT Charter. In the minutes of the negotiations of the text of the Nuremberg Charter, Robert Jackson, the lead prosecutor on behalf of the USA, referring to the list of crimes, acknowledged that it had been proposing to him by an eminent jurist specializing in international law.[22] Jackson himself did not give a name, but it is somewhat universally believed[23] to have been Hersch Lauterpacht, with whom Jackson had held multiple consultations.[24]

Here, one can notice Lauterpacht's distance from Lemkin's concept of genocide, which had embraced a different perspective, one concentrating mainly on the protection of individual population groups from annihilation. Hersch Lauterparcht's review of *Axis Rule* in the *Cambridge Law Journal* revealed his scepticism towards the competing perspective. Lauterpacht raised concerns that group protections could undermine the protection of individuals.[25] In a conversation with Philip Sands, Hersch Lauterpacht's son, Elihu conjectured that his father did not regard Lemkin too highly, viewing him as a compiler rather than thinker, for which reason he may have been acting on his disappointment with the intrusion of a personal concept such as 'genocide' in international law without sufficient backing in practice.[26]

The source queries by Andrzej Bryl, however, deny Lauterpacht's authorship of the whole phrase and concept, suggesting that the inclusion of crimes against humanity as one of the charges in the Nuremberg indictment would be attributed to the World Jewish Congress activist, Jacob Robinson, or alternatively Herbert Pell, or the Czechoslovak members of the UNWCC,[27] and in a subsequently published doctoral dissertation to President Franklin Delano Roosevelt.[28] As for the Czechoslovak trail, one must remember that Ečer's predecessor in the Commission had, of course, been Stefan Glaser, who must have had an influence on the Commission's works and its subsequent direction.

22 *Report of Robert H. Jackson United States Representative to the International Conference on Military Trials* (London 1945): 416 (LIX: Minutes of Conference Session of 2 August 1945: Discussion of return of prisoners to the scene of their crimes, appointment of officers to carry out tasks designated by Tribunal, headquarters of Tribunal and place of first trial, order of trial, definition of "crimes").

23 Schabas (2012): 51; more von Lingen (2014): 477.

24 Lauterpacht (2010): 271–272. Cf. Bryl (2021): 67ff.

25 H.L. (1945): 140.

26 Sands (2018): 145.

27 Bryl (2018): 52–53.

28 Bryl (2021): 67ff.

Hersch Lauterpacht himself regarded crimes against humanity as criminal offences regardless whether they had been committed in accordance with or obedience to the defendant's domestic law or not. He regarded them as acts violating the *'sanctity of human personality'* to an extent making irrelevant any reliance on domestic law commanding them.[29]

In this context, the principal question is how to understand the term, 'humanity.' Two possible meanings have been suggested – the people of the world as a whole and human or 'humane' feeling.[30] Thus is the physical aspect juxtaposed with the ethical angles.[31]

It is also fitting to emphasize that the language of the Nuremberg Charter did not cover all crimes against humanity committed in Germany. It should also be recalled that the representatives of the USSR had initially attempted to limit the definitional scope of crimes against humanity only to acts of fascist (Nazi) or racist nature, so as to direct the attention exclusively towards the Third Reich's activities.[32]

Of crucial importance to the definition and, more broadly, development of the concept, of crimes against humanity was the Law no. 10 enacted on 20.12.1945 by the Control Council for Germany. It provided the basis for the prosecution of war criminals and perpetrators of similar offences who were not subject to the jurisdiction of the IMT. Its Article II corresponded to the analogous provision (Article 6) of the Charter of the IMT, although the language used to define crimes against humanity reflected some differences going beyond simple redaction and including the removal of the clause: 'in execution of or in connection with any crime within the jurisdiction of the Tribunal.'[33] In that manner, crimes against humanity were made independent from any necessary connection with the other international crimes prosecuted before the IMT. From the Polish perspective, that was of crucial importance with regard to the scope of extradition and possibility of a trial before the domestic courts. A broad definition of these crimes, including genocide, was also incorporated in the Convention on the Non-Applicability of Statutory Limitations,[34] which was adopted as a result of the marked insistence of Polish diplomacy (more extensively see Chapter 10).

29 Lauterpacht (1950): 36.

30 Bramson (1948): 77.

31 Cf. Basak (1998): 350.

32 Basak (2018): 263.

33 Cyprian, Sawicki (1948b): 434ff.

34 Convention was adopted by GA on 26.11.1968; 754 UNTS 73; Dz.U.1970.26.208.

The proceedings before the Supreme National Tribunal (NTN) did not provide any guidelines as to crimes against humanity, dealt with jointly with genocide.[35] In the trial of Fischer, Leist, Meisinger and Daume, the NTN found crimes against humanity to be: 'any persecution on political, ethnic, racial or religious grounds, in connection with any crime of the first two categories [crimes against peace and war crimes] and not only during the war but also before its outbreak.'[36] The above aligned itself with the general trend of collective treatment of terms such as genocide and crimes against humanity, the legal classification of which was taken from domestic law.

In 1946, the International Association of Democratic Lawyers adopted a resolution containing the following definition:

> Guilty of crimes against humanity and as such responsible therefor are those who carry out the extermination of or persecute individuals or groups of individuals on account of their nationality, ethnicity, race, religion or outlooks. Such crimes will be punished even where committed by an individual or organization acting in the capacity of organs of a state, with the state's encouragement or toleration; crimes against humanity are independent from the notion of the state of war.[37]

Moreover, the following was emphasized: 'the perpetrators of crimes against humanity should be judged in the state in whose territory or against whose nationals the crimes were committed. Where the penalty cannot be imposed by a domestic tribunal, those guilty shall be remanded to the international criminal jurisdiction. The extradition of the criminals shall be mandatory.'[38]

The above definition of crimes against humanity, taking a shape similar to the provisions of the Control Council for Germany Law no. 10, unquestionably marks clear progress compared to the language of the IMT Charter.[39] Similarly to the Law no. 10, it disconnects crimes against humanity from war.

It must be noted that, to Manfred Lachs, the point of departure for coining the concept of human rights was found precisely in the norms of

35 Grzebyk (2014): 623f.

36 Cyprian, Sawicki (1962c): 57.

37 Międzynarodowe Kongresy Prawnicze (1947): 10 DPP 2; Cyprian, Sawicki (1948b): 439.

38 The general resolution reproduced in: (1946): 11–12 DPP 26. The Association was founded by a group of lawyers with ties to the Résistance, including Poles. In its founding congress, papers on crimes against humanity were delivered by Muszkat and Sawicki. During the Cold War period, the Association was controlled by the USSR.

39 *Ibidem.*

international criminal law. In the definition of fundamental human rights, he saw a role to play for the IMT and a special criminal classification of crime against humanity. He viewed the Nuremberg tribunal's judgment as the: 'first chapter of the charter of human rights.' Lachs believed that in the IMT, 'in convicting those guilty of the above crimes w[ould] thereby determine for the first time on the international plane what constitutes an international crime.' He emphasized that crimes against humanity could also be committed in peacetime, and thus their nature was, 'unlimited in time.' In his opinion, the Nuremberg judgment: 'in determining the punishment, w[ould] also determine the interests protect by law, the violation of which will in the future constitute a criminal offence.' That is where the precedential character of Nuremberg manifested itself, and by joining it to the design of human-rights charter, we would: 'receive legal norms ready for codification in the form of an international obligation concerning the inviolability of a human being as a human being.'[40] He went on to write that the: 'first part of the [human-rights] charter,' would be: 'sanctified in Nuremberg with the judgment of the international tribunal.'[41] In that outlook, human rights constituted a sort of mirror reflecting the prohibitions of international criminal law.[42]

In the first ICUCL after war, in Brussels in August 1947, one of the main topics to be discussed was the problem of the statutory definition of crimes against humanity. The subject and the object of the crimes were discussed. The Polish delegation presented an alternative perspective, accentuating not the detailed considerations but the establishment of international guarantees for elementary human rights – protected by the criminal statutes of all civilized states and pertaining to equality irrespective of racial, national, ethnic or religious affiliation – and campaigning for reforms to ensure such equality.[43] Eventually, the conference ended with the adoption of a resolution largely adhering to the Polish position: 'Any taking of a life or any act leading by its nature to the death of a human person or a group of people, on account of their race, nationality, ethnicity, religion or political views – whether in wartime or in peacetime – constitutes a crime against humanity and ought to be prosecuted as homicide.'[44] As can be seen, a crime against humanity was eventually treated as a *sui generis* common crime, which was

40 Lachs (1946b): 240.

41 *Ibidem*: 241.

42 Karska (2011): 384.

43 *8th conference* (1947): 10 DPP 4–5.

44 *Ibidem*.

accompanied by the recommendation for its inclusion in the future international criminal code and the criminal codes of the various states.[45]

Here, it will be expedient to recall Lemkin's communication prepared for the 1947 Brussels conference for the unification of criminal law, in which he asserted that, due to their very nature, crimes against humanity were not, nor could they become, crimes of the law of nations. He seconded Henri Donnedieu de Vabres on that if one should establish any and all sorts of persecution as crimes against the law of nations, an unacceptable situation would be created in international relations, especially considering that crimes against humanity were to be subject to the jurisdiction of domestic military occupation courts or even international ones.[46]

It would be difficult not to concur with Jerzy Sawicki, who noted that if the IMT were to judge the defendants solely for war crimes *stricto sensu*, then it would not be possible to speak of any realistic progress in international law or of the developmental opportunities opened by crimes against humanity. Sawicki also believed that the new type of crimes, through its dual nature of a crime under international and a crime under domestic law: 'open[ed] new horizons to the taxonomy of law.'[47] In this context, the principle of legality once again comes to the fore, and one must recall Glaser's strongly resonating article titled *Nullum Crimen Sine Lege*, published in the *Journal of Comparative Legislation and International Law*,[48] as well as the evolution his position had undergone.

The early activities of the ILC referred primarily to the Nuremberg principles.[49] The *Formulation of the principles recognized in the Charter of the Nuremberg Tribunal and in the judgment of the Tribunal* ultimately adopted by the ILC in 1950 on the basis of UNGA Resolution 177(II)[50] was

45 Waszczyński (1986): 70.

46 Actes de la Conférence, Paris 1948: 174.

47 Sawicki (1947): 30.

48 Glaser (1942): 29.

49 The Nuremberg principles formulated in the Nuremberg Charter were subsequently affirmed by UNGA Resolutions 3(I) of 13.02.1946 and 95(I) of 11.12.1946; neither made any direct or concrete reference to the categories of crimes. The latter, however, called for the Committee on the Progressive Development of International Law and its Codification (before the creation of the International Law Commission) to formulate the Nuremberg principles.

50 Confirmed by the GA as 'Murder, extermination, enslavement, deportation and other inhuman acts done against any civilian population, or persecutions on political, racial or religious grounds, when such acts are done or such persecutions are carried on in execution of or in connexion with any crime against peace or any war crime.'

met with diverging receptions, from determined defence[51] to categorical characterization as a mistake.[52] In that dispute, Poland, with the other socialist states, argued from the position of a need for the complete eradication of fascism and racism from modern international relations.

Once again, the matter of the definition of crimes against humanity surfaced in connection with the works on the Code of Offences, and thereafter Code of Crimes against Peace and Security of Mankind (Code of International Crimes). The ILC worked on the draft in 1949–1954 and subsequently in 1982–1996. Thus, during his term in office, Manfred Lachs did not have the opportunity to influence the ILC's works on the topic. During the next attempt, special rapporteur Doudou Thiam called for crimes against humanity to be given, 'their rightful place.'[53] Stanisław Pawlak's term in office coinciding with the years 1987–1991 did not reveal any particular interest in the matter. From a more general perspective, however, it will be fitting to note that the 1991 version of the Draft Code completely forwent the use of the term, replacing it with: 'systematic or mass violations of human rights.' Nevertheless, the final draft of 1996 resumed the use (and definition) of the term, 'crimes against humanity.'[54]

In turn, the delegations negotiating the Statute of a permanent international criminal court (the ICC) agreed that crimes against humanity were punishable under customary international law but also that the precedents to date did not add up to a cohesive understanding of the problem.[55] Despite the existing definitional, 'fluctuations,'[56] the situation also changed with regard to the method of arriving at the definition – negotiation rather than imposition by the justice of the victors (IMT) or unilaterally by the Security Council.

Thus, the Rome Conference decided for the creation of a separate definition rather than the incorporation of existing ones.[57] The intention was not at all to design a revolutionary innovative solution but rather to compile the

51 Cyprian, Sawicki (1956b).

52 Baxter (1968): 148.

53 Thiam, *Seventh report on the draft Code of Crimes against the Peace and Security of Mankind,* YILC (1989) Vol. II(1): 86 (§31,39).

54 UN GAOR, 51st Sess., Supp. No. 10, U.N. Doc. A/51/10 (1996), Art. 18: 'A crime against humanity means any of the following acts, when committed in a systematic manner or on a large scale and instigated or directed by a Government or by any organization or group: (...)'.

55 Robinson (1999): 43.

56 Doria (2009): 645.

57 Płachta (2004): 381.

previous solutions developed by the *ad hoc* tribunals in an attempt to reflect the customary norms of the time.[58]

The codification of the crimes in the Rome Statute is regarded as necessary but insufficient.[59] Analysis of the *travaux préparatoires* does not yield examples of any separate initiatives of the Polish delegation diverging from the main current of the negotiations. Once again, however, one has to note the lack of separate positions taken by the representatives of the Republic of Poland as one of the group of 'like-minded states.'[60] In principle, things were similar with the subsequent works on crimes against humanity; again, the Polish diplomacy's rather passive stance is visible.

On the basis of the above, one can conclude that the core of the definition of crimes against humanity is well anchored in international customary law, though agreement may be lacking as to the various details.[61] The regulation is fragmented – suffice to note that separate treaties deal with detailed references to such crimes against humanity as apartheid,[62] torture[63] or forced disappearances[64]. In those more detailed aspects, traces of Polish influence are easier to be found.

Polish involvement is also noticeable with regard to the enactment of the International Convention on the Elimination of All Forms of Racial Discrimination of 1966. The latter was ratified by the Council of State of the Polish People's Republic, though with a reservation excluding the application of Article 22 (concerning the referral of disputes to the ICJ).[65] In October 1997, the Polish government withdrew the reservation.

58 The following matters in particular had to be accounted for: the special form of *mens rea*, the existence of an armed conflict, the occurrence of a wide-sweeping or systematic attack, the qualification of the perpetrator's potential victims as civilians or a largely civilian population, and the implementation of a plan or state policy or organizational policy – see Iwanek (2015): 193.

59 Sadat (2018): 385.

60 Schabas (2011): 18f.

61 Dinstein (1996): 896.

62 International Convention on the Suppression and Punishment of the Crime of Apartheid of 1973, 1015 UNTS 243 (Dz.U.1976.32.186).

63 Convention against Torture and Other Cruel, Inhuman or Degrading Treatment or Punishment of 1984, 1465 UNTS 85 (Dz.U.1989.63.378).

64 International Convention for the Protection of All Persons from Enforced Disappearance of 2006, 2716 UNTS 3, signed but still unratified by Poland.

65 Dz.U.1969.25.187. The reservation: 660 UNTS 195.

2 Towards Independent Treaty Regulation

The lack of treaty regulation of crimes against humanity blurs this category of crimes, leading to conflation with other crimes (crimes against peace, war crimes or even genocide). One has to bear in mind a 'subtle' difference in the *mens rea* (intent): in the case of genocide, the perpetrator acts with the intention of eradicating a group, whereas in the cases of the other crimes, the perpetrator commits the acts on account of the victim's affiliation with a specific group.[66] In other words, whereas genocide focuses on the collective nature of the victims, crimes against humanity cover acts committed collectively.[67]

However, in this context, it is worth remembering that the above is not merely a definitional matter calling for a higher degree of detail and separation, but also a question of the direction to be taken by the continued development of the sources – a question undertaken not only within the ILC. The key problem is the sense of conducting works on the creation of a more general convention on international crimes or updating the Genocide Convention.[68] Crimes against humanity appear to meet all of the criteria adopted by the Commission for the inclusion of a topic in its agenda – they reflect the states' needs with regard to the progressive development and codification of international law, there is a sufficient corresponding practice of the states, and the subject itself is sufficiently concrete and feasible.[69] The participation of Poland's representatives in the ILC and in the Sixth Committee was not significant. We recall also that when, during the Commission's 64th session in 2012, Sean D. Murphy (USA) suggested crimes against humanity as the next topic, Zdzisław Galicki had no longer been a member of that body. Following Murphy's four reports as special rapporteur, which served as the basis for the Commission's works, and following comments from the states (Poland did not take an individual position), as well as international organizations, a draft of articles and was adopted in the second reading on 22.05.2019 and subsequently the text of the comments, in the summer session. Simultaneously, in accordance with Article

66 Glaser (1970): 109.

67 Stahn (2018): 52.

68 Kreß, Garibian (2018): 956.

69 UN Doc. A/52/10 (1997) – see: YILC(1997), vol. II(2): 72 (§238). Additionally, 'in the selection of new topics, the Commission should not restrict itself to traditional topics, but could also consider those that reflect new developments in international law and pressing concerns of the international community as a whole'.

23 of its Statute, the ILC forwarded to the UNGA its Draft articles on Prevention and Punishment of Crimes Against Humanity, recommending the preparation of a Convention by the UNGA or in an international conference on the basis of the draft.

It is only to a limited extent that the lack of submission of a Polish position to the Committee can be explained with the fact of indirect support *via* the international organizations of which Poland was a member. A more active, though not necessarily specific, stance was exhibited by Poland's representatives within the Sixth Committee. Anna Wyrozumska spoke in its 70th session in 2015, supporting the adoption of a formula based on Article 7 of the Rome Statute and highlighting the importance of an approach accounting for the perspective of the victims, especially children.[70] In the years that followed, the same argument was raised by the Director of Polish MFA's Legal Department, Andrzej Misztal, recommending several changes to improve the clarity of the text and emphasizing that the domestic criminal jurisdiction ought to be exercised without the violation of the applicable norms of international law.[71] In the 2019 session, the Department's new director, Konrad Marciniak, congratulated the Commission on the completion of the works on the topic, expressed satisfaction with the regulation of prevention and punishment and reserved the option to submit more detailed comments at the later stages of the works.[72]

The International Law Commission's activities with regard to the codification of crimes against humanity appear to be complementing the works on the substantive part of international criminal law. As was observed in the comments annexed to the draft adopted in the second reading, the purpose of the articles was not only to codify the thereunto applicable customary law but also to prepare effective regulations acceptable to the states on the basis of then-existing solutions.[73] Despite the Polish diplomacy's merely token involvement, those reflect the core dilemmas of the general development of international law and in particular international criminal law.

70 Statement by Professor Anna Wyrozumska, Adviser to The Ministry of Foreign Affairs, 70th United Nations General Assembly, Agenda Item 83, https://www.un.org/en/ga/sixth/70/pdfs/statements/ilc/poland_2.pdf

71 https://www.un.org/en/ga/sixth/71/pdfs/statements/ilc/poland_23.pdf, https://www.un.org/en/ga/sixth/72/pdfs/statements/ilc/poland_1.pdf.

72 https://www.un.org/en/ga/sixth/74/pdfs/statements/ilc/poland_1.pdf.

73 ILC Report, A/74/10(2019) 23, §3.

3 Polish Legislation

In Polish law, the situation paints an altogether different picture. In Article 4 of the PKWN Decree of 31.08.1944, the term 'crimes against humanity' was used, but only in reference to acts committed during war operations. Thus, they for the most part fell within the category of war crimes,[74] putting in question the logic of the separation. In the view of Cyprian and Sawicki, for the purposes of Polish legislation and court decisions: 'the concepts of war crimes and crimes against the integrity of the Polish state, as the domestic counterpart of the crime against peace, had been entirely sufficient.'[75]

In the Decree of 13.06.1946 (Small Criminal Code), apart from the calls to ethnic conflict regulated in Article 30 or the violations of bodily integrity or mild bodily injury on account of national, ethnic, religious or racial affiliation regulated in Article 31(2), particular attention is drawn to Article 32:

> Whoever commits a criminal act directed against a group of the population or an individual person on account of national, ethnic, religious or racial affiliation, if resulting in death, severe bodily injury, disruption of the normal course of public life, or a threat to public safety, shall be liable to no less than 3 years' imprisonment, or life imprisonment, or the death penalty.

In the draft of the Criminal Code of 1969, the norms governing the penalization of international crimes were found in the chapter titled *Crimes against peace, humanity and international relations*. In the course of parliamentary works, however, that chapter was removed. Its absence from the final text of the Code was the product of the assumption that the matter ought to be regulated by a separate statute, which, however, never came to be. The crimes dealt with by the deleted chapter were criminalized by the provisions governing common crimes. In this context, Leszek Kubicki's remark on criminalization by, 'tacit implementation of treaty obligations,' comes to mind.[76]

The first statutory definition of crime against humanity and mention of crimes of genocide appeared in the amendment of the Act on the Chief Commission for the Investigation of Nazi Crimes in Poland – Institute of National Remembrance, of 1991.[77] Its Article 2b(2) provided:

---

74 Cyprian, Sawicki (1948b): 428.

75 *Ibidem*: 427.

76 Kubicki (1961): 335.

77 Dz.U.1991.45.195).

> Crimes against humanity shall in particular be crimes of genocide within the meaning of the Convention on the Prevention and Punishment of the Crime of Genocide, of 9 December 1948 (Dz.U.1952.2.9), as well as other serious persecutions on account of the persecuted persons' affiliation with a specific national, ethnic, political, social, racial or religious group, if carried out by state authorities or inspired or tolerated by the same.

The Supreme Court referred to this definition in a resolution of 13.05.1992,[78] viewing it as fragmentary and partially divergent from the understanding of the term in international law. Interesting, the Supreme Court found the crime of genocide to be universally recognized in international law as a special form of crime against humanity. A similar view was taken in the 1968 Convention on the Non-Applicability of Statutory Limitations but also in Article 43 of the Polish Constitution of 1997, where the two categories of crimes are not treated separately, either. The lack at that time of independent definitions of crime against humanity and genocide led to their penalization on the basis of the applicable provisions protecting life, health, etc.

The new Criminal Code of 1997 already included Chapter XVI *Crimes against peace, crimes against humanity and war crimes*. As emphasized in the explanatory memorandum published in 1994, the criminal offences dealt with by the chapter: 'are in modern circumstances directed against the universal circumstances of humanity, not only the national but directly the universal human community.'[79]

Article 105(1) of the Criminal Code provides for the exclusion of statutes of limitations with regard to those crimes. The implementation of prohibition of crimes against humanity into Polish law was to be achieved by Article 118a, added to the Criminal Code by an amendment of 20.05.2010.[80] However, the new article does not contain a typical definition of crime against humanity, omitting a number of its elements mentioned in the Rome Statute, while incorporating elements suggesting amalgamation with genocide.[81]

The sentencing limits were changed with the amendment of 7.07. 2022.[82] The present wording is:

78 I KZP 39/91, OSP 1993.3.6.

79 Explanatory memorandum to the project of Criminal Code (1994): 58.

80 Dz.U.98.626.

81 See Grzebyk (2023): 23.

82 Dz.U.2022.2600.

(1) Whoever, participating in a mass attack or at least one of repeat attacks targeted against a group of the population, undertaken for the purpose of implementing or supporting the policy of a state or organization:

(1) commits homicide;

(2) causes severe damage to human health;

(3) creates for persons belonging to a population group living conditions threatening their biological existence, especially by deprivation of access to food or medical care, calculated on their extermination, shall be liable to no less than 12 years' imprisonment or life imprisonment.

(2) Whoever, participating in a mass attack or at least one of repeat attacks targeted against a group of the population, undertaken for the purpose of implementing or supporting the policy of a state or organization:

(1) causes a person to be reduced to slavery or continue in slavery;

(2) deprives a person of freedom for a time exceeding 7 days or with especial torment;

(3) uses torture or subjects a person to cruel or inhuman treatment;

(4) commits rape or, by violence, unlawful threat or deceit otherwise violates a person's sexual freedom;

(5) by violence, unlawful threat or deceit causes a woman to become pregnant with the intention of affecting the ethnic composition of a population group or commission of other serious violations of international law;

(6) deprives a person of freedom and refuses to provide information concerning the person or the person's whereabouts or provides false information concerning the person or the person's whereabouts, with the intention of depriving such person of legal protection for an extended time, shall be liable to from 5 to 25 years' imprisonment.

(3) Whoever, participating in a mass attack or at least one of repeat attacks targeted against a group of the population, undertaken for the purpose of implementing or supporting the policy of a state or organization:

(1) in violation of international law, forces persons to change their lawful place of habitation;

(2) commits the serious persecution of a population group on grounds recognized as inadmissible by international law, in

> particular political, racial, national, ethnic, cultural or religious grounds, or on the ground of the lack of a religion, or on the ground of worldview or gender, resulting in the deprivation of fundamental rights, shall be liable to 3 to 20 years' imprisonment.

Article 118a of the Criminal Code contains only a catalogue of acts falling within the scope of the term. It employs a number of vague terms and does so without regard to the language of the Statute of the ICC. The reference to a mass attack is not the only cause of interpretative difficulties. The adaptation of Article 118a to the other provisions of the chapter is doubtful.

The next iteration of crimes against humanity in the Polish Criminal Code is the Article 119(1) offence of persecution as a special subtype of crime against humanity. It penalizes the use of violence or unlawful threat against a group of persons or an individual person on account of their national, ethnic, racial, political or religious affiliation or lack of religious affiliation. As observed by Tomasz Iwanek, the comparison of the two provisions of the Polish Criminal Code reveals disproportions with regard to the degree of unlawfulness and gravity of the acts.[83]

The year 1998 saw the creation of the Institute of National Remembrance – Commission for the Prosecution of Crimes against the Polish Nation,[84] whose tasks include the prosecution of criminal offences committed between 8.11.1917 and 30.07.1990.[85] The statute establishing the Institute used the definition of crime against humanity almost identical in wording to the amendment of the Act on the Chief Commission for the Investigation of Nazi Crimes in Poland – Institute of National Remembrance of 1991, discussed above. The above leads to a number of problems, not only with

83 Iwanek (2015): 190.

84 *Ustawa z 18.12. 1998 r. o Instytucie Pamięci Narodowej – Komisji Ścigania Zbrodni przeciwko Narodowi Polskiemu*, Dz.U.1998.155.1016, as amended.

85 The original wording of Article 2, defining communist crimes, referred to a different timeline: 'Communist crimes within the meaning of this Act are acts committed by officials of the communist state during the period from 17 September 1939 to 31 December 1989, consisting in repression or other forms of violation of human rights with regard to individuals or groups of population or in connection with repression, constituting crimes according to the Polish criminal law applicable at the time of their commission.' The change came with the Act of 29.04.2016 amending the Act on the Institute of National Remembrance – Commission for the Prosecution of Crimes against the Polish Nation and certain other Acts (Dz.U.749).

the penalization of crimes committed during Martial Law (12.12.1981–22.07.1983).

4 Polish Scholarship

The problem of crimes against humanity has been met with strong interest by Polish scholarship. Monographs bearing the fruit of doctoral studies in this range of topics have been published by Tomasz Iwanek (2015), Michał Jan Filipek (2020), Krzysztof Masło (2020) and Andrzej Bryl (2021).

An indefatigable advocate of the fight on racial discrimination was Jan Balicki. Having survived the nightmare of Nazi genocide in Poland, he participated, in 1950, as a member of the Polish delegation, in the 5th session of the UNGA, actively taking a position on racial discrimination in South Africa. The year after saw the publication of his monograph titled *Rasizm w Afryce Południowej* ('Racism in South Africa'), which was subsequently translated into several languages. Balicki remained faithful to his chosen topic for decades to come. In 1967, he published *Apartheid, studium prawno-polityczne rasizmu w Afryce Południowej* (1967) ('The apartheid: a politico-legal study in racism in South Africa'). In connection with the UN International Year for Action to Combat Racism and Racial Discrimination, he published another monograph, titled *Dyskryminacja rasowa w świetle prawa międzynarodowego* (1972) ('Racial discrimination in the light of international law'). In the 80s of the 20th century, he went on to write: *Historia Burów – geneza państwa apartheidu* ('A history of the Boers – genesis of the apartheid state') and *Afrykanerzy, Afrykanie, apartheid* and, ultimately, *Dyskryminacja rasowa przeszłość i teraźniejszość* (1986) ('Racial discrimination. The past and the present').

The above remarks are, of course, very rudimentary, mentioning only monographs and omitting shorter forms, the latter often dealing with a number of detailed issues.

Last but not least, in the context of the Polish perspective and legacy on crimes against humanity, one cannot ignore the topic of the classification of the Katyń Massacre as a mass and manifestly inhuman murder, thereby meeting the characteristics of a crime against humanity, as emphatically noted by Adam Basak.[86]

86 Basak (1998): 350. Cf. Basak (1993) concerning the Soviet efforts to include that massacre in Hermann Göring's indictment.

5 Conclusions

The works on the definition and prosecution of crimes against humanity took a different course compared to works on other international crimes. On the one hand, the reference to human dignity implies the fullest and most evident demand for penalization, but at the same time one should not lose sight of the realities of international politics, having translated into a more modest, non-autonomous definition of the category in the IMT Charter. We are still experiencing the joint, not fully separate treatment of crimes against humanity with the crime of genocide.

Notwithstanding the controversy as to the authorship of the term, the concept of crimes against humanity has unquestionably been influenced by Stefan Glaser and Jerzy Litawski. The circumstances, however, brought the Czechoslovak involvement to the fore. The aftermath of WWII also yielded important findings in the proceedings before the Supreme National Tribunal. Studies into crimes against humanity in their various forms (e.g. the apartheid) and from a more general perspective have attracted (and continue to attract) Polish scholars, constituting an interesting subject of analysis if only because of its accompanying definitional differences revealed with the participation of Polish diplomatic representatives in the codification works within the ILC.

CHAPTER 9

The Crime of Genocide

1 Axis Rule in Occupied Europe

Lemkin defined genocide (creating the term on the basis of the Greek *genos*, denoting a tribe or race, and the Latin *occidere*, meaning to kill) in a book published in 1944 in Washington, D.C., under the title *Axis Rule in Occupied Europe: Laws of Occupation. Analysis of Government, Proposals for Redress*.[1] He wrote it without knowing his own family's fate. Himself, he successfully fled Europe and made it to the United States of America in 1941 thanks to the help of many people, including the American professor, Malcolm McDermott, who was his friend. It was McDermott who helped Lemkin find employment with Duke University.[2] Lemkin was able to publish the aforementioned book with the assistance of George Finch, director of the international-law department of the Carnegie Endowment for International Peace. Finch wrote a preface, in which he focused not on the innovative concept of genocide but on the documents having found their way into the book, noting their broad accessibility thanks to it (as Lemkin had translated them into English); to Finch, they probably constituted the main asset of the publication.

The main point of reference and object of study in Lemkin's book is the Nazi policy towards the occupied states and in particular the Jews. That was the community, as he noted, selected for complete eradication.[3] Lemkin was not yet aware of the scale of the Holocaust at the time and could not predict that the Shoah would claim six million victims[4] (out of which nearly three million Polish Jews, including nearly his entire family), almost wiping the Jewish culture off the map of Europe. He was in receipt of reports

1 Lemkin (1944), online: https://gallica.bnf.fr/ark:/12148/bpt6k9443228/; it is worth noting that the introduction, in which the author uses the term, 'genocide,' is dated to 1943.

2 Already since 1942, in addition to his academic duties as a lecturer at Duke University and guest lecturer at the Department of War's School of Military Government, he had served in the capacity of chief consultant at the Board of Economic Warfare (later renamed to Foreign Economic Administration) in Washington, D.C. Lemkin (2018): 183; Szawłowski (2020): 288.

3 Lemkin (1944): 81.

4 Norman Davies (2008) cited an estimate in between five and six million victims.

DOI:10.1163/9789004712690_011

describing the treatment of the Poles and the Jews. He knew the latter were extremely ill-treated, with starvation food rations; he knew of mass executions and was aware of their being the main target of the Nazi extermination aimed at the complete eradication of their nation.[5] In his book, he analysed the various aspects of Nazi rule, describing the occupation techniques with regard to the administration, police, law, courts, property, finance, labour, legal status of the Jews, and genocide. He devoted some parts of his book also to the situation in the various occupied countries. The third part, entitled *Laws of Occupation*, is a collection of German legislative enactments pertaining to the situation of seventeen occupied countries in 1938–1942, translated into English. Lemkin referred to them as death-bringing legislation.[6]

Lemkin defined genocide in the first part of Chapter IX of his book, where he described the origin of the term, the stages of the crime, and the various genocidal techniques in the political, social, cultural, economic, biological, physical, religious and moral spheres.[7] In that chapter, he also referred to the Madrid Conference of 1933, to which he had sent a paper on vandalism and barbarity, as well as the universal jurisdiction to repress them. He developed on that thought also in respect of the newly coined term, 'genocide,' which he derives from barbarity and vandalism.[8] Lemkin believed that genocide should have the rank of a *delictum juris gentium* and be met with universal repression.[9]

He defined the new term as the destruction of a national or ethnic group. In his opinion, that did not have to denote the immediate destruction of an entire nation, unless such was the intent behind mass crimes. It could simply mean a co-ordinated plan with the intention of undertaking activities leading to the destruction of the group.[10] The goal of such plan was to be the destruction of the bases of group's existence, its institutions, language, culture, religion, etc. The result was to be the annihilation of the entire group, though it could be targeted against individuals as members of a specified group. Lemkin distinguished two phases of genocide – in the first one, the destruction of the group's national pattern took place; in the second

5 Lemkin (1944) 81, 87, (2020): 188.
6 Lemkin (2020): 187.
7 Lemkin (1944): 82ff.
8 Extensively see Irvin-Erickson (2019): 218.
9 Lemkin (1944): 91–94.
10 *Ibidem*: 79.

one, it was replaced with the oppressor's pattern. Moreover, he described what genocide consisted in in the various spheres of the group's life.[11]

In the political sphere, genocide began with the introduction of German administration; replacement of toponyms with German ones; induction of inhabitants into the so-called *volkslist*, conferring entitlement to concrete privileges; or the bringing of German settlers into occupied territories, offering them tax facilitations.

In the social sphere, the genocide was grounded in the prohibition of local laws and courts and introduction of German institutions instead. The intelligentsia and civil servants were also targeted and coerced into forced labour.

Cultural genocide consisted in the prohibition of the native language in schools and in the press. In Poland, for example, the study of fine arts was banned, while trade schools remained open in order to prepare future employees for work in German industry. Artistic activity was subjected to strict controls, and persons occupied with arts (painting, sculpture, etc.) were required to obtain a licence in order to be able to continue in their activities. Archives, libraries and museums were destroyed (Lemkin mentioned the burning down of the Great Library of the Jewish theological seminar in Lublin – in practice, the same fate befell hundreds of libraries throughout the country).[12]

Lemkin described economic genocide through the prism of literal fighting for bread, as the occupier's goal was to create such living conditions as to achieve the destruction of the economic bases of the group's existence. Control was seized over banks and the deposits of the civilian population, and especially the Jews were left with no means of supporting themselves, leading to the gradual depletion of their resources.

In the biological sphere, the genocide took place by reducing the birth rates in the occupied countries. For example, marriage permits were required, and women were separated from men at forced-labour sites.

The genocide of physical nature was intended to lead to the physical weakening and even annihilation of the members of the group and was achieved by racial discrimination in nutrition, as well as imposition of life-threatening conditions and mass killings, especially with regard to Poles, Russians and Jews.[13]

---

11 *Ibidem*: 82–87.

12 Precious museum collections were looted and simply taken to Germany; more extensively see Waltoś (2015) and the literature cited therein.

13 E.g. on the basis of the data available to him, Lemkin (1944: 88) compared the food rations received by the Germans, the Jews and the Poles.

Religious genocide consisted in the pillage and destruction of the temples, persecutions of the clergy and assassinations of the religious leaders.

For the purpose of weakening the resistance among the occupied nations, in order to divert attention from moral or ethnic problems, a moral genocide was being carried out, which – in Lemkin's opinion – was intended to satisfy the group's primordial instincts through the mitigation or loosening of various moral principles. The consumption of alcohol was encouraged, pornographic materials were distributed, and the curfews were relaxed for casino guests.

Chapter IX of Lemkin's book ended in recommendations for the future. Lemkin believed in the necessity of prosecuting genocide irrespective of whether it was committed in peacetime or wartime. He believed that international law should be revised on account of the German practices, so barbarous that no one had previously thought them possible. He reminisced also about the internationalization of the crimes of barbarity and vandalism, proposed in 1933, and noted that had a convention penalizing those acts already been adopted at the time, there would have been no difficulty with judging the German crimes on its basis.[14] With regard to genocide itself, he was of the opinion that its definition should be included in the Hague Regulations,[15] the provisions of which should reflect the development of international law. As Lemkin was aware that the Regulations were applicable to wartime, he also wanted for the prosecution of genocide to be guaranteed by domestic law; to that end, in his view, the necessity was to adopt an international convention providing the basis for penalization in domestic law.[16]

Lemkin developed upon the ideas from his book and phrased them in more precise terms in several articles published shortly thereafter. In his *Genocide – a Modern Crime*, published in 1945, he wrote that the perpetrator of the crime of genocide needed to have the intention of eradication or degradation of a specific group. He mentioned national, religious and racial groups as protected groups.[17] As can be noted, he did not include ethnic groups and also omitted political and cultural groups.

Poles did not have a good reputation in the United States at the time,[18] and thus Lemkin's biographic note came with the following caveat: 'Raphael

14 Lemkin (1944): 91–92.

15 He meant Hague Regulations of 1907 (Dz.U.1927.21.161).

16 Lemkin (1944): 94, see also Lemkin (1947): 145.

17 Lemkin (1945): 39–43.

18 That was probably the effect of the great emigration in 1880–1920, comprising waves of poorly educated manual workers, with no command of English, who took up all

Lemkin is Polish but his viewpoint is international and his understanding of the Nazi menace is of more than recent date.'[19]

Thanks to Lemkin's determination, even though a convention penalizing genocide as an international crime, the term itself had already been used in the Nuremberg trial, as well as a number of publications and international documents.[20] It was also invoked during the trials before the Polish Supreme National Tribunal, as discussed in Subchapter 3.5.2. In this context, the responses to the book, and its reception in academic circles, paint an interesting picture.

Unfortunately, similarly to how George Finch's preface to the book emphasized the importance of the materials included in it, so did the first reviews, as if without regard to the innovative character of the term coined by Lemkin. Even Hersch Lauterpacht (under the initials 'H.L.') in his very brief review referred to genocide only laconically, not appreciating the importance of the concept, as it were, and focusing instead on Lemkin's provision of interesting materials for the, 'scholarly historical record.'[21] Although Hans Kelsen's review is equally short, he still noted the political (not legal!) significance of the term[22] and observed that the facts described constituted crimes that could be viewed in the light of either domestic or international law, although the only sanctions available would be those already provided for by existing law. More similarly brief and not particularly insightful reviews followed.[23] The legal potential of the new term was not appreciated.[24] Only the materials gathered by Lemkin were discussed.

Nevertheless, 3.12.1944 saw the publication, on the pages of the *Washington Post*, of an editorial in which the word 'genocide' was used. That could be one of the most insightful of the 'reviews' of Lemkin's writings during that period, though originally relating not to his book but to the report submitted to the War Refugee Board.[25] The report concerned the crimes that

sorts of low-paying jobs. The *Polish jokes* ridiculed Polish stubbornness, tenacity and bigotry, even when Poles had already begun to join the ranks of the middle class – Pulera (2004): 99.

19 Lemkin (1945).

20 See http://www.unwcc.org/wp-content/uploads/2017/04/unwcc-history.pdf.

21 Lauterpacht (1945): 140.

22 Kelsen (1946): 271–272.

23 E.g. *NY Times Book Review* note of 17.11.1944 but also: Mander (1945): 117–120.

24 This is described in more detail by Szawłowski (2020): 307–313 and Power (2013), chapter: *The crime with a name*.

25 The text, titled: *German Extermination Camps – Auschwitz and Birkenau*, was first published in whole in English on 25.11.1944 by the U.S. War Refugee Board. The document

took place in Auschwitz-Birkenau camp, involving the gassing of almost two million Jews. The report proclaimed: 'There were unspeakable atrocities in Auschwitz-Birkenau. But the point about there killings is that they were systematic and purposeful. The gas chambers and furnaces were not improvisations, they were scientifically designed instruments for the extermination of the entire ethnic group'.[26] When referring to those crimes, the editorial used the word, 'genocide,' which had been known only for several months at the time, citing Lemkin's book and his definition. And later: 'Jews were gassed at Birkenau and Aryan Poles and Russians and Slovenes were otherwise butchered not for any crime or any resistance to Axis authority but because the Nazis wished to exterminate the ethnic group to which they belonged.' Quoting Lemkin's words, the editorial ended with a reference to universal repression and the necessity of taking steps towards the adoption of an international convention to enable the punishment of the crime. The penalization of genocide would gain a legal basis.

It appears that Lemkin could not possibly have dreamt for any more effective popularization of his concept at the time.

2 Genocide in the Nuremberg Trial

In May 1945, President Harry Truman appointed Robert Jackson, an associate justice of the U.S. Supreme Court, the head of a team of counsel tasked with preparing the indictment to be brought before the IMT (Jackson later became the Chief Prosecutor in the Nuremberg trial).

John Barrett suggests that Lemkin's book influenced the Nuremberg trial more than meets the eye.[27] He claims the book accompanied Jackson to Nuremberg (UNWCC also received the copies of the book[28]). Barrett believed that Lemkin's discussion of the activities of the SS, Gestapo and various other organizations of the NSDAP as criminal organizations became the basis for the action plan designed by Murray C. Bernays of the

combined the materials based on information from Slovak fugitives from the camp, Rudolf Vrba and Alfred Wetzler, with the reports of two other fugitives, Arnost Rosin and Czesław Mordowicz, as well as the even earlier report ('Polish Major's report') by Jerzy Tabeau, a medical student who managed a successful escape from Auschwitz. Together, the documents are known as the Auschwitz Protocols. They were filed into evidence at Nuremberg as exhibit 022-l.

26 Editorial *Genocide* in: Washington Post, 3.12.1944.

27 Barrett (2010): 38–39.

28 Flemming (2022a): 242.

Department of War, who was of the opinion that the organizations had to be judged for conspiracy. The plan was approved by Secretary of War Henry L. Stimson and subsequently by Secretary of State Cordell Hull and Attorney General Francis Biddle. It also lay at the foundation of the tactic chosen by Jackson and solutions adopted in the London Agreement and therewith in the IMT Charter.

Murray Bernays, who served on Jackson's team of lawyers, prepared a document titled *Planning Memorandum*, describing the evidence of the crimes; he enumerated: '[d]ecimation of racial minorities and subjugated populations' by methods including '(1) underfeeding; (2) depriving them of clothing, shelter, fuel, sanitation, medical care; (3) deporting them for forced labor; [and] (4) working them in inhuman conditions.' On the document submitted on 16.05.1945 to the Supreme Court, Jackson added the word 'genocide' by handwriting. In effect, the phrase received the following wording: 'genocide, sterilization, castration, or destruction of racial minorities and subjugated populations by such means and methods as (1) underfeeding; (2) depriving them of clothing, shelter, fuel, sanitation, medical care; (3) deporting them for forced labor; [and] (4) working them in inhuman conditions.'[29]

The *Memorandum* was subsequently shared with the Allied states during the works in London from June to August 1945. Thus, the term 'genocide' must have been known to the delegations of the Allied states taking part in the Nuremberg trials. It did not find its way to the London Agreement, however. Nevertheless, there can be no doubt that the provisions of Articles IX and X of the IMT Charter took their origin from Lemkin's book, in which, embarking on an assessment of the criminal conduct of the SS and Gestapo, he wrote: 'mere membership in such groups should be treated as an offence, and all the members of the Gestapo and S.S. should be punished for the sole reason that they are carrying out such functions in occupied countries'.[30]

For comparison, Articles IX and X of the Charter allow an organization to be found to be criminal, with the following repercussion: 'In cases where a group or organization is declared criminal by the Tribunal, the competent national authority of any Signatory shall have the right to bring individuals to trial for membership therein before national, military or occupation courts.'

Already in May 1945 Lemkin met with a member of Jackson's legal team named Sidney Alderman and subsequently went to work for the

29 Barrett (2010): 40.

30 Lemkin (1944): 23.

Department of War as an informal member of Jackson's team of sorts himself. He only came to Europe in August 1945, arriving in London. He was not well received by Jackson's collaborators, perhaps because – as Barrett conjectures – of having independently contacted the members of the UNWCC, interfering with the plans of the U.S. representative, Joseph V. Hodgson.[31]

The indictment featured the term 'genocide' in the section on war-crime charges, using the following language: 'They conducted deliberate and systematic genocide, viz., the extermination of racial and national groups, against the civilian populations of certain occupied territories in order to destroy particular races and classes of people and national, racial, or religious groups, particularly Jews, Poles, Gypsies and others.' The term resurfaced in the closing speeches of the British and French prosecutors, who made direct references to the extermination of millions of human beings.[32]

The fact that the term appeared in the indictment was a great success of Lemkin, for which he incidentally claimed direct credit. For as he claimed in his biography: 'I included genocide in the indictment.'[33] What he could not achieve was including genocide in the judgment, despite the great deal of effort on his part.[34]

3 UNGA Resolution 96(I)

Lemkin participated in the first session of the United Nations General Assembly held at Lake Success in New York State. He endeavoured to persuade the international community to take up the subject of the crime of genocide.[35] As he mentioned, he had written a draft resolution on genocide, for which he undertook to garner support, so that it could be tabled before the UN.[36] His adherents included the foreign minister and former president of Panama, Ricardo Alfaro; Cuban ambassador, Guillermo Belt; World Alliance of Women President Margery Corbett Ashby; and head of the Indian delegation, Vijaya Lakshmi Pandit.[37] He also won over the Czechoslovak foreign minister, Jan Masaryk, who in turn secured the support of the USSR

31 Barrett (2010): 45–46.
32 Barrett (2010): 49.
33 Lemkin (2018): 124.
34 Barrett (2010): 50–51.
35 Elder (2009): 36.
36 At the time, Lemkin was on leave from the U.S. Department of War.
37 Concerning his quest for support, Lemkin (2018): 196–210.

foreign minister, Andrey Vyshinsky. The Belgian, French and British delegations also came on board.

In the end, the draft was sponsored in the UNGA by India, Cuba and Panama. The text of their version, as well as that of the eventual resolution, emphasized that genocide was a: 'denial of the right of existence of entire human groups.'[38]

The draft was subsequently sent to works in the UNGA's Sixth Committee. The United Kingdom, India, the USSR, France, Saudi Arabia, Chile and Poland, however, proposed certain amendments. Generally speaking, the paramount question, on which the states were unanimous, was the recognition of genocide as a crime of international law. Citing Lemkin's *Axis Rule*, the representative of Saudi Arabia enumerated the necessary characteristics of a crime in order to qualify as a crime of international law.[39]

Following the incorporation of the amendments, the document gained the support of a variety of states, including Poland, whose representative, let it be recalled, Lemkin officially was not. Manfred Lachs, the Polish delegate at the UN, highlighted the necessity of adopting of a resolution condemning genocide and thereafter taking all possible measures to denounce the crime. According to him, it had to be precisely defined in written law. Lachs, moreover, stressed the duty to penalize the propaganda as well, invoking the Polish experience in that regard.[40] He reiterated the necessity of such a convention also in 1948 as Chairman of the Legal Committee of the UNGA,[41] emphasizing also the need for the states to exercise universal jurisdiction to punish the crime, and for the creation of an international court.

The text of the resolution was prepared by a subcommittee[42] and the draft, approved by the Sixth Committee, was voted by the UNGA.

38 Abtahi, Webb (2008): 3.

39 *Ibidem*: 14.

40 Sixth Committee, A/C.6/96, 2.12.1946, Sawicki (1949): 35.

41 United Nations, Radio interview: https://media.un.org/en/asset/k16/k16k2t7qbw, 8.10.1948.

42 Incorporating the representatives of Saudi Arabia, Chile, Cuba, France, India, Panama, Poland, the USSR, the United Kingdom and the USA; see: Sixth Committee, A/C.6/96, 2.12.1946. The subcommittee considered Poland's proposal concerning the treatment of the propagation and dissemination of hate towards nations, ethnicities, races and religious groups as a preparatory stage preceding the commission of the crime and to be penalized. The subcommittee received that as an interesting proposal deserving to be mentioned in the report and left for consideration in connection with the draft convention or the studies completed for the purpose of the adoption of the resolution – ANNEX 15e, UN Doc. A/C.6/120.

On 11.12.1946, it passed as Resolution 96(I). The Resolution affirmed genocide as a crime of international law condemned by the civilized nations. It encouraged the states to adopt suitable legislation to prevent and punish the crime, recommending interstate co-operation in that regard, and eventually directed the ECOSOC to undertake the necessary works to design a draft convention and present it in the session of the General Assembly. Accordingly, the states' amendments were far-reaching, for the draft submitted by Cuba, India and Panama did not voice a call for a convention. The Resolution, terming genocide a crime in international law, classified it as a *delictum juris gentium* and moreover did not tie its commission to an armed conflict.

4 The Works on a Convention

In pursuance of the UNGA Resolution of 28.03.1947, the ECOSOC adopted a resolution directing the UN Secretary General to undertake studies as to the feasibility of the compilation and submission of draft convention on genocide. The works on feasibility were to take place with the participation of experts[43] in criminal law and following consultations with the Committee on the Development and Codification of International Law and Commission on Human Rights, as well following the receipt of recommendations from the states.[44] The consultations in that Committee led to the majority of the states' decision to point it out to the UNGA that the implementation of the Nuremberg principles and punishment of international crimes could require the establishment of an international judicial authority to exercise the jurisdiction. Several states opposed the idea, including Egypt, Poland and the USSR. In their opinion, the matter fell outside of the scope of powers granted to the Committee by the UNGA.[45] At the same time, the Polish representative, Lachs, was drawing attention to the necessity of criminalizing the propaganda of aggressive war.[46] That was reported by the subcommittee, with the conclusion that the Polish proposal was to be reflected in the report and considered in the draft convention,[47] noting that the propagation

43 UN Doc. A/AC.10/41.

44 UN Doc. A/AC.10/29, 19.05.1947.

45 UN Doc. A/AC.10/46, 10.06.1946.

46 UN Doc. A/AC.10/46/Corr.1, 16.06.1947.

47 *Propagation and dissemination of hatred against national or racial and religious groups as a preparatory step in the effectuation of the crime*, UN Doc. A/C.6/120, 6.12.1946.

and dissemination of ethnic, racial or religious hatred was a preparatory stage for the commission of a crime. Another representative of Poland, Aleksander Bramson, highlighted two basic concerns: that the punishability of genocide could not be limited to the highest representatives of the state alone and that cultural genocide had taken place, for example, in Poland, with the destruction of 50 million books.[48] Lachs also spoke on the necessity of the adoption of a convention, although he was sceptical on the matter of the establishment of an international criminal court. In his opinion, that called for more in-depth works. He noted, however, that genocide had found reflection neither in the IMT Charter nor the IMT's judgment. He added that biological genocide had inflicted irreparable losses on humanity and repressive consequences in that regard had always been too late in coming.[49]

The preamble of the draft prepared by the Secretariat in line with the Resolution of the ECOSOC of 28.03.1947 identified genocide as the intentional eradication of human beings. The draft's Article I already stipulated that the purpose of the convention was to prevent the extermination of political, linguistic, racial, religious and ethnic groups and that genocide meant criminal acts committed against one of the aforementioned human groups for the purpose of its complete or partial destruction or for the purpose of impeding its protection or development.[50]

Article III concerned itself with the punishability of all forms of public propaganda and systematic inspiration of hatred for the purpose of leading to genocide; the later provisions of the draft established universal jurisdiction with regard to the crime and foresaw the creation of an international court. For the last-mentioned issue, two alternative solutions were introduced. One of the proposals was to establish a court for all international crimes, and the other to create a special tribunal only for genocide.[51]

Lemkin, Donnedieu de Vabres and Pella submitted their remarks on the draft. Lemkin voiced doubts as to the purpose of inclusion of political groups under the protection of the convention. On the one hand, he noted that political groups do not have that permanency and specific features as the other mentioned groups; on the other hand, he emphasized the necessity of the adoption of Genocide Convention. In his view, one had to avoid

48 UN Doc. A/AC.10/SR.29, 24.06.1947.

49 UN Doc. A/C.6/SR.41, 3.10.1947.

50 UN Doc. E/447.

51 UN Doc. A/AC.10/41.

provoking the states to reject the convention (because of the inclusion of specific groups), especially considering how history showed racial, ethnic and religious to be the most exposed to genocide out of all human groups.[52] Another expert, Donnedieu de Vabres, was opposed to the exclusion of political groups, observing that genocide was a reprehensible crime regardless of whatever groups may have fallen victim of it and that the exclusion of political groups could have the result of genocide committed on political groups being regarded as justified. Pella, in turn, was of the opinion that the protection of political groups would not include Nazi or fascist groups.[53] Lemkin was an advocate of the inclusion of cultural genocide, alongside biological and physical, in the convention. He believed that a cultural group's right to existence was warranted not only by moral considerations but also the interests of the international community on account of the cultural contribution made to civilization. According to Lemkin, the suppression of the various cultures would be equally fatal to civilization as the physical destruction of nations.[54] Pella and Donnedieu de Vabres, however, concluded that such a proposal extended the definition of genocide too far and would provide a pretext for the expansion of minority protection, which was a subject dealt with by different conventions.

Lemkin was also of the view, in the context of the draft provisions on the prosecution of individuals, that hypothetical proceedings before an international criminal court should be reserved for the major criminals and those guilty of minor crimes should be judged before domestic courts. He argued that the referral to the jurisdiction of an international court in marginal situations would leave the perpetrators unpunished due to the limitations of the jurisdiction of international courts.[55] Pella and Donnedieu de Vabres harboured no such doubts. They were, on the other hand, adherents of the concept of the creation of an international court as part of the ICJ, in which connection they invoked the AIDP draft of 1928. Contrary to their opinion, Lemkin believed the system of international criminal law not to have matured enough for that, with the creation of an international court falling outside the boundaries of the problem of the repression of the crime of genocide.[56]

52 UN Doc. E/447.
53 UN Doc. E/447.
54 UN Doc. E/447.
55 UN Doc. E/447.
56 UN Doc. E/447.

The states were urgently requested by the ECOSOC[57] for comments on the Secretary General's draft. Already in the general debate at the Council, the Polish representative, Juliusz Katz-Suchy, pointed out[58] that Poland, as a victim of genocide, was fully aware of the gravity of the crime. He specified that the Polish delegation had previously accepted various compromises designed to avoid misunderstandings and to facilitate the states in the ratification of the convention, because Poland desired swift action on the matter, meaning the adoption of a convention enjoying universal acceptance and effective implementation. Katz-Suchy noted that the Council should encourage the states to submit their comments to be used for the creation of a draft for the Council's acceptance.

By the ECOSOC's resolution of 3.03.1948, an *ad hoc* Committee was established, comprising the representatives of China, France, Lebanon, Poland, the USSR, the USA and Venezuela. The Committee was tasked with preparing a draft and submitting it to the Council for deliberation in the following session, after discussing the various problems leading to differences of opinions among the experts and among the states. For example, should genocide – besides biological and physical – also include cultural genocide, as wanted by Lemkin; should it be limited to holders of positions of authority or should it extend to the lower ranks as well; should an international tribunal be involved to judge the crime. The Committee also formulated questions of the relationship among the hypothetical text of the convention, the Nuremberg principles, and the Draft Code of Offences.[59] Because few states took a position on the secretary's draft and only seven participated in the *ad hoc* Committee, the decision was made that alternative texts could also be submitted, with the choice as to the works on the text being left to the ECOSOC. As its point of reference, the Committee took the China-sponsored draft.

The Polish representatives in the *ad hoc* Committee's works was Aleksander Rudziński,[60] a nowadays almost forgotten character,[61] who had served as the advocate and spokesman for many of the ideas that are cur-

57 UN Doc. E/573.

58 UN Doc. E/SR.139.

59 UN Doc. E/AC.25/2.

60 Fiedorczyk (2011): 484.

61 Probably because in 1950 he chose life in the West. As Fiedorczyk puts it, Rudziński: '"chose freedom" and was granted asylum,' (*Ibidem*); identically (probably after Fiedorczyk) Szawłowski (2020): 396–397.

rently found in the Convention. In many aspects, he was reiterating the remarks of his Polish predecessors. For example, he specified that genocide consisted in the physical extermination of a human group or actions leading to its progressing extermination, termed biological genocide, irrespective of the motive.[62] Cultural genocide, in turn, was closely linked to the problem of the protection of minorities. Rudziński did not want for the provisions of the convention to extend only to those in positions of authority. He noted that such a solution would have the effect of shielding co-perpetrators from punishment. On the other hand, he was an adherent of universal jurisdiction for genocide, recalling that the repression of piracy, human trafficking and drug trafficking belonged to domestic jurisdictions. In that regard, he invoked the provisions of Poland's Criminal Code of 1932, namely its Article 9, establishing universal jurisdiction for criminal offences governed by conventions to which Poland was party.[63]

Rudziński was opposed to the American proposal of linking the crime to government decisions, implying recognition of the internationality of the crime only in cases of government involvement in its commission.[64] He noted also that the protection offered by the convention should not apply to political groups, as they lacked permanence. A religious, ethnic or racial group did not disappear simply because of the elimination of its leaders.[65] Furthermore, he believed that genocide ought to extend to all aspects of the physical destruction of a group.[66] He reiterated the Polish position that genocide should extend to cultural genocide, though he appreciated the distinction between cultural and physical destruction, noting that cultural genocide should be dealt with as a preparatory act for physical genocide. He voiced the belief that public incitement to commit the crime should also be punished.

The Polish representative believed that the most important matter was for the convention to bind the states to punish the crime of genocide – such a provision would create an international obligation. Interestingly, at that stage, the Polish representatives still did not recognize the need for the creation of any sort of international criminal justice system. Rudziński noted that the states ought to report cases of genocide to the Security Council,

---

62 UN Doc. UN Doc.E/AC.25/SR.3.

63 *Ibidem*.

64 UN Doc. UN Doc.E/AC.25/SR.4.

65 UN Doc. UN Doc.E/AC.25/SR.4.

66 UN Doc. UN Doc.E/AC.25/SR.4/Corr.1.

which should be the one to respond. His attention was focused on the repression of genocide by the states.[67]

The majority of the representatives in the Committee, however, voted in favour of the establishment of an international court. For that reason, in later discussions, Rudziński, though opposed to the hypothetical creation of an international court (in line with the position taken by Poland), he opted for giving the regulation such a wording as would leave the states with the freedom to create such a body by their own decision.[68]

When the discussion moved on to the mater of the intention of extermination as an element of the crime of genocide, Rudziński took the position that such a purpose had to be distinguished from the psychological motivation of the crime.[69] He was of the opinion, however, that the incorporation of motive as element of genocide would have the effect of the addition of a subjective factor, whereas the text of a legislative instrument should be grounded in objective criteria. He proposed for the definition to specify that genocide was the result of ethnic, religious or racial persecution. His argument was that genocide should not apply to isolated acts but instead be the effect of repeat persecution. According to him, persecution – comprising a number of tangible acts – was easier to prove than motive or intention. The idea was criticized both by the French representative, Pierre Ordonneau, and the Soviet representative, Platon Morozov, objecting that the evaluation of persecution would take on a subjective character and the passage of time needed in order to be able to evaluate persecution would frustrate the preventive role of the Convention. As a result, Rudziński proposed to drop the idea.[70]

In a counter to a proposal tabled by the Lebanese representative, Azkoul Rudziński asserted that the prevention of genocide did not give rise to interpretative difficulties and should not be limited to the adoption of the provisions of a convention governing the punishment of the crime. In the Polish representative's opinion, prevention could not remain a merely moral obligation of the states; instead, he called for the obligation to be given the character of a norm of law.[71]

Poland submitted a proposal relating to extradition for crimes of genocide. According to the Polish proposal, genocide should not be regarded

67 UN Doc. UN Doc.E/AC.25/SR.6, E/AC.25/SR.7, E/AC.25/SR.8.

68 UN Doc. UN Doc.E/AC.25/SR.20; E/AC.25/SR.24.

69 UN Doc. UN Doc.E/AC.25/SR.11.

70 UN Doc. UN Doc.E/AC.25/SR.12.

71 UN Doc. UN Doc.E/AC.25/SR.19.

as a political crime and should be grounds for extradition.[72] The proposal was supported by the other states (with amendments from the USA and Venezuela).

In the end, however, following a series of votes on the various aspects of the draft, Rudziński abstained. The draft was adopted on 30.04.1948 by five votes to one (the USSR against) and one abstention (Poland). Rudziński raised his doubts[73] – the draft did not mention fascist-Nazi crimes or the principles developed by the Nuremberg tribunal; nor did it stipulate the exclusion of superior orders as a justification or provide for the dissolution of organizations inciting genocide. He also concluded that the inclusion of political groups as groups protected by the convention could give a pretext for interference with the internal matters of a state; last but not least, he opposed the creation of a hypothetical international court, deeming that premature. He also voiced his discontent during the works on the *ad hoc* Committee's report.[74]

During the debates in the ECOSOC, the Polish representative, Juliusz Katz-Suchy, did not leave the Polish position (abstention) without comment, discussing the objections and doubts raised in the Committee by Rudziński. Katz-Suchy[75] voiced his great disappointment in the draft's failure to include any references to fascism or Nazism. He also wanted for the provisions of the convention to reflect that cultural genocide is always a prelude to physical and biological extermination. He consistently supported the Russian proposal for superior orders to be precluded as a justification for homicide, and he spoke unfavourably of the hypothetical creation of a criminal court, noting that the responsibility for the prevention and repression of genocide should rest with the SC. He was also of the opinion that the convention should include binding obligations for the state with regard to achieving the goals of the convention, which he viewed as extraordinarily important to the punishment of propaganda leading to racial, ethnic or religious hatred. He believed in the necessity of penalizing the acts preparatory to genocide, including incitement of genocide. Katz-Suchy recalled that genocide should not be regarded as a political crime and should be eligible for extradition. According to the Polish representative, however, the above

72 UN Doc. UN Doc.E/AC.25/SR.20.

73 Those can be found in the *ad hoc* committee E/794 report and the document from the works on the E/AC.25/SR.28 report.

74 UN Doc. UN Doc.E/AC.25/SR.26.

75 UN Doc. UN Doc.E/SR.218.

did not change the fact that the draft convention should be submitted to the UNGA, though he reserved the right to submit amendments.

In October 1948, the draft convention prepared in the *ad hoc* Committee was put on the agenda of the Sixth Committee, in which Poland was represented by Manfred Lachs. Lachs sustained all of the doubts raised on Poland's behalf by Rudziński and Katz-Suchy,[76] including the unfavourable outlook on the protection of political groups. Sweden and the USSR held the same position.[77] The representative of Czechoslovakia, Vladimir Prochazka, supported the Polish and Soviet idea of linking genocide to fascism and Nazism.[78] With regard to the punishment of propaganda, Poland had the support of the British representative, Gerald Fitzmaurice.[79] The representatives of Egypt, Wahid Fikry Raafat, and of the United States, John Maktos, emphasized the necessity of the prevention of the crime, recalling the Polish initiative in that regard.[80] Thus, the Polish representatives were neither alone nor supported only by the socialist states.

In November 1948, members of a Drafting Committee were appointed, comprising the representatives of Poland, Belgium, China, Cuba, Egypt, France, the USSR, the United Kingdom and the United States of America.

Poland was represented by Lachs.[81] Soon, he voiced his negative feelings on the hypothetical regulation of state responsibility (the proposal of Belgium and the United Kingdom). In his opinion, that matter should not be dealt with in a convention on individual responsibility. One had to avoid situations in which the perpetrators could escape justice for genocide because of the state's payment of damages.[82]

Lachs was replaced by Stefan Litauer, who sustained the previous opinions and expectations concerning the creation of an international criminal

---

76 UN Doc. UN Doc.A/C.6/SR.64.

77 UN Doc. UN Doc.A/C.6/SR.75.

78 UN Doc. UN Doc.A/C.6/SR.66 – only the analysis of the historical background can give the true context for the efforts by Lachs or Katz-Suchy for the text of the convention to include references to Nazism and fascism. In particular, one needs to take a negative view of the active participation of the diplomats of the Polish People's Republic in Soviet initiatives undertaken for the purpose of restricting the definitional scope of genocide so as for the definition to be able to cover fascist crimes only, without any avenue for holding the USSR responsible for its own crimes. In that regard, the roles of Lachs and Katz-Suchy were reduced to the carrying out of instructions arriving from the Kremlin.

79 UN Doc. A/C.6/SR.75.

80 UN Doc. UN Doc. A/C.6/SR.85.

81 UN Doc. UN Doc. A/C.6/SR.104.

82 *Ibidem.*

court and other matters. He observed that creating such a body would interfere with state sovereignty in internal matters;[83] he also emphasized the preventive value of the convention[84] and believed that genocide as a term should include cultural genocide. The Polish delegation voiced the opinion that the definition of genocide encompassed reprehensible crimes calculated on the destruction of a nation's art and culture.[85]

The Drafting Committee adopted three resolutions. Resolution A concerned the adoption of the convention, the definition of genocide, the means of prevention of the crime, and the court jurisdiction to judge it. Resolution B concerned the ILC's study on an international criminal court for the judgment of those guilty of the crime of genocide. Resolution C concerned the applicability of the drafted convention to non-self-governing territories.[86]

5 The Adoption of the Convention by the UNGA

During the UNGA session[87] on 9.12.1948, apart from the chairman, Iōannēs Spiropoulos, who reported on the works on the convention, the USSR representative, Platon Morozov, also spoke. His remarks came to dominate the subsequent discussion. He had his doubts with regard to a solution leaving the cultural aspect of genocide outside of the scope of the convention. He believed the convention should be applicable to non-self-governing territories and that the matter ought not to be left for the administrating state to decide; he also opposed the incorporation of provisions dealing with the jurisdiction of an international criminal court.[88] In his opinion, the creation of an international court would interfere with the internal matters of the states, so he criticized Resolution B and proposed the relevant amendments.

Katz-Suchy, the Polish representative,[89] criticized the lack of references to the fascist regimes of Germany and Spain in the preamble, and for that reason he withheld his support for the text of the preamble. For their absence, he faulted the American delegation, whose representative chaired

83 UN Doc. A/C.6/SR.130.

84 UN Doc. A/C.6/SR.133.

85 *Ibidem.*

86 UN Doc. A/PV.178, 811ff; UN Doc. A/PV.179, 831.

87 UN Doc. A/PV.178, 811ff.

88 The majority of the states, however, supported the proposed provisions, as did France, Egypt, Australia or the Netherlands, although India, e.g. was opposed.

89 UN Doc. A/PV.179: 831–852.

the discussions during the works on the Convention. Katz-Suchy believed that the Convention should guarantee the prevention of the crime of genocide, for which reason propaganda should be prohibited and preparations should be punished. Describing the Polish situation at the time with regard to the punishment of the criminals, he noted the problems with compliance with Polish extradition requests by the Western states. He also criticized the failure by the proposed provisions of the Convention to include cultural genocide, in which context he lent his support to the Soviet delegate. He believed that genocide had to include the destruction of culture and art. In the end, similarly to the Soviet delegate (and let us recall that our delegates complied with instructions coming from the Kremlin), he voiced his doubts concerning the text of Article VI of the proposed convention, noting that the nature of the provisions referring to an international criminal court was highly problematic, since no such court existed, and that such provisions could violate the principle of state sovereignty. Katz-Suchy also objected to the rejection of an article barring the use of superior orders or compliance with legislation to justify homicide. For that, he cited the example of Joseph Bühler's trial before the NTN, noting that Bühler had argued his own innocence due to having merely carried out the orders of a superior. Arguing in line with the Polish position, Katz-Suchy insisted that non-self-governed territories had to be covered by the Convention because otherwise no one would speak on behalf of their inhabitants.[90]

The UNGA voted on the USSR-sponsored amendments, none of which, however, gained majority. Nevertheless, the vast majority of the states voted for the adoption of all three of the Committee's resolutions – A, B and C. On 9.12.1948, the UNGA adopted the Convention unanimously.[91] At present, there are 153 state parties.

The text of the Convention narrowed the list of protected groups to racial, religious, national and ethnic. Political ones were left outside of the scope of protection; Lemkin did not believe them to be sufficient stable.[92] Although the exclusion of cultural genocide from the protection of the Convention was not to his preference (on that, his views coincided with those of the Polish delegation), he cherished at least the small success that the Convention did incorporate provisions recognizing as a genocidal act the transfer of children from one group to another. He also understood the inclusion of provisions on the jurisdiction of the international criminal

90 UN Doc. A/PV.179, 839–844.

91 UN Doc. A/RES/260 (III).

92 Lemkin (2018): 253–254.

court, which had been the subject of so much criticism from Poland or the USSR. Lemkin was a pragmatic person and realized that the insistence of France as an adherent of that solution[93] was of principal importance, especially given that France was hosting the UNGA session. Interestingly, in the session of the General Assembly on 9.12.1948, Lemkin's name was mentioned by the representative of Iran, stressing the necessity of the awakening of the public opinion to the fight on the crime of genocide.[94] During the works on the Convention, many of Lemkin's ideas fell through; regardless of that, it was unquestionably he who had been the author of the global agitation that led to the adoption of the Convention.

Poland acceded to the Convention on the Prevention and Punishment of Genocide already before its coming into force[95] but with reservations to Articles IX and XII (surprisingly, none with regard to the hypothetical ICC jurisdiction). The first reservation concerned the jurisdiction of the ICJ. Poland repeatedly criticized the hypothetical mandatory jurisdiction of the ICJ already during the works, and the reservation reflected that criticism. The Polish position was that the consent of the states party to the dispute should be required in order to refer the case to the ICJ. As for the second reservation, Poland did not agree to accept the provisions stipulating the inapplicability of the Convention to non-self-governed territories, including trust territories.[96] Interestingly, the states objecting to the reservation included colonial powers, former colonies and dominions: Australia, Belgium, Brazil, Ecuador, the Netherlands, and the United Kingdom. Poland withdrew these reservations on 16.09.1997.

6 Polish Legislation

When it comes to Polish domestic legislation on the crime of genocide, it was implemented into the national legal order somewhat late after the adoption of the Convention. The Decree of 13.06.1946 (Small Criminal Code) had come into force before the completion of the works on the Convention and thus did not make direct references to the crime of genocide. However, it contained provisions on the public revilement, derision and humiliation

93 *Ibidem*: 267.

94 UN Doc. A/PV.178, 825.

95 The Convention was ratified in accordance with the Act of 18.07.1950, Dz.U.1950.36.325.

96 Dz.U.1952.2.9.

of a population group on account of its affiliation with a specific group (Article 31(1)), violation of the bodily integrity of the members of the group (Article 31(2)) and commission of a criminal offence against members of the group on account of their affiliation with that group (Article 32). The protection of those provisions extended to national, racial and religious groups, i.e. those protected by the Genocide Convention (which also mentioned ethnic groups).

Similar provisions were found in the Criminal Code of 1969 – Articles 193(1) and 193(2) and 274. Nonetheless, the Code did not contain provisions reflecting the prohibition of genocide. Only in the Criminal Code of 1997, in its Article 118, can one find a criminal offence the elements of which suggest the penalization of the crime of genocide (the term 'genocide' was not used; in the words of Katarzyna Banasik: 'the term "crime of genocide" is alien to the Criminal Code'[97]). Article 118 provides:

> (1) Whoever, for the purpose of extermination in whole or in part of a national, ethnic, racial, political or faith-based group or a group with a specific worldview, commits homicide or causes severe damage to the health of a person belonging to such group shall be liable to no less than 12 years' imprisonment or life imprisonment.
>
> (2) Whoever, for the purpose set out in section 1, creates for persons belonging to such group living conditions threatening its biological extermination, uses measures intended to halt births within the group or forcibly removes children from persons belonging thereto shall be liable from 5 years' to 25 years' imprisonment.[98]

As one can see, the provisions of the Criminal Code expand the scope of the protected groups compared to the provisions of the Convention. A political group was added, as well as a group distinguished by worldview, and the religious group is literally a 'faith-based' rather than literally 'religious' group. Naturally, the states are free to choose the wording of their criminal provisions – the Genocide Convention does not require them to copy the exact definition into domestic legislation. However, this can give rise to some concerns, for example with regard to the use of universal jurisdiction for the genocide of a political group. While Poland has bound herself by treaty to prosecute genocide, it is difficult to predict the course of action with regard to hypothetically prosecuting a crime against a political group,

97 Banasik (2011): 69.
98 Dz.U.2022.2600.

given not having undertaken an international obligation to do so. The Polish courts have not yet judged such types of crimes independently, though the NTN, as has already been noted (see Subchapter 3.5.2.) dynamically interpreted the German policies as genocide, before the adoption of Resolution 96(1) and the coming into force of the Genocide Convention. By way of example, one could mention the trial of Amon Göth, in which the policy of extermination was expressly termed, 'genocide,[99] or the judgment in the trial of Höss, in which it was noted that the greatest genocide in the history of humanity had taken place at the camp in Birkenau.[100] Notable more recent cases, on the other hand, include the order of the Regional Court in Warsaw, which, after the acceptance of the transfer of Radislav Krstić's sentence from the ICTY to be served in Poland, had to determine the classification of the act according to Polish law, as well as the penalty and punitive measure to be served.[101] The Court determined that one of the acts fulfilled the elements of Article 118 of the Criminal Code.

Article 118a of the Criminal Code regulates crimes against humanity, the elements of which are different from those of the crime of genocide. However, it should be noted that the law is not necessarily consistent in treating the two crimes separately. In the Act on the Institute of National Remembrance, genocide falls within the definition of crime against humanity, which, after a fashion, copies the definition from the Convention on the Non-Applicability of Statutory Limitations. The consequences of this situation could include interpretative problems with the applicability of statutes of limitations with regard to those crimes, because neither Article 43 of the Constitution, nor Article 105(1) of the Criminal Code, which discuss statutes of limitations, make any direct reference to the crime of genocide. Because of the different premises, it would be difficult to concur with the view that genocide represents a special form of crime against humanity;[102] however, perhaps the lawmaker may have been guided by that view and consequently not distinguished genocide within Article 43.

This raises some doubts in the light of Article 55(3) of the Constitution, which mentions genocide in the context of extradition, although that is a provision added only by an amendment from 2006.[103] As regards Article 105 of the Criminal Code, which does not make an explicit mention of genocide,

99 Klafkowski (1968a): 17; NTN, Göth: 26–27.
100 NTN, Höss: 111; NTN, Auschwitz staff: 179.
101 Order of the Regional Court in Warsaw, 26.05.2014, VIII Kop 49/14.
102 Sroka (2016): 1077; Banasik (2011): 70.
103 Dz.U.2006.200.1471.

either, but notes the inapplicability of statutes of limitations to crimes against peace, crimes against humanity and war crimes – in this context, it will be fitting to refer to the title of Chapter XVI: of the Criminal Code in which Article 118 is situated: 'Crimes against peace, crimes against humanity and war crimes.' As observed by Banasik:

> The express exclusion of statutes of limitations with regard to crimes against humanity, as well as systemic interpretation referred to the wording of Article 105(1) of the Criminal Code and the title of Chapter XVI of the Criminal Code, imply that the crime of genocide is ineligible for statutes of limitations, which prompts the conclusion that the international criminal law regulation of statutory limitations is consistent with the norms decoded from Polish provisions.[104]

Given the above doubts concerning statutes of limitations and the separation of genocide from crimes against humanity, it is worth noting that – due to the operation of the provisions of the Rome Statute, to which Poland is party – the crimes covered by the jurisdiction of that court are excluded from statutes of limitations (which thus applies also to genocide, in the scope in which it is defined by the Statute), and in the event of a conflict with the Criminal Code, the provisions of the Rome Statute will take precedence. Thus, it would be a fitting recommendation to enact amendments to the Constitution and to the Criminal Code to account for the separation of the two categories of crimes. Doing so would result in a more complete reflection of the ICC Statute in Poland's legal system.

7 Polish Scholarship

The most important works on genocide include: Jerzy Sawicki, *Ludobójstwo od pojęcia do konwencji 1933–1948* (1949) ('Genocide, from the term to the convention, 1933–1948'); Czesław Pilichowski (ed.), *Zbrodnie i sprawcy: ludobójstwo hitlerowskie przed sądem ludzkości i historii* (1980b) ('Crimes and criminals: Nazi genocide before the court of humanity and history'); Krystyna Daszkiewicz, *Niemieckie ludobójstwo na narodzie polskim (1939–1945)* (2009) ('The German genocide on the Polish nation (1939–1945)'); Karolina Wierczyńska, *Pojęcie ludobójstwa w kontekście orzecznictwa*

104 Banasik (2011): 70.

międzynarodowych trybunałów karnych ad hoc (2010) ('The term genocide in the context of the *ad hoc* international criminal tribunals'); Dominika Dróżdż, *Zbrodnia ludobójstwa w międzynarodowym prawie karnym* (2010) ('The Crime of genocide in international criminal law'); Lech M. Nijakowski, Urszula Markowska-Manista, Beata Machul-Telus (ed.), *Krwawy cień genocydu: interdyscyplinarne studia nad ludobójstwem* (2011) ('The bloodied shadow of genocide: interdisciplinary studies into genocide'); Tomasz Iwanek, *Zbrodnia ludobójstwa i zbrodnie przeciwko ludzkości* (2015) ('The crime of genocide and crimes against humanity'); Agnieszka Zielińska, *Hate media wobec ludobójstwa w Rwandzie w 1994 roku* (2018) ('Hate media and the genocide in Rwanda in 1994'). Lemkin's canonical *Axis Rule in Occupied Europe* have been translated as *Rządy państw Osi w okupowanej Europie* (2013). Apart from works in international law, a number of works have been written in sociology, history, political science or philosophy on the subject of genocide.[105]

8 Conclusions

There can be no doubt that Lemkin played a key role in the introduction of the new term 'genocide' and thereafter in successfully pressing for the adoption of an UNGA resolution on the matter, followed by the Genocide Convention. His stubbornness and determination resulted in the international community's commencement of works on those documents. One has to take a critical view of the ultimate lack of regulation referring to cultural genocide in the Convention, despite the Polish delegates' consistent advocacy of its inclusion. Here, it is worth noting that even though the idea of the creation of a permanent ICC had not been supported by the Polish diplomats during the works on the Convention, Poland's position prior to the outbreak of World War II had been different. The initiatives undertaken by Rappaport, Lemkin and Glaser under the banner of unification of criminal law (see Subchapter 1.1.3) had the goal of the creation of a permanent court. In the aftermath of the war, the Poles also actively supported the activities of the Nuremberg tribunal. Thus, one can wonder at the cautious approach to the drafting of the Genocide

105 Deserving of particular attention here are the works of Lech Nijakowski, *Rozkosz zemsty: socjologia historyczna mobilizacji ludobójczej* (2013) ('The bliss of revenge: historical sociology of genocidal mobilization') and Zygmunt Bauman, *Modernity and the Holocaust* (2002).

Convention, with Lachs and Rudziński criticizing the inclusion of provisions for the jurisdiction of the ICC. It would scarcely be possible, however, not to make the connection between that position and the political and economic dependence of Poland on the USSR at the time. Interestingly, during the works on the Convention, Lemkin himself did not regard the establishment of a court as necessary in the context of the Convention but had come to terms with the 'function' of France as the host of the conference with the appurtenant right to propose such a solution.

CHAPTER 10

Statutory Limitations on the International Crimes

1 Polish Initiatives for the Non-applicability of Statutory Limitations

One of the most burning issues for Poland in the aftermath of WWII was to bring the Nazi crimes to judgment.[1] It turned out rather soon that statutes of limitations would present a problem.[2] Although international law did not regulate the question of the statutory limitations, a great number of domestic legal systems prescribed short limitation periods even for major crimes. For example, the German provisions stipulated only several years (5 or 10) even for Nazi crimes of the highest order of gravity, with war criminals treated on par with perpetrators of common crime.[3]

Poland took notice of the problem of statutes of limitations very soon after the war and spoke on the matter of the statutes of limitations running on the crimes in the Federal Republic of Germany already in 1960, in connection with the anticipated prescription on 8 May of crimes punishable by up to fifteen years' imprisonment (excluding homicide and certain other offences).[4] The Polish authorities pointed out the German authorities' tardiness with the prosecutions, noting that many of the criminals would outright avoid any bearing responsibility for the commission of crimes never before confronted by civilized societies.[5] Prescription was only one of the problems coming to the fore. The Allied states (including the German Democratic Republic), however, were intent on continuing with the trials,[6] and statutes of limitations could pose a bar to that, which could, for example, lead to denial of extradition requests.

A debate was ongoing in Germany, as well, with a new generation in power having no ties whatsoever to the Nazi regime, resulting in the open

1 This is reflected by the efforts undertaken already in the course of World War II, such as the Polish participation in the works of the UNWCC; see also Kochavi (1998): 231.

2 Grosescu (2019): 242.

3 Weinschenk (1997): 144; extensively on the German regulations see: Daszkiewicz (1970), (1972); Marszał (1972): 33ff., 209ff.; Klafkowski (1968b): 159; Pilichowski (1978): 27–42.

4 Symonides (1980): 25–34.

5 Klafkowski (1968b): 172ff.

6 Graven (1966): 396.

and critical discussion of the hypothetical amnesty effect on the perpetrators of the crimes.[7]

The topic of statutes of limitations on Nazi crimes continued its presence in academic discourse since the early 60s of the 20th century. Between 5–7.06.1964, on the initiative of the Polish Lawyers' Association,[8] an international conference was held in Warsaw to draw attention to the problem of statutory limitations on international crimes. That was the first international debate on the issue.[9] The conclusion adopted by the conference clearly specified that while common crimes should prescribe in domestic law for the good of all, which was regulated variously depending on the gravity of the crime, prescription should not be applicable to international crimes. There was no regulation allowing the prescription of crimes to be viewed as a universal principle; rather, prescription was applied on an exceptional basis. Attention was drawn also to the absence of any regulation on the prescription of crimes in international law.[10]

As a follow-up to the findings of the conference the French National Assembly adopted them in December 1964, proclaiming crimes against humanity to be incapable of prescription by their very nature, and the Consultative Assembly of the Council of Europe issued a recommendation on the necessity of the adoption of a convention on the non-applicability of statutory limitations.[11] The above clearly demonstrates that not only Poland had been determined to punish the perpetrators of the crimes of the World War II period.

In March 1965, Stefan Glaser published in the *Revue de droit pénal et de criminologie* a foundational article titled *Quelques observations sur la prescription en matiére de la criminalité de guerre*, in the conclusions of which he emphasized:

---

7 Weinschenk (1997): 146. On 10.03.1965 The Bundestag eventually decided, by a significant majority of the vote, to prevent murder from prescribing for another 5 years, until 1.01.1970. Extensions continued in later years, as will be discussed below, and the crime of genocide was excluded from prescription.

8 The congress was attended by Alfons Klafkowski and Mieczysław Maneli (vice-dean of the Faculty of Law and Administration of the University of Warsaw, who emigrated in 1968); members of the Association itself included Maria Regent-Lechowicz, who subsequently participated in the works on the Convention on Non-Applicability of Statutory Limitations and wrote publications on the topic: Regent-Lechowicz (1968).

9 Grosescu (2019): 242–243.

10 More on the conference and its assumptions: Rolland (1965).

11 Rolland (1965).

> Etant donné que dans le cas d'infractions d'ordre international il ne s'agit pas d'un prejudice porté aux intéréts ou aux biens d'un certain État ou de ses ressortissants, mais aux intérêts ou aux biens de la communauté internationale, il nous semble que le problème de la prescription à l'égard de ce genre d'infraction ne devraient pas être du resort des états particuliers. De même que la droit de grâce, la matière concernant la prescription même également devrait être ici du ressort du droit international, et c'est ainsi qu'il nous paraît souhaitable qu'une convention internationale en cette matière soit conclue dans un proche avenir.[12]

Glaser, who is probably on account of those conclusions reputed as the father of the convention,[13] was a prominent advocate of the establishment of a principle of non-prescribability of international crimes. He took an active participation in the works of the AIDP, in which – at the beginning of 1965 – the decision was made to prepare and distribute a questionnaire survey among the members of the association, specialists in international criminal law, to solicit answers to questions dealing with the prescription and non-prescription of crimes against peace and crimes against humanity.[14] The answers[15] were published in issue 3–4 of the *Revue Internationale de Droit Pénal* of 1966. The survey provided the opportunity to source the opinions of the most eminent experts well-versed in the literature of the time. From Poland, Jerzy Sawicki replied in co-operation with Leszek Kubicki; Stefan Glaser also sent his own reply. Glaser and Sawicki, among others, believed it to be necessary for the principle of non-prescription of the crimes to be regulated on a convention level.[16] Glaser was not in favour of the inclusion of provisions on statutes of limitations in other, detailed conventions.[17] Likewise, Sawicki believed that the provisions excluding statutes of limitations should be grouped in a single convention and cover certain crimes.[18] Both gave similar answers that the principle of non-applicability of statutory limitations should be proclaimed in international law.[19]

---

12 Glaser (1965): 530.

13 Cieślak (1985): 106, similarily Kubicki, interview of 13.01.2020, in the authors' possession.

14 Graven (1966): 393–450, 394, 401.

15 *Ibidem*: 393–450, 401.

16 Glaser (1966): 475; Sawicki (1966): 554.

17 Glaser (1966): 475.

18 Sawicki (1966): 554.

19 Sawicki (1966): 556; Glaser (1966): 480–481.

In connection with the anticipated prescription of Nazi crimes in numerous countries, Poland initiated works on the topic at the United Nations. In the 21st session of the CHR, Poland pointed out the need to prevent the impunity of such perpetrators as had not been apprehended to date and accordingly proposed to commence works on a convention to regulate the non-applicability of statutes of limitations to the crimes.

In 1965, already before the ILC meeting, Poland prepared a memorandum and a draft resolution[20] dealing with the problem of bringing war criminals to judgment. At the United Nations, they were submitted on 5.03.1965 by Bohdan Lewandowski, the permanent representative of the Polish People's Republic at UN at the time. The Commission concurred with the Polish initiative, as many states saw the problem. France proposed to extend the problem also to crimes against humanity, not only war crimes as indicated by the Polish memorandum, and the suggestion was accepted.[21]

The Polish memorandum referred to the situation in the Federal Republic of Germany, where on 8.05.1965 prescription was anticipated to run its course on aggravated murders. It also noted Poland's adoption of the Act of 22.04.1964 on Halting the Course of Prescription in Respect of the Perpetrators of the Gravest Nazi Crimes Committed in the Period of the WWII, which came into force on the day of publication. The Act was very concise. It contained only a single article dealing with the merits and a short preamble specifying the purpose of its adoption, which was to prevent the avoidance of criminal responsibility by those Nazi criminals who had committed the gravest crimes during World War II. In its Article 1, the Act stopped prescription in its course on those perpetrators of the crimes specified in the so-called August Decree in respect of whom proceedings had not been brought due to the non-detection or non-apprehension of the perpetrator or due to the non-extradition of a perpetrator staying abroad.[22] Unquestionably, the Polish statute, being one of the first documents relating to the matter, constitutes an addition Polish contribution to the development of international criminal law with regard to the prosecution of the perpetrators of international crimes. It also provided the impulse for the other states to take similar actions.

20 The Question of Punishment of War Criminals, Communication from the Permanent Representative of Poland to the United Nations, UN Doc. E/CN. 4/885.

21 *Ibidem*: 7.

22 Dz.U.1964.15.86.

2 Participation of Poles in the Works of UN Bodies

In the aforementioned draft resolution tabled by Lewandowski, Poland proposed that the Commission on Human Rights – having regard to the use by some states of the institution of prescription on the crimes and the fact that many perpetrators of Nazi crimes had not yet been apprehended and judged – call on all states not having yet done so to continue their efforts for all war criminals guilty of crimes committed during World War II to be apprehended and punished by the competent courts, and to adopt the necessary measures to prevent the termination of the prosecution of those crimes, and also to accede to the Genocide Convention of 1948.[23]

Most importantly, however, the proposed resolution included the suggestion for the following session to consider the adoption on a convention on the non-applicability of statutes of limitations to grave crimes.[24] The latter proposal did not find its way to the final text of the resolution but was accepted a year later.

The CHR adopted Resolution 3(XXI) on 9.04.1965. The Resolution proclaimed that the United Nations had to contribute to the resolution of the problems arising after the commission of war crimes and crimes against humanity and especially to study possible solutions to establish a principle that prescription was not to apply to such crimes in international law. The resolution also incorporated a request to the ECOSOC to admonish the states to continue in their efforts to prosecute the criminals and bring them to judgment before the competent courts. The issue of the ratification by the states of Genocide Convention was also raised. The resolution included, among other things, the obligation for the UN Secretary General to prepare a study concerning the prescription of war crimes and crimes against humanity.

The Secretary General's study submitted in February 1966[25] was based, among other sources, on information and communications from several dozen states,[26] including Poland. It referred not only to the non-application of statutes of limitations to war crimes or crimes against humanity but

23 UN Doc. E/CN. 4/885.

24 Question of punishment of war criminals and of persons who have committed crimes against humanity, E/4024 E/CN, 4/891, 133; the works on the future convention are described by: Symonides (1980), Resich (1969), and Dąbrowa (1971) and Pilichowski (1971b).

25 UN Doc. E/CN.4/906.

26 Klafkowski (1968b): 175ff.

also to crimes against peace, which was found to be necessary in order to ensure the thoroughness of the study, especially as those crimes had been mentioned in the IMT Charter. The study also observed that statutes of limitations should not be applicable to the crime of genocide, emphasizing, among others, that the Convention appeared to exclude any possibility of a prescription period.[27]

In the CHR, where the problem of statutes of limitations was discussed, Poland was represented by Zbigniew Resich and Sławomir Dąbrowa.[28] The report of the 22th session of the Commission included the resolution of which the adoption had been recommended by Poland at the time, referring to the Secretary General's study and mentioning the necessity of the United Nations' making of an effort to resolve the problems relating to the judgment of war crimes and crimes against humanity, and especially to contribute to the introduction of the just principle that there should be no period of limitation in international law for such crimes.[29]

In August 1966, the ECOSOC issued a resolution[30] largely copying the Polish proposals with only editorial changes. It emphasized the necessity of affirming that statutes of limitations should not apply to war crimes and crimes against humanity, and encouraged the states to continue in their efforts to arrest, extradite and judge those guilty of the crimes. The ECOSOC requested the Commission to prepare a draft convention for the 23th session of the Commission and requested the Secretary General's co-operation in that regard. The working group to analyse the draft convention prepared by the Secretary General with suggestions from the debate included Maria Regent-Lechowicz.

In the 23rd session of the Commission, Poland proposed to adopt another resolution intended to ask the Secretary General to invite all states to share their opinions on the codification of the principles applicable to the crimes in international law, in particular how the matter should be addressed in that regard outside of the convention on the non-applicability of statutory limitations and it what form the matter should be embodied (e.g. convention or declaration).[31] Many states were, however, diffident with their comments on the Polish proposal of a broader codification.

27 UN Doc. E/CN.4/906, §§184–190.

28 Besides him, Poland was represented in the works on the Convention at the UN by Maria Regent-Lechowicz and Władysław Neneman.

29 UN Doc. E/CN.4/916, 55.

30 UN Doc. E/RES/1158(XLI).

31 UN Doc. E/4322, E/CN.4/940, 54.

Some noted that the codification mentioned in the request would be a highly complex task requiring the investment of a great deal of time. Their concern was also that the attention given to the issue could have an adverse effect on the matter of the urgent preparation of a convention on the non-applicability of statutory limitations. In their opinion, the adoption of that convention could be seriously endangered if that specific point were to be linked to the problem of undertaking the works on the codification mentioned in the Polish draft resolution.[32] As a result, Poland agreed to postpone the debate on the subject of a codification of the crimes of international law.

In March 1968, in the 24th session of the Commission, Poland once again proposed the adoption of the resolution. The suggestion was for the CHR to request the Secretary General to submit a study on guaranteeing that those responsible for war crimes and crimes against humanity would be arrested, extradited and punished, as well as the exchange of documentation and inclusion of a study dealing with the mater of appropriate compensation for the victims of the crimes.[33] In the opinion of the Polish representatives, the matter of appropriate compensation was an extraordinarily pressing issue demanding, 'urgent and careful study,' as the majority of the victims of Nazi terror had not yet received any compensation.[34]

The CHR Resolution no. 13(XXIV) diverged only to an insignificant extent from the Polish draft, observing that the Secretary General's study should consider the matter of the determination of the criteria for the assessment of compensation for victims of war crimes and crimes against humanity.[35] One year later, in the 25th session, already after the adoption of the Convention, the Secretary General submitted to the Commission a study as regards ensuring the arrest, extradition and punishment of persons responsible for war crimes and crimes against humanity and the exchange of documentation relating thereto, together with remarks on the criteria for the determination of compensation for victims of such crimes. Poland (at that time, together with the USSR) suggested the adoption of another resolution, submitting to deliberation the thought that the ECOSOC should recommend to the UNGA the adoption of a resolution calling on the states to adopt measures enabling the detection of war crimes and crimes against humanity, as well as arrests and extraditions of those guilty of the crimes, and calling

32 *Ibidem.*

33 UN Doc. E/4475, E/CN.4/972: 118.

34 *Ibidem*: 121.

35 *Ibidem*: 159.

on the states to adopt a convention on the non-applicability of statutory limitations.

As for the CHR, it was to address a request to the Secretary General for the preparation of a more complete study after sourcing information from the states on the criteria for the determination of compensation for victims of war crimes and crimes against humanity.[36] Those proposals, which would have allowed the matter of the punishment of those responsible for the crimes to be dealt with in more detail, were defeated in the states' discussion.[37]

In the Secretary General's report prepared on the basis of the resolution, Poland raised the matter not only of judgment for the perpetrators but also compensation for the victims, which had not yet been regulated by international law, as was observed.[38] Poland also highlighted the principles that should be followed in the determination of compensation, mentioning, among others, the non-prescribability to claims for compensation for crimes.[39] The problem of compensation for the crimes committed has to this day not been resolved in international law.

During the next, 26th session, Poland (once again together with the USSR) proposed the adoption of a resolution expressing deep concern with the continued commission of war crimes and crimes against humanity in modern circumstances in various parts of the world: 'as a consequence of aggressive wars and politics and practices of racism, apartheid and colonialism, as well as other similar ideologies and practices.' The term 'aggressive war' was criticized as being insufficient because, according to the representatives of certain states, international law called for the condemnation of all wars. Several representatives also expressed the view that the resolution would not have much sense, were it to refer only to offences committed in the past. According to them, it was imperative for the UN to offer a firm

36 UN Doc. E/4621, E/CN.4/1007: 82ff.

37 *Ibidem*: 186.

38 UN Doc. E/CN.4/1010: 35–42. That was a very current problem in the Polish politics of the time, due to the perspective of establishing relations with the Federal Republic of Germany. Intensified gathering of documentation to provide the basis for talks on compensations for the effects of World War II took place. After several rounds of such talks, Prime Minister Cyrankiewicz appointed on 6.05.1970 a Commission for the Study of the Problem of German Compensation, led by Zbigniew Resich with Czesław Pilichowski as his deputy; see: https://inwentarz.ipn.gov.pl/archivalCollection?id_a=15924.

39 UN Doc. E/CN.4/1010, 24.11.1969: 40–42. See: Dąbrowa (1971): 35.

condemnation of all wars.[40] Some states objected the wording of Article 1, which dealt with the non-prescribability of the crimes and had already been adopted in the Convention, on the grounds of imprecision in the definitions of war crimes and crimes against humanity.[41] The contention was mainly that the definitions of crimes against humanity had been extended too far compared to the IMT Charter.

In the end, not one of the aforementioned Polish proposals was incorporated in the resolution.[42] In the following session, Poland once again (together with the USSR) proposed to adopt a resolution in connection with the coming into force on 11.11.1970 of the Convention on the Non-Applicability of Statutory Limitations. At that time, the Polish-Soviet draft resolution was adopted almost without discussion. The resolution mentions the adopted Convention, UNGA Resolution no. 2712(xxv),[43] where attention was drawn to the fact that many criminals were avoiding prosecution under the protection of certain states. Emphasis was also placed on the need to make efforts on behalf of the extradition of criminals and their judgment in the states in whose territories the crimes had been committed, as well as the states' duty to intensify their activities for the detection, apprehension, extradition and judgment of the perpetrators; it was noted that the states should also adopt the Convention on the Non-Applicability of Statutory Limitations.

In subsequent sessions, the Commission's active interest in the matter of the punishment of war criminals was minimal,[44] and in 1972, Poland's term in the CHR ended.

3 The Coming into Force of the Convention

The Convention on the Non-Applicability of Statutory Limitations to War Crimes and Crimes Against Humanity was adopted in the UNGA session on 26.11.1968[45] and came into force on 11.11.1970, upon gaining ten ratifications. In accordance with its Article 8. Poland signed the treaty on 16.12.1968 but ratified it on 14.02.1969, being the first state to do so. Poland also submitted

40 UN Doc. E/4816, E/CN.4/1039: 14.
41 *Ibidem*: 15; see also: Grosescu (2019): 254ff.
42 UN Doc. E/4816, E/CN.4/1039, 76.
43 GA Res. 2712(1970).
44 UN Doc. E/4949, E/CN.4/1068, 62.
45 GA Res. 2391(1968).

reservations[46] to Articles V and VII of the Convention, as to what states could become parties to the Convention. At that time, membership in the UN was not universal among the states, and the provisions referred to states already belonging to the UN or one of the specialized agencies, or of the ICJ. That, according to Poland, was discriminatory. Just as had been the case during the works on the Genocide Convention, Poland consistently advocated for the dependent territories. At present, due to almost all states being party to the United Nations and thus eligible to acceded to the Convention, the problem no longer exists.

Although there are only 56 states party to the Convention, many non-party states have adopted provisions for the non-applicability of statutory limitations to the relevant crimes in their domestic legal systems.[47]

The European Convention on the Non-Applicability of Statutory Limitation to Crimes against Humanity and War Crimes, adopted in 1974,[48] had even less luck. It entered into force in 2003, having gained three ratifications, but until now the number of states party does not exceed 10, and Poland is not among them. It is, moreover, worth emphasizing that Article 29 of the ICC Statute[49] excludes the applicability of statutory limitations to the most serious crimes specified in that document. As the Statute currently enjoys 124 states party, it is not difficult to draw the conclusion that many of those, despite not having acceded to the Convention on the Non-Applicability of Statutory Limitations, are still bound by the obligation to prevent the prescription of the most serious crimes under the Rome Statute.

It will be expedient to note, however, with regard to the adoption of the UN Convention on the Non-Applicability of Statutory Limitations, that Poland has undertaken the mission of convincing other states to ratify the Convention. As recounted by Symonides, the Poles were not only active in the UN forum but also endeavoured to lobby for the new convention elsewhere; Symonides underscored the Polish participation in the

46 'The Polish People's Republic considers that the dispositions of articles V and VII of the Convention on the Non-Applicability of Statutory Limitations to War Crimes and Crimes against Humanity, adopted by the General Assembly on the 26th of November 1968, make it impossible for a number of States to become parties to the Convention and are therefore of a discriminatory character which is contradictory to the object and aims of this Convention. The Polish People's Republic is of the opinion that, in accordance with the principle of sovereign equality of States, the Convention should be open to all States without any discrimination and limitation.'

47 Kok (2007); Grosescu (2019): 251ff.

48 ETS No. 082, accepted on 25.01.1974, entered into force on 27.06.2003.

49 Dz.U.2003.78.708.

subsequent conferences in Warsaw (1967), Moscow (1969) and Frankfurt am Main (1969).[50]

Near the end of the 70s of the 20th century, Polish initiatives on behalf of the non-prescription of war crimes and crimes against humanity were visible mostly on the intergovernmental level. The then-justice minister, Jerzy Bafia, raised the issue of statutes of limitations during official visits both to the German Democratic Republic and to the Federal Republic of Germany, as well as in the joint conference of ministers of justice of the socialist states in Berlin, in 1978. The appeal for the exclusion of prescription with regard to the Nazi war crimes and crimes against humanity, drafted by the Chief Commission for the Investigation of Nazi Crimes in Poland, was an important Polish voice. The appeal, expounding the necessity of the adoption of the principle of time-unlimited prosecution of the crimes, was widely circulated by the Polish justice minister, to, among others, the Western states, UNESCO, UNICEF, non-governmental organizations, and the prosecutor general's offices of the socialist states. It resonated broadly in Western press,[51] and the activities of the Chief Commission's director, Czesław Pilichowski, found an echo as well.[52]

Germany acceded to the Convention on the Non-Applicability of Statutory Limitations in 1973. Nevertheless, many suspected criminals never faced the domestic justice system.[53] As a result of international pressure, on 3.07.1979, the German parliament adopted an amendment to the Criminal Code, excluding the applicability of statutes of limitations to the crimes under §220a, genocide, and §211, aggravated murder, as well as enabling the time-unlimited prosecution of suspects in the gravest crimes. The statute of 2002 introducing the Code Against International Crimes (*Völkerstrafgesetzbuch*), provides for the non-application of statutes of limitations to any international crimes committed in the future.[54]

50 Symonides (1980): 29–30.

51 *Ibidem*: 32.

52 Monson (1982): 618.

53 The German historians, Hans-Christian Jasch and Wolf Kaiser, conclude that the vast majority of German criminals have avoided punishment for war crimes, extensively: Jasch, Kaiser (2018), also: Monson (1982): 619.

54 BGBL. I S. 2254, Act to Introduce the Code of Crimes against International Law of 26.06.2002 https://casebook.icrc.org/case-study/germany-international-criminal-code; also: Krzan (2022): 29.

4 Polish Legislation

As mentioned on 22.04.1964, Poland adopted the act on halting the course of prescription in relation to the perpetrators of the gravest crimes committed during the WWII. Chapter XIV of the Criminal Code of 1969[55] included provisions relating to prescription, such as Article 105(1)(1), which provided for a twenty-year limitation period on the punishability of felonies with the lower sentencing limit of three years' imprisonment or higher, whereas the provisions of the Code of Criminal Procedure[56] regarded prescription as a procedural obstacle, due to which no new proceedings were to be brought and pending proceedings were to be discontinued once the statute of limitations had run its course. The 1969 Code excluded the applicability of statutes of limitations to international crimes. Its Article 109 provided for the exclusion of war crimes and crimes against humanity from the statutes of limitations.

The Criminal Code of 1997 also contains a whole chapter devoted to statutes of limitations (XI), wherein Article 105 stipulates their non-applicability to crimes against peace, crimes against humanity, and war crimes.

As noted above (Subchapter 9.6), a similar underlying assumption is manifested in the Polish Constitution. Its Article 43[57] proclaims the exclusion of war crimes and crimes against humanity from statutes of limitations; genocide is dealt with as a qualified form of crime against humanity. A very interesting wording has been given to Article 44: 'The statute of limitation regarding actions connected with offences committed by, or by order of, public officials and which have not been prosecuted for political reasons, shall be extended for the period during which such reasons existed.' It envisions the possibility of holding e.g. the President or ministers responsible. In principle, previous constitutions did not regulate the matter of statutes of limitations. The non-prescribability of war crimes and crimes against humanity is also regulated by the Act on the Institute of National Remembrance (IPN) (see more: Subchapter 4.5).

55 Dz.U.1969.13.94.
56 Dz.U.1969.13.96.
57 Dz.U.1997.78.483.

5 Conclusions

The efforts of Resich, Regent-Lechowicz, Dąbrowa and others in the UN bodies, as well as Glaser and Sawicki in the AIDP, have led to the adoption of the Convention on the Non-Applicability of Statutory Limitations. When summarizing Poland's UN activities at the time, it is an easy conclusion to make that, although they referred to Poland and the postwar situation of Polish citizens, they also had a broader universal perspective. The principle of non-prescribability of international crimes and the necessity of judging them and paying compensation for them are the goals the international community should promote tirelessly, as the states confront these problems after every armed conflict. From the above perspective, Poland has not only campaigned for her own interests but also the interests of the international community as a whole. The matter of compensation for the crimes has to this day not been regulated in international law.

CHAPTER 11

Criminal Jurisdiction and Its Exercise

1 The Relationship between Individual and State Responsibility

The discussion of the relationship between the responsibility of the state and that of the individual has a long history, which intensified especially in the aftermath of WWII. Authors having written on state responsibility include Hersch Lauterpacht. The topic has gained its greatest influence thanks to inclusion in the seventh edition of originally Lassa Oppenheim's treaty on international law, edited by Lauterpacht,[1] and in the monograph titled *International Law and Human Rights* (1950).

An additional impulse for the consideration of topic came from the ILC's works on state responsibility, both on the occasion of the report submitted by the Commission's first rapporteur, Francisco V. Garcia-Amador,[2] and in the 70s of the 20th century, with regard to the celebrated draft of Article 19 of Roberto Ago's *Draft articles on Responsibility of States for Internationally Wrongful Acts*. The activities of both of the special rapporteurs coincided with a period in which the Commission did not have a Polish member.

The finalization of the works – an unquestionable success of James Crawford – occurred during the ILC membership of Zdzisław Galicki. The Polish professor voiced his doubts as to the possibility of holding heads of states responsible before an international criminal court, for which reason he suggested putting the discussion of state crimes temporarily on hold.[3] In the course of the later discussions, Galicki came to view Article 19 of the *Draft articles* as the greatest enemy of the concept.[4]

In state comments, Poland expressed satisfaction with the inclusion in the *Draft articles* of reference to individual criminal responsibility.[5]

To Polish scholarship, the topic of international responsibility has been the object of fascination for a long time. Authors publishing in-depth studies

1 Lauterpacht (1948): 321, (1952): 567. Cf. Symonides (1971): 63.

2 YILC (1957), vol. 1: 157.

3 Summary records of the meetings of the fiftieth session, Summary record of the 2534th meeting: 114.

4 Summary record of the 2540th meeting: 154–155.

5 UN Doc. A/CN.4/515 and Add.1–3 Comments and observations received from Governments, YILC (2001), vol. II(1): 95.

 DOI:10.1163/9789004712690_013

in the former half of the 20th century included Rundstein and Król, who, however, focused primarily on the responsibility of states. That was a consequence of the problem of international subjecthood; not being a subject of international law, the individual was not a particularly interesting subject of study. It will be fitting to mention here Cezary Berezowski's Hague lecture under the title of *Les sujets nonsouverains du droit international*.[6] Although the view denying international subjecthood to individuals continued to prevail for decades to come, it is worth noting the important findings of a study titled *Czy jednostki są podmiotami prawa międzynarodowego?* ('Are individuals subjects of international law?') by Witold W. Warkałło[7] or the more globally influential findings of Marek Stanisław Korowicz.[8]

It was universally believed that because only states were subjects of international law, only states could consequently be the subjects of criminal offences in international law. Ehrlich, in turn, proclaimed the theory recognizing in the individual a subject of international law to be the music of the future. As was persuasively argued in a study bearing the signature of Zenon Goryński: 'the existence of international criminal law cannot be seriously questioned because of the individual's not having been universally recognized as a subject of international criminal law.'[9] On the other hand, he stipulated the caveat that taking on the topic of the collective responsibility of the German nation would constitute a foray into politics.[10]

In Józef Giebułtowicz's opinion, the perpetrator of a war crime could be, depending on the specific type of the offence, either the state as a whole or an individual, alternatively a group of individuals. He accentuated the difficulties with the separation of the two circles of potential subjects and wondered to what extent an individual could act in a functional abstraction from the state. In his opinion: 'the role of individuals as subjects of law is restricted in international relations to that the state, as an abstract legal creation, cannot act without the individual as the messenger or executive organ of that will.'[11] In a later part of his reasoning, he concluded: 'the construct of attribution to the state (…) of the character of a criminal offender may incur reservations due to the association of personal criminal

6 Berezowski (1938).

7 Warkałło (1932).

8 Korowicz (1938), and, above all, Korowicz (1959).

9 Goryński (1944): 39.

10 *Ibidem*: 11.

11 Giebułtowicz (1945): 40.

responsibility with the term.'[12] The basis for the narrowing down of the offender's criminal responsibility may come from the applicable domestic system of criminal law.[13] As opposed to states (only capable of material responsibility), individuals could be held responsible under domestic provisions either civilly (materially) or criminally. The material responsibility could turn out to be a fiction, so criminal responsibility remained.

In Polish scholarship, the theory of state criminal responsibility had an ardent supporter first and foremost in Emil Stanisław Rappaport. Already in 1930, he wrote about the renascence of the: 'question of responsibility not only civil, also before everything else criminal, not only of individuals but of collectives – legal persons, and in particular states, for any attempts on the new *Pax Mundi*, founded on the solidarity of strictly co-equal – greatest, large, small and tiniest – afterwar states.'[14] Echoes of that concept can be found subsequently with Hersch Lauterpacht, who, however, did not venture as far as Rappaport had. In 1945, Rappaport published a printed manifesto-monograph, *Naród-zbrodniarz* ('The nation-criminal'), in which he expounded his theory of the personal-collective responsibility of all Nazi Germany for the crime of aggressive war.[15]

That important work was met with a very critical reception. His theses were denounced as products of a fascination with Lombroso, even though one needs to render justice unto Rappaport and acknowledge that he addressed the plane of individual guilt and made the express proviso for the need to consider all doubts. In his published work, Rappaport saw error in the exclusive reliance on the individualistic concept of criminal responsibility, contradistinguished from collective responsibility. It will be expedient to quote his exact words:

> The new responsibility of all the Germans for the guilt of the criminal aggressive war under Hitler's command only amplifies the principle (minuscule exceptions to be accounted for prove the rule) of the personal responsibility of every German for their own guilt of either intentionally implementing or unintentionally tolerating all of the totalistic crimes tied to the conduct of that war.[16]

12 *Ibidem*: 44.

13 *Ibidem*: 70.

14 Rappaport (1930): 11.

15 Rappaport (1945).

16 *Ibidem*: 39.

He developed upon that thought and narrowed it down in the later parts of his book, incurring much criticism:

> Such plenary toleration of the collective crime of one's own Nation without a shade of even a secretly harboured objection is precisely, in the mildest terms, the unintentional backing of it and thus, in the present-day new understanding as expounded by me, assistance – punishable in the territory of international justice – in the crime of the German war aggression against the continuity of modern culture on both hemispheres of the world.[17]

Realizing the impossibility of punishing all Germans, Rappaport advocated for a: 'protective supervision with a view to a special personal-collective criminal pedagogy and prophylaxis,' explaining with more precision that what he had in mind was a: 'new influence, this time a positive one.'[18]

The above-cited position aligns with Rappaport's previously expressed view when he had been dealing critically with the treatment of the responsibility of legal persons as a purported return to: 'the most regressive, the most primitive epochs of criminal law, with its collective responsibility of a whole clan for the actions of an individual, member of the clan, directed against foreign individuals and clans.'[19] He acknowledged, of course, that the assignment of culpability for the attributed criminal act was tied to the concept of individuality, but also to international criminal law, to the extent necessary for the natural recognition of the acts of the individual natural persons connected with the criminal offences of collectives, i.e. specific states. In the last-mentioned context, he substituted for the repressive sanction a preventive one, i.e. protective measures (*środki zabezpieczające*) as: 'the only means of social defence proper with regard to criminal states.'[20] He professed the conviction that: 'the new sanction, the only sanction in the interstate criminal code when it comes to the crimes of collectives, will also align itself logically and harmoniously with the full picture of modern means of criminal prevention and repression.'[21] Rappaport saw an intelligent amalgamation of realism and idealism in Vespasian Pella's *La*

17 *Ibidem*: 40.
18 *Ibidem*: 45.
19 Rappaport (1930): 20.
20 *Ibidem*: 19.
21 *Ibidem*.

criminalité collective des Etats et le droit pénal de l'avenir, preceding the second edition.[22]

A strong hint as to the Polish position on the relationship between state responsibility and individual responsibility can be found in the opening speech delivered by prosecutor Jerzy Sawicki in the trial of Ludwig Fischer and others before the Supreme National Tribunal. He took on the problem of: 'when the judge has the right to lift the team veil and the obligation to move past the fiction of, "impersonal action"'. Borrowing from Fuller's thought, Sawicki concluded the above ought to be done: 'always (...) whenever the individual attempts to hide behind the screen of an impersonal criminal cartel, trust or other corporation,' mentioning the SS and the NSDAP in the context. Simultaneously, he made the following proviso:

> The prosecution will under no guise submit to the Tribunal's advisement the matter of the responsibility of the German nation as a whole and defendants as members of that nation. We do not extend the indictment as far as that, in the name of what I recognized as the equitable purpose of the law, because we do not recognize the inequality of people on account of origin or nationality. For such a disposition of the matter would comprise the eternal damnation of the Germans, their inability to lift themselves up. Such an indictment would, therefore, be merely the inversion of the principles applied to us by the defendants. Were we to be guided by such principles, we would have to demand the eternal damnation of a certain nation as a whole, which is incompatible with our worldview and belief. It is no accident that many of those who currently speak words of condemnation of the entire German nation had once been theorists of fascism – from their works the Nazis had drawn inspiration.[23]

The text of the NTN's judgment in Albert Forster's case, however, permits the observation that part A of the opinion[24] is limited solely to considerations of the state responsibility, which markedly demonstrates the difficulty of achieving the standard demanded by prosecutor Sawicki.

To Marian Muszkat, the collective criminal responsibility manifested by the concept of state criminal responsibility was a denial of elementary

22 Pella (1926): CXXIII–CXXV.

23 Cyprian, Sawicki, Siewierski (1962): 125–126.

24 NTN, Forster case: 268–274.

human rights.[25] He emphasized that a human person could not be held criminally responsible for the activities of a collective in which the membership is not dependent on the individual's will, even though the activities might be criminal. On that account, he postulated the expediency of the complete separation of the international criminal responsibility of an individual from the matter of the responsibility of the state, even for such a type of violation of international obligations as bore every mark of a criminal offence.[26]

In the view of Ludwik Gelberg and Stanisław Pławski, the concept of criminal responsibility of a state and nation was unrealistic, outright erroneous in law, and highly dangerous politically, as it struck a heavy blow against state sovereignty.[27]

A wider-ranging response was provoked by Stefan Glaser's analysis of the possibility of holding a state criminally responsible. On the basis of a systematic review of the literature, he distinguished three tendencies. In the first order, he invoked the prevailing theory of fiction, excluding – in line with the thought of Friedrich Carl von Savigny – the possibility of the commission of a delict by the state or, more specifically, the hypothetical responsibility of a legal person.[28] Next, citing the teachings of Otto von Gierke, he recalled the doctrine according to which the capacity to commit a delict, or even capacity for criminal responsibility, was admissible.[29] Last, Glaser described an intermediate position assuming the capacity of legal persons of a delict but excluding the criminal character of responsibility.[30] Himself, he excluded the responsibility of legal persons, regarding it as the upshot of collective criminal responsibility and maintaining that there could no punishment without culpability.[31] At last, Glaser allowed for the criminal responsibility of a state in connection with international crimes but only in the person of representatives or organs, not in a collective sense. With that, he opted solely for the individual criminal responsibility of the persons truly bearing the guilt, i.e. acting in the name and on behalf of the state. The state itself, on the other hand, as a corporate entity, could be held

25 Muszkat (1949): 308.
26 *Ibidem.*
27 Gelberg, Pławski (1950): 30.
28 Glaser (1949): 428.
29 *Ibidem*: 430.
30 *Ibidem*: 434.
31 *Ibidem*: 436ff.

civilly responsible or be the target of certain administrative measures.[32] At the same time, Glaser, excluded the possibility of invoking the act-of-state doctrine to justify the lack of individual responsibility of those acting on a state's behalf, which he viewed as incompatible with the ideal of justice and inadmissible from the perspective of modern international law.[33]

In his monograph *International Law and Human Rights*, a somewhat more recent publication, Hersch Lauterpacht embarked on proving that the original subject of an international obligation was the human factor, which gave motion to the criminal offence, while the criminal responsibility of the state was of only subsidiary nature.[34]

The most reverberating international echo belonged to Krystyna Marek's article titled *Criminalizing State Responsibility*, which she published in the *Revue Belge de Droit International*.[35] There, she emphasized that, in a contradistinction to contractual civil responsibility, criminal law evidently was not one of the branches of the law capable of serving as a reservoir for international law to draw new solutions or norms from.[36]

The cited author was of the opinion that international law did not have two systems of responsibility, one limited to reparations and one based on sanctions. In her opinion, there existed only one system covering both compensation and sanctions.[37] She recalled that the legal relationship between the parties arising from a tort had been replaced in domestic law with a relationship between the author of the unlawful act and the state vested with the central power and with the monopoly on adjudication and compulsion. The replacement of that orderly process with a relationship in international law between the author of the unlawful act and the indeterminate international community was tantamount not to the replacement of the wronged party by the state acting through its courts within all guarantees of the law but to an invitation to mob justice.[38] Marek also noted that a mechanism structured in such a way would provide the great powers with impunity.[39] It will be expedient, first and foremost, to quote the warning given by the eminent internationalist in her article:

32 *Ibidem*: 451–452.
33 Glaser (1950): 13.
34 Lauterpacht (1950): 43.
35 Marek (1978): 460.
36 *Ibidem*: 464
37 *Ibidem*: 479.
38 *Ibidem*: 481.
39 *Ibidem*: fn 81.

> Internarional law is a fragile legal order. The restraints it has built up, the institutions it has developed are the outcome of long, patient, difficult labours. Compared with municipal law, they remain modest and limited. But such as they are, they ensure a minimum of security and decency in international relations. It is the prime duty of those concerned with international law – scholars, statesmen and legislators alike – to improve or, at least, to preserve them, but certainly not to contribute to their progressive disintegration.[40]

The above is one of the most oft-cited legal arguments. Should one even regard Pierre Klein's enthusiasm[41] for Marek's article as an exaggeration, the absence of any reference to her work in the doctoral dissertation on the topic[42] or especially in the seventh report of special rapporteur Gaetano Arrangio-Ruiz on the international responsibility of states is legitimately surprising.[43] The above is not the only example of foreign literature's omission of the important findings of Polish authors.[44]

The essence of the matter was aptly encapsulated by Wojciech Radecki: from the commission of an international crime arises the international responsibility of an individual, whereas from the commission of a criminal offence punishable by virtue of international treaties but not constituting an international crime such responsibility does not arise in international law.[45]

Near the end of the 80s of 20th century, Stanisław Pławski prepared the French report for an AIDP questionnaire survey. With regard to the criminal responsibility of a state and the associated reservations, he accentuated state sovereignty and the responsibility of legal persons. As for the first reservation, he warned against embracing myths by operating on an understanding characteristic for authoritarian states viewing sovereignty as the

40 *Ibidem*: 483.

41 Klein (2015): 302.

42 Malekian (1985).

43 Seventh report on State responsibility, by Mr. Gaetano Arangio-Ruiz, Special Rapporteur, UN Doc. A/CN.4/469 and Add.1 and 2.

44 By way of a negative example, one could mention that the Polish authors cited in Bonafè's monograph *The Relationship Between State and Individual Responsibility for International Crimes* include, apart from Glaser, only the French-language work of Stanisław Plawski, *Etude des principes fondamentaux du droit international pénal*, and the study into reprisals by Remigiusz Bierzanek – see: Bierzanek (1980).

45 Radecki (1981): 29.

omnipotence of the state, capable of acting without any limitations whatsoever, with supreme egoism leading to manifest injustice. He invoked the example of the persecution of the Jews in the Interwar period, which, in the name of Germany's sovereignty in its own territory, was left unpunished. Despite the fulfilment of all of the elements of a crime against humanity, that persecution was not met with punishment by the Nuremberg tribunal for the sake of respecting the sovereignty of the Nazi state. Pławski noted, however, that the 19th-century understanding of sovereignty was no longer usable.[46] Concerning the responsibility of legal persons, Pławski cited the position of the defence in the Nuremberg trial, who raised the issue of state and head-of-state responsibility, which did not lead to the exemption of natural persons and criminal organizations from responsibility in the Tribunal's judgment. In Pławski's opinion, entering a criminal conviction against a state would be unjust and unrealistic. It would spark wars instead of protecting peace among the nations. He emphasized that every state had a right to defend itself from aggression but never to embark on a repressive war. State responsibility could not be transformed into government responsibility but only translate into the criminal responsibility of individuals.[47] The above aligns perfectly with the *dictum* of Nuremberg – according to the IMT:

> Crimes against international law are committed by men, not by abstract entities, and only by punishing individuals who commit such crimes can the provisions of international law be enforced. [...] individuals have international duties which transcend the national obligations of obedience imposed by the individual state.[48]

The consideration of the criminal responsibility of legal persons is usually grounded in the lack of individual will and, in the end, the lack of culpability as a necessary precondition of responsibility.[49] The above corresponds to attributing the capacity for the commission of an act exclusively to an individual. The criminal responsibility of collective entities (corporations) was discussed in the 2nd International Congress of Penal Law in Bucarest in

46 Pławski (1989): 568.

47 *Ibidem*: 569.

48 International Military Tribunal (Nuremberg), Judgment and Sentences, October 1, 1946 quoted after (1947) 41 AJIL 221.

49 Rogacka-Rzewnicka (2013): 214.

1929. Poland's national report for that congress was written by Mieczysław Ettinger.[50]

The IMT Charter did not adhere to the concept of criminal responsibility of states but permitted the indictment of groups and organizations. As emphasized by Gardocki, the IMT's recognition of a group or organization as criminal in nature (Article IX) constituted a *sui generis* corporate conviction, with far-reaching practical ramifications.[51] Namely, in accordance with Article X, it had the lawmaking effect of authorizing domestic or occupation courts to judge individuals for membership in such a group or organization alone. The second sentence of that Article reads: 'In any such case the criminal nature of the group or organisation is considered proved and shall not be questioned.'

No analogous construct was used in the proceedings before the Tokyo Tribunal or before the more recent international criminal tribunals; however, the IMT experience clearly affirms the possibility of judging subjects other than individuals.[52] Joanna Nowakowska-Małusecka, on the other hand, while analysing the creation of *ad hoc* tribunals, observed that restricting the jurisdiction to natural persons alone had not been so obvious in the light of the preceding exploration of the topic of the functioning of criminal organizations and criminal activities as grounds of responsibility for violations of humanitarian law.[53]

Lastly, the responsibility of legal persons is foreseen also by Article 10 of the United Nations Convention Against Transnational Organized Crime.[54] In accordance with sections 2 and 3 (respectively) of that Article, on terms set forth by the legal principles of the state party: 'the liability of legal persons may be criminal, civil or administrative,' and: 'shall be without prejudice to the criminal liability of the natural persons who have committed the offences.'

The problem of the responsibility of legal persons resurfaced in the negotiations of the International Convention on the Suppression and Punishment of the Crime of Apartheid.[55] The latter's Article III established the international criminal liability of, among others, members of organizations and institutions committing acts listed in Article II of the

50 Ettinger (1929): 141.
51 Gardocki (1985): 38ff.
52 Karski (2007): 244.
53 Nowakowska-Małusecka (2000): 58ff.
54 Dz.U.2005.158.18.
55 Dz.U.1976.186.32.

Convention, who participate in such acts and incite them directly or conspire to commit them or support, encourage or co-operate in the crime of apartheid.

Lastly, one must note the overview and recapitulation of the literature and its findings in the later period in the ICJ judgment on the genocide in Bosnia,[56] of crucial importance to the parallel operation of state and individual responsibility in international law.[57] It is even more difficult to draw the line between state and individual responsibility for the crime of aggression, also demonstrated convincingly in Polish literature.[58]

2 The Domestic Forum

A special place in the doctrinal discussion belongs to the exercise of criminal jurisdiction, also for acts committed abroad.

One could hardly disagree with Rappaport's assertion that the evolution of the concept of international criminal law:

> consists in the increasing overlap of the criminal-law relationship of intra-state nature and the increasingly tight weave of the interests of no longer the national but the international community heaping up on both sides of that barricade of state sovereignty in the classical understanding of the word, which is the state's sovereign power and supremacy *stricto sensu* over an independent state territory of the various members of the international community.[59]

Rappaport considered the transformations undergone by international relations throughout centuries in the field of criminal acts and corresponding repression as confronted with the requirements of life. He succeeded in convincingly demonstrating the increase in importance of the principle of the territorial principle (territoriality) as the: 'leading principle in the fight on both home and foreign crime.'[60]

56 Application of the Convention on the Prevention and Punishment of the Crime of Genocide (Bosnia and Herzegovina v. Serbia and Montenegro), Judgment, 27.02.2007, ICJ Rep. 43.

57 Wierczyńska (2009): 363ff, (2017b).

58 Grzebyk (2013a) 199.

59 Rappaport (1934).

60 *Ibidem*: 5.

An interesting outlook on this range of problems was presented by Zygmunt Cybichowski, who defined international criminal law as part of private international law dealing with criminal law.[61] In his view, the principle of territoriality presupposed the following necessary conditions for the fruition of criminal law: the violation of the criminal law of a given state and the criminal's presence in the state's territory.[62] He also outlined the historical evolution of the principle. The jurisdiction of the courts to punish foreign crimes could be defined through general principles contraposed to the principle of territoriality. Those are usually: personality, universality, and the real (protective) principle.[63]

Similarly to many other authors contemporary or even subsequent to him, Cybichowski distinguished the original and derivative right to inflict punishment. The original *jus puniendi* of a state is stand-alone and independent from that of any other state. For that reason, a foreign act, though not criminal in foreign law, could still justify criminal proceedings in-country. A derivative *jus puniendi*, on the other hand, denotes the right to punish crimes on behalf of another state.[64] He distinguished between the imperative (*jus cogens*) and semi-imperative (*jus dispositivum*) norms and further distinguished the absolute binding force of the *jus cogens* binding solely on nationals from that binding also on foreigners. Already at that point he recognized that the *jus cogens* constituted a provision of the international public order imposed by the state on everyone within the state's power, without allowing the application of separate foreign laws.[65] The derivative *jus puniendi* extinguished with the original one on which it had depended, e.g. upon serving the punishment abroad, pardon, discontinuance or prescription; the principle of *ne bis in idem* marked its presence.

The topic was the subject of Kopek Mikliszanski's doctoral dissertation defended under the tuition of Henri Donnedieu de Vabres: *Le droit pénal international d'après la législation polonaise*.[66] In its main part, the author distinguished the overarching principles of Polish criminal international law: from the territorial, through the personal (active and passive), the protective and the subsidiarity principles to the universal principle. Mikliszanski devoted a separate part of the work to the foreign co-operation of

61 Cybichowski (1927a): 16.

62 *Ibidem*: 22.

63 *Ibidem* 35.

64 *Ibidem*: 40; cf. Kusz (1933): 346.

65 Cybichowski (1927a): 41.

66 Mikliszanski (1935).

Poland's criminal justice system. The dissertation, though met with critical reviews,[67] is deserving of particular interest on account of its systematization and above all the bringing of the normative solutions of Polish law closer to a broader audience. Mikliszanski observed:

> The competence to assign delicta iuris gentium to *iudex deprehensionis* is not merely subsidiary or optional. This competence must have priority and be mandatory, which will enable it to be exercised on behalf of the entire international community. (...) Criminal judges represent one and the same justice. It follows that *iudex deprehensionis*, although it applies its own law, does not act only for its own country, but also for other countries.[68]

From the above review of the positions taken in Interwar literature follows clearly the strong conviction that the domestic courts were primarily intended to be authorized, to have the right to judge international crimes. Lech Gardocki noted that criminal law, in the shape taken in the 19th and 20th centuries, had a substantially closed, national character, as its provisions were created with a view to the protection of the interests of states and societies and constituted internal jurisdictional norms. Such a state of affairs corresponded to the situation in international relations in the 19th century with its nationalism and tendency for walling off within nation-states.[69] Similarly to other scholars in criminal law, Gardocki noted that the territorial principle accentuated state sovereignty and ensured the equal treatment of defendants regardless of nationality. He thus regarded the principle of territoriality as closer to justice than the principle of nationality. That does not mean he was oblivious to the various inconveniences entailed by the principle of territoriality.[70]

As argued convincingly by Ludwik Ehrlich, in an expert opinion commissioned by the NTN: 'it is a certainty that the law of nations presents no obstacle to the punishment of individuals for [violations of international law] on the basis of domestic law.'[71]

67 Kuczma (1937): 259, Preuss (1936): 178.
68 Mikliszanski (1936b): 338–339.
69 Gardocki (1979): 9.
70 *Ibidem*: 15.
71 Ehrlich, Agresja III Rzeszy Niemieckiej na Polskę – pogwałcenie norm prawa międzynarodowego ('The aggression of the German Third Reich on Poland – a violation of the norms of international law'), in: Czesław Pilichowski (1979): 1 *Ekspertyzy i orzeczenia przed Najwyższym Trybunałem Narodowym* ('Expert opinions and judgments

Referring to the outbreak of WWII, Ehrlich asserted forcefully:

> From the perspective of the legislative and judicial practice of various states, especially the judgment of the Permanent Court of International Justice in the Lotus case, of 1927, it follows that there is no such norm of the law of nations as would prohibit a state from judging in its territory, through its courts, the nationals of another state who, outside the borders of that state, acted in manner contrary to the interests and at once violating the laws of a state imposing a punishment for such activities. (...) Hence, the provision of Article 8 of Polish Criminal Code, which mandates the application of the Polish criminal statute to persons having committed abroad a criminal offence against the internal or external security of the Polish State or against the officials and authorities of the Polish State – a provision included in the Criminal Code of 1932, therefore five years after the Lotus incident, did not incur even the slightest objection either in the theory or in the practice of the law of nations.[72]

In the famed France v. Turkey case concerning the French steamer *Lotus*, the PCIJ, referring to the legal basis for the exercise of extraterritorial jurisdiction, found that the states could not contravene the jurisdiction limits arising from international law but at the same time ruled that limitations on the freedom of states to act outside their borders must be express, not implied.[73] In other words, any limitations had to arise from specific prohibiting norms by which the states have consented to be bound. The principles distinguished on the plane of the exercise of penal jurisdiction are the principles of territoriality, active and passive personal jurisdiction, protective jurisdiction and universal jurisdiction.

---

before the Supreme National Tribunal') 39, adding: 'In particular, the German Reich, having abjured and condemned war, could not possibly regard its rights as infringed if Poland were to hold someone criminally responsible for such actions before her courts on the basis of her domestic law.' Similarly, a different opinion of his (*Procesy przed Najwyższym Trybunałem Narodowym, ibidem,* 102) contained a very pointed remark: 'from the perspective of the law of nations, there is no obstacle for a Polish court, on the basis of Polish provisions, to judge those defendants for the acts charged by their indictment.'

72 Ehrlich, Wybuch II wojny światowej ('The outbreak of World War II'), in: Czesław Pilichowski, Ekspertyzy i orzeczenia przed Najwyższym Trybunałem Narodowym, vol. 1, Warszawa 1979, 70.

73 The Case of S.S. "Lotus", 7.09.1927, PCIJ Ser. A, No. 10, 18ff.

Adequate penal response, however, will not always be forthcoming on the domestic levels. The influence of international law on the scope of the exercise of penal jurisdiction can on the one hand be restrictive, through the prohibition of interference with the affairs of other states, and on the other hand, it can be expansive, on account on the international (treaty-based or customary) obligations to penalize specific types of acts as international offences (crimes).

A breakthrough in the perception of the responsibility for international crimes occurred in the face of the World Wars – no longer the state as an ideal creation was to be punished but the individual responsible for the commission of the specific acts, who was thereby barred from the escape route of collective responsibility due to becoming a specific subject of international law. As opposed to the responsibility of states, the responsibility of individuals had the nature of criminal responsibility. The ideal of meting out punishment for international crimes, though not foreign to classic international law, nevertheless sparked wide systemic and terminological controversies and doubts, as well as controversies and doubts regarding sources and scopes.

The problem of the exercise of penal jurisdiction, also with regard to acts committed abroad, was dealt with the first chapter of the general part of the Criminal Code of 1932. Article 3 proclaimed the principle of territoriality; however, in accordance with Article 4, the principle of personality was applicable to Polish nationals. In that manner, all foreign felonies and misdemeanours of Poles and persons of dual or multiple nationality were prosecutable, even if they had acquired their Polish nationality after the commission of their crime. Article 5 of the Criminal Code, on the other hand, provided for the punishment of foreigners for the commission of crimes abroad against the welfare or interests of the Polish State, of a Polish national or Polish legal person. In principle, foreign infractions were not punished, unless a special provision mandated otherwise.[74] Article 6 clearly expounded the derivative *jus puniendi*, making the prosecution conditional on punishability according to law of the place where the crime was committed and providing for the application of the *lex mitior*. The original *jus puniendi* was expressed on the one hand in Article 8 of the Criminal Code of 1932, in the form of crimes against the external and internal security of the Polish state, Polish authorities or officials, as well as false testimony given before state authorities, and on the other hand, the principle of

74 See Article 3 of the Code of Petty Offences of 1932.

universality. Article 9 dealt with universal repression and mentioned among the relevant crimes: piracy; counterfeiting of coin, banknotes or securities; slave trade; trafficking in women or children; drug trafficking; trafficking in pornography; use of means capable of causing a general danger, as well as other crimes provided for by international treaties.

The Criminal Code of 1969 regulated the responsibility for crimes committed abroad in Chapter XVI. In accordance with Article 114(1) of the Criminal Code, the Polish criminal statute was applicable to foreigners having committed a crime abroad, on condition of the recognition of such an act as a criminal offence also by the law applicable at the place where the act was committed. The following provision foresaw the application of the Polish statute regardless of the provisions applicable at the place of the commission of the offence in the case of foreigners having committed a crime prosecuted pursuant to international treaties (Article 115(1)). In such cases, the prosecution was dependent on an order of the Prosecutor General (Article 116). Article 118 of the Criminal Code, on the other hand, prohibited the extradition of a Polish citizen to another state, as well as the extradition of a foreigner granted asylum. It is worth noting that in a linguistic interpretation of Article 118 of the Criminal Code, there were no obstacles to recognizing the admissibility of handing a Polish national over to the competent supranational organizations (the bodies of such organizations).[75]

The present Criminal Code of 1997 adheres to the principles of territoriality (Article 5) and active personality (Article 109). A foreigner can be held responsible for committing abroad an act directed against the interests of the Republic of Poland, a Polish national, Polish legal person or Polish organizational entity without legal personality, or a crime of terrorist nature, or an offence for which the Polish criminal statute allows more than two years' imprisonment, where the perpetrator is in the territory of the Republic of Poland and the decision was made against extradition. In order for an individual to be held responsible for a crime committed abroad, Article 111 of the Criminal Code requires that the act be recognized as a criminal offence also by the law applicable at the place where the act was committed. There is an exception for responsibility based on the protective principle. It will be expedient to recall that the latter category included the crime of defaming the Polish nation.[76] However, by the judgment of the Constitutional

75 Pałka (1996).

76 Article 112(1a) added by Article 37(1) of the Act of 18.10.2006 on the Disclosure of Information Concerning Documents of the Organs of the Security of the State from Years 1944–1990 and the Contents of Such Documents (Dz.U.218.1592), as from 15.03.2007.

Court of 19 September 2008, the relevant provisions of the Code were found to be unconstitutional and accordingly repealed.[77]

The principle of universal repression is dealt with by Article 113 of the Criminal Code, jointly for cases of commission, by either Polish national or a foreigner who is not to be extradited, of a crime the Republic of Poland is bound to prosecute by an international treaty or a crime specified by the Rome Statute of the ICC.

Of course, the lack of the perpetrator's presence within the borders of the prosecuting state may present a problem. When discussing **extradition**, we are looking at one of the oldest legal institutions having played an important role in international relations over centuries.[78] Writing in 1882, Gustaw Roszkowski described it as follows: 'the rendition by a state, upon an express demand, of fugitive criminals in its territory to the state competent to judge them for that act,' and emphasized its official (relating to the state) rather than private character, having the goal of: 'supporting foreign states in the administration of justice,' as well as recognizing: 'the solidarity of mutual interests in that the punishment be just and humane but at once that no crime go unpunished.'[79] In a later period, Ehrlich defined extradition as the act of a state consisting in the rendition, subject to specific terms, of a person found in its territory to the authorities of another state for the purpose of holding such a person responsible before a court of law or for the purpose of serving a penalty already imposed by a court judgment.[80]

Initially, universal jurisdiction was derived from the construct of treaty-based crimes and the mechanism of *aut dedere aut judicare*, accepting the terminological inexactitude manifesting itself in the universality of jurisdiction not extending to all states.[81] The exercise of universal jurisdiction is a power grounded in customary law and not merely an alternative obligation arising from even numerous treaties. It is worth noting the topic was taken on by the IDI, and the Institute's respective resolution was passed in 2005 in a session in Cracow organized by Kazimierz Lankosz.[82]

---

77 K 5/07, OTK-A 2008/7/124.

78 Flemming (1970): 524.

79 Roszkowski (1882a): 146–147.

80 Ehrlich (1958): 86.

81 Ostropolski (2008): 40.

82 La compétence universelle en matière pénale à l'égard du crime de génocide, des crimes contre l'humanité et des crimes de guerre, https://www.idi-iil.org/app/uploads/2017/06/2005_kra_03_fr.pdf.

It should be recalled, however, that the Polish diplomacy had manifested its active involvement in this field much earlier on. One could hardly omit to mention the International Law Association conference in Warsaw from 9 to 16.08.1928. The product of that conference, chaired by Cybichowski, was a Draft Convention on Extradition and Rules for the Government of Territory Occupied by Hostile Forces (London 1929).

Several decades later, on 19.05.1978, in Berlin, the socialist states signed a Convention on the transfer of persons sentenced to depriva tion of liberty to serve their sentence in the State of which they are citizens.[83]

In studies conducted for his doctoral dissertation under Karol Wolfke's tuition,[84] Leon Szpak identified core principles of universal or at least very wide application, such as the principles of non-extradition of political criminals, non-extradition of own nationals, bilateral punishability, and speciality (limited prosecution).[85] It would be difficult to disagree with Szpak's conclusion that in the aftermath of World War I the problem of the punishment of German war criminals was dealt with on the plane of theoretical assumptions and not that of practical implementation.[86] In turn, following the end of WWII, the extradition and punishment of war criminals was regulated not in one but in several legal instruments. The Polish experience is discussed more extensive in an earlier, third chapter of this book.

Krzysztof Poklewski-Koziełł mentioned several cases of denial of Polish extradition requests concerning: 'such notorious war criminals as Manstein, Rundstedt, Dehring or Bohun-Dąbrowski.'[87] He anticipated that the activities of the International Association of Democratic Lawyers on behalf of the punishment of war criminals would unquestionably gain prominence, especially with the functions of the UNWCC drawing to an end. In that connection, he expounded the importance of the establishment by the Association's Prague Congress of a permanent commission for war crimes, which would have the following tasks: (1) draw, by 1.01.1949, a list of war criminals whose extradition was to be demanded by the states entitled to make such a demand in accordance with the Moscow Declaration; (2) take care that the extradition should not be delayed by unilateral orders contrary to the Moscow Declaration and the resolution of the United Nations; (3) take care that the judgments of the courts in the cases

83 1211 UNTS 66.
84 Szpak (1974).
85 Szpak (1972–1973): 153–170, cf. Szpak (1984): 153–176.
86 Szpak (1979): 7.
87 Poklewski-Koziełł (1949): 36.

of war criminals conform to international treaties, the progress achieved in the field of international law, and the interests of the protection of peace and democracy. The resulting list of 47 people was submitted on the basis of an exhaustive compilation made by the Chief Commission for the Prosecution of Nazi Crimes in Poland.[88] It is worth noting that the attached explanation emphasized that, in addition to individual refusals, extraditions were denied by general orders.

The procedure for the extradition of the Nazi criminals evolved over time. During the first period, i.e. until October 1947, the victim state was fully entitled to demand the extradition of persons entered on the UNWCC's list and submitted to the CROWCASS, created in Paris in 1944. In accordance with Article IV of the Law no. 10 of the Allied Control Council for Germany, *Punishment of Persons Guilty of War Crimes, Crimes Against Peace and Against Humanity*, the military governor of an occupation zone was required to comply with such a request as long as another state had not previously requested the extradition of the same person. Since the autumn of 1947, unilateral changes were introduced to the procedure in the British and American occupation zones, manifested by restrictions (both with regard to the number of persons to be extradited and a deadline for requests) and by a greater degree of formalism, as well as taking on the nature of judicial proceedings, e.g. through the requirement that proof of guilt be offered again with regard to persons included in the UNWCC and CROWCASS registries.[89]

Such restrictions were met with objections, for example in the form of the joint declaration of the governments of Poland, Czechoslovakia and Yugoslavia, adopted in Prague on 18.02.1948,[90] or a resolution of the Association of Democratic Lawyers.[91] After 1949, the extradition practice with regard to Nazi criminals was based on the same terms as for common criminals. Thus, all of the same restrictions were applied, rendering extradition less accessible and oftentimes outright impossible.[92] Similar problems did not occur with the French and Soviet zones, and the matter of extradition

88 *Ibidem*: 38–40.

89 Szpak (1974): 124ff.

90 Reproduced in "Głos Ludu" 49 (1152) 19.02.1948.

91 See Resolution on the punishment of war criminals adopted by the Third Congress of the International Association of Democratic Lawyers (1948) 9 DPP 13.

92 Szpak (1974): 151ff.

was approached without such difficulties.[93] The last extraditions of Nazi criminals to Poland proceeded by the end of 1950.[94]

In the UN forum, Poland consistently advocated for the adoption of resolutions referring to the extradition and punishment of war criminals. Such was the dimension of Resolution 3(I), adopted by the UNGA on 13.02.1946, recommending: 'that Members of the United Nations forthwith take all the necessary measures to cause the arrest of those war criminals who have been responsible for or have taken a consenting part in the above crimes, and to cause them to be sent back to the countries in which their abominable deeds were done, in order that they may be judged and punished according to the laws of those countries.' A similar appeal was made to non-UN member states. The following year's UNGA Resolution 170 (II), of 31.10.1947, contained the recommendation for the member states to: 'continue with unabated energy to carry out their responsibilities as regards the surrender and trial of war criminals,' as well as the recommendation for: 'Members of the United Nations, which desire the surrender of alleged criminals or traitors (that is to say nationals of any State accused of having violated their national law by treason or active collaboration with the enemy during the war) by other Members in whose jurisdiction they are believed to be, to request their surrender as soon as possible and to support their request with sufficient evidence to establish that a reasonable *prima facie* case exists as to identity and guilt.' The opportunity was seized to reassert: 'that trials of war criminals and traitors, like all other trials, should be governed by the principles of justice, law and evidence.'[95]

With the European Convention on Extradition, done at Paris on 13.12.1957, Poland attached a declaration to the effect that asylum recipients in Poland were to be treated as Polish nationals (due to their extradition being barred). Under the Criminal Code of 1969, that mechanism was incorporated in Article 119, whereby a foreigner could not be surrendered to any other state if granted asylum in Poland. It should be borne in mind also that before joininf the Council of Europe Poland consented to be bound by the protocols additional to the European Convention on Extradition of 1975 and 1978.[96]

At the request of the Commission on Human Rights, the UN Secretary General compiled a *Study as regards ensuring the arrest, extradition and*

93 Cf. Klafkowski (1968b): 260–261.

94 *Ibidem*: 267.

95 UN Doc. A/RES/170(II).

96 Dz.U.1994.70.308–310.

punishment of persons responsible for war crimes and crimes against humanity and the exchange of documentation relating thereto,[97] published on the basis of Resolution 1158 (XLI) of the ECOSOC of 5.08.1966.

However, one should note the relationship between the surrender of persons and asylum as the inverse of extradition. Documents precluding the grant of asylum to war criminals were prepared already during World War II. By way of example, one could invoke the Universal Declaration of Human Rights, of which Article 14, which deals with asylum, precludes it from being granted: 'in the case of prosecutions genuinely arising from non-political crimes or from acts contrary to the purposes and principles of the United Nations.' During the vote on its adoption, Poland abstained.

In the works on a resolution on territorial asylum, which had started in 1962, the Polish representative called for the categorical reinforcement of the ban on asylum for perpetrators of international crimes, previously recommended by Belgium.[98] The final text of the Declaration on Territorial Asylum, adopted by the UNGA on 14.12.1967, incorporates the corresponding amendments. Article 1(2) of Resolution 2312 (XXII) provides: 'The right to seek and to enjoy asylum may not be invoked by any person with respect to whom there are serious reasons for considering that he has committed a crime against peace, a war crime or a crime against humanity, as defined in the international instruments drawn up to make provision in respect of such crimes.'

From the perspective of Polish contribution to the development of extradition rules, particular attention is drawn to the Convention for the Suppression of Unlawful Seizure of Aircraft, adopted in the International Conference on Air Law at The Hague, which took place on 1–16.12.1970 under the auspices of the International Civil Aviation Organization.

The Polish-Soviet proposal[99] to bind the asylum-granting state to extradite the perpetrator to the aircraft's state of registration and allow them to be judged (*judicare*) only where the perpetrator was a national of the registration state, was rejected by 47 against, with 10 in favour and 8 abstaining. The motions tabled by the USA and New Zealand, to the effect that judgment in the asylum state would only be possible in the case of certain bars to extradition, were similarly withdrawn during the course of the discussions.

---

97 UN Doc. E/CN.4/983.

98 Resich (1980): 803–804.

99 SA Doc. No. 33 Rev. 2, proposed by Poland and the Union of Soviet Socialist Republics (ICAO, International Conference of Air Law, The Hague, December 1970, vol. II: Documents 82).

The ultimately adopted Article 8(2) envisages a modest solution: 'If a Contracting State which makes extradition conditional on the existence of a treaty receives a request for extradition from another Contracting State with which it has no extradition treaty, it may at its option consider this Convention as the legal basis for extradition in respect of the offence. Extradition shall be subject to the other conditions provided by the law of the requested state.'

In Polish law, the institution of the surrender of criminals was regulated by Articles 642–650 of Chapter VII, Book XI, of the Regulation of the President of the Polish Republic of 19.03.1928 – Code of Criminal Procedure. As noted in the literature, the goal placed before themselves by the authors of the relevant provisions of the Code of Criminal Procedure of 1928 (Rappaport first and foremost) was for the Polish criminal procedure to reflect the mechanisms functioning in contemporary Europe. Their intention was not to introduce innovative solutions – on the contrary, they preferred to rely on a well-tested model, hoping that, with time, Poland would manage to enter into a greater number of extradition treaties.[100]

In its Article 526(2), the Code of Criminal Procedure of 1969 contained an atypical[101] solution: where Poland was the extradition-requesting state, the principle of restricting the prosecution and punishment to the offence for which the extradition was granted should be applied only at the express will of the requested state. The Code did not make any reference to the principle of speciality, where Poland was the state called on to extradite an individual. It is worth recalling that the Criminal Code of 1969 prohibited, in Article 118, the extradition of a Polish national to a foreign state.

The present Code of Criminal Procedure of 1997 refers both to active extradition – in Chapter 64 *Requesting the surrender or transfer of prosecuted or convicted individuals staying abroad or the surrender of items*, and passive extradition, regulated by Chapter 65 *Surrender and transfer of persons prosecuted or convicted or the surrender of items at the request of foreign states*. In accordance with Article 593 of the Code of Criminal Procedure, an active extradition request may concern not only the surrender, by a foreign state, of a person against whom criminal proceedings have been instituted; or the surrender of a person for the purposes of carrying out the judicial proceedings; or the service of an imposed prison sentence; but also the consent of a foreign state (other than the extraditing state) to the transfer of a prosecuted or convicted person through the territory of that state; it can

100 Pokoj (2019): 218.

101 Wierzbicki (1982): 119.

also take the form of a request for the surrender of physical evidence or items obtained by the perpetrator (who is to be extradited) as a result of the criminal offence.

The matter of co-operation with the ICC is regulated by Chapter 66e of the Code of Criminal Procedure. Here, it will be necessary to discussion the controversial relationship with surrender, which led to an amendment of Article 55 of the Constitution of the Republic of Poland.[102] The first of only two amendments to the Polish Constitution enacted to date resulted not only from a conflict with the Rome Statute of the ICC but was first of all compelled by the judgment of the Constitutional Court of 27.04.2005 in *P 1/05*, concerning the European Arrest Warrant.[103] In its judgment, the Constitutional Court found Article 607t(1) of the Code of Criminal Procedure to be unconstitutional in the scope in which it applied to Polish nationals. It will be expedient to recall that, towards the end of the discussions in the Rome Conference, the Polish delegation demanded that a distinction be drawn between the two terms – surrender and extradition.[104] 'Surrender' was defined as: 'the delivering up of a person for whom a warrant of arrest has been issued by the Pre-Trial Chamber under Article 58(3), or who has been convicted by the Court, by a State to the Court, pursuant to this Statute'; 'extradition' as: 'the delivering up of a person for the purpose of trial or service of a sentence, by one state to another as provided by treaty, convention or national legislation.' There had already been previous comments asserting that there was no inconsistency between the Constitution and the Rome Statute because of the use of different terminology.

Article 55 was amended by the addition of section 3, which does not require the conditions set forth in section 2: 'if an extradition request is made by an international judicial body established under an international treaty ratified by Poland, in connection with a crime of genocide, crime against humanity, war crime or a crime of aggression, covered by the jurisdiction of that body.' Thus, it applies directly to the surrender of persons to the ICC. Additional guarantees are provided by section 4 of Article 55, which prohibits the extradition of a person suspected of the commission of

102 Dz.U.200.1471.

103 Judgment concerning the constitutionality of Article 607t(1) of the Code of Criminal Procedure, which permits the transfer of a Polish national to a European Union member state pursuant to a European Arrest Warrant (EAW), 27.04.2005, P 1/05, Dz.U.2005.77.680.

104 See: Doc. A/CONF.183/C.1/L.93, Poland: proposal regarding article X, 17.07.1998, United Nations Diplomatic Conference of Plenipotentiaries on the Establishment of an International Criminal Court Rome, 15.06–17.07.1998, OR, vol. III: 335.

a criminal offence for political reasons without the use of force; likewise an extradition violating human and civil freedoms and rights. According to the new section 5 of the same Article, extradition is to be decided by a court of law.

The analysis of topics relating to extradition was the subject of lively interest in **scholarship.** Stefan Glaser titled his inaugural lecture of 12.01.1924 at the Stephen Báthory University in Vilnius: *Zasada extradycji w odniesieniu do przestępców politycznych*[105] – 'The principle of extradition with regard to political criminals.' In it, he clearly professed himself in favour of recognizing extradition as: 'an act of justice and a legal obligation and not an act of international comity (*comitas gentium*) or a merely moral obligation on the part of the states.'[106] He cited Franciszek Kasparek's *O wydawaniu przestępców* ('On the delivering up of criminals') of 1882. In the footsteps of Carlos Calvo, he saw the source of that obligation in the: 'necessity for every state to contribute to the rule of law on earth.'[107] One can thus identify a progressing trend for the recognition of extradition not as a political instrument of the exercise of power but one primarily in the service of justice.[108]

According to Glaser, the most important reason for the different treatment of political criminals in extradition law arises from the differences, even opposites, among the various systems of government and political systems and the lack of confidence in the impartial administration of criminal justice in a state whose interests were violated by the act.[109] Glaser further expounded on the topic in a series of several articles published near the end of the 20s of the 20th century, on the pages of the *Palestra*.[110]

The literature exploring the subject of extradition has identified the following characteristics of it: the existence of an agreement between the states, the change of territorial sovereignty in respect of the person to be extradited, and the purpose of the transfer being to enable the administration of justice – the conduct of criminal proceedings or the service of a penalty imposed by a legally binding judgment.[111]

105 Glaser (1924).
106 *Ibidem*: 11.
107 *Ibidem*.
108 Wierzbicki (1982): 101.
109 Glaser (1924): 24.
110 Glaser (1929a–e).
111 Wierzbicki (1982): 95–96.

The most complete review of the various views expressed in the literature of the Interwar period can be found in Zygmunt Cybichowski's *Międzynarodowe prawo karne. Kompetencja sądów do ścigania przestępstw zagranicznych* (1927a) ('International criminal law. The jurisdiction of the courts for foreign crimes.') Cybichowski emphasized that: 'the purpose of not extraditing [one's own] subjects is not to provide them with impunity.'[112] He went on to add:

> If a state believes its subject to be governed by domestic law even abroad, it will not extradite the subject for a crime committed there but will punish them on its own. (…) When the state has no confidence in foreign judiciary, the principle of non-extradition of own nationals is fair; otherwise, it cannot be justified. If the states cling to the principle regardless, that must be explained before everything else by aversion to analysing the level of foreign jurisdictions.

As underscored, on the other hand, by Rappaport, other states recognized that sovereign right of a state to its own exercise of penal powers. In return, however, they demanded the recognition of their own rights in analogous cases, which means they demand legal assistance to exercise their *jus puniendi* from the state in whose territory the fugitive criminals have found refuge. Emerging gradually from these foundations of reciprocity in interstate co-operation is the institution of the delivery of criminals and extradition proceedings. Rappaport regarded extradition as the manifestation of an aspiration to transcend the boundaries of the domestic fight on crime, along with: 'the necessary extrastate supplementation of the principle of nationality.' Last but not least, he mentioned the third leading principle of international criminal law, i.e. the principle of universal criminal jurisdiction. He derived it from Bartolus de Saxoferrato, who was an adherent of the concept of prosecuting the *hostes generis humani* of his era at the place of apprehension, regardless of the person and of the place of the commission of the crime.

On the basis of reciprocity, as well as the requirements arising from sovereignty and rule of law, the works devoted to the topic of extradition expounded the principle of double (dual) criminality. That principle sets forth the 'common denominator' to which, despite the differences in the

112 Cybichowski (1932): 522.

penalization of the various acts and the degree of their suppression, the criminal law of the various states can be reduced.[113] Whereas, in extradition law, the condition of double criminality consists in affording primacy to one's own law, in substantive law, the principles of one's own justice system are applied after taking foreign law into account.[114]

Glaser was critical of double criminality, noting:

> according to contemporary views, extradition is no longer to be reputed as act of international comity or courtesy but is of importance to the states' co-operation with their common interest in mind – the pursuit of the administration of justice. A violation of even one state's legal order is regarded as infringing on the common interest and, therefore, all states are called upon to co-operate so that the perpetrator cannot escape the deserved punishment. Accordingly, it should be an immaterial circumstance what legal classification, if any, the legislative provisions of the other states attribute to the act, as long as it can be verified that the act is regarded as a crime according to the law of the state of its commission.[115]

At present, too, the requirement of double criminality is viewed as: 'a sort of cuckoo's egg planted in uncertain circumstances on the penal lawmaker.'[116]

The principle of double criminality will not be applicable for reasons justified by the particular geographic location of the states. For example, crimes relating to maritime navigation – where the requested state has no access to the sea and no specific provisions relating to the navigation of the seas.[117] The most important international crimes are another exception.

The principle of speciality, in turn, is explained by the necessity of providing the extraditing state with some measure of control over the administration of justice in the requesting state and to prevent the boundaries of the extradition request from being exceeded, as well the protection of the extradited individual's rights.[118] Calls are made for the restrictions imposed by this principle to be abolished in the interest of the effectiveness of the

113 Knypl (1975): 83; Gardocki (1996): 69.
114 Płachta (1989): 111; Brodowski (2015): 34.
115 Glaser (1929c): 298.
116 Piskorski (2005): 266.
117 Wierzbicki (1982): 109.
118 Roszkowski (1882a): 289.

international co-operation,[119] similarly to Stefan Glaser's critique several decades prior.

There is a noticeable general trend to expand the scope of the principle of speciality, which is manifested in restricting the receiving state's freedom to extradite the individual further to a third state, as well as the type of punishment and type of court.

The principle of non-extradition of political criminals causes problems primarily on account of the difficulties relating to the meaning of the term 'political crime' itself. That problem was explored, among others, by Glaser[120] and Bogdan Wierzbicki, the latter of whom wrote a monograph on the topic.[121] Of course, the basis for the recognition of a given crime as a political one will be found in the type of the protected and infringed interest. Sometimes, relative political crimes and crimes of dual nature are distinguished, the latter usually also classified as common crime. Igor Andrejew observed that, although the criminal law of the Polish People's Republic did not employ the term, 'political crime,' its scope was, in principle, as far as domestic affairs were concerned, exhausted by the crimes covered by Chapter XIX of the Criminal Code of 1969.[122]

In Polish literature, recommendations were made for that principle to be supplemented with the *aut dedere aut poenam persequi*, i.e. either deliver the criminal or see to it that the penalty is enforced.[123] The postulated expansion would have made it possible to get the state to enforce in its own territory the penalty adjudicated by the court of another state (the requesting state) if refusing to deliver the convict in accordance with the extradition request. In that way, the adverse consequence of the ban on the extradition of one's own nationals could be averted. The meaning of it is reducible to the proverbial final touch, as it extends the scope of applicability of *aut dedere aut punire* from defendant (suspect) to convict, covering also the stage of service of the penalty.[124]

Realizing the need for change in domestic legislation, Płachta points out the corresponding benefits, such as the lack of costs to be incurred by the state in instituting the new proceedings, difficulties extracting evidence from abroad, as well as avoidance of the risk of divergent decisions coming

119 Piskorski (2005): 266.

120 See also Glaser (1948): 766, (1959): 16.

121 Wierzbicki (1979).

122 Andrejew (1978): 102.

123 Płachta (1993): 1991; cf. Płachta (2003c): 229.

124 See extensively, Płachta (2015): 15.

down from the courts of different states. The problem of the convict's consent proved to be a more controversial issue – there, Płachta was opposed to requiring such consent.[125] He also took on several topics relating to extradition,[126] such as the matter of Lockerbie.[127] It is worth noting that in the context of the events unfolding in 1960, Płachta discussed Eichmann's abduction in a monograph titled *Kidnaping międzynarodowy w służbie prawa*[128] ('International kidnapping in the service of the law'), continuing, as it were, on Dominik Lasok's previous study of the Nazi criminal's trial.[129]

In the ILC, the principle of *aut dedere aut judicare* was mentioned as a potential topic of discussion as early as 1949. However, the problem was included in the Commission's long-term agenda only in 2004, at the 56th session, as subsequently affirmed by UNGA Resolution 59/41 of December of the same year.

In August 2005, Zdzisław Galicki was appointed special rapporteur.[130] The precedential character of the event has to be emphasized – never before had a Pole been appointed special rapporteur for the Commission's works. Special rapporteur Galicki's first report, of preliminary character,[131] laid out a plan of action. It covered issues such as the formulation of the analysed rule and the sources from which it was derived. Moreover, he highlighted the need for analysis of the detailed obligations flowing from the *aut dedere aut judicare*, as well as other related institutions of international law.

As regards the formulation of the maxim, the special rapporteur cited three variants:[132] extradite or punish; extradite or prosecute; or, lastly, extradite or punish or deliver to an international tribunal. The nature alone of the alternative could already appear to the controversial, coming down to the question of its nature as a primary or secondary, substantive or formal rule, as well as the extent to which it could be accepted as a peremptory norm.

Galicki's first report as special rapporteur revealed the existence of a highly accentuated customary basis, which duly prompted the question of

125 *Ibidem.*
126 Płachta (2000): 34–42; *idem* (2001a), *idem* (1998): 94–105.
127 Płachta (2001b): 125–140.
128 Płachta (2000).
129 Lasok (1962): 355.
130 Confirmed by UN Doc. A/60/22 (2005).
131 UN Doc. A/CN.4/571, Preliminary report, by Mr. Zdzislaw Galicki, Special Rapporteur.
132 UN Doc. A/CN.4/585: 18.

the peremptory status of the norm (§61). As observed by Grzebyk: 'the rapporteur's enthusiasm for the customary character was, however, not shared by the majority of the states, all the less so when it came to the *jus cogens* status of the norm.'[133] Poland's state commentary recommended in-depth studies into the problem.[134] Concerning the content of the obligation, already in his first report (§§5 and 6) did the special rapporteur discuss transformations of Grotius's alternative of *aut dedere aut punire*[135] by replacement of the second element with judgment (*judicare*), which would not necessarily result in punishment.[136] Thus, *aut judicare aut prosequi* would suffice, and sometimes even the finding of a pretext to deny the request (*aut tergiversari*).[137]

However, Galicki also noted that both of the obligations could be complied with if the state were to judge and convict the perpetrator on its own and subsequently extradite them to another state to serve the penalty.[138] In that manner, the principle took the form of *aut dedere aut poenam persequi.* It is worth noting that a title of jurisdiction would suffice without need for the alleged perpetrator's presence in the territory of a given state.[139]

Polish literature has pointed out the misunderstanding involved in the treatment of the *aut dedere aut judicare* as a customary norm or at least verification of the extent to which it is so. It is viewed, for example, as a sort of technical solution rather than a norm as such, which is the reason given for the failure of the ILC's works.[140]

On the basis of the recommendation offered by the special rapporteur and the ILC as a whole, the UNGA called upon the states to provide information as to their law and practice.[141] Only a modest response was forthcoming, which translated into the second report repeating the identified aspects and the information provided. In the second record, the rapporteur

133 Grzebyk (2013c): 138.

134 UN Doc. A/CN.4/648, Fourth report on the obligation to extradite or prosecute (aut dedere aut judicare), by Mr. Zdzislaw Galicki, Special Rapporteur, §81.

135 YILC (2006), vol. II(1): 261f.

136 UN Doc. A/CN.4/603, Third report on the obligation to extradite or prosecute (aut dedere aut judicare), by Mr. Zdzislaw Galicki, Special Rapporteur, §36.

137 UN Doc. A/CN.4/571, Preliminary report, §7, In a later study, Galicki proposed the following liberal translation: demur and look for justification – Galicki (2015): 80.

138 UN Doc. A/CN.4/571, Preliminary report, §7, 49.

139 UN Doc. A/CN.4/585, Second report on the obligation to extradite or prosecute (aut dedere aut judicare), by Mr. Zdzislaw Galicki, Special Rapporteur, §96.

140 Saganek (2014): 435.

141 UN Doc. A/61/34 (2006).

proposed the wording of an Article 1 defining the scope of application of the draft articles.

In the next, third report, he incorporated further information and comments and moreover proposed to supplement Article 1 of the draft articles (by emphasizing the legal character of the alternative obligation). An important novelty was the suggestion for Article 2 to define the key terms for the topic range, which was not accompanied, however, by any realistic proposal as to the implementation of that task. The third of the articles proposed by the special rapporteur identified the treaty basis or bases for the solution, which was rightfully subjected to criticism.[142]

In order to expedite the works and provide support for Galicki as special rapporteur, the ILC decided, near the end of July 2008, to create a working group led by Alain Pellet. In a study prepared for the working group,[143] the special rapporteur asked three basic questions the group was tasked with answering, viz. the legal bases for the obligation; its substantive scope and content; relationship with other rules; conditions for triggering the obligation; its implementation; and the connection between the obligation either to extradite or to prosecute and the delivery of the perpetrator to the competent international criminal court. The first oral findings, reported by Enrique J.A. Candotti in the 62th session of the ILC, revealed the need to account for the practice of the states, which in practical terms meant there was no chance of expediting the works on the subject.[144]

Galicki's last report arrived in 2011, professing the lack of significant progress on the works. The above markedly demonstrates the lack of a universal consensus as to the general grounds of extradition and, furthermore, invites the conclusion that the topic Poland had kept raising since the time of WWII continued to suffer from neglect. Galicki recommended the adoption of a new Article 2, referring to the obligation to co-operate from the perspective of averting impunity, though that gave rise to doubts concerning its placement (the preamble was suggested instead). In turn, in Article 4, the special rapporteur suggested the inclusion of a reference to the customary basis for the obligation to extradite or prosecute with regard to serious violations of international humanitarian law, genocide, crimes against humanity or war crimes as derived from: 'general international law accepted and

---

142 Grzebyk (2013c): 133.

143 Bases for discussion in the Working Group on the topic "The obligation to extradite or prosecute (aut dedere aut judicare)", Paper prepared by Mr. Zdzislaw Galicki, Special Rapporteur, UN Doc. A/CN.4/L.774, 24.06.2010.

144 Grzebyk (2013c): 134.

recognized by the international community of States (*jus cogens*), either in the form of international treaty or international custom, criminalizing any one of acts (…).'[145] Galicki's reports (I and II) as special rapporteur incorporate extensive references to the works published in European academic journals by Michał Płachta.

The literature, especially Polish, met the ILC's works with somewhat of a critical reception.[146] In the ILC elections in the autumn of 2011, Zdzisław Galicki was not re-elected.[147]

In 2012, in lieu of appointing another special rapporteur, the ILC created another open-ended Working Group on the obligation to extradite or prosecute, led by Kriangsak Kittichaisaree. Its task was to evaluate the progress made in the Commission's works on the topic and explore potential options available to the Commission for the future. No special rapporteur was appointed in Galicki's place, and Galicki himself was no longer a member of the Commission. The works were finalized in the 66th session in 2014, when the commission created another working group on the *aut dedere aut judicare* obligation led by Kriangsak Kittichaisaree. The working group proceeded with the evaluation of the works done on the subject, especially in the light of the remarks submitted in the Sixth Committee at the 68th session of the UNGA in respect of 2013 working group's report. Appearing on behalf of Poland in the Sixth Committee, Zdzisław Galicki highlighted the link and codependency between universal jurisdiction and the principle of *aut dedere aut judicare*, emphasizing that the principle of universal jurisdiction had played a key role in giving full effect to it.[148] The Working Group held two sessions – on 6.05 and on 4.06.2014. At the session on 7.07.2014, the Commission considered the Working Group's report,[149] which considered, among other things, the recommendation for the Commission to accept the reports for 2013 and 2014 and end the exploration of the subject of: 'The obligation to extradite or prosecute (*aut dedere aut judicare*).'

---

145 Art. 4(3) – this approach appears, on the one hand, to comply with the requirements of the principle of legality (prohibition against customary punishment) with the naturally customary character of peremptory norms.

146 See e.g. Saganek (2014): 432.

147 As for the possible causes, see: Grzebyk (2018): 130 (rather critical reception of Galicki's reports by the states, as reflected by the discussion in the Sixth Committee).

148 See The scope and Application of the principle of universal jurisdiction, Agenda item 86, Statement by Professor Zdzislaw Galicki, Adviser to the Ministry of Foreign Affairs of the Republic of Poland, New York, 18.10.2013, https://www.un.org/en/ga/sixth/68/pdfs/statements/universal_jurisdiction/poland.pdf.

149 A/CN. 4/L.844.

At the session on 7.08.2014, the Commission accepted the Final Report on the Obligation to Extradite or Prosecute (*aut dedere aut judicare*) and decided to end the exploration of the topic. It also expressed its profound gratitude to Chairman Kittichaisaree for his contributions and for his effective and efficient work. The Commission also expressed gratitude for the work of the former special rapporteur, Zdzisław Galicki.

By Resolution 69/118 of 10.12.2014, the General Assembly considered the Final Report on the Obligation to Extradite or Prosecute (*aut dedere aut judicare*) in §65 of the ILC's report and encouraged its broadest possible distribution.

Once the subject had been closed, Zdzisław Galicki acknowledged: 'The obligation to extradite or judge (prosecute or punish) cannot be regarded as a traditional topic.' He recognized its evolution, emphasizing its development as an effective tool against the increasing threats posed to states and individuals by criminal offences. He reported the processes as a: 'reflection of new development trends in international law and burning needs of the international community.'[150] He also complained:

> the answers requested by the Committee had been slow to arrive and revealed significant differences among the states. While in the initial period there had even existed a certain optimism in the Commission and among the states within the Legal Committee supervising its work in respect of the possibility of the articulation of appropriate customary norms based on a concordant and universal practice of the state with regard to the application of the principle of *aut dedere aut judicare*, an increasing number of states, as the time passed, approached the hypothetical recognition of the existence of a customary principle of international law in that regard with a certain reserve.[151]

One can thus conclude that *aut dedere aut judicare* does not have a stable position with regard to the terminology, as well as matters of the substance, or in the normative, adjudicatory or scholarly layers.[152] The practice does yield strictly unequivocal evidence of a universal obligation to extradite or judge in respect of international crimes. And it is from the peremptory character of the norms dealing with international crimes[153] that the legal

150 Galicki (2015): 80.
151 *Ibidem*: 84.
152 Płachta (2015): 15.
153 Wolfke (1972): 206, cf. more cautiously – Wolfke (1974): 158.

obligation of co-operation and mutual assistance with the prosecution of war criminals is derived.[154]

3 The International Forum

When defining international criminal law, the accent is often placed on the adjudication factor, i.e. the individual responsibility of natural persons exacted before international judicial bodies. Such an outlook reduces the development of international criminal law to the history of the law applied by the international criminal tribunals – first the military ones, then those created by the Security Council, and ultimately the permanent ICC.

Nor can one ignore the initiatives aimed at the establishment of an international tribunal to judge communist crimes, which have not been publicized and the dearth of information available presents an obstacle to closer analysis.[155]

The institutional aspects from the perspective of diplomatic initiatives and scholarly studies were discussed in the preceding chapters of this work. Here, it will be expedient to note, however, that the lack of perspective for the creation by the Security Council of more *ad hoc* tribunals, as well as the limited scope of jurisdiction of the permanent ICC have forced the international community to create alternative methods of enforcement of international criminal responsibility. One interesting solution is the institution of hybrid tribunals, with a mixed international-domestic jurisdiction and composition.[156]

Notwithstanding the prospects of setting parallel international criminal jurisdictions in motion, it must be borne in mind that it is not the task of an international criminal court to replace domestic courts and, consequently, divest the states of their obligation to prosecute specific crimes in domestic law. Nevertheless, Article 9 the ICTY Statute and the identically drafted Article 8 of the ICTR counterpart provided for concurrent jurisdiction and the primacy of the international tribunals above the domestic courts. Due to concerns with regard to the impartiality of the domestic courts in the former Yugoslavian republics and the destruction of the justice system in Rwanda, the tribunals could at any stage of international proceedings demand that the domestic courts submit to their jurisdiction. Such a

154 Szpak (1979): 19; Pilichowski (1980c): 67.

155 Masło (2022): 113.

156 An excellent overview of the available mechanisms: Stasiak (2012).

hierarchical structure was reaffirmed in the ICTY judgment in the *Tadić* case: 'the sovereign rights of States cannot and should not take precedence over the right of the international community to act appropriately as they affect the whole of mankind and shock the conscience of all nations of the world.'[157] In the context of the strategy for the winding up of the operations of both of the *ad hoc* tribunals, there was an increasingly perceptible trend for returning the jurisdiction to the domestic courts by focusing exclusively on so-called major perpetrator, while cases of moderate and minor gravity were conducted before the domestic courts.

The existence of the ICC, too, should contribute to the strengthening of the domestic system for the punishment of the crimes falling within the Court's purview. The adoption of the complementarity principle (Article 17 of Rome Statute) respects state sovereignty in a greater degree and assumes the commencement of the ICC's activities only in the face of inaction by state, either due to unwillingness (e.g. when the proceedings are pending for the purpose of protecting the suspect from responsibility for crimes covered by the ICC's jurisdiction) or because of the inability of the individual states to judge the matter (e.g. as a result of the complete or significant disintegration of the domestic legal system).

The topic range of the relationship between the domestic and the international justice systems has been the subject matter of multiple monographs.[158]

Polish scholarship has not avoided the study of the procedural rules, not only from the positions of the general theory of international organizations[159] but also from the perspective of the international court system.[160] Among other topics, the internationalists have focused their efforts on finding the answer to the question of who wields the power to enact procedural rules, addressing simultaneously, as it were, the problem of the separation of substantive and procedural rules in international law. The aforementioned matters had already been the subject of interest of Hersch Lauterpacht's, who emphasized that procedural rules contained within themselves an element of substantive justice.[161] As observed on the home ground by Jan Kolasa, the decisive criterion for the division of the system of norms of international law among substantive and procedural norms is their

157 IT-94-1-T (10.08.1995), §42.
158 Socha (2004), Milik (2012), Wierczyńska (2016a).
159 Kolasa (1965), (1987b).
160 Kolasa (1987a), (1985).
161 Lauterpacht (1958): 209.

difference in functional character – substantive and procedural norms each have a different function. This comes with a warning against the use of analogies from domestic law.[162]

The source of competence to create rules of procedure could also be found in the common-law principle of judge-made law, as well as an established principle of customary international law.[163] As observed by Kolasa: 'the placement of this power within the context of the international practice gives it a more defined and strictly international character. This is not without significance in a situation demanding interpretation and a search of analogies in doubtful matters.'[164] With that, he referred to the pioneering findings of his habilitation work.[165]

In accordance with Article 2 of the London Agreement of 1945:[166] 'The constitution, jurisdiction and functions of the International Military Tribunal shall be those set out in the Charter annexed to this agreement, which Charter shall form an integral part of this Agreement.' The Charter is sometimes dubbed the: 'first code of international criminal law,'[167] as it contains *tout le droit écrit sur lequel se base le Tribunal*.[168] When it comes to the procedural rules, in turn, a higher degree of definition can be observed. Those absorb the brunt of the provisions of the Charter.[169] Furthermore, Article 13 made the Tribunal competent to create its own procedure, albeit with the proviso that the rules so created were not to be contrary to the provisions of the Charter. The task of the preparation and submission to the Tribunal for approval of draft procedural rules as provided by Article 13 was, pursuant to Article 14(e), entrusted to the signatories' Chief Prosecutors acting as a committee. According to the same article, the Tribunal was to accept the drafted rules (with or without amendments) or reject them.

162 Kolasa (1987b): 60.
163 Kolasa (1988): 60.
164 *Ibidem*.
165 Kolasa (1967): 67–70, 191–192.
166 Dz.U.1947.63.367.
167 Descheemaeker (1947): 11.
168 *Ibidem*: 17,56.
169 In particular the provisions of the Chapter IV, dealing with procedural guarantees for the defendants and the most voluminous Chapter V, devoted to the Tribunal's powers and its mode of proceeding. Separate attention is deserved by Article 19, whereby the Tribunal was: 'not bound by technical rules of evidence.' The cited article required the Tribunal only to adopt and apply as 'expeditious and non-technical procedure' as possible and admit any evidence the Tribunal itself deemed to be of probative value. Subsequent chapters deal with the judgment and sentence (Chapter VI) and the expenses (Chapter VII).

The development and proliferation of procedural rules having at least potential impact on proceedings before international courts, and, from the perspective presented here, primarily the ICC, affirm the decades-old thesis of the existence of a proportional relationship to the progressing institutionalization.[170]

Especially the last decades have abounded with works by internationalists exploring procedural issues as well.[171] Procedural studies have also been conducted by specialists in criminal procedure. Hanna Kuczyńska's habilitation dissertation published in English is deserving of particular recognition in this regard.[172] Evidence is also a popular subject matter of study.[173] Wojciech Jasiński has on multiple occasions discussed issues of admissibility of evidence in his habilitation monograph titled *Nielegalnie uzyskane dowody w procesie karnym: w poszukiwaniu optymalnego rozwiązania* ('Unlawfully obtained evidence in criminal trial: in the search of the optimal solution'), as well as publications with a more global audience.[174] In this last context, it will be expedient to recall the recommendations submitted by Poland in the course of the Rome Conference, concerning the possibility of denial of admission of evidence obtained in violation of or without compliance with an order or recommendation of the Pre-Trial Chamber.[175] Poland also participated in the works of an informal working group dealing with the bringing of proceedings in a situation in which the prosecutor finds the lack of a sufficient basis to institute the proceedings.[176]

4 Enforcement of Penalties

Last but not least, one has to discuss the enforcement of the penalty imposed. It would be impossible not to mention the achievements of the

170 Kolasa (1987b): 76.
171 Wierczyńska (2016a); Krzan (2009).
172 Kuczyńska (2015).
173 Kremens (2010).
174 Jasiński (2016); Krzan (2021).
175 See UN Doc. A/CONF.183/C.1AVGPM/LJ1, Poland: proposal to clarify the relationship between article 57, paragraph 3, and 69, paragraph 6, 29.6.1998, 15.06–17.07.1998, OR, vol. III: 294.
176 See Doc. A/CONF.183/C.1/WGPM/L.18, United Nations Diplomatic Conference of Plenipotentiaries on the Establishment of an International Criminal Court Rome, 15.06–17.07.1998, OR, vol. III: 294.

eminent professor and scholar of criminal law, one of the pioneers of Polish penology, Bronisław Wróblewski.[177] He also published abroad.[178] Already before WWII, together with his most diligent student, Witold Świda, who would go on to become the dean of the Law Faculty of the University of Wrocław, he published a pioneering work on the subject of sentencing in the light of questionnaire surveys.[179]

When considering the enforcement of penalties from the penitentiary perspective, one can hardly ignore the importance of the findings made by Leon Radzinowicz (until 1934, Rabinowicz),[180] who studied in France, Switzerland and Italy and, after returning to Poland in the 30s of the 20th century, lectured at the University of Warsaw. At the Third International Congress of Penal Law, he delivered a paper on the expediency of having a separate enforcement/executive code.[181] Before the outbreak of the war, he was dispatched by the Polish Republic's justice ministry to the United Kingdom to study the penal system there. He settled in Cambridge, where, until the end of the 40s of the 20th century, he led the Department of Criminal Science,[182] for which he is primarily known.[183]

Rappaport made a significantly smaller imprint on criminal enforcement law (executive criminal law) than on international criminal law. Nevertheless, one could hardly ignore his *Nowy system kodyfikacji ustawodawstwa kryminalnego: kodeks karny wykonawczy* (1930) ('The new system of codification of penal legislation: the Executive Penal Code'). Other specialists in in penitentiary law from the later period are less known (Stanisław Pławski, Stanisław Walczak, and Józef Wąsik). From the perspective of international visibility and impact on the international development of the discipline, it will be fitting to recall that Jerzy Śliwowski delivered the national report titled *De l'intervention de l'autorité judiciaire dans l'exécution des peines et des mesures de sûreté* in the 4th International Congress of Penal Law.[184]

What is of principal significance to our discussion here is the death penalty and its admissibility. The Interwar legislation of the Second Polish Republic provided for the death penalty, and so did the law enacted after the war. The last public execution was ordered by the Minister of Justice for

177 Wróblewski (1926).
178 Idem (1928): 64.
179 Wróblewski, Świda (1939).
180 E.g. Rabinowicz (1933), (1932a).
181 Rabinowicz (1932b): 54.
182 In 1960, he became the director of the pioneering Institute of Criminology.
183 Radzinowicz (1977).
184 Śliwowski (1937): 617.

Greiser and took place on 21.07.1946 on the slope of Fort Winiary in Poznań. Due to concerns of a possible lynching, the execution of Rudolf Höss was rescheduled from 15.04.1947 to one day later. Pursuant to instructions from the Ministry of Justice, the execution was not to be held in public; still, approximately a hundred people were in attendance.[185]

The Act of 12.07.1995 amending the Criminal Code and the Executive Criminal Code, and Raising the Lower and Upper Limits of Fines and Punitive Damages in Criminal Law[186] established a five-year statutory moratorium on capital punishment, which had already *de facto* ceased to be carried out several years prior – the last execution took place by hanging on 21.04.1988. On the wave of systemic changes, on 7.12.1989, the Sejm declared an amnesty, commuting adjudicated death penalties to 25 years' imprisonment.[187] With the coming into force of a new Criminal Code in 1997, the death penalty in Poland was abolished, and convicts already sentenced to it received a commutation to life imprisonment. The above does not necessarily translate into the formal elimination of death penalty from the Polish legal system. The August Decree on the Sentencing Guidelines for Fascist-Nazi Criminals is still in force and provides for the death penalty, which only cannot be carried out. Until 2013, the death penalty was admissible in wartime. Following ratification by the President of Poland, in 2014, of Protocol no. 13 to the European Convention on Human Rights[188] and the second optional protocol to the International Covenant of Civil and Political Rights,[189] the death penalty has been abolished in all circumstances.

The statutes of international criminal tribunals only provide basic sentencing guidelines. They do not define the mutual interrelations among them, and thus it is not possible to determine the importance and weight of each of the individual factors. Unlike in domestic law, there are no upper and lower sentencing limits.

The PKWN Decree of 31.08.1944 specified death as the only penalty for those guilty of the acts set out in its Article 1.[190] Subsequent provisions of

185 *Ostatnie dni komendanta Auschwitz Rudolfa Höβa*, https://krakow.ipn.gov.pl/pl4/edukacja/przystanek-historia/95478,Ostatnie-dni-komendanta-Auschwitz-Rudolfa-Ha.html.

186 Dz.U.1995.95.475.

187 Dz.U.1989.64.390.

188 Dz.U.2014.1155.

189 Dz.U.2014.891.

190 Actions taken in the interest of the German state or a state allied thereto, consisting in: (1) participating in the killings of civilians, military personnel or prisoners of war;

the Decree provided alternative, less severe penalties. It is worth repeating after Cieślak and Waszczyński that Article 1 of the Decree is the sole case of death as the only penalty available for an offence.[191] Moreover, it should be recalled that in line with Article 7 of the Decree, upon conviction of a criminal offence set out in it, the court was also to impose the loss of public rights and honorary civil rights, as well as confiscation of all property.

Almost in parallel with the August Decree, the Decree on Special Criminal Courts for Cases of Fascist-Nazi Criminals came out on 12.09.1944, providing for the establishment of special courts. Those followed a simplified procedural path intended to expedite the proceedings. Death was the usual penalty imposed. It was adjudicated in the Lublin trial of the staff of the Majdanek concentration camp and carried out one day later.

In the trials before the NTN, thirty-one out of a total of 49 defendants received the death penalty, but Bolesław Bierut granted clemency to Johann Paul Kremer and Arthur Breitwieser, commuting it to life imprisonment. Twenty-nine convicts were thus executed. The rest were given prison terms ranging from three years to life. The penalties imposed demonstrate irrefutably that the proceedings before the NTN cannot be regarded as show trials. On the contrary, they supply proof of conscientious administration of justice.

The amnesty commemorating the Constitution of 22.07.1952 did not extend to persons guilty of crimes under Articles 1, 3, 5, 6, 7 or 13 of the Decree of 13.06.1946 (Small Criminal Code), as well as Article 1 or 4 of the PKWN Decree of 31.08.1944.[192] Following the amnesty of 1956,[193] the majority of the German prisoners were let out of Polish prisoners, and of those, the majority returned to Germany, mainly the Federal Republic. Both Johann P. Kremer and Arthur Breitwieser left Polish prisons in 1958 and departed for the Federal Republic of Germany.

Pursuant to Article 8 of the Amnesty Act of 1956, the offences under Article 1(1) of the August Decree were exempted.[194] The next amnesty act, commemorating the twenty-fifth anniversary of the Polish People's Republic, exempted all (sic!) of the offences under the Decree of 31.08.1944, as well as

---

(2) acting, through denunciation or apprehension, to the injury of persons wanted or persecuted by the authorities for political, national, ethnic, religious or racial reasons.

191 Cieślak, Waszczyński (1989): 437.

192 Dz.U.1952.46.309, art. 9.

193 Dz.U.1956.11.57.

194 Similarly, 1974 Amnesty Act (Dz.U.1974.27.159).

the offences of sabotage and espionage set out in Article 7 of the Small Criminal Code.[195] It will be expedient to note that the next amnesty after that, pursuant to the Decree of the Council of State of the Polish People's Republic of 18.07.1977,[196] similarly exempted the crime defined in Article 1(1) of the August Decree of 1944 but the exemption was extended also onto other international crimes, by adding to Article 4(1) the words: 'or to other war crimes or crimes against humanity.'

The problem of the permissibility of granting amnesty to the perpetrators of international crimes sparks much controversy, belonging to the most disputed issues in public international law. Besides less voluminous analyses,[197] it has been the subject of a monographic study.[198]

In the course of the works on the Code of Crimes against Peace and Security of Mankind, Poland advocated for the inclusion of collective sentencing limits for all crimes, simultaneously recommending a minimum one (10 years' imprisonment) and a maximum one (35 years or life).[199] It was argued that where a strictly delimited prison term is imposed, parole should not be possible.[200]

Article 24 of the ICTY Statute, similarly to Article 23 of the ICTR Statute, defined the punishments and provided for imprisonment as the principal penalty. When determining the terms of imprisonment, the Trial Chambers were to consider the respective general practice of the courts of the former Yugoslavia and of Rwanda.[201] The second paragraph more narrowly provided that the sentencing: 'should take into account such factors as the gravity of the offence and the individual circumstances of the convicted person.' One should remember that the Chambers could also adjudicate the return

195 Dz.U.1969.21.151.

196 Dz.U.1977.24.102.

197 Płachta (2003a), (2003b).

198 Holy (2015).

199 Doc. A/CN.4/448 and Add.1, YILC (1993), vol. II(1): 95.

200 *Ibidem*.

201 The ICTY noted that "Trial Chambers are not bound by the practice of courts in the former Yugoslavia in reaching their determination of the appropriate sentence for a convicted person" (ICTY, Prosecutor v. Zejnil Delalić, Zdravko Mucić aka "Pavo", Hazim Delić and Esad Landžo aka "Zenga", Judgment, IT-96–21–A, 20.02.2001, §816). Such position may be also extrapolated onto the ICTR since 'a Trial Chamber, whilst not bound by the sentencing practices ofthe former Yugoslavia or of Rwanda is obliged to explain the sentence imposed and any divergence from the sentencing limits of either the former Yugoslavia orof Rwanda – ICTR, The Prosecutor v. Laurent Semanza, Judgement, ICTR-97–20-A, 20.05.2005, §377.

of any property acquired through the crime to its rightful owners, as provided by paragraph of the cited article.

The adjudicating practice of the *ad hoc* tribunals has not been the subject of published works in Polish scholarship.[202] In accordance with Article 27 of the ICTY Statute, prison terms are to be served in a state selected by the tribunal from a list of states having communicated to the Security Council their willingness to accept the transfer of the convicts for that purpose.[203] The imprisonment follows the law of the host state, under the international tribunal's supervision.[204] Radislav Krstić's service of his prison term in Poland was especially widely commented on.[205] That was the first such case, and thus it set the procedural standard for the transfers of prison terms imposed on persons convicted by an international tribunal.

5 Conclusions

A breakthrough in the perception of the responsibility for international crimes occurred in the face of the World Wars – no longer the state as an ideal creation was to be punished but the individual responsible for the commission of the specific acts, who was thereby barred from the escape route of collective responsibility due to becoming a specific subject of international law. As opposed to the responsibility of states, the responsibility of individuals had the nature of criminal responsibility. The ideal of meting out punishment for international crimes, though not foreign to classic international law, nevertheless sparked wide systemic and terminological controversies and doubts, as well as controversies and doubts regarding sources and scopes.

Poland has extensive achievements in the field of exercise of criminal jurisdiction with regard to perpetrators of international crime. Especially in the Interwar period, the Poles took an active participation in the international academic discourse, as well as diplomatic initiatives. The prosecution and punishment of international crimes was regulated by domestic

202 Krzan (2020b): 345.

203 UN Doc. S/RES/827 (1993).

204 "Imprisonment shall be served in a State designated by the International Tribunal from a list of States which have indicated to the Security Council their willingness to accept convicted persons. Such imprisonment shall be in accordance with the applicable law of the State concerned, subject to the supervision of the International Tribunal".

205 See, e.g. Kuc (2012): 315ff.

law and debated vividly by academics. Nor could one possibly ignore the judicial achievements of the Supreme National Tribunal. The postwar period revealed a determined distrust against the institutionalized prosecution of international crimes, which, however, corresponded to the general impasse only broken after the conclusion of the Cold War. The support for *ad hoc* tribunals (including the enforcement of the penalties imposed by the ICTY) was accompanied by diplomatic involvement on behalf of the creation of a permanent ICC. The impact on the adjudication is visible due to the fact that it has eventually been possible to achieve the appointment of a Pole as a judge of an international criminal tribunal, with Professor Piotr Hofmański who even served as the President of the ICC.

CHAPTER 12

The Principles of Individual Criminal Responsibility

1 Modes of Responsibility

There can be no doubt that the responsibility for international crimes is not reducible to the direct perpetrators alone. Such are the specifics of macro-criminality. This responsibility eludes the traditional rules of attribution of criminal liability. The problem of collective perpetration has, of course, been studied in the Polish literature of criminal law.[1] For the purposes of the analysis of complex perpetration, one has to determine the context of the unlawful act. While Hannah Arendt's analyses will be the natural point of reference for this problem on the universal level from the perspective of philosophy and ethics, in our context one could hardly ignore Polish author Zygmunt Bauman's study into the mechanisms of diffusion of responsibility.[2]

The following levels of individual criminal responsibility are distinguished:[3] (1) perpetration, co-perpetration, indirect perpetration; (2) instigation (incitement); (3) aiding and abetting; (4) contribution to the commission of international crimes by a group of individuals acting for a common purpose. From the perspective of the international criminal court system, special forms of responsibility for participation in collective crime are of substantial importance.

Already during the works on the Code of Offences against Peace and Security of Mankind, the Polish delegation, in a letter of 7.01.1950, highlighted the necessity to: 'stress the prevention of those crimes because criminal repression alone cannot give satisfactory results, neither in the material nor in the moral sphere. Such prevention should be envisaged as broadly as possible and should punish not only acts directed immediately toward the commission of the crime, but should also counteract any activity which creates favourable conditions for the commission of those crimes

1 E.g., Rejman (1972).
2 Bauman (2002).
3 Królikowski (2011): 217.

 | DOI:10.1163/9789004712690_014

and, therefore, must be from this point of view treated as a preparatory act.'[4]

From the perspective of our discussion, one should take notice of the originality of Juliusz Makarewicz's contribution to the topic of criminal co-perpetration. During the initial period of his activity, Makarewicz published his studies in German (such as the oft-cited *Einführung in die Philosophie des Strafrechts auf entwicklungsgeschichtlicher Grundlage*[5] – 'Introduction to the philosophy of criminal law'), but after the restoration of Polish independence, he published mostly in Polish, which can explain the limitations of his influence on the development of the discipline. In this regard, we can notice the paradox that a tangible impact is currently wielded primarily by the German authors publishing in the latter half of the 20th century, whereas the extent of citations from 19th-century luminaries of criminal law such as Liszt is markedly limited.

Makarewicz was the author of the original theory of forms of perpetration of a criminal offence as a complication of the concept of uniform perpetration (*Einheitstätersystem*) and participation in someone else's act (*Teilnahmesystem*).[6] It was based on four main assumptions: autonomous responsibility; individualization of guilt; independent responsibility; and individualization of responsibility.

The natural starting point will be to draw the distinction between the general theories of perpetration – the broad one and the narrow one. In the broad theory, a perpetrator is one who contributes to the materialization of the elements of a defined type of offence. The narrow understanding of perpetration, on the other hand, regards as a perpetrator only one who with their own conduct fulfils the statutory set of elements of a defined type of offence. The latter entails the distinction between perpetration and participation (other forms of criminal co-operation).

For Makarewicz's concept, the natural starting point was the assumption of the individualization and autonomous nature of the responsibility of the co-participating/co-operating persons, with the distinction drawn among the various forms of co-operation. The concept referred solely to forms

4 YILC (1950), vol. II: 250.

5 Makarewicz (1906).

6 See a dispute in "Gazeta Sądowa Warszawska" between Juliusz Makarewicz (author of the work entitled *Wykładnia kodeksu karnego. Sprawca pośredni* [Interpretation of the Penal Code. Indirect perpetrator]) and Stefan Glaser, who in the sama journal published a study entitled *Sprawstwo pośrednie a polski kodeks karny* [Indirect perpetration and the Polish Penal Code].

other than perpetration, i.e. to instigation and aiding and abetting. Perpetratory forms of co-operation did not pose a problem because Makarewicz regarded perpetration as the most basic form of commission of a crime, the original form, consisting simply in the fulfilment, by a given person, of the essence of the act. For that reason, the Criminal Code of 1932 (dubbed *Lex Makarewicz*) did not regulate the perpetratory forms of commission of crime in the general part of the Code.[7]

In Makarewicz's opinion, all of the form had the same value from the perspective of criminal unlawfulness as content.[8] Despite breaking up with making the aider and abettor or the instigator's responsibility contingent on the principal perpetrator's, Makarewicz at the same time rejected making perpetratory forms of commission of the crime out of all forms of co-operation in the commission of a crime, which was characteristic of the uniform-perpetration model. For a certainty, Makarewicz's theory did not constitute a variant of the uniform-perpetration concept; however, it also clearly rejected the assumptions of the participation theory (such as by rejecting an accessory nature of responsibility).[9] Accordingly, his concept can be regarded as an intermediate solution, characterized by elements proper to both of the competing models and supplemented with elements not appearing in either.[10]

Makarewicz regarded the construct of participation in someone else's offence as an incompetent attempt to break with the principles of collective responsibility[11] or responsibility based on the *kumplot/komplot* principle, which he saw as not having a chance to survive in the long term.[12] This refers to the term *le complot*, considered in French scholarship since the 18th century and introduced to the French *Code pénal* of 1810. It was used for determinations of co-perpetration in homicide in the context of the intensification of the activities of all sorts of brigands and marauders. At the time, such a construct of conspiracy entailed punishability only in exceptional situations, with regard to crimes against the external and internal security of the state. Thus, *le complot* denoted a plot as a resolution to act agreed and established among two or more persons. Subsequently (in the 19th century), two new terms of key importance for criminal co-operation

7 Kardas (2017): 922.
8 Makarewicz (1938): 129.
9 Liszewska (2004): 16ff.
10 Kardas (2002): 80.
11 Makarewicz (1906): 330.
12 *Ibidem*: 336, 340.

developed out of *le complot* – the construct of participation in a crime, as well as the construct of a plot as a punishworthy collusion (relating to a criminal offence against the state), which, however, did not culminate in the commission of a criminal offence. Later, French law introduced the punishability of creating a band or acting within it, and ultimately the punishability of a criminal association.[13]

Makarewicz's writings show a marked tendency in the development of criminal law from collective to individual responsibility. At the onset, the culpability of all members of a given collective was presumed, but that presumption of guilt could be refuted by delivering up the perpetrator of the offence. The subsequent *le complot* concept limited the responsibility to only those persons who had struck the agreement to commit the crime, and the distinction among the roles of the various co-participants was abandoned, so that they were all held responsible as co-perpetrators. The shortcomings of that concept led to the formulation of another concept – that of participation in the crime, in which the roles of perpetrators are distinguished from those of participants.[14]

With regard to corporate responsibility (the responsibility of collectives), Makarewicz, who was opposed to the creation of a separate division devoted to it in the Code, preferred criminal-administrative responsibility.[15] This involves the foundation of the concepts of the philosophy of criminal law, wherein any manifestation of criminal activity must be individualized, i.e. resulting from the evaluation of a specific act of a specific person, not the conduct of another. In his commentary on the 1932 Code, Makarewicz wrote:

> It must be accepted as a principle that there is no share in the criminal offence of another but that all who contribute to the commission of a criminal offence are responsible for a criminal offence of their own. The conduct of an instigator and an aider is not only the precondition of a change in the external world, as the old theory had it, but is the cause of it, in the same way as the principal perpetrator's conduct. Thus, one must reject the very name of, 'participation in a criminal offence.'[16]

13 Wójcik (2011): §2.2.
14 Makarewicz (1938): 127.
15 Makarewicz (1906): 357.
16 Makarewicz (1938): 179.

Makarewicz's concept, therefore, aimed to build a third way, providing for the individualization of the responsibility of each of those participating in the commission of a criminal offence but without making the various contributors' responsibility contingent on the central responsibility of the perpetrator. Makarewicz did not make a complete break with the concept of participation, as he did not completely abandon the separation of instigation and aiding and abetting,[17] consistently regarding them, similarly as perpetrator, as technical forms of commission of a criminal offence. The lack of consistency in this theoretical approach was noted.[18]

Makarewicz strongly criticized his contemporary luminaries of criminal law, such as Władysław Wolter and Stefan Glaser, for diminishing the Polish legacy of scholarly achievement and ignoring the Polish legal culture, which, in his opinion, did not fall short of the solutions used throughout the world.[19] Thus, it was difficult for him to accept that when commenting on the solutions of the Criminal Code, the authors relied on German constructs without accounting for the characteristics separating them.[20]

In this context, it will be once again fitting to recall the 1943 decree on the responsibility for war crimes, which had been issued before the start of the UNWCC's works and before the Moscow Declaration. It was the first normative formulation of principles of criminal responsibility for the crimes of WWII, transcending the traditional dispositions of criminal law to base the responsibility on the act's unlawfulness in international law. Neither the perpetrator's official position, nor acting on superior orders excluded responsibility for an act incompatible with international law.

A determined approach was also taken in the PKWN Decree of 31.08.1944. It served as the basis of the trial of KL Majdanek staff in Lublin. Criminal responsibility was already pursued before the end of the war and before the London Agreement. The constructs used preceded the Nuremberg principles. It must be noted clearly, however, that this specific model was not based on Soviet inspirations in the adoption of a less nuanced formula with regard to either aiders and abettors or instigators. It is difficult, in this context, to speak of distinctions as to the degree of culpability. The later developments are discussed primarily from the perspective of the influence of the constructs of conspiracy and criminal co-operation.

17 Zoll (1998): 57ff, (1996): 275ff.

18 Zoll (2009): 175.

19 Makarewicz (1933): 51.

20 Rejman (2005): 116.

2 The Constructs of Conspiracy and Joint Criminal Enterprise

Articles 9 and following of the IMT Charter allowed an organization or group to be declared criminal, as a result of which criminal sanctions could be imposed on the members. Where the Tribunal had found a group or organization to be criminal, the competent authorities of each signatory had the right to put the members before domestic or occupation courts on charges of participation in such a group or organization. Article 10 stipulated: 'In any such case the criminal nature of the group or organisation is considered proved and shall not be questioned.' Thus, the parties had the obligation to adhere to the IMT's findings as to the criminal character of such organizations. Pursuant to Article 11 of the IMT Charter, members of organizations found to be criminal could be held responsible before domestic courts. Upon conviction, in the sentencing, they could be given a penalty independent from and addition to the one imposed by the IMT for participation in the criminal activities of such an organization or group.

The practice of the courts, especially the NTN, was of crucial importance. Let us recall that the NTN's first trials (those of Arthur Greiser and Amon Göth) completed already before the IMT's judgment. Greiser's indictment included charges of: 'participation in a joint criminal enterprise.' The Polish tribunal made a reference to the role of the 'intellectual perpetrator' – an instigator inciting another individual or group of individuals to commit a crime. With that, it made the following clarification:

> this is not about creating some new collective responsibility for the guilt of another (defendant Greiser's responsibility for 'leader' Hitler's guilt), it is not about departing from the basic individualized position of personal responsibility within the limits of one's own guilt, but about taking into consideration the indubitable fact that a whole line-up of modern crimes are committed by narrower or wider circles of criminals – in a collective – with differing natures and intensities of direct co-operation (instigators, physical perpetrators, aiders and abettors).[21]

The literature emphasized the NTN's innovativeness but also its diligence in holding the war criminals accountable for their actions. As opposed to the

21 NTN, Greiser case: 16 (§13).

proceedings in other countries (e.g. the Netherlands), those were not show trials.[22]

Kubicki noted that the concept of criminal conspiracy as a criminal offence *sui generis*, foreign to continental law, found acceptance at Nuremberg and made a foray into Polish law.[23] Greiser's indictment included the charge of participation in a joint criminal enterprise, although the notion of conspiracy from the Nuremberg indictment denotes a different meaning. Nevertheless, the opinion with the NTN's judgment uses the term with the meaning adopted during the Nuremberg trial.[24] Under the applicable criminal law, the NTN could classify the act as the crime under Article 93 in conjunction with Article 97 of the 1932 Criminal Code. Let us recall that the judgment in Greiser's trial came down on 8.07.1946, and thus almost a quarter before the publication of the Nuremberg judgment. Out of necessity, it referenced attempting to deprive Poland of independence and part of the territory.[25]

In Greiser's case, the NTN explicitly recognized the principle expressed in Article 6 of the IMT Charter with regard to the leaders or organizers participating in the design or implementation of a general plan or conspiracy for the purpose of committing crimes falling within the Tribunal's jurisdiction, who bore responsibility for the actions of all individuals acting as the executors of such a plan.

In respect of all leadership positions within the NSDAP, it provided the grounds for the conclusion that the Polish authorities (including the courts) were bound by the IMT's positive findings but were free to venture beyond the negative ones.[26] The list in Article 4(3) of the August Decree following the amendment of December 1946 was merely an exemplification allowing the courts to declare other organizations criminal, too, exceeding the scope specified in the IMT's judgment. Sawicki argued that the Polish court should not be bound by the IMT's decision acquitting certain groups or organizations on the charge of criminality; in such a case, according to him, the Polish ought to have the: 'full right – and not obligation – to declare such an organization criminal for the scope of the court's jurisdiction.'[27]

22 Prusin, Finder (2018): 130.

23 Kubicki (1987): 33.

24 NTN Greiser case: 20.

25 Kubicki (1987): 33.

26 Szerer (1948a): 30.

27 Sawicki (1948): 56.

Article 166 of the Polish Criminal Code of 1932 envisaged responsibility for participation in a union designed for the purpose of committing a crime, so the construct did not spark controversy among Polish lawyers and jurists. Doubts, on the other hand, arose with regard to the list of criminal organizations and scopes of participation in them. In its original wording, the August Decree did not contain any reference to responsibility for participating in a criminal organization. The relevant changes came only with the amendment of 10.12.1946.[28] The new Article 4 established participation in a criminal organization as a criminal offence *sui generis*. Its §1 provided for at least three years' imprisonment or life imprisonment or death penalty for one guilty of: 'participating in a criminal organization created or recognized by the authorities of the German state or of a state allied thereto or by a political association acting in the interest of the German state or of a state allied thereto.'

Section 2 defined a criminal organization as follows: 'group organization: (a) having the purpose of crimes against peace, war crimes or crimes against humanity; or (b) while having a different purpose, pursuing it through the commission of the crimes set out in letter a.' The next section criminalized membership especially in: (a) the National Socialist German Workers' Party (National Sozialistische Deutsche Arbeiterpartei – NSDAP) on all tiers of leadership; (b) Protection Squadrons (Schutzstaffeln – SS), (c) Secret State Police (Geheime Staats-Polizei – Gestapo), (d) Security Service (Sicherheitsdienst – SD).

Previously, the provision established the punishability of attempting, instigating, aiding or abetting, which was viewed[29] as a superfluous repetition because Article 6 of the Decree referenced the general part of the Criminal Code, in which attempt was regulated in Articles 23–25 and instigating, aiding and abetting in Articles 26–30 of the Criminal Code.

Initially, the Polish courts took a broad view of the matter, including in this category the: 'leadership of any organizational group, even the smallest,' as long as the leader's activities and initiative were in a position to provide the group with, 'style and direction of work.'[30]

The Supreme Court noted that the IMT, in its judgment, found – among other organizations – the leadership of the NSDAP to be criminal, deciding

28 Dz.U.1946.69.376.

29 See Sawicki, Walawski (1945): 17.

30 Judgment, 16.07.1947, K 766/47 after: Kubicki (1963): 141. The finding made in the judgment of 10.09.1947 in *K 924/47* was that the language of the decree referred to all positions with names incorporating the word *Leiter* – *Ibidem*.

that it included the party's so-called Reichsleitung, the Gauleiters and Kreisleiters, Ortsgruppenleiters and office heads in Reichsleitung, Gauleitung and Kreisleitung staffs. The Supreme Court not observed also that other persons were excluded. It decided:

> the following positions have to be regarded as leadership positions within the National Socialist German Workers' Party within the meaning of Article 4(3)(a) of the Decree of 31 August 1944: Reichsleiters, Gauleiters, Kreisleiters and Ortsgruppenleiters, members of the Reichsleitung and office heads in the clerical staffs of Reichsleitung, Gauleitung and Kreisleitung tiers, whereas the position of Ortsgruppenkassenleiter [is] not a leadership position within the meaning of the above-cited provision.'[31]

In its reasons, the Supreme Court emphasized the importance of the adjudicatory link arising, from treaty, between the adjudication of the Polish courts and the international adjudication with regard to the punishment of war criminals, as well as the aforementioned background of Article 4 of the Decree, i.e. the aspiration to bring the domestic legislation to conformity with the principles of international criminal law. In the later part of the reasoning, the justices found:

> Article 4(3)(a) of the Decree of 31 August 1944 leads to the conclusion that the Polish lawmaker, when formulating the factual hypothesis of that provision, enacted after the publication of the above-cited judgment of the International Military Tribunal, in criminalizing membership in the National Socialist German Workers' Party, contemplated only the positions found to be positions of leadership by the International Tribunal.

Furthermore, it expressly emphasized: 'the close adjudicatory link between domestic and international adjudication in this field allows the Polish courts to have recourse to the International Tribunal's judgment for the interpretation of the Polish statute based on that judgment.' The above marked a departure from the recommendations of the scholars.[32]

---

31 SN, Decision (7 judges), 23.02.1948, K 949/47, OSN(K) 1948/1/1.

32 Szerer (1948a): 30; Sawicki (1948): 56–57.

In an analogous way, the Supreme Court followed the IMT's judgment in delineating the scope of responsibility for membership in the SS.[33] When it comes to membership in the Gestapo, by contrast, the Polish courts decided on a broader scope than the one arising from the Nuremberg judgment. While the IMT excluded the responsibility of the technical personnel, the Polish Supreme Court did not decide to distinguish any nuanced categories of Gestapo staff. Instead, for example, the Supreme Court's judgment of 26.11.1952 held the following position:

> The type of activities performed by a participant of the 'Gestapo' criminal organization may either justify additional responsibility for the crimes committed in such capacity or influence the sentencing within the limits of Article 4 of the Decree of 31 August 1944. There is, however, no justification for the view that service in the Gestapo in the capacity of a prison guard does not entail criminal responsibility under Article 4 of said Decree.[34]

Sometimes, when determining responsibility for membership in the Gestapo, the manner of exercise of a given function by the defendant was taken into account.[35] The participation of confidential informants in the Gestapo's activities proved to be an especially difficult mater,[36] though in the end it was held that for the responsibility to arise there was: 'no need of any particular form of accession, nor for the holding of an organizational function, as it suffice[d] to have manifested the will to collaborate with that organization and (…) awareness of its tasks and goals.'[37] In this regard, the Polish judiciary went beyond the framework set by the IMT's judgement.

---

33 SN, Decision, 15.03.1948, K 1112/47, OSN(K) 1948/2/31.

34 SN, Judgment, 26.11.1952, II K 181/52, OSNCK 1953/1/11.

35 SN, Judgment, 6.06.1950, K 576/50, OSN(K) 1950/2/8: 'Serving in the Gestapo as the censor of outgoing letters from the prisoners to their families and ones incoming to the prisoners from their families constitutes participation in the Gestapo criminal organization within the meaning of Article 4 of the Decree of 31 August 1944 (Dz.U.R.-P.1946.69.377), as it meant the direct performance of activities falling within the scope of the Gestapo's operation. Discharging the functions of a censor in such circumstances was a manifestation of the will to collaborate with that organization. Discharging the function of an interpreter at Gestapo, in turn, may indicate participation in that criminal organization within the meaning of Article 4 of the aforementioned Decree, depending on findings as to the manner of the discharge of such functions.'

36 Kubicki (1963): 144ff.

37 SN, Judgment, 10.11.1947, K 1570/47, OSN(K) 1948/2/41. The Supreme Court further specified: 'Accepting the duties of a Gestapo informant without developing any specific

Likewise, criminal organizations were treated more broadly, by including the leadership of the Generalgouvernement administration,[38] the Ukrainian Insurgent Army (UPA),[39] the Ukrainian SS formation, the concentration-camp organization, and Selbstschutz ('self-protection') units.

As for the concentration camps, one should first of all note the Auschwitz trial before the NTN in Cracow. That was an occasion to consider the significance of the Nuremberg judgment with regard to criminal organizations. When addressing that matter, the NTN emphasized the development of international law and referred to the IMT's judgment as: 'undoubtedly the first step forward towards a codification of international criminal law,' although with the simultaneous caveat that the judgment was: 'not a criminal code in the sense of the competent courts not being able to regard actions not covered by it as not criminal offences.' That allowed the Tribunal to draw the following conclusion: 'From the perspective of international law, therefore, there are no obstacles to supplementing the legal principles contained in the Nuremberg judgment with new principles not contrary to it.'[40]

While analysing the August Decree against the background of the Nuremberg judgment, the NTN found: 'The facts in the Nuremberg judgment do not constraint the Polish lawmaker, who is free to regard as punishable in Poland actions not covered by the Nuremberg judgment, as long as the latter does not expressly find them not to be punishable,' along with the lack of any conflict between the Polish statute and the Nuremberg judgment. Furthermore, it was noted: 'the interpretation of the Polish statute must not be contrary to the express language of the Nuremberg judgment,' and – more importantly: 'the Polish courts are not authorized to examine the compatibility of Polish statutes with the Nuremberg judgments but have the

criminal activity by itself fulfils the elements of the criminal offence under Article 4 of the Decree of 31 August 1944 on the Sentencing Guidelines for Fascist-Nazi Criminals (Dz.U.R.P.1946.69.377), as participation in a criminal organization mentioned in Article 4(3)(c).'

38 Cf. Rybicki (1947).

39 SN, Judgment, 22.09.1950, K 1147/50, OSN(K) 1951/2/18: 'The Ukrainian Insurgent Army (U.P.A.), created by the "Ukrainian National Committee" political association acting in the interest of Nazi Germany, had the purpose of suppression of the Polish element and anti-fascist forces within the territory of Ukraine, as well as fighting against the Soviet Union with the backing of the German Reich, in the light of which it constitutes a criminal organization within the meaning of Article 4 of the August Decree.'

40 NTN, Auschwitz trial case: 250–251.

right and obligation to refer to that judgment when interpreting the Polish statute based on it.'[41] Neither did the NTN harbour any doubts as to that:

> the organization of the German concentration camps [wa]s a criminal organization within the meaning of both the Nuremberg judgment and Article 4 of the [August] Decree, for the purpose of those camps was the unlawful deprivation of freedom, health, property and life of specific individuals and groups of the population on account of their racial (Jews, Roma), national (Poles, Czechs), religious (Judaists) or political (socialists, communists, anti-Nazis) affiliation. The German concentration-camp organization was thus an organization having the purpose of committing crimes against humanity, which were simultaneously crimes under the criminal codes of all civilized nations and war crimes, with regard to Soviet prisoners of war.[42]

It will be expedient to take a closer look at the definition coined in the NTN's judgment:

> By the concentration-camp organization one has to understand the camp's German authorities, administration and crew, with the exclusion of prisoners compelled to serve in various administrative roles, as the latter can only be held responsible for their individual activities, for they did not belong to the organization in the sense attributed to it by the Nuremberg judgment, i.e. they were not tied to it by the common purpose that was the commission of crimes against humanity. Those people did not have ideological ties to the camp organization but were used as an instrument for the commission of the individual crimes. That does not protect them from punishment for those individual actions, but it does not allow them to be held guilty of membership in a criminal organization as a standalone criminal offence.[43]

The literature underscored the importance of the NTN's judgments not only due to the enormous and precise documentation but also the diligence of its legal reasoning and argument.[44] The Supreme Court, in turn, emphasized that the responsibility for being part of the camp crew should not be treated

41 *Ibidem*: 251.

42 *Ibidem*: 253 margin no. 191, para. 14.

43 *Ibidem*: 254, margin no. 193, para. 19.

44 Klafkowski (1968a): 16.

automatically. The following caveat was made: 'merely formal and compulsory membership in the camp crew, given effect in a manner contradicting the goals and tasks of such a camp and the duties incumbent on the members of its crew cannot be regarded as a punishable – within the meaning of Article 4 – participation in a criminal organization.'[45]

One should note the phrasing – 'participation' rather than, 'membership.' According to Kubicki,[46] the above attests to the existence of a deliberate aspiration to base the criminal responsibility not only on formal but first and foremost on substantive grounds. Such was also the way in which the courts dealt with participation in an organization, looking at the perpetrator's organic ties to the organization's apparatus, consisting in readiness at all times to carry out its instructions.'[47] The duration of one's membership in the organization was immaterial.[48] It was also assumed that formal membership was not a necessary prerequisite for participation, which could consist in *de facto* participation, i.e.[49] the systematic carrying out of functions normally undertaken by the members of the organization. The responsibility for participation in a criminal organization was autonomous, i.e. irrespective of the perpetrator's activities within the organization. It arose from the membership itself, though the *mens rea* requirement could not be ignored, which precluded responsibility in a case of joining an organization with a clear lack of intention of collaborating with the occupation authorities (*reservatio mentalis*).[50]

In Fischer's case, the NTN emphasized: 'anyone who, knowing the programme and method of operation of a party or body, accedes to them, undoubtedly at least foresees the actions of the party or body and accepts them, in accepting the organizational duty of participation, assistance and obedience, in leadership positions even of initiative and active representation, in line with the party or body's by-laws and programme.' Thus: 'who accedes to bodies, accepts the full responsibility for what such a body does.' The NTN took the position that although the responsibility for collective activities was of a superior order, it still remained the individual responsibility for one's own guilty and thus not the responsibility of a guiltless person.

45 SN, Judgment, 1.10.1948 (Cracow session), Kr K 1254/48, OAIPN Kraków/IPN Kr 502/1232 https://truthaboutcamps.eu/ftp/baza-ss-oswiecim/wyroki/SN_Kr_K_1254_48_01_10_1948.pdf.

46 Kubicki (1963): 152.

47 SN, Judgment, 28.05.1950, K 538/50, quoted after: Kubicki (1963): 152–3.

48 SN, Judgment, 29.03.1949, Lu K 110/49, quoted after: Kubicki (1963): 153.

49 Kubicki (1963): 153; Pasek (2002): 108ff.

50 Kubicki (1963): 155; Pasek (2002): 109.

Superior order was also precluded from posing a bar to criminal prosecution. It was noted, pointedly: 'if (...) an individual joins a certain body, which obliges the individual to absolute obedience and discipline; if the individual accepts the body's worldview and methods of operation, the individual thereby accepts up front the responsibility for carrying out such a body's orders.'[51]

One should note the attempts to declare the Home Army a criminal organization,[52] which were ultimately abandoned.[53]

On the basis of variable court judgments, one could also consider the various categories of a joint criminal plan.[54] Firstly, this may involve a situation in which all of the perpetrators acted according to a plan, having one common purpose, that of committing a criminal offence (without necessarily performing the same actions, as the common purpose is what counts). Secondly, one has to mention the camp cases, discussed by Kubicki,[55] and thirdly, the separate category of the existence of a common plan and the perpetration of acts not being part of the plan (when one of the perpetrators exceeds the limits of the common plan) but constituting its natural consequence.[56]

Similar constructs have been relied on primarily by the ICTY and hybrid tribunals. The permanent ICC does not apply them, relying instead on the German concept of having authority over the act (*Tatherrschaft*), coined by Claus Roxin. It has become the object of substantial analysis in Polish literature.[57]

The topic of perpetration is the subject-matter of multiple studies and analyses. As far as the construct of conspiracy is concerned, considerable importance belongs to Stanisław Pomorski's study titled *Conspiracy and Criminal Organization*, included in *The Nuremberg Trial and International Law*,[58] edited by Ginsburgs and Kudriavtsev. Last but not least, one could not possibly ignore Michał Królikowski's monograph *Odpowiedzialność karna jednostki za sprawstwo zbrodni międzynarodowej* (2011) ('The criminal

51 NTN Fischer case: 58

52 SN Judgment (no specification) PiP 10/1950 191.

53 See Pasek (2002): 110.

54 Wierczyńska (2009): 79

55 Kubicki (1963): 93.

56 The form of intent consists in that the perpetrator accepted or was indifferent to the risk of causing obvious and foreseeable consequences, for which reason this is the most controversial of all categories – see Kuczyńska (2008): 606.

57 Królikowski (2011); Olewiński (2015); Nieprzecka (2022).

58 Pomorski (1990): 213.

responsibility of an individual for the perpetration of an international crime'), since it offers a comprehensive examination of the topic.

It is notable that coursebooks in international criminal law discuss this topic (in varying degrees) by reference to Article 25 of the Rome Statute.[59] In this context, it will be expedient to cite the excellent summation offered by Judge Christine Van den Wyngaert. In the case of Mathieu Ngudjolo Chui, she viewed Part III of the Rome Statute as an eclectic amalgamation of sources originating from numerous domestic legal traditions and certain international instruments, with Article 25 itself being of a multivarious origin and a compromise among different legal traditions.[60] Concurring with the acquittal, she viewed the ICC's importation of the control theory derived from the German scholarship and the findings of Claus Roxin as problematic and noted: 'Considering its universalist mission, the Court should refrain from relying on particular national models, however sophisticated they may be.'[61]

In the Criminal Code of 1969, Article 276 penalized participation in a criminal union or organized group having the purpose of the commission of a criminal offence sanctioned with one year's imprisonment or a more severe penalty; an aggravated subtype involved an armed union or group. Founding or leading a union or organized group had its own separate section (§3 of Article 276). Article 278 of the Code of 1969, on the other hand, referred to a union whose existence, organization or purpose was intended to be kept secret from the authorities of the state or one that had been dissolved or denied legalization. Article 278(3) regulated leadership activities in a dissolved union or one denied legalization, and Article 278(4) provided an exemption from punishability in the case of voluntary withdrawal from participating in the union.

The current Criminal Code of 1997 regulates participation in an organized group or union having the purpose of the commission of a criminal or fiscal-criminal offence in Article 259, with an aggravated subtype in Article 259(2) for an armed group or union or one having as its purpose the commission of a criminal offence of terrorist nature.

To explain the distinction between Article 258(1) and the construct of criminal union, one should note that the unlawfulness of the relevant

59 Hofmański, Kuczyńska (2020): 96ff.

60 ICC-01/04–02/12–4, Judgment pursuant to Article 74 of the Statute – Concurring Opinion of Judge Christine Van den Wyngaert, 18.12.2012, §13.

61 *Ibidem*: (5).

conduct is triggered not so much by the existence of a common criminal plan as membership itself in the group.

3 Command Responsibility/Immunities

The lack of responsibility of persons holding the most important functions in states was justified with the sovereign equality of states and the act-of-state doctrine, which provided immunity.

After WWI, the topic was explored during the works of the Commission on the Responsibilities. In its report, the Commission: 'desire[d] to state expressly that in the hierarchy of persons in authority, there is no reason why rank, however exalted, should in any circumstances protect the holder of it from responsibility when that responsibility has been established before a properly constituted tribunal.'[62] And in the very next sentence: 'This extends even to the case of heads of states.'[63]

The authors of the report referenced the domestic importance of immunities (effective before a domestic court) but noted the differences from the perspective of international law. The Report's argument was quite pungent: 'If the immunity of a sovereign is claimed to extend beyond the limits above stated, it would involve laying down the principle that the greatest outrages against the laws and customs of war and the laws of humanity, if proved against him, could in no circumstances be punished. Such a conclusion would shock the conscience of civilized mankind.'[64]

In the course of the UNWCC's works, certain doubts surfaced with regard to exacting responsibility from the highest representatives of a state. The autumn of 1944 saw the beginning of the discussion of the issue of so-called arch-criminals – the main war criminals.[65] Previously, the predominant view within the Commission had been that – in line with the Moscow Declaration – the punishment of the major war criminals was to be the task of the leading Allied powers. Despite the efforts undertaken by Poland and Czechoslovakia, the prevalent position was against intruding on the competences reserved to the political decision of the great powers.[66] On 26.09.1944, in the course of a discussion on the matter of the major

62 (1920) 14 AJIL 95, 116.

63 *Ibidem.*

64 *Ibidem.*

65 Cyprian, Sawicki (1948b): 130.

66 *Ibidem*: 131.

criminals, the Polish delegate (Cyprian) tabled the motion to put Hitler on the list. He won the support of the Dutch delegate and sparked a discussion in the aftermath of which the decision was made to enter on the list of war criminals the entire German government, high command, the most important persons in the NSDAP, Gestapo and SS, rather than waiting for the initiative of the governments in pursuance of the Moscow Declaration.[67]

On 24.04.1945, the UNWCC adopted its 'seventh list' with names of holders of leadership positions in the government, in the military and in the various organizations. That list was of key importance to determining the circle of potential culprits. Its adoption, furthermore, marked a break from the previous practice of investigating and approving the accusations submitted by the various states, so that the Commission took on the role of a co-accuser. Thus, from a mere fact-finding body, it became a co-driving force of international justice alongside the national prosecutor.[68] Following a heated discussion, the eventually unanimously adopted seventh list covered those holding positions of leadership in the German government, armed forces and various organizations.[69]

Article 7 of the IMT Charter expressly provided that the defendants' positions as heads of state or responsible officials in the government could not exempt them from the responsibility or mitigate their punishment. Hence, there can be no surprise in the third Nuremberg principle: 'The fact that a person who committed an act which constitutes a crime under international law, acted as Head of State or responsible government official, does not relieve him from responsibility under international law.' The above is not the sole example of the International Law Commission's taking of a position on the matter.

The irrelevance of a public function found confirmation in the judgments of the NTN following the trials of Greiser, Forster and other high officials of the occupation administration. The very prerequisite for the ability to commit a war crime was to hold a function in German military or civil service or that of a state allied to Germany.[70] As rightly pointed out by Kubicki, especially in reference to the unlawful actions of the Nazi-created Ukrainian police force: 'the principles of international law were applicable to all officials and functionaries in an identical degree, regardless of their ethnicity,

67 UNWCC Doc. M 33 (26.09.1944).

68 Cyprian, Sawicki (1948b): 142.

69 UNWCC Doc. M 57, 24.04.1945.

70 Kubicki (1963): 133.

nationality and their circumstances of joining the service.'[71] By contrast, Poles holding official positions within whatever Polish administrative structures had been preserved by the occupying authorities were in a position to commit the criminal offence of collaboration, not war crimes. In their later judgments, the courts did not regard the exercise of administrative functions alone in itself as fulfilling the elements of the offence of collaboration. Punishability required excessive zeal for the exercise of the duties.[72] The criminal offences defined by the August Decree could only be committed intentionally. They had to be committed: 'in the interest of the German occupation authorities.'

In its judgment against Greiser, the NTN expressly recognized the principle that found its way to Article 6 of the IMT Charter, i.e. the responsibility of managers or organizers participating in the design or implementation of a general plan or plot for the actions of all individuals who were the executors of such a plan. It is worth quoting the relevant portion of the text of the judgment, in which the judges noted the necessity of: 'judging justly the collective perpetrators of the brutal depredatory aggression against Poland, explicable neither by economic need nor even political expansion,' and emphasized: 'there exist managers and organizers of a criminal conspiracy on a global scale, the culprits of the most monstrous instigation of thousands of executors to crimes against the culture and civilization of humanity known to history.'[73] In response to the following question: 'should the managers or organizers who participated in the design or implementation of a general plan or plot directed towards the commission of all sorts of crimes against peace, against the laws and customs of war, or against humanity, be held, in line with the principles of the law of nations and demands of the international conscience, responsible for the actions performed by all the individuals having been the executors of such a plan?.'[74]

The NTN fully accepted the merits of the affirmative response given by Professors Ehrlich and Peretiatkowicz.[75]

---

71 *Ibidem*.

72 See SN, Judgment, 20.04.1947, K 2492/47: 'Discharging the function of a village foreman in the occupying power's service does not in itself contain the qualities of criminal activity. The function of a village foreman entails a certain scope of powers and duties and only excessive zeal in the performance of such duties could possibly be punishable in line with the provisions of the Decree' – quoted after Kubicki (1963): 133–134.

73 NTN Greiser case: 20.

74 *Ibidem*: 21.

75 *Ibidem*: 20–21.

In Höss's trial, the NTN judges held that the defendant had assumed full responsibility for all things happening at the camp.[76] The trial demonstrated that:

> he was not only the blind executor of Himmler's orders, in his position as camp commandant and later as a special plenipotentiary for the so-called *Aktion Höss*; he contributed his own initiative, venturing far beyond the camp regulations and the orders or recommendations of his superior authorities. In the excess of his SS zeal, he was not only an excellent executor but also the embodiment of all those virtues that the criminal regime had expected of its faithful servants.'[77]

The Supreme National Tribunal emphatically and categorically rejected the defendant's reliance on the circumstances of acting on superior orders (as: 'an outright mendacious and ridiculous claim'). 'an order does not provide exemption from responsibility; one may not, after all, rely on an order given by an authority that commits crimes itself. There can be no such escape from responsibility here. The defendant could only have avoided that responsibility if he had distanced himself from that criminal plot by explicitly leaving it.'[78] The NTN further developed upon the above rationale in the Auschwitz trial, in which, with regard to Liebehenschel, the judges concluded: 'one cannot surmise that it all was happening without the defendant's knowledge, against his will; on the contrary; one must hold that the defendant participated in all those killings on account of his position in the hierarchy.'[79]

In the scholarship, a similar line of argument against the applicability of immunity or privilege, including diplomatic immunity or privilege, was represented by Giebułtowicz. He noted the undermining of the logical system of the existence of law (in general, not only international law) if diplomatic privileges were to justify goals contrary to the law.[80] He wrote: 'a head of state or diplomatic representative may be under the protection of the law for as long as their conduct follows the path indicated by the law; they lose the protection of the law if their activity is contrary to the law.'[81] He viewed

76 NTN Höss case: 132.
77 *Ibidem*: 134.
78 *Ibidem*: 135 (§63).
79 NTN, Auschwitz case: 197 (§98).
80 Giebułtowicz (1945): 48.
81 *Ibidem*: 49.

the principle of personification as a relic of absolute monarchy, on par with vestiges of sacrality. For elected officials, he assumed a different mechanism, excluding any privileged position. He referenced the political solution in the case of Napoleon Bonaparte but above all Article 227 of the Treaty of Versailles as a *novum* in international relations and the beginning of the formation of a norm on the basis of which Adolf Hitler could be held responsible.[82] As he noted: 'where the responsibility [for war crimes] is not exacted by the domestic organs of the criminal's state of nationality, the one who had the duty to bring the case and to watch over the respect of the law of nations must, in turn, be held responsible.' By following on the above reasoning, one can arrive at the responsibility of the head of state, who is tasked to watch over the state's compliance with its obligations. When the latter is not forthcoming, the head of state can become a war criminal responsible for the violation of the law of nations and incurring the highest responsibility for it.[83] The responsibility of members of the government, on the other hand, according to Giebułtowicz, was of an intermediate nature between head-of-state responsibility and the responsibility of the executive organs.[84]

Command responsibility also features as Article 11 of the Draft Code of Crimes, debated within the ILC in 1988.[85] It was retained in the document adopted in 1996.[86] The statutes of the *ad hoc*[87] tribunals also framed it in similar terms.

In its commentary on Article 6 *Responsibility of the superior* of the Code of Crimes, the ILC stated: 'Military commanders are responsible for the conduct of members of the armed forces under their command and other persons under their control.'[88] That, however, was a time when the Commission had no Polish members.

Our discussion of the topic would not be complete without mentioning the ILC works relating to the immunity of state officials from foreign criminal jurisdiction. The works began during Zdzisław Galicki's term as Commission member. In his reports, special rapporteur Roman Kolodkin included references to works by Franciszek (or Frank) Przetacznik.[89]

82 *Ibidem*: 51.
83 *Ibidem*: 52.
84 *Ibidem*: 53.
85 UN Doc. A/43/10, YILC (1988), Vol. II(2): 71.
86 YILC (1996), vol. II(2): 26.
87 ICTY Statute, Art. 7; ICTR Statute, Art. 6.
88 UN Doc. (A/51/10).
89 Przetacznik (1983); *idem* (1991): 52.

Poland submitted a single comment as a product of a session of the Advisory Legal Committee of the MFA. The extensive opinion explores the scope of the relevant immunities. In line with the IDI resolution, 'personal immunity' and 'functional immunity' were the terms recommended for use. The immunities accorded to heads of state, heads of government and ministers of foreign affairs were deemed ready for codification in the form of an international instrument, as opposed to the immunities – unfortunately, likewise referred to as *ratione materiae* – applicable to other state representatives (with a corresponding lack of the *opinio juris*). The opinion, furthermore, highlighted the need to regulate the personal inviolability of the holders *ratione personae* immunities after the fashion of Article 29 of the Vienna Convention on Diplomatic Relations;[90] the following wording was suggested: 'The person of a head of state, head of government or minister of foreign affairs shall be inviolable. Such persons shall not be liable to any form of arrest or detention. Other states shall, within their territories, treat such persons with due respect and shall take all appropriate steps to prevent any attack on such persons, their freedom or dignity.'

When considering *ratione personae* immunity, reference was made to the previous Polish position as to the consequences of the non-recognition of a state or government. Those remarks were not directly reflected in the articles adopted in the first reading. In the light of the earlier plan to indict Hitler, such positions appear to fall markedly on the conservative side.

In the *Bemba* case, the ICC's Pre-Trial Chamber found Article 28 of the Statute to reflect a different form of criminal responsibility compared to the one provided by Article 25(3)(a), in the sense that a superior could be held responsible for the prohibited conduct of subordinates in the form of responsibility for failure in the duty to prevent or suppress such unlawful conduct of subordinates or refer the case to the competent authorities.[91] Questions are rightly asked as to the position assigned to the giving of orders and, as it were, degradation of the responsibility specified in the following paragraphs of the same article.[92] The Appellate Chamber's judgment did not discuss the subject; however, judges Van den Wyngaert and Morrison concurring,[93] as well as judges Monaseng and Hofmański dissenting,

---

90 500 UNTS 95.

91 ICC, PTC II, Decision Pursuant to Article 61(7)(a) and (b) of the Rome Statute on the Charges of the Prosecutor Against Jean-Pierre Bemba Gombo, ICC-01/05-01/08-424, 15.06.2009

92 Grzebyk (2013b): 218.

93 See ICC-01/05-01/08-3636-Anx2, 8.06.2018.

delivered their separate opinions.[94] Judges Monaseng and Hofmański's dissent is worth noting because of its unequivocal emphasis on that holding a commander criminally responsible for crimes falling within the Court's jurisdiction committed by subordinates is, 'only justified and indeed justifiable if there is a personal nexus between the crime and the superior'. The judges categorically underscored: 'it would be irreconcilable with basic tenets of criminal law if a superior were to be held responsible for crimes to which he or she has no connection.'[95]

4 Responsibility for Carrying Out Orders

Much attention has been devoted in the Polish literature to the matter of military orders.[96] The essence of an order comes down to a unilateral act of will creating an obligation for a specific entity; accordingly, this has two defining characteristics: unilaterality and creation of an obligation-imposing norm.[97]

The cornerstone of military discipline is the obedience of subordinates to the orders given by superiors; however, there exist principles setting some limits on obedience to orders. The intervention of criminal law manifests itself in the establishment of rules of criminal responsibility arising from the execution of an order. In domestic legislation, in principle, one can notice a high degree of convergence in attributing the responsibility to the person issuing an unlawful order. Different constructs are possible here – the issuer of an unlawful order can be held responsible as an instigator of the criminal act committed by a subordinate, as a soliciting perpetrator, managerial perpetrator or even principal (direct) perpetrator.

The 'blind (i.e. unthinking) bayonets' doctrine assumes that orders are absolutely binding and that superiors cannot, by definition, issue orders violating the law. Military discipline is given priority before other potentially protected interests. The executor of an order cannot oppose the order but is protected in return. A scathing critique of that approach was offered in his analysis of Austrian criminal law at the beginning of the 20th century by Edmund Krzymuski. He argued: 'it would be a highly improper thing if we

94 ICC-01/05-01/08-3636-Anx1-Red, 8.06.2018.

95 *Ibidem*: §334.

96 Ziewiński (1986).

97 See Czyżak (2010): 97, referring to S. Cheliński *Pojęcie rozkazu w świetle ogólnej teorii norm* published in "Czasopismo Prawnicze i Ekonomiczne", nr 1–12/1925.

were to concede to the order of a superior the power to bind a person subordinate thereto to commit acts contrary to the general norms of law.'[98] Decades later, Antoni Landau disputed the claim that: 'with the intention of protecting the law, it is good to turn to lawlessness.'[99]

The doctrine of 'thinking bayonets' assumes, by contrast, the subordinate's right to evaluate independently the legal character of the order received. The soldier gains the right to refuse to execute the order if executing it would violate the applicable law. With that, the soldier *eo ipso* has a duty to evaluate the legality of the order and the freedom to refuse to carry it out, which entails varying degrees (absolute or relative) of responsibility in the event of commission of a criminal act.

The Jurists Committee operating since the spring of 1941 in Cambridge, composed of eminent specialists employed by the University of Cambridge Faculty of Law, as well as those hailing from the occupied states, also took the matter of acting on orders into consideration. The problem was addressed in a questionnaire prepared under Lord McNair's leadership. The responses arriving reflected the opinion that the circumstance of acting on orders should be considered only in certain cases, taking into account the criminal's position or rank and the intensity of coercion exerted on them.[100] The later works on the subject, primarily comparative studies, were conducted by a special subcommittee chaired by the Belgian, de Moor, with the participation of Professors Arthur Lehman Goodhart and Hersch Lauterpacht. A comparison of the various systems revealed that only Polish and Czechoslovak law did not recognize acting on orders as a justification for unlawful acts. The law and practice of a majority of the analysed states revealed that the justification would be warranted if the act had been permitted by law and ordered by the competent authority. Even soldiers, however, could not be bound to obey manifestly unlawful orders. It was found, furthermore, that refusal to rely on superior orders could lead to the relaxation of discipline also in the Allied armed force.[101]

Matters of the corresponding responsibility were also considered as part of the works of the London International Assembly, in which Poland was represented by Bohdan Winiarski and Zygmunt Nagórski. The recommendations developed in the course of those works were for the order of a superior to commit a criminal offence to be unable to exempt responsibility in itself

---

98 Krzymuski (1901): 204 (§109).

99 Landau (1947): 320.

100 Goold Adams (1948): 98.

101 *Ibidem*: 102.

but for the circumstance of acting under compulsion to provide the basis for acquittal or for the mitigation of punishment. Simultaneously, the possibility of relying on orders was excluded for acts so manifestly reprehensible that the average person would be unable to commit it without shocking their own conscience, as well as in the cases of defendants belonging to organizations requiring their members to carry out criminal orders.[102] The latter can be viewed as the beginning of the separate, special treatment of fascist organizations.

Within the UNWCC, the matter of orders was the province of Committee III (the Legal Committee). The prevailing view in the discussion was that acting on orders could not justify the commission of a crime violating international law; nevertheless, the Commission did not adopt such a position with that wording but recommended that the decision be left to the court, albeit revealing the unanimity among the Commission's members as to that superior orders could not provide an exemption from responsibility.[103] In that manner, the conditions of responsibility were implicitly rejected (i.e. the requirement that the act committed by the executor of the orders be reprehensible).[104] The matter of acting on the orders of a criminal organization was not successfully addressed.

Article 8 of the IMT Charter provided: 'The fact that the Defendant acted pursuant to order of his Government or of a superior shall not free him from responsibility, but may be considered in mitigation of punishment if the Tribunal determines that justice so requires.' In the light of the Nuremberg judgment, the circumstance that the perpetrator had been acting on the order of a superior did not automatically provide an exemption from the responsibility for the acts committed.[105]

It should be noted that the Polish Criminal Code of 1932 did not regulate the responsibility of the executor of an order. The Military Criminal Code of 19.03.1928, on the other hand, copied – in its Article 30 – the German solution. According to the Article's §1, a soldier committing an act in pursuance of an order in matters of the service was not liable to punishment. An exception was provided in §2 if: '(a) the criminal offence arose as a result of exceeding the order; or (b) the perpetrator knew that the order concerned an act constituting a felony or misdemeanour.' In the above cases,

102 De Baer (1948): 8–9; cf. Ziewiński (1986): 179.
103 UNWCC Doc. C83, 15.3.1945.
104 Ziewiński (1986): 182.
105 Cyprian, Sawicki (1948b): 352.

the court was empowered to resort to extraordinary mitigation of the punishment.

Article 9 of the Military Criminal Code, in turn, provided: '(1) A solider committing an act being the execution of an order in matters of the service shall not be liable to punishment. (2) The provision of §1 shall not apply if: '(a) the criminal offence arose as a result of exceeding the order; or (b) the perpetrator knew that the order concerned an act constituting a felony or misdemeanour. In the above cases, the court may apply extraordinary mitigation of the punishment.'

The London Decree of March 1943 on the Criminal Responsibility for War Crimes provided, in its Article 10: 'both he who orders the commission of the act (…) and he who carries out such order (…) shall be liable to the punishments (…).'

In the August Decree, Article 3 contained the following language: 'having committed the crime set out in Article 1 or 2 of the Decree in the service of the hostile occupying power or upon the order thereof or compulsion therefrom shall provide no exemption from the responsibility.' In December 1946, Article 3 received a new §2 enabling the extraordinary mitigation of punishment on account of the person of the perpetrator or the circumstances of the act.

The PKWN decree of 23.09.1944 – Crime Code of the Polish Armed Forces[106] introduced the duty of absolute obedience. A fighting order, however, was distinguished from an order given in matters of the service. In accordance with Articles 118(1) to 118(3), a soldier failing to carry out a fighting order was liable to the death penalty. For failing to perform, exceeding or changing an order in matters of the service, the upper sentencing limit was three years' imprisonment. Cyprian and Sawicki believed that the duty of absolute obedience applied only to an act classifiable as a domestic crime but could not be applicable to any international crime.[107] Thus, the PKWN's Criminal Code of the Polish Armed Forces provided a soldier committing a crime by carrying out an order in matters of the service with a complete exemption from responsibility.

In Greiser's case, the NTN emphasized:

> According to modern theory and practice of criminal law, not every 'order of a superior' may freely be executed by a subordinate. In military law, German among others, obedience in the foundation of a

106 Dz.U.1944.6.27.

107 Cyprian, Sawicki (1948b): 3499.

> soldier's position. But even in that rigorous military law, the discipline of obedience cannot be put in terms of some blind obedience (some *Kadavergehorsam*) to any and all orders, but orders compatible with the law, not inciting the commission of a crime. Such a criminal order from a superior will always constitute a special crime, *delictum sui generis*, for the execution of which the perpetrator will be held responsible on par with the issuer of the order.[108]

By resolution of the Criminal Chamber of 25.06.1949 in *K.923/49*, the Supreme Court found, with regard to Article 5 of the August Decree:

> the lawmaker proceeded from the assumption (…) in respect of the occupier and the occupier's organ, that the latter had first and foremost the obligation to comply with international law in dealings with the population of the occupied territories and to place the interests protected by international law on a higher level than another personal interest, even though the latter might be exposed to danger in the event of failure to carry out the unlawful regulations or orders of the occupying authorities.[109]

The Interwar scholarship had also been universally opposed to the doctrine of blind obedience. Particular attention in this context is drawn by Stefan Glaser's paper written for the 1st Conference of Jurists of Slavic States in Bratislava in 1933.[110] He expounded upon the theory of responsibility for the execution of an unlawful order according to the principle of proportionately balancing (*stosunkowanie*) the interests and the obligations. Glaser argued that the judge faced the necessity of evaluating the proportion between both of the legally protected interests. That required: 'gradation of the interests and making the choice according to the proportion thereof.'[111] However, his later work titled *L'ordre hiérarchique en droit pénal international*[112] created more resonance.

The topic was still discussed in the afterwar period and continues to be discussed to the present day. Emphasis is placed on that: '[m]ilitary discipline must yield before any interest legally protected with the threat of

108 NTN, Greiser case: 16 (§12).
109 Reproduced in 8/1949, PiP 137.
110 Glaser (1933).
111 Wilk (2002): 6.
112 Glaser (1953b).

criminal sanction, whereas all legal interests not protected by criminal sanction must yield before military discipline.'[113] The topic also surfaced during the works on reports for the AIDP and the questionnaire survey. In the opinion of Gardocki, the paramount concern is to answer the question whether the particular character and gravity of international crimes *stricto sensu* justify the special, more severe regulation of the responsibility for the execution of an unlawful order. On the one hand, he does not dispute that the international community may place a greater demand on the recipient of an order; on the other hand, the exclusion of the ability to raise the defence of superior orders could mean depriving the individual of any protection whatsoever, which would be neither just nor moral.[114]

The Criminal Code of 1969 penalized refusal to carry out an order in Chapter XXXIX – *Offences against the principles of military discipline*. In accordance with Article 290(1), a soldier who committed a prohibited act through the execution of an order did not commit a criminal offence except when knowing or at least accepting that a criminal offence was committed by carrying out the order. Pursuant to Article 309(1) of the Criminal Code, a soldier who failed or refused to carry out an order or carried it out inconsistently with its meaning was liable to up to five years' imprisonment. For an analogous criminal offence in a fighting situation, the penalty was imprisonment for at least five years or death. Article 313 provided for aggravation of the penalty where the refusal was together with other soldiers or in the presence of gathered soldiers. Article 314, in turn, penalized entering into an understanding with other soldiers for the purpose of committing that crime.

The present Criminal Code of 1997 defines an order, in Article 115(18), as the instruction of a specific action or omission issued to a soldier by a superior or by an authorized higher-ranking soldier in the path of service.

Article 343(1) mandates: 'a soldier who fails or refuses to carry out an order or carries it out inconsistently with its meaning shall be liable to military arrest or up to three years' imprisonment.' The next section of the same article defines the aggravated subtypes of the offence. Article 318 of the Criminal Code excludes the criminal responsibility of the executor of the order: 'a soldier who commits a criminal offence through the execution of an order does not commit a criminal offence save were intentionally committing a criminal offence by executing the order.' And thus the soldier can be held responsible to the extent their actions or omissions were intentional. In accordance with Article 344(1) of the Criminal Code, a soldier who

113 Wąsik (2021): 68.

114 Gardocki (1989a): 99.

refuses or fails to execute an order instructing them to commit a criminal offence not commit a criminal offence. Furthermore, Article 344(2) provides that in the case of executing the order referred to in Article 344(1) inconsistently with its meaning for the purpose of significantly reducing the harm done, the court may resort to extraordinary mitigation of the punishment or refrain from punishment.

Even though both of the provisions (Article 318 and Article 344 of the Criminal Code) refer to the exemption of the recipient of an order from criminal responsibility in the situation of a conflict between the duty to carry out an unlawful order and the duty to act in accordance with the applicable law, they concern two different stages of the legal evaluation of the act constituting the execution of an unlawful order.[115] The Supreme Court's judgment in WA *13/04*, of 11.10.2004, defined an order instructing the recipient to commit a criminal offence as follows: 'an unlawful order the object of which is an action or omission corresponding to the description contained in the objective elements of any type of criminal offence, leaving aside elements defining the effect or consequence of the perpetrator's conduct.'[116] The soldier who gives a criminal order, in turn, will be responsible not as an instigator but as a perpetrator, irrespective of the executor's responsibility, as criminal law regards the issuer as a soliciting perpetrator, whether the executor is also criminally responsible or exempted under Article 318 or 344 of the Criminal Code.[117]

A wide response was attracted by the incident at the Afghan village of Nangar Khel, where, in August 2007, forces belonging to the Polish contingent attacked the alleged Taliban position as ordered, but one of the houses in the nearby village was caught in the fire. As a result, six Afghan citizens died. The case was extensively analysed in the literature.[118] In March 2012, the Supreme Court upheld the acquittals of three of the defendants, while reversing and remanding the Regional Military Court as to the other four.[119] On remand, the RMC held them responsible for having executed the order inconsistently with its meaning and with the rules governing the use of weapons by the Polish Military Contingent in Afghanistan. That judgment was, in turn, upheld by the Military Chamber of the Supreme Court, which emphasized that not in every situation could Article 318 of the Criminal

115 Skrzypek (2016): 21.

116 SN, Judgment,11.10.2004, WA 13/04, OSNWSK 2004/1/1747.

117 Klepner (2002).

118 Zajadło, Zajadło (2008); Wasiński (2008).

119 SN, Judgment,14.03.2012, WA 39/11.

Code exempt a soldier from the responsibility for an act arising from the execution of an order. A situation of intentionally committing a criminal offence was cited as an exception. The lawmaker had not recognized the 'blind bayonets' doctrine, which was unfit for modern times, and with it the absolute obedience to an order regardless of its nature.[120] As a result, the improper execution of orders could be relied on to avoid being held responsible for war crimes.

5 Conclusions

Naturally, exacting international criminal responsibility on an individual requires the attribution of that responsibility. International criminal courts and tribunals have relied on a variety of constructs in order to respond to the lack of collective responsibility and reconcile the requirements of the determination of individual involvement in the commission of crimes. Initially, the conspiracy figure was used, subsequently successfully developed into the concept of joint criminal enterprise (JCE) or, recently, control over the act. Each such construct has potential; however, for it to be used correctly, one must realize the consequences of its application. The topic range of remote perpetration attracts the interest of Polish researchers, who largely – at least within the context of Polish literature – draw upon the legacy of Juliusz Makarewicz. Though certain unquestionable similarities exist, domestic mechanisms of criminal law are difficult to translate into international criminal law. Here, one cannot ignore the dangers of an automatic projection of domestic constructs onto international law. The idiosyncratic nature of such an approach is perfectly visible on the example of the abandonment of immunities, where the Polish calls to indict Hitler, although not followed in the UNWCC's works, decidedly corresponded to expectations not fully satisfied several decades later.

Last but not least, one cannot ignore the scholarly, diplomatic and practical (through judgments) contributions with regard to constructs of command and other superior responsibility, of key importance to macro-crime.

---

120 SN, Judgment, 17.02.2016, WA 16/15. Cf. Kleczkowska (2016): 267.

Conclusion

The development of international criminal law is the responsibility of both states and judges, including judges of international courts and tribunals. Nor is the scholarship of negligible importance.

As a way of summarizing our discussion, it should be noted that the approach taken to the phaenomenon of international crime in general and specific crimes in particular has been undergoing an evolution of a kind. The relevant topics have not been and are still not free of controversy. Initially, the attention of the scholarship and the international practice had concentrated on acts termed *delicta juris gentium*. The Poles' participation in that discourse, especially throughout its initial stages, was not only noticeable but even significant. With time, the gravity centre shifted towards international crimes *stricto sensu*. In that field, too, the initiatives and contributions of Polish diplomacy, scholarship and judiciary have played a considerable and occasionally leading role. Without question, one can hardly ignore Rappaport's contribution to the penalization of aggressive war and certain other crimes, Lemkin's to the concept of genocide but not only that, or Glaser's to the topics of crimes against humanity and war crimes. The times that followed did not spell the end of active Polish involvement, although the Soviet dominance, restrictions imposed on travelling, and the limited reach of publications in the Polish language have undoubtedly left their marks. The usually weakened official involvement also has its own negative consequences. All of the above taken together results in the diminished visibility of Polish achievements and contributions.

Of course, the principal importance belongs to diplomatic initiatives. A marked regression can be seen in this regard compared to the activity in the Interwar period. At present, supporting, inspiring or implementing concrete initiatives presents a much more modest picture than in preceding analysed periods, during which, in a way, a reaction was forced by very difficult circumstances (the reacquisition of independence, problems of the Interwar period, activities of the government-in-exile following the outbreak of World War II, or the activities of the UN War Crimes Commission, etc.). Personal experiences and sacrifices translated into greater involvement and commitment, with powerful examples such as the St James Conference or the initiatives relating to the non-applicability of statutory limitations, in addition to those already mentioned. When comparing the present times with the preceding decades, one can scarcely resist – with rare exceptions such as organized crime – the impression of a certain passivity and unoriginality. Our visibility in official bodies does not encourage any excessive optimism, either. The above holds especially true if we acknowledge that, in comparison to the preparatory works on the additional protocols to the Geneva Conventions or even the Rome Statute, the recent period marks a diminished involvement of experts in works in the international forum.

Neither would it be appropriate to ignore the achievements of the judiciary, especially of the Supreme National Tribunal. The latter was partially the product of the specific situation facing Poland in the period before, during and immediately after WW II. It should be borne in mind that the NTN was the first venue of proceedings completely devoted to genocide and aggression,[1] and its judgments were also cited by the *ad hoc* tribunals. The decisions of the Supreme Court and of the common courts are not without significance, either.

An international echo (not always favourable) can be generated also by legislative initiatives, as clearly demonstrated by the hasty amendment of the Act on the Institute of National Remembrance. Moreover, one should remember that the implementation of specific treaty solutions into the domestic legal order can sometimes be slow, as was the case, for example, with the belated amendment of the Criminal Code in 2010. The prior Codes either did not regulate the corresponding topics at all or did so in a fragmentary manner.

When analysing the contributions made by the judiciary, one cannot ignore the international criminal justice system. There, too, the protracted absence of Poles from strictly international criminal court has played a role. One can hope that Judge Piotr Hofmański's service as President of the International Criminal Court could be rightly considered a catalyst of change generating greater diplomatic involvement on behalf of Polish presence in the international criminal judiciary. That would mark a return to the good traditions of the past decades of long or even natural presence, interrupted by the withdrawal of Krzysztof Skubiszewski's candidacy to the position of a judge of the International Court of Justice. Polish participation in hybrid mechanisms paints a much better picture.

The clarification and ordering of the theoretical outlook on the evolving normative reality are much needed and will make a positive contribution to the international practice with regard to the definition of *ratione materiae* and *ratione personae* jurisdiction or the necessary involvement of the state. As for the influence wielded by scholars, one cannot omit to cite Manfred

---

1 Klafkowski (1968a): 17.

Lachs on that is about: 'influence on a better understanding of the law, its application by the government apparatus, by states, groups of states, international organizations, even the international community as a whole.'[2]

In international law, the relationship between theory and practice is stronger than in many other disciplines.[3] In reality, one could not possibly imagine a comparable legal system with such a pronounced influence of scholars on the principles and rules.[4] It is not difficult to identify frequent examples of combining the two roles.

Not infrequently, the subject literature ends up being: 'unduly theoretical, insufficiently practical, and prone to over-simplification.'[5] It has even been admitted that: 'subjective factors enter into any assessment of juristic opinion and individual writers will tend to reflect national and other prejudices.'[6] In a similar vein, Hersch Lauterpacht has pointed out that: 'the divergence of view among writers on many subjects as well as apparent national bias may often render citations from them unhelpful.'[7] In this context, it will be expedient to recall the words of Judges Higgins, Kooijmans and Buergenthal from their separate opinion in the ICJ's *Yerodia* case, of 11.04.2000:

[the writings of eminent jurists], important and stimulating as they may be, cannot of themselves and without reference to the other sources of international law, evidence the existence of a jurisdictional norm. The assertion that certain treaties and court decisions rely on universal jurisdiction, which in fact they do not, does not evidence an international practice recognized as custom. And the policy arguments advanced in some of the writings can certainly suggest why a practice or a court decision should be regarded as desirable, or indeed lawful; but contrary arguments are advanced, too, and in any event these also cannot serve to substantiate an international practice where virtually none exists.[8]

Already after Nuremberg, Georg Schwarzenberger distinguished a number of diverse meanings of the term 'international criminal law' to conclude, in the end, that international criminal law in a narrow substantive meaning

2 Lachs (1986): 206.
3 Yusuf (2017): 604.
4 Jennings (1996): 413.
5 Parry (1965): 105.
6 Crawford (2012): 43.
7 Lauterpacht (1958): 24.
8 ICJ Rep. 2002, 3, Joint Separate Opinion of Judges Higgins, Kooijmans and Buergenthal, 63, 75, §44.

does not exist.[9] Almost in parallel, in Polish scholarship, Alfons Klafkowski categorically denied the existence of international criminal law as a special branch of international law.[10] Assessing the situation at a later time, Janusz Gilas noted the weak emancipation position of international criminal law as an autonomous branch of international law.[11] It will be fitting, however, to quote the pointedly accurate judgement of Renata Sonnefeld:

> The idea of international crimes and of a right to punish them was not foreign to classic international law and has never been abandoned in the theory of international law, even though the concept of international crimes and international criminal law belongs today to highly contentious concepts. Controversies are sparked by almost everything: systemic classification, terminology, definition, sources, subject scope and object scope.[12]

Fortunately, the above problems and doubts have by now been dispelled. Were one to measure the force of impact with the number of coursebooks available, one could see that enormous improvement has been made. In Poland's publishing market, the pioneering monograph penned by Lech Gardocki had long held a monopoly. In the current century, besides an updated and expanded version of that work, one can also find other works, among which particular distinction belongs to the study Michał Królikowski, Paweł Wiliński and Jacek Izydorczyk's study and to Piotr Hofmański and Hanna Kuczyńska's coursebook. This influence, however, can only have a limited reach. There is a natural obstacle in the form of the language barrier. It would be a truism to say that the English language has become the *lingua franca* of present-day academic (and not only academic) discourse.[13] The above does not change the base trend whereby only

---

9 Schwarzenberger (1965): 35.

10 Klafkowski (1968b): 40. It is worth noting that Klafkowski's position on the topic had evolved to become stronger, for his opinion published a decade earlier had been more cautiously worded: 'the term itself "international criminal law" – extensively used after WW II – does not hold an adequate share in public international law. At the most, one could say that the so-called international criminal law is in a nascent stage' – see: Klafkowski 1959: 88. In both of the works, he spoke in favour of invoking specific international treaties rather than using the term.

11 Gilas (1981): 96–97. Similar but less categorical was the position voiced by Schwarzenberger (1967): 115.

12 Sonnenfeld (1984): 62.

13 Bohlander (2014): 513.

initiatives undertaken in one of the congress languages have any chance of impact. This rule is only becoming narrower. Thus, all the greater admiration is owed to the jurists of the Interwar period, who truly played a serious role in the development of the discipline thanks to their foreign publications. The influence exerted by personages such as Glaser or Rappaport does not need any further evidence. Even though that influence was or still is considerable, however, it is also sometimes forgotten or outright ignored. In the case of French- or English-language publications, increasingly accessible in a day of digitized collections, this manner of reproach cannot be levied solely at the domestic researchers but must be stretched more expansively. This sad conclusion refers especially to the omnipresent manner of contenting oneself with a shallow, highly simplified search through the most resent sources, without accounting for the earlier findings, which ill-contributes to the elucidation of the objective state of affairs and the pace of progress, not to mention the superfluous reinventing of the wheel. There can be no doubt, however, that the mutual distrust between the adepts of criminal and international law is also to blame. Oftentimes, the authors not only do not cite one another, they do not even read one another. Once again, Oscar Schachter's warning shows its weight; writing about the, 'invisible college of international lawyers,' he warned against becoming locked up in personal domains with the resulting compartmentalization.

It is frequently emphasized that, as a discipline, international law needs renewal and departure from an exclusively doctrinal approach.[14] The unduly theoretical nature of studies and analyses in international criminal law is recognized as a serious problem.[15] The influence of German dogmatics is clearly noticeable and often challenged here. A parody of Winston Churchill's Battle of Britain quip is sometimes invoked.[16]

Without in any way disputing the contributions of German (or German-language) scholarship, one could wonder at the readiness to reference scholars such as Claus Roxin (to mention only the matters of perpetration) but not the earlier luminaries of criminal law, such as Liszt or Makarewicz. This is not done even by those Poles who have a real impact on the development of international criminal law. However, one would be mistaken to assume that citing the scholarly or judicial achievements should only be

14 Sliedregt (2020): 275.

15 Sliedregt (2016): 1.

16 Simpson (2020): 843 – "Never have so many written so much great stuff about so little".

the task or right of compatriots. From this perspective it appears to be very important for scholars in international law to resist the parochial temptation of incessantly transplanting their own domestic legal doctrines onto the international plane.[17] This is about preserving the cosmopolitan character of the diplomatic, judicial and scholarly activities. Suffice to recall that the Supreme National Tribunal's opinions were cited in the judgments of the *ad hoc* tribunals.

The purpose of this book was not only to highlight the main diplomatic initiatives or the efforts of the Polish judiciary but also to offer a panoramic view of Polish studies in international criminal law. More and more works are written in this discipline and often use as dissertations submitted for the purposes of academic advancement. The photograph of Polish jurists studying international criminal law is not limited to a narrow circle of individuals. One can even notice the progressing specialization manifested sometimes in the outright predominance of this current of research in the professional lives of some of the scholars. This ending remark warrants a degree of cautious optimism, though not without the caveat of confronting the findings with the practice and not without calling for greater openness and internationalization in the research. Only then could one attempt to transpose Schachter's invisible college of specialists in international criminal law (with Polish participation in it).

17 Kreß (2014): 26.

References

Abraszewski Andrzej (1975), *Polska w Organizacji Narodów Zjednoczonych (1945–1975)*, Interpress.

Abtahi Hirad, Webb Philippa (2008), *The Genocide Convention. The Travaux Préparatoires*, Martinus Nijhoff Publishers.

Ajnenkiel Andrzej (1997), *Józef Piłsudski – Naczelnik Państwa 1918–1922*, 4/3(9) Niepodległość i Pamięć 51.

Aleksandrow Georgiĭ Nikolaevich (1974), *Norymberga wczoraj i dziś*, GKBZHwP.

Amado Gilberto (1952), *La question de la définition de l'agression*, 2 Revue de Droit International de Science Diplomatiques et Politiques 147.

Andrejew Igor (1978), *Polskie prawo karne w zarysie*, 5. edition, PWN.

Andrejew Igor, Kubicki Leszek, Waszczyński Jan (ed.) (1985), *System Prawa Karnego. O przestępstwach w szczególności*, vol. IV, PAN, Ossolineum.

Appleman John Alan (1971), *Military Tribunals and International Crimes*, Greenwood Press Publishers 1954, reprint 1971.

Armitage David, Jennifer Pitts (2022), *"Ten współczesny Grocjusz": Życie i myśl C.H. Alexandrowicza (1902–1975)*, in: Przyborowska-Klimczak et al. (2022b): 23.

Aroneanu Eugène (1958), *La définition de l'agression. Exposé objectif*, Les Editions Internationales.

Baer Marcel de (1948), *Prace przygotowawcze nad represją zbrodni wojennych 1914–1943*, 3 PiP 5.

Bajerski Artur (2017), *Szkolnictwo wyższe międzywojennej Polski. Ujęcie geograficzne*, Wydawnictwo Naukowe UAM.

Balcerzak Michał (2022), *O Wileńskiej Szkole Prawa Międzynarodowego (1919–1939)*, in: Przyborowska-Klimczak et al. (2022b): 177.

Balicki Jan (1952a), *O definicji agresji*, 7 PiP 48.

Balicki Jan (1952b), *Pojęcie agresji w prawie międzynarodowym*, Wydawnictwo Prawnicze.

Balicki Jan (1967), *Apartheid, studium prawno-polityczne rasizmu w Afryce Południowej*, PWN.

Balicki Jan (1972), *Dyskryminacja rasowa w świetle prawa międzynarodowego*, Zakład Narodowy im. Ossolińskich.

Balicki Jan (1986), *Dyskryminacja rasowa przeszłość i teraźniejszość*, Wydawnictwo Lubelskie.

Banasik Katarzyna (2011), *Karnoprawne normy przedawnienia w prawie międzynarodowym*, 7–8 Prokuratura i Prawo 56.

Banasik Katarzyna (2012), *Od zbrodni przeciwko pokojowi do zbrodni agresji*, 5–6 Palestra 101.

Barcik Jacek (2018), *Z dziejów nauki prawa międzynarodowego na Uniwersytecie Śląskim*, 11(19) Z Dziejów Prawa 71–85.

Barcikowski Wacław (1946), *Les Nations Unies et l'organisation de la répression des crimes de guerre*, 17 (3–4) Revue international de droit pénal 156.

Barrett John Q. (2010), *Raphael Lemkin and 'Genocide' at Nuremberg 1945–1946*, in: Christoph Safferling, Eckart Conze (ed.), *The Genocide Convention Sixty Years after its Adoption*, T.M.C. Asser Press: 38.

Bartoszkiewicz Marian (1946), *Artur Greiser. Rozważania w przededniu procesu*, 4 Przegląd Zachodni 301.

Basak Adam (1993), *Historia pewnej mistyfikacji: zbrodnia katyńska przed Trybunałem Norymberskim*, WUWr.

Basak Adam (1998), *Katyń. Problem odpowiedzialności karnej sprawców w świetle Norymbergi*, XXI Studia na Faszyzmem i Zbrodniami Hitlerowskimi 325.

Basak Adam (2009), *Problem ludobójstwa "kulturalnego" a spór polsko-rosyjski o kwalifikację prawną zbrodni katyńskiej*, 64(2–3) Śląski Kwartalnik Historyczny 429.

Basak Adam (2018), *International Custom and the Experience of Nuremberg*, in: *Essays in Memory of Professor Karol Wolfke*, 8/2 Wroclaw Review of Law, Administration & Economics: 258.

Baskow Władimir I. (1987), *Pierwszy proces w historii prawa międzynarodowego*, GKBZHWP-IPN 124.

Bassiouni M. Cherif (2011), *Crimes against Humanity: Historical Evolution and Contemporary Application*, CUP.

Bassiouni M. Cherif (2013), *Introduction to International Criminal Law*, 2. edition, Martinus Nijhoff Publishers.

Bassiouni M. Cherif (2017), *Investigating War Crimes in the Former Yugoslavia War 1992–1994 The United Nations Commission of Experts Established Pursuant to Security Council Resolution 780 (1992)*, Intersentia.

Bauer Ela (2010), *Jan Gottlieb Bloch: Polish cosmopolitism versus Jewish universalism*, 17(3) European Review of History: Revue europeenne d'histoire 415.

Bauman Zygmunt (2002), *Modernity and the Holocaust*, Cornell University Press.

Baxter Richard R. (1968), *The Effects of Ill-Conceived Codification and Development of International Law*, in: *Recueil d'études de droit international en hommage à Paul Guggenheim*, Faculté de droit de l'Université de Genève – Institut universitaire de Hautes études internationales: 146.

Berezowski Cezary (1927), *O polskim projekcie międzynarodowego prawa karnego*, Drukarnia "Gazety Administracji i Policji Państwowej".

Berezowski Cezary (1938), *Les sujets nonsouverains du droit international*, 65-III RCADI 5.

Berezowski Cezary (1948), *Ochrona prawno-międzynarodowa zabytków i dzieł sztuki w czasie wojny*, Automa.

Białecki Antoni (1875), *Zadanie prawa międzynarodowego i obowiązki stron wojujących*, "Kronika Rodzinna" J. Jaworski.

Biegański Zdzisław (2003), *Sądownictwo i skazani na śmierć z przyczyn politycznych w województwie pomorskim (bydgoskim) w latach 1945–1956*, Wydawnictwo Akademii Bydgoskiej im. Kazimierza Wielkiego.

Biegański Zdzisław (2004), *Kara śmierci w orzecznictwie Specjalnych Sądów Karnych w Polsce (1944–1946)*, v Echa Przeszłości 175.

Bielawski Wacław (1980), *Wizje lokalne w latach 1964–1979 sądów przysięgłych RFN w Polsce*, in: Pilichowski (1980b): 854.

Bieniek Beata (2010), *Pranie pieniędzy w prawie międzynarodowym, europejskim oraz polskim*, Wolters Kluwer.

Bieńczyk-Missala Agnieszka, Dębski Sławomir (ed.) (2010), *Rafał Lemkin: A hero of Humankind*, PISM.

Bieńczyk-Missala Agnieszka, Kuźniar Roman (ed.) (2020), *Dziedzictwo Krzysztofa Skubiszewskiego w polityce zagranicznej RP*, Wydawnictwo Naukowe Scholar.

Bierzanek Remigiusz (1956), *Les crimes contre la sécurité de la navigation aérienne*, 27/3–4 RIDP 215.

Bierzanek Remigiusz (1958), *Ekstradycja w traktatach zawieranych przez państwa hetyckie*, Poznańskie Towarzystwo Nauk.

Bierzanek Remigiusz (1960), *Sur les origines du droit de la guerre et de la paix*, 38(4) Revue historique de droit français et étranger 83.

Bierzanek Remigiusz (1968), *Le status juridique des partisans et des mouvements de résistance armée: évolution historique et aspects actuels*, in: Vladimir Ibler (ed.), *Mélanges Offerts à Juraj Andrassy, Essays in International Law in Honour of Juraj Andrassy*, Martinus Nijhoff : 54.

Bierzanek, Remigiusz (1970), *Definicja agresji w świetle prac Komitetu Specjalnego ONZ*, 23 SM 77.

Bierzanek Remigiusz (1972), *Prawa człowieka w konfliktach zbrojnych*, MON.

Bierzanek Remigiusz (1975), *Protection of civilians and belligerents against the effects of modern conventional weapons*, 4 Studies on International Relations 60.

Bierzanek Remigiusz (1978), *Represalia w świetle prac nad rozwojem prawa konfliktów zbrojnych*, 4 SM 129.

Bierzanek Remigiusz (1980), *Reprisals as a Means of Enforcing the Laws of Warfare: The Old and the New Law*, in: Antonio Cassese (ed.), *The New Humanitarian Law of Armed Conflict*, Editoriale Scientifica: 232.

Bierzanek Remigiusz (1982), *Wojna a prawo międzynarodowe*, MON.

Bierzanek Remigiusz (2006), *Przez wiek XX. Wspomnienia i refleksje*, Wyższa Szkoła Handlu i Prawa.

Bierzanek Remigiusz, Kukułka Józef (ed.) (1965/1967/1968), *Sprawy polskie na konferencji pokojowej w Paryżu w 1919 r. Dokumenty i materiały*, vol. I–III, PWN.

Bílková Veronika (2014), *Post-Second World War Trials in Central and Eastern Europe*, in: Morten Bergsmo, Cheah Wui Ling, Yi Ping (ed.), *Historical Origins of International Criminal Law: Volume 2*, Torkel: 697.

Birt Marcin (2019), *Dekret sierpniowy PKWN z 1944 roku jako instrument legalizacji władzy komunistycznej w Polsce*, 41(4) Studia nad Autorytaryzmem i Totalitaryzmem 65.

Bloch Jan (1899), *Przyszła wojna pod względem technicznym, ekonomicznym i politycznym. Wnioski ogólne z dzieła*, Gebethner i Wolff.

Bloch Jan Gottlieb (2015), *Przyszła wojna pod względem technicznym, ekonomicznym i politycznym*, PISM.

Bogusz Józef, Wolter Władysław (1970), *Wyrok wraz z uzasadnieniem Amerykańskiego Trybunału Wojskowego nr 1 w Norymberdze w procesie lekarzy hitlerowskich z dnia 19–20.08.1947 r.*, Biuletyn Głównej Komisji Badań Zbrodni Hitlerowskich, vol. 20: 19.

Bohlander Michael (2014), *Language, Culture, Legal Traditions, and International Criminal Justice*, 12 JICJ 491.

Boister Neil (2003), *Transnational Criminal Law?*, 14(5) EJIL 953.

Bouffałł Bronisław (1930), *Wyjęcie wojny z pod prawa w pakcie Kellogga*, 10 (4) RPEiS 502.

Bramson Aleksander (1948), *Pewne aspekty prawa norymberskiego*, 5–6 PiP 74.

Bramson Aleksander (1952), *Definicja agresji a ustawy o obronie pokoju*, 3(60) SM 68.

Brewing Daniel (2022), *In the Shadow of Auschwitz: German Massacres against Polish Civilians, 1939–1945*, Berghahn.

Brodowski Lidia (2015), *Zasada podwójnej karalności czynu w kontekście ekstradycji*, 1(61) Studia Prawnicze KUL 31.

Broms Bengt (1968), *The Definition of Aggression in the United Nations*, Turun Yliopisto.

Bryl Andrzej (2021), *Zbrodnie przeciwko ludzkości w doktrynie i orzecznictwie międzynarodowych trybunałów karnych*, Wydawnictwo Naukowe Scholar.

Bogucki Kazimierz (1973), *Z badań nad działalnością Specjalnego Sądu Karnego w Gdańsku (1945–1946)*, 2 Koszalińskie Studia i Materiały 235.

Brownlie Ian (1968), *International Law and the Use of Force by States*, OUP.

Burczyk Dariusz (2014), *Specjalny Sąd Karny w Gdańsku (1945–1946): przyczynek do monografii*, 7 Przegląd Archiwalny Instytutu Pamięci Narodowej 289.

Burczyk Dariusz (2022), *Renegaci przed sądem. Specjalny Sąd Karny i Prokuratura Specjalnego Sądu Karnego w Gdańsku (1945–1946)*, IPN.

Buczyński Roman (1872), *O jurysdykcji karnej w stosunkach międzynarodowych*, Drukarnia S. Orgelbranda i Synów.

Buerghenthal Thomas (2006), *Louis B. Sohn (1914–2006)*, 100(3) AJIL 623.

Callahan Michael (2018), *The League of Nations, International Terrorism, and British Foreign Policy (1934–1938)*, Palgrave Macmillan.

Ciechański Jerzy (1998), *Międzynarodowy Trybunał Karny do spraw Zbrodni w byłej Jugosławii*, 51 (3) SM 113.

Cieślak Marian (1985), *Stefan Glaser (1895–1984)*, 4 PiP 105.

Cieślak Marian, Waszczyński Jan (1989), *Rapport nationaux / National reports: Pologne*, 60 RIDP 419.

Cox Graham (2014), *Seeking Justice for the Holocaust: Herbert C. Pell Versus the US State Department*, 25 CLF 77.

Crawford James (2012), *Brownlie's Principles of Public International Law*, OUP.

Crowe David M. (ed.) (2019), *Stalin's Soviet Justice*, Bloomsbury.

Cryer Robert (2005), *Prosecuting International Crimes. Selectivity and the International Criminal Law Regime*, CUP.

Cybichowski Zygmunt (1914), *Międzynarodowe prawo wojenne z uwzględnieniem przesilenia bałkańskiego*, Gubrynowicz i Syn.

Cybichowski Zygmunt (1915), *Prawo narodów. System Prawa Międzynarodowego*, Gubrynowicz i Syn.

Cybichowski Sigismond (1926), *La compétence des tribunaux a raison d'infractions commises hors du territoire*, 12 RCADI 247.

Cybichowski Zygmunt (1927a), *Międzynarodowe Prawo Karne. Kompetencja Sądów do Ścigania Przestępstw Zagranicznych*, Wydawnictwo Seminarjum Prawa Publicznego (Państwowego i Międzynarodowego) Uniwersytetu Warszawskiego.

Cybichowski Zygmunt (1927b), *O kompetencji sądów do ścigania przestępstw zagranicznych*, 2 Gazeta Administracji i Policji Państwowej 97.

Cybichowski Zygmunt (1927c), *Zagadnienia Okupacji*, 4 Gazeta Administracji i Policji Państwowej 1.

Cybichowski Zygmunt (1928), *Prawo międzynarodowe publiczne i prywatne*, 3. edition, Wydawnictwo Seminarjum Prawa Publicznego Uniwersytetu Warszawskiego.

Cybichowski Zygmunt (1932), *Prawo międzynarodowe publiczne i prywatne*, 4.edition, Zakłady Graficzne "Bibljoteka Polska".

Cybulski Bogdan (1986), *Polska wobec przestępstw wojennych popełnionych w I Wojnie Światowej*, Studia nad Faszyzmem i Zbrodniami Hitlerowskimi X, 765 Acta Universitatis Wratislaviensis 317.

Cybulski Bogdan (1987), *Ściganie przez Polskę zbrodni wojennych popełnionych w czasie I wojny światowej*, GKBZHwP-IPN 249.

Cybulski Bogdan (2014), *Umowy polsko-niemieckie w sprawie amnestii z lat 1919–1922*, CCCXVI/2 Acta Universitatis Wratislaviensis 3602, Prawo 161.

Cyprian Tadeusz (1948a), *Obóz koncentracyjny organizacją przestępczą*, 1 DPP 19.

Cyprian Tadeusz (1948b), *Zbrodnia przeciw pokojowi*, 3 PiP 21

Cyprian Tadeusz (1960), *Komisja stwierdziła ...* , MON.

Cyprian Tadeusz (1971), *Wehrmacht. Zbrodnia i kara*, MON.

Cyprian Tadeusz (1977), *Faktyczna i prawna sytuacja delegacji polskiej na proces norymberski*, in: *Norymberga – nadal otwarty rozdział w historii. W XXX rocznicę wyroku Międzynarodowego Trybunału Wojskowego*, Ministerstwo Sprawiedliwości: 110.

Cyprian Tadeusz, Rothert Edward, Sawicki Jerzy (1961), *Nazi Rule in Poland*, Polonia Publishing House.

Cyprian Tadeusz, Sawicki Jerzy (1946), *Prawo polskie w walce z hitleryzmem i kolaboracjonizmem*, 11–12 DPP 13.

Cyprian Thaddee, Sawicki Georges (1947), *Le droit polonais dans la lutte contre l'hitlérisme et la "collaboration"*, in: Marian Muszkat, Tadeusz Cyprian, Jerzy Sawicki, *Le droit polonais au service de la paix dans la lutte contre les criminels de guerre*, GKBZNwP.

Cyprian Tadeusz, Sawicki Jerzy (1948a), *Materiały norymberskie*, Spółdzielnia Wydawnicza "Książka".

Cyprian Tadeusz, Sawicki Jerzy (1948b), *Prawo norymberskie. Bilans i perspektywy*, Wydawnictwo E. Kuthana.

Cyprian Tadeusz, Sawicki Jerzy (1948c), *Przestępstwa międzynarodowe*, Czytelnik.

Cyprian Tadeusz, Sawicki Jerzy (1949), *Procesy wielkich zbrodniarzy wojennych w Polsce (Najwyższy Trybunał Narodowy)*, Spółdzielnia Wydawniczo-Oświatowa Czytelnik.

Cyprian Tadeusz, Sawicki Jerzy (1956a), *Sprawy polskie w procesie norymberskim*, Instytut Zachodni.

Cyprian Tadeusz, Sawicki Jerzy (1956b), *Walka o zasady norymberskie (1945–1955)*, PWN.

Cyprian Tadeusz, Sawicki Jerzy (1960), *Nie oszczędzać Polski!*, Iskry.

Cyprian Tadeusz, Sawicki Jerzy (1962a), *Przed Trybunałem Świata (refleksje – wspomnienia – dokumenty), Część I–II*, Książka i Wiedza.

Cyprian Tadeusz, Sawicki Jerzy (1962b), *Siedem wyroków Najwyższego Trybunału Narodowego*, Instytut Zachodni.

Cyprian Tadeusz, Sawicki Jerzy (1965), *Nieznana Norymberga; dwanaście procesów norymberskich*, Książka i Wiedza.

Cyprian Tadeusz, Sawicki Jerzy (1967a), *Ludzie i sprawy Norymbergi*, Wydawnictwo Poznańskie.

Cyprian Tadeusz, Sawicki Jerzy (1967b), *Nuremberg in Retrospect. People and Issues of the Trial*, Western Press Agency.

Cyprian Tadeusz, Sawicki Jerzy, Siewierski Jerzy (1962), *Głos ma prokurator …*, Iskry.

Cyprian Tadeusz, Sawicki Jerzy, Światkowski Henryk (1946), *Agresja na Polskę w świetle dokumentów*, PIW.

Czapliński Władysław (1993), *Skutki prawne nielegalnego użycia siły w stosunkach międzynarodowych*, INP PAN.

Czapliński Władysław (2006), *Jus Cogens and the Law of Treaties*, in: Christian Tomuschat, Jean-Marc Thouvenin (ed.), *The Fundamental Rules of the International Legal Order: Jus Cogens and Obligations Erga Omnes*, Brill.

Czapliński Władysław (2007–2009), *Zbrodnia agresji jako przestępstwo przeciwko prawu międzynarodowemu*, XXIX–XXX Archiwum Kryminologii 815.

Czyżak Mariusz (2010), *Odrębność polskiego prawa karnego wojskowego wobec prawa karnego powszechnego*, Wydawnictwa Akademickie i Profesjonalne.

Daszkiewicz Krystyna (1970), *Przedawnienie zbrodni wojennych i zbrodni przeciw ludzkości w prawie karnym NRF. O roli i funkcji par. 50 ust. 2 k.k. z 1871 r.*, GKBZKWP, Wydawnictwo Prawnicze.

Daszkiewicz Krystyna (1972), *Zbrodnie hitlerowskie w prawie karnym Niemieckiej Republiki Federalnej*, Instytut Zachodni.

Davies Norman (2008), *No Simple Victory: World War II in Europe, 1939–1945*, Penguin Books.

Dąbrowska Maria (1936), *Doroczny wstyd*, "Dziennik Popularny", 14.11.1936.

Dąbrowa Sławomir (1971), *Konwencja ONZ o nieprzedawnieniu zbrodni wojennych – stan i perspektywy realizacji*, 5 SM 24.

Dębski Ryszard (2013), *Kilka uwag o kryminalizacji i o ustawowej określoności czynów zabronionych*, in: Anna Błachnio-Parzych et al. (ed.), *Problemy wymiaru sprawiedliwości karnej. Księga jubileuszowa profesora Jana Skupińskiego*, Wolters Kluwer: 31.

Dembiński Henryk (1930), *Król M., Dr.: Odpowiedzialność państw w prawie Narodów, Wilno 1929*, 3 RPEiS 497.

Dembiński Henryk (1935), *Wojna jako narzędzie prawa i przewrotu*, Towarzystwo Naukowe KUL.

Descheemaeker Jacques (1947), *Le Tribunal Militaire Internationale des grands criminels de guerre*, Pedone.

Deryng Antoni (ed.) (1935), *La sécurité collective. Mémoires présentés par le Comité Central des Institutions polonaises des Sciences Politiques à la VIII-e Conférence des Hautes Études Internationales à Londres*, Lwów.

Diamandesco Jean (1935), *Le problème de l'agression dans le droit international public actuel. Deux aspects de l'organisation répressive: Définition de l'agression et détermination de l'agresseur*, Éditions A. Pedone.

Dijk Boyd van (2022), *Preparing for War. The Making of the Geneva Conventions*, OUP.

Dinstein Yoram (1996), *Crimes against Humanity*, in: Jerzy Makarczyk (ed.), *Theory of International Law at the Threshold of the 21st Century: Essays in Honour of Krzysztof Skubiszewski*, Kluwer: 891.

Dinstein Yoram (2005), *War, Aggression and Self-Defence*, 4. edition, CUP.

Długołęcki Piotr (2022), *Documents on the Polish Government-in-Exile's Policy Concerning Jews 1939–1945*, PISM.

Donnedieu de Vabres Henri (1947), *Le jugement de Nuremberg et le principe de la légalité des délits et des peines*, 26 (10/1947) Revue de droit pénal et de criminologie 833.

Doria José (2009), *Whether crimes against humanity are backdoor war crimes*, in: Jose Doria et al. (ed.), *The Legal Regime of the ICC: Essays in Honour of Prof. I.P. Blishchenko*, Nijhoff: 645.

Drozdowski Marian M. (2019), *Blaski i cienie Traktatu Wersalskiego z 28 czerwca 1919* in: Skoczek Tadeusz (ed.) *Stulecie Traktatu Wersalskiego 1919–2019*, Wydawnictwo Muzeum Niepodległości w Warszawie.

Dróżdż Dominika (2010), *Zbrodnia ludobójstwa w międzynarodowym prawie karnym*, Wolters Kluwer.

Drumbl Mark A. (2013), *'Germans are the Lords and Poles are the Servants': The Trial of Arthur Greiser in Poland, 1946*, in: Kevin J. Heller, Gerry Simpson (ed.), *The Hidden Histories of War Crimes Trials*, OUP: 411.

Dynia Elżbieta (1999), *Przestępstwa prawa międzynarodowego: odpowiedzialność prawnomiędzynarodowa jednostki*, Studia i Materiały, Polska Fundacja Spraw Międzynarodowych.

Ehrlich Ludwik (1927), *Prawo narodów*, Nakład i Własność K.S. Jakubowskiego we Lwowie.

Ehrlich Ludwik (1955), *Polski wykład prawa wojny XV wieku*, Wydawnictwo Prawnicze.

Ehrlich Ludwik (1958), *Prawo międzynarodowe*, Wydawnictwo Prawnicze.

Elder Tanya (2009), *What you see before your eyes: documenting Raphael Lemkin's life by exploring his archival papers, 1900–1959*, in: Dominik J. Schaller, Jürgen Zimmerers (ed.), *The Origins of Genocide: Raphael Lemkin as a historian of mass violence*, Routledge: 100.

Epstein Catherine (2010), *Model Nazi: Arthur Greiser and the Occupation of Western Poland*, OUP.

Erpelding Michel (2019), *Upper Silesian Mixed Commission*, Max Planck Encyclopedia of International Procedural Law, OUP.

Ettinger Mieczysław (1929), *Pologne*, 6 RDIP 141.

Ferencz Benjamin B. (1975), *Defining International Aggression. The Search for World Peace. A Documentary History of and Analysis*, t. 1–2, Oceana Publications.

Ferencz Benjamin B. (1980), *An International Criminal Court. A Step Toward World Peace – A Documentary History and Analysis, Volume I – Half a Century of Hope*, Oceana Publications.

Fiedorczyk Paweł (2011), *Polscy prawnicy emigracyjni o sowietyzacji prawa cywilnego*, XXXIII Studia nad Faszyzmem i Zbrodniami Hitlerowskimi 484.

Filipek Michał Jan (2020), *Koncepcja zbrodni przeciwko ludzkości w międzynarodowym prawie karnym*, Wydawnictwo INP PAN.

Finch George A. (1925), *The Progressive Codification of International Law*, 19 (3) AJIL 534.

Finder Gabriel, Prusin Alexander (2018), *Justice Behind the Iron Curtain: Nazis on Trial in Communist Poland*, University of Toronto Press.

Fleming Michael (2022a), *In the Shadow of the Holocaust. Poland, the United Nations War Crimes Commission, and the Search for Justice*, CUP.

Fleming Michael (2022b), *Symposium on the UNWCC: War Crimes Against Culture – Poland's Charge File Submissions to the UNWCC*, Blog Opinio Iuris, 5.05.2022.

Flemming Marian (1970), *Ekstradycja dezerterów*, 4 WPP 524.

Flemming Marian (1994), *Międzynarodowe sądownictwo karne. Nowe perspektywy*, 2 WPP 140.

Flemming Marian, Wojciechowska Janina (1999), *Zbrodnie wojenne. Przestępstwa przeciwko pokojowi, państwu i obronności. Rozdział XVI, XVII, XVIII Kodeksu karnego. Komentarz*, C.H. Beck.

Fooner Michael (2009), *Interpol, Issues in World Crime and International Criminal Justice*, Plenum Press.

Franczyk Bernard, Staszko Krzysztof (1980), *Problem ścigania zbrodniarzy wojennych w świetle zasad ekstradycyjnych ONZ*, in: Pilichowski (1980b): 819.

Fripp Eric (2016), *Nationality and Statelessness in the International Law of Refugee Status*, Bloomsbury.

Galicki Zdzisław (1981), *Terroryzm lotniczy w świetle prawa międzynarodowego*, WUW.

Galicki Zdzisław (1995), *Pojęcie zbrodni przeciwko ludzkości zgodne z prawem międzynarodowym oraz teorią prawa polskiego*, 3/17 Biuletyn Ekspertyzy i Opinie Prawne 105.

Galicki Zdzisław (2015), *Zasada aut dedere aut judicare w pracach Komisji Prawa Międzynarodowego Organizacji Narodów Zjednoczonych*, in: Karol Karski (ed.), *Kierunki rozwoju współczesnego prawa międzynarodowego*, Bellona.

Galicki Zdzisław, Kamiński Tomasz, Myszona-Kostrzewa Katarzyna (ed.) (2011), *Manfred Lachs – wybitny prawnik świata*, Stowarzyszenie Absolwentów Wydziału Prawa i Administracji Uniwersytetu Warszawskiego.

Gańczak Filip (2020), *Jan Sehn. Tropiciel nazistów*, Czarne.

Gardocki Lech (1979), *Zagadnienia internacjonalizacji odpowiedzialności karnej za przestępstwa popełnione za granicą*, WUW.

Gardocki Lech (1985), *Zarys prawa karnego międzynarodowego*, PWN.

Gardocki Lech (1989a), *Legal Problems Emerging from the Implementation of International Crimes in Domestic Criminal Law*, 60 RIDP 89.

Gardocki Lech (1989b), *Subsydiarność prawa karnego oraz in dubio pro libertate – jako zasady kryminalizacji*, 12 PiP 59

Gardocki Lech (1990a), *Das Problem des Umfangs der Strafbarkeit in der polnischen Gesetzgebung, Rechtsprechung und Strafrechtslehre*, in: Klaus Lüderssen et al. (ed.), *Modernes Strafrecht und ultima-ratio-Prinzip*, PeterLang: 17.

Gardocki Lech (1990b), *Zagadnienia teorii kryminalizacji*, PWN.

Gardocki Lech (1996), *Podwójna przestępność czynu w prawie ekstradycyjnym*, in: *Problemy nauk penalnych. Prace ofiarowane Profesor Oktawii Górniok*, WUŚ.

Gardocki Lech (1997), *Igor Andrejew (1915–1995)*, 34 Studia Iuridica 217.

Gardocki Lech (2005), *Kriminalisierung – zwischen Theorie und Praxis*, in: Jörg Arnold Et al. (ed.), *Menschengerechtes Strafrecht. Festschrift für Albin Eser zum 70. Geburtstag*, Beck: 1335.

Gardocki Lech, Gardocka Teresa, Majewski Łukasz (2017), *Prawo karne międzynarodowe. Zarys systemu*, PWN.

Garcia-Salmonez Rovira Monika (2013), *The Project of positivism in international law*, OUP.

Garrod Matthew (2016), *The British Influence on the Development of the Laws of War and the Punishment of War Criminals: From the Grotius Society to the United Nations War Crimes Commission*, in: Robert McCorquodale, Jean-Pierre Gauci (ed.), *British Influences on International Law, 1915–2015*, Brill Nijhoff: 349.

Gauden Grzegorz (2019), *Lwów – kres iluzji. Opowieść o pogromie listopadowym 1918*, Universitas.

Gawęda Stanisław (1986), *Uniwersytet Jagielloński w okresie II wojny światowej 1939–1945*, Wydawnictwo Literackie.

Gawrońska-Garstka Magdalena (2016), *Uniwersytet Stefana Batorego w Wilnie. Uczelnia ziem północno-wschodnich Drugiej Rzeczypospolitej (1919–1939) w świetle źródeł*, Wydawnictwo Rys.

Gawryszewski Andrzej (2005), *Ludność Polski w XX wieku*, Instytut Geografii i Przestrzennego Zagospodarowania Im. Stanisława Leszczyckiego PAN.

Gelberg Ludwik, Pławski Stanisław (1950), *Problem odpowiedzialności karnej państwa*, 7 PiP 18.

Gelberg Ludwik (1956), *Piractwo na morzach chińskich: próba analizy*, PWN.

Gelberg Ludwik (1978), *Die Nürnberger Prinzipien und das moderne Völkerrecht*, 2 Demokratie und Recht 177.

Gelewski Tadeusz Maria (1976), *Zbrodnie wojenne na morzu w drugiej wojnie światowej*, Wydawnictwo Morskie.

German Crimes against Poland. Official Report of the Polish Government to be submitted to the International Military Tribunal (1945), The Republic of Poland.

Giebułtowicz Józef (1945), *Odpowiedzialność przestępców wojennych w świetle prawa narodów*, Spółdzielnia Wydawnicza Czytelnik.

Gilas Janusz (1981), *Systemy normatywne w stosunkach międzynarodowych*, PWN.

GKBZHwP-IPN (1987), *Wyrok Norymberski. Sesja w 40. rocznicę (22 i 23 września 1986 r.). Referaty – Komunikaty*, GKBZHWP-IPN.

Glennon Michael (2001), *Limits of Law, Prerogatives of Power: Interventionism after Kosovo*, Palgrave.

Glaser Stefan (1924), *Zasada ekstradycji w odniesieniu do przestępców politycznych: wykład inauguracyjny wygłoszony na Uniwersytecie Stefana Batorego dnia 12 stycznia 1924*, Gebethner i Wolff.

Glaser Stefan (1929a), *Nowe kierunki w międzynarodowym prawie karnem a ekstradycja*, 3–4 Palestra 134.

Glaser Stefan (1929b), *Nowe kierunki w międzynarodowym prawie karnem a ekstradycja*, 5 Palestra 215.

Glaser Stefan (1929c), *Nowe kierunki w międzynarodowym prawie karnem a ekstradycja*, 6–7 Palestra 260.

Glaser Stefan (1929d), *Nowe kierunki w międzynarodowym prawie karnem a ekstradycja*, 8–9 Palestra 354.

Glaser Stefan (1929e), *Nowe kierunki w międzynarodowym prawie karnem a ekstradycja*, 12 Palestra 542.

Glaser Stefan (1933), *Wiążący bezprawny rozkaz*, Księgarnia Powszechna.

Glaser Stefan (1934), *Normatywna nauka o winie*, Drukarnia Rolnicza.

Glaser Stefan (1937a), *Pologne – Est-il désirable que le juge puisse retenir et punir un fait qui ne rentre pas expressément sous les termes d'une disposition légale?*, 14 RIDP 340.

Glaser Stefan (1937b), *Prawo karne na kongresach międzynarodowych (Paryż, Haga)*, 10 Palestra 874.

Glaser Stefan (1938), *Międzynarodowe zwalczanie handlu żywym towarem a polski kodeks karny*, 9 Gazeta Sądowa Warszawska 129.

Glaser Stefan (1942), *Nullum crimen sine lege*, 24(1) Journal of Comparative Legislation and International Law 29.

Glaser Stefan (1948), *Les infractions internationales, les délits politiques et l'extradition*, 28/8 RDPC 766.

Glaser (1949), *L'État en tant que personne morale est-il pénalement responsable?*, 29 RDPC 425.

Glaser Stefan (1950), *«L'acte d'état» et le problème de la responsabilité individuelle*, 31 RDPC 1.

Glaser Stefan (1952), *Vers une juridiction criminelle international*, 3 Revue Pénale Suisse 251.

Glaser Stefan (1953a), *La guerre d'agression a la lumière des sources du droit international*, Verlag Pedone.

Glaser Stefan (1953b), *L'ordre hiérarchique en droit pénal international*, 33/4 RDPC 283.

Glaser Stefan (1954), *Introduction à l'étude du droit international pénal*, Bruylant & Librairie du Recueil Sirey.

Glaser Stefan (1957), *Infraction internationale. Ses éléments constitutifs et ses aspects juridiques. Exposé sur la base du droit pénal comparé*, LGDJ.

Glaser Stefan (1959), *The conception of political delict*, Indian Yearbook of International Affairs 16.

Glaser Stefan (1960), *Culpabilité en droit international pénal*, 99 RCADI 467.

Glaser Stefan (1961), *"Agression spatiale" à la lumière du droit international pénal*, 77 Schweizerische Zeitschrift für Strafrecht 129.

Glaser Stefan (1965), *Quelques observations sur la prescription en matiére de la criminalité de guerre*, 6 RDPC 511.

Glaser Stefan (1966), *Réponse de M. Stefan Glaser*, 3–4 RIDP 475.

Glaser Stefan (1970), *Droit international pénal conventionnel*, vol. I, Bruylant.

Glaser Stefan (1974), *Urywki wspomnień*, Odnowa.

Glaser Stefan (1978), *Droit international pénal conventionnel*, vol. II, Bruylant.

Glaser Stefan (2008), *The Charter of the Nuremberg Tribunal and New Principles of International Law Perspectives on the Nuremberg Trial*, in: Guénaël Mettraux (ed.), *Perspectives on the Nuremberg Trial*, OUP: 55.

Głogowska-Balcerzak Anna (2019), *Standardy zwalczania handlu ludźmi w prawie międzynarodowym*, WUŁ.

Gondek Leszek (1981), *Polskie misje wojskowe 1945–1949. Polityczno-prawne, ekonomiczne i wojskowe problemy likwidacji skutków wojny na obszarze okupowanych Niemiec*, MON.

Gondek Leszek (1984), *Polskie cywilne sądownictwo podziemne 1942–1944 (Zarys, geneza, struktury)*, 4 Studia Historyczne PAN 650.

Gondek Leszek (1988), *Polska karząca 1939–1945. Polski podziemny wymiar sprawiedliwości w okresie okupacji niemieckiej*, Instytut Wydawniczy Pax.

Goold Adams M.E. (1948), *Praca Międzynarodowej Komisji w Cambridge do rekonstrukcji i rozwoju prawa karnego nad zagadnieniem ukarania zbrodni wojennych*, 3 PiP 96.

Goryński Zenon (1944), *Zbrodnie wojenne. Szkic prawny*, APW.

Gouttes Paul des (1930), *La Convention de Genève du 27 juillet 1929. Commentaire*, Comité International de la Croix-Rouge.

Góras Michał T. (2019), *Profesor Wacław Komarnicki, poseł na sejm RP, jeniec obozu w Kozielsku, ocalony*, 51(2) Dzieje Najnowsze 265.

Górbiel Andrzej (1993), *Prawnomiędzynarodowe aspekty terroryzmu*, in: Karol Sławik (ed.), *Terroryzm: aspekty prawno-międzynarodowe, kryminalistyczne i policyjne. Materiały sympozjum zorganizowanego przez Wydział Prawa Uniwersytetu Szczecińskiego, Szczecin, 29–30.XI.1991 r.*, Ławica: 22.

Górniok Oktawia (2004), *Przestępstwo o charakterze terrorystycznym w art. 115 §20 k. k.*, 10 Przegląd Sądowy 3.

Gumkowski Janusz, Kułakowski Tadeusz (1961), *Zbrodniarze hitlerowscy przed Najwyższym Trybunałem Narodowym*, Wydawnictwo Prawnicze.

Górbiel Andrzej (1970), *Konieczność wojskowa w prawie międzynarodowym*, Zeszyty Naukowe Uniwersytetu Jagiellońskiego, Prace Prawnicze, vol. 44.

Graven Jean (1950), *Les Crimes contre l'Humanité*, 76 RCADI 427.

Graven Jean (1966), *Projet de convention sur les crimes de guerre, les crimes contre la paix et les crimes contr' l'humanité, Introduction et questionnaire*, 3–4 RIDP 393.

Grosescu Raluca (2019), *State Socialist Endeavours for the Non-applicability of Statutory Limitations to International Crimes: Historical Roots and Current Implications*, 21 Journal of the History of International Law 239.

Grzebyk Patrycja (2010), *Odpowiedzialność karna za zbrodnię agresji*, WUW.

Grzebyk Patrycja (2013a), *Criminal Responsibility for the Crime of Aggression*, Routledge.

Grzebyk Patrycja (2013b), *Odpowiedzialność za wydanie rozkazu popełnienia zbrodni międzynarodowej*, IV Międzynarodowe Prawo Humanitarne 205.

Grzebyk Patrycja (2013c), *Prace Komisji Prawa Międzynarodowego Organizacji Narodów Zjednoczonych dotyczące obowiązku wydania lub ścigania sądowego (aut dedere aut iudicare)*, in: Elżbieta Mikos-Skuza, Katarzyna Myszona-Kostrzewa, Jerzy Poczobut (ed.), *Prawo międzynarodowe – teraźniejszość, perspektywy, dylematy. Księga jubileuszowa Profesora Zdzisława Galickiego*, Wolters Kluwer: 129.

Grzebyk Patrycja (2014), *The Role of the Polish Supreme National Tribunal in the Development of Principles of International Criminal Law*, in: Morten Bergsmo, Cheah Wui Ling, Yi Ping (ed.), *Historical Origins of International Criminal Law*, Volume 2, Torkel: 603.

Grzebyk Patrycja (2017), *Amendments of January 2018 to the Act on the Institute of National Remembrance – Commission for the Prosecution of Crimes against the Polish Nation in Light of International Law*, 37 PYIL 287.

Grzebyk (2017b), *The Annexation of Crimea in the Light of the Definition of Aggression. Does Prohibition of Aggression Apply to Russia?*, in: Władysław Czapliński, Sławomir Dębski, Rafał Tarnogórski, Karolina Wierczyńska (ed.), *The Case of Crimea's Annexation Under International Law*, INP PAN, The Centre for Polish-Russian Dialogue and Understanding, Wydawnictwo Naukowe Scholar: 137.

Grzebyk Patrycja (2018), *Rzeczypospolitej Polskiej stosunek do prawa międzynarodowego*, 54 Stosunki Międzynarodowe – International Relations 117.

Grzebyk Patrycja (2019a), *Hidden in the Glare of the Nuremberg Trial: Impunity for the Wola Massacre as the Greatest Debacle of Post-War Trials*, 7 Max Planck Institute Luxembourg for Procedural LawResearch Paper Series 1.

Grzebyk Patrycja (2019b), *Unintentional or deliberate – the omission of the Wola Massacre in the Nuremberg and post-Nuremberg trials*, in: Eryk Habowski (ed.), *Wola – Nierozliczona zbrodnia a pojęcie ludobójstwa*, Instytut Pileckiego: 301.

Grzebyk Patrycja (2020a), *Emil Stanisław Rappaport: His road From Abolition to Prosecution of Nations*, in: Immi Tallgren, Frederic Mégret (2020): 93.

Grzebyk Patrycja (2020b), *Indywidualna odpowiedzialność za wojnę agresywną oraz zbrodnie wojenne w świetle ekspertyz Ludwika Ehrlicha przed Najwyższym Trybunałem Narodowym*, in: Patrycja Grzebyk, Rafał Tarnogórski (2020c): 67.

Grzebyk Patrycja (2022a), International Crimes in National Regulations of Selected States, IWS.

Grzebyk Patrycja (2022b), *Key Risks and Difficulties of Aggression Trials*, in: Stefanie Bock, Eckart Conze (ed.), *Rethinking the Crime of Aggression. International and Interdisciplinary Perspectives*, Springer: 269.

Grzebyk Patrycja (2023), *Komentarz do art. 117–126c (Przestępstwa przeciwko pokojowi, ludzkości oraz przestępstwa wojenne*, in: Michał Królikowski, Robert Zawłocki (ed.), *Kodeks karny. Tom II. Część szczególna. Komentarz do art. 117–221*, wyd. V, C.H. Beck: 3.

Grzebyk Patrycja, Tarnogórski Rafał (ed.) (2020), *Siła prawa zamiast prawa siły. Ludwik Ehrlich i jego wkład w rozwój nauki prawa międzynarodowego oraz nauki o stosunkach międzynarodowych*, PISM.

Grzegorczyk Tomasz (2009), *Współpraca Polski z Międzynarodowym Trybunałem Karnym*, 3 Prokuratura Krajowa 7.

Grzybowski Kazimierz, Pundeff Marin (1954), *Soviet Bloc Peace Defence Laws*, 46 AJIL 537

Gutekunst Włodzimierz (1959), *Studia nad sędziowskim wymiarem kary*, 1 PiP 125.

Habowski Eryk (ed.) (2019), *Wola 1944. Nierozliczona zbrodnia a pojęcie ludobójstwa. An Unpunished crime and the notion of genocide*, Instytut Pileckiego.

Hagen William W. (2018), *Anti-Jewish Violence in Poland 1914–1920*, CUP.

Hanausek Tadeusz (1980), *W sprawie pojęcia współczesnego terroryzmu*, 143 Podstawy Kryminalistyki: 30.

Haye Eve La, *War Crimes in Internal Armed Conflicts*, CUP.

Hankey Lord (1950), *Politics, Trials and Errors*, Pen in Hand.

Heller Kevin Jon (2011), *The Nuremberg Military Tribunals and the Origins of International Criminal Law*, OUP.

Herzog Jacques-Bernard (1975), *Nuremberg: un échec fructueux?*, LGDJ.

Heydecker Joe J., Leeb Johannes (2006), *Proces w Norymberdze*, Świat Książki.

Hirsch Francine (2019), *The Soviet Union at the Palace of Justice: Law, Intrigue, and International Rivalry in the Nuremberg Trials*, in: Crowe (2019): 171.

H.L. (1945), *Review: Axis Rule in Occupied Europe by Raphael Lemkin*, 9 (1) Cambridge Law Journal 140.

Hofmański Piotr, Kuczyńska Hanna (2020), *Międzynarodowe prawo karne*, Wolters Kluwer.

Holy Katarzyna (2015), *Prawo międzynarodowe publiczne wobec amnestii*, Difin.

Hołyst Brunon (1978), *Przestępczość drugiej połowy XX wieku*, wyd. II rozszerzone, Wiedza Powszechna.

Hood Roger (2001), *Leon Radzinowicz 1906–1999*, Proceedings of the British Academy, The British Academy 636.

Indecki Krzysztof (1998), *Prawo karne wobec terroryzmu i aktu terrorystycznego*, WUŁ.

Indecki Krzysztof (2005), *Zasada* nullum crimen sine lege *w prawie karnym międzynarodowym*, in: Lech Gardocki, Michał Królikowski, Anna Walczak-Żochowska (eds.), *Gaudium in litteris est: księga jubileuszowa ofiarowana Pani Profesor Genowefie Rejman z okazji osiemdziesiątych urodzin*, Liber: 139.

Indecki Krzysztof (2018), *Terroryzm – ewolucja czy stagnacja pojęcia*, 41 Studia Prawnoustrojowe 237.

Irvin-Erickson Douglas (2019), *From Geneva to Nuremberg to New York: Andrey Vyshinsky, Raphaël Lemkin, and the Struggle to Outlaw Revolutionary Violence, State Terror, and Genocide*, in: David M. Crowe (eds.), *Stalin's Soviet Justice "Show" Trials, War Crimes Trials, and Nuremberg*, Bloomsbury Academic.

Iwanek Tomasz (2013), *Zbrodnia agresji w prawie międzynarodowym. Stan po nowelizacji Statutu Rzymskiego MTK*, 11 Studia Politicae Universitatis Silesiensis 287.

Iwanek Tomasz (2015), *Zbrodnia ludobójstwa i zbrodnie przeciwko ludzkości w prawie międzynarodowym*, Wolters Kluwer.

Izdebski Hubert (2008), *Zygmunt Klemens Cybichowski 1879–1946*, in: *Profesorowie Wydziału Prawa i Administracji Uniwersytetu Warszawskiego 1808–2008*, Lexis Nexis: 99.

Jakubowski Andrzej, Wierczyńska Karolina (2017) *Individual Responsibility for Deliberate Destruction of Cultural Heritage: Contextualizing the ICC Judgment in the Al-Mahdi Case*, 16(4) Chinese Journal of International Law 695.

Jakubowski Andrzej, Wierczyńska Karolina (2020) *The Al Mahdi Case: from Punishing Perpetrators to Repairing Cultural Heritage Harm*, in: Anne-Marie Carstens, Elisabeth Varner (eds.) *Intersections in International Cultural Heritage Law*, OUP.

Jakubowski Grzegorz (2002), *Sądownictwo powszechne w Polsce w latach 1944–1950*, IPN.

Jasiński Łukasz (2018), *Sprawiedliwość i polityka. Działalność Głównej Komisji Badania Zbrodni Niemieckich/ Hitlerowskich w Polsce 1945–1989*, ISP PAN.

Jasiński Wojciech (2016), *Admissibility of Illegaly Obtained Evidence in Proceedings before International Criminal Courts*, in: Krzan (2016) 201.

Jennings Robert (1996), *International Lawyers and the Progressive Development of International Law*, in: Jerzy Makarczyk (ed.), *Theory of International Law at the Threshold of the 21st Century: Essays in Honour of Krzysztof Skubiszewski*, Kluwer Law International: 413.

Jonca Karol (1987), *Polska myśl prawnicza wobec ścigania i nieprzedawniania zbrodni hitlerowskich*, GKBZHwP-IPN 45.

Jones Elwyn (1948), *Rola delegacji polskiej w procesie norymberskim*, 3 PiP 111.

Jurewicz Justyna (2008), *Jurysdykcja przedmiotowa Międzynarodowego Trybunału Karnego*, WUŁ.

Jurewicz Justyna (2011), *Handel ludźmi w polskim prawie karnym i prawie ponadnarodowym*, WUŁ.

Kacprzak Paweł (2011), *Wysiedlenie Ludności Niemieckiej z Polski do Radzieckiej Strefy Okupacyjnej w Niemczech w 1947 roku*, LXXXV PPA 287.

Kaczmarek Tomasz (1972), *Sędziowski wymiar kary w Polskiej Rzeczypospolitej Ludowej w świetle badań ankietowych*, Zakład Narodowy im. Ossolińskich.

Kaczmarek Tomasz (1980), *Ogólne dyrektywy wymiaru kary w teorii i praktyce sądowej*, WUWr.

Kaczmarek Tomasz (1987), *Decyzja sędziego w sprawie wymiaru kary i jej psychospołeczne uwarunkowania*, WUWr.

Kaczmarek Tomasz (2009), *Racjonalny ustawodawca wobec opinii społecznej a populizm penalny*, in: Zofia Sienkiewicz, Rajnhardt Kokot (ed.), *Populizm penalny i jego przejawy w Polsce*, Kolonia Limited: 33.

Kaczmarek Tomasz (2014), *Paradygmat naruszenia (zagrożenia) dobra prawnego jako aksjologiczna podstawa kryminalizacji*, in: Zbigniew Jędrzejewski (ed.), *Między nauką a praktyką prawa karnego: księga jubileuszowa profesora Lecha Gardockiego*, C.H. Beck: 139.

Kaczmarek Ryszard (2019), *Powstania śląskie 1919–1920–1921. Nieznana wojna polsko-niemiecka*, Wydawnictwo Literackie.

Kaiser Wolf Jasch Hans-Christian (2018), *Der Holocaust vor deutschen Gerichten, Amnestieren, Verdrängen, Bestrafen*, BPB.

Kania Leszek (2021), *Góra Świętej Anny – Kędzierzyn 1921*, Bellona.

Kardas Piotr (2002), R*egulacja współdziałania przestępnego jako podstawa zwalczania przestępczości zorganizowanej*, 10 Prokuratura i Prawo 80.

Kardas Piotr (2017), *Rozwój koncepcji odpowiedzialności za współdziałanie*, in: Ryszard Dębski (ed.), *Nauka o przestępstwie. Zasady odpowiedzialności*, System Prawa Karnego, vol. 3, C.H. Beck: 880.

Karpuz Zbigniew, Korkuć Maciej, Rezmer Waldemar (2020), *Jeńcy 1920*, IPN.

Karska Elżbieta (2009), *Subsydiarność uchwał organizacji rządowych i pozarządowych w jurysdykcji międzynarodowych trybunałów karnych*, WUWr.

Karska Elżbieta (2011), *Manfred Lachs wobec ludobójstwa i zbrodni wojennych*, in: Galicki, Kamiński, Myszona-Kostrzewa (2011): 377.

Karski Jan (1944), *A Story of Secret State*, Houghton Miffin Company.

Karski Karol (1993), *Realizacja idei utworzenia międzynarodowego sądownictwa karnego*, 569(7) PiP 65.

Karski Karol (2007a), *Marian Muszkat – profesor prawa i stosunków międzynarodowych*, 4 PPD 75.

Karski Karol (2007b), *Odpowiedzialność podmiotów zbiorowych na podstawie przepisów międzynarodowego prawa karnego (uwagi* de lege lata *i* de lege ferenda), in: Jerzy Menkes (ed.), *Prawo międzynarodowe. Księga pamiątkowa Profesor Renaty Szafarz*, WSHP: 227.

Karski Karol (2008), *Juliusz Katz-Suchy 1912–1971*, in: Grażyna Bałtruszajtys (ed.), *Profesorowie Wydziału Prawa i Administracji Uniwersytetu Warszawskiego 1808–2008*, Lexis Nexis: 318.

Karski Karol (2012), *Geneza i Skutki Nowelizacji Art. 55 Konstytucji RP: Spojrzenie z Punktu Widzenia Intencji Ustrojodawcy*, 4 Kwartalnik Prawa Publicznego 7.

Kasparek Franciszek (1882), *O wydawaniu przestępców, Uchwały Akademii prawa międzynarodowego*, Nakładem Redakcyi Przeglądu Sądowego i Administracyjnego.

Kearney Michael (2007), *The Prohibition of Propaganda for War in International Law*, OUP.

Kelsen Hans (1946), *Reviewed Work: Axis Rule in Occupied Europe. Laws of Occupation, Analysis of Government, Proposals for Redress by Raphael Lemkin*, 34 (1) California Law Review 271.

Kelsen Hans (1961), *Hersch Lauterpacht*, 10 International and Comparative Law Quarterly 3.

Klafkowski Alfons (1946), *Okupacja niemiecka w Polsce w świetle prawa narodów*, WIZ.

Klafkowski Alfons (1966), *Zasady norymberskie a rozwój prawa międzynarodowego*, Zachodnia Agencja Prasowa.

Klafkowski Alfons (1968a), *Obozy koncentracyjne hitlerowskie jako zagadnienie prawa międzynarodowego*, PWN.

Klafkowski Alfons (1968b), *Ściganie zbrodniarzy wojennych w Niemieckiej Republice Federalnej w świetle Prawa międzynarodowego*, Wydawnictwo Poznańskie.

Klafkowski Alfons (1979), *Prawo międzynarodowe publiczne*, PWN.

Kleczkowska Agata (2016), *Judgement of the Supreme Court, dated 17 February 2016 (Ref. no. WA 16/15)*, 36 PYIL 267.

Klein Pierre (2015), *À propos de «Criminalizing State Responsibility» de Krystyna Marek (1978/1979–II): une préfiguration des débats théoriques de la dernière partie du XXe siècle au sein de la doctrine internationalist*, 48 RBDI 302.

Klepner Magdalena (2002), *Sprawstwo polecające*, 1 Prokuratura i Prawo 65.

Knypl Zenon (1975), *Ekstradycja jako instytucja prawa międzynarodowego i wewnętrznego*, Wydawnictwo Prawnicze.

Kobierska-Motas Elżbieta (1991), *Ekstradycja przestępców wojennych do polski z czterech stref okupacyjnych Niemiec 1946–1950*, part I, GKBZHwP-IPN.

Kobierska-Motas Elżbieta (1992), *Ekstradycja przestępców wojennych do polski z czterech stref okupacyjnych Niemiec 1946–1950*, part II, GKBZHwP-IPN.

Kobierska-Motas Elżbieta (1995), *Rząd polski na emigracji wobec problemu dokumentowania niemieckich przestępstw wojennych*, 38 Pamięć i Sprawiedliwość 175.

Kocot Kazimierz (1953), *Zagadnienie źródeł prawa międzynarodowego na tle współczesnej walki o pokój*, Wydawnictwo Prawnicze.

Kocot Kazimierz (1956), *Dział drugi: Prawa i obowiązki państw w wypadku konfliktu zbrojnego*, in: Marian Muszkat (1956): 341.

Kocot Kazimierz (1974), *Problem pojęć: reparacje wojenne, restytucja, odszkrt.wania itp. w aspekcie umowy poczdamskiej, traktatów pokojowych, umów zawartych przez NRF, wyroków sądowych i doktryny prawa międzynarodowego*, GKBZHWP.

Kocot Kazimierz, Wolfke Karol (1976), *Wybór dokumentów do nauki prawa międzynarodowego*, ed. 3, PWN.

Kochavi Arieh J. (1998), *Prelude to Nuremberg. Allied War Crimes Policy and the Question of Punishment*, The University of North Carolina Press.

Kok Ruth (2007), *Statutory Limitations in International Criminal Law*, T.M.C. Asser Press.

Kolasa Jan (1965), *Rozwój regulaminów organizacji międzynarodowych*, 3 RPEiS 81.

Kolasa Jan (1985), *Some Reflections Concerning the Evolution of International Arbitral and Judicial Rules of Procedure*, 14 PYIL 99.

Kolasa Jan (1987a), *Regulamin Stałego Trybunału Sprawiedliwości Międzynarodowej. Początki międzynarodowej procedury sądowej*, CLIX Prawo (AUWr) 69.

Kolasa Jan (1987b), *Zarys rozwoju międzynarodowego prawa procesowego*, 22 PPA 57.

Kolasa Jan (1988), *Proces Norymberski – aspekt proceduralny*, 5 PiP 55.

Kołodziejczyk Ryszard (1983), *Jan Bloch (1836–1902). Szkic do portretu "króla polskich kolei"*, PIW.

Komarnicki Wacław (1935), *La définition de l'agresseur*, in: *La sécurité collective. Mémoires présentés par le Comité Central des Institutions polonaises des Sciences Politiques à la VIII-e Conférence des Hautes Études Internationales à Londres, 3–8 juins 1935*, in: Antoni Deryng (ed.), *La sécurité collective. Mémoires présentés par le Comité Central des Institutions polonaises des Sciences Politiques à la VIII-e Conférence des Hautes Études Internationales à Londres* 73.

Komarnicki Wacław (1936), *Określenie napastnika we współczesnem prawie narodów*, in: *Księga pamiątkowa ku czci Leona Pińskiego*, vol. I, Księgarnia Gubrynowicza i Syna.

Komarnicki Wacław (1949), *La définition de l'agresseur dans le droit international moderne*, 75 RCADI 1.

Kondracka Mariola (2000), *Kobiety na uniwersytetach*, in: Anna Żarnowska, Andrzej Szwarc (ed.), *Równe prawa i nierówne szanse. Kobiety w Polsce międzywojennej*, DiG: 276.

Korboński Stefan (1991), *W imieniu Rzeczypospolitej …*, Bellona.

Korczyk Henryk (1993), *Traktat ogólny o wyrzeczeniu się wojny (Pakt Brianda-Kellogga). Geneza, zawarcie, recepcja, działanie*, Wydawnictwo Fundacji "Historia pro Futuro".

Koredczuk Józef (2011), *Znaczenie Kodeksu Karnego z 1932 r. dla Rozwoju Nauki i Prawa Karnego w Polsce w XX Wieku*, 11 (2) Zeszyty Prawnicze IV 45.

Korkuć Maciej (2020), *"Wykorzystać – jeżeli okaże się to niezbędne": Jeńcy 1920 i Anty-Katyń*, IPN.

Kornat Marek (2008), *Barbarzyństwo – wandalizm – terroryzm – ludobójstwo. O Rafale Lemkinie i idei zdefiniowania "zbrodni w obliczu prawa narodów"*, 43 PPD 79.

Kornat Marek (2010), *Rafał Lemkin's formative years and the beginning of international Career in the Inter-war Poland (1918–1939)*, in: Agnieszka Bieńczyk-Missala, Sławomir Dębski (2010): 68.

Kornbluth Andrew (2013), *"Jest wielu Kainów pośród nas". Polski wymiar sprawiedliwości a Zagłada, 1944–1956*, 9 Zagłada Żydów. Studia i Materiały 157.

Kornbluth Andrew (2021), *The August Trials. The Holocaust and Postwar Justice in Poland*, Harvard University Press.

Korowicz Marek St. (1938), *Jednostka jako podmiot Prawa Narodów*, Głos Prawników Śląskich 41.

Korowicz Marek S. (1959), *Introduction to International Law: Present Conceptions of International Law and practice*, Martinus Nijhoff.

Kos-Rabcewicz-Zubkowski Louis (1989), *Canada – Rapport National*, 60(1–2) RIDP 195.

Kowalski Grzegorz M. (2019), *Sprawa karna SS-Oberscharführera Franza Langnera, członka załogi KL Auschwitz, przed Sądem Apelacyjnym w Krakowie (1949–1952)*, 12(2) Krakowskie Studia z Historii Państwa i Prawa 223.

Kowalski Michał (2020), *Wielki nieobecny – Ludwik Ehrlich i* Powrót do Lwowa *Philippe'a Sandsa*, in: Patrycja Grzebyk, Rafał Tarnogórski (2020c): 363.

Kremens Karolina (2010), *Dowody osobowe w międzynarodowym postępowaniu karnym*, TNOiK.

Kreß Claus (2014), *Towards a Truly Universal Invisible College of International Criminal Lawyers*, Torkel Opsahl Academic EPublisher.

Kreß Claus (2018), *On the Activation of ICC Jurisdiction over the Crime of Aggression*, 16 JICJ 1.

Kreß Claus, Barriga Stefan (ed.) (2016), *The Crime of Aggression. A Commentary*, CUP.

Kreß Claus, Garibian Sevane (2018), *Laying the Foundations for a Convention on Crimes Against Humanity: Concluding Observations*, 16 JICJ 909.

Król Michał (1929), *Odpowiedzialność państw w prawie międzynarodowem*, 3 RPW 177.

Król Michał (1930), *Represalia i wyższa konieczność w prawie międzynarodowym*, 4 RPW 15.

Król Michał (1936), *Próby kodyfikacji zasad międzynarodowej odpowiedzialności państw*, 8 RPW 174.

Król Michał (1939), *Zagadnienie agresji w prawie międzynarodowym*, 10 RPW 167.

Królikowski Michał, Wiliński Paweł, Izydorczyk Jacek (2008), *Podstawy prawa karnego międzynarodowego*, Wolters Kluwer.

Krzan Bartłomiej (2009), *Kompetencje Rady Bezpieczeństwa ONZ w międzynarodowym sądownictwie karnym*, Dom Organizatora TNOiK.

Krzan Bartłomiej (ed.) (2012), *Jurisdictional Competition of International Courts and Tribunals*, WUWr.

Krzan Bartłomiej (ed.) (2016), *Prosecuting International Crimes. A Multidisciplinary Approach*, Brill/Nijhoff.

Krzan Bartłomiej (2018), *Racjonalizacja karania z perspektywy międzynarodowego i krajowego prawa karnego*, in: Ewelina Cała-Wacinkiewicz, Jerzy Menkes (eds.), *Wspólne wartości prawa międzynarodowego, europejskiego i krajowego*, C.H. Beck 337.

Krzan Bartłomiej (2019), *Substantive and procedural opportunities of avoiding responsibility utilized by the perpatrators of Wola massacre (with particular consideration of the case of Heinz Reinefahrt)*, in: Habowski (2019): 353.

Krzan Bartłomiej (2020a), *Celowość kodyfikacji zbrodni przeciwko ludzkości przez Komisję Prawa Międzynarodowego* ONZ, 42/2 Studia nad Autorytaryzmem i Totalitaryzmem 45.

Krzan Bartłomiej (2020b), *Sędziowski wymiar kary ze stanowiska międzynarodowych trybunałów karnych* ad hoc, in: Izabela Kraśnicka (ed.), *Prawo międzynarodowe: teoria i praktyka*, C.H. Beck: 345.

Krzan Bartłomiej (2021), *Admissibility of evidence and international criminal justice*, 7/1 Revista Brasileira de Direito Processual Penal 161.

Krzan Bartłomiej (2022), *German Code of Crimes against International Law: A Look from Outside*, in: Grzebyk, (2022a): 29.

Krzymuski Edmund (1885), *Wykład prawa karnego ze szczególnem uwzględnieniem ustaw austriackich*, Księgarnia Leona Frommera.

Krzymuski Edmund (1901), *Wykład prawa karnego ze stanowiska nauki i prawa austryackiego*, vol. 1, Księgarnia Leona Frommera.

Kubicki Leszek (1961), *Zbrodnie wojenne jako zagadnienie kodyfikacyjne w prawie wewnętrznym*, 8–9 PiP 335.

Kubicki Leszek (1963), *Zbrodnie wojenne w świetle prawa polskiego*, PWN.

Kubicki Leszek (1987), *Wpływ zasad norymberskich a ustawodawstwo i orzecznictwo polskie*, GKBZHwP-IPN 27.

Kuc Oktawian (2012), *Krstić Case Continued. Decision of the Circuit Court in Warsaw of 6 December 2012 (Ref. No. VIII Kop 222/12)*, 32 PYIL 315.

Kuczma Tadeusz (1937), *Recenzja [bez tytułu] książki Mikliszański Kopek dr: Le Droit pénal in'ernational d'après la législation polonaise. Paris. Recueil Sirey, 1935*, 17 (2) RPEIS 259.

Kuczyńska Hanna (2008), *Criminal Enterprise jako szczególna forma odpowiedzialności karnej przed międzynarodowymi trybunałami karnymi*, in: Jolanta Jakubowska-Hara (ed.), *Reforma prawa karnego: propozycje i komentarze. Księga pamiątkowa profesor Barbary Kunickiej-Michalskiej*, Scholar: 598.

Kuczyńska Hanna (2014), *Model oskarżenia przed Międzynarodowym Trybunałem Karnym*, C.H. Beck.

Kuczyńska Hanna (2019a), *The possibility of initiating proceedings in the case of the Wola Massacre before national institutions*, in: Habowski (2019): 317.

Kuczyńska Hanna (2019b), *Nazi Crimes in Poland: A Never-Ending Search for Justice*, 1(133) Contemporary Central & East European Law 142.

Kudelski Robert (2005), *Niemiecka grabież polskich dzieł sztuki*, 1–2 Cenne, Bezcenne, Utracone 46.

Kuisz Jarosław (2020), *Propaganda bezprawia. O "popularyzowaniu prawa" w pierwszych latach Polski Ludowej*, Wydawnictwo Naukowe Scholar.

Kulesza Jan (2014), *Zarys teorii kryminalizacji*, 11–12 Prokuratura i Prawo 87.

Kulesza Jan (2017), *Problemy teorii kryminalizacji*, WUŁ.

Kulesza Witold (2021), *Sędziowie sądów specjalnych III Rzeszy i ich "zdrowe poczucie narodowe"*, 43 (4) Studia nad Autorytaryzmem i Totalitaryzmem 253.

Kulesza Witold (2006), *Zbrodnia katyńska w procesie norymberskim – refleksje nad stenogramem rozprawy*, in: Jacek Giezek (ed.), *Przestępstwo – kara – polityka kryminalna. Problemy tworzenia i funkcjonowania prawa. Księga jubileuszowa z okazji 70. Rocznicy urodzin Profesora Tomasza Kaczmarka*, Zakamycze: 407.

Kulesza Witold, Schenk Dieter (2023), *Władca Kraju Warty Arthur Greiser. Biografia i proces*, WUŁ.

Kulski Ladislas (Władysław) (1927), *Le problème de la sécurité depuis la Pacte de la S.D.N.*, Thèse.

Kulski Władysław (1950), *The Soviet System of Collective Security Compared with the Western System*, 44(3) AJIL 453.

Kulski Władysław (1952), *Soviet Comments on International Law*, 46 AJIL 542.

Kunicka-Michalska Barbara (2013), *Postulaty przedwojennych Międzynarodowych Kongresów Prawa Karnego AIDP*, in: Anna Błachnio-Parzych, Jolanta Jakubowska-Hara, Jacek Kosonoga, Hanna Kuczyńska (eds.), *Problemy wymiaru sprawiedliwości karnej. Księga jubileuszowa Profesora Jana Skupińskiego*, Wolters Kluwer: 1063.

Kurkowska, Edyta (2012), *Podstawy prawne organizacji i zasady postępowania w sądownictwie Polskiego Państwa Podziemnego*, XV Studia z Dziejów Państwa i Prawa Polskiego 163.

Kurowski Wojciech (2006), *Pojęcie organizacji przestępczej i przestępczości zorganizowanej*, 1 Prokuratura i Prawo 26.

Kumaniecki Kazimierz (1939), *Od republiki do protektoratu (Praga – Bratislawa – Użhorod)*, Drukarnia Uniwersytetu Jagiellońskiego pod zarządem J. Filipowskiego.

Kusz Antoni (1933), *Zasady międzynarodowego prawa karnego na tle współczesnych ustawodawstw*, 6 Głos Sądownictwa 344.

Kutrzeba Stanisław (1935), *Polska Odrodzona 1914–1928*, Gebethner i Wolff.

Lachowski Tomasz (2018), *Perspektywa praw ofiar w prawie międzynarodowym. Sprawiedliwość okresu przejściowego*, WUŁ.

Lachs Manfred (1944), *War Crimes and Political Offences*, 56 Juridical Review 27.

Lachs Manfred (1945a), *The Unwritten Laws of Warfare*, New Orleans.

Lachs Manfred (1945b), *War Crimes. An Attempt to Define the Issues*, Stevens & Sons Limited.

Lachs Manfred (1946a), *Le jugement de Nuremberg*, 3/4 RIDP 207.

Lachs Manfred (1946b), *Prawne gwarancje praw człowieka,* VI/4 Nowa Polska Miesięcznik/New Poland Monthly 232.

Lachs Manfred (1948), *O problema de Genocidio,* Argumentas.

Lachs Mandred (1952a), *Walka o definicję agresji,* 3 WPP.

Lachs Manfred (1952b), *Wojna bakteriologiczna – zbrodnia przeciw ludzkości,* 3 SM.

Lachs Manfred (1986), *Rzecz o nauce prawa międzynarodowego,* Zakład Narodowy im. Ossolińskich.

Landau Antoni (1947), *Czyn przestępny popełniony w wykonaniu rozkazu wojskowego,* 4 WPP 320.

Landau Antoni, Wasilkowski Czesław (1946), *Odpowiedzialność za zbrodnie czasu wojny w prawie polskim,* 11–12 DPP 27.

Lankosz Kazimierz (1995), *Międzynarodowy Trybunał do Spraw Ścigania Osób Winnych Popełnienia Poważnych Naruszeń Międzynarodowego Prawa Humanitarnego, Popełnionych na Terytorium b. Jugosławii. Uwagi de lege ferenda,* in: Kazimierz Lankosz (ed.), *Aktualne problemy prawa międzynarodowego we współczesnym świecie. Księga pamiątkowa poświęcona pamięci Profesora Mariana Iwanejko,* Wydawnictwo Uczelniane Akademii Ekonomicznej w Krakowie 143.

Lasok Dominik D. (1962), *The Eichmann Trial,* 11 International and Comparative Law Quarterly 355.

Lauterpacht Elihu (2010), *The Life of Hersch Lauterpacht,* CUP.

Lauterpacht Hersch (1930), *La théorie des différends non justiciables en droit international,* 34 RCADI 499.

Lauterpacht Hersch (1944), *The Law of Nations and the punishment of war crimes,* 21 BYIL 58.

Lauterpacht Hersch (1945), 9(1) Cambridge Law Journal 140.

Lauterpacht Hersch (1948), *International Law: A Treatise by L. Oppenheim,* vol. 1, *Peace, Seventh Edition, Disputes, War and Neutrality,* Longmans.

Lauterpacht Hersch (1950), *International Law and Human Rights,* Stevens.

Lauterpacht Hersch (1952), *International Law: A Treatise by L. Oppenheim,* vol. 2, *Disputes, War and Neutrality,* wyd. 7, Longmans.

Lauterpacht Hersch (1958), *The Development of International Law by the International Court,* Stevens.

Lech Marcin (2014), *Ochrona prawna społeczności międzynarodowej wobec zagrożenia terroryzmem,* WUG.

Lemkin Rafał (1933), *Przestępstwa polegające na wywołaniu niebezpieczeństwa międzypaństwowego jako delicta iuris gentium (wnioski na V Międzynarodową Konferencję Unifikacji Prawa Karnego w Madrycie),* 10 Głos Prawa (Lwów) 598.

Lemkin Rafał (1935), *Teroryzm,* 41 Gazeta Sądowa Warszawska: 561–564.

Lemkin Rafał (1936), *Amnestja 1936 r. Komentarz,* Księgarnia Powszechna.

Lemkin Rafał (1937), *II Międzynarodowy Kongres Prawa Porównawczego (Haga, 4–11 sierpnia 1937 r.)*, 1(2) Głos Prawników Śląskich 178.

Lemkin Rafał (1938a), *La protection de la paix par le droit penal interne. Rapport presente au IV-e Congres International de Droit Penal (Paris, 26–31 Juillet 1937)*, 1 RIDP 95.

Lemkin Rafał (1938b), *Prawo karne skarbowe. Komentarz. Przepisy związkowe z objaśnieniami – orzecznictwo – okólniki*, Księgarnia Powszechna.

Lemkin Rafał (1939), *La régulation des paiements internationaux. Traité de droit comparé sur les devises, les clearing et les accords de paiements, Les conflicts de lois*, Pedone.

Lemkin Raphael (1944), *Axis rule in Occupied Europe: Laws of Occupation, Analysis of Government, Proposals for Redress*, Carnegie Endowment for International Peace.

Lemkin Raphael (1945), *Genocide – a modern crime*, 4 Free World 39.

Lemkin Raphael (1946), *Genocide*, 15 (2) American Scholar 227.

Lemkin Rafael (1947), *Genocide as a Crime under International Law*, 41 AJIL 145.

Lemkin Rafał (2013), *Rządy państw Osi w okupowanej Europie*, Scholar.

Lemkin Rafał (2018), *Nieoficjalny. Autobiografia Rafała Lemkina*, Instytut Pileckiego.

Leśko Teofil (1976), *Konflikty zbrojne w świetle prawa międzynarodowego*, Wojskowa Akademia Polityczna.

Leśko Teofil (1979), *Międzynarodowe prawo konfliktów zbrojnych*, Wojskowa Akademia Polityczna.

Leuprecht Peter (2001), *Minority Rights Revisited: New Glimpses of an Old Issue*, in: Philip Alston (ed.), *Peoples' Rights*, OUP.

Lewis Mark (2014), *The Birth of the New Justice: The Internationalization of Crime and Punishment, 1919–1950*, OUP.

Lingen Kerstin von (2014), *Defining Crimes Against Humanity: The Contribution of the United Nations War Crimes Commission to International Criminal Law*, in: Morten Bergsmo et al. (ed.), *Historical Origins of International Criminal Law*, Volume 1, Torkel Opsahl Academic Epublisher: 477.

Lingen Kerstin von (2014b), *Setting the path for the UNWCC: the Representation of European Exile Governments on the London International Assembly and the Commission for Penal Reconstruction and Development, 1941–1944*, 25 CLF 45.

Lingen Kerstin von (2020), *Legal Flows: Contributing of Exiled Lawyers to the Concept of "Crimes against Humanity" during the Second World War*, 17 (2) Modern Intellectual History 507.

Lisiewicz Paweł Maria (1988), *W imieniu Polski Podziemnej. Z dziejów wojskowego sądownictwa specjalnego Armii Krajowej*, Instytut Wydawniczy Związków Zawodowych.

Litawski Jerzy J. (1943), *Geopolitics as an Instrument of German Aggression*, 74 Polish Fortnightly Review.

Litawski Jerzy J. (1948a), *Developments in the concepts of war crimes, crimes against humanity and crimes against peace*, His Majesty's Stationery Office.

Litawski Jerzy J. (1948b), *Złamanie warunków kapitulacji jako zbrodnia wojenna*, 3 PiP 33.

Liszewska Agnieszka (2004), *Współdziałanie przestępne w polskim prawie karnym: analiza dogmatyczna*, WUŁ.

Lityński Adam (1999), *O prawie i sądach początków Polski Ludowej*, Temida 2.

Loeffler James (2019), *The "Natural Right of the Jewish People" Zionism, International Law, and the Paradox of Hersch Zvi Lauterpacht*, in: James Loeffler, Paz Moria (eds.), *The Law of Strangers Jewish Lawyers and International Law in the Twentieth Century*, CUP: 23.

Lorentz Stanisław (ed.) (1970), *Walka o dobra kultury: Warszawa 1939–1945: księga zbiorowa*, vol. 1–2, PIW.

Lubecka Joanna (2011), *Karanie niemieckich zbrodniarzy wojennych w Polsce*, 34 Zeszyty Historyczne WiN-u 11.

Lubecka Joanna (2019), *Der Prozess gegen Rudolf Höß. Verlauf und juristische Aspekte*, in: Enrico Heitzer et al., *Im Schatten von Nürnberg. Transnationale Ahndung von NS-Verbrechen*, Metropol.

Lubecka Joanna (2021), *Niemiecki zbrodniarz przed polskim sądem*, IPN.

Lundgreen-Nielsen Kay (1982), *Woodrow Wilson and the Rebirth of Poland*, in: Arthur S. Link (ed.), *Woodrow Wilson and a Revolutionary World, 1913–1921*, University of North Carolina Press: 105.

Łazarska Aneta (2012), *Rzetelny proces cywilny*, Wolters Kluwer.

Łopatka Adam (1980), *The Right to Live in Peace as a Human Right*, 11(4) Bulletin of Peace Proposals 361.

Łuczak Czesław (1997), *Arthur Greiser*, PSO.

Łysko Marcin (2015), *Udział kobiet w życiu publicznym II Rzeczypospolitej Polskiej*, 1 Miscellanea Historico-Iuridica 390.

Machcewicz Piotr (2018), *Przedmowa*, in: Łukasz Jasiński, *Sprawiedliwość i polityka. Działalność Głównej Komisji Badania Zbrodni Niemieckich/Hitlerowskich w Polsce 1945–1989*, ISP PAN 9.

Machnikowska Anna (2008), *Wymiar sprawiedliwości w Polsce w latach 1944–1950*, WUG.

Machnikowska Anna (1999), *Sądownictwo karne na Pomorzu Gdańskim w latach 1945–1950*, in: Tadeusz Maciejewski (ed.), *Dzieje wymiaru sprawiedliwości*, Wydawnictwo Uczelniane BWSH: 381.

Majewski Marcin (2008), *Dokumenty dotyczące Ericha Kocha w zasobie archiwalnym Instytutu Pamięci Narodowej w Warszawie*, 1 Przegląd Archiwalny Instytutu Pamięci Narodowej 41.

Majewski Piotr M. (2016), *Społeczność Akademicka 1915–1939*, in: Tomasz Kizwalter, Piotr M. Majewski (eds.), *Dzieje Uniwersytetu Warszawskiego 1915–1945 /Monumenta Universitatis Varsoviensis 1816–2016*, WUW: 141.

Majdanek. Rozprawa przed Specjalnym Sądem Karnym w Lublinie (1945), Spółdzielnia Wydawnicza Czytelnik.

Makarewicz Juliusz (1896), *Das Wesen des Verbrechens: Eine criminalsociologische Abhandlung auf vergleichender u. rechtsgeschichtlicher Grundlage*, Manz'sche k.k. Hof-Verlags- und Universitäts-Buchhandlung.

Makarewicz Juliusz (1906), *Einführung in die Philosophie des Strafrechts auf entwicklungsgeschichtlicher Grundlage*, Verlag von Ferdinand Enke.

Makarewicz Juliusz (1932), *Kodeks karny z komentarzem*, Wydawnictwo Zakładu Narodowego imienia Ossolińskich.

Makarewicz Juliusz (1933), *Realizm w prawie karnym*, 13 RPEiS 49.

Makarewicz Juliusz (1938), *Kodeks karny z komentarzem*, Wydawnictwo Zakładu Narodowego imienia Ossolińskich.

Makowski Juljan (1915), *Zasady prawa międzynarodowego*, Druk Piotra Laskauera.

Makowski Julian (1918), *Prawo międzynarodowe*, Wyd. M. Arcta.

Makowski Julian (1931), *L'organisation actuelle de l'arbitrage international*, 36 RCADI 263.

Makowski Julian (1946), *Podręcznik prawa międzynarodowego*, Książka.

Makowski Julian (1953), *Nowe konwencje genewskie*, 5–6 PiP 716.

Makowski Wacław (1931), *Przestępstwo nawoływania do wojny zaczepnej*, 15 (1–3) Przegląd Polityczny.

Makowski Wacław (1937), *Kodeks karny. Komentarz*, Nakładem księgarni F. Hoesicka.

Malekian Farhad (1985), *International criminal responsibility of states: a study on the evolution of state responsibility with particular emphasis on the concept of crime and criminal responsibility*, Stockholms Universitet.

Małcużyński Karol (1989), *Oskarżeni nie przyznają się do winy*, Interpress.

Mander Linden (1945), *Review*, 5 (1) The American Historical Review 117.

Mamolea Andrei (2010), *Vespasian V. Pella: International Criminal Justice as safeguard of Peace, 1919–1952*, in: Immi Tallgren, Frederic Mégret (2020): 49.

Marcinko Marcin (2008), *ONZ wobec terroryzmu międzynarodowego*, Fundacja Instytut Studiów Strategicznych.

Marek Krystyna (1968), *Contribution à l'étude du Jus Cogens en Droit International*, in: *Recueil d'Études de Droit International en Hommage à Paul Guggenheim*, Imprimerie de Genève: 426.

Marek Krystyna (1978), *Criminalizing State Responsibility*, 14(2) Revue Belge de Droit International 460.

Markiewicz Jerzy (2010), *Kształtowanie się polskiego systemu prawa sądowego i jego twórcy w okresie międzywojennym 1919–1939 (Wybrane zagadnienia)*, Teka Komisji Prawniczej – OL PAN 113.

Marszał Kazimierz (1972), *Przedawnienie w prawie karnym*, PWN.

Martii Philipp (2016), *Sprawa Reinefartha. Kat powstania warszawskiego czy szacowny obywatel*, Świat Książki.

Masło Krzysztof (2020), *Międzynarodowa odpowiedzialność karna jednostek za zbrodnie przeciwko ludzkości*, Wydawnictwo IWS.

Masło Krzysztof (2022), *A Polish initiative aimed at establishing an international Tribunal to judge crimes committed by the communists*, in: Patrycja Grzebyk (ed.), *The Communist Crimes Individual and State Responsibility*, Wydawnictwo IWS: 105.

Materski Wojciech, Michowicz Waldemar (2010), *Historia dyplomacji polskiej*, vol. 6, *1944/1945–1989*, PISM.

Matthäus Jürgen et al. (2013), *Jewish Responses to Persecution*, t. 3, *1941–1942*, AltaMira Press.

Mazurkiewicz Maciej Jan (2021), *Ludobójstwo Niemiec na narodzie polskim (1939–1945): studium historycznoprawne*, IPN.

McNair Lord (1961), *Hersch Lauterpacht*, 10 International and Comparative Law Quarterly 4.

Menkes Jerzy (2012), *Propter Memoriam Profesor zw. Dr hab. Renata Sonnenfeld-Tomporek (ur. 1926 – zm. 2012)*, 10 Problemy Współczesnego Prawa Międzynarodowego, Europejskiego i Porównawczego 243.

Meron Theodor (1995), *International Criminalization of Internal Atrocities*, 89 AJIL 554.

Meron Theodor (2021), *Standing up for Justice. The Challenges of Trying Atrocity Crimes*, OUP.

Michalski Maciej, Podemski Krzysztof (ed.) (2022), *Wyparte historie. Antysemityzm na Uniwersytecie Poznańskim w latach 1919–1939*, WN UAM.

Michałowska Grażyna (2000), *Odpowiedzialność jednostki w prawie międzynarodowym* 22(3–4) Stosunki Międzynarodowe 25.

Michałowska Grażyna (2017), *Odpowiedzialność karna za niszczenie dóbr kultury w czasie konfliktów zbrojnych*, 53(2) Stosunki Międzynarodowe – International Relations 35.

Michowicz Waldemar (ed.) (1999), *Historia dyplomacji polskiej*, vol. 5, *1939–1945*, PWN.

Mierzwa Janusz (2018), *Działalność Polskiego Wydziału Prawa w Oksfordzie oraz organizacji zrzeszających polskich prawników na terenie Zjednoczonego Królestwa w latach 1940–1947*, 25(3) Niepodległość i Pamięć 77.

Mik Cezary (2010), *Ius cogens we współczesnym prawie międzynarodowym*, in: Agata Wnukiewicz-Kozłowska (ed.), *Aksjologia współczesnego prawa międzynarodowego*, WUWr: 177.

Mik Cezary (2013), *Jus Cogens in Contemporary International Law*, 33 PYIL 27.

Mikliszański Kopek (1935), *Le droit pénal international d'après la législation polonaise*, Recueil Sirey.

Mikliszanski Kopek (1936a), *Le lieu du délit en droit pénal international*, 13/3 RIDP 64.

Mikliszanski Kopek (1936b), *Le système de l'universalité du droit de punir et le droit pénal subsidiaire*, Revue de science criminelle et de droit pénal comparé 331.

Mikliszanski Kopek (1938), *De quelle manière le droit pénal interne peut-il contribuer à la protection de la paix internationale?*, 15/4 RIDP 56.

Milik Piotr (2012), *Komplementarność jurysdykcji Międzynarodowego Trybunału Karnego i trybunałów hybrydowych*, Elipsa.

Minear Richard H. (1971), *Victors' Justice, The Tokyo War Crimes Trial*, Princeton University Press.

Miszewski Dariusz (2016), *Polski rząd wobec sprawy żydowskiej w czasie drugiej wojny światowej*, 2/3 Kwartalnik Opolski 63.

Moczarski Kazimierz (2018), *Rozmowy z katem*, Znak.

Mogilnicki Aleksander (1935), *Nullum delictum sine lege*, 23–24 Gazeta Sądowa Warszawska 341.

Mogilnicki Aleksander (1937), *Pologne*, 14 RIDP 1.

Monson Robert (1982), *The West German Statute of Limitations on Murder: A Political, Legal, and Historical Exposition*, 30 (4) American Journal of Comparative Law 605.

Morawiecki Wojciech (1956), *Walka o definicję agresji w prawie międzynarodowym*, PWN.

Morzycki-Markowski Mikołaj (2017), *Zamach na Kutscherę*, Bellona.

Mullins Claude (1921), *The Leipzig Trials. An Account of the War Criminals Trials and a Study of German Mentality*, H. F. & G. Witherby.

Muszalski Edward (1926), *Rozpoczęcie i wypowiedzenie wojny w prawie państwowem i prawie narodów*, Wydawnictwo Seminarium Prawa Publicznego Uniwersytetu Warszawskiego nr 6, Nakł. Księgarni F. Hoesicka.

Murzynowski Andrzej, Rezler Jan (1972), *Wymiar sprawiedliwości w Polsce w latach 1944–1970. Ustawodawstwo, organizacja i działalność*, WUW.

Muszkat Marian (1947a), *Czy wyrok norymberski pozostał bez echa?*, 3 DPP 38.

Muszkat Marian (1947b), *Les mesures de justice à l'égard des criminels de guerre et la lutte pour l'assurance de la paix*, GKBZHwP.

Muszkat Marian (1948), *Komisja Narodów Zjednoczonych do Spraw Zbrodni Wojennych*, 3 PiP 41.

Muszkat Marian (1949), *Pojęcie międzynarodowego przestępstwa*, 2 WPP 307.

Muszkat Marian (ed.) (1955), *Zarys prawa międzynarodowego publicznego*, vol. I, Wydawnictwo Prawnicze.

Muszkat Marian (1956), *Zakaz wojen agresywnych*, in: Marian Muszkat (ed.), *Zarys prawa międzynarodowego publicznego*, vol. II, Wydawnictwo Prawnicze : 321.

Muszkat Marian, Sawicki Jerzy (1947), *Les revendications allemandes sur les territoires polonais occidentaux au point de vue du droit penal international*, GKBZNWP.

Nagorski Andrew (2017), *The Nazi Hunters*, Simon&Schuster..

Nahlik Stanisław (1958), *Grabież dzieł sztuki: rodowód zbrodni międzynarodowej*, Zakład Narodowy im. Ossolińskich.

Nahlik Stanisław (1967), *La protection internationale des biens culturels en cas de conflit armé*, 120 RCADI 61.

Nahlik Stanisław (1974), *On some deficiencies of the Hague Convention of 1954 on the Protection of Cultural Property in the Event of Armed Conflict*, 44 Annuaire de l'A.A.A. 100.

Nahlik Stanisław (1978), *Belligerent Reprisals as Seen in the Light of the Diplomatic Conference on Humanitarian Law, Geneva, 1974–1977*, 42(2) Law and Contemporary Problems 36.

Nahlik Stanisław (1979), *L'extension du statut de combattant à la lumière du protocole I de Genève de 1977*, 164 RIDP 1.

Nahlik Stanisław (1984), *Le problème des sanctions en droit international humanitaire*, in: *Études et essais sur le droit international humanitaire et sur les principes de la Croix-Rouge en l'honneur de Jean Pictet = Studies and essays on international humanitarian law and Red Cross principles in honour of Jean Pictet*, Comité International de la Croix-Rouge 469.

Nahlik Stanisław (1986), *Convention for the Protection of Cultural Property in the Event of Armed Conflict, The Hague 1954: General and Special Protection*, in: *La protezione internazionale dei beni culturali = The international protection of cultural property = La protection internationale des biens culturels*, Fondazione Europea Dragan 87.

Nahlik Stanisław (1987a), *Konsekwencje niszczenia i grabieży dóbr kultury*, GKBZH-IPN.

Nahlik Stanisław Edward (1987b), *Przesiane przez pamięć. W rodzinnym gnieździe*, Wydawnictwo Literackie.

Nahlik Stanisław (1988), *Protection of Cultural Property*, in: *International dimensions of humanitarian law*, Henry Dunant Institute 204.

Nahlik Stanisław (1991), *From reprisals to individual penal responsibility*, in: Astrid J.M. Delissen, Gerard J. Tanja (eds.), *Humanitarian law of armed conflict challenges ahead: essays in honour of Frits Kalshoven*, Nijhoff 165.

Nie Jing-Bao (2004), *The West's dismissal of the Khabarovsk trial as 'communist propaganda': ideology, evidence and international bioethics*, 1(1) Journal of Bioethical Inquiry 32.

Nieprzecka Aleksandra (2022), *Odpowiedzialność karna za popełnienie zbrodni międzynarodowej w świetle koncepcji sprawstwa przyjętej w orzecznictwie MTK*, 10 Prokuratura i Prawo 93.

Nowak Celina (2012), *O pojęciu transnarodowego prawa karnego*, 12 PiP 3.

Nowak Celina (2014), *Wpływ procesów globalizacyjnych na polskie prawo karne*, Wolters Kluwer.

Nowakowska-Małusecka Joanna (2000), *Odpowiedzialność karna jednostek za zbrodnie popełnione w byłej Jugosławii i w Rwandzie*, WUŚ.

Nowakowska-Małusecka Joanna (2012), *Sytuacja dziecka w konflikcie zbrojnym. Studium prawnomiędzynarodowe*, Oficyna Wydawnicza Brandta.

Nowakowska-Małusecka Joanna, Topa Ilona (2015) (eds.), *Międzynarodowe i europejskie prawo karne – osiągnięcia, kierunki rozwoju, wyzwania*, WUŚ.

Nowotnik Norbert (2018), *IPN współpracuje z niemiecką prokuraturą w zakresie ścigania ostatnich żyjących SS-manów*, 27.12.2018, on-line at https://dzieje.pl.

Nyiri Nicholas (1989), *The United Nations' Search for a Definition of Aggression*, American University Studies, Series X, Political Science t. 22, Peter Lang.

Ogonowski Jerzy (2012), *Sytuacja Prawna Żydów w Rzeczypospolitej Polskiej 1918–1939, Prawa cywilne i polityczne*, Żydowski Instytut Historyczny.

Ogonowski Piotr (1998), *Międzynarodowy Sąd Karny – tworzenie jego podstaw*, 6 PiP 47.

Olejniczak Jakub (2010), *Propozycja definicji zbrodni agresji, warunków wykonywania jurysdykcji przez MTK i elementów definicji zbrodni agresji*, 5 Wrocławskie Studia Erazmiańskie 145.

Olewiński Mateusz (2015), *Konstrukcja związku przestępnego (joint criminal enterprise) a Statut Rzymski Międzynarodowego Trybunału Karnego*, XIX/4 Czasopismo Prawa Karnego i Nauk Penalnych 58.

Ordon Stanisław (1974), *Wojna obronna Polski w 1939 roku na wybrzeżu i morzu w świetle prawa międzynarodowego*, Zakład Narodowy im. Ossolińskich.

Orzelska-Stączek Agnieszka (2011), *Polityka zagraniczna Polski wobec wybranych kwestii spornych w stosunkach transatlantyckich (1989–2004)*, ISP PAN.

Osęka Piotr (2018), *Antyżydowskich pogromów było w Polsce lat 30. Co najmniej kilkadziesiąt*, "Polityka" 22.02.2018.

Osiecki Mateusz (2022), *International Legal Aspects of Aerial Terrorism: Methods of Law Enforcement in Aviation*, Peter Lang.

Ostropolski Tomasz (2008), *Zasada jurysdykcji uniwersalnej w prawie międzynarodowym*, Instytut Wydawniczy EuroPrawo.

Paczkowski Andrzej (2019), *Crime, Treason and Greed: The German Wartime Occupation of Poland and Polish Post-War Retributive Justice*, in: Magnus Brechtken, Władysław Bułhak, Jürgen Zarusky (eds.), *Political and Transitional Justice in Germany, Poland and the Soviet Union from the 1930s to the 1950s*, Wallstein Verlag: 143.

Pałka Sławomir, *Zakaz ekstradycji obywatela polskiego*, "Rzeczpospolita. Prawo co dnia", 18.09.1996.

Parry Clive (1965), *The Sources and Evidences of International Law*, Manchester University Press.

Parzymies Stanisław (2012), *Polska w Organizacji Narodów Zjednoczonych*, in: Stanisław Parzymies, Irena Popiuk-Rysińska (eds.), *Udział Polski w organizacjach międzynarodowych*, Wydawnictwo Naukowe Scholar: 69.

Pasek Andrzej (2002), *Przestępstwa okupacyjne w polskim prawie karnym z lat 1944–1956*, WUWr.

Pawlak Stanisław (2019), *Główne kierunki inicjatyw polskich w ONZ w latach 1945–2018*, in: *Polska w instytucjach międzynarodowych w latach 1918–2018*, Narodowe Centrum Kultury i Polskie Towarzystwo Studiów Międzynarodowych: 252.

Paz Reut Yael (2014), *A Forgotten Kelsenian? The Story of Helen Silving-Ryu (1906–1993)*, 25 (4) EJIL 1123.

Pella Vespasien V. (1926), *La criminalité collective des Etats et le droit pénal de l'avenir*, Imprimerie de l'État.

Pelt Robert Jan van (2016), *The Case for Auschwitz. Evidence from the Irving Trial*, Indiana University Press.

Piątek Przemysław (2004), *Wybrane zagadnienia odpowiedzialności karnej za zbrodnie przeciwko ludzkrt.i określone w art. 3 ustawy o IPN*, 3/2 (6) Pamięć i Sprawiedliwość 247.

Pietrzak Michał (2000), *Sytuacja prawna kobiet w Drugiej Rzeczypospolitej*, in: Anna Żarnowska, Andrzej Szwarc (ed.), *Równe prawa i nierówne szanse. Kobiety w Polsce międzywojennej*, DiG: 77.

Pikulski Stanisław, *Terroryzm a walka narodowowyzwoleńcza*, in: Karol Sławik (ed.), *Terroryzm: aspekty prawno-międzynarodowe, kryminalistyczne i policyjne. Materiały sympozjum zorganizowanego przez Wydział Prawa Uniwersytetu Szczecińskiego, Szczecin, 29–30.XI.1991 r.*, Ławica: 29.

Pikulski Stanisław (1991), *Karnomaterialne, kryminologiczne i kryminalistyczne aspekty terroryzmu*, 3–4 WPP 43.

Pilichowski Czesław (1971a), *Norymberga*, 20 Prawo i Życie.

Pilichowski Czesław (1971b), *Trybunał Norymberski i zasady norymberskie a sprawa ścigania i karania hitlerowskich zbrodniarzy wojennych w latach 1945–1971*, 11 SM 28.

Pilichowski Czesław (oprac.) (1975), *Badanie i ściganie zbrodni hitlerowskich 1944–1974*, GKBZHWP.

Pilichowski Czesław (1978a), *Ściganie i karanie sprawców zbrodni wojennych i zbrodni przeciwko ludzkości: (wybór dokumentów)*, GKBZHWP.

Pilichowski Czesław (1978b), *Realizacja konwencji ONZ o nieprzedawnieniu zbrodni hitlerowskich*, 31 SM 27.

Pilichowski Czesław (1978–1981), *Ekspertyzy i orzeczenia przed Najwyższym Trybunałem Narodowym*, GKBZHWP.

Pilichowski Czesław (1980a), *No time-limit for these crimes*, Interpress.

Pilichowski Czesław (ed.) (1980b), *Zbrodnie i sprawcy. Ludobójstwo hitlerowskie przed sądem ludzkości i historii*, PWN.

Pilichowski Czesław (1980c), *Udział Polski w badaniu i ściganiu zbrodni hitlerowskich*, in: Czesław Pilichowski (1980b): 23.

Piskorski Justyn (2005), *Tak zwany warunek podwójnej przestępności w polskim prawie karnym materialnym*, in: Izabela Gawłowicz, Iwona Wierzchowiecka (eds.), *Koncepcje suwerenności. Zbiór studiów*, LexisNexis: 260.

Plesch Dan (2011), *America, Hitler and the UN*, I.B. Tauris.

Plesch Dan, Sattler Shanti (2014), *A New Paradigm of Customary International Criminal Law: The UN War Crimes Commission of 1943–1948 and its Associated Courts and Tribunals*, 25 CLF 17.

Płachta Michał (1989), *The role of double criminality in international cooperation in criminal matters*, in: Nils Jareborg (ed.), *Double criminality. Studies in international criminal law*, Iustus 86.

Płachta Michał (1993), *Transfer of prisoners under international instruments and domestic legislation: A comparative study*, Max-Planck-Institut für Ausländisches und Internationales Strafrecht.

Płachta Michał (1998), *Extradition and the principle aut dedere aut judicare in the new Polish legislation*, 6 European Journal of Crime, Criminal Law and Criminal Justice 94.

Płachta Michał (2000), *Zasada aut dedere aut judicare w dziedzinie międzynarodowej współpracy w sprawach karnych*, 7–8 Palestra 34.

Płachta Michał (2000), *Kidnaping międzynarodowy w służbie prawa: studium prawnomiędzynarodowe i porównawcze*, Dom Wydawniczy ABC.

Plachta Michał (2001a), *Contemporary Problems of Extradition: Human Rights, Grounds for Refusal and the Principle Aut Dedere Aut Judicare*, UNAFEI Annual Report for 1999 and Resource Material Series No. 57.

Płachta Michał (2001b), *The Lockerbie case: the role of the Security Council in enforcing the principle aut dedere aut judicare*, 12 EJIL 125.

Płachta Michał (2003a), *Amnestia jako jeden ze sposobów "rozliczania" sprawców najcięższych zbrodni międzynarodowych*, LXV/4 RPEiS 7.

Płachta Michał (2003b), *Międzynarodowy Trybunał Karny a komisje pojednania narodowego i amnestie: Jak pogodzić sprawiedliwość retrybutywną ze sprawiedliwością restytucyjną?*, II/1 Ius et Lex 95.

Płachta Michał (2003c), *Przekazywanie skazanych pomiędzy państwami*, Zakamycze.

Płachta Michał (2004), *Międzynarodowy Trybunał Karny*, Zakamycze.

Płachta Michał (2009), *Status i pojęcie międzynarodowego prawa karnego*, 5 Prokuratura i Prawo 5.

Płachta Michał W (2015), *Aut dedere aut judicare w międzynarodowym prawie karnym*, in: Joanna Nowakowska-Małusecka, Ilona Topa (2015): 13.

Płachta Michał, Wyrozumska Anna (2001), *Problem ratyfikacji Statutu Międzynarodowego Trybunału Karnego (uwagi polemiczne do artykułu K. Karskiego)*, 5 PiP 87.

Płachta Michał, Zalewski Wojciech (2003), *Kontrowersje wokół pojęcia przestępczości zorganizowanej na gruncie Konwencji ONZ z 2000 r.*, 5 Przegląd Sądowy 3.

Pławski Stanisław (1950), *Proces japońskich zbrodniarzy w Chabarowsku*, PISM.

Pławski Stanisław (1972), *Étude des principes fondamentaux du droit international pénal*, LGDJ, Paris.

Pławski Stanislaw (1989), *France*, 60(1–2) RIDP 556.

Podgóreczny Marian (1975), *Proces gauleitera Alberta Forstera*, 19/9 (213) Palestra 20.

Podgóreczny Marian (1997), *Albert Forster gauleiter i oskarżony*, Wydawnictwo Morskie.

Poklewski-Koziełł Krzysztof (1949), *Międzynarodowe Stowarzyszenie Prawników Demokratów wobec zagadnienia ekstradycji zbrodniarzy wojennych*, 8–9 DPP 36.

Pokoj Jakub (2019), *Instytucja wydawania przestępców w okresie obowiązywania k.p. k. z 1928 roku*, 12 (2) Krakowskie Studia z Historii Państwa i Prawa 205.

Pol Krzysztof (2020), *Poczet Prawników Polskich*, C.H. Beck.

Pomorski Stanisław (1990), *Conspiracy and Criminal Organization*, in: George Ginsburgs, V.N. Kudriavtsev (eds.), *The Nuremberg Trial and International Law*, Nijhoff: 213.

Pospieszalski Karol Marian (1946), *Polska pod niemieckim prawem 1939–1945 (Ziemie Zachodnie)*, WIZ.

Pospieszalski Karol Marian (1948), *Wyrok norymberski (Zasady prawne)*, 2 Przegląd Zachodni 129.

Pospieszalski Karol Marian (1952), *Hitlerowskie "prawo okupacyjne" w Polsce*, part I, *Ziemie "wcielone". Wybór dokumentów*, Instytut Zachodni.

Pospieszalski Karol Marian (1958), *Hitlerowskie "prawo okupacyjne" w Polsce*, part II, *Generalna Gubernia. Wybór dokumentów*, Instytut Zachodni.

Potyrała Anna, *Współpraca państw z międzynarodowymi trybunałami karnymi a suwerenność. Studium politologiczno-prawne*, Wydawnictwo Naukowe WNPiD UAM.

Preuss Lawrence (1936), recenzja [bez tytułu], 30(1) AJIL 178.

Proces Greisera (*Sprawozdanie prawnicze*) (1946), 7 PiP 63.

Primomo John W. (2020), *Architect of Death at Auschwitz: A Biography of Rudolf Höss*, McFarland and Company.

Prusin Alexander V. (2010), *Poland's Nuremberg: The Seven Court Cases of the Supreme National Tribunal, 1946–1948*, 24(1) Holocaust and Genocide Studies 1.

Prusin Alexander V. (2013), *Polska Norymberga: Siedem procesów Przed Najwyższym Trybunałem Narodowym, 1946–1948*, 9 Zagłada Żydów. Studia i Materiały 116.

Przetacznik Frank (1983), *Protection of Officials of Foreign States according to International Law*, Martinus Nijhoff.

Przetacznik Frank (1991), *Basic principles of international law concerning the protection of the officials of foreign States*, 69 Revue de Droit International de Sciences Diplomatiques et Politiques 52.

Przyborowska Klimczak Anna (2022a), *Pierwsi wykładowcy prawa międzynarodowego publicznego na Wydziale Prawa Uniwersytetu Marii Curie-Skłodowskiej w Lublinie*, in: Anna Przyborowska-Klimczak et al. (2022b): 241.

Przyborowska Klimczak Anna et al. (2022b), *Polska nauka prawa międzynarodowego. Dziedzictwo przeszłości i wyzwania współczesności*, Towarzystwo Naukowe KUL Jana PawłaII.

Przyborowska-Klimczak Anna, Staszewski Wojciech S. (2008), *Katedra Prawa Międzynarodowego Publicznego*, in: Antoni Dębiński et al. (ed.), *Księga jubileuszowa z okazji 90-lecia Wydziału Prawa, Prawa Kanonicznego i Administracji Katolickiego Uniwersytetu Lubelskiego*, Wydawnictwo KUL: 325.

Przybylski Adam (1932), *Walka o Śląsk Cieszyński w styczniu 1919 roku*, Wojskowe Biuro Historyczne.

Pulera Dominic (2004), *Sharing the Dream: White Males in Multicultural America*, Continuum.

Pugacewicz Tomasz (2010), *Dorobek badawczy i organizacyjny Ludwika Ehrlicha na tle rozwoju nauki o stosunkach międzynarodowych w Polsce do 1950 roku*, in: Dominika Mikucka-Wójtowicz (ed.)., *Przeszłość – Teraźniejszość – Przyszłość. Problemy badawcze młodych politologów*: 133.

Pyszkowski Aleksander (1947), *Bilans działalności sądów specjalnych*, 11–12 DPP 37.

Rabinowicz Leon (1929), *Mesures de sûreté. Ėtude de politique criminelle*, Librairie des Sciences Politiques et Sociales.

Rabinowicz Leon (1932a), *Drogi więziennictwa polskiego*, 50 Gazeta Sądowa Warszawska 734.

Rabinowicz Léon (1932b), *Est-il désirable d'avoir, à côté du Code pénal et du Code de procédure pénale, un Code d'exécution des peines?*, 9 RIDP: 54.

Rabinowicz Leon (1933), *Podstawy nauki o więziennictwie*, Gebethner i Wolff.

Ramcharan Bertrand G. (2011), *Human Rights and U.N. Peace Operations: Yugoslavia*, Martinus Nijhoff Publishers.

Raczkowski Henryk (1938), *"Anschluss" a międzynarodowe gwarancje niepodległości Austrii*, 5–6 Prawo: 486.

Radecki Wojciech (1981), *Odpowiedzialność karna za naruszenie środowiska w świetle prawa międzynarodowego*, Zakład Narodowy im. Ossolińskich – Wydawnictwo PAN.

Radomski Jerzy (2013), *Misje wojskowe na Zachodzie z ramienia komunistycznych władz z Polski i ich zadania 1945–1948*, 12 Zeszyty Historyczne 419.

Radzinowicz Leon (1929), *Mesures de sûreté. Ėtude de politique criminelle*, Librairie des Sciences Politiques et Sociales.

Radzinowicz Leon (1977), *The growth of crime: The international experience*, Hamish Hamilton.

Rafałowski Franciszek (1980), *Ekstradycja zbrodniarzy hitlerowskich po II wojnie światowej*, in: Czesław Pilichowski (1980b): 833.

Rappaport Emil S. (1927), *Propaganda wojny napastniczej*, 44 Gazeta Sądowa Warszawska 609.

Rappaport Emil Stanisław (1929a), *Le problème de l'unification internationale du Droit Pénal*, Revue Pénitentiaire de Pologne, Annexe No. 12.

Rappaport Emil S. (1929b), *Zagadnienie Unifikacji Międzynarodowego Prawa Karnego*, Skład Główny w Księgarni F. Hoesicka.

Rappaport Emil Stanisław (1930), *Zagadnienie prawa karnego międzypaństwowego*, Wydawnictwo "Bibljoteka Prawnicza".

Rappaport Emil Stanisław (1931), *Delicta juris gentium*, in: W. Makowski (ed.), Encyklopedja podręczna prawa karnego, vol. 1, Instytut Wydawniczy "Biblioteka Polska": 248.

Rappaport Emil Stanisław (1934), *Tendencje rozwojowa prawa karnego międzynarodowego*, 14 RPEiS 1.

Rappaport Emil S. (1937), *IV Międzynarodowy Kongres Prawa Karnego (Paryż, 26–31 lipca 1937)*, 1(2) Głos Prawników Śląskich 172.

Rappaport Emil S. (1945), *Naród-Zbrodniarz: przestępstwa hitleryzmu a naród niemiecki: szkic analityczny przestępczości i odpowiedzialności osobowo-zespołowej*, Spółdzielnia Dziennikarska "Prasa".

Rappaport Emil S. (1948), *Ludobójstwo jako delictum iuris gentium*, 9–10 PiP 55.

Redzik Adam (2004), *Wydział Prawa Uniwersytetu Lwowskiego w latach 1939–1945*, Rocznik Lwowski, Instytut Lwowski.

Redzik Adam (2006), *Lwowska szkoła dyplomatyczna. Zarys historii Studium Dyplomatycznego przy Wydziale Prawa Uniwersytetu Jana Kazimierza we Lwowie (1930–1939)*, 6(5)(33) PPD 121.

Redzik Adam (2007), *Nauczanie i Nauka Prawa Politycznego na Uniwersytecie Jana Kazimierza we Lwowie*, 5 (82) Przegląd Sejmowy 130.

Redzik Adam (2019), *Raphael Lemkin*, in: Kasey McCall-Smith, Jan Wouters, Felipe Gómez Isa (ed.), *The Faces of Human Rights*, Hart: 88.

Redzik Adam (2020a), *Gustaw Roszkowski (1847–1915) – gorący zwolennik i szermierz pokoju*, 534 "Pauza Akademicka" 1.

Redzik Adam (2020b), *Ludwika Ehrlicha koncepcja kształcenia dyplomatów i jej realizacja – Studium Dyplomatyczne Uniwersytetu Jana Kazimierza we Lwowie*, in: Patrycja Grzebyk, Rafał Tarnogórski (2020c).

Regent-Lechowicz Maria (1968), *ONZ w sprawach nazizmu, zbrodni wojennych i zbrodni przeciwko ludzkości*, 5 Prawo i Życie.

Reginbogin Herbert R., Safferling Christoph J.M. (eds.) (2006), *The Nuremberg Trials: International Criminal Law since 1945/Die Nürnberger Prozesse: Völkerstrafrecht seit 1944*, K.G. Saur, München.

Reisman Michael (1992), *Systems of Control in International Adjudication and Arbitration: Breakdown and repair*, Duke University Press.

Rejman Genowefa (1972), *Odpowiedzialność karna za niewłaściwe wykonanie nadzoru w zespołowym działaniu*, Wydawnictwo Prawnicze.

Rejman Genowefa (2005), *Juliusz Makarewicz – polski uczony na przełomie XIX i XX wieku (1872–1955)*, w: Alicja Grześkowiak, *Prawo karne w poglądach profesora Juliusza Makarewicza*, Wydawnictwo KUL.

Resich Zbigniew (1969), *Konwencja o nieprzedawnieniu zbrodni wojennych i zbrodni przeciwko ludzkości*, 22 SM 5.

Resich Zbigniew (1980), *Ściganie zbrodni wojennych i zbrodni przeciwko ludzkości w świetle prawa międzynarodowego*, in: Czesław Pilichowski (1980a): 789.

Resich Zbigniew (1981), *Międzynarodowa ochrona praw człowieka*, PWN.

Rędziński Kazimierz (2016), *Studenci żydowscy we Lwowie w latach 1918–1939*, XXV Prace Naukowe Akademii im. Jana Długosza w Częstochowie 581.

Rhea Harry M. (2014), *The Commission on the Responsibility of the Authors of the War and on Enforcement of Penalties and Its Contribution to International Criminal Justice After World War II*, 25 CLF 147.

Rifaat Ahmet (1979), *International Aggression. A Study of the Legal Concept: Its Development and Definition in International Law*, Almqvist & Wiksell International.

Robinson Darryl (1999), *Defining "Crimes Against Humanity" at the Rome Conference*, 93 AJIL 43.

Rogacka-Rzewnicka Maria (2003), *Prawo międzynarodowe karne: Rozwój i perspektywy sądownictwa międzynarodowego w sprawach karnych*, 41 Studia Iuridica 213.

Rogacka-Rzewnicka Maria (2007), *Oportunizm i legalizm ścigania przestępstw w świetle współczesnych przeobrażeń procesu karnego*, Wolters Kluwer.

Rogalski Aleksander (1947), *The problems of guilt and the problems of future of Germany*, Poznań.

Rojowska Elżbieta (2013), *Komisja Narodów Zjednoczonych do spraw Zbrodni Wojennych i działalność Polski w ramach jej prac: zarys problemu*, 22 Studia Prawnoustrojowe 15.

Rolland Maurice (1965), *Le colloque de Varsovie et la notion d'imprescriptibilité par nature*, 79 Après-Demain.

Rostworowski Michał (1915), *Wojna a społeczeństwo polskie*, Kraków.

Rostworowski Michał (1916), *Wojna a traktat pokojowy*, Gebethner.

Roszkowski Gustaw (1881a), *O oxfordzkim projekcie prawa wojny lądowej w porównaniu z prawem francuzkiem, hollenderskiem i rosyjskiem oraz z deklaracyą brukselską*, Redakcya "Muzeum".

Roszkowski Gustaw (1881b), *O poglądach Moltkego na prawo wojny*, Dziennik Polski.

Roszkowski Gustaw (1882a), *O azylach i ekstradycji: ze szczególnym uwzględnieniem stosunków Austro-Węgierskiej Monarchii*, drukiem S. Orgelbranda i Synów.

Roszkowski Gustaw (1882b), *O najnowszych traktatach Austro-Węgierskiej Monarchji z Belgją i Holandją z 1880 i 1881 roku w przedmiocie wydawania przestępców*, Drukarnia "Gazeta Narodowa".

Roszkowski Gustaw (1887), *O Konwencyi Genewskiej*, Księgarnia Gubrynowicza i Schmidta.

Roszkowski Gustaw (1894), *O sankcji wykonawczej dla konwencji genewskiej*, 9 PPA 743.

Roszkowski Gustaw (1900), *O zmianach projektowanych w konwencyi genewskiej r. 1864*, Nakładem Senatu Uniwersytetu Lwowskiego.

Rotfeld Adam D., Ryszka, Franciszek (1965), *Przedawnienie zbrodni hitlerowskich: problem polityczny i prawny*, 18/3 SM 13.

Równy Kazimierz (2003), *Doskonalenie prawa i pokoju międzynarodowego przez 130 lat Stowarzyszenia Prawa Międzynarodowego i 80 w nim grupy polskiej (szkice dokonań i zarys działalności u progu XXI wieku)*, 1 Biuletyn Grupy Polskiej Stowarzyszenia Prawa Międzynarodowego. 80 lat istnienia grupy polskiej ILA, Elipsa 39.

Ruckerl Adalbert (1980), *Ściganie zbrodni hitlerowskich 1945–1978*, GKBZHWP.

Rundstein Szymon (1928), *Kodyfikacja prawa międzynarodowego*, 1(8) RPEiS 1.

Rundstein Szymon (1917), *Szkody wojenne a współczesne prawo narodów*, Wydział Rejestracji Strat Wojennych.

Rundstein Szymon (1916), *Szkody Wojenne Teorya Nadzwyczajnych Indemnizacyj w Prawie Publicznem*, F. Hoesick.

Rundstein Szymon (1928), *L'arbitrage international en matière privée*, 23 RCADI 327.

Rundstein Szymon (1933), *La Cour permanente de Justice internationale comme instance de recours*, 43 RCADI 1.

Rutczyński Kazimierz (1944), *Ekstradycja zbrodniarzy wojennych*, 2 Głos Prawniczy 11.

Rutczyński Kazimierz (1947), *Zbrodnie wojenne. Studjum w skali międzynarodowej*, Książnica Polska.

Rybczyński Stanisław (1947), *Kierownictwo administracji niemieckiej jako organizacja przestępcza*, 4 DPP 35.

Ryszka Franciszek (1962), *Noc i mgła: Niemcy w okresie hitlerowskim*, Zakład Narodowy im. Ossolińskich.

Ryszka Franciszek (1966), *Sprawa polska" i sprawy Polaków: szkice z lat 1944–1946*, Wiedza Powszechna.

Ryszka Franciszek (1972), *U źródeł sukcesu i klęski: szkice z dziejów hitleryzmu*, Czytelnik.

Ryszka Franciszek (1982), *Norymberga. Prehistoria i ciąg dalszy*, Czytelnik.

Ryszka Franciszek (1985), *Państwo stanu wyjątkowego*, Ossolineum.

Rzepliński Andrzej (2004), *Prosecution of Nazi Crimes in Poland in 1939–2004; The First International Expert Meeting on War Crimes, Genocide, and Crimes against Humanity, organized by International Criminal Police Organization – Interpol General Secretariat (IPSG), Lyon, France 23–25 March 2004.*

Sadat Leila Nadya (2018), *A New Global Treaty on Crimes Against Humanity Future Prospects*, in: Margaret M. de Guzman, Diane Marie Amann (eds.), *Arcs of Global Justice: Essays in Honour of William A. Schabas*, OUP: 375.

Saganek Przemysław (2014), *Aut dedere aut judicare – uwagi w świetle prac Komisji Prawa Międzynarodowego*, in: Maciej Perkowski et al. (eds.), *Człowiek i prawo międzynarodowe. Księga dedykowana Profesorowi Bogdanowi Wierzbickiemu*, Temida 2: 431.

Saldaña Quintiliano (1925), *La justice pénale internationale*, 10 RCADI 223.

Salmonowicz Stanisław, Serczyk Jerzy (2003), *Z problemów kolaboracji w Polsce w latach 1939–1941*, 14 Czasy Nowożytne 43.

Sandorski Jan (2004), *Bohdan Winiarski. Prawo, Polityka, Sprawiedliwość*, Wydawnictwo Poznańskie.

Sands Philippe (2012), *Ku pamięci sprawiedliwości: nieoczekiwane miejsce Lwowa w prawie międzynarodowym – osobista historia*, 11–12 Palestra 11.

Sands Philippe (2018), *Powrót do Lwowa. O genezie "ludobójstwa" i "zbrodni przeciwko ludzkości"*, Aspra-JR.

Sawicki Jerzy (1947), *Pewne aspekty zasady nullum crimen sine lege – Kulisy narodzin nowych stanów faktycznych*, 1 DPP 30.

Sawicki Jerzy (1948), *Prawo norymberskie a polskie prawo karne*, 3 PiP 54.

Sawicki Jerzy (1949), *Ludobójstwo od pojęcia do konwencji 1933–1948*, Księgarnia Wydawnicza Dr. L.J. Jaroszewski.

Sawicki Jerzy (1951), *Przestępstwo podżegania do wojny*, Drukarnia Ministerstwa Sprawiedliwości.

Sawicki Jerzy (1958a), *Als sei Nürnberg nie gewesen. Die Abkehr von den völkerrechtlichen Prinzipien der Nürnberger Urteile*, Deutscher Zentraverlag.

Sawicki Jerzy (1958b), *De Nuremberg a la nouvelle Wehrmacht*, Polonia.

Sawicki Jerzy (1966), *Réponse de M. Jersy Sawicki*, 3–4 RIDP 553.

Sawicki Jerzy (1968), *Przed polskim prokuratorem*, Iskry.

Sawicki Jerzy, Walawski Bolesław (1945), *Zbiór przepisów specjalnych przeciwko zbrodniarzom hitlerowskim i zdrajcom narodu z komentarzem*, Czytelnik.

Schabas William (2011), *An Introduction to the International Criminal Court*, 4ed., OUP.

Schabas William (2012), *Unimaginable Atrocities: Justice, Politics and Rights at the War Crimes Tribunals*, OUP.

Schabas William (2014), *'Ethnic Cleansing' and Genocide: Similarities and Distinctions*, in: Tove H. Malloy, Joseph Marko (eds.), *Minority Governance in and beyond Europe*, Brill: 39.

Schabas William (2015), *The Katyn Forest Massacre and the Nuremberg Trial*, w: Morten Bergsmo, Cheah Wui Ling, Song Tianying, Yi Ping (ed.), *Historical Origins of International Criminal Law*, vol. 3, Torkel Opsahl Academic EPublisher: 249.

Schabas William A. (2018), *The Trial of the Kaiser*, OUP.

Schachter Oscar (1977), *The Invisible College of International Lawyers*, 72(2) Northwestern University School of Law 217.

Schwarzenberger Georg (1950/1965), *The Problem of an International Criminal Law*, 3 Current Legal Problems 263 = G.O.W. Mueller, E.M. Wise (eds.), *International Criminal Law*, Rothyman/Sweey and Maxwell: 3.

Schwarzenberger Georg (1967), *A Manual of International Law*, 5ed., Stevens, London.

Schwelb Egon (1946), *Crimes against Humanity*, 23 BYIL 178.

Segesser Daniel Marc (2005), *On the Road to Total Retribution? The International Debate on the Punishment of War Crimes 1872–1945*, in: Roger Chickering et al. (eds.), *A World at Total War. Global Conflict and the Politics of Destruction, 1937–1945*, CUP: 355.

Sehn Jan (1956), *Obóz koncentracyjny Oświęcim-Brzezinka (Auschwitz-Birkenau): na podstawie dokumentów i źródeł*, Wydawnictwo Prawnicze.

Sellars Kirsten (2014), *Crimes Against Peace and International Law*, CUP.

Sienkiewicz Witold (2010/2011), *Niepokonani 1920. Wojna polsko-bolszewicka*, Demart.

Simpson Gerry (2020), *International Criminal Law: The Next Hundred Years*, in: Kevin Jon Heller et al. (ed.), *The Oxford Handbook of International Criminal Law*, OUP: 841.

Skubiszewski Krzysztof (1959), *The Postwar Alliances of Poland and the United Nations Charter*, 53(3) AJIL 613.

Skubiszewski Krzysztof (1989), *Definition of Terrorism*, 19 Israel Yearbook on Human Rights 39.

Siewierski Mieczysław (1965), *Emil Stanisław Rappaport*, 10 PiP 542.

Silving Helen (1988), *Helen Silving Memoirs*, Vintage Press.

Simons (1919), *L'Extradition de l'ex-Empereur d'Allemagne et la Hollande*, 46 Journal du Droit International (Période de la guerre 1914–1919) 953.

Skoczek Tadeusz (ed.) (2019), *Stulecie Traktatu Wersalskiego 1919–2019*, Wydawnictwo Muzeum Niepodległości w Warszawie.

Skrzypek Wojciech (2016), *Odpowiedzialność karna żołnierza za wykonanie i wydanie rozkazu przestępnego*, 3 (279) WPP 5.

Sliedregt Elies van (2007), *Joint Criminal Enterprise as a Pathway to Convicting Individuals for Genocide*, 5 JICJ 184.

Sliedregt Elies van (2016), *International Criminal Law: Over-studied and Underachieving?*, 29 Leiden Journal of International Law 1.

Sliedregt Elies van (2020), *International Criminal Justice: A Bubble About to Burst?*, in: Elisa Hoven, Michael Kubiciel (eds.), *Zukunftsperspektiven des Strafrechts: Symposium zum 70. Geburtstag von Thomas Weigend*, Nomos: 253.

Sliwowski Georges Ladislas (1937), *Pologne – De l'intervention de l'autorité judiciaire dans l'exécution des peines et des mesures de sûreté*, 14 RIDP 617.

Sławik Karol (1993), *Terroryzm (próba oceny zjawiska i zarysowanie zagrożeń)*, in: Karol. Sławik (ed.), *Terroryzm: aspekty prawno-międzynarodowe, kryminalistyczne i policyjne. Materiały sympozjum zorganizowanego przez Wydział Prawa Uniwersytetu Szczecińskiego, Szczecin, 29–30.XI.1991 r.*, Ławica: 5.

Smirnowa Leona, Zajcew Jewgienij (1983), *Przed tokijskim trybunałem*, MON.

Socha Elżbieta (2004), *Zbieżność a komplementarność jurysdykcji międzynarodowych trybunałów karnych i sądów krajowych*, WUWr.

Sonnenfeld Renata (1984), *Pojęcie "międzynarodowego prawa karnego publicznego"*, 3 PiP 62.

Spotowski Andrzej (1981), *Ściganie zbrodni hitlerowskich w świetle prawa karnego RFN*, in: Jan Barcz, Przemysław Maćkowiak (eds.), *Przedawnienie i ściganie zbrodni przeciwko pokojowi, zbrodni wojennych i zbrodni przeciwko ludzkości w systemie prawa RFN*, Instytut Badania Prawa Sądowego Ministerstwa Sprawiedliwości.

Sroka Tomasz (2016), *Artykuł 43*, in: Marek Safjan, Leszek Bosek (ed.), *Konstytucja RP*, vol. I, C.H. Beck: 1068.

Stachiewicz Piotr (1987), *Akcja "Kutschera"*, Książka i Wiedza.

Stahn Carsten (2018), *A Critical Introduction to International Criminal Law*, CUP.

Stasiak Kinga (2012), *Trybunały umiędzynarodowione w systemie międzynarodowego sądownictwa karnego*, Wydawnictwo KUL.

Stasiak Kinga (2016), *Prace Komisji Prawa Międzynarodowego nad zbrodniami przeciwko ludzkości a możliwe implikacje dla odpowiedzialności karnej jednostek*, in: Michał Balcerzak, Julia Kapelańska-Pręgowska (eds.), *Odpowiedzialność międzynarodowa w związku z naruszeniami praw człowieka i międzynarodowego prawa humanitarnego*, Uniwersytet Mikołaja Kopernika. Katedra Praw Człowieka: 341.

Staszewski Wojciech S. (2006), *Antoni Deryng (1901–1978)*, in: Antoni Dębiński et al. (ed.), *Profesorowie Prawa Katolickiego Uniwersytetu Lubelskiego*, Wydawnictwo KUL: 93.

Staszewski Wojciech S. (2008), *Antoni Deryng (1901–1978). Dziekan Wydziału Prawa i Nauk Społeczno-Ekonomicznych w latach akademickich 1937/1938–1938/1939*, in: Antoni Dębiński et al. (ed.), *Dziekani Wydziału Prawa, Prawa Kanonicznego i Administracji Katolickiego Uniwersytetu Lubelskiego Jana Pawła II*, Wydawnictwo KUL: 33.

Staszewski Wojciech S. (2022), *"Lubelscy" profesorowie prawa międzynarodowego w dwudziestoleciu międzywojennym*, in: Przyborowska-Klimczak *et al.* (2022b): 261.

Steinsbergowa Aniela (2016), *Widziane z ławy obrończej*, Więzi.

Stone Julius (1958), *Aggression and World Order. A Critique of United Nations Theories of Aggression*, Stevens & Sons Limited.

Strzembosz Tomasz (1983), *Akcje zbrojne podziemnej Warszawy 1939–1944*, 2ed., PIW.

Stypułkowska Maria (1994), *Trudna droga kobiet do wykonywania zawodów prawniczych*, 9–10 Palestra 141.

Sukiennicki Wiktor (1967), *Legenda i rzeczywistość. Wspomnienia i uwagi o dwudziestu latach Uniwersytetu Stefana Batorego w Wilnie*, Instytut Literacki.

Symonides Janusz (1971), *Odpowiedzialność państwa w prawie międzynarodowym*, 30 Studia Prawnicze 33.

Symonides Janusz (1980a), *Education for Peace*, 11(3) Security Dialogue 234.

Symonides Janusz (1980b), *Polskie inicjatywy dotyczące nieprzedawniania zbrodni wojennych i zbrodni przeciwko ludzkości*, 6 SM 25.

Symonides Janusz (1985), *Współpraca międzynarodowa w zwalczaniu przestępczości na morzu otwartym*, Centralny Ośrodek Metodyczny Studiów Nauk Politycznych UW.

Szafrański Jerzy (2007), *Współczesne zagrożenia terroryzmem oraz metody działań antyterrorystycznych*, Wydawnictwo Wyższej Szkoły Policji.

Szawłowski Ryszard ("Karol Liszewski") (1995), *Wojna polsko-sowiecka 1939. Tło polityczne, prawnomiędzynarodowe i psychologiczne. Agresja sowiecka i polska obrona. Sowieckie zbrodnie wojenne i przeciw ludzkości oraz zbrodnie ukraińskie*, vol. 1–2, Neriton.

Szawłowski Ryszard (2010), *Raphael Lemkin's Life Journey: From Creative Legal Scholar and Well-to-do Lawyer in Warsaw until 1939 to Pinnacle of International Achievements during the 1940s in the States, Ending Penniless Crusader in New York in the 1950s*, in: Agnieszka Bieńczyk-Missala, Sławomir Dębski (2010): 31.

Szawłowski Ryszard (2014), *Rafał Lemkin – warszawski adwokat (1934–1939), twórca pojęcia "genocyd" i główny architekt konwencji z 9 grudnia 1948 r. ("konwencji Lemkina"). W 55-lecie śmierci*, 9 Palestra 291.

Szawłowski Ryszard (2020), *Rafał Lemkin. Biografia intelektualna*, Sendo Wydawnictwo Akademickie.

Szerer Mieczysław (1948a), *Granice obowiązywania wyroku norymberskiego*, 3 DPP 30.

Szerer Mieczysław (1948b), *Udział Polski we wprowadzaniu karania zbrodni wojennych*, 3 PiP 113.

Szerer Mieczysław (1977), Wy*powiedź w sprawie referatu prof. T. Cypriana*, in: *Norymberga – nadal otwarty rozdział w historii. W XXX rocznicę wyroku Międzynarodowego Trybunału Wojskowego*, MS-GKBZHP: 122.

Szlachta Bogdan, Bieroń Tomasz (ed.) (2004), *Polish Perspectives on Communism: An Anthology*, Lexington Books.

Szmaglewska Seweryna (1945), *Dymy nad Birkenau*, Spółdzielnia Wydawnicza Czytelnik.

Szmaglewska Seweryna (1976), *Niewinni w Norymberdze*, Książka i Wiedza.

Szpak Agnieszka (2011), *Kontrola przestrzegania międzynarodowego prawa humanitarnego w orzecznictwie międzynarodowych trybunałów karnych* ad hoc, Dom Organizatora TNOiK.

Szpak Leon (1972–1973), *Extradition of Criminals in Bilateral Agreements Concluded by Poland*, 5 PYIL 153.

Szpak Leon (1974), *Ekstradycja hitlerowskich zbrodniarzy wojennych*, Wrocław (PhD thesis manuscript).

Szpak Leon (1979), *Ekstradycja hitlerowskich zbrodniarzy wojennych ze szczególnym uwzględnieniem praktyki polskiej, Ministerstwo Sprawiedliwości*, GKBZHWP, Informacja zewnętrzna nr 57.

Szpak Leon (1984), *Le Rôle Normatif de la Practique de l'Extradition de Criminels Nazis*, 13 PYIL 153.

Szreffel Michał (2010), *Bereza Kartuska jako przykład więzienia politycznego*, 6 Studia Iuridica Toruniensia 207.

Sztucki Jerzy (1974), *Jus Cogens and the Vienna Convention on the Law of Treaties. A Critical Appraisal*, Springer.

Szulc Wacław (1980), *Pomoc prawna w sprawach o ściganie zbrodniarzy hitlerowskich*, in: Pilichowski (1980b): 846.

Szymborski Grzegorz (2019), *Zbrodnia na zachętę*, "Więź", 13.03.2019.

Szymowski Leszek, *Huzarzy Śmierci*, "Rzeczpospolita, Historia", 12.08.2021.

Szyprowski Bartłomiej (2012), *Podstawy prawne i działanie sądownictwa Komendy Głównej ZWZ/AK*, 3 WPP 19.

Tallgren Immi, Mégret Frederic (eds.) (2020), *The Dawn of discipline, International Criminal Justice and Its Early Exponents*, CUP.

Targański Tomasz (2019), *Misja Czerwonego Krzyża czy szpiedzy?*, "Newsweek", 20.11.2019.

Trębacz Zofia, *Antysemityzm uniwersytecki w dwudziestoleciu międzywojennym*, https://www.jhi.pl/artykuly/antysemityzm-uniwersytecki-w-dwudziestoleciu-miedzywojennym,3634.

Tryuk Małgorzata (2014), *Ty nic nie mów, ja będę tłumaczył. O etyce w tłumaczeniu ustnym*, Wydawnictwo Naukowe Instytutu Kulturologii i Lingwistyki Antropocentrycznej Uniwersytet Warszawski.

Tryuk Małgorzata (2021), *Interpretation in the Supreme National Tribunal in Poland (1946–1948)*, 20 (2:24) Między Oryginałem a Przekładem 85.

Tylman Janusz (1965), *Zasada legalizmu w procesie karnym*, Wydawnictwo Prawnicze.

Uczkiewicz Dominika (2019), *Dekret Prezydenta Rzeczypospolitej Polskiej o odpowiedzialności karnej za zbrodnie wojenne z dnia 30 marca 1943 roku*, 41(2) Studia nad Autorytaryzmem i Totalitaryzmem 79.

Uczkiewicz Dominika (2020), Debata prawnicza jako przestrzeń wolności?, in: Alicja Bartuś (ed.), *Pola wolności*, Oświęcimski Instytut Praw Człowieka: 237.

Uczkiewicz Dominika (2022), *Problem odpowiedzialności karnej za zbrodnie wojenne w pracach rządu polskiego na emigracji (1939–1945)*, Scholar.

United Nations War Crimes Commission (1948), *History of the United Nations War Crimes Commission and the Development of the Laws of War*, His Majesty's Stationery Office, London.

Waciórski Jerzy (1939), *Le terrorisme politique*, Pédone.

Walczak M. (1995), *Ludzie nauki i nauczyciele polscy podczas II wojny światowej: księga strat osobowych*, Polskie Towarzystwo Pedagogiczne.

Waltoś Stanisław (2015), *Grabież Ołtarza Wita Stwosza*, Wolters Kluwer.

Warkałło Witold W. (1932), *Czy jednostki są podmiotami prawa międzynarodowego?*, 1 Rocznik Prawa i Ekonomii 45.

Wasiński Marek (2008), *Odpowiedzialność prawna Polski za incydent w Nangar Khel*, 8 PiP 26.

Waszczyński Jan (1986), *Zbrodnie przeciw ludzkości: (narodziny i rozwój pojęcia)*, 10–11 Palestra 63.

Waszczyński Jan (1987), *Proces Hansa Biebowa: zagłada getta łódzkiego: (akta i stenogramy sądowe)*, GKBZHwP-IPN.

Wąsik Damian (2021), *Odpowiedzialność karna żołnierza za odmowę wykonania rozkazu (art. 343 k.k.)*, 1–3 WPP 53.

Wehberg Hans (1931), *The Outlawry of War*, Carnegie Endowment for International Peace, Washington.

Weichert Michał (1948), *Odpowiedzialność władz administracyjnych w szczególności sekretarza stanu w tzw. Generalnym Gubernatorstwie, dr Buhlera*, 3 PiP 120.

Weinschenk Fritz (1997), *"The Murderers Among Them" – German Justice and the Nazis*, 3 Hofstra Law & Policy Symposium 137.

Wiak Krzysztof (2009), *Prawnokarne środki przeciwdziałania terroryzmowi*, Wydawnictwo KUL.

Wiak Krzysztof (2012), *Terrorism and criminal law*, Wydawnictwo KUL.

Widacki Jan (2019), *The Polish years of Leon Radzinowicz: A contribution to biography*, XLI (2) Archiwum Kryminologii 365.

Wierczyńska Karolina (2009), *Relacja między odpowiedzialnością państwa a odpowiedzialnością jednostek w prawie międzynarodowym*, in: Artur Kozłowski, Barbara Mielnik (eds.), *Odpowiedzialność międzynarodowa jako element międzynarodowego porządku prawnego*, WUWr: 363.

Wierczyńska Karolina (2010), *Pojęcie ludobójstwa w kontekście orzecznictwa międzynarodowych trybunałów karnych* ad hoc, Wydawnictwo Naukowe Scholar.

Wierczyńska Karolina (2012), *The Principle of Complementarity in International Criminal Law*, in: Krzan (2012): 263.

Wierczyńska Karolina (2016a), *Przesłanki dopuszczalności wykonywania jurysdykcji przez Międzynarodowy Trybunał Karny. Studium Międzynarodowoprawne*, Wydawnictwo Naukowe Scholar.

Wierczyńska Karolina (2016b), *Sufficient domestic proceedings – the standard of national criminal proceedings before the ICC in context of Art. 17 of the Rome Statute*, in: Krzan (2016): 255.

Wierczyńska Karolina (2017a), *Act of 18 December 1998 on the Institute of National Remembrance – Commission for the Prosecution of Crimes against the Polish Nation as a Ground for Prosecution of Crimes against Humanity, War Crimes and Crimes against Peace*, 37 PYIL 275.

Wierczyńska Karolina (2017b), *Responsibility of state and responsibility of individual – old problems and new challenges for international law*, 8 Czech Yearbook of Public & Private International Law 22.

Wierczyńska Karolina (2019), *Contemporary opportunities of enforcing responsibility for the Wola Massacre before international institutions*, in: Habowski (2019): 371.

Wierczyńska Karolina (2022), *International crimes in the jurisprudence of domestic courts in the light of Polish experience*, in: Patrycja Grzebyk (ed.), *Communist crimes. Individual and state responsibility*, Wydawnictwo IWS: 131.

Wierczyńska Karolina, Wierczyński Grzegorz (2020), *Stefan Glaser Polish Lawyer, Diplomat and Scholar*, in: Immi Tallgren, Frederic Mégret: 306.

Wieruszewski Roman (2019), *Tadeusz Mazowiecki. The Human Rights Envoy of the Former Yugoslavia*, in: Kasey McCall-Smith et al. (eds.), *The faces of human rights*, Hart: 238.

Wierzbicki Bogdan (1979), *Pojęcie przestępstwa politycznego w prawie międzynarodowym*, PWN.

Wierzbicki Bogdan (1982), *O azylach i ekstradycji przestępców*, Wydawnictwo Prawnicze.

Wierzbicki Bogdan (1986), *Zagadnienia współpracy państw w zapobieganiu i zwalczaniu przestępczości*, Dział Wydawnictw Filii UW.

Wilk Leszek (2002), *Nieposłuszeństwo rozkazowi wojskowemu*, 75 WPP 3.

Wilson Page (2009), *Aggression, Crime and International Security. Moral, political and legal dimensions of international relations*, Routledge.

Willis James (1976), *Prologue to Nuremberg: The Punishment of War Criminals of the First World War*, Duke University, Xerox University Microfilms.

Wilt Harmen van der (2016), *Expanding Criminal Responsibility in Transnational and International Organised Crime*, 4 Groningen Journal of International Law 1.

Winiarski Bohdan (1930), *O Kodyfikacji Prawa Międzynarodowego, wykład inauguracyjny wygłoszony w Auli Uniwersytetu Poznańskiego dnia 20 października 1929 r.*, 10 RPEiS 144.

Winiarski Bohdan (1936), *"Obrona konieczna" w prawie narodów*, Zakład Narodowy im. Ossolińskich.

Wolfke Karol (1972), *Problem norm bezwzględnie wiążących w prawie międzynarodowym*, 38 Prawo, 163 Acta Universitatis Wratislaviensis 206.

Wolfke Karol (1974), Jus cogens *in international law (Regulation and prospects)*, 6 PYIL 145.

Wolter Ladislas (1937), *Pologne – Est-il désirable que le juge puisse retenir et punir un fait qui ne rentre pas expressément sous les termes d'une disposition légale?*, 14 RIDP 357.

Wolter Władysław (1934), *Prawo karne pod znakiem swastyki*, 49 Przegląd Współczesny 231.

Wolter Władysław (1939), *Międzynarodowe prawo karne*, Nakładem Koła Uczniów i Absolwentów Szkoły Nauk Politycznych.

Wolter Władysław (1964), *Z problematyki Prawa Karnego Międzynarodowego*, in: Wacław Osuchowski et al. (eds.), *Rozprawy prawnicze. Księga pamiątkowa dla uczczenia pracy naukowej Kazimierza Przybyłowskiego*, PWN.

Wołkonowski Jarosław (2007), *Wymiar sprawiedliwości Polskiego Państwa Podziemnego na Wileńszczyźnie w latach II wojny światowej*, V Miscellanea Historico-Iuridica 121.

Wójcik Jerzy W. (2011), *Przeciwdziałanie przestępczości zorganizowanej. Zagadnienia prawne, kryminologiczne i kryminalistyczne*, Wolters Kluwer.

Wright Lord (1948), *Hitlerowska okupacja w Polsce w świetle prawa narodów*, 3 PiP 87.

Wróblewski Bronisław (1926), *Penologja: socjologja kar*, Vol. 1, Skład główny w Księgarni Kazimierza Rutskiego.

Wróblewski Bronislaw (1928), *Pénologie et sociologie des peines*, 5 RIDP 64.

Wróblewski Bronisław, Świda Witold (1939), *Sędziowski wymiar kary w Rzeczypospolitej Polskiej. Ankieta*, Skład Główny: Księgarnia Józefa Zawadzkiego.

Wyrozumska Anna (1999), *Statut Międzynarodowego Trybunału Karnego – najważniejsze rozwiązania instytucjonalne a ratyfikacja Konwencji rzymskiej przez Polskę*, 2(6) Przegląd Prawa Europejskiego 5.

Wyrwas Zdzisław, *Przestępstwa o charalterze międzynarodowym*, 57 Zeszyty Naukowe ASW 105.

Wysocki Alfred (1974), *Tajemnice dyplomatycznego sejfu*, Książka i Wiedza, Warszawa.

Yusuf Abdulqawi Ahmed (2017), *The Role of International Lawyers between Theory and Practice*, 15(3) JICJ 603.

Zajadło Jerzy, Zajadło Paulina (2008), *Na marginesie wydarzeń w Nangar Khel: respondeat superior?*, 19 Gdańskie Studia Prawnicze 63.

Zdrójkowski Dawid (2022), *The criminal trial of Adam Karol Tyczyński as an example of an unsettled judicial crime*, in: Grzebyk Patrycja (ed.), *The Communist crimes. Individual and state responsibility*, Instytut Wymiaru Sprawiedliwości: 179.

Zielińska Eleonora (2010), *Definicja zbrodni agresji w polskim kodeksie karnym w kontekście art. 8bis Rzymskiego Statutu Międzynarodowego Trybunału Karnego*, Instytut Wymiaru Sprawiedliwości.

Ziewiński Jan (1986), *Rozkaz wojskowy w prawie karnym*, MON.

Zięba Ryszard (2020), *Polska w OBWE*, 2 (XVII) Krakowskie Studia Międzynarodowe XVII/Krakow International Studies 275.

Ziorkiewicz Beata (2005), *Poland*, in: Claus Kreß, Flavia Lattanzi, Bruce Broomhall, Valeria Santori (eds.), *The Rome Statute and Domestic Legal Orders: Constitutional issues, Cooperation and Enforcement*, Il Sirente: 295.

Zoll Andrzej (1996), *Strafbare Beteiligung an Sonderdelikten im polnischen Strafrecht*, in: Kurt Schmoller (ed.), *Festschrift für Otto Triffterer zum 65. Geburtstag*, Springer: 275.

Zoll Andrzej (1998), *Alleinhandeln und Zusammenwirken aus polnischer Sicht*, in: Albin Eser (ed.), *Einzelverantwortung und Mitverantwortung im Strafrecht*, Ed. Iuscrim: 57.

Zoll Andrzej (2009), *Sprawstwo bez wykonania czynu zabronionego*, 71/2 RPEiS 175.

Žourek Jaroslaw (1974), *L'interdiction de l'emploi de la force en droit international*, A.W. Sijthoff, Institut Henry Dunant.

Żukowski Przemysław Marcin (2016), *Wydział Prawa Uniwersytetu Jagiellońskiego w Krakowie w latach 1918–1939*, Wydawnictwo Księgarnia Akademicka.

Żylicz Marek (2014), *Jurysdykcja państw w międzynarodowym lotniczym prawie karnym*, in: Zdzisław Galicki, Katarzyna Myszona-Kostrzewa (eds.), *50 lat konwencji tokijskiej: bezpieczeństwo żeglugi lotniczej z perspektywy przestrzeni powietrznej i kosmicznej: księga dedykowana Profesorowi Markowi Żyliczowi*, Stowarzyszenie Absolwentów WPiA UW: 29.

Żytnicki Piotr (2022), *Więzienie CIA bez kary. "Wyborcza" ujawnia: prokuratura umorzyła tajne śledztwo i rozgrzeszyła polskie władze*, "Gazeta Wyborcza", 24.10.2022.

Index

Printed in the United States
by Baker & Taylor Publisher Services